Handbook of Research on Cyber Law, Data Protection, and Privacy

Nisha Dhanraj Dewani
Maharaja Agrasen Institute of Management Studies, Guru Gobind Singh Indraprastha University, India

Zubair Ahmed Khan
University School of Law and Legal Studies, Guru Gobind Singh Indraprastha University, India

Aarushi Agarwal
Maharaja Agrasen Institute of Management Studies, India

Mamta Sharma
Gautam Buddha University, India

Shaharyar Asaf Khan
Manav Rachna University, India

A volume in the Advances in Information Security, Privacy, and Ethics (AISPE) Book Series

Published in the United States of America by
IGI Global
Information Science Reference (an imprint of IGI Global)
701 E. Chocolate Avenue
Hershey PA, USA 17033
Tel: 717-533-8845
Fax: 717-533-8661
E-mail: cust@igi-global.com
Web site: http://www.igi-global.com

Library of Congress Cataloging-in-Publication Data

Names: Dewani, Nisha Dhanraj, 1985- editor. | Khan, Zubair Ahmed, 1985-
    editor. | Agarwal, Aarushi, 1988- editor. | Sharma, Mamta, 1974- editor.
    | Khan, Shaharyar Asaf, 1983- editor.
Title: Handbook of research on cyber law, data protection, and privacy /
    Nisha Dhanraj Dewani, Zubair Ahmed Khan, Aarushi Agarwal, Mamta Sharma,
    and Shaharyar Asaf Khan, editors.
Description: Hershey PA : Information Science Reference, (an imprint of IGI
    Global), [2022] | Includes bibliographical references and index. |
    Summary: "This handbook examines the legislations on internet, data
    security and their effects on user engagement and cyber-crime while
    contextualizing the inter- relationship between technology and law and
    addressing the need for additional regulations to safeguard user
    identification, data and privacy"-- Provided by publisher.
Identifiers: LCCN 2021027666 (print) | LCCN 2021027667 (ebook) | ISBN
    9781799886419 (hardcover) | ISBN 9781799886433 (ebook)
Subjects: LCSH: Internet--Law and legislation. | Computer crimes--Law and
    legislation. | Data protection--Law and legislation.
Classification: LCC K564.C6 H355 2022 (print) | LCC K564.C6 (ebook) | DDC
    343.09/99--dc23
LC record available at https://lccn.loc.gov/2021027666
LC ebook record available at https://lccn.loc.gov/2021027667

This book is published in the IGI Global book series Advances in Information Security, Privacy, and Ethics (AISPE) (ISSN:
1948-9730; eISSN: 1948-9749)

British Cataloguing in Publication Data
A Cataloguing in Publication record for this book is available from the British Library.

For electronic access to this publication, please contact: eresources@igi-global.com.

Advances in Information Security, Privacy, and Ethics (AISPE) Book Series

Manish Gupta
State University of New York, USA

ISSN:1948-9730
EISSN:1948-9749

MISSION

As digital technologies become more pervasive in everyday life and the Internet is utilized in ever in-creasing ways by both private and public entities, concern over digital threats becomes more prevalent.

The **Advances in Information Security, Privacy, & Ethics (AISPE) Book Series** provides cutting-edge research on the protection and misuse of information and technology across various industries and settings. Comprised of scholarly research on topics such as identity management, cryptography, system security, authentication, and data protection, this book series is ideal for reference by IT professionals, academicians, and upper-level students.

COVERAGE

- Computer ethics
- Global Privacy Concerns
- Privacy Issues of Social Networking
- Network Security Services
- Technoethics
- CIA Triad of Information Security
- Cyberethics
- Data Storage of Minors
- Risk Management
- Electronic Mail Security

IGI Global is currently accepting manuscripts for publication within this series. To submit a proposal for a volume in this series, please contact our Acquisition Editors at Acquisitions@igi-global.com or visit: http://www.igi-global.com/publish/.

Titles in this Series

For a list of additional titles in this series, please visit: http://www.igi-global.com/book-series/advances-information-security-privacy-ethics/37157

Cybersecurity Capabilities in Developing Nations and Its Impact on Global Security
Maurice Dawson (Illinois Institute of Technology, USA) Oteng Tabona (Botswana International University of Science and Technology, Botswana) and Thabiso Maupong (Botswana International University of Science and Technology, Botswana)
Information Science Reference • © 2022 • 282pp • H/C (ISBN: 9781799886938) • US $215.00

Advances in Malware and Data-Driven Network Security
Brij B. Gupta (National Institute of Technology, Kurukshetra, India)
Information Science Reference • © 2022 • 304pp • H/C (ISBN: 9781799877899) • US $195.00

Modern Day Surveillance Ecosystem and Impacts on Privacy
Ananda Mitra (Wake Forest University, USA)
Information Science Reference • © 2022 • 242pp • H/C (ISBN: 9781799838470) • US $195.00

Ethical Hacking Techniques and Countermeasures for Cybercrime Prevention
Nabie Y. Conteh (Southern University at New Orleans, USA)
Information Science Reference • © 2021 • 168pp • H/C (ISBN: 9781799865049) • US $225.00

NATO and the Future of European and Asian Security
Carsten Sander Christensen (Billund Municipaly's Museums, Denmark) and Vakhtang Maisaia (Caucasus International University, Georgia)
Information Science Reference • © 2021 • 331pp • H/C (ISBN: 9781799871187) • US $195.00

Handbook of Research on Advancing Cybersecurity for Digital Transformation
Kamaljeet Sandhu (University of New England, Australia)
Information Science Reference • © 2021 • 460pp • H/C (ISBN: 9781799869757) • US $275.00

Enabling Blockchain Technology for Secure Networking and Communications
Adel Ben Mnaouer (Canadian University Dubai, UAE) and Lamia Chaari Fourati (University of Sfax, Tunisia)
Information Science Reference • © 2021 • 339pp • H/C (ISBN: 9781799858393) • US $215.00

701 East Chocolate Avenue, Hershey, PA 17033, USA
Tel: 717-533-8845 x100 • Fax: 717-533-8661
E-Mail: cust@igi-global.com • www.igi-global.com

Editorial Advisory Board

List of Contributors

Table of Contents

Detailed Table of Contents

Chapter 1

Yilsev Hoca, Cyprus International University, Cyprus
Deren Firat, Cyprus International University, Cyprus
Ersin Çağlar, European University of Lefke, Cyprus

Today, due to the rapid development of technology and communication, personal rights can be damaged. In particular, the electronic processing of personal data, which is a part of personal rights, may cause problems in terms of data security. Therefore, as a result of the development of technology and communication, all kinds of information should be able to move freely, and at the same time, fundamental rights dependent on the person should be protected. By clarifying the concepts of data, personal data, and data processing, the study examines the reliability of the data processed in the light of these concepts at the point of data security.

Chapter 2

Rajab Ssemwogerere, Islamic University in Uganda, Uganda
Balyejusa Gusite, Kampala International University, Uganda

Data privacy is an intricate job and is becoming a key area of research as far as cloud technologies are concerned. This is because the information is massively generated from many sources. It's collected, shared, and disseminated in many different segments. Due to this factor, countless individuals or organizations have absconded the cloud services despite the fact of their endless fruitiness benefits. Providing security to this data is a major concern. There are numerous ways this data can be protected from unauthorized users. Hence, data security and privacy are becoming very important fields of research for the future development and improvement of cloud technologies for the government, business, and industry. Data privacy protection issues are relevant to both hardware and software in the cloud architecture. Therefore, this study will review different data privacy concepts, data access protection methods, approaches to manage data privacy, data privacy techniques, challenges faced during data access, and some research trends in data privacy.

The world is filled with technology-driven systems and instruments in the present era. Artificial intelligence (hereinafter referred to as "AI") is increasingly dominating our everyday life. Deepfakes is one such AI-based technological innovation that is leading to huge concerns amongst legal and scientific experts. There have been recent instances wherein videos of statements never made and acts never done by public figures became viral on the internet. Face swap in videos is easily done for the purpose of cyber bullying and harassment of innocent victims. Since creation of these synthetic contents called deepfakes is becoming easier by the day, the growing concerns surrounding them demand immediate attention. This chapter shall specifically probe into the deepfake technology with dual objectives (i.e., to understand the causes of concern surrounding deepfakes related AI-technology and to compare effective ideas and regulatory measures of nations abroad such as US and China) in order to arrive at possible solutions to appropriately tackle this issue in India.

The proliferation of social media in Nigeria has birthed new paradigms of communication and two-way interactions among friends, family colleagues, and business associates. It has equally morphed to become a channel for money generation among enterprising youth across the nation. It cannot be denied that the merits associated with this phenomenon called social media are enviable; however, it is also arguable that cyber security is a key factor to the enjoyment of these attendant benefits. This study is anchored on the protection motivation theory and the technological determinism theory. The study identified some cyber security risks synonymous to the use of social media in Nigeria. To remedy the situation, the study recommends that education and practical training in technological best practices in formal and non-formal school settings will help mitigate the inherent risks discussed. Also, initiatives should be taken by the government and organisations to curb this serious issue.

This chapter aims to analyse pathways for global legislative formulation on AI. Part 1 of the chapter seeks to chart and analyse the development of the proposed EU regulation itself and seek to create an understanding of the rationales, practical and theoretical, that underpin the legislation and its provisions. Part 2 of the chapter seeks to analyse the present practices of key multilateral discussion forums and Asian jurisdictions on the subject and the approaches adopted by them in policy and vision documents released by various regulators to analyse their similarity or otherwise with the approach espoused by the EU. Part 3 of the chapter expands on the process of how a human-centered approach goes from strategy to regulation and explores the path the world can take on the issue given the dynamic nature of the subject and the geopolitics at play involving the issue. This section is followed by a conclusion to the chapter on what can be derived about the state of AI ethics at the moment and what shape they can take insofar as becoming global norms in the years to come.

Chapter 6

Rama Sharma, School of Law, Justice, and Governance, Gautam Buddha University, India
Anurag Singh, Meerut College, India

India is an agrarian country, and farmers are the backbone of this agriculture system. Now, when India is stepping ahead in all sectors of economy, agriculture is still lagging behind. Farmers are struggling for a minimum standard of living due to non-availability of basic infrastructure and natural calamities. According to the National Crime Records Bureau (NCRB), 10,349 persons involved in farming sector (consisting of 5,763 farmers or cultivators and 4,586 agricultural labourers) committed suicide during 2018, accounting for 7.7% of total suicide (134,516) victims. In this light, it is impertinent to see the current agricultural policies in place aiming to revive the status of farmers in India. Supply of low quality and spurious inputs is an important factor for increased cost without adequate gain in productivity. In this chapter, effort has been made to know how blockchain technology can improve the agricultural sector as well as the condition of farmers in India.

Chapter 7

Vinayak Jhamb, University School of Law and Legal Studies, Guru Gobind Singh
Indraprastha University, India
Manini Syali, Guru Gobind Singh Indraprastha University, India

One of the critical features of automated biometric recognition applications is that, unlike traditional security systems, they do not solely rely on memory or knowledge-based features like passwords and thus provide protection and identification of an enhanced form. Bio-metric recognition systems instead weigh on pattern matching. They collect biological data from an individual using sensors and match the extracted discriminatory features from the input received with the already existing data in the system. Unique identification projects do not solely pose a danger from the side of the government authorities alone, and private players have also entered the game of misusing sensitive information of the users. It would thus not be wrong to state that privacy has indeed become a commodity to be sold off for monetary gains. However, the concept of "privacy" is a contentious domain, and debates pertaining to its scope continue.

Chapter 8

Ekta Sood, HIMCAPES College of Law, India
Vibhuti Nakta, Panjab University, India

The mushroom growth of cyberspace and e-commerce has been increasingly threatening to the trademark and trademark statutes like the challenge posed to the domain names in connection with trademarks. Domain names cannot be restricted geographically with regards to access, use, and invasion, and cybersquatting is when trade name is used directly or after registration to invade the rights of the lawful user to whom the domain name belongs. The only objective is to feed upon the goodwill of a lawful owner to earn profits.

Unlike other countries, India now does not have specific legislation for the protection of domain names and resorts to the Trademarks Act, 1999. Protection of inventions and enhancing cybersecurity is the need of the hour. To conform in compliance with the WIPO internet treaties to safeguard the copyrighted works, online digital risk management (DRM) schemes were drafted in the Copyright (Amendment) Act, of 2012. Thus, the chapter aims to emphasise the need to designate cybersquatting as a cybercrime while understanding cybercrime, its nature, and judicial intent.

Sambhav Sharma, Amity Law School, Guru Gobind Singh Indraprastha University, Delhi, India
Ramayni Sood, Amity Law School, Guru Gobind Singh Indraprastha University, Delhi, India

The avatar of currency has evolved over time, and 'cryptocurrency' is its latest incarnation. Cryptocurrency is a type of digital currency that allows peer-to-peer online payments without interference of financial institutions. Though experts are impressed with its growth trajectory, its decentralized and unregulated structure has stirred insecurity amongst governments across jurisdictions that has translated into bans and indecisiveness related to its status. While the concerns are not baseless and it is susceptible to cybercrimes, the focus must be to mitigate the issues rather than imposing a blanket prohibition that would be antithetical to the fundamental spirit and purpose of financial digitization, which is to promote the free flow of funds. In this chapter, the authors, firstly, analyze the practicality of cryptocurrency in light of the legal barriers and, secondly, assess the viability of a regulatory framework that ensures minimal control from the authorities but also checks concerns including cybercrime, illegal transactions, tax evasion, and lack of accountability.

Prapti Bhattacharjee, Pailan College of Management and Technology, India
Vivek Saha, Pailan College of Management and Technology, India
Parag Chatterjee, Pailan College of Management and Technology, India

Since ancient times, currency has been an integral part of our lives. In the early times, we saw the barter system. No one really knows how currency came into the play. China created the world's first paper money in the early 7th century. Thousands of years later, we are living in the era of internet where after virtual games and friends, we have started using virtual currency. Cryptocurrency is an encrypted, peer-to-peer network for online payments directly between two parties without going through a financial institution. Bitcoin was the first and most popular cryptocurrency that was introduced in the year 2009 which created a huge surge in the market and got a lot of attention from the world. This new type of money is not likely to replace traditional flat currency, but it has the potential to change the way global markets interact with each other. Since the introduction of cryptocurrency, it has gathered a lot of appreciation and criticism. This chapter will provide in-depth discussion on cryptocurrency, its architecture, and also its pros and cons.

Swarnendu Chatterjee, Saraf and Partners, Delhi, India & Supreme Court of India, India
Shifa Qureshi, Faculty of Law, Aligarh Muslim University, Aligarh, India

Any individual who utilises public services is appropriately stressed that, in spite of organisations' earnest attempts to secure their frameworks, criminals may still access government databases and steal or manipulate records. This chapter is an attempt to analyse blockchain technology and whether this technology is effective in supporting cybersecurity. Existing research in blockchain technology tends to focus on finding what this technology is and how it can be implemented for data protection. However, there is no special study on the effectiveness of this technology, regardless of whether it actually protects population data. Therefore, the purpose of this chapter is to outline the effectiveness of blockchain technology in protecting data and the factors that may affect the effectiveness of their solutions.

Brady Lund, Emporia State University, USA

This chapter describes the author's personal experience as a member of a crypto-trading "pump-and-dump" group – groups organized on Reddit and Discord channels that use social media to spread positive misinformation about a cryptocurrency in order to temporarily inflate its value and collect huge profits. It discusses the nature of cryptocurrency marketplaces, social networking related to crypto, the pump-and-dump phenomenon, its social and economic impacts, and ethical concerns. Following the rise in the value of Bitcoin and the WallStreetBets/GameStop saga in December 2020 and January 2021, these pump-and-dump groups used the frenzy surrounding "get rich quick" investing to generate inordinate profits off of these ambitious individuals' losses. Rallying around a shared philosophy and profit motive, these groups utilized social media disinformation campaigns to fool new crypto investors in squandering their funds, often while failing to acknowledge the legal and ethical conundrum of stealing from the poor and ambitious.

Madhvendra Singh, Ministry of External Affairs, India
Nitya Jain, Panag and Babu Law Office, India

Blockchain is an indestructible ledger technology with a permanent digital footprint which is bringing about disruptions in almost every aspect of life. Since its inception, blockchain was deployed to eliminate human cost and effort and bring in decentralisation of power and control. With the overburdening of cases in national court systems, alternate dispute resolution is today the preferred mechanism for resolving private commercial disputes, outside of courts, especially arbitration. Resolution of commercial disputes plays a major role in the economic growth of any nation. Success of any system calls for a comprehensive approach consisting of five building blocks: the legal basis, the organisational setup, human excellence, communications, and management of change. It is also a hypothesis that the courts in the future will be more like a service rather than a location, with courtrooms being online/virtual, and customer-centric providers leading the market space. Resolution of commercial disputes will become more competitive and differentiated on the international front.

Abhishek Vats, MAIMS, Guru Gobind Singh Indraprastha University, India
Claudia Masoni, New York University, USA & Siena University, Italy

State surveillance is the act of using technology like sensors, social media analytics, predictive policy systems, etc. to store, monitor, and/or analyze information about the targeted individual. In the age of Big Data and AI State surveillance is an ad hoc practise. This chapter intends to inform the readers about the harmful ramifications of indiscriminate mass surveillance by Governments. This chapter sheds light on incidents like NSA Leak, Cambridge Analytica and the surveillance of Uyghur Muslims in China. This chapter also discusses the impact of mass surveillance and human rights violations and the resultant chilling effect. Finally, this chapter recommends that to regulate surveillance, universal regulations striking a balance between privacy rights and surveillance coupled with strong domestic laws could be instrumental in preserving human rights.

Jayapradha J., Department of Computing Technologies, SRM Institute of Science and
*   Technology, Kattankulathur, India*
Prakash M., Department of Data Science and Business Systems, SRM Institute of Science
*   and Technology, Kattankulathur, India*

Big data deals with massive amounts of data with various characteristics and intricate structures. The vast amount of data collection in big data has led to lots of security and privacy threats. Big data evolution and the need for security and privacy in big data have been covered in the study. Big data taxonomy framework, the privacy laws, and acts have also been analyzed and studied. Various privacy-preserving data publishing models and their attack models have been thoroughly studied under the categories of 1) record linkage model, 2) attribute linkage model, 3) table linkage model, and 4) probabilistic model. Furthermore, the trade-off between privacy and utility, future directions, and inference from the study have been summarized. The study gives insights into various techniques in privacy-preserving data publishing to address the problems related to privacy in big data.

Unanza Gulzar, NorthCap University, India

Despite the shift in e-commerce in India, there are inadequate laws to protect a person over the internet. The chapter highlights that the Information Technology (Amendment) Act, 2008, incorporated Section-A, which validates just e-commerce including e-shopping but does not include attendant principles of its formation, which gave rise to a number of questions. The chapter also discusses the loopholes and lacunas in the Information Technology Act relating to online consumers and the Indian Contract Act for formation of contracts that cannot be made equally applicable to online contracts, leaving consumers in a position where they cannot bargain. Further, the author has evaluated and analysed cases filed by consumers in terms of challenges they face. Lastly, the chapter came up with certain suggestions keeping in view unfilled space.

The OTT platform is a new market in itself. The growth of this new internet-based industry has brought atrocious competition in the broadcast industry. They effort to distinguish them from their competitors by getting exclusive content from the creators. This exclusivity though not per se appears to be anti-competitive but it raises apprehensions of its negative effect on the market. In fact, these agreements demonstrate interdependence of market players to sustain and reach consumers in the market. The competition laws of many jurisdictions refer to the anti-competitive nature of vertical agreement as ex post unlike cartel (horizontal agreements) which are per se void. The chapter discussed the distribution chain where vertical relationship in the form of agreement or integration is generally developed. The present chapter explains the nature of exclusive distribution agreement or exclusive screening license in the broadcast industry.

The courts have gone on a discourse starting from admissibility of CDs as evidence to the latest being that of WhatsApp Chats. The author of this chapter will map the changing discourse of electronic evidence in India and its evolution in India. The author will discuss the normative discourse with respect to electronic evidence and its applicability, which will be followed by the legal dynamics during such evolution and in the third part argue the current trend of decisions. The author will further provide for the current policy and future changes which need to be imbibed in order to make the law more robust.

The internet is a tremendous tool. It allows users to chat, read, play, and be entertained while viewing content from around the world. It's vibrant, diverse, and provides instant access to knowledge on any topic. Although the internet has many advantages, it still has some drawbacks. The internet can be a dangerous place for anyone, but children and teenagers are particularly at risk. Online dangers can have severe, expensive, and even tragic consequences, ranging from cyber bullies to social media posts that can come back to haunt them later in life. Children can unintentionally expose their families to cyber attacks by downloading malware that gives cyber criminals access to their parents' bank accounts or other sensitive information. The internet can be a dangerous place for children due to cyberbullying, sexual communication, identity theft, scams, and exposure to adult content. The chapter is an attempt to view in detail the possible menace of cyber crime, its types, and the national and international conventions and legislations on the same.

Chapter 20

We currently live in the "big data" era in which we have the ability to collect massive amounts of data that are too onerous for a single individual to process. Artificial intelligence has already proven to be beneficial in a variety of industries, including technology, banking, marketing, and entertainment. For example, transportation, including the transition to self-driving, or autonomous cars, has been one of the most transformative transformations. Another example is that of Amazon. It suggests other clothes or products you might like based on some of your searches. Even Netflix predicts which movies you may like to watch next. AI is also being used in a variety of sectors that we aren't aware of, such as credit card fraud detection and mortgage loan approval, with more uses on the way. Artificial intelligence is beginning to have an impact on our lives in a variety of ways. Thus, this chapter will analyse the important issues and challenges in the area of AI.

Foreword

In the modern world, cyberspace is as relevant as the virtual space that an individual occupies. However, even as the average person lives and transacts online as easily as they do offline, they are not being regulated and held accountable in the same manner. As more and more of our daily lives migrate online, accelerated in a large amount by the recent COVID-19 pandemic and rapidly developing technology. In an interconnected world, each jurisdiction has developed its own security and data protection regime and procedures. The privacy of personally identifiable information is an increasingly sensitive and important issue across industries, as the labyrinth of state, federal and international privacy, data protection and security laws with which businesses must contend grows ever more complex. It is increasingly becoming the rule that entities engaged in the collection, use or disclosure of personally identifiable information will be required by law to protect the privacy and security of that information. Cyber threats to sensitive data are immediate and real, as massive data breaches are making headlines with alarming frequency.

The discourse on Cyber Law, Data Protection, and Privacy goes through paradigm shift, the topics covered in the book such as information security, including information assurance, data privacy, cyberspace, Online shopping, ICT and ODR, Blockchain Technology and cryptocurrency are going to be of contemporary relevance and would hit sensitive chords of issues and challenges faced in the cyber-security domain. This research work in the form of a handbook is bridging an approach for readers to understand the significance of different principle of data privacy and cyber concerns and challenges faced by different countries. Mostly chapters are presented and explained by describing various methods and techniques. Moreover, there are numerous helpful examples to reinforce the reader's understanding and expertise with these techniques and methodologies. This book has incorporated specific territorial case studies with cutting-edge research in the field of data privacy and cyber law. The book not only grips with the problems but also provides insights into how all these problems can be dealt effectively. The book, with its accessible style, is an essential companion for all security practitioners and professionals who need to understand and effectively use both information hiding and encryption to protect digital data and communications. It is also suitable for self-study in the areas of programming, data privacy, security, and its legality.

Viney Kapoor Mehra
Dr. B.R. Ambedkar National Law University, India

Viney Kapoor Mehra is the founder Vice Chancellor of the Dr. B.R. Ambedkar National Law University, Rai, Sonepat, India. She was previously the State Information Commissioner of Punjab, India. She has also served at Guru Nanak Dev University,

Amritsar, where she headed the Department of Law. Prof. Mehra was a member of the syndicate and senate of GNDU between 2008 and 2014. She was also a member of the national committee for the commemoration of the 350th birth anniversary of Guru Gobind Singh headed by the Prime Minister of India. She is associated with various social organisations in India. Prof. Mehra is also an expert on cyber research and human rights issues. She has many authored books in her credit. Prof. Mehra has several research articles published in reputed national and international journals.

Preface

As Bill Gates rightly pointed out: "The intersection of law, politics and technology is going to force a lot of good thinking", the interdisciplinary study of law and technology in cyberspace always has brand new avenues to offer for research and innovation in the legal systems of various nations and at the international level as well. Since technology is ever-changing and law is perpetually trying to keep pace with it, the perpetual tussle between the two requires incessant efforts on the part of legal researchers as well as technological experts. Contrastingly, law and policymaking are also largely dependent on technological innovations and know-how in today's neoliberal times. The pandemic world has witnessed that jobs, processes, learning and even the legal and judicial system have become largely reliant on digitization through technology.

With the emergence of the latest technological miracles such as blockchain, cryptocurrency, NFTs and digital data protection in cyberspace at a global level, it becomes pertinent to keep a check on the adequacy of laws or lack of it to tackle the socio-legal issues that emerge alongside these technologies. It is when the new technology is at a nascent stage that legal experts are required to delve into its possible impact on the society at large. For instance, the rising NFT wave is combined with copyright violations and huge scope for money laundering as the sellers tend to form communities to sell and buy from each other to increase the value of their piece in the digital world. Another technology capable of misuse at a huge level is deepfakes, which can lead to spread of misinformation and revenge porn. Technological misuse often leads to grave human right violations. On several occasions, it has also resulted in infringement of the right to privacy of innocent victims who fall prey to it.

Through this book titled *Handbook of Research on Cyber Law, Data Protection, and Privacy*, an attempt has been made to provide research-based pieces of work of eminent academicians, erudite scholars and experienced professionals from all around the world covering the various aspects of amalgamation of law and technology in the cyber world and identifying the pros and cons of each. Based on their analysis from a critical lens, the authors have highlighted the limitations of certain law and/or technology.

The 20 chapters in this edited book attempt to highlight the inadequacy or absence of laws to deal with technology-based issues in various nations. They also attempt to reflect upon the possible effects of upcoming laws on the societal setup. It is only through timely deliberations and brainstorming that we can arrive at solutions to adverse impacts that the application of a particular law or technology may have on the society at large. The following is the list of all chapters included in the book, briefly stating the objective of each chapter for the readers to go through immediately.

Chapter titled "Principles of Data Privacy and Security in Cyber World" authored by Ms. Yilsev Hoca, Ms. Deren First, and Prof. (Dr.) Ersin Çağlar provides an insight of security breaches in the cyber world, which may ultimately lead to violation of the right of privacy of netizens. The author also extensively reflects on the various principles of data privacy that have gained legal recognition in the cyber world.

Chapter titled "Data Access, Privacy, Protection Methods, and Challenges: A Systematic Literature Review" authored by Mr. Rajab Ssemwogerere and Mr. Balyejusa Gusite deals with the ever-increasing collection of the data on online platform and have also dealt with different data privacy concepts, data access protection methods, approaches to manage data privacy, data privacy techniques, challenges faced during data access, and some research trends in data privacy.

Chapter titled "Privacy and Other Legal Concerns in the Wake of Deep-Fake Technology: Comparative Study of India, US, and China" authored by Ms. Purva Kaushik exhaustively covers the process of deepfake creation through artificial intelligence and the adverse effects of this technology such as privacy violations, social security concerns and the menace of revenge porn. Since India is yet to have a law to regulate deep-fake technology, the author has suggested legal borrowings from US and China.

Dr. Desmond Okocha, Mr. Damilare J. Agbele in their chapter titled "Social Media and Cyber Security: Investigating the Risk in Nigeria" specifically analyses the case of Nigeria and delves into an in-depth study of the issues concerning cyber security breach on and via social media platforms.

Mr. Charitarth Bharti analyses pathways for global legislative formulation on AI in his chapter titled "The European Union's proposed Artificial Intelligence Legislation and the Path Ahead for Asian Approaches to Artificial Intelligence". The author has also dealt with the ethical aspect involved in the said are and the legal prospects for AI to become a legal entity.

Chapter titled "Blockchain technology in Agricultural Supply Chain: A Case Study of India" authored by Dr. Rama Sharma and Dr. Anurag Singh indulges in discussion of the lowering contribution of agriculture in Indian economy. The authors suggest the importance of Block chain technology in improving the agricultural sector and standard of living of farmers in India.

Chapter titled "Gauging the Scale of Intertwinement: Juggling Between the Use of Bio-Metric Data and Right to Privacy" authored by Mr. Vinayak Jhamb and Ms. Manini Syali have dealt with the excessive use and collection of the data in form of bio-metrics and the possible breach of right to privacy.

Chapter titled "Cybersquatting: Need for Protection of Domain Names in Realm of Cyberspace" authored by Ms. Ekta Sood and Ms. Vibhuti Nakta have highlighted how mushroom growth of cyberspace and e-commerce has been increasingly threatening to the trademark and trademark statutes like the challenge posed to the domain names in connection with trademark. The authors have emphasised the need to designate cybersquatting as a cybercrime.

Chapter titled "Evolution of Cryptocurrency: Analysing the Utility, Legality, and Regulatory Framework in India" authored by Mr. Sambhav Sharma and Ms. Ramayani Sood highlighted the evolution and growth of cryptocurrency as alternate currency. The authors have also shed light over the possible misuse of the same for cyber-crimes, tax avoidance etc.

Chapter titled "Cryptocurrency: A Detailed Study" authored by Ms. Prapti Bhattacherjee, Mr. Vivek Saha and Prof. Parag Chatterjee have dealt with how this new type of money is not likely to replace traditional flat currency, but it has the potential to change the way global markets interact with each other.

Swarnendu Chatterjee and Shifa Qureshi took the concept ahead in their chapter titled "Blockchain Technology Efficiently Managing Information and Cyber Security" and have dealt with the concept of Block chain Technology and its effectiveness in protecting data and the factors that may affect the effectiveness of their solutions.

Chapter titled "The Cryptocurrency 'Pump-and-Dump': Social Media and Legal and Ethical Ambiguity" authored by Dr. Brady Lund discusses the nature of cryptocurrency marketplaces, social networking related to crypto, and the pump-and-dump phenomenon, its social and economic impacts, and ethical concerns. The author has also highlighted how this mechanism keep the new crypto investors mostly on the losing end.

Chapter titled "Considerations for Blockchain-Based Online Dispute Resolution" authored by Mr. Madhvendra Singh and Ms. Nitya Jain have dealt how Blockchain method can prove to be an effective means to be adopted for alternate dispute resolution to ease the burden of the regular courts.

Chapter titled "A Decade in Pixels: Analyzing Incidents of State Sponsored Surveillance from the Last Decade" authored by Mr. Abhishek Vats and Dr. Claudia Masoni, deals with the aspect of intermediaries and the use of technology as tools of State surveillance in various nations and its effect on the basic rights including Right to Privacy.

Chapter titled "A Survey on Privacy-Preserving Data Publishing Models for Big Data" authored by Ms. Jayapradha J and Dr. Prakash M have analysed Big Data taxonomy framework, the privacy laws, and acts. The chapter also deals with various privacy-preserving data publishing models and their attack models.

Chapter titled "Critical Appraisal of Challenges to Online Consumers Fissures in Information Technology Law in India" authored by Dr. Unanza Gulzar has dealt at length with the loopholes in the legislative framework which deals with online shopping and has also suggested remedial measures to fill those gaps.

Chapter titled "OTT Platforms and Their Distributorship Agreement With Content Maker: A Study From the Perspective of Competition Law and Policy in India and Other Jurisdictions" authored by Dr. Swati Bajaj Seth reflects upon the competitive interests of OTT platforms in today's age.

Chapter titled "Mapping the Changing Contours of Electronic Evidence in India" authored by Mr. Utkarsh Maria and Dr. Anant Vijay Maria has successfully attempted to map the changing discourse and the legal dynamics of the admissibility of the electronic evidence in the Indian courts and has suggested measures to make the procedural law compatible with the advance in the technology.

Chapter titled "Vulnerability of Children in Cyberspace" authored by Mrs. Vibhuti Nakta and Mrs. Ekta Sood shows at length how the cyberspace is and shall be a consistent threat to the children and teenagers. The authors have expressed the concern over the lack of effective laws and the unmonitored world i.e., cyber space that can be a breeding ground for the bullying, online harassment etc.

Chapter titled "Artificial Intelligence: The Need of an Hour" authored by Mr. Ramit Rana and Ms. Apurva Bhutani deals with the role of Artificial Intelligence in day-to-day life including selection of food items, clothes, transportation, etc., and the challenges that shall be attached with it.

Acknowledgment

We are indebted to all the chapter proposers and full chapter contributors. Without their excellent contributions, this book would not have taken the shape of such an insightful work. Constant interaction with them through multiple rounds of emails enabled us to know all of them and their cooperative and instant response made the entire process smooth and productive.

We are grateful to all especially invited chapter reviewers and authors who not only contributed but also reviewed the assigned chapters to meet the required standard for the publication. Without their critiques and constructive comments and suggestions, the double blinded review could not be realized in a timely manner.

Special thanks are also given to the Editorial Advisory Board members. Their professional guidance, suggestions and cooperation on this book project encouraged and inspired us throughout the arduous development process.

During the year-long development process, we were provided with ongoing support by the IGI Global staff. I appreciate, Ms. Katie McLoughlin, the Editorial Assistant, Development Division of IGI Global, who assisted us in organizing ideas, identifying contributing authors, reviewing contributions, and publishing throughout each step of the development process.

In the successful completion of this book project, the efforts and contribution of every reviewer, Editorial Advisory Board member, every contributing author, and the publisher, IGI Global, are most cordially appreciated.

Nisha Dhanraj Dewani

Zubair Ahmed Khan

Aarushi Agarwal

Mamta Sharma

Shaharyar Asaf Khan

Chapter 1
Principles of Data Privacy and Security in a Cyber World

Yilsev Hoca
Cyprus International University, Cyprus

Deren Firat
https://orcid.org/0000-0002-3570-0854
Cyprus International University, Cyprus

Ersin Çağlar
European University of Lefke, Cyprus

ABSTRACT

Today, due to the rapid development of technology and communication, personal rights can be damaged. In particular, the electronic processing of personal data, which is a part of personal rights, may cause problems in terms of data security. Therefore, as a result of the development of technology and communication, all kinds of information should be able to move freely, and at the same time, fundamental rights dependent on the person should be protected. By clarifying the concepts of data, personal data, and data processing, the study examines the reliability of the data processed in the light of these concepts at the point of data security.

INTRODUCTION

The whole world has entered into a new era with the unstoppable development of technology and internet. Hence, the individuals as well as countries started to live in the cyberspace created by such information systems. While social media and communication are the leading individual information systems, countries have introduced e-government or e-voting. Additionally, transnational information systems have become available as well.

Based on this fast development and various uses, individuals and countries encountered with many new challenges, one of which is the possibility to violate private rights. A number of potential problems may arise with regard to the data security particularly with the processing of private data as the part of

DOI: 10.4018/978-1-7998-8641-9.ch001

private rights on the e-media. Therefore, fundamental private rights should be prevented as all kinds of information have free circulation due to the development of technology and internet.

The development of technology improved technological opportunities allowing suppliers and service providers perform their activities via internet. Because of the internet processes, service providers can collect and process large amounts of private data, which makes storage, access and transfer of private data easier. However, the collection and use of that many data introduced a different concept on information technologies called big data. Software and hardware systems should be much stronger and modern in order to work on and store big data. In addition to the necessary systems, security is also an important issue since data loss or data corruption many cause the collapse of whole system. Not only data corruption but also the use of data for malicious people may also be possible. Consequently, the collected and processed data may also cause tangible or intangible damages for people.

Unauthorized use of private data by other parties virtually or in daily life is illegal. However, the fast momentum in technology equally increases the chances for malicious people called hackers to have access or corrupt such data. Technology makes it also difficult to detect such people, and in some circumstances, it is not even possible to identify the crime. Hence, the significance of data security becomes prominent due to the nature of such cybercrimes. Private data that are shared by the individuals based on trust should be secured by the related institutions and organizations, and such data should be backed up to prevent a potential data loss.

The goal of this study is to identify the level of security in the prevention of private data based on the data security principle, evaluate the influence of technological developments on data security and reflect the legal and technological measures against the private data breach. This study also goals to clarify the concepts of private data and private data prevention, and analyse the reliability of data processed based on such concepts. Within this framework, the international practices by the United Nations, European Commission and European Union would be assessed, and the data prevention principles and their significance would be indicated. This study would also discuss the international conventions and European Union Directives on private data prevention and data security through giving examples regarding the existing practices. Additionally, the improvement opportunities for the information systems of each country would be analyzed based on the infrastructure facilities. Moreover, this study would also discuss the needs for developing countries with regard to the information system use or security improvement.

The fundamental rights and freedoms are affected adversely where the private data are shared without any authorization upon being generated and processed with information technologies. Hence, private data prevention is not only related with the right to privacy but also all of the fundamental rights and freedoms. The aspects data security, which is one of the crucial aspects on the private data prevention, has become a vital aspect where private data are acquired by third parties in the way of exceeding private data privacy. All countries should work in cooperation to take effective measures for data security and prevention of private data towards the circumstances that the boundaries of private data go beyond the privacy limits with the popularity of internet use. Hence, this study would indicate the required phases in the realization of data security efficiency.

The data that are processed within the field of private data prevention and data security shall be utilized in a transparent and balanced manner by informing the related party without going beyond the privacy boundaries. Any other different practice would lead data breach. Deterrent and preventive measures should be taken to highlight cybercrimes and data hack, and to raise awareness respectively. Such measures may vary by the information systems and infrastructure. Each country uses different security measures for its own information systems. Such measures are called the Privacy Enhancing Measures (PEMs).

Additionally, blockchain systems are one of the available techniques used in the prevention of data. For instance, blockchain is used for the prevention and anti-corruption of private data in electronic voting.

However, ensuring an improvement in the area of information and technology is not sufficient for the accomplishment of preventive measures. Additionally, such measures should foresee the effects and potential dangers of private behaviours within the privacy boundaries. Moreover, each person to use information systems should have a good level of computer and internet literacy. Users should have knowledge on information sharing on cyberspace as well as keeping their information updated too. Users should also know how to keep their private data secure, have awareness on cybercrimes and inform other users accordingly.

Therefore, the preventive measures can be successful if individuals are informed about data security so that they would not suffer from their own behaviours since the security measures become meaningless without internet and computer literacy regardless of the most state-of-art security infrastructure. The lack of computer and internet literacy would make data access or data corruption easier.

In this context, the last part of this study would cover some recent examples of private data breaches from various countries as well as measures against private data breaches. Moreover, this study also analyses the security measures taken by the countries to eliminate the possibility of such breaches, and data recovery systems following any breaches.

This study is foreseen to guide developing countries in the use of information systems and data security from the legal and technological perspective.

PRIVATE DATA

The explanation of the terms of private data is made similarly in national and international regulations. For example, due to the Data Prevention Directive, "an identifiable person who can be identified, directly or indirectly, by reference to one or more factors specific to his or her physical, physiological, mental, economic, cultural or social identity or to an identification number; identified or identified shall mean any information relating to a natural person who can be identified". (Directive, 1995). Many countries have transferred the definition of private data to their domestic laws, but since the definition is broad in content, it has led to different interpretations. (Ayözger, 2016). In the light of these definitions, in addition to the information that precisely determines the people such as ID information data containing a concrete content such as expressing the financial, cultural, social or psychological identity of the persons, and any information such as identity, social security number, passport number, telephone number. All of the data that will make people identifiable as a result of associating them with a record is expressed as private data. (Korkmaz, 2016).

The popularity of information technologies is increasing due to the rapidly increasing development. This rapid development and popularity seriously affects the usage areas of information technologies and the demands of users. At the beginning of these usage areas are cloud computing, internet of things, e-commerce (e-business), big data systems. Increasing demand for usage areas has revealed the idea of collecting, processing, transferring and preventing information very quickly.

The information used in electronic media has also brought the concept of electronic data to the literature. Electronic data is the basis of information systems and refers to information converted into a certain format.

Today, due to the increasing demand for the opportunities provided by information technologies, billions of people around the world share or transfer too many information to be counted using electronic media. Figure 1 shows the numbers of social media users in 2019. Almost all social media users are sharing or transferring information. (Clement, 2020).

Information stored on the internet through social media or other platforms may collect some private data without the user's knowledge and/or consent in order for the internet to function. IP addresses of devices such as computers, tablets and mobile phones used by any internet user to connect to the internet environment are recorded in the traffic logs. This registration process is completely outside the user's knowledge. Unauthorized IP addresses are a unique address that identifies a device on the internet or local network. In other words, IP addresses contain the location information of the device connecting to the internet and make that device accessible for communication in the internet environment. For this reason, even a stand-alone IP address is often private data, at least on public internet sites. Because, thanks to the IP address information, the owner of the internet line or the person using the internet line can be identified and other shared information can be accessed.

Figure 1. Number of social media users

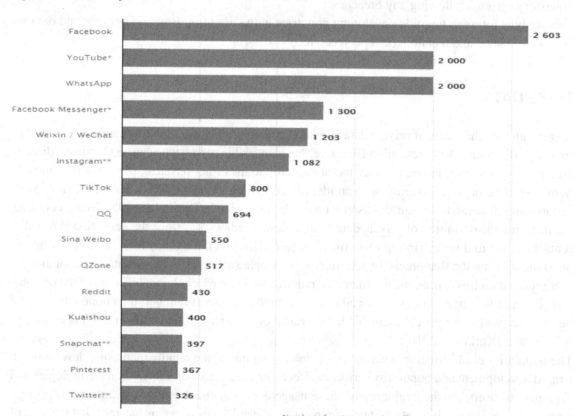

The fact that private information, including user or device information, is shared or processed very quickly and unannounced on the Internet brings with it a number of concerns and sometimes problems.

PREVENTION OF PRIVATE DATA AND CYBER ENVIRONMENTS (PART 1)

There are many opinions regarding the prevention of private data. According to one of these views, the concept of private data includes; information that directly or indirectly identifies, identifies or may indicate someone, ethnic origin, physical factors, health-related information, education information, residential address information, bank or credit card information, communication information with others, beliefs and ideological views. enters (Bozkurt, 2019).

With the development of technology and mass media, people make their private data available in all kinds of electronic media. Many technological systems developed and widely used record the user's phone number and the date they are connected to that system as soon as they meet with the user. Electronic media often tend to access more than the desired private data. For example, when we look at the Android applications that are widely used today, the data owner is asked for permission to access private data such as phone book numbers, messages and conversation details of the person who wants to install an application on their mobile device, while data owners grant access to install and use the application. The methods of obtaining private data change day by day. The widely used data access method is access with the explicit consent of the person in connection with the private data prevention provisions regulated in the legislation of the states. (Habip, 2013).

Today, with the dramatically changes of technology, it has become easier to collect and store data using electronic devices, and to transfer it between individuals, between institutions and organizations, even between countries. Sharing information in such an easy way disrupts the balance of interests between the people who store private data and the data owners and develops to the detriment of the data owners. With the ease of access to people's data, data owners began to suffer material and moral damage, and at some point it became clear that their interests needed to be prevented. However, people's access to data and the need to take measures that can best prevent the privacy of private life while providing this access have formed the agenda of developed countries that attach great importance to human rights. Basic aspects regarding the processing of private data do not set concrete and strict rules; however, it introduces rules regarding compliance with regulations on data prevention. From this point of view, violation of basic aspects will result in illegality in the processing of data. If the data controllers act in accordance with the general principles while processing the data, there will be no illegality in processing the data. The general principles of data prevention interact with each other and in some cases it may be impossible to distinguish them from each other. (Küzeci, 2019).

Although this important issue has not been fully clarified, it has been accepted by the "datenschutz", that is, the data prevention principle, invented by the Germans, and has been the subject of national and international regulations. (Karimi and Korkmaz, 2013). Regulations in general, article 12 of the UN Universal Declaration of Human Rights of 1948 "No any person shall be subjected to arbitrary interference with his private life, family, home or correspondence, nor to attacks upon his/her honor and reputation. Everyone has the right to the prevention of the law against such interference or attacks." Article 5 of the European Convention on Human Rights states that "Everyone has the right to respect for his private and family life, his home and his correspondence. (Assembly, 1948). Any interference by a public authority with the exercise of this right shall only be prescribed by law and to the extent necessary in a democratic society in the interests of national security, public safety, the economic well-being of the country, the prevention of peace and order, the prevention of crime, the prevention of health or morals, or the rights and freedoms of others. may be in question provided that (Frowein, 1950).

Within the scope of international law, private data is a subject of a private right that must be prevented, but also an economic value. For this reason, it is possible to divide the international legal regulations on private data into two different categories. The first is the international treaties that regulate the articles on the privacy of private life, which is a fundamental right. The said articles have been interpreted as covering the right to the prevention of private data in the following years. The second is the regulations on the prevention of private data, which emerged as a result of the rapid development of information and communication technologies. However, despite the regulations made, states can display a preventive attitude by claiming that the standards on data prevention include national differences and risks related to national security. This, in turn, risks the deepening of the differences between national regulations and the operability of national regulations by agreeing on international standards. The UN has accepted access to the internet, a global communication network, as an important right both related to global development and enabling the effective use of fundamental rights and freedoms. (LaRue, 2011).

INTERNATIONAL REGULATIONS (PART 2)

With the aim of determining the standards for the prevention of private data, the UN's Guidelines on Computerized Private Data Files numbered 45/95 in 1976 were prepared. The publication of this document only took place on 14 December 1990. This text, which took a long time to be published, formed the basis for different arrangements in the period between its preparation and publication. (Gür, 2019).

The first of these regulations is the "Guiding Principles on the Prevention of Private Life and Cross-Border Transfer of Private Data" published by the Organization for Economic Cooperation and Development (OECD) in 1980. This document, which is advisory in terms of countries and does not carry any binding, is expressed as the first international document published. Another aspect of the guiding principles is that they specifically addressed the issue of data transfer abroad. Considering that the OECD is an economic organization, it can be said that it looks at the issues primarily from an economic perspective, and therefore, the transfer of private data abroad has begun to be seen as an international economic value. Referring to the guiding principles in the OECD Council Recommendation, it is stated that the transfer of private data across borders will have a positive effect on the social and economic development of states, and national regulations on the privacy of individuals' private lives may hinder cross-border data transfers (OCED, 1980).

In Article 16 of the document, it is foreseen that there will be no restrictions on data transfers between OECD member countries and on data movements that will take place by passing through the national jurisdiction. In Article 17, it is accepted that the restriction is only applied in cases where the OECD member country to be transferred does not act in accordance with the guidelines, the data transferred is data subject to special regulation and there is no equivalent prevention in the country to be transferred, or the transfer to a third country may result in evasion of the state's legislation. has been done. In Article 18, it is emphasized that it is necessary to act on the basis of proportionality, considering that the regulations on private freedoms and the prevention of private life may impose restrictions on cross-border data transfers (OCED, 1980).

Chapter 2 of the OECD Guiding Principles talks about the "Core Principles of National Practice". The principles in this section set out the basic principles to be considered in private data processing activities. These principles are:

- Limited Information Collection: There should be certain limitations in the collection of private data. While collecting data for legal reasons and means, the data owner should be informed about the collection and informed consent should be obtained.
- Data Quality: Private data should be as accurate, complete and up-to-date as possible, provided that it is related to the purpose for which they will be used.
- Purpose Specificity: The purpose of collecting private data should be determined and this data should be used only for the specified purpose. If the purpose of use changes after the time the data was collected, or if there is a possibility that the data processing activity may harm the data owner in accordance with the new purpose, the data owner should be informed.
- Limitation of Use: The collected data cannot be spread, kept or used for other purposes other than the purposes determined by the principle of "purpose-specificity". Exceptions to the usage limitation; conscious consent of the data owner and legal authority.
- Security Precautions: The collected data should be prevented against potential dangers (loss, unauthorized access, damage, alteration, use, disclosure) with reasonable security measures.
- Openness Principle: There should be a general openness principle regarding developments, practices and policies regarding private data; individuals should be given the right to easily access these privacy policies of institutions and organizations that hold data about them.
  - Participation of the Individual (Consent): Data should not be made accessible and disclosed without the consent of the data subject. However, the data owner;
    - The data controller should have the right to receive information about whether he or she has data about him.
    - The right to contact the controller with regard to data relating to him within a reasonable time, at a reasonable fee, by means of clear and understandable means should be provided.
    - If an application made for the reasons written in (a) and (b) above has been rejected, it should have the right to appeal against it.
    - If the objection is accepted, the right to request the deletion, change or correction of the data should be provided.
- Accountability: It should be possible for data subjects to hold accountability against data collectors within the framework of the above principles.

In later years, OECD adopted the 1985 "Declaration on Transboundary Data Transfer" and the 1998 "Ministerial Declaration on the Prevention of Global Network Privacy".

"Convention on the Prevention of Individuals Against Automatic Processing of Private Data" (Convention No. 108), signed by the members of the Council of Europe in 1981, is the second text on data prevention within the framework of international law. (Cemil, 2011).

The right to prevent private data is also considered within the goal of privacy in the regulations made by the United Nations. However, with the development of technology, the violation of this right through computers becomes widespread. (Dülger, 2018). Accordingly, the United Nations General Assembly published "Guidelines for the Regulation of Computerized Private Data Files" (Assembly, 1990) and made the first regulation regarding the right to prevent private data directly, regardless of the United Nations' right to privacy. In terms of the prevention of private data, the document, which contains 10 articles, aims to meet a minimum standard by using the member states' own initiatives. Therefore, these principles are important for the prevention of private data. These principles are:

- Legality and honesty: Private data should not be collected in unlawful and dishonest ways, and the collected data should not be used contrary to the principles regarding fundamental rights and freedoms for the purpose of collection.
- Accuracy: While collecting data, their accuracy should be checked and updated to ensure that the data is retained correctly and completely throughout the period it is stored.
- The purpose should be specific and justified: While collecting private data, it should be determined which legitimate purpose is based on at the beginning, and this purpose should be clearly communicated to all concerned.
- The right of access of the relevant persons: Provided that they prove their identity, the persons should be able to learn about the transactions that the information collected about them has been subjected to, and they should be able to obtain a copy of them without excessive expense and loss of time.
- Avoiding discrimination: Information on sensitive issues such as a person's ethnicity, race, sexual life, religious or philosophical beliefs should only be collected in justified and necessary cases permitted by law.
- Authority to make exceptions: The authority to depart from the measures related to the principles of legality and honesty, accuracy, specific and justified purpose, and the right of access of the persons concerned, in order to prevent national security, public order, public health, public morals or not to harm the rights and freedoms of other persons, is authorized by the competent authorities. available. However, the scope and limits of this authority should be clearly defined in the relevant law. However, exceptions to the principle of avoiding discrimination should not be contrary to fundamental rights and freedoms.
- Security: All institutions and persons responsible for the collection, storage and processing of private data should take every precaution to prevent this data against natural disasters, accidents and the dangers of human error, fault and crime.
- Audit and sanction: The responsibility of applying the principles and rules stipulated in the regulations on the prevention of private data, taking the necessary precautions and performing the necessary audits should be given to an impartial, competent and fair authority.
- Cross-border data transfer: In order to transfer private data from the country where it is stored to another country, the national legislation of both countries must first allow this transfer. In addition, the prevention provided by the country to which the data will be sent should not be less than the prevention provided in the country where the data is located.
- Field of Application: Although the current principles cover private data processed via computer for the public and private sectors, manually processed private data can be optionally included. In case the data of legal entities contain private data of natural persons, this data may optionally be included in the scope of private data.

Looking at the previously issued documents, the UN's Guiding Principles is the first international law document that envisages the establishment of an authorized and independent data prevention body to oversee the implementation of the principles on the prevention of private data.

It is accepted that article which is 17th of the International Covenant on Private and Political Rights regarding the right to privacy also covers this right. In this convention, negative obligations such as respecting the privacy of private life and not violating this right arbitrarily or unlawfully have been brought to the state, and positive obligations such as taking measures to prevent this right have also been introduced. (No, 1988).

Regulations on Data Prevention under the Council of Europe

The Council of Europe has been working on the prevention of private data since the 1970s. The "Convention on the Prevention of Individuals Against Automatic Processing of Private Data", which opened for sign in 1981 as a result of the studies, entered into force in 1985. Since it was prepared by the EC, this convention, which mostly EC member countries are parties to, is also ready for sign by non-member countries. The main purpose of the Convention, also known as the Convention No. 108 today; is to secure the fundamental rights and freedoms of real persons, regardless of their nationality or residence, in each member state, and their right to private life, especially against the automatic processing of private data concerning them. In this context, the Convention prohibits the collection and processing of sensitive data relating to real persons, such as race, sexual orientation, criminal record, without taking appropriate measures. Another important right included here is that the relevant persons can learn the data collected about them and make corrections if they are incomplete or incorrect. Article 7 of the Convention states that "In order to prevent private data recorded in automatic files, appropriate security measures are taken against accidental or unauthorized destruction or accidental loss or their unauthorized acquisition, modification or distribution". As such, it regulates the minimum requirements similar to the guidelines prepared by the OECD and the UN. In the following years, new developments in communication technologies, the spread of data economy-based business models, the ability to easily transfer data across borders, store and process it in regions falling under the jurisdiction of different countries led to the preparation of an additional protocol to the Convention No. 108. Thus, the Protocol No. 181 on the "Convention on the Prevention of Individuals Against the Automatic Processing of Private Data (Additional Protocol) on Supervisory Authorities and Transnational Data Flow" was created.

Two goals have been set with this protocol. First, it has been stipulated by the parties to establish a supervisory authority that will carry out their duties independently within the field of the prevention of private data. Thus, the supervisory authorities will be able to take an active role in the legal process as well as having the authority to investigate and intervene. Again, as is often seen in such institutions, it is expected that the concerned persons have the authority to examine the complaints they make. Secondly, while there is no provision regarding the transfer of private data to countries that are not party to the Convention No. 108, this shortcoming has been eliminated with Article 2 of this protocol. According to this, the parties will be able to allow the transfer of private data to the non-party countries only after they are sure that the relevant state or organization will provide an equivalent prevention. In 2018, the modernization of the Convention No. 108 was completed. The new text was adopted with Protocol No. 223. While making changes, the basic principles of the contract were adhered to. On the other hand, the scope of the contract was expanded by raising the prevention standards envisaged. (Rouvroy, 2018). Another important development is the strengthening of the structure for auditing compliance with the contract. (Greenleaf, 2018).

Although the European Convention for the Prevention of Human Rights and Freedoms (ECHR), which was prepared by the Council of Europe and entered into force in 1953, does not contain a direct regulation on the processing of private data, the European Court of Human Rights has prevented private data with its case law. These decisions undoubtedly have an impact on the decisions of the local courts. In this context, it is foreseen that the states will not make any acts that would violate this fundamental right. It has also been recognized that states have a positive obligation to provide this prevention. In short, the ECtHR has adopted a similar approach with the interpretation of the International Covenant on Civil and Political Rights.

Regulations on Data Prevention under the European Union

In 1995, the European Parliament and European Council Directive on the Prevention of Private Data No. 95/46/EC on the Prevention of Private Data in the European Union. The main purpose of the directive is to harmonize the regulations on the prevention of private data in the member states of the European Union. According to Article 17 of the Directive; "Member States shall take appropriate organizational and technical measures necessary to prevent private data against unauthorized disclosure or access, alteration, accidental loss or accidental or unlawful destruction, when the processing requires the transferring of data in network and against all other illegal forms of processing, the controller's application they will provide." In EU Law, directives do not directly replace domestic legislation. In the same way, this Directive has left room for differentiation to the member states by regulating the basic issues. It has not been ignored in the text of the directive that the EU members are already party to the Convention No. 108, and it is stated that the directive will strengthen and increase the prevention provided by this contract.

The right to prevention of private data is not an unlimited right as it has exceptions and limitations regarding its basic principles. It is seen that the restrictions and exceptions introduced occur especially in cases where the public interest is in question (Korkmaz, 2016). These exceptions and limitations are mentioned in Article 13 of Directive 95/46/EC on the security of private data. Accordingly, member states that take measures to limit the rights and obligations set forth in Articles 6/1, 10, 11/1, 12 and 21 will be deemed acceptable. The specified exceptions and limitations are as follows:

1. national security,
2. defense,
3. public safety,
4. prevention, investigation, detection and prosecution of ethical violations of certain regulated professions or criminal offenses,
5. The economic or financial interest of the European Union and/or its member state,
6. In the cases mentioned in c, d and e, the regulatory function or monitoring, inspection, even occasionally connected with the execution of the official authority,
7. the prevention of the rights and freedoms of others or the data subject.

Another important development was the recognition of private data prevention as a constitutional right during the same period. This right, which is included in Article 8 of the EU Charter of Fundamental Rights, gained a constitutional right with the entry into force of the Lisbon Treaty in 2009. (De Búrca, 2013). In addition, Article 16 of the Treaty on the Functioning of the EU has brought an obligation to the EU Parliament and the EU Council to determine the rules regarding the processing of private data. The recognition of the Prevention of Private Data as a constitutional right separate from the prevention of private life has emerged as an EU-specific approach.

In the Directive, it is stated that data to be transferred outside the EU borders will only be allowed to be transferred to countries that have passed the "conformity check". Therefore, considering the national regulations and/or international commitments, it is required that the European Commission has decided that adequate prevention will be provided. Although this is the rule, it has been deemed necessary to introduce exceptions, taking into account the difficulty of dissemination of compliance control, private preferences and the requirements of economic life. Even in the absence of adequate prevention within the framework of these exceptions, the explicit consent of the data subject, the fact that the data transfer is necessary for the performance of a contract to which the relevant person is a party or to fulfill other obligations arising from a contract, social benefit or legal obligation to perform the transfer, proof of legal rights It is considered appropriate to transfer data to third countries in cases where it is necessary or compulsory for the prevention, defense, prevention of the interests of the person concerned.

The EU Private Data Prevention Directive, which has been in effect since 1995, was repealed on 25 May 2018 and was replaced by the European Union General Data Prevention Regulation (GDPR). GDPR is the most comprehensive legislation on private data when looking at the current supranational and international documents. It imposes heavy responsibilities on all public and private institutions dealing with private data. For this reason, EU members have been granted a transition period of 2 years in order to comply with the GDPR provisions.

In the preparation of the GDPR, two main objectives were emphasized. The first is to improve the data prevention rights of the data subjects, and the second is to facilitate data transfer within the scope of the activities of public institutions and commercial enterprises by eliminating the differences in legislation between EU members. (File, 2012). In this context, not only the private data flow between EU members, but also the conditions for data transfer beyond EU borders are regulated. The provisions regarding the data to be transferred outside the EU borders and to international organizations are basically discussed in the 5th section of the regulation. This section leaves no major changes to the general restrictions imposed by the Directive on data transfer. In Article 45, the conditions to be sought in the compliance audit are defined in more detail and it is added that the compliance audit will be repeated every 4 years and the compliance decision can be canceled if the conditions change. One of the important differences between the two legislations is that although not included in the Directive, the prevention measure 'binding company rules', which is widely used in practice, is recognized and regulated in detail by GDPR. In addition, the model contract provisions remained as a safeguard in the GDPR, but the requirement for approval by the supervisory authority was also removed. Purpose-oriented contracts are also recognized as a preventive measure in the GDPR, as in the Directive, but this method is required to pass through the "compliance mechanism" process of independent supervisory and regulatory institutions. It is thought that with the arrangement of different preventive measures alternatives, it will provide a remarkable relief in practice. As a matter of fact, the exceptions in the directive are also recognized by being defined in more detail in the GDPR, at the same time compelling legitimate interests of the data controller are added to these exceptions. However, the requirement for the consent of the person concerned in article 26/1-a of the Directive has been changed to express consent in article 49/1-a of GDPR.

In GDPR, it is regulated by the 5th paragraph of article 49 that certain categories of data to be transferred outside the EU may be restricted by member states for reasons related to social interests. It has been pointed out that this practice may threaten harmony within the union and have a negative impact on commercial life. When looking at article 3 on how GDPR is reflected in the EU's internal market and the EU's external relations, it is regulated that even if data processing activities are carried out outside the European Union, the processed data will also be applied in non-member lands if the person or persons located in the EU territory. It is clear that the Regulation applies regardless of whether any data processing that takes place in the context of the entity's activities is within the EU. GDPR article 3/1 has two main differences from 95 Directive 4/1-a: The first is that GDPR imposes responsibility not only on the data controller, but also on the data processor. Secondly, contrary to Directive 95, data processing does not have to take place within the borders of the European Union according to GDPR (Alsenoy, 2017). With the GDPR article 3/2, "target place basis" has been adopted. The focus on the prevention of private data has been shifted from the data processing activity and the data controller to the person or persons affected by the data processing activity with the Regulation. After the GDPR came into effect, one of the most discussed issues has been its application area. According to Article 3/2 of the Regulation, the processing of data belonging to persons within the European Union makes it possible to apply it even if the processors are outside the European Union. The debate on the EU's use of extraterritorial jurisdiction has grown with the Google v. Spain Case and flared up with the adoption of GDPR. It can be argued that the legal and legitimate ground for the extraterritorial application of GDPR stems from the cross-border feature of the internet. However, this causes legal problems due to the rule of sovereign equality of States, and economic problems due to the burden on foreign trade. (Dal, 2019).

Ensuring data security is primarily an obligation of the data controller. However, it is important that the owner of the data also contributes to the prevention activity. The data owner can help this prevention by using the best encryption techniques for the products (credit card, smart cards, etc.) obtained due to technological developments. (Hatipoğlu, 2019).

Legal regulations do not specify exactly what private data includes by making a general definition. However, it is important that the person processing the data and the data controller know exactly what the concept of private data includes. Looking at the international (European Commission, European Council, OECD) regulations on data security, it is seen that some common principles have been adopted.

States collect information about individuals by citing some reasons such as public order, public security, social state practices. The collection of private information has gained a new dimension with the development of technology and mass media. Combining data stored in complex situations in previous years, establishing a connection between data and using effective methods for data analysis led to discussions about the violation of privacy at the point of prevention of private data. The basis of the discussions is the prevention of private freedoms against the public interest of the state. In a society where private life is not prevented, it will not be possible to talk about a liberal-democratic state-society structure (Ketizmen and Ülküderner, 2007).

Privacy comes in two different forms. On the one hand, while preventing the privacy of private life is an important issue, on the other hand, it is necessary to carry out public activities and therefore some activities that may cause a violation of the privacy of private life should be carried out. From this point of view, it is not always correct to prevent the privacy of private life absolutely on the basis of the prevention of private data, that is, not to process private data due to the privacy of private life. The processing of private data for public and/or private reasons causes the collected data to become accessible to unauthorized persons and raises the obligation to prevent the unlawful disclosure of data. This means ensuring data security at the point of preventing private data (Bygrave, 1998). Ensuring data security imposes a lot of obligations on the data processors. The most important of these obligations is undoubtedly to take measures to prevent private data from falling into the hands of unauthorized persons. Accordingly, the nature of the measures is directly related to the nature of the private data and the purposes of its processing. The use of some information systems that allow easy access in the world has become widespread. The use of these systems has led to an increase in the processing of private data by storing them in digital media. However, the programs for the transfer of private data to such systems by citizens and the intensive use of this information by storing it in the digital environment continue to increase day by day. The increase in the electronic storage and processing of private data has begun to threaten the security of the data. For this reason, systems that process people's data so much have allowed data security violations to be seen frequently and these violations to cause a practical problem instead of being theoretical. Public and private sector institutions work towards this problem and want to take some measures to eliminate the security vulnerabilities they harbor or, at best, to ensure the security of access to data over the internet. However, the problem that will arise here is that each institution, whether private or public, will try to take measures with its own methods. Measures to be taken within the scope of the principle of private data prevention and data security or company policies in this direction are not decisions that institutions can take individually (Ayözger, 2016). Therefore, a certain standard application must be regulated for the practices of all public and private sector institutions and organizations. The changes in information technologies in the historical process have also caused changes in the quality of the stored data, and this has made it necessary to share the responsibilities to be taken in terms of security measures to be taken. How effective is data security; Questions such as how the private data is obtained, by whom it is processed, what is the purpose of processing the data, where and how the data is stored, by whom and how the data for which the purpose of use is terminated is destroyed should be able to be answered clearly. Within the framework of the data security policy, a stronger security will be created if each individual who shares the responsibility above fully fulfills the responsibilities they have assumed. Therefore, the data security policies to be created for this information, which is defined by the law and provides a high level of prevention, should also include information containing private rights (Henkoğlu, 2017).

In the process from the rapid development of technology to the present, the development and widespread use of computer networks is said to be the most effective tool in the formation of security risks and the commission of cyber crimes. In order to ensure data security more effectively, it is necessary to examine the data management stages and eliminate the deficiencies. Accordingly, the following steps should be carried out for the effectiveness of data security (Henkoğlu, 2017):

- Important data to be prevented needs to be identified.
- Threats to this data should be listed and evaluated.
- The most ideal method for data prevention should be determined.
- Methods that will provide comprehensive and effective prevention should be applied.

Identification of the important data that is envisaged to be prevented is the most basic element. Defining important data and updating it at regular intervals have a very important role in detecting possible threats and determining the administrative or legal measures to be taken against these threats.

In order to ensure the security of the data, it is aimed to determine the confidentiality, integrity and usability elements in an advanced manner. Confidentiality is the prevention of changes and deletion of private data by non-data owners. The element of integrity is the continuous and uninterrupted availability of data or data systems. The usability element is the authentication of the user during access to the data. However, when the security of data in digital environments is mentioned, it can be said that the elements of confidentiality and integrity come to the fore. Therefore, the balance between data accessibility and data security should be taken into account and security policies should be developed accordingly. For example, with the arrival of 2021, WhatsApp, one of the most used communication applications, announced to its users that they have made some changes in their privacy policies to prevent the privacy of people's data and that users must approve new privacy terms in order to continue using the application. After this statement, many people who doubted the privacy of their private data deleted the application and started to use alternative applications. In a statement made by the company executives after the criticisms regarding data privacy, it was stated that all data processed over WhatsApp is prevented with end-to-end encryption, therefore the data cannot be accessed by third parties.

While the development of technology provides easy access to data, it has also revealed risks such as cyber attacks. Therefore, maintaining the integrity of information by ensuring the security of data stored in electronic media is more difficult than data stored in written media. For this reason, keeping the data in electronic media in an original way and keeping it unharmed for many years causes doubts. It was mentioned that there are some risks in terms of preventing the integrity of the data stored in electronic media. The existence of these risks raises the issue of austerity measures being implemented in some institutions. The prohibitions on printing out data in electronic media, which are implemented under the name of saving measure (Henkoğlu, 2017), reveal the necessity of preventing the data that is envisaged to be prevented not only within the framework of certain administrative measures and data security policies, but also in terms of legal responsibility.

MEASURES TO BE TAKEN AGAINST PRIVATE DATA VIOLATIONS (PART 3)

Considering the statistics obtained as a result of the researches on data security breaches in 2015 (Index, 2018); It can be said that 43% of the data processed in public institutions and 19% of the data processed for health services are violated data. Considering these results, it shows that especially private data is preferred when data is violated, and this shows that more attention should be paid in terms of measures to prevent private data while applying data security measures. By 2018, it was realized that adequate measures were not taken to prevent private data and therefore the data was too accessible. Even large and important institutions such as Facebook, Aadhar and Google have been in a difficult situation by being exposed to data breaches due to security vulnerabilities. This shows that information technology systems cannot provide adequate service in the prevention of private data (Aktan, 2018). Considering the many violations experienced in 2019, such as Dunkin Donuts Data Breach, Toyota Data Breach, Walmart Email Data Breach, it is seen that the data obtained illegally is again based on private data and mostly concentrates on important information such as private identity information and account information (Bilir, 2021).

Internet networks and data security issues are intertwined in practice with cybercrime, laws on the prevention of private data and telecommunication regulations. For this reason, it is not possible to consider the precautionary policies for the prevention of data security independently of the existing telecommunication, data prevention provisions and policies on cybercrime. Prevention of private data is one of the most important data that states should prevent within their data security policies. Private data is very important and sensitive information for the data owner. Therefore, such important information should be prevented from being seized by unauthorized persons, and it should be ensured that it is used in accordance with its purpose only by persons with access authorization.

According to researches, technological measures (software, firewalls, etc.) cannot fully provide security elements consisting of confidentiality, integrity and usability. Transactions performed using electronic devices and the increase in the variety of these transactions day by day have led to the necessity of taking new and more advanced measures to prevent data and ensure confidentiality (Çobansoy, 2020).

In recent years, deterrent and preventive measures have been taken to draw attention to cybercrime and data theft and to raise awareness on this issue. However, in order for preventive measures to be successful, it is not only sufficient to develop in the field of information and technology, but also the effects of one's behavior in the field of private privacy and the dangers that one may face should be foreseen. For this reason, it is important for individuals to be informed in order to ensure the security of their data so that they do not suffer victimization as a result of their behavior, and to be conscious about this issue, in the success of preventive measures.

Today, technologically widespread measures are generally about identity verification and prevention of material damage, and are implemented through electronic signatures and smart cards. Basic precaution to prevent data; Privacy Enhancing Technologies (PET). PETs are an Information Communication Technology (ICT) system that destroys, reduces, or prevents undesired use of data while maintaining the functionality of data systems (Acarer, 2020). These technology systems give the data controller the chance to control the data against the danger of making it public, spreading and using it on the internet.

In order to ensure privacy, security must also be well-prevented. Therefore, there is a close relationship between security technologies and PETs. PETs are generally designed for the use of consumers who provide their information to institutions and businesses in order to perform a transaction, but some types are designed by institutions and businesses to help prevent corporate privacy. "Electronic signature" and "smart cards" are the most widely used technologies among the PET types. Electronic signature is a technology that allows the parties to transfer their identities to each other via electronic media without touching the essence of the information. It is an important issue to verify the identity of the parties while carrying out legal proceedings. Especially in a transaction that will take place in an electronic environment, the most reliable methods should be preferred for identity verification. Smart cards, on the other hand, are hardware that are frequently used in the infrastructure of electronic signature and prevention of data confidentiality during data transfer (Acarer, 2020). Smart cards can be used for transferring private data, as well as for electronic encryption or encryption of GSM phones or credit cards. Although these cards are used in some encryption applications for the confidentiality of electronic signature, they are also considered quite reliable in terms of services that require authentication.

Despite the regulations and foreseen measures against data breaches, data security breaches have not decreased today, on the contrary, breaches have changed in size with the advancement of technology day by day. In recent years, the following events can be given as examples of violations where the private data of millions of people have been obtained unlawfully and unfairly used.

Adobe

In October 2013, Brian Krebs who is security blogger, reported an Adobe announcement that encrypted credit card information of nearly 3 million users had been stolen and many accounts had been accessed.

In the same month, Adobe made a statement that the identity and passwords(encrypted) of active users (38 million) were compromised. Krebs later published that "there are 150 or more million accounts and password(encrypted) retrieved from Adobe." A long investigation, it was understood that the attack exposed users identities information, passwords, and bank account information.

A settlement in August 2015 required Adobe to pay users around one million dollar in official fees and an hidden amount to resolve allegations of violations of the Customer Records Act and unjustified business practices. 2016 of November, it was reported that the amount paid to customers was $1 million.

LinkedIn

LinkedIn becomes an open target for hackers looking to conduct attacks. At the same time, LinkedIn has been an open target of user data leaks in the past.

LinkedIn announced that 6.5 million unrelated passwords(encrypted) to be seized by hackers and the information was published in a hacker forum in 2012. However, details of the incident did not emerge until 2016. Same hacker(s), who also published and sold MySpace's data, was found to have given away the account details of nearly 165 million LinkedIn users for a small amount of money such as 5 bitcoins. Upon these developments, LinkedIn accepted that it was aware of the attack and announced that it had renew the passwords of the accounts affected by the situation.

Zynga

Zynga, the creator of Farmville, once one of the giants of the Facebook gaming world and most popular gamers in the mobile gaming arena, with millions of gamers all around the world.

In 2019, hacker who is Gnosticplayerski, argued that to have hacked Zynga's database of "Draw Something for Your Friends to Guess", where he also claimed to have access to 218 million accounts that were registered. The Zynga accepted and stolen.

Facebook

In 2019, another hacker team revealed that two third-party Facebook app information and data were exposed to the public Internet.

Cultura Colectiva, which weighs around 146 gigabytes and contains more than half billion records detailing likes, comments, account names, reactions, Facebook IDs, and more. It is seen that the similar kind of combination in a same concentrated form has been a cause for concern.

MGM Grand Data Breach

Hackers try to access to guest recordings (10 millions) from MGM Grand. The recordings revealed the contact details of former hotel guests, including famous singer Justin Bieber, and many government officials.

According to the statement made by MGM Grand, it was ensured that no user account data was exposed in the breach.

Sociallarks Data Breach

It has been understood that Sociallarks, has made a massive data leak through the insecure ElasticSearch database. Sociallarks' server had no password prevention mechanism, was unencrypted, and was a public entity. In other words, any user who knows the server information details can easily access the leaked sensitive data.

The breached database found to store data of Facebook, Instagram, and Linkedin users (more than 200 million). Published records contained mobile phone numbers, locations, email account details, profile details, names, connected social media account login names, and LinkedIn profile links.

CONCLUSION

The development of technology and information systems with increasing momentum has led to a significant change in the life of humanity. The Internet is one of the most important informatics factors that provide this change. With the introduction of the internet into the life of humanity, the workforce has decreased and great savings have been achieved in time. Thanks to these opportunities provided by the internet, the presence of people in their lives have become indispensable. However, besides these conveniences and advantages provided by the internet, there were also bad effects. At the beginning of these bad effects was that the private information of internet users became accessible and even usable by others.

Today, private data of individuals are used in many fields such as scientific, public, security and public interest, with the widespread use of technology. The use of these data has also brought up the necessity of being clear in terms of interfering with the privacy of individuals and drawing the limits of use. The sharing of data obtained and processed using information technologies without the permission of the person adversely affects the use of all of the fundamental rights and freedoms of the person. Therefore, the prevention of private data is related not only to the privacy of life, but also to all fundamental rights and freedoms. The principle of data security, which is the most important of the principles regarding the prevention of private data, gains great importance in terms of obtaining private data by third parties in a way that goes beyond privacy. After the widespread use of the Internet, all countries in the world should make effective arrangements for data security and prevention of private data in cooperation with the situations where private data exceeds the privacy limits.

Today, such crimes committed through information systems and the internet are at a scale that concerns the whole world. The number of internet users exposed to such attacks is increasing day by day. However, systems that provide full prevention against this great threat that concerns the whole world continue to be developed. In addition, the drafting or enactment of legal laws for these crimes around the world has not been fully realized.

REFERENCES

Acarer, T. (2020). Ülke Güvenliğimizde Alınabilecek Makro Siber Güvenlik Önlemleri. *Uluslararası Bilgi Güvenliği Mühendisliği Dergisi*, *6*(2), 61–71.

Aktan, E. (2018). Büyük veri: Uygulama alanları, analitiği ve güvenlik boyutu. *Bilgi Yönetimi*, *1*(1), 1–22. doi:10.33721/by.403010

Alsenoy, B. V. (2017) Reconciling The (Extra)Territorial Reach Of The GDPR With Public International Law. Data Prevention And Privacy Under Pressure Transatlantic Tensions, EU Surveillance, And Big Data, 77-100.

Assembly, U. G. (1948). Universal declaration of human rights. *UN General Assembly*, *302*(2), 14–25.

Assembly, U. G. (1990). *Guidelines for the regulation of computerized private data files*. Academic Press.

Ayözger, A. Ç. (2016). *Elektronik Haberleşme Sektöründe Kişisel Verilerin Korunması*. İstanbul Üniversitesi Sosyal Bilimler Enstitüsü, Doktora Tezi.

Bilir, F. (2021). Kişisel Verilerin Korunması Kişinin Kendisinin Korunmasıdır. *TRT Akademi, 6*(11), 172–181.

Bozkurt, H. (2019). *Kişisel verilerin işlenmesinin hukuki boyutu.* Kadir Has Üniversitesi, Yüksek Lisans Tezi.

Bygrave, L. A. (1998). Data prevention pursuant to the right to privacy in human rights treaties. *International Journal of Law and Information Technology, 6*(3), 247–284. doi:10.1093/ijlit/6.3.247

Cemil, K. (2011). Avrupa Birliği veri koruma direktifi ekseninde hassas (kişisel) veriler ve işlenmesi. *Journal of Istanbul University Law Faculty, 69*(1-2), 317–334.

Clement, J. (2020). *Number of social network users worldwide from 2010 to 2023.* Academic Press.

Çobansoy, G. (2020). *İnsan hakları açısından kişisel verilerin korunması sorunu* (Master's thesis). Maltepe Üniversitesi, Sosyal Bilimler Enstitüsü.

Dal, U. (2019). Article. *Kişisel Verileri Koruma Dergisi, 1*(1), 21–33.

De Búrca, G. (2013). After the EU Charter of Fundamental Rights: The Court of Justice as a human rights adjudicator? *Maastricht Journal of European and Comparative Law, 20*(2), 168–184. doi:10.1177/1023263X1302000202

Directive, E. U. (1995). 95/46/EC of the European Parliament and of the Council of 24 October 1995 on the prevention of individuals with regard to the processing of private data and on the free movement of such data. *Official Journal of the EC, 23*(6).

Dülger, M. V. (2018). İnsan hakları ve temel hak ve özgürlükler bağlamında kişisel verilerin korunması. *İstanbul Medipol Üniversitesi Hukuk Fakültesi Dergisi, 5*(1), 71-144.

File, I. (2012). *Proposal for a Regulation of the European Parliament and of the Council on the Prevention of Individuals with Regard to the Processing of Private Data and on the Free movement of Such Data (General Data Prevention Regulation).* General Data Prevention Regulation.

Frowein, J. A. (1950). European Convention on Human Rights. *Encyclopedia of Public International Law, 2*, 188-196.

Greenleaf, G. (2018). 'Modernised' Data Prevention Convention 108 and the GDPR. *Data Prevention Convention, 108*, 22-3.

Gür, B. A. (2019). Uluslararası Hukuk ve AB Hukuku Boyutuyla Kişisel Verilerin Yurt Dışına Aktarılması. *Marmara Üniversitesi Hukuk Fakültesi Hukuk Araştırmaları Dergisi, 25*(2), 850–872.

Habip, O. (2013). Elektronik Ortamda Kişisel Verilerin Korunması, Bazı Ülke Uygulamaları Ve Ülkemizdeki Durum. *Uyuşmazlık Mahkemesi Dergisi,* (3), 1–38.

Hatipoğlu, S. (2019). *Kişisel Verilerin Korunması ve İdarenin Sorumluluğu, Trakya Üniversitesi Sosyal Bilimler Enstitüsü, Yüksek.* Lisans Tezi.

Henkoğlu, T. (2017). Kişisel Verileriniz Ne Kadar Güvende? Bilgi Güvenliği Kapsamında Bir Değerlendirme. *Arşiv Dünyası,* (18-19), 36–47.

Index, B. L. (2018). *Data breach database*. Academic Press.

Karimi, O., & Korkmaz, A. (2013). Kişisel Verilerin Korunması. *XViIII. Türkiye'de İnternet Konferansı*, 193-199.

Ketizmen, M., & Ülküderner, Ç. (2007). E-devlet uygulamalarında kişisel verilerin korun (ma) ması. *XII. Türkiye'de İnternet Konferansı*, 8-10.

Korkmaz, İ. (2016). Kişisel Verilerin Korunmasi Kanunu Hakkinda Bir Değerlendirme. *Türkiye Barolar Birliği Dergisi*, (124), 81–152.

Küzeci, E. (2019). *Kişisel Verilerin Korunması. Turhan Kitapevi. Yenilenmiş ve Gözden Geçirilmiş 3. Baskı*.

LaRue, F. (2011). *Report of the Special Rapporteur on the promotion and prevention of the right to freedom of opinion and expression*. Frank La Rue. UN.

No, G. C. (1988) *16: The right to respect of privacy, family, home and correspondence, and prevention of honour and reputation* (Art. 17). UN Doc HRI/GEN/1/Rev, 1.

OCED. (1980). *OECD (Organization for Economic Co-operation and Development) guidelines on the prevention of privacy and transborder flows of private data*. Author.

Rouvroy, A. (2018). *Bureau Of The Consultatıve Commıttee Of The Conventıon For The Preventıon Of Indıvıduals Wıth Regard To Automatıc Processıng Of Private Data* [ETS 108]. T-PD-BUR.

Chapter 2
Data Access, Privacy, Protection Methods, and Challenges:
A Systematic Literature Review

Rajab Ssemwogerere

iD https://orcid.org/0000-0002-9786-8898

Islamic University in Uganda, Uganda

Balyejusa Gusite

Kampala International University, Uganda

ABSTRACT

Data privacy is an intricate job and is becoming a key area of research as far as cloud technologies are concerned. This is because the information is massively generated from many sources. It's collected, shared, and disseminated in many different segments. Due to this factor, countless individuals or organizations have absconded the cloud services despite the fact of their endless fruitiness benefits. Providing security to this data is a major concern. There are numerous ways this data can be protected from unauthorized users. Hence, data security and privacy are becoming very important fields of research for the future development and improvement of cloud technologies for the government, business, and industry. Data privacy protection issues are relevant to both hardware and software in the cloud architecture. Therefore, this study will review different data privacy concepts, data access protection methods, approaches to manage data privacy, data privacy techniques, challenges faced during data access, and some research trends in data privacy.

INTRODUCTION

Data privacy and data protection are fundamental issues in contemporary societies, they prevent the dissemination of sensitive information of individuals (Gellert & Gutwirth, 2013). Computer Law & Security Review that privacy and data protection are products of discrete practices of pronunciation, such as politics, law, and ethics (Gellert & Gutwirth, 2013). Anonymous data breaches worry the general public

DOI: 10.4018/978-1-7998-8641-9.ch002

about how third parties protect the privacy of individual entities, states, organizations, institutions, and companies during this digital era. This has raised general concerns over the legal safeties of electronic data in many national states (Mulligan et al., 2019). Many data breaches have happened since the year 2020. For example, SolarWinds company in the United States of America, thousands of large private companies, and high-security governmental departments' data were left vulnerable to Russian hackers (December 2020). Another data breach happened on Facebook in April 2021, where over 533 million users information was posted online by a hacker.

Data access is based on the ability to retrieve, update, copy data from centralized storage. Data is the collection of raw facts in a form a computer can process e.g. experimental or clinical measurements, words, observations from surveys, interviews, questionnaires, modeling, or simulation among others. It's generated from various sources, but the primary sources are **social networks** that provide human-sourced information (Nambobi et al., 2021), like Facebook, Twitter, emails, blogs, etc., **traditional business transaction systems** that offer customer services like banking, e-commerce, credit cards, medical records, etc., and increasing **internet of things** (IoT) devices like wireless sensors, security surveillance cameras among others. In most cases, the storage media of the data collected from different sources is the cloud. Providing security to this data is a major concern. There are numerous ways of how this data can be protected from unauthorized users. In this paper, we will highlight some of the data access protection methods and the challenges faced during data access.

Data is a very important aspect as an organization or individual, it's organized for analysis, making decisions and is also used to produce research outputs such as research journals, papers, and publications (Payne, 2007). Users use different mechanisms of accessing their data. Data access defines the various procedures or mechanisms through which individuals or users can access, manipulate, retrieve stored data in datasets. A dataset is an electronically stored collection of data associated with files (Alsahafi & Gay, 2018; Withers, 2005). Data access generally involves activities like data cleaning, storage, retrieval, and data protection (Ganti & Sarma, 2013; Rahm & Do, 2000). Data protection specifically involves mechanisms of safeguarding sensitive information from being compromised or losing it (Danezis et al., 2015; Makulilo, 2016).

Intended attacks into government, individual, private organizational networks, and insufficient privacy and cybersecurity practices have exposed the government, individual, and private data to unauthorized personnel. Since recent years, these practices have been evolving and have been accelerated to date, due to the improvements in internet technologies that regularly progress. This makes many individuals, organizations, government agencies, health sectors transmit their data on the internet at a very high rate than before, exposing their data to third parties behind scenes. As an impact, the data breaches and privacy violations of this data have arisen as a foremost problem, raising national concerns over legal protection regarding internet or electronic data and how private sectors have to control and protect government, individual, and private organizational data stored in the cloud. Some of the related concepts about data access, its protection methods, and challenges have been discussed in this chapter.

Information Security

Information security covers methods, safeguards that are mapped together towards achieving major practices like access control (Borky & Bradley, 2019; Höne & Eloff, 2002). This determines who gets access to the data, which operation can be performed and how such data is kept in respect to the key security elements that are confidentiality, integrity, and availability. Information security also defines the state of how information is protected against unauthorized users. Here the main focus is specifically electronic data, or the measures derived to achieve information security. The basic fundamental principles of information security are CIA. They are abbreviated as confidentiality, integrity, and availability sometimes termed as reliability. These principles are meant to be implemented by any program or software, or any security control developed should at least achieve one or more of those principles.

Confidentiality measures in data security are designed to prevent unauthorized disclosure of data or information against unintended groups of people. This principle is meant to ensure that unexposed information to the public remains private and only accessed by rightful individuals required to complete their job duties with that information. Integrity measure defines the protection of information from unauthorized modifications such as adding, deleting, or changing. The principle is designed to ensure that information or data is trusted to be accurate, excluding it from the thinking or attempts that it has not been inappropriately changed (Cho et al., 2016; Huang et al., 2017; Lei & Yucong, 2021). Availability measures are meant to protect the functionality of support systems and ensure data is fully available at the point in time (or period requirements) when it is needed by its users. In many other studies, the availability principle is commonly termed the reliability principle. The major objective of this principle is to provide a guarantee that data will be available to be used at any time when needed to make intended decisions.

Furthermore, authorization, authentication, and non-repudiation are paramount in shaping a secure and authentic data/information management environment. Information security has to do with networks or configurations made on our computers like setting up firewalls, password patterns, facial recognition. Information security has to do with physical security and cybersecurity.

Technologies Used in Data Security

Data backup and recovery possibility due to the ever upgrading complexities that are created within networks, hardware and software failures. Data backup is creating a copy of the original data or information. Regular data backup is a very important aspect because the backup copy of data can be recovered and restored in the event of a primary data failure. Primary data failures can be the consequence of hardware or software failure, data corruption, or a human-caused event, such as a malicious attack, or accidental deletion of data (G.-Z. Sun et al., 2010).

Network monitoring devices like the firewalls, Hypertext transfer protocol forward proxies or intrusion detection systems for monitoring the outbound traffic and correspondence reports about the sensitive organization's information against malicious activities like data exfiltration (Kumar & Deepamala, 2010).

Using data encryption techniques, data is encoded and can only be decrypted by a person having permission or key to this data using encryption tools like Tor, KeePass, and TrueCrypt among many others (Agrawal & Mishra, 2012). Data can be encrypted using asymmetric and symmetric techniques as shown in figure 2.1.

Blockchain technology is a new and promising data encryption mechanism for big data security management that ensures unique data elements, time-stamped, data stored on a block of chain with unique private keys improving the level of data security. This technology further provides an overall solution for systematic security about data safety (Ren et al., 2021).

Data masking, confidential data is masked such as the first twelve digits of a credit card against exposure to reduce risks of data breaches and raise levels of data privacy and assurance. Data masking's objective is to encrypt sensitive data from the external world full of hackers ready to sabotage it (Sarada et al., 2015).

A data risk assessment or Data auditing is normally performed to identify security vulnerabilities and take immediate steps to fix such serious security risks (Hawkins et al., 2000). Data auditing involves assessing how an organization's data is fit for a given purpose. This mechanism is so important because it helps to monitor each interaction with the data and log it to an audit trail.

Data real-time alerts, most organizations spend several months to discover data security breaches, real-time monitoring and alerts can prevent unauthorized access to personal data and can trigger alert actions on a per-result basis.

Physical Security

Habitually, the physical security component has not been treated with maximum attention for people put a lot of emphasis on cybersecurity, thus laying strategies to the process of managing secure data packets delivery over the network. Well thumbs up for this, but, what about if we can't even migrate data to the network? probably because of burglary attacks on computer laboratories, offices, homes, or even internet cafés. This, therefore, implies modeling, implementing, and always revising the security mechanism both at the network and physical level.

On the physical part of it, hardware components of the computer, storage mediums like external hard disk drives, compact disk, and flash disks need physical security to ensure the major physical security elements are detective, deterrent, and preventive (DDP). The physical security outline is composed of three main mechanisms: access control, surveillance, and testing (Ouaddah et al., 2017).

The access control mechanism is a key mechanism of maximizing an organization's data or information physical security measures. This is done by limiting and controlling what people have access to and should be allowed to access sites centered with the organization's data such as server rooms and data centers, including facilities and materials and devices containing organization data such as laptops, tablets, cell phones among others. Access control encompasses the measures taken to limit exposure of devices having the organization's data or information to only authorized personnel. Examples of these corporate barriers include displaying department Identification badges to security guards, using Radio Frequency Identification systems (Nambobi et al., 2020), installing biometrics such as fingerprint scanners, iris, voice, and facial recognition systems (Dargan & Kumar, 2020), door locks and keypads. Also confiscated technological access controls like smart ID card scanners, embedded near-field communication (NFC) microchips below the skin of their authorized individuals, and NFC ID cards have evolved to verify the identities of individuals incoming and departing various data facilities (Michael, 2016; Olenik et al., 2021). Others include passwords, pins, hidden patterns, security questions, and answers plus many more.

Surveillance mechanism is another important physical security component for both prevention and post-incident recovery. This mechanism can monitor activities happening at different real-world locations and facilities using surveillance Closed circuit television (CCTV) cameras, sensors, and notification systems. The benefit of this mechanism is that, provides visual evidence of perpetrators and their tactics.

Cyberspace

This is a virtual space environment created by interconnected networks and computers on the Internet that directly or indirectly interconnects systems, and other infrastructures critical to society's needs (Parn & Edwards, 2019). A good example of cyberspace is the home of Facebook Google, Gmail, and Yahoo.

In cyberspace, data in transit or data traffic happen to go through different layers of data transfer like physical layer, data link layer, Network layer, transport layer, Session layer, and presentation layer (Clark, 2010; Uma & Padmavathi, 2013). For routed data, it still undergoes Cisco's hierarchy network model that consists of the Access layer, Distribution, and core layer. Different international bodies have come up to draft laws and principles that should be tolerated/ recognized in cyberspace. Some of these include:

- The Cybercrime Program Office (C-PROC) is under the council of Europe (de Arimatéia da Cruz, 2020). This unit aims at laying a framework for combating, restoring, and responding to the different cybersecurity violations in different countries across the globe. A specialized computer security incident response team (C-SIRT) at this point is paramount for attempts to sabotage further data acts and privacy violations by the cybercriminals (de Arimatéia da Cruz, 2020). Sequentially, this involves several steps namely; preparedness, which renders the capability to detect attacks and analyze at that point, then blocking or containing such malicious activity, and finally carry out a post-attack patching/activities to prevent further attacks.
- Computer Crime and Intelligence Property Section (CCIPS) (Finnell, 1979). This is a United States federal government agency that operates under the department of justice. It primarily seeks to locate and prosecute intellectual property rights violations across the globe.
- The Electronic Crime Task Force (ECTF) (Stol et al., 2013). The electronic crime task force is a body under the department of homeland security, particularly in secret services. Its motivation lies in eradicating cyber law violations like email systems attacks, intrusions, and theft in cyberspace.
- Anti-Phishing Working Group (APWG) (Oest et al., 2018; Sharma et al., 2017). The anti-phishing working group is a non-government entity that focuses on eradicating phishing and email spoofing. A report by APWG 2020, indicates that there have been more attacks on the industrial sector than any other sector (Sharma et al., 2017).
- International Telecommunication Union (ITU) (Union, 2001). This Union has through the global security agenda and partnership advocated for cybersecurity improvement. One of its best principal practices of the use or embedding of secure technical standards so as to achieve security. There are several cybersecurity unions in place across the globe, all primarily drafting and implementing procedures of exacting a safe cloud of communications.

RELATED STUDIES

(Byun & Li, 2008), discussed the comprehensive approaches for privacy, and addressed the problem of how to determine the purpose for which certain data are accessed by a given user. Guarda, Paolo & Zannone, Nicola, made a reference base for the development of methodologies tailored to design privacy-aware systems to be compliant with data protection regulations. (Bieker et al., 2016), examined the new requirements in detail and inspected behaviors for their fruitful implementation and endorsing the suitable attention to important rights as warranted by the General Data Protection Regulation incorporating the legislation's new requirements.

(Parn & Edwards, 2019), presented a complete review of cyber-threats challenging critical infrastructure asset management depends upon a joint data setting to enlarge building information modeling implementation. (Cashell et al., 2004) described the difficulties that attend the measurement of cyber-risk. They stated the difficulties such as lack of data about the severity of cyber-attacks, secondly, the inherent difficulty in determining costs that may be subject to countless contingencies. (Zhu et al., 2011), scientifically identified the possible cyber attacks including cyber-induced cyber-physical attacks on Supervisory Control and Data Acquisition systems (SCADA). They further defined exclusive challenges posed to securing SCADA systems versus traditional Information Technology systems.

(Li et al., 2012) defined smart grid goals, tactics, and also presented a three-layer smart grid network architecture, elaborated on smart grid cybersecurity issues, and described a classification of basic cyber attacks, upon which sophisticated attack behaviors may be constructed. They finally presented important security techniques that could achieve full safety against the existed and future sophisticated security attacks. (Hathaway et al., 2012), identified the need for a complete legal outline at both the domestic and international levels to successfully address cyber-attacks inform of a new international regulation about cyber-attack.

(Hua & Bapna, 2013) compared the fatalities caused by cyber terrorists and common hackers. Their study reviewed Information system security, game-theoretical models of Information system security, cyber terrorism, and cyber deterrence. Their findings advised organizations to shield their planned information systems against cyber terrorists who tolerate characteristics of long-term goals.

(Kindt, 2016) deeply examined from a legal viewpoint the various privacy and data protection risks fashioned by the use of biometric technology for considering possible interference with the data subject's rights, and proposed proposals and recommendations on an outline for providing complete legal protection about data subjects. (Song et al., 2012), explored a new cloud platform architecture called Data Protection as a Service, which dramatically decreases the per-application development energy required to offer data protection.

(Somani et al., 2010), evaluated Cloud Storage Methodology and Data Security in the cloud by the Implementation of digital signature with Rivest–Shamir–Adleman (RSA) algorithm. Additionally, he provided insight on data security features for Data-in-Transit and Data-at-Rest, based on all the stages of Software as a Service (SaaS), Platform as a Service (PaaS), and Infrastructure as a Service (IaaS).

Issues of Cyber Attacks on the Private Sector

A store of data comprising credentials of over 360 million accounts and 1.25 billion email addresses was sold on an online black market (Kaur et al., 2018). So far, this is considered the largest and strangest data breach in history. The enormous data collected by cyber attackers was attained through attacks on, Gmail, Microsoft, Yahoo, and Google plus others for three weeks. This data breach is indicative of an increasingly threatening trend of actors employing cyber-attacks that caused significant damages to the private sector and also threatened personal, national, and economic security (Watkins, 2014).

The institute of Ponemon reported 6 countries and 234 multinational companies were wounded of malware outbreaks and about 57% experienced Distributed Denial of Service (DDoS) (Ponemon Institute, 2013). These companies were breached 1.3 times a week at an annual cost of about $7.2 million. This made these companies and their countries suffer a significant loss.

Best Practices Encountered in Data Privacy and Data Protection

Data Privacy: several studies have been conducted on how data can be privately kept against unauthorized users. For example, (Mehmood et al., 2016) provided a complete summary of the data privacy preservation mechanisms about big data using various existed mechanisms, they further illustrated the infrastructure of big data and the state-of-the-art data privacy-preserving mechanisms in each stage of the big data life cycle. (Yao-Huai, 2020) also reviewed changes in China, showing how modern notions of data privacy in China constitute a dialectical synthesis of both traditional Chinese emphases on the importance of the family and the state and more Western emphases on individual rights including the right to data privacy.

Data privacy seeks to avail an environment in which only the intended, authentic parties gain access to information and also cautions them to treat such data with utmost good practices. This means therefore that data should be as private as negligible to unauthorized parties whether employees or external stakeholders. Data is a paramount asset that computer users like companies, organizations, factories, and universities have to be properly managed. Data determines the success or failure of an entity. Many tools, techniques, and methods or approaches like machine learning, Artificial intelligence, data mining, online analytical processing (OLAP), among others can be used to create business intelligence out of daily data generated by Operational systems. The above paragraph justifies the need for data, hence ensuring its privacy is crucial. Different companies and organizations at this point should not tolerate data privacy violations like disclosure.

Data Protection: This is the major concern to be addressed nowadays. If proper mechanisms are not provided properly for data access by different users then data is at high risk. Several consequences can happen due to poor data protection mechanisms, they are often severe and can have a long-lasting effect in four key areas; financial (Companies usually face substantial financial losses, including regulatory fines and settlement payments.), legal (when a breach happens concerning any personal information, companies are likely to face class action lawsuits), reputation (it's hard to estimate the damage a breach does to a company's reputation) and lastly, operational (some breaches lead to loss of important and sensitive data). To solve and eliminate these risks you have to understand where risk is coming from. They occur from devices and people; people have to be granted access to sensitive information but their mistakes and actions lead to data breaches. Devices are another factor, they store sensitive information but they are susceptible to being either lost or stolen. It's hard to extend security controls to these devices. One clear solution is to come up with a clear data access protection method that can combine these two risk factors routes.

Data protection in this perspective points out all kinds of safeguards mapped towards ensuring the intactness of the information or data in question. According to the data protection and privacy act, 2019, the major aim is to protect the privacy of individuals and personal data by regulating the collection and processing of personal information, to provide for the rights of the persons whose data is collected and the obligations of data collectors, data processors and data controllers to regulate the use or disclosure of personal information and for any related matters (Determann, 2019).

Data protection is one of the most important things any company, firm, or organization should be well versed with and implement regularly, in case your organization is engaged in processing personal data (Bygrave, 2002; Voigt & Von dem Bussche, 2017). The main motive behind this is to ensure the safety of personal data. Below are some of the data protection principles that need to be observed as a control measure of computer resource protection or security.

1. **Setup a data usage policy.**

The data policy in a given setting like a company, points out the different data types held, the specific kind of people with access to it, and the kind of operations that can be performed depending on the privileges. Note that, failure to observe that rules and regulations by the policy have consequences to whoever does so.

2.   Implement an access control functionality.

Access control is one in which an employee has privileges and also ensures that rights or privileges are appropriately assigned according to the purpose or operations to be performed. For example, write, read-only, modify. Access control is at different levels thus to say; those that must be followed by all employees being administrative level, then the access control level were operations that transform data state and configurations like for firewalls, data routing, among others being technical level and lastly at the physical level.

Access Control policies guarantee three main functions; authentication, authorization, and audit (Stallings & Brown, 2008). Authentication verifies that the identifications of the user or an entity are valid, authorization grants a right to a user trying to access a specific system resource like a web application. Audit reviews system records and activities to ensure compliance with established policy and operational procedures to recommend any indicated changes in control, policy, and procedures. An access control mechanism arbitrates between a user and system resources, such as applications, operating systems, firewalls, routers, files, and databases (Stallings & Brown, 2008). The system must first authenticate a user seeking access. Typically, there are three different types of access control policies; Discretionary Access Control (DAC), Mandatory Access Control (MAC), Role-Based Access Control (RBAC), and Attribute-based access control (ABAC). DAC controls access to a resource based on the identity of the requestor and access rules stating what the requestor is supposed to do. It's used in small business places or basic applications. DAC is termed discretionary because a user might have access rights that permit him or her enable another user to access some resource, MAC Controls access based on comparing security labels with security clearances, RBAC Controls access based on the roles that users have within the system, ABAC Controls access based on attributes of the user, the resource to be accessed, and current environmental conditions (Stallings & Brown, 2008). If, however, you have highly confidential or sensitive data on your business platform, MAC or RBAC are two options that you may need to highly consider.

3.   Harnessing and employing cryptographic technologies (data encryption)

These technologies render data useless and meaningless unless decrypted with the challenge-response key assigned to authentic users of such data. Data Cryptography, this method is mentioned among the best methods of data protection in the GDPR, it is a security method where data is encoded and ready to only be accessed by authenticated or authorized users with the correct encryption key and access rights. Encrypted data, also known as ciphertext, appears scrambled or unreadable to a person or entity accessing without permission. This method prevents careless parties from accessing sensitive data. Encryption has two types symmetric and asymmetric. An asymmetric or public key uses two keys to encrypt a plain text using a public key by anyone who might want to send you a message and decrypting the ciphertext using a secret key that is kept private. Symmetric key encryption involves only one secret key to encrypt and decrypt information. It's an old and best-known technique. It uses a secret key that can either be a number, a word, or a string combined with the plain text message to modify the content in a specific way, here the sender and the receiver must recognize the secret key used to encrypt and decrypt the messages.

The most common architecture is Blowfish. The main disadvantage of symmetric key encryption is that all parties involved have to exchange the key used to encrypt the data before they can decrypt it. Figure 2.1 illustrates Asymmetric and Symmetric encryption techniques.

Figure 1. Illustrates asymmetric and symmetric encryption techniques

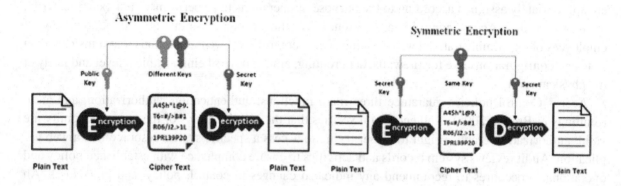

4.   Running regular data back-ups

This is a recommended habit, whereby timely back-ups are made either automatically or manually according to the desire of the data owners. This helps in disaster times whereby at least a copy of such data is residing on certain different servers somewhere. One can perform a full backup, incremental back-up, or differential back-up. Backups are as a result of making a copy of original files, documents, folders saved to some other safe place to be able to restore them in case of any data loss or corruption which may happen due to viruses, hardware failures, fire, theft, and any other unpredictable situation. It's so important to regularly update sensitive data and to always encrypt this data before it is backed up. Never store sensitive data in the cloud, since there is no built trust between the cloud service providers and consumers despite the fact of several proposed data protection techniques proposed by researchers to attain the highest degree of data security in the cloud (Y. Sun et al., 2014).

5.   Using genuine Hard-wares and soft-wares that are up-to-date and also upgrading regularly.

Sometimes systems fail not necessarily due to hacking or viruses, outdated and counterfeit (pirated) technologies also pose a big challenge due to lack of standard guarantee of performance.

6.   Synchronize a load balancing and clustering strategy for the company's systems.

Companies run more than one system thus the need to cluster different computers, this renders high processing power, zeroing down the response time thereby providing full-time resource access and re-dundancy just in case it is needed.

7.   **Pseudonymization** is a data de-identification technique of personally identifiable information fields within a data record being replaced by one or more artificial pseudonyms. This makes the

data record less identifiable while remaining suitable for data analysis and data processing. It's also identified as another way of complying with the GDPR demands for increasing data security and privacy securing for data storage of sensitive identifiable personal information.

8. **Data destruction,** sometimes data may need to be destroyed because it's being protected against unauthorized recovery and access by specific individuals. This is also stated under GDPR, that under such circumstances, you have the obligation and right to delete the databasing on how sensitive this data is to some individuals or companies, using more comprehensive destruction methods like data overwriting, degaussing, physical destruction like disk shredding and melting. Overwriting is one of the most common ways of the destruction of data using some specific software that is addressed to all the physical data storage areas. However, it takes a long time to overwrite an entire high-capacity drive and it might also fail to sterilize some highly protected specific areas, still making data recoverable to some extent. Physical destruction gives an assurance of absolute destruction of data but is not considered to be an effective method. Physical Hard drives are most often destroyed, while documents like reports, journals, articles, Compact Drives, and tapes are torn into very tiny pieces (Winter, 2013). This is recommended for sensitive data. But for Encrypted data, can be simply deleted by destroying the decryption keys, this assures that data can no longer be unreadable.

9. **Data Risk Assessments**, sensitive data should always be highly protected as compared to the low-risk data that may require less protection. The major motive for these assessments is the cost-benefit. However, it is necessary to understand what data needs to be highly protected. Data risk assessments identify critical data that is exposed and put a plan in place to avoid security breaches. These proactive measures provide timely prevention of Data loss that may later result to information breaches (Teymourlouei & Jackson, 2016).

10. **User Authentication** verifies whether the credentials of the user are valid like password authentication, two-factor authentication, and many more. Once you have these credentials are set by the authorized people like the database administrators. Passwords are the most basic form of authentication, however, even secret passwords are vulnerable to hacking by cybercriminals that use programs to generate several potential passwords to gain access. To lessen this risk, users have been tasked to choose secure passwords having both letters and numbers, upper and lower case, special characters i.e. (P@w0rd2020), and also avoid using shorter passwords. Two-factor authentication builds on passwords to create a more robust significantly protective solution to our data. It requires both a password and at point possession of a specific physical device like a mobile phone to gain access and login into the application for example latest update of WhatsApp mobile phone application, apple iCloud account login among many others.

OTHER DATA PROTECTION PRINCIPLES

According to the Data regulations in the European Union, they set the main principles that establish how data processing is performed, the privacy principles include;

1. **The lawfulness of Data Processing and Fair Processing:** Data must be processed lawfully, fairly, and transparently about the data subject. An individual or organization involved in data collection must identify valid grounds under the GDPR, the mission, and the purpose for collecting and us-

ing personal data. This means you must not process the data in a way that is unduly detrimental, unexpected, or misleading to the individuals concerned (Malgieri, 2020).

2. **Data transparency:** Personal data shall be processed lawfully, fairly, and transparently about the data subject ("lawfulness, fairness and transparency")). Data transparency means utilizing data with integrity so that data objects know what data is collected, the third parties involved during its storage process, who have access to it, and how they're able to interact with it. The Ag Data Transparent (ADT) organization has a mission to increase data transparency (Hong et al., 2015).

3. **Purpose Limitation:** Personal data shall be collected for specified, explicit, and legitimate purposes and not further processed in a method that is unsuited with those purposes; further processing for archiving purposes in the public interest, scientific or historical research purposes or statistical purposes shall.

4. **Data Minimization:** Personal data shall be adequate, relevant, and limited to what is necessary concerning the purposes for which they are processed. When an organization applies data minimization, any data processing performed will become so easy and will use the least amount of data necessary. Also, the data collected should not be used for any other purpose without agreement from the data subject from whom the data was collected.

5. **Data Storage Limitation:** Personal data shall be kept in a form that permits identification of data subjects for no longer than is necessary for the purposes for which the personal data are processed; personal data may be stored for longer periods insofar as the personal data will be processed solely for archiving purposes in the public interest. Organizations shouldn't keep personal data for longer than it is needed, else they should be able to justify why they need to store that personal data longer and have a data retention policy.

6. **Accuracy:** Personal data shall be accurate and, where necessary, kept up to date; every reasonable step must be taken to ensure that inaccurate personal data, having regard to the purposes for which they are processed, are erased or rectified without delay.

7. **Integrity and Confidentiality:** Personal data shall be processed in a manner that ensures appropriate security of the personal data, including protection against unauthorized or unlawful processing and accidental loss, destruction, or damage, using appropriate technical or organizational measures.

CHALLENGES OF DATA ACCESS, PRIVACY, AND PROTECTION

Several challenges have evolved since the 1980s of how we can access our data through different critical applications like WhatsApp (Determann, 2019; Kindt, 2016). A number of them have been addressed struggling to fulfill the needs of the megatrends like Big Data and Cloud Computing.

The development of Relational database systems started with structured Query Language (SQL) that was standardized and could support transactions in a very reliable fashion through what was called "ACID" compliance (Atomicity, Consistency, Isolation, and Durability), it provided a very reliable way dealing with data. Despite the fact, "ACID" compliance was not optimized neither to handle large transaction requests nor handle huge volumes of transactions. This was the greatest challenge in the 1980s.

In the 1990s and early 2000s with the advent of "NoSQL", multiple applications were used to access a database with new requirements for performance, scalability, and volume. The structure of their databases used to employ one of these several different storage models; key-value that was designed to handle massive amounts of data and Bigtable that was based on Google technology, these databases were scalable, but they were not standardized for optimized access methods like SQL. There best way to query was through the Representational State Transfer Application programming interface (REST API) and Web services. Each NoSQL database usually required an appropriate method to be accessed, this caused frequent API changes to applications when dealing with multiple databases.

Currently, multiple applications requiring access to multiple databases using alternate data storage models and different access methods are required. This introduced NewSQL to fulfill the gaps uncovered by NoSQL with better support for ACID transactions while retaining the performance and scalability characteristics. The greatest challenge is rewriting the means of how we access the data in the database. The current access method is a hybrid SQL that will require effort before more vendor tools and middleware drivers support it.

According to the National Academies Press (Council, 2003). They reviewed some of the technological methods for data management and storage that could advance the capability of users to search, query, subset, and access data, including some of the possible challenges in data availability and access. Among these challenges include;

1. The process of acquiring environmental data for research use was still problematic because users must first seek out the data they need, which is time-consuming and hard because there is no complete list of or universal access point to all state data holdings, hence high chances of missing key datasets.

2. Data search is not straightforward because query terms and measures differ from center to center, for users less knowledgeable about the datasets they want, will require help from the centers' customer service representatives.

3. Another challenge of data access for data centers is to distribute data only requested by the user, neither more nor less. This may be archived by performing sub-setting. Sub-setting involves extracting portions of data, such as time slices or spatially defined sections. It is particularly important in large datasets, such as those generated by remote sensing. However, despite consistent user demand, there continues to be a shortage of sub-setting tools (Council, 2003).

4. Obtaining data from users requires complex skills. Although frequent users typically become skillful at manipulating the infrastructure, access and retrieval methods differ from center to center, so even skilled users may be familiar with only one center's approach. Inexperienced users and investigators using several dissimilar data sources require a substantial investment of time to obtain data. Data centers offer multiple approaches of retrieving data in their holdings (for example file transfer protocol, which permits users to copy files stored on data center computers). This provides flexibility but confuses the retrieval process (Council, 2003).

5. Interdisciplinary users face the real challenge of assimilating dissimilar datasets usually obtained from diverse data centers. Data interoperability remains problematic because standards, formats, and metadata were selected to optimize the practicality of a particular dataset, rather than a collection of diverse data.

SOME NEW RESEARCH TRENDS IN DATA PRIVACY

Data privacy issues are a major concept especially in cloud platforms motivating some companies to build their clouds to escape these issues (Sen, 2015). The introduction of cloud computing introduced several risks, opportunities, and possibilities for innovations. These are defined as the new trends in data privacy. Under these research trends in data privacy, we focused on some of the relevant future solutions or developments that have been developed and their long-term effects. Common security issues around cloud computing are divided into four main categories (Sengupta et al., 2011), cloud infrastructure, data, access, and compliance. Our major focus is data privacy, focusing on data integrity, data lock-in, data remanence, provenance, data confidentiality, and user privacy-specific concerns.

Authentication and identity management: Users can easily access their personal information and make it available to various services across the Internet using an identity management (IDM) mechanism, it can authenticate users and services based on their credentials and characteristics. The existing password-based authentication systems have a limitation and pose significant risks. But an IDM-based system protects private and sensitive data or information related to users and processes (Sen, 2015).

Access control and accounting: Access control services should be flexible enough to capture dynamic, context, or attribute-or credential-based access requirements and to enforce the principle of least privilege. Such access control services might need to integrate privacy-protection requirements expressed through complex rules. It's important that the access control system employed in clouds is easily managed (Sen, 2015) and its privilege distribution is administered efficiently.

Consumer activism: Consumer awareness and involvement will create more meaning about data privacy, how it has been or will be applied and implemented in the future research trends. Consumers will become more eager to know how organizations or companies got their data i.e. how a consumer's email has been compromised to start receiving spam emails. Data breaches and data misuse court cases have all eroded the trust that individuals place in for-profit and non-profit entities. I firmly believe that this damage can be repaired, but it will take work on the part of organizations to win trust through transparency.

Ethical questions around automation: Data privacy around the automated disruptive technologies like IoT, mobile and wearable devices combined with machine learning and artificial intelligence is still encountering difficulties. In a way that some organizations are still profiting from the use of a person's information i.e. Facebook. Secondly, an ethical dilemma around anonymized data i.e. wearable health devices that track data patterns of an individual's healthy activity pattern, these results are analyzed anonymously by healthcare researchers using AI. If one of these researchers finds a correlation between a certain reading and a healthcare risk, is there an ethical obligation to then inform users who exhibit this pattern? But of course, if the data is all anonymized, this should not be possible.

CONCLUSION

Choosing the right data access protection method that is most suitable for your organization is highly paramount and may consider several factors basing on your organization. Additionally, implementing a data destruction policy is a must for all organizations for an assurance of free from data breaches. The challenges identified in this study require more advanced innovative solutions and technologies such as the logic used in blockchain technologies. In this chapter data access protection methods and some of the possible challenges have been provided to ensure secure data access. Information security should be considered and strategies laid before a company procures such gadgets and software environments. Once a secure platform is well laid, with considerations from physical security, then the road map to secure systems seems clear. In this, having a well-trained technical team is paramount and highly recommended for managing security on the individual hardware components, data residing on external media, software, configuring, and managing server requests among others. Once these kinds of safeguards are practiced, then a certain level of security is at least attained.

REFERENCES

Agrawal, M., & Mishra, P. (2012). A comparative survey on symmetric key encryption techniques. *International Journal on Computer Science and Engineering, 4*(5), 877.

Alsahafi, A. Y. A., & Gay, B. V. (2018). An overview of electronic personal health records. *Health Policy and Technology, 7*(4), 427–432. doi:10.1016/j.hlpt.2018.10.004

Bieker, F., Friedewald, M., Hansen, M., Obersteller, H., & Rost, M. (2016). A process for data protection impact assessment under the European general data protection regulation. *Annual Privacy Forum*, 21–37.

Borky, J. M., & Bradley, T. H. (2019). Protecting information with cybersecurity. In *Effective Model-Based Systems Engineering* (pp. 345–404). Springer. doi:10.1007/978-3-319-95669-5_10

Bygrave, L. A. (2002). *Data protection law*. Wolters Kluwer Law & Business.

Byun, J.-W., & Li, N. (2008). Purpose based access control for privacy protection in relational database systems. *The VLDB Journal—The International Journal on Very Large Data Bases, 17*(4), 603–619.

Cashell, B., Jackson, W. D., Jickling, M., & Webel, B. (2004). The economic impact of cyber-attacks. Congressional Research Service Documents, CRS RL32331, 2.

Cho, H., Im, J., & Kim, D. (2016). A metadata service architecture providing trusted data to global food service. *2016 IEEE World Congress on Services (SERVICES)*, 64–67. 10.1109/SERVICES.2016.39

Clark, D. (2010). Characterizing cyberspace: Past, present and future. *MIT CSAIL. Version, 1*, 2016–2028.

Council, N. R. (2003). *Government data centers: Meeting increasing demands*. National Academies Press.

Danezis, G., Domingo-Ferrer, J., Hansen, M., Hoepman, J.-H., Le Metayer, D., Tirtea, R., & Schiffner, S. (2015). Privacy and data protection by design-from policy to engineering. *ArXiv Preprint ArXiv:1501.03726*.

Dargan, S., & Kumar, M. (2020). A comprehensive survey on the biometric recognition systems based on physiological and behavioral modalities. *Expert Systems with Applications, 143*, 113114. doi:10.1016/j.eswa.2019.113114

de Arimatéia da Cruz, J. (2020). The Legislative Framework of the European Union (EU) Convention on Cybercrime. The Palgrave Handbook of International Cybercrime and Cyberdeviance, 223–237.

Determann, L. (2019). Privacy and Data Protection. *Московский Журнал Международного Права, 1*, 18–26.

Finnell, K. O. (1979). Computer Crime-Senate Bill S. 240. *Mem. St. UL Rev., 10*, 660.

Ganti, V., & Das Sarma, A. (2013). Data cleaning: A practical perspective. *Synthesis Lectures on Data Management, 5*(3), 1–85. doi:10.2200/S00523ED1V01Y201307DTM036

Gellert, R., & Gutwirth, S. (2013). The legal construction of privacy and data protection. *Computer Law & Security Review*, *29*(5), 522–530. doi:10.1016/j.clsr.2013.07.005

Hathaway, O. A., Crootof, R., Levitz, P., Nix, H., Nowlan, A., Perdue, W., & Spiegel, J. (2012). The law of cyber-attack. *California Law Review*, 817–885.

Hawkins, S. M., Yen, D. C., & Chou, D. C. (2000). Disaster recovery planning: A strategy for data security. *Information Management & Computer Security*, *8*(5), 222–230. doi:10.1108/09685220010353150

Höne, K., & Eloff, J. H. P. (2002). Information security policy—What do international information security standards say? *Computers & Security*, *21*(5), 402–409. doi:10.1016/S0167-4048(02)00504-7

Hong, H., Pradhan, B., Xu, C., & Bui, D. T. (2015). Spatial prediction of landslide hazard at the Yihuang area (China) using two-class kernel logistic regression, alternating decision tree and support vector machines. *Catena*, *133*, 266–281. doi:10.1016/j.catena.2015.05.019

Hua, J., & Bapna, S. (2013). The economic impact of cyber terrorism. *The Journal of Strategic Information Systems*, *22*(2), 175–186. doi:10.1016/j.jsis.2012.10.004

Huang, Z., Su, X., Zhang, Y., Shi, C., Zhang, H., & Xie, L. (2017). A decentralized solution for IoT data trusted exchange based-on blockchain. *2017 3rd IEEE International Conference on Computer and Communications (ICCC)*, 1180–1184.

Kaur, R., Singh, S., & Kumar, H. (2018). Rise of spam and compromised accounts in online social networks: A state-of-the-art review of different combating approaches. *Journal of Network and Computer Applications*, *112*, 53–88. doi:10.1016/j.jnca.2018.03.015

Kindt, E. J. (2016). *Privacy and data protection issues of biometric applications* (Vol. 1). Springer.

Kumar, P. R., & Deepamala, N. (2010). Design for implementing NetFlow using existing session tables in devices like Stateful Inspection firewalls and Load balancers. *Trendz in Information Sciences & Computing*, 210–213.

Lei, Y., & Yucong, D. (2021). Trusted Service Provider Discovery Based on Data, Information, Knowledge, and Wisdom. *International Journal of Software Engineering and Knowledge Engineering*, *31*(01), 3–19. doi:10.1142/S0218194021400015

Li, X., Liang, X., Lu, R., Shen, X., Lin, X., & Zhu, H. (2012). Securing smart grid: Cyber attacks, countermeasures, and challenges. *IEEE Communications Magazine*, *50*(8), 38–45. doi:10.1109/MCOM.2012.6257525

Makulilo, A. B. (2016). *African data privacy laws* (Vol. 33). Springer. doi:10.1007/978-3-319-47317-8

Malgieri, G. (2020). The concept of fairness in the GDPR: a linguistic and contextual interpretation. *Proceedings of the 2020 Conference on Fairness, Accountability, and Transparency*, 154–166. 10.1145/3351095.3372868

Mehmood, A., Natgunanathan, I., Xiang, Y., Hua, G., & Guo, S. (2016). Protection of big data privacy. *IEEE Access: Practical Innovations, Open Solutions*, *4*, 1821–1834. doi:10.1109/ACCESS.2016.2558446

Michael, K. (2016). RFID/NFC implants for bitcoin transactions. *IEEE Consumer Electronics Magazine, 5*(3), 103–106. doi:10.1109/MCE.2016.2556900

Mulligan, S. P., Freeman, W. C., & Linebaugh, C. D. (2019). *Data protection law: An overview.* R45631. Congressional Research Service. Https://Crsreports. Congress. Gov/Product/Pdf

Nambobi, M., Ruth, K., Alli, A. A., & Ssemwogerere, R. (2021). The Age of Autonomous Internet of Things Devices: Opportunities and Challenges of IoT. *Challenges and Opportunities for the Convergence of IoT, Big Data, and Cloud Computing,* 1–16.

Nambobi, M., Ssemwogerere, R., & Ramadhan, B. K. (2020). Implementation of Autonomous Library Assistants Using RFID Technology. In *Emerging Trends and Impacts of the Internet of Things in Libraries* (pp. 140–150). IGI Global. doi:10.4018/978-1-7998-4742-7.ch008

Oest, A., Safei, Y., Doupé, A., Ahn, G.-J., Wardman, B., & Warner, G. (2018). Inside a phisher's mind: Understanding the anti-phishing ecosystem through phishing kit analysis. *2018 APWG Symposium on Electronic Crime Research (ECrime),* 1–12. 10.1109/ECRIME.2018.8376206

Olenik, S., Lee, H. S., & Güder, F. (2021). The future of near-field communication-based wireless sensing. *Nature Reviews. Materials, 6*(4), 1–3. doi:10.103841578-021-00299-8 PMID:33680503

Ouaddah, A., Mousannif, H., Abou Elkalam, A., & Ouahman, A. A. (2017). Access control in the Internet of Things: Big challenges and new opportunities. *Computer Networks, 112,* 237–262. doi:10.1016/j.comnet.2016.11.007

Parn, E. A., & Edwards, D. (2019). Cyber threats confronting the digital built environment. *Engineering, Construction, and Architectural Management, 26*(2), 245–266. doi:10.1108/ECAM-03-2018-0101

Payne, S. (2007). Qualitative methods of data collection and analysis. *Research Methods in Palliative Care,* 139–161.

Ponemon Institute. (2013). 2013 Cost of Cyber Crime Study: Global Report. Technical Report October, Ponemon Institute.

Rahm, E., & Do, H. (2000). Data cleaning: Problems and current approaches. *IEEE Data Eng. Bull., 23*(4), 3–13. http://wwwiti.cs.uni-magdeburg.de/iti_db/lehre/dw/paper/data_cleaning.pdf%5Cnpapers2://publication/uuid/17B58056-3A7F-4184-8E8B-0E4D82EFEA1A%5Cnhttp://dc-pubs.dbs.uni-leipzig.de/files/Rahm2000DataCleaningProblemsand.pdf

Ren, W., Wan, X., & Gan, P. (2021). A double-blockchain solution for agricultural sampled data security in Internet of Things network. *Future Generation Computer Systems, 117,* 453–461. doi:10.1016/j.future.2020.12.007

Sarada, G., Abitha, N., Manikandan, G., & Sairam, N. (2015). A few new approaches for data masking. *2015 International Conference on Circuits, Power and Computing Technologies [ICCPCT-2015],* 1–4. 10.1109/ICCPCT.2015.7159301

Sen, J. (2015). Security and privacy issues in cloud computing. In *Cloud technology: concepts, methodologies, tools, and applications* (pp. 1585–1630). IGI Global. doi:10.4018/978-1-4666-6539-2.ch074

Sengupta, S., Kaulgud, V., & Sharma, V. S. (2011). Cloud computing security—trends and research directions. *2011 IEEE World Congress on Services*, 524–531. 10.1109/SERVICES.2011.20

Sharma, H., Meenakshi, E., & Bhatia, S. K. (2017). A comparative analysis and awareness survey of phishing detection tools. *2017 2nd IEEE International Conference on Recent Trends in Electronics, Information & Communication Technology (RTEICT)*, 1437–1442.

Somani, U., Lakhani, K., & Mundra, M. (2010). Implementing digital signature with RSA encryption algorithm to enhance the Data Security of cloud in Cloud Computing. *2010 First International Conference On Parallel, Distributed and Grid Computing (PDGC 2010)*, 211–216. 10.1109/PDGC.2010.5679895

Song, D., Shi, E., Fischer, I., & Shankar, U. (2012). Cloud data protection for the masses. *Computer*, *45*(1), 39–45. doi:10.1109/MC.2012.1

Stallings, W., & Brown, L. (2008). Computer security: Principles and practice. Pearson Education.

Stol, W., Leukfeldt, R., & Klap, H. (2013). 5 Policing a Digitized Society. *Cybercrime and the Police*, 61.

Sun, G.-Z., Dong, Y., Chen, D.-W., & Wei, J. (2010). Data backup and recovery based on data de-duplication. *2010 International Conference on Artificial Intelligence and Computational Intelligence*, *2*, 379–382. 10.1109/AICI.2010.200

Sun, Y., Zhang, J., Xiong, Y., & Zhu, G. (2014). Data security and privacy in cloud computing. *International Journal of Distributed Sensor Networks*, *10*(7), 190903. doi:10.1155/2014/190903

Teymourlouei, H., & Jackson, L. (2016). Detecting and preventing information security breaches. *Proceedings of the International Conference on Security and Management (SAM)*, 304.

Uma, M., & Padmavathi, G. (2013). A Survey on Various Cyber Attacks and their Classification. *International Journal of Network Security*, *15*(5), 390–396.

Union, T. (2001). International telecommunication union. *Yearbook of Statistics 1991–2000*.

Voigt, P., & Von dem Bussche, A. (2017). *The eu general data protection regulation (gdpr). A Practical Guide* (1st ed.). Springer International Publishing. doi:10.1007/978-3-319-57959-7

Watkins, B. (2014). The impact of cyber attacks on the private sector. *Briefing Paper. Association for International Affair*, *12*, 1–11.

Winter, R. (2013). SSD vs HDD–data recovery and destruction. *Network Security*, *2013*(3), 12–14. doi:10.1016/S1353-4858(13)70041-2

Withers, K. J. (2005). Electronically stored information: The December 2006 amendments to the federal rules of civil procedure. *Nw. J. Tech. & Intell. Prop.*, *4*, 171.

Yao-Huai, L. (2020). Privacy and data privacy issues in contemporary China. In *The Ethics of Information Technologies* (pp. 189–197). Routledge. doi:10.4324/9781003075011-14

Zhu, B., Joseph, A., & Sastry, S. (2011). A taxonomy of cyber attacks on SCADA systems. *2011 International Conference on Internet of Things and 4th International Conference on Cyber, Physical and Social Computing*, 380–388. 10.1109/iThings/CPSCom.2011.34

Chapter 3
Privacy and Other Legal Concerns in the Wake of Deepfake Technology:
Comparative Study of India, US, and China

Purva Kaushik

Amity Law School, Guru Gobind Singh Indraprastha University, Delhi, India

ABSTRACT

The world is filled with technology-driven systems and instruments in the present era. Artificial intelligence (hereinafter referred to as "AI") is increasingly dominating our everyday life. Deepfakes is one such AI-based technological innovation that is leading to huge concerns amongst legal and scientific experts. There have been recent instances wherein videos of statements never made and acts never done by public figures became viral on the internet. Face swap in videos is easily done for the purpose of cyber bullying and harassment of innocent victims. Since creation of these synthetic contents called deepfakes is becoming easier by the day, the growing concerns surrounding them demand immediate attention. This chapter shall specifically probe into the deepfake technology with dual objectives (i.e., to understand the causes of concern surrounding deepfakes related AI-technology and to compare effective ideas and regulatory measures of nations abroad such as US and China) in order to arrive at possible solutions to appropriately tackle this issue in India.

INTRODUCTION

The goal of this chapter is to understand the potential risks involved in the use of deepfake technology. There is an old saying - "Seeing is believing". However, in the wake of the advancing deepfake technology, it could be dangerous for individuals as well as society to believe in what they view. Considering the fact that detection and regulatory measures concerning deepfakes are still in their nascent stage throughout the world, it is pertinent to be well aware of our technological and legal capabilities in the fight against this hazard. For the same purpose, the laws and regulatory frameworks of US and China

DOI: 10.4018/978-1-7998-8641-9.ch003

shall also be analysed since these nations have proactively taken techno-legal measures to curb the havoc that deepfakes are capable of creating. Based on our critical understanding of these measures, we would be better equipped to look for solutions in the Indian set-up.

In order to reach solutions, we need to first understand the problem at hand. It all starts with the increasing involvement of social media platforms in the preceding decade. As a result, uploading of digital images and videos is trending worldwide. This has further led to creation of a significant number of new image/video-altering techniques and apps. In the given backdrop, deepfake origination took place.

Deepfakes have a close nexus with Digital Image Forensics Research Field. The term "deepfakes" is derived from a deep understanding of the technology that is required for creation of very realistic fake videos and images. Original faces, expressions and even voices are mimicked, altered and replaced by fake ones, thereby breaching social trust and creating privacy and other legal concerns. A deepfake is a product of AI and advanced machine learning algorithm called *deep learning*. It utilizes Generative Adversarial Networks (hereinafter referred to as "GAN") for morphing original content. Simply understood, the role of GAN is to train two neural net architectures i.e., a generator (decoder) and a discriminator in an adversarial relationship (Smith & Mansted, 2020). Once the encoder has extracted the latent features of original face images, the generator (decoder) reconstructs the images and the discriminator detects whether or not the image created by generator is extremely real looking.

In this way, the generator-discriminator paired algorithms constantly compete against each other and constantly evolve. As a result, any defects in a deepfake can be instantly detected and corrected, thereby making this technology difficult to combat. Recently, multi-task Convolutional Neural Networks (hereinafter referred to as "CNN") have been developed to increase the stability of face detection and reliability of face alignment in deepfakes. It involves image mapping wherein initially the algorithms used to work on massive data sets to extract, train and create content (Gerstner, 2020). However, with the constant advancements in this technology, now even a single image can be used to render a high quality deepfake which is difficult to detect by humans as well as machines. Another characteristic of this technology is that it requires very little skill and renders quick results in the form of extremely deceptive fake content.

Morphed images and videos are not new to this world, but extremely real looking ones are a recent development. It wasn't until 2017, when the first public example of deepfakes surfaced that experts from the technological and legal field started viewing them as a threat. In this case, the faces of Hollywood celebrities were extracted from original images and superimposed onto faces of pornographic actresses by some anonymous users of the online platform of Reddit. Apart from that, certain non-pornographic deepfakes were also created by swapping the face of Nicholas Cage into numerous movie videos, though this was purely meant for entertainment purposes. This led to widespread circulation of deepfakes, thereby turning it into a new trend. In 2018, apps such as DeepNude and FakeApp surfaced which provided both free and paid platform to users for creating deepfakes and thereby harassing, blackmailing, bullying targets and spreading fake news (Schick, 2020). In the past 4 years, multiple apps have been created and made easily available to the public at large for creating deepfakes.

Deepfakes can be broadly divided into four categories based on the method of creation employed, namely – (1) *Image deepfake* which employs the method of face and body swapping;

(2) *Audio deepfake* which employs text-to-speak and voice swapping methods; (3) *Video deepfake* which employs face-morphing and face-swapping methods; and (4) *Audio-visual deepfake* which employs lip-syncing in addition to the abovementioned methods (Kietzmann, McCarthy & Lee, 2019). Some other categories of audio-visual manipulations include '*cheap fakes*' and '*shallow fakes*'. Contrastingly, the process of creation of fake contents like cheap fakes and shallow fakes does not involve the utilisation

of AI. These are created by humans through software editing tools which use techniques of speeding up, slowing down, recontextualizing the images or audio-visual content to deceive the target audience.

BACKGROUND

In this section, some crucial causes of concern surrounding deepfake technology have been extensively discussed and substantiated by real instances that occurred in the recent past. These concerns are based on both, public and private interests of society and individuals.

Causes of Concern Surrounding Deepfake Technology

The fast emergence of new and advanced technologies including apps such as Reface, Avatarify, Wombo have made it quite easy for anybody, even any iphone/ android user, to create deepfake videos. As a result, it becomes extremely difficult to detect such videos since the law fails to keep pace with the advancing technologies. A fake video created by deepfake technology cannot be banned or regulated unless detected. That is a major concern in the legal arena. It is further pertinent to mention that it is extremely difficult to detect the perpetrator who originally created a viral deepfake video. Some particular concerns which make the society fearful of deepfakes are as follows -

Privacy Concerns

Since deepfakes are so realistic, people can easily trust and rely on the information provided by fake persons in such videos, thereby persuading the victims to loosen up their guard and reveal private data and information to the perpetrator. Even detection techniques invented to deal with the deepfake menace tend to infringe upon the privacy of the internet users at large. In 2019, one of the first effective solutions to the issue of deepfakes was invented and publicised by Danielle Citron and Robert Chesney in Boston University, US. This was famously called the "authenticated alibi service." Theoretically, the purpose of this service is to disprove the claims made via deepfakes. This service creates digital life-logs which track the individuals and their online activities (Jing & Murugesan, 2020).

This means that the online activities of the individuals would be under constant surveillance. On the same grounds, it was met with global criticism as it tends to violate individuals' right to privacy in lieu of a potential solution to misinformation spread through deepfakes. The thought behind this idea was further indicative of how the concerned authorities are willing to compromise the privacy of individuals to evade the potential risks posed by deepfakes. In India, the right to privacy is recognized as a fundamental right impliedly present in Article 21 of the Indian Constitution. The Apex court in the landmark case of *Justice K.S. Puttaswamy (Retd.) v. Union of India* (2017 10 SCC 1) upheld that "informational privacy" in specific is part and parcel of the right to privacy under Article 21.

This means that every individual would have control over the circulation of any material which is personal to him/her. This further means that informational privacy would cover digital privacy as well, thereby providing a protective shield to individuals as regards their right to privacy on digital platforms. It is only after obtaining their consent that any digital content, original or manipulated, can be created and disseminated on social media.

Pornography Concerns

Face swap in pornographic content can easily create fake porn that can appear chillingly realistic, thereby harming the reputation of innocent victims. All that the perpetrator requires is a video/ image of the victim to be merged, combined or superimposed on a video to make it appear authentic. The original videos/images which are required to create deepfakes can be easily accessed from the social media account of the targeted victim. You will come across deepfake pornography mainly bifurcated into two categories – *Firstly*, celebrities' faces swapped onto pornographic videos they never participated in. This serves the audiences having celebrity fetish. There are thousands of such fake celebrity porn clips on various porn sites created using deepfake technology and depicting Hollywood and Bollywood actresses.

Secondly, revenge porn as the name suggests is created with the purpose of seeking revenge from the person depicted in such videos. It involves face swapping to make it appear as if the victim was part of a pornographic content, though he/she was not. Anyone with a fair understanding of AI can now create deepfake porn using the software apps freely available for this purpose today. To prevent widespread uploading and downloading of malicious deepfake porn, Google followed the lead of Twitter and Reddit in September, 2018 and added "involuntary synthetic pornographic imagery" to its ban list (Gieseke, 2020). It further permitted the persons depicted in such video clips containing their deceptive sexually explicit footage, to report such content so that it can be promptly blocked.

A classic example of revenge porn can be cited from India in 2018. A famous Indian journalist Rana Ayyub was threatened, harassed and humiliated by swapping her face onto a pornographic clip and making it appear as if she had acted in that clip, though she had not. Apparently, this sexually explicit video slip was virulently circulated because she had criticized some local BJP leaders of Jammu for supporting the accused persons in the gang rape case of an 8-year-old girl child, famously known as the *Kathua rape case* in Kashmir. In addition to the heinousness of the crime, religious differences and outrage had seeped into the case as the rape victim was a Muslim girl and the accused persons were Hindus by religion.

National and Social Security Concerns

The spread of fake news created through AI-based deepfake technology can be a threat to national security and social order. Statements depicted to have been made by a public figure/ Government official in a deepfake video can trigger war crimes with enemy nations and even internal disturbance/ armed conflicts within the nation. With the bona fide purpose of demonstrating the potential risks and future of fake news in the wake of deepfake technology, Buzzfeed used the voice of the American writer and director, Jordan Peele to create a fake manipulated video depicting the former President of US, Barack Obama as cursing and calling out the then sitting President of US, Donald Trump. They immediately revealed that the video clip was synthetically created by using AI-enabled deepfake technology. Through the means of deepfake technology, terrorists and insurgent groups can portray their adversaries as making statements that might hurt the sentiments of certain religious or caste-based communities (Vaccari & Chadwick, 2020). Such an issue would adversely affect the law-and-order situation in the society.

Concerns Relating to Authenticity of Video Evidence

In the wake of deepfake videos and the uncertain accuracy of detecting techniques, it becomes extremely difficult to determine the authenticity of video evidence produced in legal proceedings. The "Silent

Witness Theory" permits the courts to accept photographic/video evidence even without verification of its genuineness by eye-witnesses, provided that the process used to create it is reliable. Tampering with videos and morphing their content is easily enabled in today's age of AI. This further opens the door for genuine cases with legitimate video-recorded evidence being looked down upon with suspicion. This technology not only erodes the probative value of video evidences in court proceedings, but it also reduces the trust of the courts in the genuine and authentic pieces of digital evidence that might have otherwise proved to be quite crucial to the proceedings in court (Maras & Alexandrou, 2019).

The existence of deepfake technology would be a treat for the advocates of real perpetrators as it would allow them to grab the opportunity to falsely claim that the authentic pieces of video evidence produced digitally are either forged or morphed or synthetically created. It could act as a serious threat to the law and justice enforcement machinery as spotting the difference between real and fake evidence would become close to impossible, considering the constantly evolving technology used in deepfakes which produces high quality fake content that is getting better by the day.

Legal Measures Undertaken by US and China

In this section, an attempt will first be made by the author to discuss the reasons behind reluctance on the part of nations to outrightly ban deepfakes altogether. Thereafter, we shall delve into the existing legal measures that have been imposed by US and China. It is pertinent to deeply study such laws in order to decide if the same or similar laws could possibly be implemented in India in the near future to avoid threat to social stability and national security. The possibility of meaningful deterrence via imposition of civil and/or criminal liability will also be ventured in this section.

Issues with a Blanket Ban

When it comes to technological tools, outrightly imposing a blanket ban on particular activities is never the best solution. Instead, it is through effective regulatory measures that the socio-legal issues can be tackled most efficiently. In the case of deepfake technology and its usage, there are three extremely significant considerations which are convincing enough against a complete ban, namely – *Firstly*, it is highly difficult to distinguish between original content and deepfake content. As a result, detection becomes close to impossible. Unless detected, any legal measure banning deepfakes wouldn't be fully operational and effective; *Secondly*, a complete ban on deepfake content would be violative of the freedom of expression of individuals at large. Article 19 of the Universal Declaration of Human Rights (hereinafter referred to as "UDHR") and International Covenant on Civil and Political Rights (hereinafter referred to as "ICCPR") provide for the right to freedom of expression to individuals globally; *Thirdly*, like any other tool, deepfake technology is not causing harm in all cases, but rather it has proven to have beneficial utility in some situations. It plays a key role in routine modifications thereby improving the overall clarity of content on the digital platforms.

Nowadays, audio-visual deepfakes involving lip-syncing can be created, thereby allowing the conversion of advertisements and other videos in different languages without the efforts of re-shooting several times. For instance, David Beckham's announcement for the 'Malaria Must Die campaign' was created in nine different languages using deepfake technology to increase the reach of the message. This is a perfect example to show that deepfakes have made the issue of bad dubbing and language barriers a thing of the past with its high quality real looking content creation skill. Furthermore, deepfakes can be used as a double-edged sword to give the video gamers and movie audience an excellent experience by providing a platform for the creation of videos and video games with high quality VFX technology at an accelerated speed and pocket-friendly costs (Smith & Mansted, 2020). By democratizing the extremely costly VFX technology in this manner, deepfakes can make it a win-win situation for both the creators and the audience.

Another advantage of deepfakes is that it can allow the viewers to experience watching and interacting with famous fictional or dead personalities as if they were alive. The entertainment and cultural industry can flourish by the usage of deepfakes as happened in the Dali Museum, Florida wherein people brought the famous Spanish artist Salvador Dali back to life with the help of deepfake technology and allowed the museum visitors to watch, interact and click pictures with the long-gone famous artist. Similarly, Mona Lisa was also brought to life using this AI-generated synthetic technology in Samsung AI laboratory, Moscow, thereby astonishing the visitors (Kietzmann, McCarthy & Lee, 2019). For the same reasons, no country has imposed a complete legal ban on deepfakes as yet. In the following section, the legislative actions of US and China against misuse of deepfakes have been critically analyzed in detail.

Existing Legal Measures in US

One of the major problems with the pace with which technology grows and develops is that it is always ahead of the present laws. However, that shouldn't stop the state authorities from creating laws to deal with violation of rights and offences caused via technology. Currently, no law in India or abroad puts a flat ban on deepfake creation and distribution. Laws must be drafted after extensive deliberations, opinion sharing and research, especially when the intent is to deal with an emerging technology. US is one of the first few nations to respond to the issue of deepfakes.

In the US, until now, the age-old law of *Communications Decency Act, 1996* under its Section 230 provided immunity from liability to digital media platforms, with few exceptions as in the case of violation of intellectual property laws, the criminal laws and the Electronic Communications Privacy Act. Recently, the US government has passed certain laws to regulate the use of deepfake content, but these Federal legislations were made hurriedly and the same is evident in their poorly drafted provisions. The *Malicious Deep Fake Prohibition Act, 2018* passed by the US Senate is one such law. This Act makes it an offence to create a deepfake with the malicious intent to facilitate a criminal or tortious conduct and to distribute it with the same intent. The purpose could be related to conducts of this nature under the Federal, State, local or even Tribal law. The issue with this law is that the conduct proposed to be prohibited by this law is already prohibited under the existing laws in US. The only additional step taken by this Act is to make the punishment more severe (O'Donnell, 2021).

Furthermore, the *DEEPFAKES Accountability Act, 2019* (acronym for "Defending Each and Every Person from False Appearances by Creating Exploitative Subject to Accountability Act") is another legislation added to combat the menace of deepfakes. Even the title of the act appears to be vague and uncertain in nature. Under this Act, the creators of any AI-based fake content are required to mention their name and disclose the fact of its fakeness very prominently for the viewers to know. One major problem with this law is that it fails to take into account the obvious fact that the creators who would voluntarily add their name to the content and also make a declaration regarding any manipulation using AI are not the kind of creators we must be worrying about. This law would tend to target the beneficial or harmless deepfakes created by youtubers, digital artists and videographers, etc.

Evading this law would still be possible for the creators of malicious deepfakes who create pornographic or political deepfakes meant to incite violence or violate the privacy rights of individuals. However, this doesn't bring us to the conclusion that the *DEEPFAKES Accountability Act* serves no purpose at all. It does bring on record for the public to know and understand as to what is permissible and what is prohibited. Detection of malicious deepfakes might be close to impossible since law is always two steps behind technology. However, if and when a malicious deepfake is detected, this law gives the authorities a high level of certainty regarding the legal provisions that the creator and distributor of deepfakes may be charged under and made liable. Several states such as Texas, California and New York have introduced State legislations dealing with deepfakes. California is the first state in US to pass laws to regulate the use of deepfake technology.

In California, two State bills were signed into law by Governor Gavin Newsom in 2019, namely - Assembly Bill No. 602 (hereinafter referred to as "AB 602") and Assembly Bill No. 730 (hereinafter referred to as "AB 730"). The purpose was to give a legal recourse to victims of pornographic and political deepfakes respectively. AB 602 provides a private cause of action to victims of deepfakes with pornographic/sexually explicit content against the creator of such content. AB 730, on the other hand, is added to the California Election Code to target deepfakes created with malice to spread fake political news. More specifically, AB 730 gives a cause of action to candidates on the ballot within 60 days of their election, in case the deepfake was created and distributed with the malicious intent to injure the reputation of such candidate or to deceive the voters to vote/refrain from voting in favor of such candidate (Citron & Chesney, 2019). The new law in Texas relating to use of political deepfakes is quite similar to the AB 730 in California, with but one point of distinction i.e., the Texas law provides a cause of action to candidates on the ballot within 30 days of election, instead of 60 days.

Existing Legal Measures in China

China also took proactive steps to control the fast developing and unregulated use of deepfake technology. Deepfakes were already infamous in China for their notorious nature, but the incoming of an app named Zao further added to the havoc. This app allowed the people in China to swap their faces with those of celebrities not only in images, but in videos as well. Eventually, people noticed that the terms and conditions of Zao app were a cause of privacy concerns since it permitted the developers of the app to use and share any content created by users on the app with third parties without the consent of users. Further, the smile-to-pay service of Alipay app permitted bank transactions based on face recognition. As a result, any user of both the apps i.e., Zao and Alipay could easily become a victim of financial frauds if a third party who got access to the user's image through Zao uses it to make payments on Alipay (Zhao, Ge, Li, Wang & Ming, 2019).

Considering the nuisance caused abruptly by millions of deepfakes created using the Zao app in China, the Cyberspace Administration of China (hereinafter referred to as "CAC") passed the law criminalizing deepfakes in 2019. According to this law, deepfake creation, publication and distribution is made a criminal offence, if done by any person without appropriate disclosure (Hao, 2021). This essentially means that every person publishing a synthetically created fake footage, including deepfakes was required to clearly notify the viewers regarding its fakeness. The rule became effective from the beginning of 2020. The Government of China can now prosecute both the online platforms and the users in case they fail to abide by the law. However, enforcement related questions still remain unanswered as deepfakes are notoriously difficult to detect. Unless detected, culpability is questionable.

Another criticism of this law is that it might not be effective against the actual malicious deepfakes, since those deepfake creators who intend to cause harm would nevertheless intentionally skip the step requiring declaration of fakeness. The target of this law would be limited to harmless deepfakes intended for bona fide purposes such as art, entertainment, education, etc. So, it would tend to fail in fulfilling the main objective for which it is designed, i.e., taking down harmful deceptive synthetic content created using deepfake technology.

Unregulated Use of Deepfake Technology in India

India is a country with very diverse religions, cultures, castes and languages. To maintain peace and tranquility is a challenge for the government at times. In such a socio-cultural set up, fake news which is spread like wild fire in the age of social media, can trigger violence and riots. Fake news circulation is quite rampant at the time of political election campaigns. India is already battling a baggage of fake news which are mostly spread through WhatsApp. As the number of WhatsApp users increases in India, so does the fake news. Such news can trigger enmity between the communities and thereby trigger violence and disrupt the law-and-order situation. Considering this situation, it gives all the more reason for Indian law-makers to give more importance to regulation of deepfake circulation. However, the use of deepfake technology is still clearly going unregulated.

No new laws have been introduced to tackle the misuse of deepfake technology. The already existing laws i.e., the *Information Technology Act, 2000* (hereinafter referred to as the "*IT Act, 2000*") and rules made thereunder, the criminal laws and the tort law are struggling to provide legal recourse to the aggrieved persons. In this section, the author shall highlight the present laws providing legal recourses, though insufficiently, against the misuse of deepfakes in India. The most relevant legislation in this regard is the *IT Act, 2000*. Any instances of misuse of digital media with malicious intent falls under its purview. Any publication of sexually explicit material in digital form is made punishable under Section 67 and 67A of the *IT Act, 2000*. These provisions would cover deceptive deepfakes with celebrity faces swapped and revenge porn as well (Chadha, Kumar, Kashyap & Gupta, 2021).

If the individual depicted in the pornographic deepfake is a child, it becomes an offence under section 67B of the *IT Act, 2000*. Section 67C of the Act is attracted if the malicious deepfake contains the electronic signatures or any other similar unique identification feature of a person, provided that the same is obtained dishonestly/ fraudulently. Under this provision, the perpetrator would be held liable for identity theft. Further, Section 66D is attracted if the deepfake video is enabling the creator to commit cheating by impersonation. The Central Government can also intervene under the Act and direct the intermediary platform to block the public access of any malicious deepfakes if it deems it necessary to protect sovereignty of India, security of the state, public interest and friendly relations with neighboring countries.

Additionally, the victims of malicious deepfakes can also seek civil or criminal remedy for defamation. Under the *Indian Penal Code, 1860* (hereinafter referred to as "*IPC*"), Section 499 is attracted to make the perpetrator liable for defamation. The tort law also provides for civil remedy against defamation in the form of damages to the victim. Section 468 of the *IPC* which makes forgery punishable is also attracted if the deepfakes are created by turning the original content into its forged versions, thereby harming the reputation or property of the victim with a malicious intent. Despite all these legal remedies, the cases of misuse of deepfakes still remains unregulated for two simple reasons – *Firstly*, detection of deceptive deepfakes require expert supervision and surveillance. Until that is achievable, the role of any legal provisions meant for establishing the culpability and liability stand redundant.

Secondly, deepfakes have technical advancements to such an extent that even post-detection, regular cyber laws will not suffice to establish culpability and liability. This is so because the evidentiary value of proofs submitted, witness reliability, proof of mens rea, etc. all require specialist treatment and deepfake-specific techno-legal know-how in the entire course of legal proceedings. Therefore, advanced and specialized laws meant solely for the regulation of deepfakes is the need of the hour. To cater to the privacy concerns in India, the Personal Data Protection Bill, 2019 is also pending in the Parliament. A Joint Committee of Parliament has been set up to submit its report on the Bill. The Bill seeks to regulate the usage of individual's data by the private companies as well as the Government authorities. This means that personal data including the original images and videos of the individuals in electronic form would be protected under the provisions of the Bill, if passed by the Parliament. This further means that the Bill would protect individuals against the creation and dissemination of manipulated forms of their personal images and videos created through deepfake technology.

The rampant use of deepfakes can be witnessed in the fake pornographic clips depicting the A-list Bollywood celebrities and revenge porn victims circulated across the globe on several adult content sites. These deepfakes are concerning and extremely powerful since they seem to be very real. The fast-paced deepfake technology has recently disturbed the Indian politics and election campaigns as well. Though deepfakes haven't adversely affected the Indian politics to a great extent, its high potential is such that its misuse cannot be underestimated. The first ever case of use of deepfakes in Indian elections was witnessed during the Delhi Assembly elections in 2020.

In this case, two deepfake video clips (one in English and the other in Haryanvi, to increase the reach of the video to several potential voters) of the BJP member, Manoj Tiwari were created by the Delhi BJP IT cell with assistance from political communications firm Ideaz Factory. The purpose was to make it appear as if he was criticizing his opponent, the Chief Minister of Delhi, Arvind Kejriwal for all the false and unfulfilled promises made in his election campaigns. In the original video, Manoj Tiwari was actually speaking in Hindi and that too on an altogether different issue. In a public interview, Neelkant Bakshi, the co-incharge of Delhi BJP IT cell, even praised the deepfake technology for its positive role in the election campaigns. He added that it helped a great deal in approaching the target audience (potential voters of Delhi who spoke English or Haryanvi) even though the depicted candidate for election did not actually speak in those languages. This got the political leaders and technological experts deeply worried about the future flood of deepfakes and the chaos it was capable of creating.

SOLUTIONS AND RECOMMENDATIONS

Advanced detection techniques clubbed with stringent regulatory laws are the only tools for the containment of the ever-expanding deepfake technology, its misuse and adverse effects.

Advanced Detection Techniques

Earlier, when the deepfake technology had not advanced enough, detection of fakeness was even possible by the naked eye upon close examination. Pattern recognition was one of the most commonly used methods for deepfake detection a few years back. Significant difference in facial expressions could be caught between two adjacent frames in deepfake videos. There used to be no visibly natural transformation. Furthermore, any manipulation by synthetic media was quite evident. But as the deepfake technology has advanced for creation, the detection techniques have necessarily become advanced. Today, the detection techniques also involve the assistance of AI and deep learning. The techniques of detection can be categorised into learning-based and biological signal-based in nature. A few subtle indicators of deepfake have been suggested by the Media Forensic Experts as well, such as lighting inconsistencies, blurred edges, unnatural eye direction and blurred/missing facial features.

In 2018, David Guera and Edward Delp theorized that there are often inconsistencies between frames in deepfake videos. In order to detect such discrepancies, they proposed a structure for the study and processing of the frame sequences in the videos, commonly known today as *Temporal Sequential Analysis*. Another detection technique for deepfakes, the *Capsule Networks*, though invented long back in 2011, was improved in 2018-19 by Hinton and others, thereby making it more all the more effective. *Blockchain technology* can also act as an effective tool to detect deepfake content and further regulate its use (Fairfield, 2021). Apart from detection techniques, the users of social media platforms must be asked to keep their original content recorded so as to avail the alibi service by providing the recording as evidence and seeking deniability from the deepfake.

Stringent Regulatory Laws

Putting a blanket ban on deepfake content would be directly hit by Article 19(1)(a) in Part III of the Indian Constitution which provides for the fundamental right to freedom of speech and expression. Instead of banning deepfakes, the more feasible and constitutionally permissible option is to make stringent and effective regulatory laws. Of course, it would be difficult to detect deepfakes for proper regulation, but it won't be impossible.

Based on the comparative study of Indian laws with those of US and China, it becomes aptly clear that the present laws available in India would not suffice to deal with the cases concerning malicious deepfakes. Therefore, in addition to the need to frame separate laws to regulate deepfakes, the law agencies must also hold the social media platforms accountable. This would promote responsibility in posting content on social media (Fairfield, 2021). It would then create a shared responsibility between the users and the social media platform provider. These platform providers would then proactively keep a check on the content being posted by their users, and get rid of it as soon as some suspicious content is detected. Such a step would enhance the accountability of both the direct party as well as the indirect party, thereby reducing the risk posed by deepfakes to a great number of people.

The new IT rules of 2021 try to create liability of digital media platforms and OTT platforms in cases of violation of users' rights. These rules provide for appointment of a Resident Grievance Officer who would closely and actively monitor the content on such platforms. There are two additional problems that would be resolved to a great extent, given that the digital platform providers are also held liable to the extent that they permitted circulation of illegal content on their platform. To explain the first problem, if the distributors of deepfake content are careful enough, they tend to circulate it while maintaining their own anonymity. For the purpose of anonymous circulation, they use technologies such as *Tor*, but not limited to it. Now the use of these technologies is met with the result that the IP addresses that have a nexus with the posts is often lost, thereby making it impossible to trace the post back to the originating party (Feeney, 2021). In such cases, the victims of deepfakes have no practical legal recourse against the creator. So, they are left with no choice, but to prosecute the social media platform provider for the violation of their rights.

The second obstacle that would be overcome by holding the intermediary platforms liable relates to jurisdictional issues. This arises when the creator or digital platform provider is outside the jurisdictional limits of the particular nation wherein the cause of action has arisen. As a result, the legal process prescribed for providing relief to the victim cannot be effectively utilized against the perpetrator, even though their identity is well-known to the legal authorities. Such is the global reach of deepfakes, at times far and beyond the scope of legislative outreach. At least, the social media platform which allowed the dissemination can be held accountable in such cases. The Indian Parliament must learn from the mistakes made by the legislative authorities of US and China. Based on legal borrowings from these and other countries, the law-making agencies in India must draft a specific legislation (in addition to the present laws including the new IT Rules, 2021), which would particularly deal with the various concerns surrounding deepfakes. It must extensively clarify the doubts regarding definitions and concepts, the stakeholders involved, rights and duties of such stakeholders, authorities and agencies responsible and the offences and penalties.

FUTURE RESEARCH DIRECTIONS

In this chapter, the author has essentially focused on constitutional and criminal law violations. Issues related to privacy concerns, national security concerns, concerns relating to deepfake pornography and those relating to video evidence production in courts have been discussed. The domain of intellectual property rights, more specifically copyright infringement concerns has not been ventured. However, they are also extremely significant since the source images and videos altered using deepfake technology are subject to copyright at times. Based on the interests of future researchers, copyright infringement aspect of deepfakes might be explored and potential solutions in the form of regulatory framework and legal recourse might be suggested.

Presently, not many nations have particularly addressed the misuse of deepfakes since it is in its nascent stage and surrounded with uncertainty. Therefore, the scope for comparative research would undoubtedly increase in the coming future, for researchers to derive the most suitable technological and legal borrowings. As the new technological innovations come about, the detection techniques and regulatory laws will also evolve. Future researchers may soon have a plethora of new data to analyze and come up with conclusions regarding the future prospects of this infamous technological revolution.

CONCLUSION

It is well settled that deepfakes are nothing more than lies which have had a technological twist. They may cause harm to individuals and society at large in an extremely magnified form. In order to become well-equipped with information about deepfakes, this chapter has shared some significant insights for a clear understanding of the process of deepfake creation. The author has highlighted the technological and legal concerns surrounding deepfakes. The effect of deepfakes on politics, social media, etc. have been discussed. It can be concluded that deepfakes depicting political news might not really deceive the public, but it does bring uncertainty and confusion into their minds, which further reduces their general trust on the news circulated in social media, even if it is authentic. That said, it is pertinent that we keep a check on the content shared on digital platforms for viewers to see. Thereafter, a general overview of methods of detection employed for regulating the misuse of deepfake technology have been discussed.

Additionally, the legal rules and regulations provided in US and China to fight against deepfakes have been critically analyzed in order to come up with innovative and effective legal measures to be implemented in India for the prevention of large-scale adverse effects of deepfakes. Like any other technology-driven tool, deepfakes as extensively discussed in this chapter, have both positive and negative impacts. The suggestions and recommendations given in this chapter would be helpful in detection and regulation of deepfakes. However, this constantly evolving technology motivates the law-makers to bring new legislations to keep up with its pace. They are required to specially target only that sub-category of deepfakes which has the effect of inflicting harm upon individual rights or social security through morphed pornographic video clips, political deepfake dissemination or the like.

Apart from the technological and legal solutions to malicious deepfakes, on an individual level, we must sensitize the public about the existence of such a technology on the one hand. We must teach the youth not to blindly trust any news or video we see on social media unless it is coming from an authentic source or is verified by an authentic source. On the other hand, we must bear in mind that our right to freedom of expression ends where it starts infringing upon the right to privacy of other individuals.

REFERENCES

Chadha, A., Kumar, V., Kashyap, S., & Gupta, M. (2021). Deepfake: An Overview. In *Proceedings of Second International Conference on Computing, Communication, and Cyber Security* (pp. 557-565). Springer. 10.1007/978-981-16-0733-2_39

Citron, D. K., & Chesney, R. (2019). Deep Fakes: A Looming Challenge for Privacy, Democracy, and National Security. *California Law Review, 107*, 1753–1801.

Fairfield, J. A. T. (2021). *Runaway Technology: Can Law Keep Up?* Cambridge University Press. doi:10.1017/9781108545839

Feeney, M. (2021). *Deepfake Laws Risk Creating More Problems Than They Solve*. Regulatory Transparency Project of the Federalist Society. https://regproject.org/wp-content/uploads/Paper-Deepfake-Laws-Risk-Creating-More-Problems-Than-They-Solve.pdf

Gerstner, E. (2020). Face/Off: "Deepfake" Face Swaps and Privacy Laws. *Defense Counsel Journal, 87*(1), 1–14.

Gieseke, A. (2020). "The Weapon of Choice": Law's Current Inability to Properly Address Deepfake Pornography. *Vanderbilt Law Review, 73*(5), 1479–1516.

Hao, K. (2021). Deepfake Porn is Ruining Women's Lives. Now the Law may finally ban it. *MIT Technology Review*. https://www.technologyreview.com/2021/02/12/1018222/deepfake-revenge-porn-coming-ban/

Jing, T. W., & Murugesan, R. K. (2020). Protecting Data Privacy and Prevent Fake News and Deepfakes in Social Media via Blockchain Technology. In *International Conference on Advances in Cyber Security* (pp. 674-684). Springer.

Kietzmann, J., McCarthy, I. P., & Lee, L. W. (2019 in press). *Deepfakes: Trick or Treat*. Kelley School of Business, Indiana University Press.

Maras, M. H., & Alexandrou, A. (2019). Determining Authenticity of Video Evidence in the Age of Artificial Intelligence and in the Wake of Deepfake Videos. *International Journal of Evidence and Proof*, *23*(3), 255–262. doi:10.1177/1365712718807226

O'Donnell, N. (2021). Have We No Decency? Section 230 and the Liability of Social Media Companies for Deepfake Videos. *University of Illinois Law Review, 2021*(2), 701–ii.

Schick, N. (2020). *Deep Fakes and the Infocalypse: What You Urgently Need to Know*. Octopus Publishing Group.

Smith, H., & Mansted, K. (2020). What's a Deep Fake. Australian Strategic Policy Institute.

Vaccari, C., & Chadwick, A. (2020). Deepfakes and Disinformation: Exploring the Impact of Synthetic Political Video on Deception, Uncertainty and Trust in News. *Safe Journal*, *6*(1), 1–13. doi:10.1177/2056305120903408

Zhao, Y., Ge, W., Li, W., Wang, R., Zhao, L., & Ming, J. (2019). Capturing the Persistence of Facial Expression Features for Deepfake Video Detection. In *International Conference on Information and Communications Security* (pp. 630-645). Springer.

KEY TERMS AND DEFINITIONS

Artificial Intelligence (AI): The programming of machines in such a manner which allows them to study human intelligence through absorption of huge amounts of data and copy it in their actions.

Deepfakes: Deceptive fake digital content created using AI and deep learning, which allows manipulation of original content. It may be for a positive or negative use.

Disinformation: A subset of misinformation, this is false information that is created and circulated with the malicious intention to deceive/ mislead the audience.

Generative Adversarial Networks (GAN): An advanced form of AI used for the creation of deepfakes. It involves the use of two neural networks (generator and discriminator) on previous data to compete against each other, thereby improving upon the output of each other and creating real looking morphed images and videos.

Misinformation: False information that is created and circulated, with or without a malicious intention to deceive/ mislead the audience.

Morphed Image/Video: Changing an original image or video into another image or video with the assistance of seamless transition using computer-based techniques,

Silent Witness Theory: A rule of the law of evidence which allows acceptance of photo evidence even without verification by eye witnesses, if such evidence is produced through a reliable process which assures accuracy.

Chapter 4
Social Media and Cyber Security:
Investigating the Risk in Nigeria

Desmond Onyemechi Okocha
https://orcid.org/0000-0001-5070-280X
Bingham University, Nigeria

Damilare J. Agbele
Bingham University, Nigeria

ABSTRACT

The proliferation of social media in Nigeria has birthed new paradigms of communication and two-way interactions among friends, family colleagues, and business associates. It has equally morphed to become a channel for money generation among enterprising youth across the nation. It cannot be denied that the merits associated with this phenomenon called social media are enviable; however, it is also arguable that cyber security is a key factor to the enjoyment of these attendant benefits. This study is anchored on the protection motivation theory and the technological determinism theory. The study identified some cyber security risks synonymous to the use of social media in Nigeria. To remedy the situation, the study recommends that education and practical training in technological best practices in formal and non-formal school settings will help mitigate the inherent risks discussed. Also, initiatives should be taken by the government and organisations to curb this serious issue.

INTRODUCTION

Social media is one out of the platforms provided by the evolution of new media technologies. It is perhaps the most popular and people identify with it owing to its capacity to generate user-defined contents, facilitate two-way communication without the problem of time and boundaries. Social media encompasses all platforms founded of the web 2.0 technology – the technology that expedites the generation and exchange of contents (texts, images, videos, and sounds) by users. It is affirmed that social media hinges on either mobile or web-based technologies to create conversational network/groups where

DOI: 10.4018/978-1-7998-8641-9.ch004

individuals and communities share, comment, discuss and modify user-generated contents (Toivo-Think Tank, 2012) classified social media into six categories, they are:

- Social Networks, e.g., Facebook, Google+, Myspace, and LinkedIn
- Media Products Community/Content sharing, e.g., YouTube, Flickr, and SlideShare
- Blog Services, e.g., Wordpress, Blogger, and Twitter
- Information Community/Collaborative communities, e.g., Wikipedia and Wikispaces
- Virtual Communities. These are also called Virtual Game Worlds
- Link Sharing Services, e.g., Digg and Diigo

Social media exists in the form of smartphone applications and websites and some of the most utilized in Nigeria are Facebook, WhatsApp, Instagram, and Telegram. Asides from the ease of communication made possible by the social media, it has also evolved to become marketing channel whereon enterprising Nigerian youths advertise/market their products and services. Thus, the medium is a communication cum marketing platform.

The statistics (2021) estimates that as of January 2021, Nigeria has estimated 33 million social media users. This explains the large number of people who visit social media platforms to link-up with friends and to sustain connections, be it professional or personal reasons. Scholars have argued that as much as social media platforms have provided many opportunities for transformation and advancement of humanity in the society through interactive information exchange, it has also created catalogue of challenges that the society is presently contending with (Agbawe, 2018). Popular among these challenges is the issue of cyber threat, i.e., threats to the safety and security of social media users. These threats can be direct or indirect and they take different forms. Some of the common ones are account cloning, access to private information, hacking, phishing among other things. Social media companies, organizations and individual users are becoming more concerned about how to reduce the risk of unauthorized access and loss of their private information, hence more attention to cyber-security. This discussion will examine social media and its penetration in Nigeria and the cyber breaches common to social media. Two landmark cases of cybercrimes in Nigeria in recent years will be examined, as well as strategies to mitigate against cyber security breaches in a developing nation like Nigeria.

RESEARCH OBJECTIVES

The underlining aim of the study is to improve the available body of research works related to social media and cyber security in Nigeria. The driving specific objectives are:

1. To review the history of social media in Nigeria
2. To examine cyber breaches common to social media in Nigeria
3. To identify strategies to mitigate against cyber security breaches in Nigeria

RESEARCH METHODOLOGY

This study adopted the qualitative desk research approach. It critically reviewed secondary data from academic papers and published print materials (online and hardcopy) that are peculiar to the discourse. Eight cases of cyber-related crimes committed by Nigerians were profiled in the study.

Theoretical Framework

This study is hinged on Protection Motivation Theory (PMT) and Communication Privacy Management Theory (CPMT). The protection motivation theory (Rogers, 1975) explains that the intention of an individual to protect him or herself depends on four perceptions, these are; the severity of a threatening situation, the probability of occurrence, the efficacy of the commended preventive behavior by the individual, and the individual's self-efficacy. Social media platforms have tendencies of exposing users to a variety of online security threats that requires them to activate safety mode. PMT predicts the utilization of protective technologies which help users escape harm from negative technologies by practicing healthier behaviors when dealing with issues that are security-related (Boss, Galletta, Lowry, Moody, & Polak, 2015). This study adopts PMT because it helps to understand behaviors that guarantee safety in the context of social media use.

Communication Privacy Management Theory was developed by Sandra Petronio in 1991, it explains the believe that people have ownership rights to their private information but somehow miss the part that when they disclose any information to others, they have made themselves vulnerable in a way or another. Petronio (2004) explains the need for controlling private information. Petronio notes that once private information is shared with others, ownership of such information is not secured anymore, and one can't decide what happens to the information after such information has been shared on social media. Social media users interact with each other and share private and public information. The theory encourages social media users to build privacy boundaries by knowing whom they disclose their private information to. This study adopts the communication privacy theory because it helps social media users understand the importance of information privacy when setting up and/or using social media platforms, and to be conscious of building privacy boundaries to avoid issues of vulnerability.

SOCIAL MEDIA IN NIGERIA: HISTORY, PENETRATION AND USAGE

Social media adoption in Nigeria can be attributed to the growth of Information Communication Technologies (ICTs) which began in the 1990s. Golub (2018) notes that the very first technological evolution seed sown into the Nigerian soil was in 1995 when UNESCO-sponsored the Regional Informatics Networks for Africa (RINAF) project. The project had the objectives of ensuring that new information and telecommunication technologies favour exchanges between African countries; remedy the isolation of development and research institutions in African countries and facilitate dialogue between researchers, academics, and industrialists; develop an operative process for the coordination, integration and upgrading of African networks, as well as exchange with other international networks. In the same year, the Nigeria Internet Group (NIG) was formed as a non-governmental organization, and the group held workshops around the country to increase the level of awareness on benefits of Internet for Nigeria. In 1996, internet officially penetrated Nigeria after the Nigerian Communications Commission (NCC) agreed to issue license to internet service providers. Linkserve Ltd. was the first licensed Internet provider and it started operations on January 1, 1997. Between the year 1996 to 2000, more internet service providers gained licenses from the NCC, these brought about greater access to the internet as more internet exchange points were built around the country.

Figure 1. Rate of Internet Penetration in Nigeria

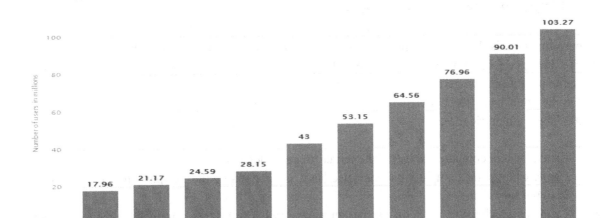

Nigeria opened up its borders for ICTs and eventually came up with information technology policy to improve the use of technology for development in the late 1990s and the beginning of the millennium (Igyuve and Agbele, 2016). This development allowed ICT and its ancillary technologies to gain footings in Nigeria as people were able to communicate virtually from computer systems and the internet-enabled phones, starting with emails. The internet user figure in Nigeria stands at 104.4M as at January 2021 (Kemp, 2021), Statistica (2021) notes that there an estimated 33 million social media users in Nigeria as of January 2021 and projects that the figures will hit 43M by the end of the year (See chart). This statistic explains how social media continues to permeate the lives of Nigerians. At present, it seems that one could hardly find a place in Nigeria, where people do not use social media.

After year 2000, more user-friendly social networking sites sprang up and become known in Nigeria, the likes of Myspace, Facebook, 2go are examples. This greatly enhanced two-way and instant communication between/among people and groups who share common interest. Today we have more conventional social media platforms that Nigerians are registered in which they engage to communicate, transact, and socialize. Some of these platforms are Wikipedia, Friendster, LinkedIn, Hi5, Instagram, WhatsApp, Tik-Tok, Triller, Snapchat, and Telegram. Other social media platforms were purely Nigerian-oriented, hence, they catered specifically for the need of Nigerians, some of these are NaijaPals and NairaLand (Uwem, Enobong, and Nsikan, 2013).

A Pew Research Centre survey in March 2021 revealed that social media engagement has a correlation with having network of diverse friends and connections, especially in economies that are emerging. This exposition explains the primary utility of the social media which is to allow people keep in touch with family and friends. The use also attempts to do more formal forms of communication such as business discussions and networking. People also use social media platforms to source for career opportunities, connect people with like interests across the globe, and share insights. Asides from the basic communication, social media is also engaged for marketing purposes, building brands & online presence and disseminate new stories. Akanni (2012) also discovered that social media serve as a tool for socialization, enhances learning opportunities, communication, entertainment, political participation, and instant messaging as the uses of social network sites among Nigerians.

CYBERCRIME: CASES IN NIGERIA

Cybercrime entails the use of computers, network device(s) or a network to further illegal/fraudulent course. In Nigeria, cases of cybercrimes are no longer new. Cases of arrest of cybercriminals are becoming quite popular in the media too. Two popular cases are profiled below.

On the other hand, the US Department of Justice divided cybercrime into three categories (Brush, 2020). These categories are;

- Crimes where computer gadget is the target (to gain illegal access).
- Crime wherein the computer gadget is used as a weapon (using the computer for credit card fraud or cyber terrorism).
- Crime in which the computer is used as an accessory to crimes (e.g., storage of illegal document).

The necessity of internet connectivity and heavy social media presence has enabled and increased the volume and pace of cybercrime in recent years. Cybercrimes can be planned and executed by an individual or a group and the aim is to exploit the vulnerability of social media users.

The Hushpuppi Case and Others

News broke on June 20, 2020, that popular Nigerian and social media influencer popularly known as Ray Hushpuppi had been arrested in Dubai where he lived. Until his arrest, he lived a luxurious life and had followership of about 2.5M on Instagram. Hushpuppi (38yrs) usually posts videos of himself playing with wads of cash and flaunting wealth but had always maintained that he was a real estate developer. CNN reported that a Federal affidavit alleged Hushpuppi's extravagant lifestyle was financed through hacking schemes. The affidavit further alleged that Hushpuppi stole millions of dollars from companies in USA and Europe. His flamboyant posts on the internet left digital trails of evidence that investigators used to link him to the cybercrimes. Hushpuppi was arrested in Dubai and was extradited to the United State to face trail for conspiring to launder millions of dollars through cybercrime. Hushpuppi is alleged to lead a global network of cyber criminals that use business email compromise, money laundry, and computer intrusions strategies to steal from individual and companies. Hushpuppi was arrested along with 11 cohorts and investigators were reported to have seized items worth 41 million US Dollars, 13 luxury cars worth 6.8 million US Dollars, smartphones and computer evidence, Dubai Police said in a statement. Email addresses of nearly 2 million possible victims on phones were uncovered, computers, and hard drives. (Source: CNN News, 2021). The trial is currently on in the USA soil and Hushpuppi has pleaded guilty to his crimes.

Another case was published by the Interpol in November 2019 when the InterPol declared the arrest of three Nigerians in Lagos for cybercrime investigation. The suspects were arrested following a joint taskforce operation by the Group-IB, INTERPOL and Nigeria Police Force following a year-long investigation with the code-named 'Operation Falcon'. The three Nigerians are believed to be members of a wider organized crime group – a group responsible for carrying out phishing campaigns, distributing malware and extensive business email compromise scams. It was alleged that the suspects developed phishing links, domains, and mass mailing campaigns through which they impersonated representatives of different organizations. Through this fraudulent mailing campaigns, 26 malware programmes were disseminated through spyware and remote access tools. These programmes were used to penetrate exiting cyber securities and monitor the systems of individuals and victim organizations. Afterwards, scams were launched, and funds were syphoned. The gang is believed to have compromised government establishments and private sector companies in more than 150 countries since 2017 (Source, The Interpol).

The security agency in charge with investigating related cybercrimes in Nigeria is the Economic and Financial Crimes commission and the Lagos zonal headquarter of the Agency reported that they have arrested 44 suspected internet fraudsters in Lagos, during different operations in some parts of Lagos State between June 1, 2021, and June 3 (The National News, 2021). The BBC in February 2021 also reported the 10 years sentence judgement of 33yearsd old Nigerian, Okeke Obi (also known as Invictus Obi) by the East Virginia District Judiciary. Okeke Obi was sentenced after being found guilty of cyber fraud that has led to the theft of about 11million US Dollars (equivalent to 8 million British Pounds). Obi primarily used Nigerian-based companies to defraud people in the US. According to the report, Obi was part of a group which engaged in cybercrimes between the years 2015 to 2019. Obi was also accused of working with conspirators to create profiles of hundreds of victims including people in the US's Eastern District of Virginia. In one phishing attack in 2018, Obi and his gang gained access to the email of a manager at Unatrac Holding Limited, the export sales office for Caterpillar's heavy industrial and farm equipment. Thereafter, fraudulent wire transfers to the tune of nearly $11m was made and the funds was moved overseas.

In November 2019, the US Department of justice charged ten Nigerians in the US with conspiracy to launder proceeds that were fraudulently obtained from Nigerian romance scam operation targeting multiple victims. The indictment alleged that since 2017, the co-conspirators coordinated with unknown individuals in Nigeria who assumed false identities on online dating sites and social networking sites to defraud unsuspecting victims. The individual told the victims they were U.S. residents working abroad and thereafter, romantic relationships were formed. At the early stage, victims would receive requests of gift cards and cell phones. As the relationships continued, the requests would develop into increasingly larger sums of money intended to complete projects or to return to the United States.

The victims were directed by the online romance scammers to send funds to the defendants' bank accounts. The defendants concealed the proceeds of romance scam operations by moving money between and among multiple bank accounts that were opened using fraudulent identity documents to obscure the source of the funds and the identities of the co-conspirators. They also purchased salvaged vehicles and car parts to export overseas, usually to Nigeria, to conceal the sources. As published on the US department of justice website, their names are Afeez Olajide Adebara, (34 years) U.S. citizen; Oluwaseun John Ogundele, (30 years) U.S. citizen US; Joshua Nnandom ditep, (25 years) Nigerian citizen; Paul Usoro, (25 years) Nigerian citizen; Chibuzo Godwin Obiefuna Jr, (26 years) U.S. citizen; Jamiu Ibukun Adedeji, (23 years) Nigerian, residing in Norman, Oklahoma; Tobiloba Kehinde, (27 years) Nigerians.

The last three names were unknown as they were still at large as at press time, but they were confirmed to also be residing in the US as at the period of the crimes, just like the first seven.

Another 52 internet fraudsters were arrested by operatives of the Benin Zonal Office of the Economic and Financial Crimes Commission (EFCC) on May 11, 2021 (Premium Times, 2021). The anti-graft Agency indicated that the suspects were involved in romance scam on social media, using fake identities of Caucasian men or women to defraud unsuspecting victims of their hard-earned monies. Items recovered from the suspects at the time of arrest include fake identity cards, six exotic cars, laptop, mobile phones, and documents.

Similarly, two Nigerian youths were convicted of cybercrimes and sentenced to two years imprisonment by the Edo State High Court in Benin City, Edo State. on July 19, 2021 (Channels TV, 2021). The defendants, known with the monikers Frank Mark (real name being Noah Omoregbe) and William Scot (real name being Destiny Efewengbe) were arraigned on one count charge each of impersonation and fraudulent intentions, contrary to section 484 of the Criminal Code Law Cap 48 Laws of defunct Bendel State of Nigeria (as applicable in Edo State) 1976.

The Federal High Court in Port Harcourt, Rivers State also convicted and sentenced two Internet fraudsters, Jonathan Collins and Godspower Ofonime, to six years imprisonment each for internet fraud after being arraigned by the EFCC. One of the charges against Collins stated that Jonathan Collins (Alias Janis Louise Hughes; Allan Carmack Calluk; Dr. James Lattimore) fraudulently impersonated one Janis Louise Hughes, a white man from Glenville, North Carolina, USA with the intent to obtain money from unsuspecting men and women. (Francis and Naku, 2021). Ofonime met his waterloo when verified intelligence by the EFCC linked him with scam emails to foreigners.

Popular Nigerian newspaper, Daily Post also reported the arrest and conviction of two Nigerians internet fraudsters (Tolani Bakare and Alimi Sikiru) by the Lagos State High Court following a suit by the Economic and Financial Crimes Commission (EFCC) in August 2021. Bakare, claimed his forte is business email compromise and confessed to have hacked into different companies outside the shores of Nigeria and the accounts of KLM Airline, Turkish Airline and British Airways. The second defendant, Sikiru, in his statement to the EFCC, admitted that majority of the funds found in his account were from the first defendant, Bakare. The convicts forfeited over N200 million and properties in the upscale Lekki axis of Lagos to the Federal Government. These cases explain the rate at which cybercrimes continue to increase in Nigeria, hence the need to seek ways to address the situation.

SCHEMES UTILIZED BY CYBERCRIMINALS

Cybercriminals can be described as people who engage in criminal activity by using computers and internet (Oxford Dictionary, 2021). Some of the schemes employed by cybercriminals are:

- **Cyberstalking:** This is the use of the internet connectivity and other computer-based technologies to harass or stalk other persons in the online space (Gordon, 2021). Cyberstalking has a fixated pattern and obsessions behaviour by the cybercriminals, it is intrusive, causes fear and endangers alarm in victims. The Cyber Helpline (2020) list some of the common stalking activities of cyber stalkers to include; unsolicited messages, information gathering, surveillance, unauthorized access to online accounts and spread of misinformation. Victims of cyberstalking are usually known persons to the cyber stalker. Cyber stalkers could be an ex-lover, colleague or known crush. In some cases, the cyberstalker could be an unknown person totally.

- **Phishing Attack:** This is a kind of cybercrime where a malicious link or attachment file is sent by the intruder to harvest personal information from the victim's system, once clicked on - information such as username and password, credit card information, online banking information. Baykara and Gurel (2018) also mentioned that people who commit this crime often gather background information from social media platforms and other public information resources such as Twitter LinkedIn or Facebook about victim's personal work history interests and activity. When the study is completed friend requests are sent to the victim or they are followed online sometimes the links or messages just come out of the blue.

- **Cyberbullying:** Adeniran (2020) & Balogun et al (2017) observed that's cyberbullying is becoming a common phenomenon in Nigeria and that it is rampant on social media platforms where a lot of people are subscribed. Cyber bullying is that trolling, catfishing, blatant harassment, and mistreatment of people online (Iyanda, 2020). Cyber bullying is the utilization of smartphones or social media platforms to embarrass other persons. It is carried out in various ways, one of which is posting the naked picture of someone online, projecting a part or type of body of someone on the social media for the purpose of embarrassment (popularly called body shaming), revealing personal information about someone without their consent (also called doxing), this could be photos, documents, phone numbers, and addresses.

- **Cross-Site Scripting (XSS):** Cross-site scripting is one of the most common forms of attack on web-based applications (Almarabeh & Suleiman, 2019). In cross site scripting, harmful codes are inserted into sites or applications to be opened in system browser. The intention is to remotely steal cookies (that is text files with small pieces of information, e.g., username and passwords), modify the websites, capture clip boards contents, scan ports and download (Raman, 2008). This also leads to account hacking.

- **Clickjacking:** This is an attack that tricks social media users to click on hidden elements such as unintended links so they would end up on malicious websites or download viruses and disruptive software. As mentioned by Lundeen and Rhodes (2011), cybercriminals can use the hardware of user computers such as camera and microphone to record their activities.

- **Account Cloning:** This is it a technique used by cybercriminals to create a fake profile by using personal information, images and/or video stolen from the profile of targeted social media users (Almarabeh, 2015). This can be done manually or automatically (through written programme codes). In most cases, accounts that are cloned are usually set as public, so all information of the user are available to everyone, including the cybercriminal. Through cloned accounts, cybercriminals send messages to targeted audience most times for money extortion.

- **Harvesting of Private Information:** Cybercriminals can also set out to harvest private information of social media users to harm them. Social media users who are more susceptible to it are those who usually reveal their health status, show-off their wealth in the social media space, reviewed all their locations publicly, bank details and information that are sensitive. Leakage of this sensitive information could hold negative implications for social media users. Maremot (2010) cited an example of insurance companies who now use social media data to distinguish between risky and safe clients.

- **Romance Scam:** This is one of oldest cybercrime approach known in Nigeria. It is a situation where cyber criminals create fake profiles on social media with the intention of swindling lovers.

Cyber criminals in this case play on emotional triggers to get partners to provide them with money gifts or personal information.

CYBERCRIMES IN NIGERIA: CAUSES AND EFFECTS

Statistics shows that a significant proportion of cybercrimes are perpetuated by youths (Ibrahim, 2019). Cybercrime can be attributed to factors such as high youth unemployment, negative role-modeling, desire for wealth, weak implementation of cyber laws, poor education of internet users on cybercrimes, corruption, the vulnerable nature of the internet and the laissez faire attitude of individuals and businesses regarding cyber security (Hassan, Lass & Makinde, 2012).

Causes of Cyber-Crimes in Nigeria are discussed below.

- **Unemployment and Poverty:** This is perhaps the major causes of cybercrime in Nigeria. Unemployment rate in Nigeria stood at 33%, as at the last quarter of 2020 (Olurounbi. 2021). High rate of unemployment has consequential effects, some of which are socioeconomic, political, and psychological consequences. The issue of unemployment automatically increased the rate at which people take part in criminal activities for their survival. Unemployment encourages the development of cybercrime among youths who constitutes a large percentage of the unemployed workforce. There is a connection between unemployment and poverty as one who is not gainfully employed will most likely be poor. The 2019/2020 Nigerian living standards survey released by the National Bureau of Statistics, NBS, shows that 82.9 million (40.1 per cent of the population) Nigerians are poor. A poverty-stricken person may very liable turn to crime for survival.
- **The 'Quest for Wealth' Culture:** The culture of hard work, honesty and integrity are fast failing in the Nigerian society. Nowadays, youths tend to be greedy and are not ready to start small; they strive to level up with their rich counterparts by engaging in cybercrimes (Ibrahim, 2019 and Omodunbi, Odiase, Olaniyan & Esan, 2016).
- **Negative Role Modeling and Corruption:** Meke (2012) notes that parents transmit criminal tendencies to their children through the process of socialization. This means that some children pick up criminal tendencies from their parents. Additionally, Nigeria, at the end of the year 2020 ranked 149 on the global ranking of corrupt countries after surveys by the Transparency International (Vanguard Newspaper, 2021). The Nigerian society also celebrates wealth without care or question on the source of such wealth. This misguided disposition encourages the get-rich-quick mindset that can be fed through cybercrimes as younger ones tend to model their lives after celebrated 'criminals' in the society.

Brush (2018) adduced that the true cost of cybercrime is difficult to assess accurately. This implication of this statement is that the effect of cybercrimes on the society cannot truly quantify as it cuts across different spheres of the nation and indeed the social media users. Starting with the social media user, users who are online victims of cyber-attacks suffer from emotional trauma, which could lead to depression and acute stress disorder (Lynn, 2007). In most psychological cases, victims of cyber-attack feel they are to be blamed for the attack because they let their guards down, they therefore prefer not to involve anyone, live in isolation, and not even report the case.

• **Ill-equipped Law Enforcement Agencies and Implementation of Cybercrime Laws:** African countries have received constant criticism for inadequately handling the implementation of policies. This appears the same for Nigerian Cybercrimes (Prohibition and Prevention) Act, 2015. The Act makes provision for the protection of people, property, and the government against unethical internet practices (Uba and Agbakoba, 2021). However, it saddens that Nigeria continues to experience great effects of cybercrime. Internet fraud appears to be everyday job of some Nigerians owing to weak implementation by agencies managing the Act's implementation. These agencies are trying but in some ways some perpetrators get off the hook when apprehended. This in a way encourages offenders to commit more crime, knowing that they can always escape the wrath of the law.

Asides from the above listed, cybercrimes in Nigeria can also be attributed to poor education of social media users on the issue. A good number of social media users don't read terms and conditions, especially with regards to privacy when registering on social media sites. Kumar et al (2013) observed that some social media users put themselves at risk of cybercriminals too as the amount of personal information they leave as public on their social media platforms can give them away. People also tend to read less about new methods used by cybercriminals and what to do to avoid them, as disseminated by the mass media. The relaxed attitude of individuals and businesses towards online security is also a challenge. Aladenusi, a cyber risk expert attributed the rise in cyber frauds to insufficient skilled resources, deficiency in awareness, rapidly changing technology landscape and weakness in cyber security controls (All Africa News, 2021).

Ogunjobi (2020) also advanced other effects of cybercrime, some of which are huge cost required by organizations to fix damages caused by cybercriminals with a view to preventing a repeat of such. Other effects are reputational distrust, loss of creditworthiness for people whose have suffered identity theft. The kind of life that cybercrime provides, e.g., lavish lifestyle, flaunting of wealth on social media, clubbing, and other social pump gatherings have also reduced the love for true education and hard work among youths. Youths today go as far as withdrawing from school to join the pyramid of cybercriminals. A lot of youths who would have contributed meaningfully to the nation are now recruited, trained, and mentored by the godfathers in internet fraud.

Another major effect of cybercrime is revenue losses to nations and social media users. Allogo (2021) reported that Nigeria lost 5.5 trillion Naira to fraud and cybercrimes in the last 10 years. Cybercrimes disruption of business causes profit pilferage, and welfare losses. Cybercrime also have national security implications; therefore, manpower and funds are channeled to the government to avoid a collapse of the nation to external hackers. During the #EndSars protest in October 2020, popular hacking group called *'Anonymous'* claimed via its Twitter handle, that it had infiltrated some Nigerian government and business organisation websites (Adeshina, 2020) in support of the protest that took over many cities in Nigeria. This protest evolved following calls for the disbandment of the special police unit called the Federal Special Anti-Robbery Squad (FSARS). The group was reported to be involved in the abduction, harassment, extortion, and murder of innocent Nigerian victims. It was alleged that the 'Anonymous' group infiltrated a popular Telcom operator in Nigeria and gave 1000 NGN credit to all users. The Telecom Company came out to deny this breach.

CYBERSECURITY - MITIGATING AGAINST CYBER BREACHES IN NIGERIA

Cyber security is a practice of keeping computer systems, networks, and programmes safe from cyber-attacks. Eweniyi and Frank (2013) gave a scholarly definition of the term cyber security. To them, cyber security is the collection of tools, policies, security concepts, security safeguards, guidelines, risk management approaches, actions, training, best practices, assurance, and technologies that can be used to protect the cyber environment and organization and user's assets. As discussed earlier in this study, social media users, be its private persons or business organizations are susceptible to various forms of calculated cybercrimes therefore steps must be taken to ensure security. Cisco (2019) is of the opinion that cybersecurity approach that would be successful would have multiple layers of protection that spread across the computers networks programs or data that one intends to keep safe. This means that addressing cybercrime is not a one-way affair, it is a multilayered approach. There is a need to involve people, processes, and technology. This study believes that mitigation of cybercrime is a role of three, entities namely, the individuals (social media users), organisations (social media companies and other organizations and the government.

At the social media user level, Kumar et al (2013) advised users to protect themselves online by reducing personal information put online so that chances of cybercriminals piecing together one's routine becomes limited. Social media are expected to be comfortably safe about what they post online. If possible, users should google themselves and see if very personal information like address, phone number or places regularly visited is public. If this information are public, find a way to bring them down by contacting the site. Also, social media users should reduce the use of third-party applications that makes their way around the major applications like cameras and beautifying applications. Almarabeh & Suleiman (2019) gave some tips regarding social media safety in the wake of cybercrimes, they suggested that social media users take the advantages of all update notifications on the site and applications which are continuously developed to improve the level of data security. Users should carefully review any social media users' terms before accepting them. Many social media platforms use GPS tracking to tag user location to posts and photos, this can be turned off in the settings. Social media users who feel stalked should not hesitate to tell those around and report such to the right authorities. Self-security and privacy consciousness is important.

The government and organizations should also embark on cybercrime literacy campaigns. Tayouri (2015) believes proper training can raise necessary awareness and personal responsibility to help prevent social media cybercrimes. Organizations should also provide effective security trainings for staff on best practices in social media use, threats, precautions, policy and how to report when there is breach. On the part of organization, Organizations should beef up IT systems and protect critical information infrastructure. Chi (2011) suggested that organizations should ensure the internet security firewalls are up to date, that anti-virus and anti-spy software are installed on employees' systems and other devices they use. Finally, the Nigerian government should also strengthen her agencies so that more can be achieved in the fight against cybercrime. Cyber legislation can also be constantly reviewed so that new trends in cybercrime can be addressed as they evolve.

CONCLUSION

Social media has offered novel ways of interaction and communication, similarly it has brought about new security and privacy challenges. These challenges include cyberstalking, phishing attacks, cyber bullying, cross-site scripting, cyber jacking, account cloning, harvesting of private information and romance scam. Equally, the study revealed that cybercrime is a problem in Nigeria and various factors have sustained the challenge. The study mentioned some of these factors/challenges; they are poverty, unemployment, wrong modeling and societal values, desire for wealth pop culture, ill-equipped law enforcement agencies and implementation of cybercrime laws, poor education about cybercrimes, weak structures of organization internet systems. Cybercrimes effect also cut across the political, economic, social, technology domains of Nigeria. Large amounts of money is lost to cybercrimes every year while victims also suffer losses, even their lives sometimes. In order to reduce the risk of Cybercrimes in Nigeria in the social media, strategic measures should by every stakeholder in the social media industry, i.e., the social media users, the government, and the social media companies. The government should create jobs as the idle hand is the devil's workshop. An enabling environment for job creation by youths and entrepreneur will help to tackle unemployment and poverty considerably, thereby help reduce crime rates, especially cybercrime. Stringent laws that reduce the participation of youths in cybercrime should be enacted and enforced by the government of the day in Nigeria. Parental, families and the society should revert to the teaching of virtues such as integrity and hard work, this will help to produce better individuals in the society. Parent and people in positions of authority/influence should stand as good role model to Nigerian youths. There should be massive education on cybercrimes and how to avoid them by organizations, social media companies and the government, as this will help social media users.

REFERENCES

Adediran, A. (2020), Cyberbullying in Nigeria: Examining the Adequacy of Legal Responses. *International Journal for the Semiotics of Law - Revue internationale de Sémiotiquejuridique*, (34), 29.

Adeshina, O. (2020). *Popular Hacking Group "Anonymous" Allegedly Hacks Nigerian Government Websites*. https://nairametrics.com/2020/10/15/endsars-popular-hacking-group-anonymous-allegedly-hacks-nigerian-govt-websites/

Almarabeh, H., & Suleiman, A. (2015) The Impact of Cyber Threats on Social Networking Sites. *International Journal of Advanced Research in Computer Science, 10*(2).

Alogo, U. (2021). *West Africa: 'Nigeria Lost N5.5 Trillion to Cybercrimes in 10 Years*. Retrieved from https://allafrica.com/stories/202104260948.html

Ayakoroma, F. B. (2008). #Endsars: Popular Hacking Group, Anonymous Allegedly Hacks Nigerian Govt. Websites Reinventing the Pollical Process in Nigerian Video Films: A Critical Reading of Teco Benson's "The Senator". *Nigerian Theatre Journal., 14*(2), 1–21.

Balogun, N. A., Awodele, T. A., Bello, O. W., Oyekunle, R. A., & Balogun, U. O. (2017). Impact of Social Networks on the Increase of Cyberbully Among Nigerian University Students in Ilorin Metropolis. *Journal of Science and Technology, 8*(2), 102–111.

BBC. (2021). *Obinwanne Okeke: Nigerian Email Fraudster Jailed for 10 Years in US*. Available at https://www.bbc.com/news/world-africa-56085217

Bertot, J. C., Jaeger, P. T., & Hansen, D. (2012). The Impact of Polices in Government Social Media Usage; Issues, Challenges And Recommendations. *Government Information Quarterly, 29*(1), 30–40. doi:10.1016/j.giq.2011.04.004

Boss, S. R., Galletta, D. F., Lowry, P. B., Moody, G. D., & Polak, P. (2015). *What Do Systems Users Have to Fear? Using Fear Appeals to Engender Threats and Fear that Motivate Protective Security Behaviors*. Rochester, NY: Social Science Research Network. Retrieved from https://papers.ssrn.com/abstract=2607190 doi:10.25300/MISQ/2015/39.4.5

Chai, S., Bagchi-Sen, S., Rao, H. R., Upadhyaya, S.J., & Morrell, C. (2009). Internet and Online Information Privacy: An Exploratory Study of Preteens and Early Teens. *IEEE Transactions on Professional Communication, 52*(2), 167-182. doi:10.1109/TPC.2009.2017985

Channels, T. V. (2021). *Court Sends Two Internet Fraudsters to Two Years in Prison*. Available at https://www.channelstv.com/2021/07/19/court-sends-two-internet-fraudsters-to-two-years-in-prison/

Chiemela, Q. A., Ovute, A. O., & Obochi, C. I. (2015). The Influence of the Social Media on the Nigerian Youths: Aba Residents Rxperience. *Journal of Research in Humanities and Social Science, 3*(3), 12–20.

Cisco. (2019). *What is cybersecurity?* Available at https://www.cisco.com/c/en/us/products/security/what-is-cybersecurity.html#~how-cybersecurity-work

CNN. (2020). *He Flaunted Private Jets and Luxury Cars on Instagram. Feds Used His Posts to Link Him to Alleged Cybercrimes*. Available at https://edition.cnn.com/2020/07/12/us/ray-hushpuppi-alleged-money-laundering-trnd/index.html

Cyber Help Line. (2019). *Cyber Stalking*. https://www.thecyberhelpline.com/guides/cyber-stalking

Daily Post Newspaper. (2021). *Two Internet Fraudsters Convicted in Lagos, Forfeit Assets to FG*. Available at https://dailypost.ng/2021/08/09/two-internet-fraudsters-convicted-in-lagos-forfeit-assets-to-fg/

Francis, O., & Naku, D. (2021). *Man Bags Two-Year Jail Term For Currency Counterfeiting*. Available at https://punchng.com/two-internet-fraudsters-jailed-six-years-in-rivers/

Gaolub, K. (2018). *History of Social Media in Nigeria and the World*. https://www.legit.ng/1209780-history-social-media-nigeria-world.html

Gordon, S. (2021). *What Is Cyberstalking?* https://www.verywellmind.com/what-is-cyberstalking-5181466

Ibikunle, F. & Eweniyi, O (2013). Approach to Cyber Security Issues in Nigeria: Challenges and Solution. *International Journal of Cognitive Research in Science, Engineering and Education, 1*(1).

Internet Society. (2000). *History of Internet in Africa*. Available at https://www.internetsociety.org/internet/history-of-the-internet-in-africa/

Kemp, S. (2021). *Digital 2021 Nigeria*. Available at https://datareportal.com/reports/digital-2021-nigeria

Kumar, A., Gupta, S. K., Rai, A. K., & Sinha, S. (2013). *Social Networking Sites and their Security Issues* (Vol. 3). International Journal of Scientific and Research Publications.

Ogunjobe, O. (2020). *The Impact of Cybercrime on Nigerian Youths*. Retrieved from https://www.researchgate.net/publication/347436728_THE_IMPACT_OF_CYBERCRIME_ON_NIGERIAN_YOUTHS

Olurounbi, R. (2021). *Nigeria Unemployment Rate Rises to 33%, Second Highest on Global List*. Available at https://www.bloomberg.com/news/articles/2021-03-15/nigeria-unemployment-rate-rises-to-second-highest-on-global-list

Petronio, S. (2004). Road to Developing Communication Privacy Management Theory: Narrative in Progress, Please Stand By. *Journal of Family Communication, 4*(3/4), 193–207. doi:10.120715327698jfc0403&4_6

Premium Times. (2021). *52 Suspected Internet fraudsters Arrested in Benin, Six in Abuja*. Available at https://www.premiumtimesng.com/news/top-news/460807-52-suspected-internet-fraudsters-arrested-in-benin-six-in-abuja.html

Rogers, R. W. (1975). A Protection Motivation Theory of Fear Appeals and Attitude Change. *The Journal of Psychology, 91*(1), 93–114. doi:10.1080/00223980.1975.9915803 PMID:28136248

Scroxton, A. (2019). *Three Cyber Criminals Arrested in Nigerian BEC Investigation*. Available at https://www.computerweekly.com/news/252492711/Three-cyber-criminals-arrested-in-Nigerian-BEC-investigation

Tade, O. (2021). *Poverty and Widening Inequality in Nigeria*. Available at https://www.vanguardngr.com/2021/07/poverty-and-widening-inequality-in-nigeria/

The Interpol. (2020). *Three Arrested as INTERPOL, Group-IB and the Nigeria Police Force Disrupt Prolific Cybercrime Group*. Available at https://www.interpol.int/en/News-and-Events/News/2020/Three-arrested-as-INTERPOL-Group-IB-and-the-Nigeria-Police-Force-disrupt-prolific-cybercrime-group

The National News. (2021). *More Than Email Scams: The Evolution of Nigeria's Cyber-Crime Threat*. Available at https://www.thenationalnews.com/world/africa/2021/07/22/more-than-email-scams-the-evolution-of-nigerias-cyber-crime-threat/

The US Department of Justice. (2019). *10 Men Involved in Nigerian Romance Scams Indicted for Money Laundering Conspiracy*. Available at https://www.justice.gov/opa/pr/10-men-involved-nigerian-romance-scams-indicted-money-laundering-conspiracy

Toivo-Think Tank. (2012). *Social Media- The New Power of Political Influence*. Centre for European Studies.

Uba, J., & Agbakoba, O. (2021). *Cybercrimes and Cyber Laws in Nigeria: All You Need To Know*. https://www.mondaq.com/nigeria/security/1088292/cybercrimes-and-cyber-laws-in-nigeria-all-you-need-to-know

Uwem, A., Enobong, A., & Nsikan, S. (2013). Uses and Gratifications of Social Networking Websites among Youths in Uyo, Nigeria. *International Journal of Asian Social Science, 3*(2), 353–369.

Vanguard Newspapers. (2021). *Nigeria Drops in Transparency International Corruption Perceptions Index, ranks 149 out of 183 countries*. https://www.vanguardngr.com/2021/01/nigeria-drops-in-transparency-international-corruption-perceptions-index-ranks-149-out-of-183-countries/

Chapter 5
The European Union's Proposed Artificial Intelligence Legislation and the Path Ahead for Asian Approaches to Artifical Intelligence

Charitarth Bharti

National University of Singapore, Singapore

ABSTRACT

This chapter aims to analyse pathways for global legislative formulation on AI. Part 1 of the chapter seeks to chart and analyse the development of the proposed EU regulation itself and seek to create an understanding of the rationales, practical and theoretical, that underpin the legislation and its provisions. Part 2 of the chapter seeks to analyse the present practices of key multilateral discussion forums and Asian jurisdictions on the subject and the approaches adopted by them in policy and vision documents released by various regulators to analyse their similarity or otherwise with the approach espoused by the EU. Part 3 of the chapter expands on the process of how a human-centered approach goes from strategy to regulation and explores the path the world can take on the issue given the dynamic nature of the subject and the geopolitics at play involving the issue. This section is followed by a conclusion to the chapter on what can be derived about the state of AI ethics at the moment and what shape they can take insofar as becoming global norms in the years to come.

INTRODUCTION

One of the key aspects of emerging technologies is their ability to cut across borders in their application and transferability. The field of Artificial Intelligence (AI) has witnessed the expanding reach of such technology at a breakneck speed with countries in a cut-throat competition to develop AI capabilities and to harvest the windfall winner takes all gains that such groundbreaking use cases and innovations

DOI: 10.4018/978-1-7998-8641-9.ch005

bring to the nation states, economically and geopolitically. While there is no one definition of what constitutes AI, there have been efforts to get some consensus around the idea. Simply put, AI has been defined as a system that performs intelligent operations (which may have some autonomy) in response to environment and input (European Commission, 2018). It's no longer a remote futuristic projection to predict the ubiquity of AI across sectors especially with the rollout of new technologies like Internet of Things and 5G (Taulli, 2020). While the advantages of AI are rather evident, there has also been a lot of discussion (European Parliament, 2017) around its dangers and ethical issues associated with its use cases. The EU Parliament adopted a resolution to this effect in 2017 where it asked the Commission for "a proposal for a legislative instrument on legal questions related to the development and use of robotics and AI foreseeable in the next 10 to 15 years, combined with non-legislative instruments such as guidelines and codes of conduct". The need for a comprehensive regulation on the subject has hence been felt for a long time now.

While several governments have adopted AI strategies the EU has traditionally been the leader in setting standards on human rights jurisprudence with rights associated with emerging technologies. In addition to the EU wide plan, the States were also encouraged to develop their own national AI strategies. Another key document released encapsulating the European approach to AI has been the European Commission's communication titled "Artificial Intelligence for Europe" (European Commission, 2018). The three key goals of the communication were as follows:

1. To boost the EU's technological and industrial capacity and AI uptake across the economy, both by the private and public sectors.
2. To prepare for socio-economic changes brought about by AI
3. To ensure an appropriate ethical and legal framework.

Subsequently, the EU entered the fray on a proper pan-European commercial strategy when in 2018 it adopted the Coordinated Plan on Artificial Intelligence developed together with its Member States with a goal to maximise the investments on an EU and National level (European Commission, 2018). Established under the Commissions Communication, the High-Level Expert Group (HLEG) on AI presented Ethics Guidelines for Trustworthy Artificial Intelligence published the first draft of the Ethics guidelines for trustworthy AI (AI HLEG, 2018). The Guidelines put forward 7 key requirements that AI systems must meet to be deemed trustworthy. The European approach to AI has released its 2021 review of the Coordinated Plan on Artificial Intelligence (European Commission, 2021). Other documents released by the HLEG were Policy and Investment Recommendations for Trustworthy AI, Assessment List for Trustworthy AI (ALTAI) and Sectoral Considerations on the Policy and Investment Recommendations (AI HLEG, 2020). The updated Coordinated plan, in conjunction with the White Paper, puts down concrete joint actions for the EU and its various member states to pursue in order to achieve the goals of AI integration in the economy while also aiming to ensure that the approach remains human-centric, sustainable, secure, inclusive and trustworthy. As per the plan, the EU member states need to (European Commission, 2021):

- accelerate investments in AI technologies to drive resilient economic and social recovery facilitated by the uptake of new digital solutions;
- act on AI strategies and programmes by implementing them fully and in a timely manner to ensure that the EU reaps the full benefits of first-mover adopter advantages; and

- align AI policy to remove fragmentation and address global challenges

In addition, as of late 2021 by the time of the publishing of the AI Watch Report – a publication of the European Commission tracking the National AI strategies of the EU member states, 20 member states had published their National Strategies while 7 were in the final drafting phase. Simultaneous to the release of the updated Coordinated Plan, the Commission also adopted the AI package which included the proposal for a first of its kind legal framework on AI which professes a risk based approach to AI putting EU on the path towards leading the jurisprudential movement on the subject (European Commission, 2021). Since removing fragmentation and ensuring standardization is one of the goals espoused under the plan, a key trend to follow would be to see how, if at all, the present legislation and standards are diffused across Asia, as other legislative frameworks have, over the years (Greenleaf, 2018).

THE RELATIONSHIP BETWEEN DATA PROTECTION LAWS AND ARTIFICIAL INTELLIGENCE

Learning needs information, and the machines are no different from the humans in that domain. At the very heart of the technological wonder that is Artificial Intelligence and Machine Learning, is the information that it processes to learn. This information is consumed in the form of data collected from systems and devices across the digital ecosystem and the collection of this data is governed by the various data protection laws in place which seek to protect the consumers' privacy, set in place rules for the collection, storage and processing of the information sought to be so collected.

The General Data Protection Regulation (GDPR) is the most landmark legislation in the domain of data protection enacted in the European Union in 2016 and in force since 2018. The GDPR has set the ball rolling on the adaptation of key principles espoused therein by various jurisdictions across the world in their own legislations on data protection (Greenleaf, 2018). Over the years, despite not being the leading economic power across the globe or the hub of technology investment, the European Union has established itself as a central authority on digital jurisprudence and regulation of emerging technologies and the present legislative proposal for governance of Artificial Intelligence is another such endeavor. In what the EU hopes would be another case of the "Brussels effect" – a theory which seeks to explain the EU's unilateral power to regulate global markets and influence the business environment without resorting to international institutions (Bradford, 2020).

While the GDPR and other laws modeled around it don't specifically deal with AI, and in GDPR's case, there is no mention of it either, the provisions therein have a bearing on AI development and deployment. Article 4(7) differentiates the roles of Data Controllers and Processors and places the onus of proper data handling on the Controller to ensure the data is not sent out to third parties without due consent. It also places the onus on the Controller to specify the purposes for collection and to collect only as much data as is reasonably needed for the purpose specified. Similarly, Article 5 details the principles of lawfulness, fairness and transparency protecting citizens from automatic processing in conjunction with the right against automated decision-making and profiling under Article 22. This implies the right to demand that the data be processed with a human in the loop, or not at all (TRPC, 2018).

The European Parliamentary Research Service has also commissioned a report on the subject of the impact of the GDPR on Artificial Intelligence and examines the extent to which the GDPR aligns with the emerging technological needs of AI discussing the tensions and proximities. In particular, it points to two principles of GDPR and data protection in general which have had a deep impact on AI – data minimization and purpose limitation. Discussing automated decision-making as well, it concludes that while AI can be deployed in a manner consistent with the GDPR, GDPR needs to provide more detailed guidance to controllers on the subject and some of its prescriptions need to be expanded and concretised. It also stresses that the gaps in the GDPR can also be bridged by Data Protection Authorities and the Board guidances on the subject amongst other recommendations (European Parliament, 2020).

THE PROPOSED EU REGULATION AT A GLANCE

Like the GDPR on its introduction, the recent release of the EU Commission's updated draft proposal for Regulation of AI (European Commission, 2021) ("Regulation") has marked a sea shift in the jurisprudence in the field and has the potential to set the tone for other jurisdictions. The Regulation covers a broad sweep of software and processing activities within the ambit of what it defines an "AI system". Under the Regulation, an "AI system" as a "software that is developed with one or more of the techniques and approaches listed in Annex I and can, for a given set of human-defined objectives, generate outputs such as content, predictions, recommendations, or decisions influencing environments they interact with."

Within the realm of what it defines as an "AI system", however, it takes a calibrated risk-based approach to the AI systems splitting its regulatory approach into four broad tiers based on the impact the use case might have on citizens and society. The Regulation proceeds to outright prohibit certain AI practices while deeming some activities high risk and the remainder as being limited or minimal risk activities which are subject to no or significantly lesser oversight mechanisms as compared to the "high risk" tier (European Council, 2020). Title II establishes the list of prohibited AI. These include exploitative and manipulative practices where human behavior is sought to be influenced through subliminal messaging or choice architecture, live and large scale biometric identification and surveillance and social scoring and classification of population based on behavior. Title III contains rules for high-risk systems. This forms the bulk of the legislation and is seemingly a direct result of the European Council meeting – *Special meeting of the European Council (1and 2 October 2020) – Conclusions* EUCO 13/20, 2020 which called for a clear determination of the AI applications that should be considered high-risk.

Minimal risk systems are expected to cover most systems like spam filters and video games which pose minimal or no risk to user safety. Limited risk systems will be subject to transparency obligations where the user must be made aware of the AI system at work allowing them to make informed decisions (European Commission, 2021). Examples of these systems can be where a user sees a "deep fake" video or when interacting with an AI chatbot or chat assistant - an area fraught with concerns on AI development and deployment (Deloitte, 2018).

The high-risk systems, though not outrightly banned, bear the burden of being trained on high-quality unbiased data set, being transparent and subject to human oversight, as well as "robust" and accurate (Clarke, 2021). The Regulation splits the governance of high-risk systems by charting out two broad categories for these systems (European Commission, 2021):–

- AI Systems intended to be used as safety component of products that are subject to third party ex-ante conformity assessment.
- Stand-alone AI systems with mainly fundamental rights implications

While the majority of the obligations as regards the proposed legislation apply to high-risk systems, the framework provides for a measure of algorithmic transparency in cases where the AI systems are meant to interact with individuals. Overall, the framework has placed bias mitigation, algorithmic transparency and a human oversight centric approach front and center for every conversation around AI henceforth.

While the Regulation has covered users of AI systems as well, the bulk of its focus has been on the providers with it suggesting fines to the tune of €20 million, or up to 4% of total annual turnover of the AI provider for non-compliance for high-risk systems. For non-compliance with the mandate on prohibited AI systems, the fines extend up to 6% of total annual turnover of the AI provider or €20 million, whichever is higher.

Although the Regulation has largely been lauded as a remarkable first step in the direction of putting down concrete rules on the subject of AI by most civil rights groups, it has also received flak from competing quarters for missing the mark on several key issues that were expected to be covered in the latest draft. Advocates of digital rights bemoan what they describe as the half-hearted measures on banned and high-risk systems leaving room for maneuvering and possible circumvention of the norms. This is on account of the conformity assessments which subject high-risk systems to self-assessment models (with the exception of biometric recognition systems which are subject to third-party assessments. The carving out of "public security" exceptions to definitionally banned AI has been seen as an unwelcome compromise by advocates of digital rights (European Digital Rights, 2021). Concerns have been voiced around loopholes by key actors no less than the European Data Protection Supervisor itself, emerging from vagueness of the language used for exploitation and detriment and who becomes the arbiter of truth on such subjective terms (European Data Protection Supervisor, 2021). On the other hand, advocates of a more open system - for the sake of technological competitiveness - have complained of the definition being myopic in a way that may be resistant to technological change and operate in a rigid structure. The report of Commission releasing the Regulation, however, clarifies that the list of high-risk systems as compiled in Annex III to the Regulation is subject to expansion as new and currently unforeseen technologies materialize. Another key criticism emerging against the Regulation is that it does little in the name of measures to support innovation putting it on a backfoot in the race for AI dominance. Seemingly anticipating this criticism coming the legislation's way, the drafters of the legislation included Title V, Articles 53-55 of the Regulation to cover "Measures in support of Innovation" and encourages national authorities to set up regulatory sandboxes and sets a basic framework in terms of governance, supervision and liability. It also goes on to provide priority sandbox access and dedication communication channels for smaller operators under Art. 55 (European Commission, 2021). How that will be implemented and whether it will go far enough to bridge the gap between EU and the rest of the world on AI, remains to be seen.

Margrethe Vestager, the European Commission's Executive Vice-President, laid out the value proposition behind the Regulation succinctly saying that when it comes to *"artificial intelligence, trust is a must, not a nice to have"* (European Commission, 2021). With the present draft of the Regulation, Europe has made a conscious and an arguably tough choice on AI in a world where moving fast and breaking things seems to be the motto behind technology and innovation. Taking a leaf from the GDPR playbook with its extra-territorial operation, Article 2(1)(a) of the proposed AI Regulation ensures that the Regulation applies to any providers based outside the EU who make their AI systems available in the EU (European Commission, 2021). Akin to the GDPR which also embodies the same extra-territorial operation principle and imposes obligations on service providers handling/processing data of European Citizens whether from within the EU or without, the provision is also likely to have a profound impact on

Regulations across the globe (European Commission, 2021) in another display of the "Brussels Effect" discussed above. explain similar to the GDPR plan in 2018, the Commission is seeking to set down a basic level of public trust with strident safeguards against misuse and user/societal harm. Similar to the effect the GDPR had on the data protection legislations across the world (Deloitte, 2020), the EU hopes to build out a "third way" focusing on the development of AI in a human centric manner and hopes that the world follows suit (Atlantic Council, 2020).

A LEGISLATIVE FIRST AMIDST A SEA OF "STRATEGIES"

With the new model, the EU stands in stark contrast to every other jurisdiction on AI Regulation. Since Canada published the very first AI strategy in 2017 (Since then, the Pan Canadian Artificial Intelligence Strategy set up with a grant of $125 million to the Montreal Institute for Learning Algorithms (MILA), the Alberta Machine Intelligence Institute (AMII) in Edmonton, and the new Vector Institute for Artificial Intelligence, based in Toronto), more than 30 other countries have come out with AI strategies (Zhang et al, 2021). While the US and China are undoubtedly the leaders in the AI race, their strategies and those of other jurisdictions remain primarily innovation focused with a discussion around the broad strokes of ethical AI being discussed and largely left to the researcher's discretion. As the balance of AI supremacy shifts towards Asia – largely but not entirely because of China – A brief overview of the AI strategies in key jurisdictions in Asia would be insightful to understand their focus on AI ethics and social safeguards for research and development (Forbes, 2021). It would also shed light on their alignment with the EU principles espoused in the proposed Regulation and give a clearer picture of the potential domino effect that the EU Regulation could have, if any.

China

Since 2013, China has published several national-level policy documents, which reflect the intention to develop and deploy AI in a variety of sectors. For example, in 2015, the State Council released guidelines on China's 'Internet +' action. Other examples are the 10-year plan 'Made in China 2025' and the 13th 5-year plan (Roberts et al, 2021). On 20th July, 2017, China's State Council (The Highest organ of state administration in China consisting of the Premier, Vice-Premiers, State Councilor, Ministers in charge of ministries and commission, the Auditor-General, and the Secretary-General) released its most ambitious AI strategy with targets through to 2030 (State Council of China, 2017). While there had been previous strategies on the subject, they treated AI as one of the technology focus areas for China while the present strategy envisions China becoming "the world's primary AI innovation center" by 2030 (Roberts et al, 2021). Analysis of the strategy document (written in mandarin) reveals scant attention to ethical issues in AI and focuses, instead, on creating innovation clusters with an open source and collaborative approach creating synergies between industry, academia and research (Webster et al, 2017).

The Chinese Communist Party (CCP) seeks to leverage AI towards national competitiveness and discusses a range of applications in what it calls "social governance" to protect public security and "social stability" by "grasping group cognition and psychological changes in a timely manner" (State Council of China, 2017). In this introductory backdrop, the strategy goes on to list research on legal, ethical, and social issues related to AI, and establishment of laws, Regulations and ethical frameworks to ensure the healthy development of AI as one of the priority areas (State Council of China, 2017). China's focus on the rapid expansion of and innovation in AI also seems to be reaping dividend in practice as it most recently overtook the US in AI Journal Citations (The Verge, 2021). A strategy document entitled "Principles Of Next-Generation AI Governance - Responsible AI" was also released in 2019 along with the "Beijing AI Principles" by the Beijing Academy of Artificial Intelligence(BAAI) and touch upon the key principles of ethical AI (Laskai et al, 2019). However, with the practical aspects of AI research and implementation in China being far removed from these principles, it has received scant attention within and without and has been relegated to the domain of lip service.

In a shift away from its traditional model of doing things, China has also accepted and recognized that the era of AI would be led by entrepreneurship rather than its usual statist flavor thus nominating its corporate champions for this battle. China gave Baidu, Alibaba, Tencent, iFlytek and SenseTime "privileged positions for national technical standards setting and also was intended to give the companies confidence." (Allen, 2019). Most recently, investment in Chinese firms has surpassed that of the investment received by US firms (The Verge, 2021). The CCP's focus on AI as a tool for social construction and the use of its "smart cities" model to create a panopticon has a potential for state surveillance, censorship and oppression with grave implications for human rights and privacy (Kania, 2021) (Anderlini, 2019). It therefore makes the EU's AI Regulation a necessary balancing force or at the least, an alternative model as China lays the groundwork for a generational advantage in AI development (Allison and Schmidt, 2021).

Japan

The Japanese have placed AI front and center of not only its economic goal, but from holistic societal point of view as well. AI is looked at as an important method for the future design of the nation known as "Society 5.0" (Government of Japan – Cabinet Office, 2019). Proposed by the 5th Science and Technology Basic Plan, the idea follows the chronology of hunting society (Society 1.0), agricultural society (Society 2.0), industrial society (Society 3.0), and information society (Society 4.0). In the Japanese idea of Society 5.0, "a huge amount of information from sensors in physical space is accumulated in cyberspace. In cyberspace, this big data is analyzed by artificial intelligence (AI), and the analysis results are fed back to humans in physical space in various forms." With AI being a critical aspect of this ideal futuristic society, Japan's Sixth Basic Plan pledges efforts to realize concrete goals set forth in its AI Strategy 2019 (Government of Japan – Cabinet Office, 2021) (Integrated Innovation Strategy Promotion Council, 2019). Like most other comprehensive strategies, Japan's AI Strategy also addresses ethical bounds in which the research must be conducted to minimize harms from the negative aspects of AI as specified in section IV of the Strategy. The Document goes further in vision setting and includes an initiative on a multilateral framework on the social principles of AI to prevent the practice of ethics dumping i.e., conducting unethical research in countries/regions where ethics rules are loose. To remedy this and to encourage local research and testing of technologies before they're released on the market, Japan has leveraged regulatory sandboxes in order to avoid being ethically blindsided.

The Cabinet office in Japan also laid out the Social Principles of Human-centric AI document in March, 2019 whereby core principles of what must constitute a Human-centric approach for an "AI Ready Society" were laid down (Government of Japan – Cabinet Office, 2019). Under the AI R&D and Utilization principles section of the same document, the document also mandates that developers and business operators of AI should establish and comply with the AI development and utilization principles based on the fundamental philosophy and social principles of AI outlined below:

1. Human-Centric,
2. Education/Literacy,
3. Privacy Protection,
4. Ensuring Security,
5. Fair Competition,
6. Fairness, Accountability, and Transparency,
7. Innovation basic philosophy

The document lists the above principles under the basic philosophy of Dignity, Diversity & Inclusion and Sustainability: A sustainable society as the key values behind the society that Japan must aspire to be. Furthermore, a draft of "Guidelines for AI Development for International Debate" was published in July 2017, in which the Committee proposed AI development principles addressing AI developers, and a draft of "AI Utilization Guidelines" was published in August 2019, which provides a guidance for AI users, including but not limited to AI service providers and users (businesses) of AI systems (Ministry of Internal Affairs and Communications, 2017) (Ministry of Internal Affairs and Communications, 2019). The latest Integrated Innovation Strategy also promises to anticipate domestic and overseas trends while investigating the strengthening of the industrial competitiveness of Japan and the forms of AI governance, such as Regulations, standardization, guidelines, audits, etc. that contribute to the improvement of the social acceptance of AI (Government of Japan – Cabinet Office, 2019). In this backdrop and in light of Japan's own the EU's AI Regulation is bound to strengthen any multilateral efforts to push the principles embodied in the Regulation and also have a positive impact on Japan's push for its own municipal legislation in this regard.

Singapore

In stark contrast to the large datasets advantage of China and simply by cleverly positioning itself as the gateway of Asia with its nearly 6 million odd population, Singapore has also featured front and center in the race for AI in Asia. It's National Artificial Intelligence Strategy launched in November 2019 envisions Singapore as the "leader in developing and deploying scalable, impactful AI solutions" (The Smart Nation and Digital Governance Office, 2019).

The Strategy defines key sectors to focus the efforts on and sets down an AI deployment loop. To this effect, it has announced 5 National AI projects which will guide investment in AI research which include Intelligent Freight Planning, Seamless and Efficient Municipal Services, Chronic Disease Prediction and Management, Personalised Education through Adaptive Learning and Assessment, and Border Clearance Operations (The Smart Nation and Digital Governance Office, 2019). More importantly though, the Strategy puts a human-centric approach front and center. Under the section entitled "Ecosystem Enabler 4: Progressive and Trusted Environment", the Key Thrust 4.1 hopes to establish citizens' trust on the responsible use of AI and leads with the establishment of an industry-led Advisory Council on the Ethical Use of AI and Data to advise the Government (Infocomm Media Development Authority, 2018).

January 2019 also saw the publishing of Asia's first Model AI Governance Framework (First Edition) at the 2019 World Economic Forum Annual Meeting in Davos, Switzerland on 23rd January, 2019 by the Personal Data Protection Commission (PDPC) of Singapore thereby providing detailed guidance to the private sector for development and deployment of the technology (PDPC, 2019). A second edition of the Framework with additions was also released on 21st January, 2020.The Framework establishes two broad guiding principles underpinning AI research (PDPC, 2020) –:

1. Decisions made by or with the assistance of AI are explainable, transparent and fair to consumers; and
2. Their AI solutions are human-centric.

Section 3.1 of the Framework lists out these core principles form the basis of the four areas of guidance provided by the Framework which include the following (PDPC, 2020):

1. Internal governance structures and measures
2. Determining the level of human involvement in AI-augmented decision-making
3. Operations management
4. Stakeholder interaction and communication

Overall, the Framework contains robust and detailed ethics measures, a self-assessment guide, and two volumes of use case libraries developed with industry consultation setting up a risk management approach for tackling AI deployment risks (Granzen, 2021).

The Singapore PDPC had also released a discussion paper titled "Artificial intelligence (AI) and Personal Data – Fostering Responsible Development and Adoption of AI" which suggested an accountability based framework on the ethical, consumer protection and governance angles pertaining to AI which seeks to strike a balance between maximizing the benefits of AI without compromising privacy and accountability (PDPC, 2018). The paper prescribes the trifecta of explainability, transparency, and fairness for AI decision-making and also promisingly requires the systems to be human-centric. In a very promising sign, the paper also discussed a framework which was sector agnostic and widely applicable on principles defined above. However, the discussion paper from the beginning circumscribed its approach to the subject by taking a view that governance frameworks shall be technology neutral and "light touch" so that AI "can develop in a direction that is not hindered or distorted by prescriptive rules that are laid down prematurely. While in principle, this is an innocuous statement, how the present EU framework would be looked at and whether it would qualify as "light touch" from the Singapore perspective or not is a question yet to be answered. Contrary to the EU framework though, the proposed framework here made clear that the it does not does not set out to address specific questions of legal liability or apportionment of damages (PDPC, 2018). However, some indications of how Singapore might see this can be gathered in its treatment of data protection on a legislative level – a connected issue in case of AI, as discussed above.

Singapore has also collaborated with the World Economic Forum on its Model AI Governance Framework and in general, is an extremely sensitive to the market sentiments around the globe with its economy anchored on foreign investment and it being the hub for Asia headquarters for most major organisations. In that light, it is likely that any work on a potential legislation is bound to consider an international outlook and hence the EU's Regulatory landscape. However, its propensity to bend to market sentiment can also drive it away from too strictly regulating AI as well in order to avoid stifling research and economic prospects from the technology. An indication of this can be seen from the subtle but key differences that Singapore's Personal Data Protection Act has maintained in comparison to the GDPR with its lack of differentiation between sensitive and non-personal data within the legislation. Its most recent amendment, for instance, brought in "exceptions to consent" which now allows businesses to use, collect, and disclose data for "legitimate purposes", business improvement, and a wider scope of research and development.

The country being the finance hub for Asia, Singapore's Monetary Authority has also shown leadership in setting down responsible use principles of Fairness, Ethics Accountability and Transparency (FEAT) in the Finance sector aptly named 'Veritas' (Monetary Authority of Singapore, 2019). As Singapore seeks to project itself as a test bed for AI solutions seeking external validation internationally (See key thrust 5.2 in the National Strategy document), it is essential for it to protect its population from the potentially harmful use cases of AI (The Smart Nation and Digital Governance Office, 2019). While its model framework is largely aligned with the principles imbibed by the EU Regulation, some key differences remain. Singapore has traditionally retained its focus on economic factors over those of rights jurisprudence – as is also evident from its data protection laws aligning more towards facilitating AI research than ensuring human rights (Future for Privacy Forum, 2020). Hence, while it covers ethics within its strategies and frameworks, it remains to be seen whether it would heed Europe's call for the same human-centric approach in any future legislation on the subject, and if so, to what degree.

Taiwan

Taiwan announced its four-year "Taiwan AI Action Plan" in January 2018 with a view to leverage its Information Technology and Semiconductor edge to build AI capabilities (Government of Taiwan, 2021). The country has put down a massive investment of around 338.3 Million USD. The Strategy delineates the 5 national initiatives to further its AI goals until 2021.

1. To nurture advanced AI Research and Development talent locally and attract foreign talent in the field as well with its separate AI Talent Program (Government of Taiwan, 2021);
2. Set up a new Pilot project based on DARPA in the US and SIP in Japan (Government of Taiwan, 2021);
3. Setting up an AI International Innovation Hub with the aim of fostering 100 AI related start-ups (Government of Taiwan, 2021).
4. Testing of Open Data Fields and Flexible Regulations to support AI development (Government of Taiwan, 2021);
5. Demand driven talent cultivation for pairing with the Governments 5+2 Industrial Innovation push (Government of Taiwan, 2021).

Taiwan's AI policy comes in at a time where it has rapidly lost out its technological edge to Personal Computers manufacturing which moved away to China. Its primary focus on retaining its technological prowess is also vested in its security concerns with China (Carnegie Endowment for International Peace, 2020). Taiwan has placed scant focus on its ethics and regulatory framework so far, though as has also been noticed and documented by the European Parliament as of 2020 (European Parliament, 2020). Under its initiative for Flexible regulations to support AI development, areas of Consumer Protection for AI Applications, Open Data, Regulations for AI Applications and Rights and Obligations derived from AI Applications are merely listed as "to be evaluated and analysed". Apart from the above, the Ministry of Science and Technology (MoST) All Vista Healthcare Sub-Center (MAHC) - one of two sub-centers of the MoST Joint Research Center for AI Technology and All Vista Heathcare (AINTU).

It is located at the National Taiwan University (NTU) - has a project on "Ethical, Legal and Societal Issues in Artificial Intelligence assisted Medical Care" which seems to sum up its efforts in this regard (Netherlands Enterprise Agency, 2021).

South Korea

The "Mid-to Long-term Master Plan in Preparation for the Intelligent Information Society: Managing the Fourth Industrial Revolution" published by the Korean Ministry of Science, ICT and Future Planning (MSIP) is the AI Development Strategy guiding Korea's path on the technology (Ministry of Science and ICT, 2016). It builds on the Intelligent Information Society Strategy of January 2016 and considers the role of AI, amongst other technologies, in building South Korea's future. The policy specifically envisages devising and implementing a balanced policy regime that encompasses technologies, industries, and society and shapes the development of a more humane society. Over the years, South Korea has reposed a lot of faith and money in the industry making it increasingly visible as far as AI potential and investment initiatives are concerned (Chawla, 2020).

The recently released "National AI Strategy" involves plans to implement nine strategies and 100 initiatives in the three main areas of AI identified – establishment of AI ecosystem, utilisation of AI, and creation of human-centered AI by 2030 (Diplomat, 2019). The Strategy broadly looks at issues of investment and talent crunch and has more of an innovation focus than a human-centric bent. However, the Strategy also specifically includes identifying major pieces of legislation on key common issues across all areas as well as those that are specific to certain fields, and coming up with measures to establish or amend the existing legal system to avoid the adverse effects of AI and in line with the incoming AI era. The Strategy specifically looks to engage the industry in the process of Regulation and very wisely, perhaps, urges AI related companies to not press ahead with business without factoring in the regulatory measures which ensure ethical standards of research (Government of the Republic of Korea, 2019). A section within the strategy is dedicated to the "Realization of People-centered AI" which specifically deals with the prevention of dysfunction and establishing of AI ethics. The strategy specifically sets out establishing AI ethical standards that are consistent with global norms by identifying and analyzing the AI Code of Ethics and discussion trends in international organizations and major countries as a key deliverable (Government of the Republic of Korea, 2019).

India

India's policy on AI is defined by its National Strategy for Artificial intelligence released by the Government think tank Niti Aayog. The strategy identifies five focus areas where AI development could enable both growth and greater inclusion. The areas so identified are:

1. Healthcare;
2. Agriculture;
3. Education;
4. Urban-/smart city infrastructure; and
5. Transportation and Mobility

The strategy also seeks to identify present and potential barriers to be addressed

India took some early steps in 2018 setting up a Task Force on Artificial Intelligence established by the Ministry of Commerce and Industry to leverage AI for economic growth to come up with a policy framework for development of deployment of AI in the country. The Task Force's report looks at answering the following questions which shed considerable light on the long-term approach India will take on AI:

- What are the areas where government should play a role?
- How can AI improve quality of life and solve problems at scale for Indian citizens?
- What are the sectors that can generate employment and growth by the use of AI technology?

Defining the scope of the report as above, the report also specifically mentions how AI should not just be looked at as an economic booster but also as a technology for solutions. The Report goes on to identify 10 specific "domains of relevance" to india which include Manufacturing, FinTech, Agriculture, Healthcare, Technology for the Differently-abled, National Security, Environment, Public Utility Services, Retail and Customer Relationship, and Education. It also identifies certain problems in the specific context of India which might hinder uptake and deployment such as infrastructural barriers, managing scale and innovation, and the collection, validation and distribution of data.

On the aspect of AI ethics, the Task Force suggests various measures such as promoting explainability, transparency and auditability for biases. The report goes on to identify the need for new standards for AI deployment as well as industrial standards for robotics. The report also touches upon the need for ensuring privacy in this context but fails to go beyond recognising the importance of this sector and does not chart out any path towards aligning that with AI development and deployment. The report has received criticism on its failure to address ethical concerns on privacy and AI, (for instance issues of data minimization and purpose limitation – which are key issues for AI development) within what was supposed to be an expansive examination of the AI landscape in the country. On the domain of security for instance, one that the report identifies as being "relevant", the Report does not go beyond cost and capacity and does not touch upon the need for accountability in light of privacy and freedom of speech issues identified therein by several experts (Manheim et al, 2019). However, the report has been lauded for it's democratization of development and equal access as well as assigning ownership and framing transparent rules for usage of the infrastructure (Niti Aayog, 2018).

Outside of the two broad policy structures above, India has also taken a leaf out of Japan's playbook in promoting regulatory sandboxes to encourage thorough testing to uncover and weigh the possible downsides, social or otherwise, of emerging technologies with Telecom Regulatory Authority of India setting up one such sector wide sandbox and pointing to how sectoral leadership can go above and beyond national approaches in this regard (Telecom Regulatory Authority of India, 2017). The Indian Data Protection Bill, which is in the draft stage, has also been said to be requiring some updates in order to catch up with the AI age and structural protections to ensure fairness and transparency in automated profiling have been recommended (Medianama, 2020).

HUMAN-CENTRIC APPROACH: FROM STRATEGY TO LEGISLATION

As is evident from a brief snapshot of each major jurisdiction above, most strategies have focused on the rapid research and development or addressing talent shortages in AI. While that is the case by and large, the AI race has not been completely oblivious to the possible social pitfalls of AI development and deployment. The issue has even been a part of multilateral negotiations and discussions around digital economy for APAC Nations going forward featuring prominently, if not meaningfully, in the agendas of most nations (European Parliament, 2020). The G20 Ministerial meeting – which counts China, Australia, Japan, South Korea, Indonesia and India as members and hosted Singapore as a guest also adopted a set of non-binding AI principles to ensure AI is developed in a human-centric manner (G20, 2019). The OECD – which also counts Japan and South Korea as members (and counts Singapore as an adherent in this case) – adopted the OECD principles on AI and has made strident efforts to help members formulate consistent public policy approaches to AI (OECD, 2019). The Recommendations includes two substantive sections - Principles for responsible stewardship of trustworthy AI; and National Policies International co-operation for trustworthy AI (as available on the OECD AI Policy Observatory which collates data on various trends, data and country initiatives amongst other things). The most significant development so far on the subject is coming from the United Nations Educational, Scientific and Cultural Organisation (UNESCO) which has made considerable headway in bringing a measure of consensus to this otherwise polarized field. In the run up to its General Conference in November, 2021, AI ethics have been a key focus area for UNESCO when its newly minted recommendations – the result of months of dialogue and negotiations with stakeholders and UNESCO Member States leading to agreement on the draft text (UNESCO, 2021). The importance of the draft text of the Recommendation's cannot be overstated for it promises to truly achieve some consensus on AI ethics in what the EU's framework hopes to over time – standardization and benchmarking. The key difference between the two efforts being the legal backing that the EU brings to the harmonized ethical standards which UNESCO seems to be closing in on. It promises to be a reference point on how to control the risks and pitfalls associated with AI development and deployment. On the 2nd of July, the text was agreed upon and is now set to be adopted by the General Conference at its 41st session in November, 2021 (UNESCO, 2021).

Another key point that emerges from the analysis of the various AI strategies is the differences within the APAC region in approaches to regulating the technology. Three broad approaches to AI in the region include National/overarching AI strategies, Sector-specific/Industry-driven AI strategies, and Foundational Guidelines, Principles, and Standards on AI (International Institute of Communications, 2020). While efforts to harmonise these policy approaches have been long underway as discussed above, the EU Regulation throws key considerations of legislative direction and clarity into the mix.

The Regulation is the very first proposed AI legislation as opposed to AI strategies that most countries have developed and will likely serve as a draft and benchmark for other jurisdictions in the months and years to come. In its vision for the "Digital Decade" shortly preceding the release of the AI Regulation, the bloc puts a human-centric vision of the digital economy and society front and center (European Commission, 2021). The signaling within the Regulation itself also clearly reflects its disapproving stance on the current state of affairs and AI use cases adopted by other countries while charting its own different vision for AI. For instance, the inclusion of AI systems "that allow for 'social scoring' by governments" is also a direct reference to the Chinese social scoring system which the Regulation which the Regulation proclaims "may lead to the detrimental or unfavourable treatment of natural persons or whole groups thereof in social contexts" (European Commission, 2021).

While accepting the need for a human-centric policy, skeptics of the EU AI strategy have expressed their reservations about the harsher measures adopted by EU. The perception is that the Regulation would cripple AI development in the region while the rest of the world leaps forward (TechCrunch, 2021). Such fears around the Regulation are reminiscent of the competitiveness doomsday scenarios projected at the time GDPR was being implemented as well (International Association of Privacy

Professionals, 2019). However, Europe has chosen to double down on its bet for a rights-based regime with the present Regulation. It also released an in-depth report on the compatibility of GDPR with AI development concluding that the two were compatible and clarifications and expanded prescriptions for developers were required instead of sweeping changes suggested by critics of the EU digital rights regime (European Parliament, 2020). However, it is pertinent to point out that the EU's February 2020 white paper points out that efforts need to be made to bridge the AI funding gap between the EU and the rest of the world. It notes that "3.2 billion [euros] were invested in AI in Europe in 2016, compared to around 12.1 billion [euros] in North America and 6.5 billion [euros] in Asia" while noting that in the three years "EU funding for research and innovation for AI has risen to 1.5 billion [euros], i.e. a 70% increase compared to the previous period," (European Commission, 2020) (Carnegie Endowment for International Peace, 2020). Increasingly, the opinion on the interaction of the two is coming to a consensus on the two being lifelong partners with the GDPR helping create the trust necessary for AI adoption as AI and data-specific Regulations arise globally along the EU model (Spyridaki, 2021). Over the years since the enactment of the GDPR, Asia has seen an increasing adoption and inspiration from the principles and provisions of the GDPR (Deloitte, 2020). This is crucial, since the EU inspired data protection legislative mandates or processes already in place in these jurisdictions are likely to anchor these jurisdictions to at least some, if varying, form of human-centric approach on AI given how the same data is the fuel of any AI development.

A crucial factor in the uptake and international acceptance of the legislation and its standards would be the way the United States – the West's AI powerhouse reacts to it. While some quarters within the US have expressed their reservations for the EU's "third way" between China's state led and US's open regulatory regime, the EU has been keen on signaling that its third way is not opposed to the US approach but rather similar to it (Politico, 2021). The Transatlantic AI Accord pitched by the EU is an effort to reconcile these differences to present a united front against the Chinese approach (European Commission, 2020). Another key factor in this debate that is likely to transcend National Governments is the fact that major tech giants have voluntarily extended EU technical and legal standards to their users across the world with an eye towards creating user trust – a key metric for companies (The Verge, 2018).

While the jury is still out on whether the EU's approach has yielded the best outcomes for AI, if the GDPR is an example, and it argued above that It can be on account of the common thread of rights-based jurisprudence connecting them and the nature of the technology, the adoption of EU's AI model is likely to be adopted in Asia. While the US response the EU rulebook will be crucial, the Regulation already builds on a variety of past and ongoing multilateral efforts discussed above to harmonize the AI strategies and regimes across jurisdictions (OECD, 2020).

CONCLUSION

In its essence, a common understanding derived from the reading of the above AI strategies is the promise of economic growth that most nations are banking upon with stellar estimates running into hundreds of billions if not trillions of dollars in value addition to economy and as much as 26% growth to the GDP amounting to nearly $15.7 Trillion with a 50% reduction in government costs by in the next decade or so (PwC, 2021). Hence, naturally, the AI strategies have paid little attention to the ethics of AI development and most only provide lip service to the very essential element, if at all. The European Union's proposed legislation and human centric cautionary approach has rather predictably been a contentious move against this backdrop of reckless focus on AI commercialization at the cost of propriety in development. Several observers have also predicted very stark scenarios for the EU's AI development and leadership prospects with predictions of it estimated losses attributed to the legislation allegedly running as high as 10.9 billion euros per year by 2025, or 31 billion euros over the next five years (Center for Data Innovation, 2021). Working on the basis of these impending compliance costs calculated by the center itself, it also seems to suggest that the investment in European AI companies could see a reduction by about 20 percent. The report also goes on to say that only 7% of the non-financial businesses in the EU use AI but about 1/3rd of the non-financial businesses (by value) would be designated as high risk by the Regulation thereby placing an unnecessary cost on the businesses. While critiquing the analysis by the center and the numbers associated with it is beyond the scope of this paper, it is indisputable that there will be additional costs to compliance (Center for Data Innovation, 2021).

On that front, while one may differ on the numbers, the argument that ballooning compliance costs can be a problem with any emerging technology is isn't really an argument as much as it is a statement of fact. Perhaps a better lens to look at this issue calls for an analysis of the necessity of the compliance burdens placed on these emerging technologies – a factor the report does not consider - and a repetition of the oft repeated quote of "Just because we can, doesn't mean we should" – a thought that probably should be at the forefront of every AI researcher/developer's mind. Examples of deepfakes, biased AI, facial recognition error are rampant in the AI industry and have been causes for concern in a range of industries including healthcare, autonomous driving, education, lending, legal and law enforcement (European Parliament, 2021). Inevitably, the technology is bound to be the mainstay of almost every digitised industry as it complements the very idea of "machines" – that of reducing human effort. However, its rapid adoption is no guarantee of its accuracy. A study by Gartner has found that nearly 85% of all AI implementations will fail by 2022 leaving the accuracy of any AI derived insights at 15% (Gartner, 2018). The dreadful impact of these often opaque and automated decision-making has on a real person cannot be overstated. Devoid of its own moral compass, AI borrows it from the developers who cannot point out the anomalies and biases in algorithms like they could have regular software code thanks to deep learning. From discrimination on account of faulty facial recognition (Najibi, 2020), to dubious ethical foundations in driverless cars (New York Times, 2021) and Amazon firing employees who actually worked as expected of them (Business Standard, 2021), the concerns related to improperly developed and deployed AI are aplenty. Hence, what becomes important to understand is that AI doesn't only scale solutions – it also scales risk (Harvard Business Review, 2020).

Several instances of poor AI ethics translating to reputational, regulatory and legal risks with instances of organisations being investigated for algorithms that encourage nurses and doctors to pay more attention to white patients and those that grant larger credit limits to men over women. The discussions on AI ethics which were largely limited to academic and non-profit spheres have now been mainstreamed to the likes of Google, Amazon, Microsoft and Facebook since the ground reality is that it impacts the bottom line. Most major suppliers of facial recognition softwares had already banned sales to police departments before the European Data Protection Board (EDPB) and European Data Protection Supervisor Issued a statement calling for the ban of the use of such technologies in public spaces. Similar actions have already been taken by major cities in the USA. A recent case in point in this regard is the AI ethics researcher Timnit Gebru's exit from Google – which has since become a PR scandal that threatens to derail the credibility and equity of its groundbreaking research on large language models and has shed light on the environmental cost and social effects of such models.

Whether the legislative first that is the EU's Artificial Intelligence legislative proposal, will take hold in the global landscape for AI remains to be seen. However, the above analysis shows that if the EU's history of being the focal point of digital jurisprudence and the recent consolidation on AI principles on a multilateral organizational level is anything to go by, the world seems to be on track to slowly come around to regulating the risks of unchecked AI development, on similar ethical lines as the EU's bold legislative proposal. The view of Europe's pivotal role in promoting trustworthy AI and aligning the AI and other emerging technologies with economic, social and environmental goals, such as the SDG's and the proposal is a manifestation of those expectations to fill the ethics vacuum in research (Centre for European Policy Studies, 2019). While the proposal itself is also a work in progress and has received a lot of flak from social/ethical activists and the proponents of self-regulation alike, the proposal is likely to evolve over time before and after its enactment and is most certainly an unprecedented move to nudge conversation and research on ethical AI.

REFERENCES

Allen, G. (2019). *Understanding China's AI Strategy*. The Center for a New American Security (CNAS). https://www.cnas.org/publications/reports/understanding-chinas-ai-strategy

Allison, G., & Schmidt, E. (2020). *Is China Beating the U.S. to AI Supremacy?* Belfer Center for Science and International Affairs. https://www.belfercenter.org/publication/china-beating-us-ai-supremacy#footnote-027

Anderlini, J. (2019). How China's smart-city tech focuses on its own citizens. *Financial Times*. https://www.ft.com/content/46bc137a-5d27-11e9-840c-530737425559

Beijing, A. I. (2019). Principles. *Datenschutz Datensich*, *43*(10), 656. doi:10.100711623-019-1183-6

Benjamin, M. (2021). *How much will the Artificial Intelligence Act cost Europe?* Center for Data Innovation. https://www2.datainnovation.org/2021-aia-costs.pdf

Blackman, R. (2020). *A Practical Guide to Building Ethical AI*. https://hbr.org/2020/10/a-practical-guide-to-building-ethical-ai

Boxall, L. (2020). *Exceptional Exceptions to Consent*. Data Protection Excellence Network. https://www.dpexnetwork.org/articles/exceptional-exceptions-consent/

Bradford, A. (2020). *The Brussels Effect: How the European Union Rules the World*. Oxford University Press. doi:10.1093/oso/9780190088583.001.0001

Brattberg, E., Csernatoni, R., & Rugova, V. (2020). *Europe and AI: Leading, Lagging Behind, or Carving Its Own Way?* Carnegie Endowment for International Peace. https://carnegieendowment.org/2020/07/09/europe-and-ai-leading-lagging-behind-or-carving-its-own-way-pub-82236

Brethenoux, E., Dekate, C., Hare, J., Govekar, M., Chandrasekaran, A., & Rich, C. (2018). *Predicts 2019: Artificial Intelligence Core Technologies*. Gartner. https://www.gartner.com/en/documents/3894131

Cabinet Office of Japan. (2019). *Social Principles of Human-centric AI*. https://www8.cao.go.jp/cstp/stmain/aisocialprinciples.pdf

Castro, D., & Chivo, E. (2019). *Want Europe to have the best AI? Reform the GDPR*. International Association of Privacy Professionals. https://iapp.org/news/a/want-europe-to-have-the-best-ai-reform-the-gdpr/

Chawla, V. (2020). Why We Shouldn't Underestimate South Korea In The Race To AI Supremacy. *Analytics India Mag*. https://analyticsindiamag.com/why-we-shouldnt-underestimate-south-korea-in-the-race-to-ai-supremacy/

Clarke, L. (2021). *The EU's leaked AI Regulation is ambitious but disappointingly vague*. https://tech-monitor.ai/policy/eu-ai-Regulation-machine-learning-european-union

Daws, R. (2021). *Amazon will continue to ban police from using its facial recognition AI*. Artificial Intelligence News. https://artificialintelligence-news.com/2021/05/24/amazon-continue-ban-police-using-facial-recognition-ai/

Deloitte Asia Pacific Limited. (2020). *Deloitte Asia Pacific Privacy Guide 2020-21*. https://www2.deloitte.com/mm/en/pages/risk/articles/ap-privacy-guide-2020-2021.html

European Commission. (2018). *Coordinated Plan on Artificial Intelligence (COM(2018) 795 final)*. https://eur-lex.europa.eu/resource.html?uri=cellar:22ee84bb-fa04-11e8-a96d-01aa75ed71a1.0002.02/DOC_1&format=PDF

European Commission. (2018). *Communication From The Commission To The European Parliament, The European Council, The Council, The European Economic And Social Committee And The Committee Of The Regions 25th April, 2018. COM(2018)237*. https://eur-lex.europa.eu/legal-content/EN/TXT/PDF/?uri=CELEX:52018DC0237&from=EN

European Commission. (2020). *EU-US: A new transatlantic agenda for global change*. https://ec.europa.eu/commission/presscorner/detail/en/IP_20_2279

European Commission. (2020). *On Artificial Intelligence: A European Approach to Excellence and Trust*. https://ec.europa.eu/info/publications/white-paper-artificial-intelligence-european-approach-excellence-and-trust_en

European Commission. (2020). *Communication from the Commission to the European Parliament and the Council - two years of application of the General Data Protection Regulation*. https://ec.europa.eu/info/law/law-topic/data-protection/communication-two-years-application-general-data-protection-regulation_en

European Commission. (2021). *Proposal For A Regulation Of The European Parliament And Of The Council Laying Down Harmonised Rules On Artificial Intelligence (Artificial Intelligence Act) And Amending Certain Union Legislative Acts*. https://digital-strategy.ec.europa.eu/en/library/proposal-Regulation-laying-down-harmonised-rules-artificial-intelligence

European Commission. (2021). *Coordinated Plan on Artificial intelligence Review* (COM(2021) 205 final). https://eur-lex.europa.eu/resource.html?uri=cellar:01ff45fa-a375-11eb-9585-01aa75ed71a1.0001.02/DOC_1&format=PDF

European Commission. (2021). *Communication: 2030 Digital Compass: The European way for the Digital Decade. Brussels, 9.3.2021 COM(2021) 118 final.* https://eur-lex.europa.eu/legal-content/en/TXT/?uri=CELEX%3A52021DC0118

European Commission, Directorate-General for Communication. (2018). *A definition of AI: Main capabilities and scientific disciplines.* https://digital-strategy.ec.europa.eu/en/library/definition-artificial-intelligence-main-capabilities-and-scientific-disciplines

European Commission – Press Release. (2021). *Europe fit for the Digital Age: Commission proposes new rules and actions for excellence and trust in Artificial Intelligence.* https://ec.europa.eu/commission/presscorner/detail/en/ip_21_1682

European Data Protection Board. (2021). *EDPB & EDPS call for ban on use of AI for automated recognition of human features in publicly accessible spaces, and some other uses of AI that can lead to unfair discrimination.* Press Release statement 2021_05. https://edpb.europa.eu/news/news/2021/edpb-edps-call-ban-use-ai-automated-recognition-human-features-publicly-accessible_en

European Digital Rights. (2021). *Open letter: Civil society call for the introduction of red lines in the upcoming European Commission proposal on Artificial Intelligence.* https://edri.org/wp-content/uploads/2021/01/EDRi-open-letter-AI-red-lines.pdf

European Parliament. (2017). *European Parliament resolution of 16 February 2017 with recommendations to the Commission on Civil Law Rules on Robotics.* Resolution No. P8_TA(2017)0051 dated 16th February, 2017. https://www.europarl.europa.eu/doceo/document/TA-8-2017-0051_EN.html

European Parliament, Panel for Future of Science and Technology. (2020). *The impact of the General Data Protection Regulation (GDPR) on artificial intelligence.* https://www.europarl.europa.eu/RegData/etudes/STUD/2020/641530/EPRS_STU(2020)641530_EN.pdf

European Parliament, Panel for Future of Science and Technology. (2020). *The ethics of artificial intelligence: Issues and Initiatives.* https://www.europarl.europa.eu/RegData/etudes/STUD/2020/634452/EPRS_STU(2020)634452_EN.pdf

European Parliament. (2021). *Tackling Deepfakes in European Policy.* Panel for Future of Science and Technology. https://www.europarl.europa.eu/RegData/etudes/STUD/2021/690039/EPRS_STU%282021%29690039_EN.pdf

European Parliament, Panel for Future of Science and Technology. (2020). *The ethics of artificial intelligence: Issues and Initiatives.* Author.

Evans, M., & Mathews, W. (2019). New York Regulator Probes UnitedHealth Algorithm for Racial Bias. *The Wall Street Journal.* https://www.wsj.com/articles/new-york-regulator-probes-unitedhealth-algorithm-for-racial-bias-11572087601

Feigenbaum, E. (2020). *Assuring Taiwan's Innovation Future.* Carnegie Endowment for International Peace. https://carnegieendowment.org/files/2020-Feigenbaum-Taiwan_Innovation.pdf

G20 Ministerial Statement on Trade and Digital Economy. (2019). https://www.mofa.go.jp/files/000486596.pdf

Government of Japan. (2020). *Integrated Innovation Strategy 2020*. https://www8.cao.go.jp/cstp/english/strategy_2020.pdf

Government of Japan, Cabinet Office. (2021). *Sixth Science, Technology and Innovation Basic Plan*. https://www8.cao.go.jp/cstp/english/sti_basic_plan.pdf

Government of Japan, Cabinet Office. (n.d.). *The 5th Science and Technology Basic Plan, Human-centered society that balances economic advancement with the resolution of social problems by a system that highly integrates cyberspace and physical space*. https://www8.cao.go.jp/cstp/kihonkeikaku/5basicplan_en.pdf

Government of Taiwan. (n.d.a). *AI for Industrial Innovation*. https://ai.taiwan.gov.tw/actionplan/ai-for-industrial-innovation/

Government of Taiwan. (n.d.b). *AI International Innovation Hub*. https://ai.taiwan.gov.tw/actionplan/ai-international-innovation-hub/

Government of Taiwan. (n.d.c). *AI Pilot Project*. https://ai.taiwan.gov.tw/actionplan/ai-pilot-project/

Government of Taiwan. (n.d.d). *AI Talent Program*. https://ai.taiwan.gov.tw/actionplan/ai-talent-program/ Last Accessed 24th July, 2021.

Government of Taiwan. (n.d.e). *Cabinet plans to develop the Nation's AI Industry*. https://ai.taiwan.gov.tw/news/cabinet-plans-to-develop-the-nations-ai-industry/

Government of Taiwan. (n.d.f). *Test Fields and Regulatory Co-creation*. https://ai.taiwan.gov.tw/action-plan/test-fields-and-regulatory-co-creation/

Granzen, A. (2021). *How will Singapore ensure responsible AI use?* GovInsider. https://govinsider.asia/digital-gov/achim-granzen-forrester-ai-drives-the-evolution-of-technology-and-data-governance/

GreenleafG. (2018). *Global Convergence of Data Privacy Standards and Laws: Speaking Notes for the European Commission Events on the Launch of the General Data Protection Regulation (GDPR) in Brussels & New Delhi, 25 May 2018*. UNSW Law Research Paper No. 18-56. Available at https://ssrn.com/abstract=3184548 doi:10.2139/ssrn.3184548

Hao, K. (2020). *We read the paper that forced Timnit Gebru out of Google. Here's what it says*. https://www.technologyreview.com/2020/12/04/1013294/google-ai-ethics-research-paper-forced-out-timnit-gebru/

Heikkila, M. (2021a). *Europe throws down gauntlet on AI with new rulebook*. Politico. https://www.politico.eu/article/europe-throws-down-gauntlet-on-ai-with-new-rulebook/

Heikkila, M. (2021b). *Ex-Google chief: European tech 'not big enough' to compete with China alone*. Politico. https://www.politico.eu/article/ex-google-chief-eric-schmidt-european-tech-not-big-enough-to-compete-with-china-alone/

Hickok, E., Mohandas, S., & Paul Barooah, S. (2018). *The AI Task Force Report - The first steps towards India's AI framework*. The Center for Internet and Society. https://cis-india.org/internet-governance/blog/the-ai-task-force-report-the-first-steps-towards-indias-ai-framework

High-Level Expert Group on Artificial Intelligence (AI HLEG). (2019). *Ethics Guidelines for Trustworthy AI.* https://digital-strategy.ec.europa.eu/en/library/ethics-guidelines-trustworthy-ai

High-Level Expert Group on Artificial Intelligence (AI HLEG). (2020a). *Policy and investment recommendations for trustworthy Artificial Intelligence.* https://digital-strategy.ec.europa.eu/en/library/policy-and-investment-recommendations-trustworthy-artificial-intelligence

High-Level Expert Group on Artificial Intelligence (AI HLEG). (2020b). *Assessment List for Trustworthy AI (ALTAI).* https://digital-strategy.ec.europa.eu/en/library/assessment-list-trustworthy-artificial-intelligence-altai-self-assessment

High-Level Expert Group on Artificial Intelligence (AI HLEG). (2020c). *Sectoral Considerations on the Policy and Investment Recommendations.* https://digital-strategy.ec.europa.eu/en/library/assessment-list-trustworthy-artificial-intelligence-altai-self-assessment

Hopland, C., Dorwart, H., & Zanfir-Fortuna, G. (2020). *Singapore's Personal Data Protection Act shifts away from a consent-centric framework.* Future of Privacy Forum. https://fpf.org/blog/singapores-personal-data-protection-act-shifts-away-from-a-consent-centric-framework/

Infocomm Media Development Authority. (2018). *Composition of the Advisory Council on the Ethical Use of Artificial Intelligence ("AI") and Data.* https://www.imda.gov.sg/news-and-events/Media-Room/Media-Releases/2018/composition-of-the-advisory-council-on-the-ethical-use-of-ai-and-data

Integrated Innovation Strategy Promotion Council Decision. (2019). *AI Strategy 2019.* https://www.kantei.go.jp/jp/singi/ai_senryaku/pdf/aistratagy2019en.pdf

International Institute of Communications. (2020). *Artificial Intelligence in the Asia-Pacific Region.* https://www.iicom.org/wp-content/uploads/IIC-AI-Report-2020.pdf

Jarmanning, A. (2020). *Boston Bans Use Of Facial Recognition Technology. It's The 2nd-Largest City To Do So.* WBUR News. https://www.wbur.org/news/2020/06/23/boston-facial-recognition-ban

Joshi, D. (2020). *India's Privacy Law Needs To Incorporate Rights Against The Machine.* Medianama. https://www.medianama.com/2020/05/223-indias-privacy-law-needs-to-incorporate-rights-against-the-machine/

Kania, E. (2018). *China's ambitions an Artificial Intelligence: A challenge to the future of democracy?* https://www.power3point0.org/2018/08/08/chinas-ambitions-in-artificial-intelligence-a-challenge-to-the-future-of-democracy/

Khanna, A., & Khanna, P. (2020). Where Asia is taking the world with AI. *Forbes.* https://www.forbes.com/sites/insights-ibmai/2020/05/21/where-asia-is-taking-the-world-with-ai/?sh=3669da577947

Laskai, L., & Webster, G. (2019). *Translation: Chinese Expert Group Offers 'Governance Principles' for 'Responsible AI'.* https://perma.cc/V9FL-H6J7

Loucks, J. (2018). Deepfakes and AI: Questioning artificial intelligence ethics and the dangers of AI. In *State of AI in Enterprise* (2nd ed.). Deloitte. https://www2.deloitte.com/us/en/pages/technology-media-and-telecommunications/articles/deepfakes-artificial-intelligence-ethics.html

Manheim, K., & Kaplan, L. (2019). Artificial Intelligence: Risks to Privacy and Democracy. *Yale Journal of Law and Technology, 21*(106). https://www.trai.gov.in/consultation-paper-privacy-security-and-ownership-data-telecom-sector

Minevich, M. (2021). *European AI needs strategic leadership, not overregulation.* TechCrunch. https://techcrunch.com/2021/05/15/european-ai-needs-strategic-leadership-not-overRegulation/

Ministry of Internal Affairs and Communications. (2017). *AI Utilisation Guidelines.* https://www.soumu.go.jp/main_content/000499625.pdf

Ministry of Internal Affairs and Communications. (2019). *AI Utilisation Guidelines.* https://www.soumu.go.jp/main_content/000658284.pdf

Ministry of Science and ICT, Government of Taiwan. (2016). *Mid-to Long-term Master Plan in Preparation for the Intelligent Information Society: Managing the Fourth Industrial Revolution.* http://english.msit.go.kr/cms/english/pl/policies2/__icsFiles/afieldfile/2017/07/20/Master%20Plan%20for%20the%20intelligent%20information%20society.pdf

Monetary Authority of Singapore. (2019). *MAS Partners Financial Industry to Create Framework for Responsible Use of AI.* https://www.mas.gov.sg/news/media-releases/2019/mas-partners-financial-industry-to-create-framework-for-responsible-use-of-ai

Mueller-Kaler, J. (2020). *Europe's third way.* Atlantic Council. https://www.atlanticcouncil.org/content-series/smart-partnerships/europes-third-way/

Najibi, A. (2020). *Racial Discrimination in Facial Recognition Technology.* Blog, Science Policy, Special Edition – Science Policy and Social Justice. Graduate School of Arts and Sciences, Harvard University. https://sitn.hms.harvard.edu/flash/2020/racial-discrimination-in-face-recognition-technology/

Netherlands Enterprise Agency. (2020). *Artificial Intelligence; an overview of policies and developments in Taiwan.* https://www.rvo.nl/sites/default/files/2020/04/AI-Developments-in-Taiwan.pdf

Ong, T. (2018). *Facebook announces new European privacy controls, for the world.* The Verge. https://www.theverge.com/2018/4/18/17250840/facebook-privacy-protections-europe-world-gdpr

Organisation for Economic Cooperation and Development. (2019). *Committee on Digital Economy Policy, Recommendation of the Council on Artificial Intelligence adopted on. OECD/LEGAL/0449.* https://legalinstruments.oecd.org/en/instruments/OECD-LEGAL-0449

Personal Data Protection Commission. (2018). *Discussion Paper on Artificial Intelligence (AI) and Personal Data - Fostering Responsible Development and Adoption of AI.* https://www.pdpc.gov.sg/-/media/Files/PDPC/PDF-Files/Resource-for-Organisation/AI/Discussion-Paper-on-AI-and-PD---050618.pdf

Personal Data Protection Commission. (2020). *Model Artificial Intelligence Governance Framework – Second Edition.* Accessible at: https://www.pdpc.gov.sg/-/media/Files/PDPC/PDF-Files/Resource-for-Organisation/AI/SGModelAIGovFramework2.pdf

Pietsch, B. (2021). 2 Killed in Driverless Tesla Car Crash, Officials Say. *The New York Times.* https://www.nytimes.com/2021/04/18/business/tesla-fatal-crash-texas.html

PwC. (2017). *Sizing the prize: PwC's Global Artificial Intelligence Study: Exploiting the AI Revolution.* https://www.pwc.com/gx/en/issues/data-and-analytics/publications/artificial-intelligence-study.html

Roberts, H., Cowls, J., Morley, J., Taddeo, M., Wang, V., & Floridi, L. (2021). The Chinese approach to artificial intelligence: An analysis of policy, ethics, and Regulation. *AI & Society*, *36*(1), 59–77. doi:10.100700146-020-00992-2

Soper, S. (2021). Amazon employee fired by a robot: It's you vs machine's algorithm. *The Business Standard.* https://www.business-standard.com/article/international/amazon-employee-fired-by-a-robot-it-s-you-vs-machine-s-algorithm-121062801581_1.html

Spyridaki, K. (2021). *GDPR and AI: Friends, foes or something in between?* SAS Europe. https://www.sas.com/en_us/insights/articles/data-management/gdpr-and-ai--friends--foes-or-something-in-between-.html

Stangarone, T. (2019). COVID-19 Underscores the Benefits of South Korea's Artificial Intelligence Push. *The Diplomat.* https://thediplomat.com/2020/12/covid-19-underscores-the-benefits-of-south-koreas-artificial-intelligence-push/

State Council of China. (2017). *A Next Generation Artificial Intelligence Development Plan.* New American. https://na-production.s3.amazonaws.com/documents/translation-fulltext-8.1.17.pdf

Taulli, T. (2020). *How 5G will Unleash AI.* https://www.forbes.com/sites/tomtaulli/2020/05/08/how-5g-will-unleash-ai/?sh=59235be448c3

Telecom Regulatory Authority of India. (2017). *TRAI's Consultation Paper on Privacy, Security and Ownership of the Data in the Telecom Sector.* https://trai.gov.in/sites/default/files/CIS_07_11_2017.pdf

Telford, T. (2019). *Apple Card algorithm sparks gender bias allegations against Goldman Sachs.* https://www.washingtonpost.com/business/2019/11/11/apple-card-algorithm-sparks-gender-bias-allegations-against-goldman-sachs/

The Declaration of the International Panel on Artificial Intelligence facilitating international collaboration on AI led in the most part by Canada and France. (n.d.). https://www.canada.ca/en/innovation-science-economic-development/news/2019/05/declaration-of-the-international-panel-on-artificial-intelligence.html

The Smart Nation and Digital Governance Office, Government of Singapore. (2019). *National Artificial Intelligence Strategy.* https://www.smartnation.gov.sg/docs/default-source/default-document-library/national-ai-strategy.pdf?sfvrsn=2c3bd8e9_4

TRPC. (2018). *Privacy in the Age of Artificial Intelligence.* Briefing Paper. https://trpc.biz/old_archive/wp-content/uploads/IIC.Singapore-AI.BriefingPaper.20Nov.pdf

United Nations Educational, Scientific and Cultural Organisation (UNESCO). (2021). *Draft Text of the Recommendation on the Ethics of Artificial Intelligence.* https://unesdoc.unesco.org/ark:/48223/pf0000377897/PDF/377897eng.pdf.multi

Van Roy, V., Rossetti, F., Perset, K., Galindo-Romero, L., & Watch, A. I. (2021). National strategies on Artificial Intelligence: A European perspective, 2021 edition, EUR 30745 EN. Publications Office of the European Union. doi:10.2760/069178

Vincent, J. (2021a). *China overtakes US in AI start-up funding with a focus on facial recognition and chips.* The Verge. https://www.theverge.com/2018/2/22/17039696/china-us-ai-funding-startup-comparison

Vincent, J. (2021b). *Artificial intelligence research continues to grow as China overtakes US in AI journal citations.* The Verge. https://www.theverge.com/2021/3/3/22310840/ai-research-global-growth-china-us-paper-citations-index-report-2020

Wang, W. (2019). *Reflecting on Chinese Artificial Intelligence and National Responsible Innovation.* https://cyberbrics.info/wp-content/uploads/2019/10/Reflecting-on-Chinese-Artificial-Intelligence-and-National-Responsible-Innovation.pdf

Webster, G., Creemers, R., Triolo, P., & Kania, E. (2017). *China's Plan to 'Lead' in AI: Purpose, Prospects, and Problems.* New America. https://www.newamerica.org/cybersecurity-initiative/blog/chinas-plan-lead-ai-purpose-prospects-and-problems/

Zhang, D., Mishra, S., Brynjolfsson, E., Etchemendy, J., Ganguli, D., Grosz, B., Lyons, T., Manyika, J., Carlos Niebles, J., Sellitto, M., Shoham, Y., Clark, J., & Perrault, R. (n.d.). *The AI Index 2021 Annual Report.* AI Index Steering Committee, Human-Centered AI Institute, Stanford University. https://aiindex.stanford.edu/wp-content/uploads/2021/03/2021-AI-Index-Report_Master.pdf

Chapter 6
Blockchain Technology in the Agricultural Supply Chain:
A Case Study of India

Rama Sharma

School of Law, Justice, and Governance, Gautam Buddha University, India

Anurag Singh

Meerut College, India

ABSTRACT

India is an agrarian country, and farmers are the backbone of this agriculture system. Now, when India is stepping ahead in all sectors of economy, agriculture is still lagging behind. Farmers are struggling for a minimum standard of living due to non-availability of basic infrastructure and natural calamities. According to the National Crime Records Bureau (NCRB), 10,349 persons involved in farming sector (consisting of 5,763 farmers or cultivators and 4,586 agricultural labourers) committed suicide during 2018, accounting for 7.7% of total suicide (134,516) victims. In this light, it is impertinent to see the current agricultural policies in place aiming to revive the status of farmers in India. Supply of low quality and spurious inputs is an important factor for increased cost without adequate gain in productivity. In this chapter, effort has been made to know how blockchain technology can improve the agricultural sector as well as the condition of farmers in India.

INTRODUCTION

Adverse climate, long-term environmental degradation, and cost increases in the input and commodity markets are all risks to farmers around the world. Furthermore, peasant farm households face many obstacles, both natural (soil quality, precipitation, etc.) and human (infrastructure, fiscal policies, marketing, information, and innovation). Better credit, better quality, and less expensive data sources are required for harvests, provide valuable weather information to agricultural producers for the suspicious design of their crop yields, eliminate intermediaries by connecting farmers directly to consumers/retailers, and

DOI: 10.4018/978-1-7998-8641-9.ch006

improve cultivating productivity to ensure farmers' budgetary strength are all goals of an e-agriculture scenario (Alam, 2020). The development of information and communication technology (ICT) over the last decade has opened up a slew of new options for overcoming some of agriculture's challenges. Growing use of mobile-broadband access devices, the Internet - of - things (IoT), unmanned aerial vehicles, communications protocol, potential for big data analytics, and AI i.e., artificial intelligence, among other technological advancements, have created crucial tools and technologies for agricultural stakeholders to develop production, marketing, and development processes. (Ahmad, 2021), e.g. When it comes to ICT technology used by farmers, the Imperial Tobacco Company of India (ITC) Ltd.'s e-Choupal initiative, which connects directly with rural farmers via the Internet for the announcement of agriculture and aquaculture products such as Soyabean wheat coffee and prawns, is a good example. Similarly, in rural India, the performance enhancing Web access kiosks to provide farmers with access to marketing and agricultural information, allowing them to make better-informed decisions and potentially boost their revenue by better matching farm produce to market demand (Trendov, 2020).

Blockchain technology is a hybrid of ancient and modern technologies that have been restructured. When we mention "block" and "chain," we're referring to digital data (the "block") that is stored in a public database (the "chain"). On the blockchain, "blocks" are made up of digital information. As the name implies, blockchain is made up of a series of interconnected blocks. It is a distributed ledger for preserving the history of a digital transaction that is shared and unchanged cryptographically. On the blockchain system, each participant (stakeholder) stores copies of all past transactions ever conducted using the provided system. However, the fact that a party/node has no single owner suggests that it is not a centralized system (Laurence, 2019). When Blockchain technology was announced through the paper titled *"Bitcoin: A Peer-to-Peer Electronic Cash System"* by Satoshi Nakamoto in 2008, it was an innovative mix of public key cryptography (invented in the 1970s), cryptographic hash functions (born in the 1970s) and proof-of-work invented in the 1990s (Nakamoto, 2008). A variety of financial technology (FinTech) applications, distributed leisure technology (DLT) applications with peer-to-peer electronic cash transactions and more than thousands of crypto currencies are being used for Blockchain. The most famous crypto currency is Bitcoin. Blockchain has now shifted from electronic cash to other applications in government, supply chain management, healthcare, agriculture, real estate international development and almost any database application that can be replaced with a safer, persistent, responsive, accessible and trust-based database (Sam Goundar, 2020) The main objective of this chapter is to analyze the mindset of different stakeholders, to technology in general, involved in the agricultural sector and to illustrate how smart contracts of blockchain can provide an electronic record of a product's background to the retail store. This will give buyers more trust in the goods they purchase, and it is also an opportunity to reward farmers who grow their produce using good and sustainable agricultural practices (Swan, 2015).

FARMERS' ISSUES AND NECESSITY OF BLOCKCHAIN TECHNOLOGY

Although India is an agricultural country, with half of the population employed in the sector, agriculture is also ingrained in their culture. The vicious cycle of poverty, built by a decline in production, a failure of the economy and restricted access to credit, traps the vast majority of farmers. Agriculture's challenges are also compounded by the intensified demand to generate more food from dwindling means while preserving the environment's balance (Goundar, 2020). Here are some issues that are facing by the agriculture community in India (Mishra, 2019)

1.   Smaller operational holdings

Agriculture is a family business in India, with assets distributed among the generations, resulting in smaller land holdings passed down through the generations. The lower holding size restricts both the magnitude of the activity and the farmer's capacity.

2.   Erratic climatic changes:

Climate change has had a negative impact on Indian agriculture and farmers because they rely significantly on the rainfall for agriculture. Irrigation is hampered by variable weather patterns and irregular rainfall, resulting in yield variances (Wassenaer, 2021).

3.   Deviating youth and labour in agriculture:

Agriculture has been left with limited agricultural workers as more and more young people migrate to cities and work in manufacturing and construction. The less rural agricultural workers and inflation have led to higher wages.

4.   Poor Quality inputs:

A large number of firms, through a vast network of distributors and retailers, supply inputs to farmers with agricultural soil, seeds, climate, supply, distribution, market information etc. At various stages, the consistency of inputs is compromised from producer to retailer due to insufficient knowledge of handling and often purposely. Manufacturers' incentives to distributors and retailers often contribute to the prescription of incorrect inputs, sacrificing yield at the end of farmers.

5.   Inadequate marketing facilities:

Marketing is critical for every business, and agriculture seems to be not different. Farmers' revenues are jeopardized due to a lack of marketing facilities and a long chain of intermediaries. Fear of crop failure combined with insufficient storage facilities has resulted in a large number of distressed agricultural commodity transactions.

6. Farmers' debt and loan:

Farmers in the country take advantage of both institutional and non-institutional credit sources. More structured institutional sources need proper paper work that, in particular, cannot be supplied by landless workers, diverting them to non-institutional sources of credit.

7.   Lack of Information:

The govt. and a number of other organizations have worked tirelessly through various schemes and programmed to empower farmers. However, due to inappropriate contact, most of these structures and services are not capable of percolating to guide the farmers. The government has adopted a variety of steps to spread information, including farmer's fairs, digital technologies such as mobile applications, text messages, and toll-free numbers, while the farming community's active engagement is critical to the success of these projects.

8.   **Minimum Support Price:**

Every year, the government sets a minimum support price for main crops cultivated to help farmers, but the agricultural industry contends that the cost of production measured for this reason is not the same as the actual cost.

The study on blockchain technology can be directed to following angles:

1.   How will agricultural precision practices be implemented with blockchain technology to optimize it?
2.   In general, various agro-supply chain stakeholders such as agriculturists are not very friendly to technology and therefore it will make a lot of difference how effectively different stakeholders could be provided with the blockchain-based solution?
3.   One field may provide an effective solution for the convergence of the blockchain with current network of the food supply chain.
4.   Compliance with regulatory concerns with the blockchain-based framework must be discussed (Yadav, 2019).

BLOCKCHAIN TECHNOLOGY: HOW IT WORKS?

A blockchain is made-up of permanent data blocks, each block contains a transaction list and a unique relation to the block of its predecessor. In order to preserve consistency between each block and its ancestor, powerful cryptographic techniques are employed. A blockchain, in simple terms, is a linked chain that stores auditable data in units known as blocks. For individuals with the relevant authorization, this simplifies the dissemination and verification of blockchains. Blockchain can also be referred to as a distributed ledger, and is also commonly referred to as a form of distributed specialized database. In the digital world, distributed ledgers are a multi-purpose technology designed explicitly to be spread across a network of multiple locations, geographies or organizations. Records are kept in a ledger that is always growing (Bindra, 2019). The information on the ledger is protected by a cryptographic approach that gives each person two' keys'–one is kept private, while the others are made public–that work together like the two-key system used to unlock a safety deposit box. Like a password or PIN, the private key allows the user to 'lock' or 'unlock' their data and control when and by whom it is accessible. Other trustworthy 'nodes' on the network will subsequently be given a public key, allowing them to view the opened information and double-check that it truly originates from the user.

The installation of blockchain technology entails a list of records known as blocks that continues to increase as new data is added. The cryptographic hash (a 'hash' is a unique, mathematically produced identifier that automatically binds each new record to the entry that came before it) is used to connect these blocks. Each block holds the hash of the previous block, providing a chain of functions (Alam, 2020). A math function converts digital data into a string of numbers and letters, resulting in hash codes. The hash code changes if that information is changed in any way. This ensures that a single record on the blockchain cannot be edited, erased, or replicated by another person without affecting all of the other entries in the chain, making fraud obvious to anybody looking at the ledger. This fundamental invention assures that the data saved on the blockchain is essential, and it assists users in reaching a consensus that each record is correct and immutable. Once a block is placed to the end of blockchain, it is quite difficult to go back and change the contents of a block.

Figure 1. Block

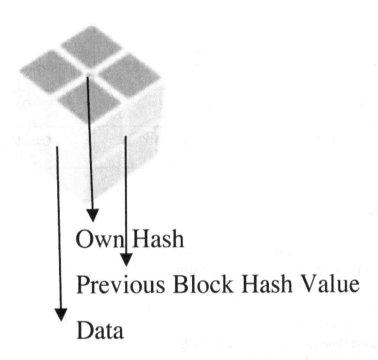

Own Hash

Previous Block Hash Value

Data

A proof-of - work consensus model is used by Blockchain, in which a node gets the right to connect to the next block by solving a computer exhaustive puzzle. It is easy to check the outcome of the calculation and thus allows different nodes to quickly authenticate and upgrade the blockchain. "The" reward "is won by the node that solves the computational puzzle and this method is called" mining.

Figure 2. Block chain

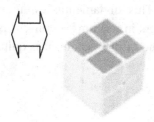  

BLOCK -I	BLOCK-II	BLOCK – III
Previous Hash: 0	Previous Hash: A1B2	Previous Hash: C4D2
Data: ABC	Data: XYZ	Data: PQR
Own Hash: A1B2	Own Hash: C4D2	Own Hash: M2L4

A blockchain can be developed as -

1.Identify a Suitable Use-case that makes business sense.
2.Select the Most Appropriate Consensus Mechanism
3.Select the Most Appropriate Platform
4.Creating the Nodes
5. Create a Blockchain Instance
6.Creating Application Programming Interfaces (APIs)
7.Create the administrative and user interfaces
8.Incorporating Future Technology

A blockchain cannot access data from outside its structure by default, to create the blockchain, data is supplied by a specified entity known as an oracle. An oracle is a crucial link between the physical world and blockchain. An oracle might be based on hardware, software, or consensus. This type of decentralized system provides confidence because each operation in the system is accessible and auditable by all stakeholders. Oracle is a trustworthy intermediate and an important part of the smart contract network, providing data feeds to the blockchain ecosystem. Blockchains are all about trust in technology and the absence of third parties or brokers (Holbrook, 2020).

DOES A BLOCKCHAIN WORKS IN AGRICULTURAL SUPPLY CHAIN?

Visible distortions haunt the modern supply chain in agriculture. On the supply end, farmers do not receive reasonable compensation for their produce. On the demand side, rising food prices make it difficult for consumers to maintain a balanced diet. The main advantage of blockchain technology is that it allows farmers to connect directly with manufacturers or customers at the end of the supply chain. This would not only encourage farmers to increase their income by bypassing intermediaries who are responsible for their fewer earnings, but would also normalize the consumer's inflationary tendencies. Blockchain technology, according to industry start-ups, would help farmers negotiate better pricing while also allowing customers to build trust in the quality of the products they buy. Traditional roadblocks to blockchain-based applications include a lack of or shoddy infrastructure, interoperability issues, and other technological issues. While the trend now is to try the implementation of conventional processes based on blockchain, this introduces needless overheads in most cases and does not deliver any tangible benefits. What it promises is that an open, decentralized, protected transaction mechanism will be delivered and transaction costs can be minimized (Bashir, 2018). In case of blockchain technology in agriculture, the most frequent thing is small land ownership. In the agricultural arena, this modest ownership, along with self-executing smart contracts and automatic payments, will be a game changer. Smart contracts are the most common application of blockchain technology in agriculture. Smart contracts are contracts that execute themselves (Omohundro, 2014).

Smart contracts could be highly useful in a variety of situations, including agriculture insurance, green bonds, and traceability. Agricultural insurance based on blockchain with key weather events and related payouts drawn up on a smart contract, connected to mobile wallets with weather data generated regularly by field sensors and correlated with data from nearby weather stations will encourage immediate payouts in the event of a drought or flooding in the region. However, in order to ensure smart contracts' maximum efficacy, the mechanisms for fostering such innovation, such as high-quality data, enabling policies, and legislation, must be addressed first (Swan, 2015). Smart contracts are self-executing contracts that are activated based on predetermined and negotiated events. The "smart" part of a smart contract stems from the fact that the contract's provisions are checked and the needed code is run without human intervention. Transactions in smart contracts are automatically initiated when the contract's pre-agreed conditions are met (Mathis, 2016). The contract's terms and conditions will be written in the form of decentralized blockchain codes. (Currently, global firms who acquire agricultural produce from farmers make payments through locally involved third party service providers.) The contract is executed based on the information put on the blockchain and is irreversible. This results in higher costs for businesses and poorer pay for farmers. Direct payments can be made by companies to their suppliers via mobile phones with the help of blockchain technology. The smart contract has a role, an association, and interactions with each involved entity. The seven participating units are Seed Company, Farmer, Grain Elevator, Grain Processor, Distributor, Retailer and Customer. How ICT can be used in agriculture is shown in the chart below (FA0, 2019)

Table 1. Use of ICT in agriculture

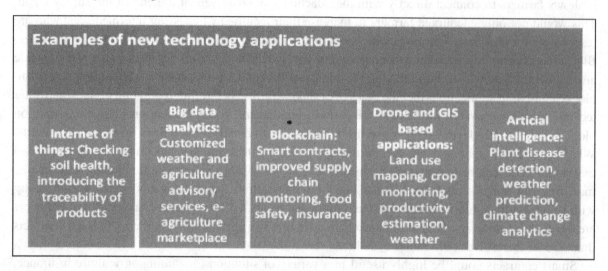

Improving the traceability of goods at any point of the supply chain is another exciting blockchain application. The un-falsifiable data reported on the supply chain at any point would give the customers trust that the product they got is the one they paid for. It will also be possible for customers to make educated decisions about the items they want to purchase. The product origin, the environmental conditions for cultivation, and the type of inputs used in its cultivation may all be provided in real time using blockchain.

Blockchain technology facilitates the immutable storage of essential details on the agriculture, processing and transport of agricultural commodities. Blocks for blockchain technology can be developed as:

Table 2. Blocks for blockchain technology

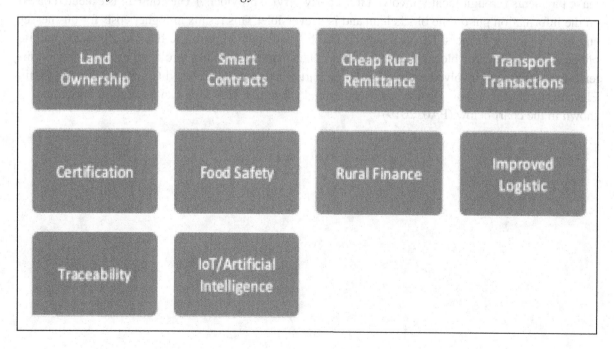

Blockchain technology is useful for tracking, auditing, and controlling the food supply chain. It has been found to be beneficial in enhancing supply chain performance for suppliers, consumers, and supervisory departments (government agencies). The blockchain provides a reliable source of truth about the state of agricultural crops, inventories, and contracts in an industry where data processing is typically prohibitively expensive (Wassenaer, 2021).

Table 3. Role of ICT in agriculture

Role of ICT in Agriculture							
Agricultural Extention and Advisory Services	Promote Environmentally Sustainable Farm Practice	Disaster Managem ent and Early Warning System	Enhanced Market Access	Food Safety and Transfera bility	Insurance and Risk Managem ent	Capicity Develop ment and Empower ment	Regulator y and Policy

Food may be certified using blockchain technology, which can help to ensure food quality and safety while also fostering trust between producers and customers. Suppliers benefit from the adoption of blockchain technology because it allows them to build a trusting relationship with customers and improve the reputation of their products by transparently storing specific product information in the blockchain. Customers benefit from the blockchain because it makes real and verifiable information about how food is prepared and exchanged public. This helps to resolve the question of customers about food protection, quality and environmental friendliness (Xiong, 2020). For certain aspects of these issues, blockchain technology may provide suitable solutions:

a) **Data security**: Blockchain technology provides private key encryption, a versatile technique for establishing authentication criteria.
b) **Supply chain management**: Blockchain technology may make supply chain management more efficient than traditional monitoring systems by cutting signaling costs for each entity.
c) **Payment methods**: A decentralized payment solution with zero rates is offered by the blockchain. In addition, the use of crypto-currency in agricultural commodity transactions would reduce the cost of transactions more significantly (Bashir, 2018).

d) **Consumer confidence**: The blockchain distributed accounting system is time-stamped thanks to the decentralized process, making all chain information public and un-modifiable.

e) **Reduce the cost of farmers**: Due to the low volume of transactions and restricted availability, traditional e-commerce is unwilling or unable to provide services for them, thus excluding them from the market. Blockchain technology has the potential to significantly lower transaction costs and reintroduce them into the market.

BLOCKCHAIN IN FOOD SUPPLY CHAIN

Food supply chains have grown longer and more complex than ever before as a result of greater globalization and increased competitiveness in the industry. Food supply chain challenges such as food traceability, food safety and sustainability, food trust, and supply chain inefficiency represent significant hazards to society as a whole, as well as to the environment and human health. For both theoretical and practical applications, blockchain technology in food supply chains involves agricultural insurance, smart farming, and agricultural commodities exchanges.

Table 4. Issues in food supply chain

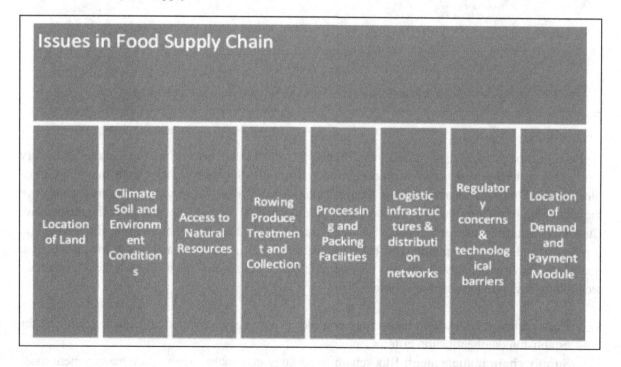

The main stages of food supply chain are:

1. **Production**: All agricultural activities carried out within the farm are represented by the development process. To grow crops and livestock, the farmer uses raw and organic materials (fertilizers, seeds, animal breeds and feed). The activities of production can be classified as follows:
   a. **Distributor:** Details on the crops, pesticides and fertilizers used, and machinery involved, among other things. The producer/dealings farmers are documented.
   b. **Producer:** Details on the farm and the farming methods used. It is also feasible to include additional information on the crop cultivation process, weather conditions, or animals and their care.
2. **Processing:** This stage entails the conversion of the original product into one or more secondary products, either completely or partially. Following that, a packaging stage is planned, in which each package is uniquely recognized by a production batch code that includes information such as the date of manufacture and the raw materials utilized.
3. **Distribution**: Until the product is packed and numbered, it is released for distribution. Delivery times might be set within a certain range depending on the object, and inventory could be stored for a period of time.
4. **Retailing**: The products are sent to merchants at the end of the distribution process, where they are sold (Retailers). The end-user of the chain will be the client who purchases the product.
5. **Consumption**: The consumer, who is the chain's end user, buys the product and requires traceable information on quality criteria, place of origin, manufacturing procedures, etc.

Blockchain and the above measures could favor medium-sized growers, as they form a group clearly distinct from that of large companies. On the other hand, either small-scale or medium-scale farmers could form cooperatives and they could become very large organizations representing tens or hundreds of farmers. For such cooperatives, Blockchain may be very useful, and the confidentiality of the details involved may help to settle farmers' disagreements and conflicts in a fairer manner for all. Farmers (i.e., cooperative members) could benefit from insurance policies that protect them from unpredicted weather conditions that harm their crops, as well as other hazards such as natural disasters.

CHALLENGES AND RISKS INVOLVED IN BLOCK CHAIN

In the distributed Blockchain system, each flow of transactions is registered in the ledger. The entry in the ledger is immutable, so that the transactions cannot be manipulated or adjusted by the entity. Providers (of raw materials, such as seeds and nutrients, as well as pesticides, and other chemicals), producer (usually the farmer, responsible for actions from planting to harvesting), processor (perform various actions, from simple packaging to more complex processes), distributor (responsible for moving the output of the processor (e.g., from seeding/planting to harvesting), processor (responsible for moving the output of the processor- the final element of the chain). The proposed framework incorporates advantage of the increasing technologies provided by modern smart devices that can be used directly as complete networks of the implementation of our layered blockchain, thus enhancing the entire network's resistance, devolution, protection and trust. Blockchain reflects about 80 percent shift in the business process and 20 percent adoption of technology. It reflects a complete move away from the conventional ways of doing things. This also extends to sectors that have already undergone a big change from emerging technology. In a decentralized network, it places trust and authority rather than in a powerful central institution. It's still unknown who will be most affected by the adoption of blockchain technology and which industries will be most affected. As a result, a more "imaginative" approach is required to grasp opportunities and how things may improve (Bashir, 2018).

The Blockchain technology in Agriculture food Supply chain can provide real-time traceability from 'farm to fork'. Thus, blockchain technology in the food supply chain helps to build and retain digital product records, including farm origin data, batch numbers, plant and processing information, product quality and quantity, expiry dates, storage and transport system temperatures, shipping details for the final product and includes the process of reaching in the hands of consumers. All of these data are related digitally and at each point of the process, the information is fed into the Blockchain. The data collected at each level is visible to all supply chain participants, and by consensus, the data becomes a permanent, unalterable record. This information aids in food safety and allows manufacturers to provide a more accurate estimate of a product's shelf life. Blockchain technology has the ability to revolutionize the supply chain by generating value for each supply chain partner. To assure authenticity and transparency, blockchain can facilitate transactions involving authentication, settlement, exchange, signature, or validation. The Blockchain aids in the authentication of critical parts of supply chain data and transactions, resulting in increased consumer loyalty. There are lot of opportunities and benefits in applying blockchain to the agriculture supply chain but with certain challenges and barriers in its adoption. Some of them are discussed herewith.

Table 5. Opportunities and benefits; challenges and barriers

Opportunities and potential benefits	Challenges and barriers
In value chains, traceability is important.	This technology is not suitable for small businesses.
Small-scale farming assistance	Small SME have less expertise
Financing and insurance for farmers in rural areas	High levels of uncertainty
Financial transaction facilitation in poor nations	Platforms for education and training are limited.
Pricing that is more equitable across the entire value chain	There are no rules in place.
To serve as a platform for efforts to reduce emissions.	Policymakers and technical specialists don't comprehend each other. Scalability difficulties and unanswered technological questions The developed and developing worlds have a digital divide.
Better privacy and security	Privacy isn't merely protected by the government.

Blockchain-based applications do face conventional obstacles, such as a lack of or weak infrastructure, interoperability failures, and other problems with technology. To determine whether a problem you face could benefit from a blockchain-based solution, first define usage, then establish the main guiding principles (including regulatory criteria, stakeholders, legal structure, interoperability with the current system, scale, and other key requirements) to determine whether a problem you face might benefit from a blockchain-based solution, and finally determine what technology or design will help address the system's challenges. Currently, the most significant obstacles to Blockchain adoption in supply chains are: (Banerjee, 2018):

1. **Infrastructure and network**: Blockchain is based on a robust internet-connected network with the necessary IT infrastructure, which can be difficult to adapt to emerging economies. The technical scalability of the network, which is a blockchain technology difficulty, might place a burden on the adoption process, especially for public blockchains. This lack of scalability is less of an issue with private blockchain networks because network nodes are designed to handle transactions in an ecosystem of trusted parties, which makes financial sense.

2. **Inadequate Professionals and Interoperability**: Despite the fact that the demand for professional blockchain workers is skyrocketing, there is a critical scarcity of appropriately qualified and competent individuals in the blockchain landscape for building and managing the intricacies of peer-to-peer networks. Because to their complex, encrypt, and distributed nature blockchain technologies can be slow and inconvenient. However, blockchain technology necessitates more knowledge and expertise. Businesses in the supply chain will only adopt blockchain if it can integrate with existing IT systems and allow the company to run smoothly.

3. **Lack of regulatory clarity**: Legislative uncertainty and regulatory vagueness is a major hurdle in widespread use of blockchain technology. Regulations are never in position to keep up with technological development. One of the challenges (which was also one of its original motivations) of the blockchain solution is that it eliminates oversight.

4. **Data storage cost (data per transaction) on Blockchain:** The information generated in the Blockchain is saved on the cloud and requires a lot of storage space because the data must be stored permanently and eternally. In the early stages, the supply chain partners must be integrated in the system, which can cause costs and for its machinery is needed.

5. **Data validation latency**: The blocks in the chain would only be valid if they were verified by all of the miners participating. This process takes 8 to 19 minutes to finish, but it could take longer. But if the food supply chain wants to use this blockchain technology, this delay can be reduced to seconds.

6. **Payload size restriction**: Another impediment to blockchain adoption is the lack of payload standards, which is mostly related to network and infrastructure issues.

7. **Regulatory and legal acceptance**: A major issue that supply chains that have attempted to incorporate this technology have encountered is the lack of a regulatory framework. This is a difficult topic to tackle since it might cause trust issues among the chain's partners.

8. **Trust**: Trust is one of the supply chain's key factors that often proves to be a difficulty in implementing the blockchain. In the supply chain, the implementation of blockchain technology will improve visibility and traceability. But it is very important that supply chain partners should have faith so that they are able to share their data.

9. **Identity and security**: Public blockchains carry out transactions using an individual's public and private key, but they do not keep track of the identity associated with the key. This poses security concerns for law enforcement and applications that rely on identities.

ASSURANCE OF TRANSPARENCY AND ACCOUNTABILITY VIA BLOCKCHAIN IN AGRICULTURE SUPPLY CHAIN

Agriculture and food supply chains are closely linked since agricultural goods are virtually always employed as inputs in a multi-actor distributed supply chain, with the consumer as the final client. Blockchain technology provides a number of benefits, including the ability to provide a safe, distributed method of conducting transactions amongst many untrustworthy parties. Supply chain management, food safety, trade finance, agricultural financial services, market information, land registries, and agricultural agreements are just a few of the applications in agriculture. The blockchain policy and regulatory system is in its infancy and thus carries elevated risks. Supply chain information is to be collected from sourcing, warehousing, manufacturing, distribution and transport. Blockchain is a network-replicated database that uses consensus to assess what is true and what is not. As a result, the share ledger provides permanent and verifiable data inputs, reduces the number of intermediaries, and allows for real-time transactions. Farmers' low proportion of the consumer rupee is frequently blamed on middlemen, who are accused of exploiting them. The ability to recall all information about a food product's origin, often known as the "one step back, one step forward" approach, is known as traceability. It provides past information starting from the purchase of seeds to reach in the hands of consumers.

Information and Communication Technologies (ICT) can help in finding the intermediaries (agents, wholesalers, distributors and retailers) and trace the reason behind why the price received by the farmer is so low and the price paid by consumer is so high. In using ICT, Distributed Ledger Technologies (DLTs) can be used to provide information needed by creating blocks for each intermediary. It can provide a safe platform to share data. DLT can improve the interchange of value and knowledge by increasing transparency, traceability, performance, accountability, and confidence. Blockchain can disintermediate transactions in agricultural supply chains since DLTs and smart contracts produce similar results in trade finance and agricultural financial services (payment services, agricultural insurance, credit, and derivatives). As a result, smallholders and MSMEs have easier access to financial services, and sellers and banks have cheaper transaction costs (Swan, 2015).

When blockchain tracking is combined with artificial intelligence, it is possible to estimate the epidemic's direction, speed, and even economic impact. Artificial Intelligence under blockchain operates on the basis of the neural network includes extracting knowledge from different sources of the database, which is then analyzed to gain different insights. The main application of artificial intelligence is Internet of Things. The Internet of Things can be used in the agricultural supply chain to determine an efficient marketing system, which means the availability of quality inputs and outputs at the desired location, at the right time, and in the appropriate form, which is not possible without strong infrastructure support, efficient transportation (to monitor the quality of fresh foods, especially perishables), processing, grading, and storage facilities in compliance with food safety requirements, thereby minimalizing foodborne illness. The perishable nature of these agricultural products necessitates strict temperature control, visibility, and supply chain transparency. With the assistance of RFID (radio-frequency identification) and other sensors, IoT will help with this need. RFID (Tags given by RFID have various information like weight, harvest date, harvested field, moisture level temperature, and nutritional information) is used to assure traceability and accountability. These tags provide secure access, high recognition, simple integration, and bulk data storage. RFID tags are used in greenhouses to capture specific data, which aids in equipment management, documenting and measuring growth time, and people management. RFID is used to track Phytoplasma and viruses. This is one of the existing technologies that can be used to identify foods and plants that are subject to rules and regulations. In the early stages of blockchain adoption, RFID will be the most precise source of product knowledge. Protection can also be ensured by using encryption of data in the RFID tags. RFID tags are temperature resistant and can calculate temperatures below zero degrees and above 100 degrees effectively, thereby expanding their use.

Existing issues in the industrialized world, such as unjust pricing and the sway of large corporations, have historically hindered the environmental and economic viability of smaller farms. When a farmer wakes up, the first thing that comes his mind is the dangers he faces: weather, resource demand, abortion, location, biological, health, financial, political, and infrastructure risk. Blockchain could aid in more equitable pricing across the entire value chain. Blockchain can be used to track social and environmental responsibilities, improve provenance data, enable mobile payments, loans, and funding, reduce transaction fees, and provide secure and reliable real-time supply chain management. Blockchain rules may be required by the government and other tightly regulated industries. With Blockchain our young farmers can take agriculture to the new heights with the help of an incorruptible flow of data into our value chains. It can instill trust in the system from input suppliers, bankers, and crop insurers whose businesses are data-driven, all the way down to the supply chain, production, and logistics, and all the way to customers. Farmers may be able to become bankable with the help of blockchain.

HOW BLOCKCHAIN TECHNOLOGY WILL BE BENEFICIAL FOR INDIA?

In India, land/farmer data is based on paperwork and files are still heavily relied upon to store, which may be a time-consuming operation fraught with inaccuracies. In the case of farmer/land registrations in both urban and rural areas, technology could definitely come to our rescue, since blockchain could create a structured, tamper-proof digital database of land records. The records can be reliably kept after the data is effectively connected to appropriate digital IDs. This information may be utilized to conduct additional surveys, maintain correct landholding statistics in our country, and give farmers with tailored solutions based on their specific needs, all of which will aid in the promotion of sustainable farming. All parties involved can benefit from updated demand and supplier information thanks to blockchain technology. This technology makes it easier to record precise information about the crop's origin, as well as the farmer's and trader's contact information, which is critical for export purposes. Farmers will be able to set their own pricing and sell in markets as a result of these details.

The Maharashtra State Warehousing Corporation (MSWC) has directed the farmers gain retrieve to product credit faster through a pilot initiative employing blockchain technology. Financial institutions make loans in return for agricultural commodities, which is known as commodity finance. Warehouse receipts, which are issued by accredited warehouses to farmers or dealers, can be used to obtain loans. The goal is to assist farmers in obtaining a greater price for their produce while avoiding low-cost distress sales. The process of commodities finance, according to experts, is both time consuming and intricate. Farmers bring their crops to the warehouse, which prints receipts. The tangible receipts are taken to the bank, which issues loans, when the stock is validated. This takes at least seven to fifteen days, which defeats the entire purpose of the strategy. The MSWC has entered into a one-of-a-kind partnership with the Maharashtra State Cooperative Bank for this scheme (MSC). MSWC has connected 203 of its warehouses with technology developed by WHRRL Solutions, a start-up, in order to provide receipts rapidly. The platform can also be used by the bank, and the transaction can take as little as 24 hours to complete. In the fiscal year 2020-21, at least 185 farmers took part in the pilot project, with a total loan amount of Rs 3.63 crore. 423 farmers have already received the receipt this fiscal year, and Rs 9.75 crore in loans have been disbursed.

By maintaining current, precise quality assurance certificates on the blockchain and sharing them with those who need to know, food safety can be ensured. Furthermore, by sharing end-to-end supply chain information with consumers via augmented reality, it can improve their purchasing experiences. Enertech Innovations, an Indian business, has been using Blockchain to solve the problem of traceability in India. The app, dubbed 'Grotius,' aims to increase pricing transparency and eliminate middlemen's exploitation of farmers. It is bolstering the farmer collective ecosystem through heavy use of emerging technologies such as Blockchain, AI, and IoT. AgroTrust's services include quality certificates, fertilizer and pesticide usage, fair trade rules, and international standards, all of which will be established with Blockchain assistance.

To develop digital agriculture through pilot projects Mr. Narendra Singh Tomar, Union Minister of Agriculture and Farmers Welfare, signed five memorandums of understanding (MoUs) with CISCO, Ninjacart, Jio Platforms Limited, ITC Limited, and NCDEX e-Markets Limited (NeML) and also announced the launch of the Digital Agriculture Mission 2021–2025 in September 2021. The Digital Agriculture Mission 2021–2025 aims to promote and accelerate projects which are based on modern technologies such as artificial intelligence (AI), blockchain, remote sensing and geographic information systems (GIS), and the use of drones and robotics.

In August 2019, Cisco released an Agricultural Digital Infrastructure (ADI) solution that improves farming and knowledge exchange. This ADI is likely to play a key role in the data pool that the Department of Agriculture will build as part of the National Agri Stack. Kaithal (Haryana) and Morena (India) will host the initiative's pilot project (Madhya Pradesh).

The Jio Agri (JioKrishi) platform, which was introduced in February 2020, digitizes the agricultural ecosystem throughout the value chain to empower farmers. The platform's main function provides advisory using data from standalone applications; advanced functions use data from numerous sources, input the data into AI/ML algorithms, and deliver precise tailored advice. This initiative's pilot project will launched in Jalna and Nashik (Maharashtra).

Using a digital crop monitoring platform hosted on ITC's e-Choupal 4.0 digital platform, ITC has proposed creating a personalized 'Site Specific Crop Advise' service to change conventional crop-level generic advice into a personalized site-specific crop advisory for farmers. This initiative's pilot experiment will be place in Sehore and Vidisha (Madhya Pradesh).

CONCLUSION

This historical perspective on Indian agriculture aims to provide a comprehensive picture of the contemporary issues. Farmers' suicides are prevalent, and several farmers' agitation movements have sprung up around the country. According to the National Crime Records Bureau (NCRB), 10,349 people working in the agricultural sector (including 5,763 farmers or cultivators and 4,586 agricultural labourers) committed suicide in 2018, accounting for 7.7% of all suicide victims (1,34,516) (available at https://ncrb.gov.in/sites/default/files/chapter-2-suicides-2018.pdf accessed on October 2, 2020). Farmers today make up the majority of the population living in poverty. As per the data of Ministry of Statistics and Programme Implementation, 36.4 percent of all agricultural households are poor. In this context, it is important to consider the present agricultural policies in place in India, which aim to improve the status of farmers. Poor extension, a missing link with the supply chain of quality seed and plant propagation material, a lack of institutional financing in many states, a lack of investments in agriculture, and a lack of technology are the key reasons for agriculture's underdevelopment. The availability of low-quality and bogus inputs is a major contributor to rising costs without significant productivity gains. Despite its leading role in exports, the agricultural business is technologically and technically behind the times. In many areas of domestic agriculture production, the use of information technology is minimal or non-existent. Apart from emphasizing the use of modern inputs, there is a need to put in place effective mechanisms for monitoring and regulating the quality of inputs such as seed, fertilizer, and agro-chemicals. Blockchain technology will prove a prominent reform particularly in the field of the agricultural supply chain and also in rural poverty in general. The use of blockchain technology in Indian agriculture would decentralize agricultural government dramatically.

The process of moving products from the point of production to the point of consumption may be streamlined and simplified using blockchain technology, and the planting, selection, processing, and calculations of the commodity can all be tracked in real time. It provides clear advantages for all parties involved in the food supply chain. With the requisite approvals in place in many sectors of the economy, this technology has a strong chance of becoming popular not only among Indian agricultural holdings, but also among small farms producing unique or organic products.

REFERENCES

Ahmad, L., & Firasath, N. (2021). *Agriculture 5.0: Artificial Intelligence, IoT and Machine Learning*. CRC Press. doi:10.1201/9781003125433

Alam, M. A. (2020). *A Neoteric Smart and sustainable farming environment incorporating block chain-based artificial intelligence approach in Crypto Currencies and Blockchain Technology Applications*. John Wiley and Sons.

Banerjee, A. (2018). Blockchain technology: Supply chain insights from ERP. In *Advances in Computers* (Vol. 111). Elsevier.

Bashir, I. (2018). *Mastering Blockchain: Distributed ledger technology, decentralization, and smart contracts explained* (2nd ed.). Packt Publishing Ltd.

Bindra, J. (2019). *The Tech Whisperer: On Digital Transformation and the Technologies that Enable It*. Penguin Random House India Private Limited.

Biswas, P. (2021). *Maharashtra: Blockchain tech to get farmers faster finance*. The Indian Express.

FAO (Food and Agriculture Organization) of the United Nations. (2019). *International Telecommunication Union, E-agriculture in action: Blockchain for agriculture: Opportunities and challenges*. Food & Agriculture Org.

Ghode, P. (2020). *Blockchain, the doorway to transforming agri sector*. The Hindu BusinessLine.

Goundar, S. (2020). *Blockchain Technologies, Applications And Cryptocurrencies: Current Practice And Future Trends*. World Scientific.

Holbrook, J. (2020). *Architecting Enterprise Blockchain Solutions*. John Wiley & Sons. doi:10.1002/9781119557722

Laurence, T. (2019). *Introduction to Blockchain Technology*. Van Haren.

Mathis, T. (2016). *Blockchain: A Guide to Blockchain; The Technology Behind Bitcoin; Ethereum And Other Cryptocurrency*. Level Up Lifestyle Limited.

Mishra, P. K. (2019). *Sustainable Agriculture and Natural Resource Management: Issues and Challenges*. DAYA Publishing House.

Nakamoto, S. (2008). *Bitcoin: A peer-to-peer electronic cash system*. Available at https://bitcoin.org/bitcoin.pdf

Omohundro, S. (2014). Crypto-Currencies, Smart Contracts, and Artificial Intelligence. *AI Matters*, *1*(2), 19–21. doi:10.1145/2685328.2685334

Report of Indian Council of Food and Agriculture. (2020). *Agriculture and Indian Farmers: Issues and Road Ahead*. Author.

Swan, M. (2015). *Blockchain: Blueprint for a New Economy*. O'Reilly Media, Inc.

Trendov, N.M. (2019). *Digital Technologies in Agriculture and Rural Areas: Status report*. Food and Agriculture Organization of the United Nations, FAO.

Van, W. (2021). *Applying blockchain for climate action in agriculture: state of play and outlook*. Food & Agriculture Org.

Xiong, H. (2020). *Blockchain Technology for Agriculture: Applications and Rationale*. . doi:10.3389/fbloc.2020.00007

Yadav, V. S., & Singh, A. R. (2020). A Systematic Literature Review of Blockchain Technology in Agriculture. *International Conference on Industrial Engineering and Operations Management*.

Chapter 7
Gauging the Scale of Intertwinement:
Juggling Between the Use of Biometric Data and Right to Privacy

Vinayak Jhamb

University School of Law and Legal Studies, Guru Gobind Singh Indraprastha University, India

Manini Syali

Guru Gobind Singh Indraprastha University, India

ABSTRACT

One of the critical features of automated biometric recognition applications is that, unlike traditional security systems, they do not solely rely on memory or knowledge-based features like passwords and thus provide protection and identification of an enhanced form. Bio-metric recognition systems instead weigh on pattern matching. They collect biological data from an individual using sensors and match the extracted discriminatory features from the input received with the already existing data in the system. Unique identification projects do not solely pose a danger from the side of the government authorities alone, and private players have also entered the game of misusing sensitive information of the users. It would thus not be wrong to state that privacy has indeed become a commodity to be sold off for monetary gains. However, the concept of "privacy" is a contentious domain, and debates pertaining to its scope continue.

INTRODUCTION AND EVOLUTION OF BIOMETRIC DATA SYSTEM

The post-modern world has witnessed a surge in innovative and novel technological advancements across the globe. In this fast-changing technology-savvy world, everything is available at the click of our mouse. However, this ceaseless changing technology also causes incomprehensible problems for the people who are placed on the other side of the digital divide. One of the technological boons of the Contemporary world is the introduction of Biometric data in daily mundane life. It has found a due place in our lives

DOI: 10.4018/978-1-7998-8641-9.ch007

as the ultimate purpose of emerging technology is to make our lives better. Lately, this technology has been used by the government, private offices, and other organizations.

Not only this, in February 2015, the government of India required all the people to provide their information on the Biometric system for applying for a passport. The trajectory of this highly appreciated technology emanated in India after LPG in the 1990s as many Multinational Companies and Transnational Corporations came in our country with a new set of labour-intensive technology and humungous capital (Sharma, 2006). Fortunately, the domestic companies also started following the newly recognized technology so as to be at par with their foreign contemporaries. Therefore, information stored in a Biometric system has become quite a norm these days in India. Developed nations like the USA, UK, Australia, New Zealand have been practicing this technique since the 1950s. However, it is heartening to note that even Developing nations follow the 'good practices' in this modern technological setup.

Conversely, the present Chapter shall also delve into the detailed nuances of this technology and the problems emanating out of the same. It shall be not be discussing the rosy picture only, instead it shall also look into the issues of Privacy which usually become the cause of concern when it comes to Biometric data. The Chapter shall also delve into the legal imperatives in India, tackling the said issue of Intertwinement between the Right to Privacy and the use and application of Biometric Data.

History of Biometric Data System: Going Through the Prism of the 'Past'

A handful of scholars across the globe would disagree with the proposition pertaining to uniqueness of the human race. However, it has been scientifically proven that human beings demonstrate various physical, emotional and sociological traits which are completely different form their counterparts. The author is not trying to contemplate a categorical classification among the humans but the emphasis is on the uniqueness of the individuals which eventually becomes the subject matter of Biometric data system. One of the fundamental documents in the International legal paraphernalia, Universal Declaration of Human Rights, 1948 categorically states and ensures the Equality among each and every being on this Earth (Salomon, 2019). However, acknowledging the unique characteristics in each and every human being is indicative of the fact that dignity and respect should be given primary importance irrespective of similarities or dissimilarities.

Many centuries before the "automated" biometric technologies came into existence, when there were no signs of Computer based system, the scholarly men across the globe used certain categories of non-automated technological set ups which were widely prevalent back then. There has also been references pertaining to use of non-automated Biometric Data System was identified in Nova Scotia wherein certain ridge patterns were used by people for recognition as all of them had special patterns allotted as per their physical features (Shwed, 2015). Also, it has been observed by anthropologists that Fingerprint recognition was one of the oldest forms of biometric identification going back up to at least 6000 B.C. Scholars point out that the first use of Fingerprint ever recorded was done by the ancient Assyrians, Babylonians, Japanese, and Chinese for the signing of legal documents. In the ancient times, fingerprinting technique was used in clay and sand and were solely used for business transactions. Apparently, even Chinese people started using this technique which was later found by a historian named, Joao de Barros. However, one of (Reed, 2016) the most obnoxious details were put out when talked about the use of fingerprinting in Chinese culture wherein children used to write codes on their arms so that the adults in their houses can remember the patterns and get identified and recognized by kings and council.

The first ever comprehensive study on fingerprinting techniques was carried out by one of the famous Czech physiologist and Scientologist named, Johannes Evangelista Purkinje along with a committed team of professors and researchers who were working in at the University of Breslau. His team did a commendable job and a report was submitted to the Board of Academicians at the University. The report explicitly talked about the valuable functions which can be carried out for recognition as well as identification purposes. In the year 1823, he also proposed a system of "fingerprint classification" (Hann, 2017). This was obviously opposed by a lot of scholars back then owing to its limited capacity and functioning. However, these techniques got popular in no time and prevailed over in Europe quickly. Even other countries also started sing similar techniques to ensure and facilitate the identification process. The English followed the same in their colonies and commenced palm and fingerprints usage in India in July 1858, when the Governor General of India used hand-printing techniques on the back side of the Contract deeds. However, he did not use the palm printing strategy instead used the index finger as well as the middle finger.

The situation began to ease down when an Anthropologist and a part time clerk in the police office in Paris by the name, Alphonse Bertillon came up with a solution to identify and recognize repeat offenders since the human memory is limited and short. His ultimate purpose was to seek identification of the criminals based on their fingerprints and analysing the same would replace the limitation of limited human memory. Earlier, he developed a method of recognition wherein body measurements were considered a valid source of recognition. However, the method failed as it had a lot of concerns associated with it. Then, he built a system of multiple body arrangements which was essentially name after him and was known Bertillonage. This method of identifying the repeat offenders was very well received by all Criminologists across the globe and this method was soon adopted by many countries' police officials. On the contrary, some scholars in London highlighted that the lacuna of this particular method lies in the proportionality of similar body measurements and arrangements (Gupta, 2015). Even though critiqued later, this method was an overnight sensation when it came out.

Etymological References of Biometric Data System: Emanation and Origin

The term 'Biometric' is an amalgamation of two Greek words: Bio meaning life and Metric meaning measure. Therefore, etymologically the term Biometric implies measuring the lifelike characteristics of human behavioural pattern in order to identify as well as recognize them. For facilitating the human population, Biometric system has been referred to technologies measuring as well as analysing the human behaviour or physiological characteristics. These characteristics are quite personal or unique to those individuals possessing them, therefore can become a strong source of identification or recognition of the target population. *According to the USA Manual on Biometric Data Safety and Concerns*, it is defined as the art and science of capturing the personal, unique characteristics of and individual and then, subsequently using it in a system or sub-system which is primarily built for human recognition or identification. The scientologists across the globe have listed down three categories of Identification-Management carried out by Biometric Data System (Haday, 2012). These are as follows:

- Something You have Stage: The lowest level is known as "something you have" wherein you need to flash your ID badge in front of a scanner or photograph booth. Therefore, your possessions act as a source of identification through some tangible materials.

- Something You Know Stage: The next level is known as "something you know," wherein specific numbers are used as passwords or combinations of words or numbers are used in a computer log in and also includes PIN etc.
- Who you are Stage: The highest level is known as the "who you are," which entails the fundamental tenets of biometrics- the analysis of physical or behavioural characteristics of human beings for identification and recognition purpose.

Identity Management: A Critical Component of Biometric Data System

One of the most fundamental tenets of the Biometric Data System is the Identity management of various individuals whose information has been registered under the said device. It has been defined as "the registration, storage, protection, issuance, and assurance of a user's personal identifier(s) and privilege(s) in an electronic environment in a secure, efficient, and cost-effective manner." Identity management has been posed as one of the most serious concerns in offices as a lot of data which has been stored in the devices is subject to theft, decay or identity crisis. Lately, the private offices have been majorly suffering from Identity Theft as well which certainly needs management and regulation (Sungya, 2018).

According to recent statistical figures issued by FDIC, around 80 million of people living in Americans suffer from identity theft in 2019 which posed a whooping cost to business billion and also a personal and deep impact which cannot be measured in terms of money and therefore, cannot be estimated at all. This not only is a microeconomic issue but has the capacity to broaden the economic vulnerabilities and also national security issues as well. Therefore, Biometric Data System has been evolved to prevent and control the Identity theft so that Identity Management can be facilitated. Biometric Data System is used as a countermeasure to Identity theft and other similar issues.

It has been time and again noted that authentication of the people's identity is of paramount importance when it comes to matters pertaining to national security, data preservation and also safety of the public at times. Over these years, issue of maintain the identity of the individuals in an organization or so as to eliminate the plausible threats to national security and public safety protocols etc. In the light of these technological advancements, the need for Identity Management continues to be one of the most important conditions of contemporary business transactions (Shah, 2019). The organizations may be large or small but still accountability is something all of them look forward to in today's scenario. Not only accountability, other factors are also significant in this regard like security among the partners of the firm, employees and even customers. It has been pointed out that the most reliable method for dealing with identity theft issues is the centralization of Identity Management wherein all the data can be stored without any breakdown in such storage. One the contrary, if there are too many channels dealing with the stored data, there are higher chances of data being distorted and mutilated.

Biometric Data System provides one of the most efficient ways to verify that an individual's data has been authentic or not. It is usually done directly through a device or through a PIN, password, or other token. Biometric Data System is considered one of the best solutions when there is a large-scale population involved and the data for each one of them needs to be stored. It does not only entail storage of data but also encompasses other functions like identity registration, assurance, protection, issuance, life cycle management, and system management, which are equally important for best graphic results in identification of the population.

The algorithms used in this system have excellent levels of accuracy in terms of recognition and identification. All must be taken into account and integrated for the best results (see preceding graphic).

This is not only considered cost-effective as it yields long-term results but also better than the traditional way of storing the data which was susceptible to theft and decay. However, the experts also warned the organizations to deploy limited resources to this technology set up as they might face a financial crunch later. Therefore, the organizations should consider all the factors on the spectrum to decide the viability of such a technological set-up (Hamnnon, 2013)

Functioning of Biometric Data System: Analysing the Nuts and Bolts

It has been already discussed that at their most basic or fundamental level, biometric data system-based technology is usually recognition patterns that either work on image-oriented devices such as usage of scanners, cameras or even iris-based technologies. They are either visual or oral technologies which work on characteristics or human behavioural patterns. The characteristics of the individuals whose data is recorded is exclusive as well as distinctive between the users of that interface as well as the centralized agency managing the data through requisite devices.

Its functioning is considered commendable because it creates a template which is mathematical representation of human's persona and behaviour. The data in the templates is stored in a database so that the chances of theft or stealing is made minimal. They work on both-software and hardware basis which keeps decision-making a steady choice in tough times, particularly to restore the data,

This part discusses the functions of a Biometric System other than ample storage of data. Some of them have been listen above as follows:

- Data Collection and Assembling
- Data Storage and Identity Management
- Signal Processing
- Decision making based on both Software and Hardware

INTERSECTING DIMENSION BETWEEN BIOMETRIC DATA SYSTEM AND PRIVACY ISSUES

The scholars across the globe have argued that one of the critical problems associated with this ever-changing and advanced Biometric system is the privacy concerns. Human rights activists have been stressing on this fact that the multi-faceted technology is not only disparaging the existing traditional protocols but also causing privacy concerns. However, some of the scholars have also pin pointed that this new technology essentially ensures the data from any decay or theft, therefore, promotes privacy to the grassroot levels. This never-ending tussle between the two theories continues to provide a grey space for researchers to act upon this.

Privacy can be defined as the complete or utmost control of human beings over their information which is usually susceptible to decay, theft and distortion. This information van be either in the tangible form or intangible form but the ultimate goal of every individual is to protect that information from unnecessary exposure. Even the international community backs up the Right to Privacy under United Declaration of Human Rights, 1948 and states that each and every individual should be allowed to be completely free from any unwarranted intrusion whatsoever. This acts as an embargo against the states as well that they also transgress the permissible limits of entering into their citizen's life. Going by the mandate of UDHR, ICCPR and ICESCR, privacy constitutes an essential ingredient of a dignified life. Even though the Biometric Data System does prevent your information from decay or distortion, there can be tiny possibility of the information being misused by the Organization itself. Even the government in power, which is maintaining a warehouse of information can misappropriate the same as and when the time comes (Shawn, 2014). However, it is to be clarified at this juncture that exceptions pertaining to public safety and integrity of the nation are not being discussed here.

The organizations which use this Biometric Data system technique usually have a centralized agency which stores all the information and therefore, they do have the capacity to mutilate or misuse the information as and when they desire. In support of this view, many human rights activists across the globe have called for complete or else partial ban of this technology as it can lead to unwarranted intrusion by the State itself or private organizations etc. In order to tackle the challenges emanating out of such innovative technologies, three-way technique was suggested by one of temporary committees of the Economic and Social Council of the United Nations in the year 2018. Following three principles were considered to be the backbone of an effective as well as efficient Biometric Data System:

- Regulation and Control: Under this principle, the ideal Biometric Data system should include and entail a well-established watchdog which can regulate the entire technological set-up. If there is no watchdog to look out for the actions of the Organization, it can become an unruly horse amuck with power. Therefore, it is always advisable to have a well-established legal framework which can not only regulate and control but manage and maintain as well. Four sub-principles working under the domain of Regulation are as follows:
    1. Transparency of the Regulatory Authority
    2. Limiting the purpose of the Authority to Data Protection only.
    3. Security of the Personal Data against unauthorized disclosure or decay.
    4. Ensuing the quality of the data as intact.
- Practice: A common practice has been followed by the countries across the globe of making specific laws for Data Protection. Not only this, the governments in power ensured that the centralized agencies do not go astray and work under a watchdog. They do not adhere to the norms because of any sanction, instead they follow these 'good practices' owing to reputational issues in the international community.
- Familiarity with the process: In developing countries, most of the people are considered on the other side of the Digital Divide. Therefore, a lot people are not equipped with the fundamentals of technology which makes it really difficult for them to understand the nuances of Biometric Data System. When introduced in the government sector in India, it was seen that people were so lethargic that they did not even want to learn the basics of new technology, that is where the problem begins.

Addressing the Elephant in the Room: Privacy Concerns

Many people have shown concerns regarding the storage of data and its safety in the centralized system operated by any organization or even the government. The induction of new technology like the Biometric Data System brings in a lot of challenges and concerns that need an adequate solution and attention as well. Therefore, a system of "Checks and Balances" has been found to tackle this challenge effectively and efficiently. The Checks can be initiated from the perspective of people availing the novel technology. These can be summarized in deciphering the answers to the following questions:

- Why is the person's data essentially needed at all?
- What is the purpose of Data storage?
- How safe is the Biometric Data System?
- Are there any chances of my data being stolen or manipulated?

If the organization is able to fully answer the above questions, then the people who shall be providing their information under the Biometric Data System will be satisfied to a certain extent. These are known as the "Checks" of the approach discussed above. The 'Balances', on the other hand, is the vesting of responsibility on the government to ensure privacy is not violated after the data is put into the Biometric Data System. For this to happen, organizations and even the governments have started coming up with "Privacy Enhancing Technology" which is a safeguard measure against the possibility of information leaking. Therefore, this hybrid amalgamated method of "Checks and Balances" has been pin pointed as the need of the hour.

Stakeholders in the Privacy Debate

Table 1. Stakeholders of biometric data system

S.No.	Stakeholders in the Privacy Debate	Concerns and arguments
1.	Citizens and consumers	The citizens and the consumers are the beneficiaries of this novel technology. They provide the information to the system and it is stored under safety. They do express their concern over the safety of their data as it is susceptible to theft and mutilation and manipulation.
2.	Governments	The governments have a different stand altogether. When it comes to acting as a watchdog for the private entrepreneurs, they do their jobs nicely. However, wherein the data is stored under their surveillance, it can also be subject to misuse as the government can do things as per their own whims and fancies which can certainly create a problem in the long run.
3.	Regulatory bodies	The regulatory bodies have been constituted to act as watchdogs for the private entrepreneurs as well as the government in power as well. However, many times it has been seen that dereliction of duty on their part proves to be disastrous. They need to be unbiased, unfair and avoid reckless decision making.
4.	Private enterprises	The private organizations are under the clutches of the government, the regulatory authorities and even the consumers. So, there is a tripartite enforcing mechanism operating right over them. However, all this is required as well because these corporate biggies tend to go astray which is problematic.

Continued on following page

Table 1. Continued

S.No.	Stakeholders in the Privacy Debate	Concerns and arguments
5.	**Privacy Advocate Organizations**	These organizations work on finding the autocracy of the government or private entrepreneurs in the functioning of Biometric Data System. They usually go the Court of Law for such issues emanating out of this novel technological set up.
6.	**Technology Suppliers**	They are also under the radar of the government, regulatory authorities and the consumers. They need to be highly cautious while delivering the new technical set up as a minor problem in that regard can cause drastic results. Therefore, it is their primary duty to ensure that everything is pre-mediated when it comes to Biometric Data System as that would not leave any scope for treachery or theft.

LEGAL PARAPHERNALIA GOVERNING RIGHT TO PRIVACY IN INDIA

Within the Indian context it is the Part III of the Constitution which can be called the foundation stone of the entire Human Rights jurisprudence. (Das, 2020) The Supreme Court of India has rightly utilized the provisions contained therein to widen the scope of Fundamental Rights available to the citizens. In the initial years of independence, the Constitutional interpretation done by the apex court was very restrictive in nature and the court exercised restraint. The concept of balance of power gets very well demonstrated in cases like *Champakam Dorairajan vs. State of Madras and A.K. Gopalan vs. Union of India* and the court appears to be away from the function of law making. (Semwal, 2011)

This positivistic attitude of the Court, however, underwent a change in the 1970s with the initiation of the Public Interest Litigation movement in the country. Judges like Justice Bhagwati and Justice Krishna Iyer adopted a very liberal attitude and went on to lay down a Human Rights jurisprudence unique to the Indian socio-economic landscape. Cases like *MC Mehta vs. Union of India* (Oleum Gas Leak Case), *Parmanand Katara vs. Union of India, Olga Tellis vs. State of Maharashtra* etc demonstrate an extraordinary innovative spirit. Moreover, the Fundamental Rights have been treated like a pandora's box and a wide variety of rights which otherwise do not find any mention anywhere in the Constitution have emerged. A landmark ruling which brought a shift from the Austinian era in the Indian legal jurisprudence is the *Maneka Gandhi vs. Union of India* case. (Rekhi, n.d.) The case pertains to interpretation of the scope of liberties available to citizens and the court gave an upper hand to fundamental freedoms over the power of the legislative organ of the government. This multi-dimensional utilization of Article 21 in the post-Maneka Gandhi era can be stated to be the origination point after which privacy related rights started evolving in India. (Vakil, 2018)

Before discussing the evolution of Right to Privacy in detail further it becomes pertinent to discuss the meaning and scope of the word Privacy. Focus also needs to be placed on other legal systems and how they went on to recognize rights related to privacy.

At the international level it has been recognized that privacy related rights are very essential for human development and are closely linked to individual liberty. An individual can enjoy the freedoms guaranteed to him under a given legal system only when his privacy is secure. Universal Declaration of Human Rights (UDHR) and the International Covenant on Civil and Political Rights (ICCPR) which are the core human rights instruments prevailing internationally have also acknowledged Right to Privacy.

This simply portrays that in the era when technology and internet was not available in an advanced stage in a similar manner as the present day, Privacy as a human rights still had a lot of importance.

In the Art. 12 of the UDHR it has been enunciated that no individual shall be treated in arbitrary manner so as to impact his privacy. This right extends to personal as well as private life. The idea is to utilize the benefits of a human rights oriented legal system to protect citizens from unsolicited attacks on individual dignity and reputation. A reflection of the above discussed parent provision contained in the UDHR can also be found in Art. 17 of the ICCPR as well. It is pertinent to note that the two human rights covenants ICCPR and ICESCR are based on the UDHR and the only difference remains in terms of their enforceability, the latter being binding on the parties signing and ratifying them where as the former remaining a soft law instrument. (Krishnamurthy, 2020)

Further, there is also a mechanism in place for implementation of the ICCPR in the form of the Human Rights Committee which on regular intervals keeps reviewing the governmental policies in place in the jurisdictions which become parties to the Covenant. (Humble, 2020) Further, the Committee has also been accorded the function of giving General Comments on the emerging dynamics of the provisions contained in the international human rights instruments. In this regard, in the year 1988, undertook the task of reviewing increasing instances of State Surveillance across the globe. It was observed that attempts by the national governmental authorities to interfere in the private lives of individuals need to be subjected to the rule of law. Moreover, this law should be defined in clear terms and should focus on protecting the right to privacy. In the light of the same General Comment no. 16 of 1988 on Art. 17 and General comment no. 19 on the insurance of the family, the right to marriage and equality of spouses (Art. 23) of 1990 are relevant. (Rengel, 2014)

It was in the late 1980s that India had started witnessing a revolution in the sphere of Information Technology and Electronic Commerce. This was the first time the legal issues pertaining to misuse of sensitive electronic data and excessive state surveillance was witnessed for the first time. General Comment no. 17 in this regard became important which explicitly laid down a responsibility on State Parties to ensure that private information did not go into the hands of private or public authorities which otherwise were not entitled for the same. Further, the right of individuals to be aware of in whose hands their private information was going was also acknowledged by the Human Rights Committee in this comment. (Sonkar, 2021) The next step in the direction of the impact which the digital age can have on privacy of individuals was further discussed in the United Nations General Assembly Resolution on the right of privacy in the digital age, passed on December 18, 2013.

It was in the year 2018, through the Justice Puttaswamy judgement that the Indian Supreme Court explicitly recognized privacy to be an integral part of Right to Life. This happened in the light of analyzing the Constitutional validity of the Aadhar card (Unique Identification scheme of the Government of India). (Viswanath, 2018) However, in other jurisdictions the rights were acknowledged a lot earlier than this. Moreover, the extent of protection available to Right to Privacy in countries like Hungary and South Africa is such that, explicit legal provisions are available in their Constitution regarding the same. These specific rights are mostly in the form of access to and control over personal information of individuals. On the other hand, in jurisdictions like United States and Ireland, similar to the Indian scenario, protection has been granted to privacy by the Constitutional courts, when the law makers did not lay down provisions for the same.

Moreover, legal protection accorded to privacy has also been guaranteed in the form of broad normative frameworks in some legal systems. The general movement of adopting such laws was a result of the model law introduced by the Organization for Economic Cooperation and Development (OECD) and the Council of Europe. As a result of the shortcomings of the laws available and mostly because of lack of uniformity in this regard, the European Union introduced a directive for 'Protection of Individuals with regard to the processing of personal data and on the free movement of such data'. A deadline of October, 1998 was set for the members of the European Union to comply with this directive within their domestic legal systems. An important feature of this directive was that the sensitive user information of the European citizens shall be kept safeguarded while being transferred or sent outside the continent. The Directive has proved successful to a large extent and more than forty European countries have adopted national legislations in furtherance of the same.

Other than the model laws making the entire process of introduction of a domestic law easier, there are several other reasons which contributed to passing of legal frameworks by domestic law-making authorities. Some such reasons are: remedying the privacy violations undertaken by past authoritarian regimes in countries like South Africa, Latin American nations etc., Secondly, to make laws in consonance with European countries and lastly, to resolve the legal hurdles which e-commerce was creating. (Dalmia, 2017)

Taking inspiration from the international as well as regional developments discussed above, the Supreme Court of India expanded the scope of protection to life and personal liberty granted by the Indian Constitution under Article 21 so as to guarantee Right to Privacy. In the initial cases discussing the dimensions of liberty, a mention was not of privacy as we understand in the present-day era of digitalisation. However, those cases marked a beginning of a new era of individual liberty in an otherwise socialist state of affair prevailing in India.

The Supreme Court for the first time undertook this discussion in the case of *Kharak Singh vs. State of Uttar Pradesh (UP)*. Herein, the law under question was regulation 236 of the UP Police Regulation, which entitled police officials to visits the homes of 'habitual offenders. The court holding this practice of police visits at odd hours to the petitioner's household unconstitutional stated that privacy is an integral part of 'liberty' as secured by Art. 21 of the Constitution.

Next came the case of Govind vs. Madhya Pradesh in which the court reiterated the ratio of Kharak Singh. The court here invoked Art. 19(1)(a) and 19(1)(d) along with Art. 21. However, the court refused to recognise the absoluteness of this right and paved way for state surveillance, holding that larger public interest at times demands subservient status of individual rights. (Burman, 2020)

A landmark case which can rightly be stated to be the turning point in the direction of revival of natural school of legal philosophy in India is the *Maneka Gandhi vs. Union of India* case. The court in this case did not explicitly discussed right to privacy but mentioned that there are several rights which can emanate out of Art. 21 of the Constitution, out of which some also have the status of fundamental rights. Further, it was stated that liberty of individuals can only be curtailed by laws made by the parliament when there has been followed a procedure to enact that law and the procedure is not arbitrary.

The line of argument laid down in the Maneka Gandhi case was taken to another level in the Naz Foundation case in which the Delhi High Court was analysing the Constitutional validity of S. 377 of the Indian Penal Code. The court stated that there must be a private space in which there is no interference from the side of the society and the State. This private space extends to the domain of family, procreation, education etc. The most explicit recognition to Right to Privacy, however, has come in the *K.S. Puttaswamy vs. Union of India*. The judgement pertains to the constitutional validity of the Unique Identification scheme introduced by the Government of India. The court analysed the issue in the light of Right to Privacy and held the Aadhar card to be constitutionally valid, however, it diluted its mandatory character especially in case of information being asked by private companies.

For development of Right to Privacy a huge contribution indeed was that of Justice Chandrachud who in his dissenting opinion discussed individual liberty in great details. He stated that availability of sensitive user data with private companies could result into misappropriation of the same by governmental authorities as well. "These preferences could also be used to influence the decision making of the electorate in choosing candidates for electoral offices. This is contrary to privacy protection norms. Data cannot be used for any purpose other than those that have been approved." The other judges, however, did not concur with this observation and instead focused upon the benefits associated with the identification scheme, especially those arising out of the social welfare projects.

From the above discussed propositions, it can thus be stated that recognition of Right to Privacy in a social welfare-oriented country like India has taken decades. The reason behind this mainly remains state security and connected issues. However, due to changing dynamics of the concept of privacy and penetration of internet technology in almost all the spheres of human activity the importance of privacy as a human right has increased multifield. Other than constitutional and jurisprudential recognition the need of the hour is also to introduce a legislation exclusively dealing with the issue of privacy. A bill in this regard has already been introduced in India and the subsequent section of the paper will be discussing that in detail.

INTRODUCTION OF THE DATA PROTECTION BILL: A RELIEF?

In furtherance of the mandate of the Puttaswamy judgement, a committee headed by Justice B.N. Srikrishna was constituted to deal specifically with the data protection related issues impacting right to privacy. Soon after in the year 2018 itself the committee submitted its report before the Ministry of Electronics and Information along with a Draft Personal Data Protection Bill, 2018. While drafting the bill the committee also consulted a number of stakeholders and consultants. The bill is in furtherance of the Puttaswamy judgement's mandate of securing 'informational privacy' of citizens and hence lays down a preventive framework against business houses who can possibly misuse sensitive data of users. (Basu, 2020) A key feature of the bill is establishment of Data Protection Authority (DPA), a statutory body designated for framing regulations regarding taking consent while transferring information to third parties, cross-border data transfer and other allied domains. The supervisory role of the authority has been defined broadly in the Act and this remains subject to criticism given the lack of available checks and balances. The involvement of the Central Government in the regulatory functioning of the DPA is also very miniscule.

Informational Privacy is an area which is cross-sectorial in nature and applies on all domains of business activities, because of this reason the scope of the Data Protection Bill extends to all the enterprises operating within the Indian economy. The only exception provided under the bill are those which will be specifically excluded by the Central Government. The scope of the Bill is thus similar to that of the General Data Protection Regulation (GDPR). It is pertinent to note that within the European Union around 23 million small scale businesses get covered by the GDPR. (Govindrajan, 2019)

Other than the above discussed provisions, another prominent feature of the bill which can rightly be stated to be its foundation stone is 'free consent' of users. The bill states that any variety of data before being processed requires consent which should be free as well as specific. A sub category of data is sensitive data which is important from the point of view of the present research. The requisite threshold of consent is even more in cases involving data which is sensitive in nature. Further, with respect to this sensitive personal data, obligation has been imposed upon data fiduciaries to maintain records regarding "important operations in the data life-cycle.

Despite laying down such detailed provisions for protecting informational privacy there are number of problems which remain associated with the draft bill. The regulatory approach laid down under the law emphasises upon the user consent. Yet the report and the bill go on to state that the users are incapable of granting 'meaningful consent', because the consent agreements offered by service providers are highly technical in nature. Further, the drafters of the bill have also not attempted to resolve the problems which have arisen with respect to consent in other legal frameworks existing prior to the bill.

Furthermore, the protection granted to personal data under the bill is only from the side of the private entities alone and the bill contains provisions which make sensitive data to be within the reach of governmental authorities. In this regard it has been explicitly highlighted in the bill that if the state wants to provide some benefits to individuals it can access personal data without consent.

However, on Monday (21st November, 2021) the Joint Parliament Committee adopted the final draft of the Data Protection Bill of 2019 and it would be table in the coming Winter session of 2021. If passed, it would be first comprehensive law on Data Protection in India which is definitely a motivating step for the country.

From the above discussed short comings, it thus becomes clear that the protection granted by the Supreme Court to Right to Privacy is much more holistic and comprehensive in contrast to the proposed Data Privacy Bill. The actual intent of the Right to Privacy related jurisprudence has a long road ahead and for that the governmental control over sensitive data needs to be loosened up. Further, alternative mechanisms to consent also need to be laid down in the law for better legal protection. (Mandavia, 2019)

CONCLUSION AND SUGGETSIONS FOR A BETTER FRAMEWORK

This Chapter provided us a comprehensive analysis of the working of Biometric System (scientifically) and the legal paraphernalia attached to the same. Biometric data came up with a view to ease out the human operations and has been considered as one of the best technologies across the globe. Developed nations like USA, UK, Australia and other European countries have started using these technologies long back. However, the Developing nations owing to the TRIPS restrictions started using the same in the 1990s after their economies integrated with the world economy. The biometric system works on the principle of gauging the human behavioural patterns and characteristics possessed by the individuals and storing them till eternity. However, many human rights activists across the globe have pinned down major privacy concerns pertaining to the sue of Biometric Data System. Even after such concerns, its widespread usage and popularity is something note-worthy. Indian government also have been using this technique in many arenas, most prominently under the Aadhaar Program issued by the Unique Identification Authority of India. Some of the most quoted benefits of the Biometric system are summed up as follows:

- The strength and non-repudiation element
- Usage motivation after finding its quality worthy enough to invest
- Exponential increase in the convenience
- Greater inclusive facility offered by the System
- Reduced operational costs and overheads

These are some of the benefits which make the Biometric Data System quite interesting and lucrative. However, its is not like the rosy picture which shows only one side of the story and ignores the other. There are certain areas which need adequate attention as it could become one of the biggest problems emanating out of this System. Privacy, which has always been the talk of the town and found a due place in the India judicial system under the Puttuswamy Judgment is still very well in place. Even though this new technical set up was supposed to curb privacy concerns but still it has not completely eradicated the privacy issues completely. The stakeholders have also started raising fingers on the same. However, we need to find some concrete suggestions so that the technology can be used with a little adjustment either legal or extra-legal. These suggestions are purely based on the assessment of the situation of Biometric Data System in general and in India as well. These might not act as a straightjacket solution for the contemporaneous problems emanating out of the Biometric Data System but shall be a lamppost for the future advancements in the said area. Some of the plausible suggestions for a better framework can be as follows:

- Strengthening of the existing legal system: It has been time and again quoted that, countries do possess the requisite laws for tackling issues coming out of new technical advancements. The only problem seems to be the effective implementation of the norms which are already in place. Lack of effective and efficient implementation causes the organizations to go astray and therefore, it is the need of the hour that the government should not only be focussed on making such laws but also following the diktat of those laws with utmost sincerity and dedication. Also, internalization of the laws by the people is also something which should be looked at.
- Procedural safeguards: It has been relentlessly argued that organizations which maintain a Biometric Data System have a centralized agency to store that information which is susceptible to misuse and mutilation. Therefore, unbiased and impartial "Third-party agents" should be given the responsibility to closely monitor the activities of such organizations so that the consumers also feel safe about their data being protected. These "Third-party agents" should be appointed after complete scrutiny and in consultation with the consumers. These agents can also work in a similar fashion with the governments as well.
- Overcoming the challenge of Digital Divide: One of the issues is the lack of Digital literacy prevailing mostly in the Developing nations. People are not well equipped in terms of digital education are majority of them are on the other side of the Digital Divide. As a result of which, they are never comfortable with the idea of registering their data in a computerized machine as they fear of data theft and decay. The focus should be on digitizing the knowledge of the people so that are aware of nuances of this new technological set up. This way, the people should join hands with the government in furthering the cause of promoting digital education to the fullest.
- Auditing and Accountability: The Biometric Data system should be regularly monitored or audited by a set of experts which can verify the levels of accountability of the system. These auditing schemes shall vest faith in the customers who are putting their data in that system. The government should come up with well-defined protocols pertaining to auditing standards and parameters should be laid down.
- Algorithm Protection: Algorithm protection is one of the biggest issues attached to the Biometric Data system. The formulas and the equations should be made so specific and in detail that there is no scope left for any deviation and defect under the system. It is the responsibility of the organization to make the algorithm highly complex for protecting it.

Therefore, these are some of the suggestions provided to ensure a better framework of Biometric Data System. However, this does not entail an exhaustive list of all the plausible solutions which can be benefitting in the present scenario.

REFERENCES

Agrawal, S. (2019). *Government localises 'critical' & 'sensitive' personal data.* Retrieved from The Economic Times: https://economictimes.indiatimes.com/news/politics-and-nation/government-localises-critical-sensitive-personal-data/articleshow/72376594.cms?from=mdr

Basu, A. (2020). *Key Global Takeaways From India's Revised Personal Data Protection Bill.* Retrieved from Law Fare Blog: https://www.lawfareblog.com/key-global-takeaways-indias-revised-personal-data-protection-bill

Burman, A. (2020). *Will India's Proposed Data Protection Law Protect Privacy and Promote Growth?* Retrieved from Carnegie India: https://carnegieindia.org/2020/03/09/will-india-s-proposed-data-protection-law-protect-privacy-and-promote-growth-pub-81217

Dalmia, V. P. (2017). *Data Protection Laws In India - Everything You Must Know.* Retrieved from Mondaq: https://www.mondaq.com/india/data-protection/655034/data-protection-laws-in-india--everything-you-must-know

Das, P. (2020). Critical Analysis of Interpretation of Article 21 of the Constitution. *International Journal of Law, Management and Humanities.*

Govindrajan, V. (2019). *How India Plans to Protect Consumer Data.* Retrieved from Harvard Business Review: https://hbr.org/2019/12/how-india-plans-to-protect-consumer-data

Gupta, D. (2015). *Biomteirc Data: History and Evolution.* Thompson Reuters.

Haday, L. (2012, March 13). Biomteric Data: Stages and steps in the making. *Technology Bites*, 23-31.

Hamnnon, J. (2013). *Functions of Biomteirc Data: Scope redefined.* Springer.

Hann, M. (2017). *Fingerprinting and Anthropology: Connection and disconnection.* Thomson Reuters.

Humble, K. (2020). International law, surveillance and the protection of privacy. *International Journal of Human Rights.*

Krishnamurthy, V. (2020). A Tale of Two Privacy Laws: The GDPR and the International Right to Privacy. *The American Journal of International Law.*

MandaviaS. A. (2019). https://economictimes.indiatimes.com/news/politics-and-nation/government-localises-critical-sensitive-personal-data/articleshow/72376594.cms?from=mdr

Reed, K. (2016). History and Technology: Intersecting lines in the spectrum. *International Journal of Anthropology*, 23–39.

Rekhi, K. S. (n.d.). *Analytical Positivism- Indian Perspective*. Retrieved from Legal Service India-E-journal: https://www.legalserviceindia.com/legal/article-4931-analytical-positivisim-indian-prespective.html

Rengel, A. (2014). *Privacy as an International Human Right and the Right to Obscurity in Cyberspace*. *Groningen Journal of International Law*. doi:10.21827/5a86a81e79532

Salomon, A. (2019). UDHR and New Prospects. *Sustainability*, 230–247.

Semwal, S. K. (2011). Human Rights Jurisprudence in Indian Constitution. *The Indian Journal of Political Science*.

Shah, H. (2019). Biometric Data: A complex mystery to resolve. Academic Press.

Sharma, K. (2006). *Reimagining LPG in the post modern world*. Lexis Nexus.

Shawn, T. (2014). *Right to Privacy and contemporary world*. Thompson Reuters.

Shwed, K. (2015). History and its impact on technical know how. *The International Journal of Social Sciences (Islamabad)*.

Sonkar, S. (2021, May). *Privacy Delayed is Privacy Denied*. Retrieved from The Wire: https://thewire.in/tech/data-protection-law-india-right-to-privacy

Sungya, L. (2018). *Identity Management: boon or curse?* University College of London.

Vakil, R. (2018). Constitutionalizing administrative law in the Indian Supreme Court: Natural justice and fundamental rights. *International Journal of Constitutional Law*, *16*(2), 475–502. doi:10.1093/icon/moy027

Viswanath, N. (2018). *The Supreme Court's Aadhaar Judgement And The Right To Privacy*. Retrieved from Mondaq: https://www.mondaq.com/india/privacy-protection/744522/the-supreme-court39s-aadhaar-judgement-and-the-right-to-privacy

KEY TERMS AND DEFINITIONS

Bertillonage: It is the process found in the early 1800s wherein body arrangements were used for identification and recognition.

Biometric Data System: It is a new technological system wherein human beings are identified and recognized on the basis of their personality traits and characteristics.

Fingerprinting: The technique of using fingers for identification and recognition of individuals.

Identity Management: It is the process of managing the information submitted by the consumers under the Biometric Data System for keeping it safe under surveillance.

Privacy: It is s state of controlling your own information and space and one has the absolute right over the same.

Chapter 8
Cybersquatting:
Need for Protection of Domain Names in the Realm of Cyberspace

Ekta Sood

https://orcid.org/0000-0001-6627-4803

HIMCAPES College of Law, India

Vibhuti Nakta

Panjab University, India

ABSTRACT

The mushroom growth of cyberspace and e-commerce has been increasingly threatening to the trademark and trademark statutes like the challenge posed to the domain names in connection with trademarks. Domain names cannot be restricted geographically with regards to access, use, and invasion, and cybersquatting is when trade name is used directly or after registration to invade the rights of the lawful user to whom the domain name belongs. The only objective is to feed upon the goodwill of a lawful owner to earn profits. Unlike other countries, India now does not have specific legislation for the protection of domain names and resorts to the Trademarks Act, 1999. Protection of inventions and enhancing cybersecurity is the need of the hour. To conform in compliance with the WIPO internet treaties to safeguard the copyrighted works, online digital risk management (DRM) schemes were drafted in the Copyright (Amendment) Act, of 2012. Thus, the chapter aims to emphasise the need to designate cybersquatting as a cybercrime while understanding cybercrime, its nature, and judicial intent.

INTRODUCTION

In this world of globalization, a synthesis of technology and science, where life can be cherished with single a single click. In the nineteenth century, the internet brought about a revolutionary development that coincided with the industrial revolution. Internet was first created in the early 1960s as a tool for exchanging information and connecting people. But internet evolved into a crucial instrument in our lives with the advancement in technology and progress in society. They are now utilized for a variety of

DOI: 10.4018/978-1-7998-8641-9.ch008

tasks including social engagement, business transactions, online business, account maintenance, startups, and many more. It is well said that every coin has two sides, and that every invention, technology, and so on, has two sides as well, and that how the user deals with them is entirely up to him. In the field of intellectual property, duplication, copying, piracy is the key concerns. (Shalini, 2021)

The recent internet trend has driven a transformation in the commercial world. Most company groups have moved to the Internet world of commerce and marketing, giving their companies more visibility. This has sparked a detrimental competition in which people attempt to profit from other people's existing trade names to cash in on the goodwill connected with a trading name that was meticulously crafted by the owners (Deo, 2019). All reputable trademark owners may not have or do not have their domain, which could be used by a competitor. When it comes to registering a domain name, it's on a first-come, first-served basis. Cybersquatting is when someone obtains a name that is indistinguishable from a trademark and attempts to vend or rent it. In recent years, the legal challenge has been to find a mechanism to support intellectual property development on the internet while preventing its illegal use. (Ryder, 2001). With the introduction of domain names, the practice of cybersquatting was born. Because not all merchants are experts in the internet or technology, their trade name may be utilized by another trader, who may then try to vend it to the true owner of the trademark, such as a domain name. Cybersquatters can usually register any domain names, free of cost, even if a domain name with a similar name already exists. Cybersquatters frequently utilize a combination of illegal and legitimate work to get money. As a result, the legitimate owner suffers a significant loss (Shalini, 2021).

CONCEPT OF DOMAIN NAMES

Before discussing cyber-squatting and laws which deal with cybersquatting, it is very important to understand the concept of Domain systems. In an age of globalization where the internet is an integral part of our daily lives, we cannot overlook the terminologies that are linked with it. In the internet age, domain names are one example of such a concept. In the twenty-first century, life would be inconceivable without a mobile phone, and each mobile phone is assigned a unique number, which we dial when we want to communicate with someone. Our homes and offices both have addresses. Domain names, on the other hand, are nothing more than simple internet addresses. Every website on the internet has its address (Shalini, 2021).

It is necessary to dial a number on the phone when we need to speak with someone on the phone. Similarly, to reach a Web site such as http://www.facebook.com, one must type in its Internet Protocol (IP) address, which is 31.13.86.36. These IP addresses are required for computers to visit websites. However, because there are so many websites, remembering their IP addresses is challenging. As a result, domain names are created. The Domain Name System (DNS) aims to locate a Web page on the Internet by name rather than IP address. As a result, the linguistic analogous of an IP address is a domain name (Singh, 2018).

The Domain Name System (DNS) was developed to make it easier to retain these long numerical Internet Protocols. It's an internet-based system that offers an alphabetical alternative to numerical values. When a customer visits a website, this provides them with a sense of ease and comfort. Domain names are made up of numbers and letters, as well as domain name extensions like .com, .net, .org, and .in. Let us consider the website www.rise19.com, where www is the hostname, rise19 is the domain name, and .com is the domain name extension (Shalini, 2021).

Classification of Domain Names Extension

There are three levels in Domain Name System:

1.   Top-level

   After the last dot ("."), a domain name's top level is found. The top-level domain of "iprhelpdesk. eu," for example, is "eu." The top-level domain is further classified into two categories:

a.   generic Top-Level Domain (gTLD) - indicates the type of activity (for example, ".com" for all purposes or ".biz" for companies only);
b.   country code Top Level Domain (ccTLD) - denotes the nation or territory in which the domain owner desires to do business (for example, ".uk" for the United Kingdom or ".eu"3 for the European Economic Area).
2.   Second level

   A domain name's second level is positioned just to the left of the top-level domain. The second-level domain in "iprhelpdesk.eu," for example, would be "iprhelpdesk." This sort of domain is the subject of the majority of domain name disputes.

3.   Third level

   A subdomain is the third level of a domain name, which is positioned directly to the left of the second-level domain. The third level domain in "helpline.iprhelpdesk.eu," for example, would be "helpline." This level is not included in every URL since it is frequently used to distinguish between different portions of a website, which correspond to distinct divisions in large organizations (European IPR Helpdesk, 2017).

SCOPE OF PROTECTION

The exclusive right to use a domain name acquired by the owner of a domain name for the term of a contract with the registrar is usually not considered intellectual property. Domain names can be thought of as non-physical assets similar to true intellectual property rights. The first-come, first-served rule applies to domain name registration, just as it does to trademark registration. This means that anyone can buy a domain name as long as it is available, that is if it hasn't already been registered by someone else. Domain names, unlike trademarks, are not territorial. Rather, they have a global geographic reach. Individuals and businesses can register their domain names with any recognized registrar in the globe, and once registered, the domain name has a global effect (European IPR Helpdesk, 2017).

MEANING AND CONCEPT OF CYBERSQUATTING

The process of purchasing an Internet domain name that is expected to be sought by another person, business, or organization in the hopes of selling it for a profit to that person, business, or organization is referred to as cybersquatting. It entails trade names and trademarks being registered as domain names by third parties that do not own the trademarks or trade names. Simply stated, cybersquatters (also known as bad faith mimics) register third-party trade-marks, business names, trade names, and so on to deceive consumers or prospective customers and, in certain cases, sell the domain name to the legitimate owner at a profit (Singh & Associates, 2012).

The Anti-Cybersquatting Consumer Protection Act defines cybersquatting as the act of registering, trading in, or using a domain name in bad faith with the intent of benefitting on the goodwill of someone else's trademark. The cyber squatter then proposes a high sum to sell the domain to the person or company who owns the trademark in the name. It's also known as domain squatting. Squatting is defined as possessing an abandoned or unoccupied place or structure that the squatter doesn't even rent, own, or have permission to use. (Jain, 2015).

To urge the subject to buy the domain from them, some cybersquatters post nasty statements about the person or entity the name is supposed to represent. Others monetize their squatting by posting paid connections to the genuine site that the user most likely requested via advertising networks (Charan, 2015).

The case of *Manish Vij v. Indra Chugh* (2002) perfectly encapsulates the definition of cybersquatting. The court ruled that "obtaining a false registration with the intent to sell the domain name to the authorized owner for a premium" was illegal. Tata, Bennett & Coleman, McDonald's, and other international corporations were among the first victims of internet squatting.

According to the World Intellectual Property Organization, cybersquatting occurs:

1. when a domain name in which the complainant has a right is identical or fallaciously similar to a trade or service mark.
2. The domain name's owner has no legal or genuine claim to it.; and
3. The domain name has been registered and is being used in bad faith (Deo, 2019).

DIFFERENT FORMS OF CYBERSQUATTING

1. *Typosquatting*

Typosquatting is also known as "URL hijacking," "sting sites," and "fake URLs." Typosquatters take advantage of typical typos made by netizens while entering a web URL into a web page. Misspellings (e.g., www.intrenet.com), alternative phrasings of a domain name (e.g., www.internets.com), other top-level domains (www.internet.net), and the usage of Country Code Top-Level Domains (www.internet. co) are examples of such errors. Advanced typosquatting techniques take advantage of trademark visual, auditory, and hardware similarities. Homograph attacks, for example, depending on the resemblance of symbols that might be mistaken, along with letters or characters that can be mixed up, such as the misunderstanding between the letters like 'vv' and 'w' in the domain name www.bankofthewest.com (www.bankofthevvest.com) (Dimov, 2017).

2. *Identity Theft*

In most cases, true owners of domains either neglect or fail to renew their domains unintentionally which further allows a cybersquatter to obtain the web domain. Cybersquatters normally possess software that helps them to keep track of the expiration dates of those web domains in which they are interested. This allows them to trick users into thinking they are the legitimate owners of previously registered web addresses. Domain name subscriptions on the Internet are for a set time. It is important for the Domain Name Owner to re-register or renew the web domain before it expires and once the Domain Name expires, it can be acquired by anyone around the world. The registration is deemed to lapse at this time. A cyber squatter could use an automated software application to register the expired Domain name as soon as it becomes available. Extension exaggeration and alert angling are two further methods of domain name identity theft (Deo, 2019).

3. *Name Jacking*

Name Jacking is squatting which is carried out when in a top-level domain a person's name is registered. If a person's name is "Johnny Jones," for example, he can buy the domain name johnnyjones. com. The domain name buyer can earn from any searches for that name on search engines like Bing and Google by creating a website like this. These "name jacked" webpages are usually set up by persons who wish to sell elevated items such as eBooks or numerous business opportunities and only require a few payments to generate money. Jacked domains are free from most international restrictions because they are frequently created using non-trademarked names and serve a function other than simply trading the domain name back to the original owner. (Deshpande, 2020).

Stars and well-known individuals are frequently targeted by these stealers. It is the acquisition of a domain name connected with a famous person. They earn from the volume that these individuals produce in the web space. In the United States, such individuals' names are protected as trademarks. Such a connection or name has the potential to draw a large amount of traffic (Deo, 2019).

4. *Reverse Cybersquatting*

Reverse cybersquatting occurs when an effort is made to assure a lawful owner's domain name. It entails intimidating and pressuring the rightful owner to transfer ownership to an organization or individual who possesses a trademark displayed in the domain name. It's worth noting that reverse cybersquatting could be deemed an abuse of the domain name dispute resolution process. Reverse cybersquatting may be considered a misuse of the domain name dispute resolution mechanism. Under the laws of several countries, reverse-cybersquatting might well be regarded as a tort or an unfair commercial practice, entitling compensation for the losses of reverse-cybersquatters to the victims (Dimov, 2021).

POSITION IN USA

The Anti-Cybersquatting Consumer Protection Act (ACPA) prohibits cybersquatting, but domain names are routinely held on a first-come, first-served basis, so it remains a concern. Statutory damage of $1,00,000 is granted by the court for each domain name if a trademark owner can establish that the defendant: (1) possesses a distinctive or well-known mark; (2) uses, registers, or traffics in a domain name that is equivalent to or confusingly similar to the mark; and (3) had a "bad faith intent to profit" from the mark. A court can then award statutory damages of up to $100,000 per domain name, apart from that can transfer or cancel the domain name to the appropriate trademark holder, and perhaps even reimburse the plaintiff's legal fees.

In federal courts in Michigan, several cybersquatting lawsuits have been brought. *Audi AG v. D'Amato* (2006) was appealed to the Sixth Circuit of the United States Court of Appeals. In this case, Volkswagen and Audi sued an alleged cybersquatter for obtaining the domain name www.audisport.com in federal district court. The proprietor of the website appealed the district court's ruling that he had broken the rules of ACPA. The Sixth Circuit maintained the verdict, stating that while the website supplied information and items to Audi lovers, the domain name's owner does not have any right in the mark "Audi" and customers were directed to be away from Audi's genuine web page by the domain name's owner. Even though the domain name owner was not trying to convince Audi to buy the domain name from him, the court decided that he wished to profit from Audi's trademark or we can say that, the defendant's intention to profit was not good.

In the USA, a cybersquatting victim always has two have options:

1. To sue under the provisions of Anticybersquatting Consumer Protection Act (ACPA)
2. To use Internet Corporation of Assigned Names and Numbers (ICANN) is a system related to arbitration.

Because the ICANN approach does not involve the use of an attorney, it is both speedier and less expensive than the ACPA.

1. *Anticybersquatting Consumer Protection Act (ACPA)*

Congress established the Antiicybersquatting Consumer Protection Act ("ACPA") in 1999 to safeguard American businesses and consumers, promote e-commerce platforms, and establish trademark law by outlawing "cybersquatting," which is the willful, malafide, and fraudulent registration of distinctive marks as Internet domain names to profit from the goodwill of marks. The ACPA provides a remedy that is civil in nature for those who register a domain name with malafide intention to earn profit and such registered domain name must be similar to a distinctive or renowned mark. There was no apparent deterrent to cybersquatting prior to the ACPA. Despite the success of the Federal Trademark Dilution Act in combating cybersquatters, Congress concluded that additional legislation was required. As a result, in November 1999, the ACPA took effect, a law that makes it illegal to register, trade-in, or even use a domain name that is a renowned or distinct mark or confusingly similar to a famous or distinctive mark with the intent to enrich dishonestly (Mota, 2003).

Intermatic v. Toeppen (1996) and *Ponavision v. Toeppen* (1998) are considered landmark decisions in which the judge decided in the plaintiff's favor. Mr. Toeppen's activities caused trademark infringement, according to the court, because the registration of domain names like intermatic.com made it more difficult for Intermatic to distinguish and differentiate its goods and services via the internet. The court further stated that the respondent's use of a web page in the name of Intermatic detracted from the mark's legitimate value. The Anti-Cybersquatting Consumer Protection Act would not have been possible without these two crucial judgments (ACPA). This law was vital in ensuring that trademark owners were protected. The effect of the above judgments was evident in the year 2000, when John Zuccarini, a very well-known cyber squatter loses two suits because of new legislation and was forced to pay a huge amount of $500,000 as regulatory damages and attorney's fees as directed by federal courts.

The ACPA was invoked in the conventional sense of cybersquatting in *Virtual Works, Inc. v. Volkswagen of America, Inc.* (2001), when the domain name proprietor offered to sell the domain to the trademark holder, VW. In *Interstellar Starship Services, Ltd. v. Epix, Inc*, despite being the trademark infringement in the past, the ACPA was not applicable in this present case and the domain name was also not ordered to be transferred as there was a lack of evidence regarding malafide intention to take benefit.

Plaintiff Hasbro sued defendant Clue Computing in *Hasbro, Inc. v. Clue Computing, Inc.*, (1999), claiming that defendant Clue Computing's registration of "ww.clue.com" infringed and diluted plaintiff's Clue board game trademark." Clue Computing's registration was determined to be a "legitimate competing use of the domain name" that did not impede on or dilute Hasbro's trademark".

In *Lamparello v. Falwell*, 420 F.3d 309 (4th Cir. 2005), The common law trademarks "Jerry Falwell" and "Falwell" belonged to Reverend Falwell, as did the registered brand "Listen America with Jerry Falwell." www.falwell.com is the website for Jerry Falwell Ministries. Christopher Lamparello purchased the domain name www.fallwell.com, which contains extensive criticism of Reverend Falwell's ideas. Although there was no disclaimer on the inside pages of Lamparello's website, the homepage boldly indicated that the website was not linked with Jerry Falwell or his ministry. Reverend Falwell wrote Lamparello letters requesting that he discontinue using www.fallwell.com or any derivation of Reverend Falwell's name as a domain name. Lamparello eventually launched the current lawsuit against Reverend Falwell and his organizations, seeking a non-infringement declaration. Even though Lamparello and Reverend Falwell used similar marks online, the court found that Lamparello's website did not resemble Reverend Falwell's. Furthermore, Lamperello's website was created solely to provide a platform for criticizing ideas, not to steal them.

In M*icrosoft* V. M*ikerowesoft*, (2004) Mike Rowe launched MikeRoweSoft.com in 2003 to sell his web design services. He did so since the phonetic pun made him think of the word "Microsoft." The larger firm, however, requested that he transfer the domain name because it was phonetically similar to Microsoft.com. They offered him $10 in exchange for the registration fee. Microsoft issued a cease and desist letter charging Rowe with cybersquatting after he wanted $10,000 for the domain. Following widespread public outrage, the business reached an out-of-court settlement.

2. *Internet Corporation of Assigned Names and Numbers (ICANN)*

The Internet Corporation for Assigned Names and Numbers (ICANN) has overarching responsibility for DNS management. The Internet Corporation for Assigned Names and Numbers (ICANN) is a non-profit organization. The domain names can be purchased from any ICANN-accredited registrar. It oversees the domain name registration system and establishes standards and criteria for all accredited registrars to follow. ICANN is a private company that manages the distribution of unique domain names and IP addresses and maintains and organizes the domain name system. Actual domain name registration, on the other hand, is managed by several domain name registries located in different nations across the globe. The most common underlying issues in the various domain name disputes that have come before courts around the world have been cyber squatting, parody disputes, and rival conflicts (Charan, 2015).

Uniform Domain Name Dispute Resolution Policy ("UDRP")

The Uniform Domain Name Dispute Resolution Policy ("UDRP") was authorized by ICANN in October 1999 for use in all domain name disputes. All persons or organizations who register domain names with an ICANN-accredited domain registry are obligated to use the UDRP. There are no monetary awards attainable under the UDRP, unlike in litigation, particularly one involving the ACPA. Using the ICANN arbitration mechanism, the Uniform Domain Name Dispute Resolution Policy (UNDRP), rather than litigating under the Act, is likely to be speedier (Coran, 2001).

The UDRP allows anyone to file a complaint. To assert that a particular domain name in which a person has a right, is deceptively identical or similar, one must have to prove that the particular domain name owner does not have any intellectual property right or any legitimate interest in that domain name and such domain name was used and registered in breach of trust. If all these factors were established then that domain name will be terminated and transferred to the rightful owner (JUSTIA, 2018).

All generic and top-level domain names that have deliberately agreed to embrace the UDRP are affected. It is the world's first and most comprehensive virtual dispute settlement system. On a worldwide scale, it has resolved around 20,000 domain name conflicts. It is essentially a worldwide arbitration process. The major goal in developing this policy was to solve issues that arise between domain name registrants and trademark owners. The UDRP aims to create a process that is both cheaper and faster than our current legal system. Arbitrators with experience in trademark law oversee the UDRP hearings. This ensures that UDRP cases are decided by professionals, as opposed to the courts, which may or may not happen. eBay, a well-known internet firm, won one of the largest cybersquatting cases in January 2015, claiming ownership of over 1000 domains that had exploited its brand (Shalini, 2021).

World Wrestling Federation Entertainment Inc. V. Michael Bosman, [1 N.C.J.L. & Tech. 3 (2000)]. It is the first UDRP case to be decided. In this case, WWF, a US-based Federation, filed a lawsuit against Michael Bosman, a resident of California, for registering the domain name www.worldwrestlingfederation. com. Later, he proposed WWF a larger price for the domain name. The WWF alleged that the registered person was acting illegally by utilizing this domain name since it was obscurely similar or identical to a brand they had registered. The court decided that the domain name should indeed be forwarded to the World Wrestling Federation in this case.

WIPO ON CYBERSQUATTING

The first worldwide dispute settlement mechanism aimed at reducing trademark abuse on the Internet was inaugurated this week, sending a warning signal to cybersquatters. One day after the new regulations went into effect, on December 2, 1999, the first dispute under the new Uniform Dispute Resolution Policy for top-level domains (com,. net, and.org) was submitted with the World Intellectual Property Organization (WIPO) Arbitration and Mediation Center (WIPO Processes, 1999).

WIPO's anti-cyber squatting program is based on the Uniform Domain Name Dispute Resolution Policy (UDRP). In 1999, UDRP founded WIPO and is used all across the world to prevent trademark infringement in domain names by all brand owners. As of November 20, 2020, WIPO had handled 50,000 UDRP-based procedures involving parties from over 180 countries and including around 91,000 domain names. Since the majority of the world has already been working at home, businesses and consumers have been significantly reliant upon this Internet, whether to participate in their careers, online shopping, or educate oneself on how to stay safe in the current pandemic (WIPO's Anti-Cybersquatting, 2021).

A rise in the number of domain names registered has been reported by many domain name registration agencies. These can be used for media sites or to promote business development opportunities, but they can also be used to disseminate disinformation and participate in criminal and fraudulent operations, just like social networking platforms. The COVID-19 pandemic has driven a surge in cybersquatting claims filed with the World Intellectual Property Organization's Arbitration and Mediation Center, which has set a new high for WIPO filings this year. The WIPO Center handled 3,405 cases from January to October 2020, an increase of 11% over the same time in 2019 (WIPO's Anti-Cybersquatting, 2021).

In *Google Inc. v. Herit Shah (Shah)* (2009), an action relating to cybersquatting was won by Google Inc., an internet software business against an Indian teenager who had claimed the domain name googblog. com. Google claimed that the domain name was confusingly similar to its trademark. On May 15, 2009, the World Intellectual Property Organization (WIPO) directed Herit Shah (Shah), an Indian adolescent to transfer the domain's rights to Google Inc. who had been using the domain name 'googblog.com. Industry experts considered this as a case of cyber squatting, however, according to industry commentators, Google was able to effectively safeguard its intellectual property rights (IPR).

POSITION IN INDIA

Cyber-squatting is a menace that knows no bounds and is rapidly expanding. Notwithstanding the awareness of the harm and instability it posed by the rising problem of cybersquatting, India has no formal laws addressing the issue. In India, cybersquatting has wreaked havoc on several businesses, including start-ups. In contrast with the rest of the developed world, India lacks a law that protects domain names to combat cybersquatting. In India, the Trademark Act of 1999 governs matters involving domain names, making obtaining domain name protection a difficult task. Admittedly, the only law dealing with the internet and cybercrime, the Information Technology Act of 2000, has overlooked a serious crime like cybersquatting (Shalini, 2021).

In the matter of *Satyam Infoway Ltd vs Sifynet Solutions* (2004), the Hon'ble Supreme Court stated, "As far as India is concerned, there is no statute which relates to dispute settlement in connection with domain names. Although the Trade Marks Act of 1999 is not extraterritorially applicable and may not provide appropriate protection for domain names, this does not preclude domain names from being legally protected to the degree practicable under the rules governing passing off."
Victims in India are given these choices to combat cybersquatting:

1. Remedy action under the Law of Passing-Off and Trade Marks Act of 1999
2. Complaint filed under the INDRP
3. Remedy action under the Law of Passing-Off and Trade Marks Act of 1999

Even though domain names are neither defined by Indian law nor governed by any separate legislation; the Indian courts have applied the Trade Marks Act, 1999 to such cases. Two types of reliefs are possible under the Trademarks Act of 1999, as they are in other cases:

a. Infringement remedy

The Trade Mark Act only allows the owner of a trademark to seek infringement relief if the mark is registered (Singh & Associates, 2021). Infringement occurs when one trademark is used that adds to the confusion, is likely to cause confusion to, or confusingly identical to another trademark (Deo, 2019). According to Section 135 of the Trade Mark Act of 1999, legal remedies for trademark infringement include injunctions, an account of profits, damages, delivery of goods, and destruction of infringing articles as per Section 135 of the Trade Mark Act of 1999. The use of fraudulent trademarks is penalized under Section 103 by a period of infringement of not less than 6 months and up to 3 years, followed by a fine of not less than Rs. 50000 and up to 2 lacs. If a mark is registered, the owner has the common law remedy of passing off, but if his mark is registered, he also has the statutory right to launch an action for infringement under the Trademarks Act 1999 (Pandey, 2021).

b.   Remedy of passing off

If the owner plans to use the passing-off remedy, no registration of the trademark is required (Singh & Associates, 2021). In *Erven Warnink v Townend* (the 'Advocaat' case) (1979), Lord Diplock identified five characteristics that must be present to establish a viable cause of action for passing off. These were:

i.   a misrepresentation;
ii.   made by a trader in the course of business;
iii.   to prospective customers of his or ultimate consumers of goods or services supplied by him;
iv.   calculated to harm the business or goodwill of another trader (in the sense that this is a reasonably foreseeable consequence); and
v.   which either does actual damage to a trader's business or goodwill or will very certainly do so (in a quia timet suit).

JUDICIAL RESPONSES IN INDIA

In *N.R. Dongre v. Whirlpool Corporation* (1996), The Delhi High Court held that one company cannot sell those items that appear to be from another. An injunction may be granted if the trademark owner can establish that perhaps the domain name registrant did so intending to confuse the public.

Yahoo Inc. v. Aakash Arora & Anr. (2000) was the first case of cybersquatting in India in which the defendant created a website that was substantially similar to the plaintiff's well-known website and offered identical services. The judge took the side of the plaintiff, Yahoo Inc., and ruled against the defendant as they have registered a domain name, YahooIndia.com.

In *Rediff Communications Ltd. v. Cyberbooth & Another* (2000), the domain name www.radiff.com was registered by Cyberbooth. Hence, similar to the already existing domain name www.rediff.com. The High Court of Bombay ruled that domain names are of substantial importance and have a high value linked to them, making them a corporate asset. It went on to say that domain name similarities can be perplexing for the general public, especially first-time clients.

Dr. Reddy's Laboratories Limited v. Manu Kasouri (2001): Manu Kasouri (defendant) was barred from ever using the domain name "drreddyslab.com" because it was confusingly similar to the plaintiff's registered trademark. The court held the defendant guilty under passing-off since the domain name is important in the realm of e-commerce.

In *Tata Sons Limited v. Manu Kishori & Others*, (2001) The defendant was successful in registering a variety of domain names, including the well-known trademark TATA. Citing the Rediff Communication decision, the court decided in favor of the plaintiff and restricted the use of the domain name.

In *Acqua Minerals Limited. v. Pramod Borse & Another,* (2001) The defendant, Mr. Borse, registered www.bisleri.com as a domain name, that is identical to Bisleri's Indian trademark. The defendant was found guilty of trademark infringement after allowing the plaintiff to transmit the domain name to him, according to the Delhi High Court.

The plaintiff won again in *Satyam Infoway Ltd. v Sifynet Solutions*, (2004). In this case, the respondent had registered two domain names respectively, www.siffynet.com and www.siffynet.net. These domain names were quite identical to the plaintiff's domain name registered as www.sifynet.com. Plaintiff (Satyam) enjoys a good reputation in the market and had registered several names including 'Sifynet' with World Intellectual Property Organization (WIPO) and ICANN. The plaintiff invented the term 'Sify' by uniting the elements from its corporate brand 'Satyam Infoway' which has its goodwill and strong reputation in the market. Hence, as per Supreme Court's opinion corporate entities use a particular domain name so that their company's goods and services be distinguished and identified from the rest of the entities. Supreme Court also stated that all the features of the domain names are similar to trademarks only and a passing-off action can lie wherever there is an infringement of Domain Names.

Tata Sons Limited and Anr Vs Fashion ID Limited (2005): "The use of the same or similar domain name may result in a diversion of users, which could arise from such users accessing one domain name instead of another," the court said. This can happen in e-commerce because of its quick growth and prompt (and erotically endless) exposure to potential buyers and users, and it's especially true in sectors where there's a lot of overlap. Ordinary consumers/users who are looking for certain features under one domain name may be mistakenly reached to the different but almost identical website which offers similar services. It is upon those users to decide that whether the first domain name owner wrongly represented its services or goods through promotional activities and as a result, the first domain name owner can lose their business on complaint files by the users. As a result, it is clear that a domain name might have all of the features of a trademark and so be the basis for a passing off case."

In *Mr. Arun Jaitley v. The Network Solutions Pvt. Ltd.*, (2011) Mr. Jaitley is a well-known Indian politician. He was India's former Finance Minister (2014-2019). In this case, the domain name www.arunjaitley.com was registered by the defendant. Mr. Arun Jaitley made numerous attempts to purchase this domain name from the criminal, but the respondent demanded a fee well over the cost. The respondent was found guilty of objectionable registration of a popular figure as a domain name by the High Court of Delhi. Mr. Jaitley received the domain name as a result.

Complaint Filed under the INDRP

India has its own country-specific domain name extension, in the form of "in." which is also known as Country Code Top Level Domain. The National Internet Exchange of India is in charge of handling and adjudicating all disputes involving the .in top-level domain (NIXI). As a result, the .IN Dispute Resolution Policy and the Rules of Procedure of INDRP manage all domain names and cybersquatting complaints involving .in domains (Deshpande, 2020).

India is not a signatory to the UDRP. INDRP, on the other hand, was developed in accordance with UDRP, norms that are internationally accepted, and as per a few sections of the Indian IT Act 2000. The INDRP lays down the procedure for resolving a dispute regarding registration and the use of '.in'

Internet Domain Name between the Registrant and the Complainant. Whenever a complaint is filed by the complainant against the Registrant with the .IN Registry, the Registrant is required to submit himself to the arbitration proceedings as per the rules of INDRP. After receiving the complaint, an Arbitrator will be designated by the .IN Registry from the roster of arbitrators by the Registry. Within three days of receiving the complaint, notification to the Respondent must be given by the Arbitrator. Arbitration Proceedings must be conducted by the Arbitrator in accordance with the Arbitration and Conciliation Act, 1996 including the rules set forth therein. Once the arbitrator is appointed. Notification to the parties regarding appointment is given by .IN Registry. The Arbitrator will issue a reasoned award and provide a copy of the award to the Complainant, Respondent, and the.IN Registry as soon as possible. Within 60 days of the starting of arbitration proceedings, the award must be issued. In extraordinary circumstances, the Arbitrator may extend this term for up to 30 days. However, the Arbitrator must provide written justifications for the extension. The Arbitrator must determine evidence of malafide registration and use of a domain name, taking into account paragraph 6 of the INDRP, but without limitation. It is important that the Arbitrator must ensure that all copies of the papers, answers, applications, rejoinders, and orders that are passed from time to time are immediately provided to the .IN Registry to maintain records and proceedings' transparency (Khan et.al., 2015).

The policy states that no in-person proceedings (including videoconference, teleconference, and web conference hearings) will be held, provided that the Arbitrator on his sole discretion and as an extraordinary matter, requires such a hearing to be in-person proceedings to resolve the Complaint. In any case before an Arbitrator, remedies available to the Complainant's are limited such as invalidating the domain name of Registrant or assignment to the Complainant of the domain name registration of Registrant. The arbitrator can award costs to the complainant. The INDRP provides that once the proceeding is concluded, or even when the complaint is pending, Registrant is precluded from transmitting a contentious registration of domain name to some other holder for a period of 15 working days ('working days' means any other day apart from Saturday, Sunday or public holiday) unless the party agrees in writing, to whom the domain name registration is being transferred, to be bound by the decision of the Arbitration Panel (Khan, et.al., 2015).

Essential Elements under INDRP

A complainant must prove all three criteria listed below, in the order specified in Rule 4 of the INDRP, in order to succeed in a complaint under the INDRP:

- The Registrant's domain name is deceptively similar to a Complainant-owned name, trademark, or service mark.,
- The Registrant has no permitted interests in the domain name and has no rights to it. and
- The domain name of the Registrant was registered or is being utilized in bad faith (Choudhary, 2020).

Few Cases on INDRP

1. *YouTube LLC v. Rohit Kohli (2007)*

A domain name www.youtube.in was registered by the defendant and this domain name is deceptively identical to the complainant's famous trademark, YouTube LLC. Documents provided by the complainant prove that various trademark applications were filed by him in several countries that include India as well. As conceptually and phonetically both the domain names are similar, it is decided that upon the payment of the fees for the registry, the domain name would be transferred to the complainant.

2. *Vodafone Group Plc v. Rohit Bansal (2007)*

In this case, as per the Arbitrator, the Complainant's capacity to substantiate his rights in the trademark VODAFONE is sufficient to prove that there is an element of ill faith on the side of the Respondent. It is decided that registration of domain name "Vodafone.co.in" was registered by the Respondent with malafide intentions of selling it to the Complainant and to make profit from the sale. Hence, it was ordered that the domain name must be transferred to the Complainant.

3. *Bloomberg Finance L.P., (BF) vs. Mr. Kanhan Vijay (2009).*

The most important case heard by the INDRP Arbitration Panel in 2009 is this one. In this case, the disputed domain name (www.bloomberg.net.in) was registered by Bloomberg Finance L.P. The service mark 'BLOOMBERG' was registered by this company in India and overseas since 1986 and rights attached to it are trade name, trademark, and has own corporate identity with strong goodwill and reputation. Even though there is no reason for the company to adopt and register the domain name www.blooberg.net.in but still they had registered various domain names that feature the domain name as "Bloomberg". Hence, it made them the first user, registrant, and adopter. The Arbitration Panel found that respondents lacked due diligence and acted in bad faith and failed to provide proper evidence in support of their assertions. Therefore, as a result, the domain name should be assigned back to the complainant.

4. *Starbucks corporation v. Mohanraj (2009)*

The Complainant claimed that the respondent's domain name, www.starbucks.co.in was deceptively identical to its domain name i.e. www.starbucks.in. It was also claimed that there is no legitimate interest of the respondent in the domain name and he used the trademark with malafide intentions. The arbitrator determined that the domain name in the issue was deceptively similar to the trademark of the complainant's and they are the rightful owner of the claim. Further, stated that the domain name must be transmitted to the complainant as the respondent registered it in bad faith.

5. *GOOGLE Inc. v. Gulshan Khatri (2011)*

The complainant submitted the current complaint in order to prevent the respondent from registering the domain name in his or her favor. The complainant's complaint was based on the latter's adoption of an identical and similar domain name, as well as similar services provided by the respondent. The learned arbitrator determined that the disputed domain name was identical and confusingly similar to the complainant's other prior registered domain name and a registered trademark, and ordered the registry to cancel the domain name immediately and transfer it to the complainant. It is important to understand that the rules of INDRP and UDRP do not take away the authority of civil courts in India. Hence, a complaint can be made to the appropriate civil court if the aggrieved party wants to claim compensation as remedies provided under common law are extensive in nature. Under the Common Law of Passing-Off, in most cases, a civil court can issue an order granting a permanent injunction against the wrongful domain name user.

RECOMMENDATIONS AND SUGGESTIONS

1. *New Legislation*

In India, no legislation deals specifically with the issues of the domain name. hence, it is in need of an hour to establish new legislation. The courts have previously stretched the boundaries by interpreting trademark law provisions broadly responsible for domain name conflicts. There is still no sufficient defense against cyber squatters, as seen by the widespread prevalence of this threat. Miscreants come up with innovative ways to deceive and extort money from large corporations. The lack of a direct law helps them achieve their goal because they can easily find drawbacks in the law that would exempt them from prosecution. Most courts apply trademark legislation and IT Act but they have their flaws and do not provide adequate protection. The law of trademarks has been unable to address the wide range of conflicts that are continually arising in cyberspace. Furthermore, applying this ancient rule would waste a significant amount of time in the trial courts, which is extremely detrimental in the digital world where time is of the essence, and could result in the loss of the claimed right (Khan et.al., 2015).

The Information Technology Act primarily governs cybercrime and electronic signatures, with little mention of intellectual property rights, particularly concerning internet-related activities. The legislation is likewise quiet on internet squatting, which is on the rise, as documented in "Cyber Squatting: Modern Day Extortion". In many cases, Indian courts must go to English and American laws and decisions for guidance. As a result, India must enact legislation similar to the ACPA in the United States, which is in line with the UDRP's requirements.

2. *Independent Adjudicatory Body*

A counterpart body should be established in India which shall be based on the model of the National Arbitration Forum of the United States and the Czech Arbitration Court. This authority will solely hear matters involving domain name disputes, particularly cyber squatting in Indian domains. Such organizations would be more effective and more efficient as they consume less time of the parties as the parties would not have to be on standby to be assigned to the docket and to wait for the final decree to arrive.

3. *Revamping INDRP*

Instead of being merely a guiding principle, the INDRP should be made into law. The difficulty with it being a policy is that it is not required to be followed, resulting in a slack regime. The INDRP, while modeled after the UDRP, still has several flaws that limit its use and efficacy. The INDRP arbitration procedure is pervasive with extraneous formal requirements as a result of the discrepancies, and they both vary substantially on domain names. As a result, it is urgent to bring it into compliance with the UDRP and give it a legal form.

4. *Arbitration*

It is also proposed that the WIPO Arbitration and Mediation Centre's arbitration verdicts be declared binding in India under the Arbitration and Conciliation Act 1996. Just like any other arbitration judgments, WIPO judgments can also be appealed to the High Court as judgments passed by the arbitrator are also deemed to be decree under the Arbitration Act, hence, application to enforce such judgments can also be filed. In this way, the judgments from ICAAN and WIPO will benefit the overcrowded Indian judicial system.

Many cases involving cyber squatting have been adjudicated by Indian courts. Cyber squatting has piqued the interest of governments all around the world, prompting them to investigate the subject more thoroughly. Cyber squatting is still increasing with a high rate in India as well as in other countries, hence, it should be the duty of registrars to make an effort to inscribe and curb it at the level of registration only. This can be done at the initial level only when a person files his claim, at that time, conducting background checks about domain names should be done rather than just allocating them blindly. This should help a lot with cybersquatting control (Khan et.al., 2015).

CONCLUSION

Cybersquatting is a rapidly expanding threat with no territorial limits. Businesses all across the world have been affected by cybersquatters. Cybersquatting and other related actions have forced governments all around the world to take this issue extremely seriously. WIPO has been instrumental in resolving disputes and developing concrete principles in this area. Developed countries, such as the United States, have implemented stringent anti-cyber squatting legislation, such as the Anti-Cybersquatting Consumer Protection Act (ACPA).

Since the internet arrived in India, cybersquatting has become a problem for Indian businesses and trademark owners. Many cases involving cybersquatting have been handled by Indian courts, which have attempted to offer remedies under the Trademark Act and the statute of passing off. The legislature must implement a domain name protection law that addresses cybersquatting and gives proper remedy to trademark owners. The government's introduction of the.IN Dispute Resolution Policy (INDRP) is a step in the right direction.

REFERENCES

Acqua Minerals Limited. v. Pramod Borse & Another, AIR 2001 Del 463

Bloomberg Finance L.P., (BF) vs. Mr. Kanhan Vijay, INDRP/110 (2009)

Charan, P. (2015). A Survey of the Prominent Effects of Cybersquatting in India. *International Journal of Information Security and Cybercrime, 4*(1), 47–58. doi:10.19107/IJISC.2015.01.07

Chowdhury, A. R. (2020). *Domain Name Protection: Is Your Interest Legitimate?* ALG India. https://www.algindia.com/domain-name-protection-is-your-interest-legitimate/

Coran, S. J. (2001). The Anticybersquatting Consumer Protection Act' s In Rem Provision: Making American Trademark Law the Law of the Internet? *Hofstra Law Review, 30*, 169–196.

Cybersquatting Examples Everything You Need to Know. (2020). Retrieved from: https://www.upcounsel.com/cybersquatting-examples

Cybersquatting. (2018). *JUSTIA.* Retrieved from: https://www.justia.com/intellectual-property/trademarks/cybersquatting/

Deo, S. (2019). Cybersquatting: Threat to Domain Name. *International Journal of Innovative Technology and Exploring Engineering, 8*(6S4), 1432–1434. doi:10.35940/ijitee.F1291.0486S419

Deshpande, S. (2020). Cyber squatting – A study of Legal framework in India. *International Journal of Law. Management & Humanities, 3*, 1825–1835.

DiGiacomo, J. (2015). *An overview of Cybersquatting Laws.* Revision/Legal. https://revisionlegal.com/copyright/copyright-infringement/an-overview-of-cybersquatting-laws/

Dimov, D. (2017). *Latest trends in Cybersquatting.* INFOSEC. https://resources.infosecinstitute.com/topic/latest-trends-in-cybersquatting/

Ryder, D. R. (2001). Guide to Cyber Laws (Information Technology Act, 2000: E-commerce, Data Protection & the Internet). Eastern Book Publisher.

Dr. Reddy's Laboratories Limited v. Manu Kasouri, 2001 PTC 859 (Del).

Ervin Warnink v Townend, [1979] A.C. 731

European I. P. R. Helpdesk. (2017). *Domain Names and Cybersquatting.* Retrieved from: https://www.ipoi.gov.ie/en/commercialise-your-ip/tools-for-business/domain-name-and-cybersquatting.pdf

Google inc. v. Gulshan Khatri, Case no. 8 of 2011. https://www.registry.in›show-doc›id=googleein

Google Inc. v. Herit Shah (Shah), Case No. D2009-0405 (2009)

Hasbro, Inc. v. Clue Computing, Inc., 66 F. Supp. 2d 117 (1999)

Intermatic v. Toeppen, 947 F. supp 1227 (N.D.I ll. 1996)

Interstellar Starship Services, Ltd. v. Epix, Inc, 304 F.3d at 947

JainS. (2015). Cyber Squatting: Concept, Types and Legal Regimes in India. https://ssrn.com/abstract=2786474 doi:10.2139/ssrn.2786474

Khan, Z. H., Charan, P., Ansari, M. A., & Khan, K. H. (2015). Cybersquatting and its Effectual Position in India. *International Journal of Scientific and Engineering Research, 6*, 880–886.

Lamparello v. Falwell, 420 F.3d 309 (4th Cir. 2005)

Manish Vij v. Indra Chugh, AIR 2002 Del. 243.

Michigan. Audi AG v. D'Amato, 469 F.3d 534 (6th Cir. 2006)

Microsoft v. MikeroweSoft, (2004)

Mota, S. A. (2003). The anticybersquatting consumer protection act: An analysis of the decisions from the courts of appeals. *Journal of Computer & Information Law*, *21*, 355–370.

Mr. Arun Jaitley v. The Network Solutions Pvt. Ltd, 181 (2011) DLT 716.

N.R. Dongre v. Whirlpool Corporation, 1996 (16) PTC 583 (SC).

Pandey, A. (2017). *Laws against cybersquatting*. IPleaders. https://blog.ipleaders.in/cyber-squatting/

Ponavision v. Toeppen, 141 F.3e 1316 (1998)

Rediff Communications Ltd. v. Cyberbooth & Another, AIR 2000 Bom 27

Satyam Infoway Ltd versus Sifynet Solutions, 2004 (3) AWC 2366 SC, AIR 2004 SC 3540

Shalini. (2021). Cybersquatting: The Domain Name Dispute. *Law Audience Journal, 2*, 69-85.

Singh & Associates. (2012). *India: Cyber Squatting Laws in India*. Mondaq. https://www.mondaq.com/india/trademark/208840/cyber-squatting-laws-in%20india

Singh, H. P. (2018). Cyber squatting and the role of Indian Courts: A Review. *Amity Journal of Computational Sciences, 2*, 18-23. https://amity.edu/UserFiles/aijem/914%20-%202018_V02_I02_P017-021.pdf

Starbucks corporation v. Mohanraj, Case Number INDRP/118 (2009)

Tata Sons Limited v. Manu Kishori & Others, 2001 IIIAD Delhi 545

Tata Sons Limited and Anr Vs Fashion ID Limited, (2005) 140 PLR 12

Works, V. Inc. v. Volkswagen of America, 238 F.3d 264 (4th Cir. 2001) Vodafone Group Plc v. Rohit Bansal, INDRP/052. https://www.registry.in/show-doc?id=vodafone_0.pdf

WIPO Press Releases. (1999). *WIPO Processes First Case Under Cybersquatting Procedure*. Retrieved from: https://www.wipo.int/pressroom/en/prdocs/1999/wipo_pr_1999_200.html

WIPO Press Release. (2020). *WIPO's Anti-"Cybersquatting" Service: 50,000 Cases and Growing amid COVID-19 Surge*. Retrieved from: https://www.wipo.int/pressroom/en/articles/2020/article_0026.html

World Wrestling Federation Entertainment Inc. v. Michael Bosman,[1 N.C.J.L. & Tech. 3 (2000)]

Yahoo Inc. v. Aakash Arora & Anr, 2000 PTC 209 (Del.).

YouTube LLC v. Rohit Kohli, Case no. INDRP/42. https://www.registry.in/show-doc?id=youtubeco_0.pdf

Chapter 9
Evolution of Cryptocurrency:
Analysing the Utility, Legality, and Regulatory Framework in India

Sambhav Sharma

Amity Law School, Guru Gobind Singh Indraprastha University, Delhi, India

Ramayni Sood

Amity Law School, Guru Gobind Singh Indraprastha University, Delhi, India

ABSTRACT

The avatar of currency has evolved over time, and 'cryptocurrency' is its latest incarnation. Cryptocurrency is a type of digital currency that allows peer-to-peer online payments without interference of financial institutions. Though experts are impressed with its growth trajectory, its decentralized and unregulated structure has stirred insecurity amongst governments across jurisdictions that has translated into bans and indecisiveness related to its status. While the concerns are not baseless and it is susceptible to cybercrimes, the focus must be to mitigate the issues rather than imposing a blanket prohibition that would be antithetical to the fundamental spirit and purpose of financial digitization, which is to promote the free flow of funds. In this chapter, the authors, firstly, analyze the practicality of cryptocurrency in light of the legal barriers and, secondly, assess the viability of a regulatory framework that ensures minimal control from the authorities but also checks concerns including cybercrime, illegal transactions, tax evasion, and lack of accountability.

INTRODUCTION

Cryptocurrency is increasingly becoming more popular amongst not just technology enthusiasts but also people who encourage a shift from the conventional form of trading. Furthermore, with the advent of digital money and online payment, Cryptocurrency has served as a diversion from the traditional way of monetary exchange and store of value.

As and when society evolves, it tends to change the way it functions and carries out the exchange of commodities, services, and legal tender. Throughout history, it has been seen how humans first believed

DOI: 10.4018/978-1-7998-8641-9.ch009

everything to be free for all, including all resources available on earth. However, gradually, after realizing the dearth of resources, humans introduced ownership in society as one of the means of livelihood. Ownership subsequently gave rise to the barter system as a method of acquiring resources that others possess in exchange for one's own possession. Later, the advent of legal tender in the way of metal and coins replaced the barter system as a new form of acquiring resources. Finally, after decades of using precious metals and coins as means of payment, humans realized that what matters is the value ascribed to the currency and not the actual value the material possesses. Thus, came currency notes and coins as known today. Each currency in the world stores a different quantum of value, which is subject to change depending on foreign exchange and the world economy.

It wasn't until the early 2000s that people started realizing that it was time for society to progress further and enter the realm of digital and electronic currencies; as for them, the physical currency had become unnecessary owing to the advancement in technology, which allowed for the ease of trading and currency exchange with just a click of a button. One such kind of digital currency came to be known as Cryptocurrency.

This chapter, through the method of doctrinal study of literature and policies of various jurisdictions, structurally analyzes the growth trajectory of Cryptocurrency around the world, its legality and issues surrounding it. The objective is to assess the viability of this invention in the backdrop of legal and economic concerns and find solutions for the same. The chapter is relevant for economists, Information Technology experts, legal practitioners, and students interested in the growth of Cryptocurrency.

BACKGROUND

To begin, difference must be drawn between two terms: electronic money and digital currency. To put it simply, the digital equivalent of currency is electronic money. Electronic money is essentially fiat or physical money that is stored in electronic form; it is the digital equivalent to fiat money. When the device's owner makes a purchase or sale transaction, the quantity of stored monetary value is reduced or increased accordingly.

Whereas digital currency is a type of payment that exists only in electronic form, that is, there is no physical equivalent of it in the owner's possession (Ayhan, 2017). Digital currency does not have a physical form, such as coins or currency notes. Instead, transactions of digital currency are made through computer devices, with the help of electronic codes (Reserve Bank of India (RBI, 2017).

Cryptocurrency is digital currency and not electronic money, as discussed above, as they do not have a fiat equivalent to them. Essentially, it is a digital representation of value that follows its own unit of account, and is issued by private developers. (Dong He et al., 2016, pp. 7, 16-17). Unlike the electronic equivalents of fiat money, Cryptocurrency is not governed by any central financial or governmental authority. Instead, it signifies a free flow of funds, unrestricted and unregulated by government norms and policies, in the furtherance of a more democratic setup. Although it operates independently of banks, governments, financial institutions, or brokers, like various currency exchanges that exist for normal currency, Cryptocurrency also requires the use of digital exchange platforms to be operated and traded in.

Cryptocurrency operates on blockchain technology. What is Blockchain? Blockchain is a decentralized technology that manages and records transactions across a large number of computers in a distributed environment. A block is a collection of transactions carried out between users of a digital currency such as bitcoin. A chain is formed from these blocks, each of which contains the history of previous transactions. This chain can be used to establish a ledger, which can be used to verify the balance or currency that a user possesses publicly. In essence, a blockchain is a digital ledger containing all past transactions, with each block representing a new page containing all current transactions. This information is then shared across a vast network of computers associated with the blockchain. The following are the features of cryptocurrency:

Cryptocurrency as a Universal Currency

Every country has its official currency. United States accepts US Dollars (USD), India recognizes Indian Rupees (INR) as its medium for exchange, and Pounds and Yen are the currency of the United Kingdom and Japan, respectively. One cannot buy a commodity in the United States using INR or Pounds as the medium of exchange. The value of INR or Pounds or any other currency will first need to be changed into the country's currency according to an exchange rate, and only then the transaction can be concluded. Before the rise of electronic money, the conversion process was done only by financial institutions that physically exchanged one fiat currency into another according to the foreign exchange rate. With the advent of globalization and the technological era, the exchange process was simplified because of the emergence of electronic money. Fiat money stored electronically could now be transferred through a convenient online procedure. However, the same was also subjected to a process of conversion. For example, when one shops online using net banking from a website in the United Kingdom while sitting in India, the transaction amount which is stored in INR is electronically converted into Pounds, and the same then reaches the online bank of the receiver in United Kingdom. The final value debited from the account is subject to the exchange rate and a conversion fee is charged by the intermediary financial institution. Virtual currencies like Cryptocurrency aim at eliminating this divide that exists in the global economy. As cryptocurrencies are not governed by any particular country, their universal nature eliminates currency conversion hassles in cross border transactions.

The idea of a universally accepted currency is not alien to civilization. Before paper and metal currencies, gold was widely used as a mode of exchange throughout the world. In the current scenario, it is widely acknowledged that Cryptocurrency creators envisaged a digital equivalent to gold as was historically used. Such currency has the potential of eliminating the vices of currency exchange rates and serve as a universal token of exchange that anyone can possess and spend anywhere.

Anonymity of Cryptocurrency Transactions

In the beginning, it was commonly believed that cryptocurrencies such as Bitcoin were a shelter for criminals because of their anonymous and untraceable nature. To prevent being tied to a common owner, it was originally recommended in the first Bitcoin whitepaper that users must use a new address for each transaction to maintain anonymity. However, cryptocurrencies do not follow this proposed idea, and every smallest transaction in the crypto world is traceable. As organizations and the general public became more familiar with blockchain technology, it became clear that Bitcoin's public transaction record was, in reality, a gold mine loaded with information for the authorities. Trading in virtual cash is analogous to writing under a pseudonym. Whenever an author's pseudonym is attached to their identity, every activity that has ever taken place written under that pseudonym can be traced back to them. However, the question of how anonymous Cryptocurrency is, remains unanswered.

The situation cannot be described as anything other than a paradox. On the one hand, transactions related to Cryptocurrency are completely anonymous. While on the other hand, it is easily trackable and completely transparent. Crypto trading allows anonymity in the sense that one can have a crypto account without exposing anything at all about one's identity. Therefore, one person could have numerous addresses, and there will be hardly any evidence to connect them or show that the same person held them. However, some platforms have tried to remedy this issue by adding compulsory Know-Your-Customer (KYC) and Anti-Money Laundering (AML) policies that require one to disclose the correct identity. The same can even be strengthened by verifying the information provided and adding privacy settings recommended by experts that strengthen the security, such as Zerocoin, Monero, Cryptonote etc. (Greenberg, 2017).

Therefore, the question is, whether Cryptocurrencies are truly anonymous. It is a well-known fact that to achieve perfect anonymity, there must be absolute '*unlinkability*' of the transaction to the source. However, it is well known that sources can be identified from the Cryptocurrency transactions. Thus, while Cryptocurrencies are claimed to be anonymous, they are, at best, pseudonymous.

Decentralized Framework of Cryptocurrency Transactions

Trading in assets is not a new phenomenon, and in this era dominated by globalization, one can see visible growth in transactions. However, until the emergence of Cryptocurrency, trusted third parties have always regulated the trading of assets. There are two different kinds of control exercised: *firstly*, regulation by the national and international authorities on a macro level. For example, the Securities and Exchange Board of India (SEBI) is responsible for regulating the Indian securities market. Today, even though the stock market has mainly become virtual, it is not free from the control and regulation of the SEBI, Reserve Bank of India (RBI), Ministry of Finance and the stock exchanges' rules. *Secondly*, financial institutions regulate every electronic transaction. For example, money transfers using net banking or online shopping are governed by financial institutions that act as intermediaries. The financial institutions are also regulated by an umbrella organization, for example, the RBI in India.

However, this is not the case with cryptocurrencies. The very idea of Cryptocurrency was to create a version of electronic cash for purely peer-to-peer online transactions that eliminate interference from any financial institution. Allowing secure transactions across the globe even after eliminating third party institutions was the fundamental solution proposed in the introductory whitepaper on Bitcoin. The focus was to promote a system of electronic transactions that are based on cryptographic proof instead of trusting third parties (Nakamoto, 2008). Furthermore, cryptocurrencies are free from any direct control of any authority. Even though it is not completely free from regulation as the assets invested and earned are eventually connected to the national and global economies, they enjoy significant autonomy. This feature has also led to insecurities amongst national functionaries that control the economical and capital framework in the countries.

Therefore, Cryptocurrencies are the only kind of currency that guarantees the three features: pseudo-anonymity, independence and autonomy from any central authority, and security against double-spending attacks. However, experts have noted that it has taken approximately twenty-five years to ensure that all three characteristics co-exist (Narayanan et al., 2016).

KINDS OF CRYPTOCURRENCY

The Cryptocurrency ecosystem houses various kinds of exchangeable currency, which can broadly be divided into two; coins and tokens. Both kinds have similar functions, but tokens are believed to serve additional purposes.

What are Coins?

Crypto Coins are the primary form of currency that is used as a medium of exchange. These crypto-coins they are built on their own independent blockchain. Bitcoin is the primary Cryptocurrency that is considered a coin, and other coins with similar characteristics are called 'Altcoins,' i.e., Alternative Cryptocurrency Coins. In other words, Altcoins are coins other than Bitcoin. Cryptocurrencies such as Bitcoin (BTC), Polkadot (DOT), Ethereum (ETH), and Hedera Hashgraph (HBAR) are some examples of cryptocurrency coins. These currencies are powered by their native blockchain network and function independent of other blockchains. Each blockchain may differ in size, rules etc., but the fundamental principle of operation remains the same. The purpose of digital coins is identical to actual physical coins; to serve as a medium of exchange. Thus, digital coins store value are used in financial transactions. This implies that, like actual money, digital coins are also subject to the economies of demand and supply; that is, their value depends on the supply of the coin and the correlating demand in the market. However, unlike physical money, which central banks and financial institutions generally regulate, the trade of digital coins is unregulated, which results in much more volatility in their price fluctuation.

What are Tokens?

Tokens, unlike coins, are produced and distributed through an Initial Coin Offering or an ICO. Tokens can be in the following forms:

- Token of value;
- Tokens of security;
- tokens of utility.

Tokens, unlike coins, are not intended to be used as a medium of exchange. Rather, tokens are used to describe a function. Like USD, they signify value instead of possessing their own.

Common Cryptocurrencies Being Traded

The following are some popular cryptocurrencies: -

1. Bitcoin- Bitcoin was the first modern digital Cryptocurrency that was publicly traded. It was proposed by Santoshi Nakamoto for the purpose of eliminating third parties and creating a safe environment for peer-to-peer transactions. Bitcoin is currently the most popular Cryptocurrency in the market. As per the University of Cambridge, in 2017 around 2.9 to 5.8 million unique users were found using a cryptocurrency wallet holding Bitcoin (Hileman & Rauchs, 2017).

2. Bitcoin Cash- Bitcoin Cash was a result of a Bitcoin hard fork in 2017. Hard fork means a split in the existing cryptocurrency blockchain based on various factors such as user dissatisfaction, operational changes etc. Its primary purpose was to increase the individual block size to permit more transactions in a single block. It further split into Bitcoin Cash ABC, more commonly referred to as Bitcoin Cash as known today, and Bitcoin Cash SV, termed after Satoshi Nakamoto's vision for Bitcoin.

3. Ethereum- ETH is the cryptocurrency functioning on its native blockchain called 'Ethereum'. Ethereum is a decentralized ledger that records and verifies transactions. As of May 2021, ETH was the second-largest Cryptocurrency after Bitcoin in terms of its market value.

4. Meme Coins like Dogecoins- meme coins were developed primarily as a joke on cryptocurrencies. However, coins such as DOGE garnered huge interest and backing from its supporters, who refer to themselves collectively as Doge Army. The continuous enthusiasm and trading of the supporters and Tesla Entrepreneur Elon Musk resulted in the value of doge reaching very close to $1 in 2021.

MINING AS A MODE OF ACQUIRING CRYPTOCURRENCY

How is cryptocurrency obtained? one can either buy it in the traditional manner or can exchange it on a trading platform for other cryptocurrencies (for instance, one can purchase Bitcoin by paying in Etherium). Due to the growing presence of Cryptocurrency globally, certain organisations have even started compensating their employees in Cryptocurrency. However, there is another way to obtain Cryptocurrency mining. Typically, miners do not pay for their crypto directly; they earn it via their intelligence. Miners are technologically skilled investors who are often compared to the Old West's prospectors panning for gold in 1848. Cryptocurrency mining is the procedure of verifying and adding transactions for various forms of Cryptocurrency to the blockchain ledger. The voluntary coders, known as crypto miners, battle together to solve complicated mathematical problems employing high-performance computers during the crypto-monetary mining process. Each challenge is solved using cryptographic hash functions that are connected with a block holding the data for a cryptocurrency transaction. The miner who is the first to crack each code is rewarded with the ability to authorize the transaction, and crypto-miners receive modest sums of Cryptocurrency in exchange for their services. Once the crypto miner has solved the mathematical problem and verified the transaction data, the data is added to the public blockchain ledger.

Profitability of Mining

Mining was highly rewarding in the early days of bitcoin. Specifically, with Bitcoin, the first Bitcoin ever mined in 2009, received a 50-bitcoin (BTC) incentive worth roughly USD 6,000. The resources and energy needed to obtain one bitcoin were also substantially lower than they are today so that mining professionals could retain most of the reward as profit. The Bitcoin Protocol states that Bitcoin's premium lasts around four years; therefore, a single bitcoin is currently 6.25 BTC. Although the Bitcoin mining premium has declined over time, the value of each bitcoin has greatly increased. In April 2021, the price of a Bitcoin award reached a startling high of USD 333,023.75. In comparison, bitcoin mining costs have significantly increased. The cost of hardware alone ranges from hundreds to tens of thousands of USD, but the cost of electricity is substantially higher. Depending on the location and type of hardware they utilize, the total cost of bitcoin mining power usage may vary. This may indicate that the profitability of bitcoin mining and other cryptocurrencies may vary, but the revenue of crypto-mining outweighs the costs.

Furthermore, miners also create a bitcoin wallet and join a mining pool with the aim to maximize their profitability. These groups of miners combine their hashing power and resources to mine more coins. The profit generated is then evenly distributed to all members of the mining pool. Such pools are significant because they allow individuals to work together in a group and compete more efficiently and effectively against mining enterprises that are supported by heavier resources than any one individual.

EFFECT OF CRYPTOCURRENCY ON THE GLOBAL ECONOMY

The world of Cryptocurrency has made multifarious additions to the economic sphere in the world. To put it simply, with the advent of Cryptocurrency, the digital money industry has boomed. The development can be divided into direct and indirect beneficiaries. Direct beneficiaries are those who have experienced an immediate and directly consequential gain from the introduction of cryptocurrencies. This group includes traders of cryptocurrencies, financial institutions that have seen a growth in electronic funds transfer, online portals such as Coinbase, Binance and WazirX that first-hand deal with the trading in cryptocurrencies and the likes. However, there is another class of individuals that have come to benefit from the rise of Cryptocurrency, which is called the indirect beneficiaries. These are people who have no direct involvement in trading or investing in Cryptocurrency but gain profit from the direct beneficiaries. This class includes the staff working in organizations such as Binance and WazirX that provide assistance to cryptocurrency traders, Market analysts that forecast the rise and fall of Cryptocurrency and various other stakeholders that have no relation with the actual trading of Cryptocurrency.

This brings us to an important realization; Cryptocurrency has opened new gates to the development of the world economy and has introduced new ways for people to earn a livelihood. Unlike the olden times, where opportunities were limited and extremely exclusive in the world of trading, Cryptocurrency paves the way for a more liberal and flexible approach. Cryptocurrences are now responsible for running several businesses and projects such as trading and mining platoforms, leading to employment of thousands of people. Tesla, one of the biggest car manufacturers in the world, began accepting payments in Bitcoin and also started testing payments in the form of Dogecoin. Additionally, those who invested in Cryptocurrencies early, such as Bitcoin, are now reaping the benefits of the surge in their value, resulting in growing wealth. This wealth is then used as investment in businesses and projects, leading to a growth in the global economy. Cryptocurrency is governed largely by the basic economic facets of demand and supply, so much so that the industry is often termed 'volatile' due to the stark reactions it shows after a change in demand or preferences.

Blockchain technology and cryptocurrencies have allowed entrepreneurs to bypass the hurdles of cash payment or overseas transaction costs by permitting them to receive payments in the form of crypto-coins. It has proved to be a hassle free method of transacting, thus encouraging small and large businesses alike. BitPesa is an example of a corporation that assists African business owners with financial transactions with European, American, and Asian firms. Given the versatile nature of cryptocurrency payments and its growing usage all over the world. More corporations are joining the trend and paying their employees in cryptocurrency. Therefore, more and more people are now beginning to trust cryptocurrency as the new and more efficient form of payment.

Recently, an upcoming trend of behemoth organizations and entrepreneurs promoting the cryptocurrency industry in their own spheres has been seen. For instance, one of the largest Banks in the world, the Bank of New York Mellon, invested in 'Fireblocks', a cryptocurrency custody and a market leader in offering safe technology to support digital asset services in March 2021. The bank aims to provide Bitcoin and other crypto custody services to its clients and intends to employ Fireblocks' technology in conjunction with its ambition to act as a custodian for digital assets on behalf of its institutional investors.

Similarly, Visa has announced that transactions on its payment network would be permitted to be settled using the Cryptocurrency USD coin, a stable cryptocurrency whose value is fixed directly to the USD. The payments network will collaborate with a cryptocurrency platform and Anchorage, a digital-asset bank, as part of a trial initiative. Paypal, the leading American company operating an online payments system that supports online money transfers, has stated that customers in the United States can now use their bitcoin holdings to pay at its numerous online merchants throughout the world. As a result, clients who have virtual currencies in their PayPal digital wallets will be able to use them to make purchases at checkout. This checkout function complements PayPal's cryptocurrency buying, selling, and holding service.

Apart from that, the use of Cryptocurrency could alleviate the practical issues faced by users not having bank accounts attempting to participate in international trade, which is a common occurrence nowadays. Individuals and businesses could benefit from the use of Cryptocurrency to facilitate small-scale international trade (Casey et al., 2018). Using Cryptocurrency such as Ethereum allows these parties to sell products by making payments in Cryptocurrency, thereby doing away with traditional requirements such as setting up bank accounts (Scott, 2016).

Banks like Morgan Stanley have now begun to offer access to Bitcoin funds to their clients. Similarly, JPMorgan is looking into Bitcoin and cryptocurrency clearinghouse solutions, highlighting the necessity for an intermediary to sit between OTC desks and traders to create market liquidity and ensure trade enforcement.

Additionally, the easier and more efficient nature of Cryptocurrency transactions has allowed better participation of countries in expanding their participation in the global economy (Assenmacher & Krogstrup, 2018). Today, any user from the remotest corner of the world can place a purchase order for Cryptocurrency on a trading platform, or sell Cryptocurrency in exchange for goods in another jurisdiction, thereby permitting third-world countries such as India to contribute to their economic growth (Scott, 2016). Thus, a reasonable yet powerful assumption that can be drawn from these worldly developments is that Cryptocurrency as an industry has a huge bearing on all facets of the world economy. Gone are the days when banks and financial institutions were pitted against digital coins and Cryptocurrency, and one used to treat the other as a threat. The banking, entrepreneurial and cryptocurrency industries are gradually merging and collaborating for the collective advancements of the global economy, which seems to be the norm of the future.

LEGALITY OF CRYPTOCURRENCY IN VARIOUS JURISDICTIONS

The trading and investment in Cryptocurrency have been met differently by various countries. As Cryptocurrency is a relatively new asset, some countries have yet to take a stand on its validity or legality, while some have expressly accepted or prohibited its usage. The following are a few examples of countries' stances regarding the validity of Cryptocurrency.

Table 1. Major countries and jurisdictions that favour cryptocurrency

Favourable Regimes	
Region	**Status**
Australia	Classifies bitcoin as an asset for capital gains tax purposes.
Canada	Considers bitcoin a commodity. Their laws exchange of bitcoin.
El Salvador	Allows Bitcoin as legal tender.
EU	Trading digital currencies are now exempt from VAT in all member states.
USA	FinCEN, a division of the Treasury Department, has issued bitcoin guidance since 2013. The Treasury defines bitcoin as a money services business (MSB).

Table 2. Major countries and jurisdictions that do not favour cryptocurrency

Unfavourable Regimes	
Region	**Status**
Bolivia	Cryptocurrency usage is banned by The Central Bank of Bolivia.
China	Bitcoin is illegal in China. It is illegal for banks and other financial institutions to transact or deal in bitcoin. Crypto exchanges are banned. Miners are sanctioned.
Columbia	Columbia prohibits cryptocurrency usage.
Ecuador	Ecuador's national assembly voted to ban bitcoin and other cryptocurrencies.
Egypt	Dar al-Ifta, Egypt's primary Islamic legislator, has declared bitcoin transactions haram (illegal under Islamic law).
Russian Federation	Using Bitcoin to pay for goods or services is illegal in Russia.
Vietnam	Bitcoin is not regulated as a valid mode of payment in Vietnam.

CRYPTOCURRENCY IN INDIA

India's cryptocurrency saga has seen numerous ups and downs since its introduction to the Indian economy. In India, Cryptocurrency can be traded through online platforms like WazirX. To trade cryptocurrencies on WazirX, one must first register an account. Account creation is followed by a KYC (know your customer) authentication. After KYC authentication, customers can access their WazirX accounts to trade cryptocurrencies. This account accepts INR and cryptocurrencies. These currencies can also be transferred from other wallets or cryptocurrency exchanges in India to the WazirX account. The process is free with no fee on any deposits. When funds are transferred into the WazirX wallet, one can easily trade Cryptocurrency in India. The Exchange, which is available on Android, iOS, and Windows smartphones, allows users to purchase and sell currencies in real-time. Account-holders must enter the desired amount in INR and Bitcoin (BTC) to proceed with the purchase. Once the order is executed, BTC reflects in a user's WazirX wallet.

Overview of Cryptocurrency Use in India

Even after Cryptocurrency was first introduced in India through "Bitcoin: A Peer to Peer Electronic Cash System", a paper in 2008 by Satoshi Nakamoto, the first commercial transaction in Bitcoin took place only in 2010. The transaction involved swapping 10,000 Bitcoins for two pizzas. It was the first time that a monetary value was attached to the Cryptocurrency in India. 2011 saw the debuts of new cryptocurrencies, like Litecoin, Namecoin, and Swiftcoin. At the same time, Bitcoin, the originator, had come under scrutiny as allegations surfaced that it promoted illicit activity on the "dark web". Cryptocurrencies gained popularity during the next five years, owing to an increase in the number of transactions of Bitcoin, which went from around USD 5 at the beginning of 2012 to nearly USD 1,000 by the end of 2017.

Between 2012 and 2017, numerous crypto-exchanges and trading platforms opened their doors in India, adding depth and volume to the country's burgeoning crypto-asset market. Popular cryptocurrency exchanges including Coinsecure, Zebpay, Pocket Bits, Unocoin, Koinex, and Bitxoxo took advantage of the popularity wave and introduced themselves to the Indian market. Though the Indian market was introduced to Cryptocurrency much later than the rest of the world, it gained popularity faster than most expected it to.

As the value of cryptocurrencies began to skyrocket in India, and payments were being accepted in cryptocurrency, it caught the attention of the regulatory and law enforcement authorities of the world. The same was the position in India. The RBI, India's primary financial authority issued a Press warning the public against dealing in virtual currencies such as Bitcoin in 2013. However, in 2016, when the country saw demonetization, which resulted in the existing currency being replaced and old cash being banned, the public massively turned to cryptocurrency for the ease of transactions and minimal regulation.

Further, the Indian government began to give importance to online transaction and promote digital economy by campaigns such as "Digital India". This resulted in the public acceptance of previously unconventional modes of transaction, the digital transactions. Since the public was being encouraged to shift to the online method of conducting business and making payments, many turned to cryptocurrencies. This shift from the traditional modes of payment to digital ones, which also resulted in a great interest in cryptocurrency exchanges prompted the Reserve Bank of India to issue a second Press Release in 2017, reiterating its concerns about cryptocurrencies, which it had previously expressed in a Press Release in 2013.Eventually, the year 2017 saw multiple petitions being filed in the Supreme Court of India, seeking either a complete ban or introduction of regulatory mechanisms for cryptocurrencies in India.

In November 2017, the Government of India established a high-level Inter-Ministerial Committee under the chairmanship of Mr. Subhash Chandra Garg, Secretary, Department of Economic Affairs, Ministry of Finance, and consisting of the Secretary of Ministry of Electronics and Information Technology, the Chairman of the SEBI, and the Secretary of the Department of Economic Affairs in the Ministry of Deputy Governor of the RBI. The Committee was tasked with investigating various reservations about participation in crypto-trading, following which it had to make recommendations on specific measures that could be taken in response to those difficulties. In its conclusion, the Committee recommended that private cryptocurrencies should be banned in India.

Although regulators made their displeasure with cryptocurrencies very known through differing views, until March 2018, neither the Reserve Bank of India nor the Ministry of Finance had taken any legal action against cryptocurrencies or issued any official directions against them. However, all of this changed on April 6 2018, when the Reserve Bank of India issued a circular prohibiting Commercial and Co-operative Banks, Payments Banks, Small Finance Banks, Non-Banking Financial Companies, and Payment System Providers from not only dealing in virtual currencies themselves but also from providing services to any entity that deals in virtual currencies.

In December 2017, the Indian Ministry of Finance along with the RBI issued warnings to the public, outlining the risks involved in cryptocurrency transactions. The government made it clear that cryptocurrency transactions must be discouraged and that it does not favour use of cryptocurrency as fiat money. However, no definitive legal action was taken by the government and the central financial institution against the use of cryptocurrency until 2018. In 2018, the RBI prohibited Non-Banking Financial Companies, Commercial and Co-operative Banks, Small Finance Banks, and Payment System Providers from participating in virtual currency transactions. Furthermore, they were also prohibited from offering their services to any organisation or entity that dealt with cryptocurrencies. This was the first time that the Indian Government took a legal action against the use of cryptocurrency and virtual money.

As a result of the said prohibition, cryptocurrency exchanges that functioned with the aid and assistance of traditional banks and financial institutions were left high and dry, without any source of money inflow. All their operations came to a sudden halt as cryptocurrency transactions became impossible without the participation of money lending banks and institutions.

Consequently, the operations of cryptocurrency exchanges were severely hampered, and the total number of transactions on these exchanges decreased significantly. Those in possession of cryptocurrency were compelled to panic sell them, given that crypto-trading was essentially prohibited in the country. This also led to a great loss for those who had to sell their crypto-assets in light of the operations of the exchanges coming to a standstill. Trading platforms had no means to survive, and with users selling all their currency to avoid further losses, the exchanges were depleted of whatever resources and funds they were left with. To combat this existential threat, a number of exchanges that were members of the Internet and Mobile Association of India (IMAI) filed a writ petition in the Supreme Court in 2018. Consequently, in 2020 the Court struck down the Circular issued by the RBI that imposed a banking ban on crypto. One of the reasons attributed for overturning the ban was that cryptocurrencies are unregulated but not illegal in India. As a result, the decaying cryptocurrency market was startled back to life.

As a response, many exchanges collectively approached the Supreme Court of India and filed a petition challenging the prohibition by the government. Eventually, the Supreme Court observed that a blanket ban on cryptocurrency was not feasible and that while there might not exist any regulatory mechanisms in India, cryptocurrencies cannot be deemed as illegal. The Court thus struck down the circular by the RBI that prohibited the use of crypto. As of 2021, cryptocurrency transactions are not illegal in India.

Validity of a Blanket Ban on Cryptocurrency in India

In 2018, the RBI issued a "Statement on Developmental and Regulatory Policies" that became a landmark step in the history of cryptocurrency in India. This Statement was followed by a Circular dated April 6, 2018, that mandated all banks and financial institutions that are regulated by the RBI to cease and terminate their relationship with entities (individuals and businesses) that are trading in cryptocurrencies.

India faced a peculiar situation. Even though the government had not put a ban on virtual currencies themselves, their trading was sent to comatose. The Circular by the RBI cut off the lifeline that the cryptocurrency market survived on. As no financial institution or bank was allowed to deal with individuals trading in cryptocurrency, the banking interface that was used to transfer funds was disconnected.

The RBI justified its actions by saying that innumerable risks were attached to virtual currencies, and the Circular was a reaction to the ignored notices released by it in the past cautioning users of these risks. In its annual report for the year 2017-2018, it communicated its concerns regarding Bitcoin's growing popularity and price bubbles that can potentially create severe issues for consumer and investor safety, as well as market integrity. It brought to light the extremely uncertain and volatile nature of the virtual currencies by citing Bitcoin's market capitalization trajectory, which fell by approximately USD 200 billion within a short span of two months. Furthermore, it noted the hacking and operational concerns connected to digital/electronic medium-electronic wallets, which have already been seen in a few cases around the world. Another point that went against the cryptocurrency market was the absence of any established framework that allowed customers to seek recourse to their grievances. The very nature of the peer-to-peer platform was to eliminate intermediaries and central authorities, thereby also eliminating the possibility of a trusted disputes resolution mechanism within the framework. Consequently, the RBI was also insecure of its use for illegal purposes such as tax evasion and the possibility of transferring dark cash in offshore locations. Other major concerns brought by the RBI also included the following:

- The RBI argued that virtual currencies cannot be acknowledged as 'currency' as they lacked the basic characteristics that a currency must possess. It was said that cryptocurrency does not act as a store of value, and consequently it cannot be treated as a medium of exchange.
- It was a concern that the growth of cryptocurrency and other such virtual currencies will contribute to the destabilization of the Indian monetary framework.
- The very essence of this peer-to-peer model is to eliminate control of any authority. Therefore it is inevitable that this system will be prone to anonymous/pseudonymous criminal activity including but not limited to money laundering and terrorism. (Committee on Payments and Market Infrastructures – CPMI, 2015). The Financial Action Task Force (FATF) voiced a similar concern regarding the growth of financing terrorism using cryptocurrency. The FATF further proposed that global coordination is an essential to fight the vices brought by cryptocurrency.
- Many international organisations called for legislations that can regulate the cryptocurrency market. One such organisation was the Bank for International Settlements (BIS). It expressed its concerns regarding the disaster that is inevitable in the future if virtual currencies like crypto are allowed to flourish. It named the crypto market as a "hybrid of a bubble, a Ponzi scheme, and an environmental disaster". (BIS, 2018)
- Another concern that strengthened the RBI's argument was that cryptocurrency has not been given the status of a legal tender anywhere. It was argued that the response to this virtual currency has ranged from an absolute ban to a comparatively lighter response.
- The RBI noted that its response to cryptocurrency was not excessive in any way. It was further contended that the three month limit provided to the banks and financial institution provides a window to entities dealing with crypto to withdraw from the market.
- It was vehemently argued that the stance taken by the RBI with respect to cryptocurrency was motivated by public interest.
- Another contention was that the KYC norms followed by the exchange platforms were not in consonance with the general practice. Rather, the crypto exchange platforms were treating KYC norms as a mere formality.

- Allowing unregulated cross-border transactions through peer-to-peer platforms coupled with the absence of accountability will have a grave effect on the Indian monetary system that is regulated by the RBI.

Consequently, the decision of the RBI to cut off financial institutions from the entities trading in the crypto market was challenged before the Hon'ble Supreme Court of India in the case of *Internet and Mobile Association of India v. Reserve Bank of India* (2020). Certain associations filed a Writ Petition on behalf of various stakeholders in the Indian cryptocurrency market, such as the virtual trading platforms, companies dealing in crypto assets, individual traders etc. The Petitioners prayed for the quashing of the impugned Statement and Circular issued by the RBI and a direction to allow financial institutions to continue dealings with entities trading in cryptocurrency. Simultaneously, the Government of India took the view that cryptocurrency should be banned, and a bill was introduced in the Lok Sabha titled "Banning of Cryptocurrency and Regulation of Official Digital Currency Bill, 2019", to give effect to the said stance.

In a nutshell, the petitioners raised the following contentions and sought relief from the Court on the following grounds:

- The RBI lacks power to ban trading in virtual currencies.
- In any case, the mode of exercise of power by the RBI fails the tests of application of mind, Proportionality, Relevance, Colourable exercise of power etc.
- Other stakeholders, such as SEBI, Central Board of Direct Taxes, etc., have recognized the benefits of Cryptocurrency that the RBI ignored.
- Many economies of the world and international and multinational organizations have scanned Cryptocurrency and found nothing objectionable.
- The RBI turned a blind eye to the necessary precautions taken by the Petitioners that ensure safety in transactions. These precautionary steps include avoidance of transactions in cash, mandatory KYC steps, and the fact that peer to peer transactions are allowed only within India.
- The RBI's failure to acknowledge established facts that prove that all cryptocurrencies are not anonymous. The petitioners quoted a Report given by the European Parliament that discussed the two classes of virtual currencies. It was clearly mentioned that there are two kinds of cryptocurrencies anonymous and pseudo-anonymous (Houben, 2018). Therefore, it was argued that if the contention of the RBI surrounds the issue of anonymity, the option which is the least severe and invasive must be exercised. The petitioners suggested that only cryptocurrencies that are anonymous must be banned.
- The Petitioners argued that the RBI is taking a self-contradictory stance by prohibiting financial institutions to deal with entities trading in cryptocurrency. The RBI accepts blockchain technology but bans cryptocurrency transactions as the latter is based on blockchain technology.
- The Circular issued by the RBI is not based on any independent study undertaken by it.
- The Circular violates Article 19(1)(g) of the Constitution of India. The said Article guarantees freedom to practice any profession or carry on any occupation, trade or business to the Indian citizens. The Petitioners argued that even though regulation by imposing reasonable restrictions under Article 19(6) is permitted when done in the interests of the general public, a total prohibition of activity through a directive from the RBI, i.e. subordinate legislation instead of a legislature, is violative of the aforementioned fundamental right enshrined in Article 19(1)(g).

- The said Circular released by the RBI was arbitrary. It was further argued that no reasonable classification was followed and the restrictions imposed were disproportionate.

The Supreme Court in the instant case of *Internet and Mobile Association of India v. Reserve Bank of India* (2020) held that the Statement and Circular issued by the RBI that indirectly banned cryptocurrency by cutting off the financial institutions from those entities dealing with crypto to be bad in law. A detailed analysis of the same was done by the Apex Court and a variety of factors were considered. These factors such as the status of virtual currencies vis-à-vis real currency, the RBI's power to issue such a Circular and the Constitutionality of the decision have been discussed in detail hereinafter.

Does Cryptocurrency Qualify as 'Money'?

Traditionally the following three functions and services were supposed to be provided by 'money': -

1. Act as a medium of exchange
2. A store of value
3. A unit of account

However, as civilized societies became more structured and advanced, the fourth function of money was added; Money must be capable of being able to discharge debt and act as a standard of deferred payment, and this function can be fulfilled only when the government of a country confers the status of 'legal tender'. Experts around the world have argued that virtual currencies are not money as they do not fulfil the last function and have not acquired a legal tender status (Fox, 2008).

Though the Supreme Court of India noted that most regulators and governments of various countries do not accept virtual currencies to have achieved the status of a legal tender, it is almost unanimously admitted that digital currencies represent value and are capable of acting as a medium of exchange, a unit of account and/or, a store of value. It is widely accepted that digital currencies and cryptocurrencies hold value and can legitimately fulfil the abovementioned traits of 'money'. However, the Supreme Court of India has noted that governments of various countries have yet to accept this as reality.

The Apex judicial body of India has rightly equated the scenario of acceptance of virtual currencies around the globe with the proverbial cat who closes its eyes and pretends there is complete darkness. Regulators around the world are in denial of a reality that exists right in front of them also because of their insecurities. VC has all the characteristics that qualify it to be used as real money, but once it is accepted as a legal tender for all, the shift towards this unconventional form of currency will cause the authorities will lose a significant amount of control over the economic structure.

The Bench in the instant case concluded that virtual currencies could be covered under the inclusive definition of "currency", as envisaged under section 2(h) of the Foreign Exchange Management Act, 1999. It was held that as certain institutions accept virtual currencies as a payment method, it cannot be called anything otherwise.

RBI's Power vis-à-vis Crypto-Regulation

As discussed before, the central idea proposed by Santoshi was to eliminate the interference of third parties and promote a purely peer-to-peer system of online transactions. Therefore the question faced by the

Supreme Court was a clash of two radical thoughts. Does the RBI have the power to regulate, prohibit and govern such peer-to-peer transactions that do not form a part of the credit or payment structure?

Let us first understand the scope of powers and responsibilities of the RBI. In the case of *Keshavlal Khemchand and Sons Pvt. Ltd. v. Union of India* (2014), the Supreme Court of India recognized the RBI as an expert body that is entrusted with the responsibility of monitoring India's economic system. It has statutory backing under various legislations, including the 'Reserve Bank of India Act, 1934' and the 'Banking Regulation Act, 1949'.

Thus, from a perusal of the statutory provisions and observations of the Supreme Court, It can be validly concluded that the RBI's powers are fairly wide and include supervision and regulation of all activities that form a part of India's economic structure. Thus, anything that adversely affects the Indian economy must be scrutinised by the RBI and it is the responsibility of the RBI to make regulations in order to circumvent the adversities. The RBI's role and power are not contingent upon a medium of exchange acquiring the status of a legal tender.

The Bench noted that "it is ironical that virtual currencies which took avatar (according to its creator Satoshi) to kill the demon of a central authority (such as the RBI), seek from the very same central authority, access to banking services so that the purpose of the avatar is accomplished". It further opined that even though digital currency was introduced to provide a medium of exchange that is beyond the control of the central authorities, its existence cannot be free from all kinds of regulation. Therefore, the argument seeking an order to declare the Circular ultra vires was dismissed on the ground that interference becomes justified when a situation challenges the functioning of the central authority.

Constitutionality of Cryptocurrency Ban

The Supreme Court then went on to the Petitioner's contention of the Circular not being a 'reasonable restriction' and thus violating provisions of the Indian Constitution., specifically Article 19(1)(g) which provides the fundamental right to practice any profession. The unimpeachable parameters laid down in *Md. Faruk v. State of Madhya Pradesh and Others* (1969) were revisited, and it was held that the measure infringes Article 19(1)(g) on the ground that the Circular has an immediate impact on the constitutional guarantees that provide the freedom to practice an occupation of one's choosing and carry on business as desired. As financial institutions are the lifeline of any business, cutting them off implies restricting business.

With regard to the doctrine of proportionality, the Apex Court made various observations, which were as follows:-

- The RBI did not find activities of virtual currencies that adversely impact the financial institutions
- Virtual currencies have not been banned in India.
- Inter-Ministerial Committee that was constituted in 2017 initially took the view that a regulatory framework must be introduced rather than taking an extreme step to ban virtual currencies altogether.

The Court relied on the principles laid down in the case of *State of Maharashtra v. Indian Hotel and Restaurants Association* (2013) and held that owing to the absence of any supporting empirical data as evidence of the harm suffered by the activity, the measure fails the test of proportionality and is not covered by Article 19(6) of the Constitution. It was reiterated that even though the RBI has the power to take such measures, the measure fails the test of proportionality. Due to the indecisiveness of the government and the consistent stand of the RBI that virtual currencies are not banned, the impugned measure was set aside.

Therefore, pursuant to the points discussed above, the decision of the RBI to indirectly impose a blanket ban on cryptocurrency transactions by restricting financial institutions from associating with entities trading in cryptocurrency was held to be unconstitutional.

Are Cryptocurrency Transactions Subject to Indian Tax Laws?

During the global pandemic, innumerable people realized the necessity of creating a passive source of income after experiencing two lockdowns in a row. Some created their own businesses from the comfort of their own homes, while others invested in real estate and IPOs. Many people, however, opted to invest their money in cryptocurrency. As reported, 2021 has seen an influx of around 9-10 million cryptocurrency investors in India alone. Hesitation surrounding Cryptocurrency has seen a significant decline in India since the Supreme Court has decided against the RBI. However, the effect of trading in Cryptocurrency on taxation continues to be a concern amongst people (Gupta, 2021).

In March 2021, the then Indian Minister of State for Finance clarified the status of the taxability of Cryptocurrency in India. He explained that according to the Income Tax Act, 1961 (Section 5), the total income, including all income irrespective of its source and legal status, is taxable. Therefore, income earned from Cryptocurrency is taxable in India. Additionally, the supply of any service is taxable under GST unless the same is specifically exempted, and as no service linked to bitcoin trading has been exempted, the same is taxable. However, a major problem suffered by the government is the lack of a formal database that communicates cryptocurrency transactions to the government.

Cryptocurrency as an Investment

Section 2(14) of the Income Tax Act defines a capital asset as "property of any kind held by the assessee whether or not connected with his business or profession". Thus, these assets encompass all types of property that are not expressly excluded by the Act. As a result, any gains derived from trading in Cryptocurrency must be treated as capital gains if the Cryptocurrency is held for investment purposes. Depending on the time of the holding period for these assets, they would be taxed as long-term capital gains or short-term capital gains. If the asset is kept for less than 36 months, short term gain tax will apply according to the individual's income tax bracket. If, however, the crypto-assets are sold after three years, they can be classified as a long-term investment and taxed at a rate of 20%.

To understand this concept, let us take a simple example:

Table 3. Illustration on tax treatment of cryptocurrency held as investments

S. No	Particulars	Hypothetical Value in INR
1.	Number of Bitcoins purchased	100
2.	Purchase value of Bitcoin	3
3.	Total value of Bitcoin purchased	300
4.	Selling Price of Bitcoin	4
5.	Total value of Bitcoin sold	400
6.	Capital Gains (Purchase value minus selling value)	100

In case the capital assets are held for a period of less than 36 months, the capital gain that is INR 100 will be considered to be a short term capital gain and will be taxed according to individual tax slabs. However, if the assets are sold after they are held for a period of three years, the capital gain that is INR 100 will be treated as long term and be taxed at the rate of 20%, and the cost of acquisition will be computed after indexation is applied.

Crypto Services and Goods and Services Tax (GST)

Indian cryptocurrency exchanges already charge their consumers GST. This indirect tax is included by the exchange platforms in the trading fee charged for purchasing crypto assets like Bitcoin, Tether, Ethereum etc.

Further, the government requires payment of GST from the exchange platforms as part of their overall tax obligations. Recently, the Central Economic Intelligence Bureau (CEIB) proposed to the Central Board for Indirect Taxes and Customs (CBIC) that bitcoin exchanges and platforms should be subject to the GST. It has been proposed that cryptocurrency mining should also be recognized as a service because it generates bitcoin and charges transaction fees, and as such, should be classified as an intangible asset that is subject to an 18% GST. Additionally, the CEIB has proposed that taxpayers who engage in cryptocurrency mining must register for GST if their yearly turnover surpasses INR 2 million. GST will be levied on the transaction fee and/or the reward, which is the mined currency.

Mandatory Disclosure of Cryptocurrency Transactions

To ensure taxability, the Corporate Affairs Ministry has mandated that businesses dealing in virtual currencies must disclose profits and losses incurred on cryptocurrency transactions, the number of crypto assets they hold, and advances from anyone for trading in the balance sheet.

The erstwhile Finance Minister of India, Late Mr. Arun Jaitley, in his budget speech in 2018, noted that "considering that bitcoin transactions are gradually picking up in India, while, laws regulating them are significantly absent, we are hopeful that the government will come up with a notification soon to dispel the ambiguity around the legality of bitcoins, their taxability and disclosure requirement of bitcoins". The statement of the then Minister of State for Finance, and the amendment of the Companies Act that requires mandatory disclosure are steps towards the regulation of the crypto market in India.

SOLUTIONS AND RECOMMENDATIONS

Until this point, the authors have discussed the status of Cryptocurrency in various jurisdictions world-wide, with special emphasis on India. Indian crypto market and its gradual growth are a testament to the increasing acceptance of Cryptocurrency in developing countries.

In the discussion earlier, the legal position of Cryptocurrency in various jurisdictions around the world differs. While countries such as the United States have legalized it, other countries like China that were initially big stakeholders have imposed a complete ban. However, even countries that have not banned crypto assets have not conferred them with the status of a legal tender. As discussed, the observations of the Supreme Court of India in the case of *Internet and Mobile Association of India v. Reserve Bank of India* (2020) is the most plausible view of this situation. There is no doubt that crypto assets have the capability of functioning as real currency. Its characteristics of acting as a medium of exchange, a unit of account and/or a store of value makes it fully capable of replacing national currencies. When analyzing the global reaction and growth, one can conclude that its potential as real money has been noticed; however, it has not been officially accepted.

Bitcoin was only an idea in a whitepaper in 2008. The fact that cryptocurrencies have created such a global presence in this short span prepares one for a future that will be dominated by it, and as the world moves toward it at this fast pace, a need for more regulation is seen. However, regulations can only be implemented when recognition is granted. If central authorities refuse to grant it the status of real currency, it will be impossible to regulate it.

General Regulations Required to be Implemented

It is safe to state that crypto has initiated the process of creating a parallel global economy that is not controlled by any central authority directly. The crypto market can be imagined as a large multinational cooperation having bases in multiple jurisdictions around the world but without a definite headquarter. Like any other MNC that is based in various counties, the crypto market is bound to follow basic national laws that define how the cooperation must interact with the society, but it has reasonable autonomy with respect to its internal functioning. While the Criminal Codes, Cyber and Privacy laws and all other general regulations applicable to all citizens and organizations operating in the country bind the crypto market, its internal functioning is free from the control and purview of any law. Such an unregulated structure is a big shift from the erstwhile centralized trading systems followed in most jurisdictions worldwide. An example discussed earlier in the chapter must be revisited to understand this concept. SEBI regulates the securities market in India. It has its statutory basis under the SEBI Act, 1992. Its functions include safeguarding the interests of securities investors, encouraging the growth of and regu-lating the securities market, and other purposes related to or incidental to the securities market. While trading in stock exchanges such as the Bombay Stock Exchange (BSE) or the National Stock Exchange (NSE) operates according to the market forces of demand and supply, all aspects related to trading are regulated and supervised by this umbrella organization, including the by-laws of the exchanges. These stock exchanges are also subject to the general laws of the land related to economic offences, privacy and cyber laws etc., but there is an additional layer of regulation through specific statutes and bodies like the SEBI. This is absent in the cryptocurrency trade. As mentioned before, exchanges like WazirX are bound by the general laws of the land but not regulated or supervised by any specific laws that lay down an additional layer of regulation.

Recently a Court in India directed a Police Station in Delhi to file an FIR and investigate an allegation of illegal transactions of Bitcoin done online through exchange platform "Binance" in *Hitesh Bhatia v. Kumar Vivekanand* (2021). The complainant stated that he dealt with the selling and purchase of Bitcoins. The complainant further asserted that the accused had repeatedly purchased Bitcoins from him and transferred payments to his bank account in exchange. He sent the Bitcoins to the defendant's virtual wallet on the internet payment platform Binance. In June 2020, the complainant was notified that his bank accounts was suspended, and Bitcoin transactions were flagged as illegal. When confronted with the legality of the consideration against the Bitcoins, the complaint noted that the accused allegedly admitted that the payments were a "scam" and refused to refund the Bitcoins. The Court concluded that all cryptocurrency transactions must comply with general Indian laws, including the Prevention of Money Laundering Act (PMLA) 2002, Indian Penal Code, Narcotic Drugs Psychotropic Substance (NDPS) Act, Foreign Exchange Regulation Act (FERA), and tax legislation, as well as the RBI regulations involving KYC (know your customer), CFT (countering terrorist financing), and AML (anti-money laundering). Other jurisdictions around the world have also taken a similar view. For example, in USA, the Securities and Exchange Commission (SEC) prosecuted the founder of Bitcoin Savings and Trust (BTCST), Trendon Shavers, for promoting illegal Bitcoin deposits and swindling them to the tune of approximately seven hundred thousand BTC (*SEC v. Trendon Shavers* [2014]. In the case of *United States v. Ulbricht* (2014), the US Courts took cognizance of and adjudicated on contentions related to trafficking of narcotics and psychotropic substances, money laundering, and criminal conspiracy amongst other information technology breach reports.

The extension of general laws that govern the interaction of the crypto market with the mainstream economy shows some form of acceptance by the central authorities. These general laws provide the first layer of regulations.

Need for a Specific Framework for Cryptocurrency Regulation

General regulations also highlight the need for regulation as the crypto market can be a breeding ground for innumerable issues. According to a recent survey, around twenty five percent of Bitcoin users and fifty percent of the transactions involving Bitcoin have a nexus with criminal behaviour. Bitcoin facilitates around USD 72 billion in criminal activities each year (Foley et al., 2018). Cases of funding terrorist activities, narcotics and other illegal transactions are more common than one assumes it to be. The general regulations only provide a remedy to such situations, and it is contingent upon the authorities finding out about such illicit transactions. Even though crypto transactions are systematically stored in a ledger and are not completely anonymous, the central authorities do not have complete access to the digital ledger that tracks all transactions. Thus, the argument that crypto transactions are not completely anonymous falls short because regardless of its true nature, it is not under the scrutiny of any authority that makes it as good as anonymous. Furthermore, eminent international financial institutions like the International Monetary Fund (IMF) have noted their concerns regarding the potential negative impact that the growth of cryptocurrency will have on government policies across jurisdictions. The report after analyzing both sides of the coin concludes that huge cryptocurrency holdings have the power to muddle monetary policy management. While the report noted the vast list of pros connected to blockchain technology including ensuring privacy and detecting fraud, it emphasized on the cons such as tax evasion and anonymous criminality that it allows to creep in.

Therefore, there is a need for specific regulations to deal with the menaces accompanying this revolutionary technology. The regulators must aim at finding a viable solution to harmonize the goals of the crypto market and add another layer of protection for the citizens investing in the market. According to the authors, this can only be done by having access to the transactions' records and identifying illicit transactions. *Firstly*, this step will act as a deterrent, and *secondly*, it will ensure that no illicit transaction goes unpunished. For this purpose, a specialized body must be constituted. This supervisory body need not be the central authority of any one country. It can be an organization having representatives from all countries working under the aegis of eminent financial institutions that have been made to establish global cooperation amongst various economies. However, if the same cannot be done, an India specific solution would be to mandate compulsory disclosure of all transactions that are being carried out within the territory of India. Currently, only companies have been mandated to disclose such information; however, information must be sought from the online exchange platforms that act as intermediaries by facilitating these transactions. Some may argue that the same violates the users' privacy; however if this suggestion is analyzed through the lenses of the landmark judgement of *Justice K.S. Puttaswamy (Retd.) v Union of India* (2017), because it is a matter related to the interest of the society, it will withstand the touchstone of permissible restrictions on fundamental rights by meeting the *three-pronged test* of 'legality, need and proportionality'. Therefore, the State is justified to audit all transactions related to India as it is a matter of security and interest of the society, which is a legitimate State aim.

In this way, the central authorities can ensure supervision without directly regulating any transactions. However, this country-specific solution is only viable until the market does not further grow exponentially. Ultimately, an international regulatory body will have to be constituted for regulation and supervision due to the global nature of the crypto market.

Responsibility of Exchange Platforms

The authors will analyze the role and responsibilities of crypto exchange platforms, specifically under Indian laws.

Crypto exchange platforms squarely fall within the definition of 'intermediaries' as given under Section 2(w) of the Information Technology Act, 2000 (IT Act). Intermediaries are "any person who on behalf of another person receives, stores or transmits that record or provides any service with respect to that record and includes telecom service providers, web-housing service providers, search engines, online payment sites, online auction sites, online marketplaces and cyber cafes". 'Intermediaries' are typically defined as individuals who facilitate internet use. Although intermediaries provide a diverse range of services, common activities include hosting online content, evaluating scattered data, collecting information, enabling communication and information sharing, aggregating data etc.

The IT Act, 2000 (Section 79) provides a 'safe harbour' clause that excludes intermediaries from liability for third-party activities that are hosted on their site. The IT Act further under Section 79(1) extends a conditional immunity to such intermediaries with respected to any date posted by third party users of the site. The conditions are laid down under Section 79(2) and (3) of the IT Act, 2000. These conditions include due diligence, knowledge and control that the intermediary exercised over the published/transmitted information, and the scope of service rendered by the intermediary. Additionally, the IT Act, 2000 under Section 79(3)(b) establishes a mechanism in cases where objectionable data is published/transmitted. The mechanism requires the intermediary to takedown any content barred by law when it gets conscious of its existence.

As exchange platforms merely provide technical and passive services by acting as a facilitator of transactions, it will enjoy the 'safe harbour' protection offered under Section 79 of the IT Act. However, this immunity is conditional upon the aforementioned due diligence requirements under the IT Act and other Rules and Guidelines surrounding it.

Tackling Cryptocurrency Related Cyber Crimes

Owing to its online nature, the crypto market is highly vulnerable to cybercrimes. Cyber fraud, hacking, phishing, amongst various other crimes, can be committed in a country without being physically present in that country as boundaries do not deter cybercriminals. Thus, without any specific regulatory framework, several issues will arise. While general laws related to cybercrimes will apply, its adjudication will face the same issues as all other cross border cybercrimes, such as dependence on international cooperation of investigating agencies, anonymity over the internet etc. These menaces need to be tackled not only as a cure after the crime has been committed but also be prevented. This can only happen if there is global cooperation to regulate such aspects of the crypto economy.

Need for a Dispute Resolution Mechanism

There is consensus that with every passing day, the crypto economy will only grow further. This also implied that it is inevitable to avoid disputes related to those transactions, between people and between exchanges and the customers and other stakeholders. Circling back to the SEBI example in India, the regulatory body also provides the first step to accountability. Currently, there is a lack of accountability in the crypto market. This problem has its base in the lack of any formal structure that regulates the nuances of the market. The only recourse is to approach the Courts of a country that simultaneously suffer from the lack of proper training and knowledge of this relatively unconventional technology. Therefore, a specialised forum for resolution of cryptocurrency related disputes is required to ensure a sustainable and responsible participation in the digital economy.

CONCLUSION

Digitization of Money and finances is one of the most significant advancements that new technologies have added to our lives. The significance of this concept is growing more and more with each passing day. As a result, the description of digital currency, as well as its scope and limitations, become the primary concern for both scholars and individuals. The fact that people are constantly moving means that it is impossible to precisely define borders. Cryptocurrency helps abundantly in such cases where it is not bound by borders and territories. It assists traders and investors to execute real-time trades and ensure efficient flow of monetary resources.

The cryptocurrency industry is continuously evolving, with it still being in a nascent stage, presently. We have realized that cryptocurrency can eventually become a mainstream mode of exchange and store of value. Thus, countries and governments must work towards integrating Cryptocurrency with existing the financial and economic framework of the world. A blanket ban on Cryptocurrency will be counterproductive to the very essence and purpose of digitization of finance, which aims at promoting the free flow of funds. Instead, governments and banks should move towards forming a structured regulatory framework for the management of Cryptocurrency, which will further make it easier for people to get accustomed to its use. As discussed above, many countries have already begun to take favourable steps towards legalizing and normalizing the usage of Cryptocurrency. However, a worldwide acceptance is the need of the hour, which will also do away with the scepticism attached to the word 'cryptocurrency'.

REFERENCES

Assenmacher, K., & Krogstrup, S. (2018). *Monetary Policy with Negative Interest Rates: Decoupling Cash from Electronic Money*. International Monetary Fund.

Ayhan, B. (2017). *Digitalization and Society*. Peter Lang Gmbh, Internationaler Verlag Der Wissenschaften. doi:10.3726/978-3-653-07022-4

Casey, M., Crane, J., Gensler, G., Jonson, S., & Narula, N. (2018). *The Impact of Blockchain Technology on Finance: A Catalyst for Change*. International Center for Monetary and Banking Studies. https://www.sipotra.it/old/wp-content/uploads/2018/07/The-Impact-of-Blockchain-Technology-on-Finance-A-Catalyst-for-Change.pdf

Foley, S., Karlsen, J. R., & Putniņš, T. J. (2018). *Sex, Drugs, and Bitcoin: How Much Illegal Activity Is Financed Through Cryptocurrencies? Review of Financial Studies*. Published.

Fox, D. (2008). *Property Rights in Money*. Oxford University Press.

Franks, J. (2019, January). *Cryptocurrencies and Monetary Policy*. International Monetary Fund.

Greenberg, A. (2017, January 25). Cryptocurrency Monero Is Skyrocketing Thanks to Darknet Druglords. *Wired*. https://www.wired.com/2017/01/monero-drug-dealers-cryptocurrency-choice-fire/

Gupta, A. (2021, June 30). *Made gains from cryptocurrencies? Know the income tax implications*. Moneycontrol. https://www.moneycontrol.com/news/business/personal-finance/made-gains-from-cryptocurrencies-know-the-income-tax-implications-7106151.html

He, D., Habermeier, K., Leckow, R., Haksar, V., Almeida, Y., Kashima, M., Kyriakos-Saad, N., Oura, H., Sedik, T. S., Stetsenko, N., & Yepes, C. (2016, January). *Virtual Currencies and Beyond: Initial Considerations*. International Monetary Fund. https://www.imf.org/external/pubs/ft/sdn/2016/sdn1603.pdf

Hileman, G., & Rauchs, M. (2017, April). *Global Cryptocurrency Benchmarking Study*. Cambridge University Press.

Hitesh Bhatia v. Kumar Vivekanand, Case No. 3207/2020.

Houben, R. (2018, July). *Cryptocurrencies and Blockchain*. European Parliament. https://www.europarl.europa.eu/cmsdata/150761/TAX3%20Study%20on%20cryptocurrencies%20and%20blockchain.pdf

Internet and Mobile Association of India v. Reserve Bank of India, Writ Petition (Civil) No.528 of 2018.

Justice K.S. Puttaswamy (Retd.) v. Union of India (2017) 10 SCC 1.

Keshavlal Khemchand and Sons Pvt. Ltd. v. Union of India Writ Petition (Civil) No. 901 of 2014.

Md. Faruk v. State of Madhya Pradesh and Others (1969) 1 SCC 853.

Nakamoto, S. (2008, October). *Bitcoin: A Peer-to-Peer Electronic Cash System.* https://bitcoin.org/bitcoin.pdf

Narayanan, A., Bonneau, J., Felten, E., Miller, A., & Goldfeder, S. (2016). Bitcoin and Cryptocurrency Technologies: A Comprehensive Introduction (Illustrated ed.). Princeton University Press.

Reserve Bank of India. (2017, December). *Report of the Working Group on FinTech and Digital Banking.* https://rbidocs.rbi.org.in/rdocs/PublicationReport/Pdfs/WGFR68AA1890D7334D8F8F72C-C2399A27F4A.PDF

Scott, B. (2016, February). *How Can Cryptocurrency and Blockchain Technology Play a Role in Building Social and Solidarity Finance?* United Nations Research Institute for Social Development (UNRISD). https://www.unrisd.org/80256B3C005BCCF9/(httpPublications)/196AEF663B617144C1257F550057887C?OpenDocument

Securities and Exchange Commission v. Trendon T. Shavers and Bitcoin Savings and Trust, Civil Action No. Civil Action No. 4:13-CV-416 (2014).

State of Maharashtra v. Indian Hotel and Restaurants Association (2013) 8 SCC 519.

United States v. Ulbricht, 31 F. Supp. 3d 540 (S.D.N.Y. 2014).

KEY TERMS AND DEFINITIONS

Altcoin: It could also be understood as 'Alternative Coins". Essentially, it used to mean any coin other than Bitcoin. However, with the advent of mainstream coins like Ethereum (ETC), it may also mean coins other than primary cryptocurrency coins such as Bitcoin and Ethereum.

Binance: A cryptocurrency exchange domiciled in the Cayman Islands, founded in 2017.

Blockchain: It is an elaborate database and a digital ledger of transactions that is disseminated across all devices and systems connected to the network. Blockchain technology consists of various blocks and each of these blocks carries a certain amount of transactions. Each time a new transaction is given effect on a network, the record of the transaction is added to the existing list in the form of a ledger.

Coinbase: An American cryptocurrency exchange platform founded in 2012.

Cryptocurrency: A digital currency used and traded by means of cryptography. It functions in a decentralized system.

Fork: A consequence of changes made to existing rules of a blockchain. The changes result in a bifurcation of the blockchain into two parts: one remains the blockchain with the original rules and the new set of rules make a separate version of the blockchain.

KYC: Know Your Customer (KYC) is a process used by financial institutions and cryptocurrency exchanges to verifies the users' identity. It involves steps such as linking mobile number, unique identification number, address etc. to the account of the user.

Miner: The individual who executes mining of cryptocurrency.

Mining: The method by which new cryptocurrency is gained and a log of user transactions is kept.

Token: A unit of value that exists on a blockchain which serves other functions besides acting as a store or transfer of value.

Transaction: The action of buying, selling, or trading a commodity, product or service,

WazirX: Largest cryptocurrency exchange in India. It was founded in 2018 and it headquartered in the city of Mumbai, Maharashtra.

Whitepaper: It is a technical manifesto or document outlining complex issues pertaining to a product or subject proposed by the author or the issuing organisation. Its purpose is to provide the reader with detailed knowledge and information about the subject, in order to enhance the reader's comprehension on the topic. For example, the Bitcoin Whitepaper was released in 2008 by a pseudonymous author Satoshi, which explained the principles of cryptocurrency in detail for the first time.

Chapter 10
Cryptocurrency:
A Detailed Study

Prapti Bhattacharjee
Pailan College of Management and Technology, India

Vivek Saha
Pailan College of Management and Technology, India

Parag Chatterjee
Pailan College of Management and Technology, India

ABSTRACT

Since ancient times, currency has been an integral part of our lives. In the early times, we saw the barter system. No one really knows how currency came into the play. China created the world's first paper money in the early 7th century. Thousands of years later, we are living in the era of internet where after virtual games and friends, we have started using virtual currency. Cryptocurrency is an encrypted, peer-to-peer network for online payments directly between two parties without going through a financial institution. Bitcoin was the first and most popular cryptocurrency that was introduced in the year 2009 which created a huge surge in the market and got a lot of attention from the world. This new type of money is not likely to replace traditional flat currency, but it has the potential to change the way global markets interact with each other. Since the introduction of cryptocurrency, it has gathered a lot of appreciation and criticism. This chapter will provide in-depth discussion on cryptocurrency, its architecture, and also its pros and cons.

INTRODUCTION

Cryptocurrency is an electronic form of money made with technology that controls its development and preserves transactions while masking its users' identities. Crypto- is short for "cryptography" and cryptographing consists of privacy, data hiding, identity and several others. Currency literally means "money is currently being used." (Härdle et al., 2010)

DOI: 10.4018/978-1-7998-8641-9.ch010

Cryptocurrencies are a part of electronic money which is intended to be faster, cost - effective, and more credible than traditional government-issued currencies. Rather than relying on the government to produce the money and banks to deposit, transfer, and collect it, users trade directly with one another and store their own funds. Transactions are normally very cheap and fast since people can transfer money directly without going through an intermediary.

To avoid fraud and corruption, each cryptocurrency user can record and check their own transactions as well as the transactions of other users at the same time. The digital transaction records are referred to as a "ledger," and this ledger is open to the public. Transactions become more effective, irreversible, stable, and clear with this public ledger.

Cryptocurrencies do not require anyone to trust a bank to keep the money because of public records. They don't expect anyone to have faith in the person with whom they doing business to pay them. Instead, thousands of users will see the money being sent, collected, checked, and registered. There is no need for confidence in this framework. This one-of-a-kind optimistic trait is referred to as "trustless".

The story of cryptocurrency begins in the year 1983. David Chum, an American cryptographer, was the first person who developed a cryptographic electronic cash system called eCash. In 1995, he developed a similar system named DigiCash. However, the term "cryptocurrency" was coined in the year 1998. That same year Wei Dai started thinking about developing a new anonymous electronic cash system named "b-money". PayPal and rivals arose, taking a structured approach to digital transactions in existing currencies. These companies continue to play a significant role in online and international trade (Vajjhala, 2021).

A paper titled Bitcoin – A Peer to Peer Electronic Cash System was posted to a cryptography mailing list discussion in the year 2008. It was posted by someone going by the name Satoshi Nakamoto, whose identity is still unknown to this day. Next year, Bitcoin came to life and the software was made available to the public. Nakamoto was not the only one who thought of creating a new way of payment that could be decentralized and be used internationally without having any financial institution behind it. Later in 2011, Namecoin was released. Soon after, Litecoin was developed which used script as its hash function instead of SHA-256 that was originally used for Bitcoin. Peercoin, another notable cryptocurrency used a proof-of-stake hybrid (Berentsen et al., 2018).

Nakamoto wanted to create a fair, borderless and secure currency where anonymous transaction could be done in a secure way. Development of the IT industry in the field of database, cryptography and network transmission helped in the advancement of blockchain technology for what it is today. The future of cryptocurrency depends on the adoption of blockchain by the governments and by the masses around the globe with respect to the economic conditions.

As of 2021, Bitcoin is one of the most successful cryptocurrencies with a market capital of 1 trillion dollars. Due to special data storage structure, Bitcoin transaction network does not need any third party. The basic requirements to mine Bitcoin or any other form of cryptocurrency is blockchain. The technology was first proposed by Nakamoto in 2008 and later got implemented in 2009. Blockchain is more like a ledger where all transactions are stored as blocks. When a block's storage capacity is reached, it is closed and linked to the previous filled block, forming a data chain known as the blockchain. All new information that follows that newly added block is compiled into a newly formed block, which is then added to the chain once it is complete. Blockchain is decentralised, i.e., no single entity has the total control over the network. With the growing demand and usage of blockchain architecture, it is evolving greatly and improving efficiently.

BLOCKCHAIN ARCHITECTURE

Blockchain and bitcoin are some of the most trending keywords as part of today's technology. Even those who have no knowledge of cryptocurrency are quiet interested in the same. Blockchain technology has been around for a while now it is being used highly for transaction management. It is even replacing the current transaction management system.

The simple definition of blockchain technology is that it it is a *decentralized distributed* shared database containing entries that must be validated and encrypted. We will have a look at decentralized and distributed systems in the later part of the chapter.

A blockchain creationist theory is described by Abadi and Brunnermeier (2018), which means that every records can simultaneously fulfil all of the best features of any recording system – accuracy, decentralisation and cost-efficiency. However, a blockchain technology is better than a centralized, classic ledger (Babich and Hilary, 2018).

Centralized Systems

We begin with centralised systems because they are the most intuitive, understandable, and definable. In Centralised Systems, a central node is connected with one or more clients over a network. The central node has full authority over the entire network. For example, Google having full control over its users' Google Drive storage space. The user cannot extend his/her storage without the consent of Google.

Users depend on authority to complete transactions in centralised systems. Customers in banks, for example, depend on the banking system to change their account balances after transactions. The central authority in a centralised system can change the whole system by explicitly changing and modifying databases at the back-end. Since centralised services do not allow for delegation of authority, they are provided by a single service provider. Several examples of centralised processes include online payment, cloud systems, states, and courts. The use of these systems has a significant effect on incorporating the essential properties of a stable system such as fairness, accountability, openness, and confidence.

The centralized system has a significant flaw. Users will not be able to access their data even if just a single server ceases to work. Thus, the dependency on a centralised system is highly susceptible. The crashing of the central network is catastrophic and may lead to security breaches in the system.

Decentralized Systems

The polar opposite to a centralised system is a decentralised system. A decision is taken across several nodes, which is referred to as decentralised. Each node determines its own behaviour, which has an impact on the system's overall behaviour. This means that no one node has access to the whole system. We are now using a decentralised structure, which is the internet, which is governed by no single ruling body.

The internet is not really owned by anybody. Nobody is actually in charge of deciding what websites can and cannot do. But it was fairly straight forward. In a decentralized system, a server crash will not make the entire system redundant. A part of the day might be still accessible thus, not stalling the entire system. On the other hand, a centralized system is rendered redundant with the crash of the main centralised server.

Distributed System

In the same way as a decentralised organisation does not have a single parent node, a distributed system does not either. A parent node connecting all the other nodes to the system are absent here as well. The Blockchain data is distributed across millions of interconnected computers all over the world. Distributed system gives users equal access over the network and privileges can be allowed for certain parties as well. These systems can be said to be safe as the data is distributed over many computers. The World Wide Web is a common example of a distributed system. Since the framework is distributed through several nodes, distributed blockchain networks are more safe.

As a consequence of the shortcomings of other technologies, distributed systems have advanced. Many organizations prefer distributed systems over other systems because it is more secure, takes less space and is much more efficient.

Hence, it is evident that most industries will switch to distributed systems because of its sheer advantages over other systems.

Blockchain is decentralised and distributed. All data in a blockchain is distributed. No single entity can take control over the entire data. Any person trying to do so will have to alter each and every computer before making a transaction successful which is practically impossible. By disseminating everything, the evil guy will have to adjust details in all locations at the same time in order to carry out their nefarious schemes.

It might seem strange, but by opening up and making the data available to all, you are protecting it. The Blockchain is a distributed ledger that is controlled by no one, has no single point of functionality, and is distributed in nature.

Figure 1. Visualization of decentralized, centralized and distributed system
Source: Introduction to Blockchain by MURTAKI, 2019.

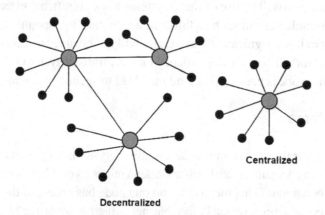

Centralized

Decentralized

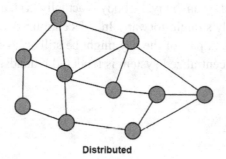

Distributed

Need for Decentralized System

The core concept behind decentralised networks is to have a fault-tolerant distributed computing environment in which authority can be distributed without relying on a central system. This guarantees a variety of other qualities, such as trust, reliability, and data security, among others. The need for blockchain is urgent in order to provide publicly open networks and achieve interoperability. It allows a vast number of untrusted users to create autonomous applications and distributed software infrastructures. The centralised system's concern is that it is vulnerable to single point malfunction, and it lacks accountability, equal access to resources, fairness, non-repudiation of transactions, and data immutability. The implementation of bitcoin and Ethereum are well-known manifestations of decentralised frameworks. (Hoffman, Ibáñez and Simperl, 2020)

How Does a Blockchain Work?

The entire concept of a blockchain is to let people transact — particularly those who do not trust one another and to exchange valuable data securely, without any alterations.
Blocks, nodes, and miners comprise the main structure of blockchain.

- **Block**

Several *blocks* constitute an entire blockchain. Each block contains three parts:

- Data of the block.
- A nonce is a 32-bit whole integer. When a block is formed, a nonce is generated at random, which then generates a block header hash.
- The hash is a 256-bit integer that is associated with the nonce. It has to begin with a large number of zeros (i.e., be extremely small).

A cryptographic hash is generated by the nonce hash when the first block of a chain is produced. If it is not mined, the data in the block is verified and indefinitely linked to the nonce and hash.

- **Miners**
  - Adding new blocks to the blockchain can be achieved by mining. Each block in a blockchain has its own unique nonce and hash, but it also pertains to the previous block's hash, making mining a block tough, typically on large blockchains. Miners implement highly specialised algorithms to solve the extremely difficult mathematical problems of generating an agreed hash using a nonce. Because the nonce is only 32 bits long and the hash is 256 bits long, there are nearly four billion nonce-hash variations to mine until the correct one is discovered. When this happens, miners are said to have discovered the "golden nonce," and their block is added to the blockchain. Any alteration made to a block will result in re-mining of the following blocks. As a result, modifications blockchain is practically impossible as mining golden nonces takes a lot of computational power, money and other resources

- **Nodes**
  - ○ One of the most important principles of blockchain technology is decentralization. A single machine or entity cannot own the chain. A node is any type of electronic system that stores backups of the blockchain and keeps the network running. The chain's nodes create a distributed ledger.

Every node has its own identical copy of the blockchain, and the network must algorithmically authenticate each newly mined block for the chain to be updated, trusted, and validated. Any behaviour in the ledger can be easily reviewed and interpreted because blockchains are transparent. A unique alphanumeric identification number is assigned to each participant, and is used to track their purchases.

The blockchain maintains transparency and builds trust among users by combining public records with a system of checks and balances. In a nutshell, blockchains are a technology that allows you to scale trust.

IMPLEMENTATION OF BLOCKCHAIN – CRYPTOCURRENCY

Cryptocurrencies are digital currencies that record and protect any transaction using blockchain technology. A cryptocurrency such as Bitcoin can be used as an e - cash source to pay for anything from restaurants to electricity bills to stocks. It can be purchased using one of the digital wallets or trading sites and then digitally exchanged after an item is purchased. In the future we may also see an influx of cryptocurrency which might replace the normal currencies of the world. Bitcoin or any other cryptocurrency can be purchased from several websites and mobile applications in exchange of money or cryptocurrency itself. The buyer's transaction is recorded on the blockchain. The entire transaction is timestamped, encrypted and stored in the public ledger thus making it highly difficult to tamper with.

Is Blockchain Secure?

The most well-known and arguable use of blockchain is in cryptocurrencies. Cryptocurrencies, such as Bitcoin, Ethereum, and Litecoin, are some of the most popular digital coins (or tokens) that can be used to purchase products and services. Crypto, like a cryptographic type of currency, can be used to purchase anything from lunch to a new home. Unlike cash, cryptocurrencies rely on blockchain to serve as both a public ledger and a stronger cryptographic authentication mechanism, ensuring that online transactions are always registered and protected.

Currently there are about almost 16,000 cryptocurrencies in the world. The total market cap of all cryptocurrencies is about $1.9 trillion approximately, with Bitcoin holding most of the market. The price of one Bitcoin is $43,000 approximately as of January 2022. Below are some of the key explanations why cryptocurrencies are unexpectedly gaining popularity:

- As each cryptocurrency has its own unique identifier and is linked to a single owner, the blockchain's dependability makes stealing far more difficult.
- Crypto reduces the need for individualized currencies and central banks. Crypto can be sent to anyone, anywhere in the world, using blockchain, without the need for currency conversion or central bank intervention.

- Investors have been pushing up the price of crypto, mostly Bitcoin, allowing some early adopters to become billionaires. If this is a success or not remains to be seen, as some critics claim that speculators aren't thinking about the long-term benefits of crypto.
- The concept of a blockchain-based digital currency for payments is gaining traction within major companies. The electric car manufacturing company, Tesla, earlier stated in February 2021 that it intends to spend $1.5 billion in Bitcoin as payment for its vehicles.

It remains to be seen if digital currencies have a future. For the time being, it seems that blockchain's meteoric growth is more than just a new trend. Blockchain is showing potential beyond Bitcoin, notwithstanding the fact that it is still making progress in this brand-new, extremely exploratory sector.

Blockchain technology deals with problems of privacy and credibility. Well first, new blocks are recorded in a linear and sequential order. This means the additional blocks are added towards the "end" of the blockchain. When looking at the Bitcoin blockchain, we can see that each block on the chain has a layout termed as "height." As of February 2022, the block's height was reported as 722766 blocks.

It's nearly impossible that a block's contents will be changed after it's been appended to the end of the blockchain unless the majority agrees. It's just because each block has its own hash, as well as the hash of the block before it and the time stamp previously listed. Hash codes are created by converting digital data into a series of numbers and letters using a mathematical formula. If the information is altered in any manner, the hash code changes. So therefore, it's important in the context of monitoring. Let's pretend a hacker wants to steal Bitcoin from the rest of the world and needs to modify the blockchain. If they made a change to their single copy, it would no longer match anyone else's copy. When other people compare their versions, they'll note how different this one is, and the hacker's chain will be brushed aside as invalid.

To be successful, the hacker will need to control and change 51 percent of the blockchain copies at the same moment, guaranteeing that their existing copy is the predominant copy and so the consented blockchain would exist. An attack such as this would cost a fortune and duration because all the bits would have to be redone because the record and hash schematics would be clearly distinct presently.

Given the size of Bitcoin's network and how quickly it is growing, the cost of completing such a task will very probably be insurmountable. Not only would this be extremely expensive, but it would also be pointless. Members of the network, who might notice such significant modifications to the blockchain, would never overlook these acts. Members of the network will then fork off to a different iteration of the chain that is static.

This would cause the value of the targeted version of Bitcoin to plunge, rendering the attack futile since the bad guy would be in possession of a worthless commodity. If a nefarious individual targeted Bitcoin's latest fork, the same thing is going to happen. It is designed in such a way so that engaging in the network is much more financially lucrative than attacking it.

Understanding The Different Types of Cryptocurrencies

Cryptocurrencies can behave like actual money, they are real money—but they exist in a digital form with no centralized authority to manage or regulate them. Cryptocurrencies are a true product of the modern age, since they run without the intervention of banks, states, or any other intermediary. However, you will almost always need to purchase and sell your digital properties through a digital currency exchange. There are more than 50 million blockchain wallet users right now.

Cryptocurrencies are encrypted (safe and secure) with advanced programming code known as cryptography, which offers protection. We already know how they are intentionally built to be difficult to solve, like a tricky puzzle (and hack). Insiders refer to it as "crypto".

As of April 2021, there are over 10,000 different types of cryptocurrency. There are two types of cryptography:

- Coins such as Bitcoins and altcoins (non-Bitcoin cryptocurrencies)
- Tokens

Crypto Tokens vs. Coins

Crypto refers to coins and tokens that have been encrypted. Altcoins or alternative crypto coins and tokens are the two types of cryptocurrency that can be mentioned.

Alternative Cryptocurrency Coins (Altcoins)

Any coin that isn't Bitcoin is referred to as an altcoin. Bitcoin is a well-known digital currency that is generated by solving difficult math problems computationally. It operates independently of any central bank or government agency (i.e., government-backed Treasury).
Some examples of alternative coins are-

- Peercoin
- Litecoin
- Dogecoin
- Auroracoin
- Namecoin

In reality, the term "altcoin" is short for "alternative to Bitcoin." Namecoin, which was launched in 2011, is widely regarded as the first altcoin.

To maintain stability and strengthen their intrinsic worth, most of the other cryptocurrencies discussed here, including Bitcoin, have a finite quantity of coins. The quantity of Bitcoins that can exist has been set at 21 million by the Bitcoin founders, yet some are still being mined. That's all there is to it until all 21 million have been used (the number varies as new blocks are mined). The only way to raise the quantity of money entering the system is for Bitcoin's protocol to enable it.

Many altcoins claim to be superior to Bitcoin despite the fact that they are based on the same core foundation.

Each method is distinct since it was created to support a wide range of objectives and applications, and it is described in many ways.

However, just a few coins employ the same open-source technology as Bitcoin. For example, the following cryptocurrencies have created their own networks and protocols:

- Bitcoin
- Ethereum
- Ripple

- Omni
- Nxt
- Waves
- Counterparty

Tokens

Unlike cryptocurrencies, tokens are created and distributed through an Initial Coin Offering (ICO), which is comparable to a stock offering. It's possible to read them as follows:

- Tokens of value (Bitcoins)
- Tokens of security (to keep your account secure)
- Tokens of utility (devoted to various purposes)

They're meant to be used to describe a purpose rather than to be exchanged for money. They have worth in the same way that American money do, but they aren't valuable in and of themselves. Tokens are long lines of numbers and letters that represent the crypto utilised in a contract like a transfer of funds or a bill payment. To conclude, tokens can have many different meanings. Crypto tokens include Bitcoin and Ether (short for Ethereum).

Few Popular Cryptocurrencies

1. Bitcoin

Bitcoin is a form of digital currency that can be defined as "internet cash." It is indeed categorized as cryptocurrency because cryptography makes Bitcoin design and transactions possible.

In the sense that its name is the most familiar and loosely aligned with the cryptocurrency scheme, it is perhaps the "Kleenex" or "Coca Cola" of all crypto. There are reportedly more than 18.5 million Bitcoin tokens in circulation, compared to a 21 million cap.

2. Bitcoin Cash

Bitcoin Cash is one of the most common forms of cryptocurrency on the market, having been introduced in 2017. The biggest difference between it and the first Bitcoin is the block size, which is 8MB. In comparison, the initial Bitcoin block size was just 1MB. For consumers, this means higher processing speeds.

3. Litecoin

Litecoin is gradually being mentioned in the same breath as Bitcoin, and it works in a similar manner. Charlie Lee, a former Google employee, developed it in 2011. He built it to be a better version of Bitcoin, with faster checkout times, lower fees, and more focused miners.

4. *Ethereum*

In contradistinction to Bitcoin, Ethereum focuses on decentralised technologies rather than digital currencies (phone apps). Ethereum can be compared to an app store. The network wants to reclaim ownership of software from middlemen and give it over to the original developers (like Apple, for instance). The original developer will be the only one who could make improvements to the app. The token in question is Ether, which is a digital currency used by both software creators and consumers.

5. *Ripple*

Ripple is one of the cryptocurrencies on the list, although it is not built on the Blockchain. It's not for private consumers as it is for bigger businesses and organisations who need to move massive amount of capital *(known as XRP) around the world.*

6. *Stellar*

It is better known for its electronic payment interface than for its cryptocurrency, XRP. This is because the scheme provides for the conversion of funds of any currency, including dollars and Bitcoin (or others). It boasts a transaction rate of 1,500 transactions per second (tps). As compared to Bitcoin, which can accommodate 3-6 tps, this is a significant difference (not including scaling layers). Ethereum is capable of 15 tps.

Stellar focuses on financial transactions, and its network is built to make them more reliable and quicker, including across national boundaries. It was founded in 2014 by Ripple co-founder Jed McCaleb and is run by Stellar.org, a non-profit organisation.

7. *NEO*

NEO, formerly known as Antshares and founded in China, is aiming to become a significant international crypto company. Its main focus is on smart contracts (digital contracts), which enable users to build *and enforce contracts without the need for a third party.*

It's aiming for the main competitor, Ethereum, but NEO lead developer Erik Zhang said in a Reddit AMA that the project has three distinct advantages: simpler infrastructure, developer-friendly smart contracts, and digital identities and digital properties for faster integration into the real world.

Ethereum, but at the other hand, does have its own programming languages that developers must first master before using it to create smart contracts.

8. *Cardano*

Cardano, or ADA, is a cryptocurrency that is used to send and receive electronic currency. It appears to be the first cryptocurrency with a "scientific theory and research-driven approach," as well as a *more equitable and sustainable environment for cryptocurrencies.*

Which implies that it is subjected to extra scrutiny from scientists and programmers. Charles Hoskinson, who is also the co-founder of Ethereum, originally established it.

9. *IOTA*

IOTA stands for Internet of Things Application, and it was first introduced in 2016. It doesn't work with a block and chain like most other Blockchain technologies; instead, it works with mobile devices on the Internet of Things (IoT). According to Coin Central, this ensures that the machines must be able to buy more power, bandwidth, storage, or data when they are required, and sell them when they are *not*.

10. *Tether*

Tether was introduced in 2014 and described itself as a "a blockchain-enabled platform designed to facilitate the use of fiat currencies in a digital manner." (Luke Conway, 2021)

Tether is characterised as a stablecoin, a fiat currency currency, the U.S. dollar in this case. Tether's concept is to combine the benefits of a cryptocurrency (for example, financial middlemen are not needed) with a self governing stable currency.

Table 1. Top 60 cryptocurrencies

Names of Cryptocurrencies (Symbols)			
Bitcoin **BTC**	Binance USD **BUSD**	Unus Sed Leo **LEO**	NEO **NEO**
Ethereum **ETH**	THETA **THETA**	Theta Fuel **TFUEL**	Aave **AAVE**
Tether **USDT**	Stellar **XLM**	Huobi Token **HT**	EOS **EOS**
Binance Coin **BNB**	Internet Computer **ICP**	Tezos **XTZ**	Monero **XMR**
Cardano **ADA**	Wrapped Bitcoin **WBTC**	Crypto.com Chain **CRO**	Matic Network **MATIC**
Dogecoin **DOGE**	VeChain **VET**	MIOTA **IOTA**	Hedera Hashgraph **HBAR**
Ripple **XRP**	Ethereum Classic **ETC**	Maker **MKR**	Dash **DASH**
USD Coin **USDC**	Filecoin **FIL**	PancakeSwap **CAKE**	Zcash **ZEC**
Polkadot **DOT**	Dai **DAI**	Cosmos **ATOM**	Telcoin **TEL**
Uniswap **UNI**	TRON **TRX**	FTX Token **FTT**	Celsius **CEL**
Bitcoin Cash **BCH**	Waves **WAVES**	Kusama **KSM**	Elrond **EGLD**
Litecoin **LTC**	Chiliz **CHZ**	Bitcoin SV **BSV**	THORChain **RUNE**
Solana **SOL**	Bitcoin BEP2 **BTCB**	Algorand **ALGO**	NEM **XEM**
Chainlink **LINK**	Terra **LUNA**	SHIBA INU **SHIB**	Digibyte **DGB**
Polygon **MATIC**	Avalanche **AVAX**	BitTorrent **BTT**	Curve DAO Token **CRV**

Source: (Crypto.com, 2021)

11. *Dogecoin*

Dogecoin initially was made a joke in fun of wild cryptocurrency speculation. It is meant to be used as a sort of digital money like bitcoin, and depicts a Shiba Inu dog as "mascot." Dogecoin, however, makes it easy to record the payments, but it does not limit the number of coins that may be minted over time.

Bitcoin- A Remarkable Cryptographic Achievement

Satoshi Nakamoto is one of the first name we came across when this chapter started. It is an important name when bitcoin is being mentioned.

In 2007, Nakamoto began coding the code for bitcoin, a peer-to-peer electronic currency system that was truly revolutionary. This code would prove the cornerstone of the cryptocurrency, which has changed how we think about the organisation of our financial institutions since its inception in 2009.

This financial phenom's name is merely an alias; it's a total fabrication. Furthermore, it's unclear if Nakamoto is a single individual or a group of persons working together under the fictional identity. Till date, the true identity of Nakamoto has been speculated to be Hal Finney, a cryptologist who was the first to use bitcoin after Nakamoto; Nick Szabo, a proponent of decentralised currencies; Dorian Satoshi Nakamoto, a libertarian scientist; or Craig Wright, a litigious professor. However, the truth is that we still don't know for sure. Bitcoin was created by Satoshi Nakamoto to work in a decentralised, peer-to-peer network that didn't require faith. However, in the past, fractional-reserve banking has relied heavily on trust.

Most commercial banks operate a fractional-reserve banking system, which is based on client deposits. These are deposits that the bank lends to borrowers; the banks only maintain a small portion of their total liabilities on hand. It's probable that withdrawals will exceed the bank's reserves, similar to the bank run sequences in It's a Wonderful Life. We just believe that our hard-earned money is secure in the hands of banks, and that those assets will be managed wisely.

This paper marked the start of the bitcoin trading network and highlighted the vulnerability of trust-based financial institutions, offering bitcoin as a potentially revolutionary alternative. Hal Finney got 10 bitcoins from Satoshi Nakamoto on January 12, 2009, in the world's first bitcoin transaction. But, for good reason, BTC's adoption did not come immediately. There were many weaknesses in the system.

On 2010, Bitcoin had its first and only security vulnerability and exploitation, when transactions weren't really carefully validated before being included in the blockchain. Over 184 billion bitcoins were created as a result of this flaw, however the transactions were wiped and the bitcoin protocol was fixed within hours. Since then, bitcoin has shown to be a trustworthy system.

It wasn't till 2013 that businesses began taking bitcoin as payment in greater numbers, and this movement was pioneered by groups that were heavily online, such as the Internet Archive. (Chohan, 2017)

However this adoption was significant because it highlighted the feasibility of a decentralised financial system that is not managed and regulated by a central authority such as a bank or a government. Many individuals believe that using money is safer because of the transparency given by blockchain technology. But, for all of bitcoin's revolutionary potential and history, it also brings with it a high level of volatility.

Bitcoin was worthless in its early years. When 10,000 bitcoins were auctioned off in 2010 at a starting price of $50 USD, no one ever bid. In the spring of 2011, however, one bitcoin was equal to one US dollar. The valuation of one bitcoin hit $1,242 on November 29, 2013. The currency began to gain traction, and as a speculative investment, this attracted additional purchasers. However, in April of 2014, prices plummeted from roughly $1,200 to $340. This drop exemplifies bitcoin's vulnerability; it took three years for bitcoin to recover and return to its November 2013 value.

Bitcoin had a spectacular year in 2017, with values rising from $1,290 to a remarkable $19,783.06 at the end of the year. However, by December 2018, BTC values had dropped to only $3,300USD during the same time period. This crash occurred due to a number of factors, including hackers and other cryptocurrencies' security weaknesses. However, a clear image emerged: while bitcoin and cryptocurrencies appear revolutionary and possibly valuable, they are also hazardous. The only way to invest securely in bitcoin is to conduct proper homework, use dollar cost averaging to reduce the exposure, and never invest more than one can afford to lose, as the history of bitcoin has taught us.

Bitcoin was worth more over $52,000CAD in January 2021. Only time can tell whether this spectacular climb is another bubble, or whether the current high valuation will continue. In any case, we know that bitcoin is both unpredictable and valuable, and that it is most likely here to stay.

Working of Bitcoin Transaction

Bitcoin (BTC) was designed as a peer-to-peer electronic cash system. It is sensible to consider how a transaction operates when you are paying or taking BTC as payment. Bitcoin transfers are digitally signed messages, similar to email, that are submitted to the whole Bitcoin Network for authentication. Transactions are anonymous and can be found on the database, a distributed ledger.
All and every BTC transaction can be traced back to the time when bitcoins were first created.

Bitcoins Exist as Records of Bitcoin Transactions

We define a bitcoin as a chain of digital signatures. Each owner transfers bitcoin to the next by digitally signing a hash of the previous transaction and the public key of the next owner and adding these to the end of the coin. A payee can verify the signatures to verify the chain of ownership.

(Satoshi Nakamoto, Bitcoin Whitepaper, 2009)

It really is important to note that Bitcoins (Bitcoin) do not "exist" by themselves. That is true! BTC in one's wallet does not have the same overt existence as currency, coins, or even stocks. There are no actual bitcoins anywhere—on a hard disc, in a spreadsheet, in a bank account, or even on a server. Consider the blockchain to be a ledger of transactions from different bitcoin addresses. As balances rise and fall, the Bitcoin network updates and distributes these transaction histories to all of its nodes. If anyone wishes to see the past as well as the entire balance of any BTC address, they can use one of the block explorers.

A Sample Bitcoin Transaction

Chandler wishes to give Joey some bitcoin. In general, a Bitcoin transaction is made up of three parts:
   An Input: It is a record of Chandler's original BTC address from which he got the bitcoin he wishes to give to Joey.
   An Amount: Chandler wants to give Joey a certain amount of BTC.
   An Output: Joey's public key, also known as his bitcoin address, is the output.

To send BTC, one must have access to the public and private keys involved with that amount of bitcoin. When someone "has bitcoins," it simply means that the person has access to a key-pair that consists of:

- a public key with which some amount of bitcoin has previously been sent
- the subsequent unique private key that permits the BTC formerly sent to the said pub-key to be sent elsewhere

Bitcoin addresses, commonly known as public keys, are randomized sequence of numbers and letters that work in the same way as an e - mail address or a social-media account username does. Since they are public, we can safely share them with others. In reality, if we want anyone to send us BTC, we must give them our Bitcoin address. The private key is a different set of letters and numbers. Digital keys, including email or other account codes, must be kept private.

Never, ever disclose your private key with someone you do not completely trust not to steal from you. Also, bear in mind to backup private keys using paper and pen and keep them someplace safe. Every Bitcoin address is like a transparent safe. Others can see what's inside, but only those with the private key can open the safe and access the cash. Chandler wishes to send some BTC to Joey in the example transaction above. To do this, he uses his private key to sign a message containing transaction-specific information. This message is then transmitted to the blockchain and contains an:

Figure 2. Figure representing a digital transaction with and without a trusted third Party
Source: The Economics of Cryptocurrencies – Bitcoin and Beyond by Jonathan Chiu, Bank of Canada, Thorsten V. Koeppl, Queen's University"

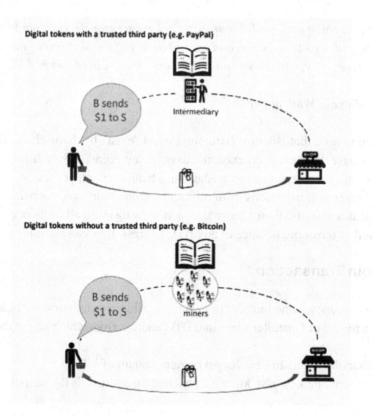

- *input:* the origin of the coins already sent to Chandler's address
- *amount:* Chandler will send some amount of BTC to Joey.
- *output:* Public address of Joey

This transaction would then be broadcasted to the Bitcoin network, where miners validate that Chandler's keys may access the inputs (i.e. the address(s) from whom he originally got BTC) that he asserts to possess. This validation procedure is known as mining since it demands computationally expensive effort and pays miners in BTC for each block solved. This is also the procedure for 'creating' new Bitcoins.

Miners on the blockchain are required to verify all Bitcoin transactions. It's important to note that miners don't mine transactions; instead, they mine blocks, which are collections of transactions. Transaction may be left out from the current block and placed on hold until the next one is put together. The Bitcoin protocol changes requirements constantly such that each block takes about 10 minutes to mine. Another factor contributing to extended confirmation times is the present Bitcoin protocol's 1MB block size restriction. Such arbitrary restriction can be raised, but for now it restricts the number of transactions that can be included in a block, significantly slowing confirmation times and, by extension, the whole Bitcoin network.

More about Inputs and Outputs of Bitcoin

Although it would be possible to handle coins individually, it would be unwieldy to make a separate transaction for every cent in a transfer. To allow value to be split and combined, transactions contain multiple inputs and outputs. Normally there will be either a single input from a larger previous transaction or multiple inputs combining smaller amounts, and at most two outputs: one for the payment, and one returning the change, if any, back to the sender.

(Satoshi Nakamoto, Bitcoin Whitepaper, 2009)

We know that BTCs exist simply as a log of blockchain transactions. This implies that several transactions are occasionally tied to a certain Bitcoin address. Say, in our wallet, we have 2 BTCs. The two BTC came from four pals, each of whom sent us. 5 BTC for birthday celebration. The wallet interface displays our holdings for convenience under "2 BTC." However, not every one of them is 'added' to our wallet. We are left with .5 BTC inputs into 2 BTC in our wallets. Instead, our wallet just monitors the four .5 BTC transactions, which total 2 BTCs individually. It is uses transaction logs with varying amounts to add up to the amount of BTC we want to spend whenever we want want to buy anything with BTC. Assuming it is a .25 BTC number, we will want to use it for a merchant buying clothes. Based on the information above, we know that with exactly .25 BTC we have no single input. The user can't divide a transaction into smaller amounts, and a transaction can only spend the total output. So, if we open our wallet and input ".25" into the amount field, then theoretically, it is one of the .5 BTC transactions that is being delivered in their entirety (from our nice buddy Chris). A fresh transaction will return the difference. The technological procedure has been broken down here:

- The *amount* due is 25 BTC for clothing.
- The .5 BTC *input* is 'sent' to the shop. (It is to be noted that all inputs have to be spent).
- The *output* is the clothing store's bitcoin address.

However, for this transaction our wallet will really produces two results:

- .25 BTC to the clothing merchant
- .25 BTC to the new wallet address to obtain a 'change' from the biz.

This could appear perplexing. The good news is that understanding this is not necessary to transmit or get bitcoin.

Transaction Fees

A number of parameters are used to compute Bitcoin transaction cost. Many wallets enable users to adjust transaction charges manually. Any part of a transaction not due to the receiver or refunded as "change" is included as a charge. Fees are paid to mine workers and may be employed by promoting miners to give priority to certain transaction to boost efficiency.

Cryptocurrency from a Legal Perspective

The development of cryptocurrency resulted in the creation of a fundamentally new form of economic relations in which asset exchanges are carried out without the involvement of centralised financial institutions or other intermediaries, and the security and dependability of transactions between counterpart companies are provided by the distributed ledger system, which is a network of blockchains.

Various legal aspects of virtual currencies must be considered depending on the country. Some countries consider them as currency and lawful, others as assets and legal, while some countries, such as India, do not label them as unlawful or legal due to a lack of legal framework. Bangladesh and Russia are two countries that create bitcoin illegally. In other countries, its position is a little more complicated. Cryptocurrencies are illegal in some countries, such as Iceland, due to current laws. However, cryptocurrencies in India, like many other nations, are still unregulated and without a legal framework. Following are some of the legal challenges surrounding cryptocurrency:

1. **Decentralized nature:** Cryptocurrencies are decentralised in nature, making it impossible for the government to regulate them. Unlike government-issued currencies (banknotes, coins, etc.) that are directly under the jurisdiction of the issuing authority and get their value from the issuing authority's guarantee and stored gold.
2. **Absence of a well-defined legal framework:** Numerous countries lack a suitable legal framework to control the worth and circulation of digital currencies both inside and outside the country, adding to the difficulty of regulating a decentralised currency.
3. **The volatility of Virtual Currencies:** Cryptocurrencies, as evidenced by recent changes in the value of the most well-known cryptocurrency bitcoin, which began with a base value of $0.30 in 2010 and has since risen to about $4000, follow a tumultuous track of highs and lows that further exacerbate market and economic volatility.
4. **Independent Wallets:** Due to the lack of any enforceable international rules, private firms construct and administer wallets that keep cryptocurrency and engage in transactions. These firms have no influence over any organisation. As a result, they are not liable for the customer's loss or any type of financial crime performed by or through the usage of such wallets.

5. **Taxation:** One of the most serious issues with cryptocurrencies is taxation. Because of their pseudo-anonymity, they may easily be utilised to hide property for tax evasion purposes if handled appropriately. The ability to take and store cryptocurrencies online makes it easier to move them over border checks and cash them out once inside the country, thereby evading border taxes. A person can exploit cryptocurrency attributes such as anonymity and absence of or obsolete or badly implemented cryptocurrency schemes due to loopholes in some nations' legal and tax schemes.

6. **Money Laundering:** While addressing Cryptocurrency, money laundering is often taken into account when building a country's legislative framework. However, many governments have struggled with money laundering issues as a result of cryptocurrencies since their inception. Money laundering is a major legal difficulty with such currencies due to their ease of movement across countries with little or no regulation. While corporations can track virtual currency acquired through banks, it's more difficult to do so when buying or selling coins with cash or other tough-to-trace methods. Other safeguards offered in relation with bitcoin trading include:

   ○ **Spoofing and Phishing Payment Information:** Phishing attacks impact cryptocurrency users in the same way they impact regular e-money users because they might be sent to a false website that needs them to input their crypto-wallet user IDs and passwords. While transaction spoofing occurs when a user attempts to copy the wallet address for a transaction, the address is substituted by malware and the user is ignorant of the modifications since not everyone is vigilant in double-checking a lengthy address copied by them.

   ○ **Error in User Address:** There is also a risk of loss if the recipient's address is incorrect, which might result in a monetary loss. In the case of Ethereum, for example, if any of the recipient address's last digits are inputted incorrectly, the money will either vanish or be sent to the precise address, but the targeted value multiplied by 256 will be transacted.

   ○ **Loss of a Wallet File:** One of the most serious problems with cryptocurrencies is the loss or theft of personal wallet documents as a result of hard disc breakdowns or other disruptions. To save local credentials, a paper wallet or a hardware wallet backup is typically advised.

   ○ **Insecure ICOs:** Initial Coin Offerings (ICOs) using virtual currencies can be used to invest in cryptocurrency-funding. In most cases, an ICO is given to increase a lump quantity of money by purchasing and selling cryptocurrency that requires an Internet connection. Another stumbling block to administering digital currencies is the lack of a risk-free access method to manage the bitcoin market and trace down and de-anonymize a payee.

   ○ **Payment Gateway Hacking:** Hacking may be done by persuading the hosting provider that they are the legitimate domain owners, and then intercepting the funds. Plenty of well-known financial services have been targeted by hackers who have used such methods.

   ○ **Fraud at the Trading Exchange:** Considering Bitcoin's growing popularity and recent price surge, new prospective exchange and trading platforms are springing up all over the world. These trading exchanges keep the public and private keys to all of their clients' wallets on their own servers. If any, a trading exchange supplier will elect to flee with all of their clients' cryptocurrency. Due to the lack of regulation and regulatory structures, there is little that can be done to combat such offences, putting all dealers in a vulnerable situation.

The legal position of virtual currencies varies greatly from country to country, and many of them are currently unclear or undergoing changes. While the usage of cryptocurrencies is not illegal in many countries, its position as money (or a commodity) varies, resulting in varying statutory repercussions.

While some countries have openly allowed its usage and commerce, others have restricted or outright forbidden it. Similarly, different government agencies, departments, and courts have different perspectives on cryptocurrency. For example, cryptocurrencies are unregulated in India, the United Kingdom, Brazil, and other countries because no legal framework has yet been established, or because their usage has been deregulated and is free to use with no or little legal restrictions. While usage is allowed in countries like France, Finland, and Germany, it is controlled for tax and other reasons, and is sometimes considered as currency. In certain countries, the usage of cryptocurrency is restricted yet permitted under specific circumstances, such as in China, where individuals may be able to transact but companies and banks are not. It is illegal to buy or trade bitcoins in Iceland, though they may be mined. Bitcoin has been explicitly outlawed in countries such as Russia, Bangladesh, and Ecuador. CME Group Inc. in the United States has launched a bitcoin futures market, while SEBI in India has formed a Financial and Regulatory Technology (CFRT) Committee to study, analyse, and advise on cryptocurrency concerns. Customers who trade bitcoin were also warned by the Reserve Bank of India about the volatile nature of cryptocurrencies. Some recommendations and safeguards for bitcoin owners and investors are listed below:

Always double-check a Web wallet's address and avoid pursuing suspicious links to a Web bank or Web wallet.

- Before completing a transaction, double-check the recipient's address, the amount submitted, and the transaction fees and additional costs.
- Recover lost or forgotten account passwords and other personal information and keep them safe and secure.
- Cryptography is a risky investment. Investing in unforeseeable situations such as diversified investment, supplier reliability, and a powerful attitude requires common methods to be followed.

The majority of cryptocurrency use around the globe is now unregulated and unregulated. Some countries have included it into their financial systems, while others have outright banned it. If the popularity of virtual currencies grows much further, it may be controlled by a growing number of countries, albeit few countries are considering outright bans. With the growing number of clients and the recent increase in the value of Bitcoin, one of the most popular virtual currencies, there are more obstacles to overcome, such as the need for a legal framework and regulatory authority, knowledge of wallet use, transaction processing, and the risks involved with digital currency transactions. As a result, cryptocurrencies have a great deal of potential to become a worldwide currency. Even in countries where the courts have prohibited its use, it is still a question of totally prohibiting its usage without internet restriction. As a result, it is clear that incorporating Virtual Currencies into legal frameworks and the present financial system offers significant development potential and benefits. Indian banking and finance are ready to use blockchain technology and distributed ledgers to speed up transaction processing. In the next years, there will almost certainly be further discussion concerning the legality and acceptance of cryptocurrencies.

Cryptocurrencies barely play a minor role in shaping the economy of third world countries. The future is solely dependent on the laws that would be implemented, as well as the sustainable growth and acceptance will follow. (Moritz Holtmeier, Philipp Sandner, 2019)

Impact of Cryptocurrency on the Global Economy

Cryptocurrencies have an impact on humanity's economic, political, cultural, and social lives. Digital money will not be a replacement for actual money, but it may serve as a catalyst for the creation of a new currency system. There is now a possibility of unscrupulous individuals surfacing on the market due to the lack of rules and warranties to safeguard bitcoin customers.

Governments sometimes wanted to prevent or restrict the use of cryptocurrencies, but today many countries are warming to the new technology. Electronic money can be sent almost anywhere in the globe at almost no cost, and it can also be exchanged using crypto signals.

The global economy will shift, and fiat currencies will be converted to virtual savings. Every day there is an increase in the number of investors, which results in much more than digital assets being evaluated.

In general, the market for cryptocurrencies is increasing and new firms and initiatives for infrastructure are emerging. And the attempted evaluation of the effects of bitcoin and other virtual currencies on economy growth by legal institutions and software development services is a favourable message. This again illustrates the multiple facets of cryptocurrency.

Figure 3. Map the cryptocurrency economy of the world as a fraction from a scale 0 to 1
Source: The 2020 Geography of Cryptocurrency Report by Chain Analysis"

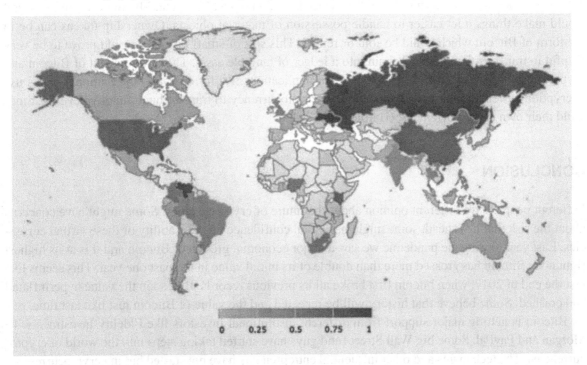

FUTURE OF CRYPTOCURRENCY

The common people, like us, has very little interest in a decentralized digital currency. In order for Bitcoin to function as an established currency, more strict regulation and customer protection is necessary. This will result in a rise of Bitcoin transaction fees and reduce its anonymity, that happens to be two of the most enticing features. Additionally, business sector has different applications for Bitcoin. The chance of insolvency, and price volatility, rises with decentralization. Bitcoin has its own limitations but it can be used to circumvent capital regulations to quiet some extent. Bitcoin cannot be uses as a primary asset but can boost investment portfolio profits and decreases the risk: however, they may aid to diversify a portfolio. Bitcoin lacks the fluidness of traditional bank notes. Cryptocurrencies are prone to code-based assaults and the theft is mostly untraceable. As a result of which Bitcoin isn't much in public's demand except for investors trying to expand their kingdom, few interested individuals hoping to find their luck with cryptocurrency, and the people on the dark web who wishes to deal anonymously in the black market. The rapid price drop of Bitcoin makes it unlikely to be uses as a purchase currency. This shows the lack of demand for bitcoin as its price is volatile and that makes it an unreliable mode of payment. Most stores don't have the option to use Bitcoin or any other cryptocurrency as payment. Looking past the down side, there is ample space for growth of cryptocurrency in this and various other industries as the idea of cryptocurrency itself is very promising. Many people wish to use the cryptographic technology of Bitcoin to claim the ownership of an object like a car. Making everything digital would make things a lot easier to handle possession of material objects. Ownership tokens can be in the form of Bitcoin which could be sold or rented. This sort of smart property would prove to be very helpful in transforming the blockchain into a ledger of tangible asset. The development of Bitcoin and cryptography might result in a wide variety of applications. As for example, international banks use encryption system similar to bitcoin and other cryptocurrency to transfer huge funds or even at times build their own cryptocurrencies. (Härdle et al., 2019)

CONCLUSION

Different people have different opinion about the future of cryptocurrency. Some might have concerns about the risk that lies ahead, some might have total confidence on the stability of these virtual currencies. Last year, during the pandemic we saw a major economic growth of Bitcoin and it is at its highest right now. Bitcoin has grossed more than double of its initial value in the past one year. This seems like just the end of 2017, when bitcoin first broke all its previous records. But, soon the value hyperinflated and crashed. Some believe that history will be repeated and the value of Bitcoin just like last time.

Bitcoin is getting major support from different institutional investors like Fidelity Investments, JP Morgan and PayPal. Some big Wall Street fund guys have started taking steps into the world of cryptocurrencies. The tech giants and other influential entrepreneurs have not started buying cryptocurrencies for themselves but are also making others aware of the future currency of this world.

The government has no fixed interest rates and do not intend on setting their own interest rates and that is one of the problems for cryptocurrencies. There are very few individuals who are genuinely interested and invested in the prospect of cryptocurrency. Companies and industries who are aware of the booming future are the major investors. With the ban of cryptocurrency in different parts of the world like China and UAE, and the fear of the risk involved lack of knowledge makes the market fearful of the outcomes, filled with limited demographics.

The innovations that come with Bitcoin have a lot of popular uses, and it's feasible that some form of cryptocurrency technology implementation and mobile-based payment system with cryptocurrency integration will be the future of everyday payment systems. Future technical developments in money and payment systems will be fascinating to watch, and while Bitcoin is unlikely to become a widely used established currency in the near future, its technology will undoubtedly have far-reaching ramifications.

REFERENCES

A Brief History of Cryptocurrency. (2020). CryptoVantage.

Abadi, J., & Brunnermeier, M. (2018). *Blockchain Economics*. Princeton University. Retrieved on the 24.01.2019 from https://scholar.princeton.edu/sites/default/files/markus/files/blockchain_paper_v3g.pdf

Árnason. (2015). *Cryptocurrency and Bitcoin: A possible foundation of future currency why it has value, what is its history and its future outlook*. Verslunarfélag Reykjavíkur.

Arya. (2018). *What Is Blockchain Technology?* [Video presentation]. Edureka. https://www.youtube.com/watch?v=QCvL-DWcojc//transaction works

Babich & Hilary. (2018b). *Distributed Ledgers and Operations: What Operations Management Researchers Should Know about Blockchain Technology*. Georgetown McDonough School of Business Research Paper No. 3131250.

Berentsen, A., & Schär, F. (2018). *A Short Introduction to the World of Cryptocurrencies*. https://www.researchgate.net/publication/322456542_A_Short_Introduction_to_the_World_of_Cryptocurrencies

Bovaird, C. (2017, September 1). *Why Bitcoin Prices Have Risen More Than 400% This Year*. Retrieved from https://www.forbes.com/sites/cbovaird/2017/09/01/why-bitcoin-prices-have-risen-more-than-400-this-year/#15d4160f6f68

Corbet, S., Larkin, C. J., Lucey, B. M., Meegan, A., & Vigne, S. (2019). *Cryptocurrency Architecture and Interaction With Market Shocks*. https://papers.ssrn.com/sol3/papers.cfm?abstract_id=3369527

DeVries, P. D. (2016). *An Analysis of Cryptocurrency, Bitcoin, and the Future. International Journal of Business Management and Commerce*.

Different types of cryptocurrencies available in the digital world. (2020). *The European Business Review*.

Dourado, E., & Brito, J. (2014). Cryptocurrency. *The New Palgrave Dictionary of Economics*. https://www.researchgate.net/publication/298792075_Cryptocurrency

Farell, R. (2015). *An Analysis of the Cryptocurrency Industry*. Wharton Research Scholars. https://repository.upenn.edu/wharton_research_scholars/13

FrankenfieldJ. (2021). *Altcoin*. https://www.investopedia.com/terms/a/altcoin.asp

Franklin, A. W. (2012). Management of the problem. In S. M. Smith (Ed.), *The maltreatment of children* (pp. 83–95). MTP.

Härdle, Harvey, & Reule. (2019). *Understanding Cryptocurrencies*. International Research Training Group 1792.

Hoffman, Ibáñez, & Simperl. (2020). *Toward a Formal Scholarly Understanding of Blockchain-Mediated Decentralization: A Systematic Review and a Framework*. doi:10.3389/fbloc.2020.00035

Holtmeier & Sandner. (2019). *Cryptocurrencies and the Future of Money*. Academic Press.

Lieure, A. (2018). *Herd behaviour and information uncertainty: Insights from the cryptocurrency market*. Academic Press.

Murphy, Murphy, & Seitzinger. (2015). *Bitcoin: Questions, Answers, and Analysis of Legal Issues*. Congressional Research Service. 7-5700.

Rossolillo. (2021). *Types of Cryptocurrency*. The Motley Fool.

Rueckert. (2019). Cryptocurrencies and fundamental rights. *Journal of Cybersecurity*. doi:10.1093/cybsec/tyz004

Shashank. (2019). *How blockchain works*. Edukera.

Singh & Chawla. (2019). Cryptocurrency Regulation: Legal Issues and Challenges. *International Journal of Reviews and Research in Social Sciences*, 365-375.

Team Mogo. (2021). *History of Bitcoin*. Author.

The Influence of Cryptocurrency on the World Economy. (2020). *The World Financial Review*. https://worldfinancialreview.com/the-influence-of-cryptocurrency-on-the-world-economy/

The Legal Nature of Cryptocurrency. (n.d.). https://iopscience.iop.org/article/10.1088/1755-1315/272/3/032166/pdf

Understanding The Different Types of Cryptocurrency. (2021). SoFi.

Vardhan. (2019). *Blockchain Technology* [Video presentation]. Edureka. https://www.youtube.com/watch?v=QQcBvfP3KBw

Zheng, Z., Xie, S., Dai, H.-N., Chen, X., & Wang, H. (2017). An Overview of Blockchain Technology: Architecture, Consensus, and Future Trends. Academic Press.

KEY TERMS AND DEFINITIONS

Blockchain: Blockchain is a shared, unchangeable database for documenting and monitoring transactions in a corporate network.

Cryptocurrency: Cryptocurrency is a kind of virtual money in simple sense. It is indeed ordinary money like dollars, pounds, euros, yen and so on but it is only available electronically.

Currency: It is money, in the form of paper or coins, authorised by a government and acknowledged as a payment option in general at its current valuations.

Decentralization: The transition from the centralized administration to a sub-national body is described as decentralisation.

Encryption: Encryption is the process of changing data to a form that cannot be recognised or "encrypted."

Hacking: An effort to breach a private computer system or network is called hacking.

Ledger: The directory provides a constant overview of all the amounts recorded in journals listing transactional data by date.

Mining: In the cryptocurrency sector, mining refers to the process of maintaining blockchain data and keeping it under control.

Peer-to-Peer: The distributed application architecture that distributes activities or tasks amongst peers is peer-to-peer (P2P) networking.

Phishing: An attacker sends a fake mail aiming to trick the victim into exposing confidential information for the attacker.

Tokens: Crypto tokens are a sort of cryptocurrency which denotes an asset or a particular use and remains on its blockchain.

Chapter 11
Blockchain Technology Efficiently Managing Information and Cyber Security

Swarnendu Chatterjee
Saraf and Partners, Delhi, India & Supreme Court of India, India

Shifa Qureshi
iD https://orcid.org/0000-0002-5860-9113
Faculty of Law, Aligarh Muslim University, Aligarh, India

ABSTRACT

Any individual who utilises public services is appropriately stressed that, in spite of organisations' earnest attempts to secure their frameworks, criminals may still access government databases and steal or manipulate records. This chapter is an attempt to analyse blockchain technology and whether this technology is effective in supporting cybersecurity. Existing research in blockchain technology tends to focus on finding what this technology is and how it can be implemented for data protection. However, there is no special study on the effectiveness of this technology, regardless of whether it actually protects population data. Therefore, the purpose of this chapter is to outline the effectiveness of blockchain technology in protecting data and the factors that may affect the effectiveness of their solutions.

INTRODUCTION

While still nascent, there is a promising innovation in blockchain towards helping enterprises tackle immutable Cyber Risk challenges such as digital identities and maintaining data integrity. - -Ed Powers, Deloitte's U.S. Cyber Risk Lead (Piscini et al., 2017, p. 4)

In 1981, before the advent of the information age, researchers were attempting to resolve various privacy, encryption, and security issues in the network that was still in its nascent stage. Despite trying countless technologies, regardless of the proposed solution, security still exists as a big issue owing to the

DOI: 10.4018/978-1-7998-8641-9.ch011

involvement of a third party (such as a credit card processor). Ten years later, after the global financial crisis, Satoshi Nakamoto, an anonymous developer, "*outlined a new protocol*" that combines distributed computing and peer-to-peer technology to create the cryptocurrency that will be called Bitcoin.

Blockchain was originally the technology behind Bitcoin but has now generally developed into a plausible network security mitigation technology. In less than ten years, Blockchain technology (BT) has seen investments from many companies, stimulating the establishment of a series of consortia. BT is a distributed, decentralised ledger mechanism that enables transactions to be recorded across several computers. There are usually no central authorities, such as a government, bank, or corporation, and it includes tamper-proof and obvious digital ledgers executed as a distributed system without a central repository. It enables community members to keep track of transactions in a shared ledger. After the transaction is released in the normal operation of the blockchain network, it cannot be changed.

But what exactly is the process of Blockchain? In other words, anytime Person1 wishes to conduct a transaction with Person2, Person1 will encode the transaction as a block. The block will be broadcast to every node in the network (Rathore et al., 2021, p. 352). As long as enough miners approve the transaction, it will be added to the blockchain. In the end, the transaction is completed (Rathore et al., 2021, p. 352).

Blockchain has evolved in years and has various versions. Version 1 of the blockchain technology was released first, and it mostly dealt with financial transfers. The blockchain was revamped in version 2 to allow for the deployment of decentralised applications (Rathore et al., 2021, p. 352). Version 3 of the blockchain is now applied to a wider scale, and the shortcomings of earlier implementations have been addressed. It is decentralised, transparent, and easier to review, as well as more reliable, preventing data tampering.

"*Blockchain is going to change how people do business, the same way how the Internet changed the way how people access information,*" says Matt Lucas. Indians are well-known around the world for their IT prowess and is the third-largest economy in Asia and the fifth-largest in the world (Rathore et al., 2021, p. 352). Though India and China have outlawed the use of cryptocurrency in government transactions, Japan has begun to regulate it. While many people think that blockchain is more about cryptocurrency, but that is not the case.

Through this chapter, the authors aim to introduce in detail the two sides of the argument related to blockchain technology. It is a great invention, but it does have its own inherent problems. After explaining the technique, the authors will analyse the effectiveness of the technique; whether in real life, it can achieve the expected result or not. No cyber defence or data framework can be considered 100% secure. In view of the lucrative nature of cybercrime and the criminal's inventiveness to look for new techniques, the so-called security of today will not be tomorrow. However, given the lack of literature, it has not been highlighted previously. In the final analysis, this chapter concludes that despite some of the blockchains' basic functions are to provide data confidentiality, integrity, and availability, just like other systems, organisations that use the blockchain in their technical infrastructure still need to adopt network security controls and standards in order to protect its organisation from external attacks.

HOW THE CYBER SECURITY THREAT LANDSCAPE IS CHANGING

Cybersecurity has a history of 20 years, but in the past five years, defenders have to protect themselves against potential vulnerabilities (such as terabytes of DDoS attacks, advanced social engineering, crypto-ransomware, zero-day exploits and multi-vector malware) (Gupta, 2018).

Cybersecurity, also known as information technology security, refers to the systems, procedures, and methods that are used to protect information- *"to prevent, detect and recover from damage to confidentiality, integrity and availability of information in cyberspace"* (Bayuk et al., 2012). Cybersecurity, according to this broad definition, encompasses not only technological but also political and legislative policies (Shad, 2019).

The 21st era is of cyberspace, due to which technological advancement has become a critical component of ongoing security-related innovation and operations (Gupta, 2018). In the era of interconnected automobiles, the Internet of Things, mobility, and cloud offers a focal point for cybercrime, targeted assaults, and industrial espionage. After the attacker discovers a vulnerability and determines how to get to the program, he has everything needed to create an exploit for this program, hence strong vulnerability management is required (Gupta, 2018, p. 7). The ability of the organisation to keep up with the emerging security threats and models is one of the important factors for the effectiveness of vulnerability management. Social engineering has been proven to be an effective approach to gain access to a target network, and security agencies confront several obstacles in detecting malicious entries (Gupta, 2018). Prior to the prominence of Facebook and LinkedIn, if an individual needed to find information about an organisation, they wouldn't get a lot of information on the Internet, so using social media platforms enabled social engineering attacks easier to perform (Gupta, 2018).

Cyber threats are clearly seen as one of the most pressing challenges of crime and social security today, as well as an incredibly difficult policy area for governments—cyberspace is the new front line.

Future Threats: What Are the Consequences of Failure to Act Now?

The threat landscape is constantly evolving. The last five years have seen a lot of transition, and the next five are likely to bring even more.

Organised Cybercrime

The latest development that cybersecurity agencies will have to address is *organised cybercrime*. It's more of an emerging threat than a potential threat (CompTIA UK, 2017). Until now, most incidents have been isolated incidents motivated by malice rather than monetary gain. However, this is changing.

According to Europol's "Serious Organised Crime Threat Assessment" published in early 2017, because data has become a commodity like money, gangs (talented and well-funded groups around the world) have officially boosted cybercrime (CompTIA UK, 2017). The majority of these gangs are driven by greed, but some have ideological agendas as well. Attack patterns are frequently based on 'Crime as a Service' models, which are common on the dark web and in which gangs hire hackers to carry out cyber-attacks.

Regardless of whether they were state-sponsored or the work of gangs, many of the recent ransomware attacks are thought to have been well-planned. Intel Security discovered 124 different ransomware types in 2016, some of which were linked to gang power. Meanwhile, a South Korean firm recently announced the world's largest ransomware payment of $1 million, demonstrating how lucrative these attacks can be (CompTIA UK, 2017). As a result, it's not surprising that the criminal community has turned its attention to this issue.

Cyber-Terror

If the physical and digital realms become increasingly interconnected, an especially troubling mode of attack may appear, based on the points raised above. The near proximity of the NHS ransomware attack and the terror attacks on London Bridge demonstrates how coordinated attacks can have catastrophic consequences.

Around 50 trusts were affected by the WannaCry attack, which stopped them from treating patients; fortunately, no one was killed (CompTIA UK, 2017). If this event had occurred in conjunction with a large-scale terror attack, the consequences might have been catastrophic, with local hospitals unable to cope with terror casualties. It would be naive to believe that a terrorist organisation would not attempt to exploit the financial possibilities of cybercrime in the same way that organised criminal organisations have.

Interstitial Attacks

Another form of vulnerability has arisen, and it's only going to get worse as we use more technology systems in tandem (CompTIA UK, 2017). A weakness that occurs in the gap between two separate systems or technologies is known as an interstitial attack. Human-computer interaction is the most common interstice, which leads to the aforementioned human error vulnerability. This happens between systems as well, and this should be a cause for concern.

For example, a few years back, several social networking sites would send a forgotten password request by SMS to the user's mobile phone. Due to the fact that SMS technology is unencrypted and does not utilise strong authentication, hackers may easily listen in and obtain a large number of different passwords.

Interstitial attacks may become more prevalent as the need to incorporate and integrate various programmes grows. Organizations are now opting for an increasing number of cloud-based services that communicate directly with their local business networks. IoT devices that communicate with email systems are another example (CompTIA UK, 2017). Both of these gaps, and several more, are actually vulnerabilities that hackers might abuse. This figure can only rise as these services become more prominent.

INTRODUCING BLOCKCHAIN

What is Blockchain Technology?

In this digital world, we never know when a financially motivated hacker is attempting to access the identities of millions of users of a popular social networking site (Hill & Swinhoe, 2021). If the hacker gains access to the servers, then it can steal a vast number of credentials. This massive credential theft can be revealed publicly, which will make an individual concerned about trust and privacy. There are many examples of such thefts; the recent Equifax 2017 Data Breach case [143 million users details compromised] followed by the Adult Friend Finder 2016 case [413 million identity thefts], Anthem 2015 case [78 million accounts hacked], and others (Hill & Swinhoe, 2021; Tunggal, 2021).

While neither of the prevention measures would guarantee complete security, identifying the issue at the right moment could prevent such instances of abuse (Tunggal, 2021). Just think what technology could accomplish if it could:

- Determine or detect who is looking at an individual's account and changing it?
- Ensure your personal information isn't misused?

This is what a blockchain accomplishes. Briefly stated, it is nothing more than a smart, secure, and constantly expanding database. It is a distributed ledger that records transactions of any value or asset in a secure manner. The blockchain network allows for the peer-to-peer transfer of any sort of value or asset between distinct entities. The primary intent of BT was to create trustworthy financial transactions between two separate parties without the intervention of a third party, such as a bank; however, many companies have since implemented blockchain to expedite their supply chain operations, KYC systems, data storage, and other processes. With the increased usage of internet banking and the volume of online purchases, consumers have to rely on third-party suppliers such as banks and payment gateway providers. As a result, the blockchain was born!

History of Blockchain Technology

Satoshi Nakamoto published a whitepaper titled *Bitcoin: A Peer-to-Peer Electronic Cash System* in 2009 to address existing financial market problems. The aim of this whitepaper was on the creation of a platform that would enable online transfers from one party to another without the use of financial institutions. One of the major difficulties addressed in the article was the double process, which is utilized to prevent double-spending (a particular difficulty with digital currency is the potential of duplicating the same amount after spending it). Since Bitcoin is digital money and it is not difficult to copy and announce digital data, double-spending occurred, and a workaround to avoid this was proposed—BLOCKCHAIN. However, the term blockchain does not appear in Nakamoto's original paper; it first appeared as block-chain in a Bitcoin source code comment.

Fundamentals of the Blockchain

One can consider the blockchain as a ledger of transactions. An actual physical ledger is normally kept up by an incorporated position, not by market participants. However, the blockchain is a distributed ledger located on each participant's device. Whenever a transaction or group of transactions completes, each individual copy is updated. The equipment of each participant or user is usually called a "node", which forms part of the node network. The blockchain is unique in light of the fact that each node in the network must authenticate every transaction. This is why, when a new node enters the network, it downloads the entire transaction record to its system (for example, for Bitcoin, this process takes more than 24 hours). From that point on, it will update the ledger together with other nodes when validating new transactions. The authentication process is based on advanced encryption technology (cryptography) and is widely regarded as inherently secure. Therefore, participants do not need to rely on third parties to ensure transparency and authenticity. Blockchain uses pure mathematics rather than trust to ensure the transparency and integrity of transactions. The types of transactions vary depending on the application of blockchain technology. For example, in Bitcoin, each transaction is a transfer of a certain amount of Bitcoin between participants, and each transaction is recorded on the Bitcoin blockchain. However, transactions can also be used for other purposes, such as fiat money transactions or real estate title transfers.

Blockchain has swiftly acquired acceptance in a multitude of industries due to its open ledger. The blockchain database makes it nearly impossible for cyber attackers to access secret data, which is ideal for a corporation that cannot afford a single point of vulnerability. Furthermore, anyone who can be trusted, whether a known or unknown organization, can manage blockchain, not just trusted administrators or developers.

A blockchain node program and blockchain-specific programs must be installed on any computer with an internet connection. The engagement of these computers may be limited based on usage cases. Bankchain, for one, is a blockchain-based ecosystem that only allows banks to operate the bankchain node client programme.

How Does It Work?

Let's take a look at how the blockchain ledger works in its most basic form. It is necessary to use multiple states of blockchain and investigate them further in order to understand the framework in its generic form:

- **Transaction preparation**: At this point, Party A generates a transaction that includes information like as the receiver's public address, a source digital signature, and a transaction message.
- **Transaction verification**: In a trustless paradigm, each node (computer running blockchain client software) receives the transaction and verifies the digital signature using party A's public key. This authenticated transaction is parked in the ledger queue after successful verification and waits for all nodes to successfully validate the same transaction.
- **Block generation**: One of the nodes in the network is responsible for generating a block, which contains all of the transactions that have been queued in the network. Bitcoins are rewarded on the Bitcoin blockchain when a Bitcoin node, also known as a miner, solves a mathematically challenging problem that results in the generation of a whole block.
- **Block validation**: The network's nodes are subjected to an iterative validation process after efficient block creation, in which the majority of nodes must achieve consensus in order for the process to be successful. Proof of Work (PoW), Proof of Stack (PoS), Delegated Proof of Stack (DPoS), and Practical Byzantine Fault Tolerance (PBFT) are four common ways to accomplish consensus. Bitcoin achieves consensus via PoW, while Ethereum achieves consensus through PoS. This system has an effect on financial issues and assures the security of all transaction activities.
- **Block chained**: The blocks are validated and applied to the blockchain after a strong consensus process.

Characteristics of Blockchains

Blockchain is distinguished by a number of main characteristics, which are mentioned below.

A Decentralised System

Blockchain's decentralised nature weakens certain features of conventional centralised entities. A conventional centralised institution in the financial sector typically verifies all buyers' and sellers' records, reserves the right to allow customers to sign terms and conditions, and preserves all transaction data. Such a centralised operating pattern will expose users' personal information, allow cyber attackers to manipulate trading information, and so on. Blockchain offers a novel way to turn a centralised operation pattern into a decentralised, autonomous pattern. Information in Blockchain is validated among all nodes in the network using a consensus system, and it is replicated at each node. Without a single agency, this mechanism is totally decentralised.

Nodes and Storages are Distributed

The autonomous and self-management of nodes is improved by blockchain. A Blockchain network's nodes are independent entities or organisations that are also geographically dispersed. Blockchain provides a distributed data management system based on a networked structure, with a copy of the ledger stored on each node of the network. When a new block (containing one or more data items) is created, it is validated by all nodes, inserted into the ledger, and synchronised between all nodes.

Consensus and Smart Contract

To construct a trustworthy fault-tolerant chain-connected network, blockchain systems require the co-operation and coordination of distributed nodes. Every decision in a Blockchain system is determined based on majority mode agreement, which is known as consensus. A number of consensus algorithms have been developed in recent years, the most popular of which being Proof of Work (PoW) and Proof of Stake (PoS).

The term "smart contract" refers to a set of software codes that define pre-determined execution conditions. The "if...then..." conditional form is often used in smart contracts. Once the delivery conditions are met, the contract will be immediately executed without the need for human involvement or third-party oversight.

Asymmetric Encryption

Although this distributed architecture is completely decentralized, ensuring network security requires the use of trustworthy encryption solutions. As a default, blockchain networks use asymmetric encryption technology. Asymmetric encryption is used to provide each node with two keys: a public key, which is communicated to all nodes in the network and also serves as the owner's ID address; and a private key, which is kept concealed and also serves as the owner's identity.

Information encryption and digital signature are two of the most common uses of asymmetric encryption in Blockchain networks. To encrypt information and broadcast it to the network, the sender node must first encrypt the information using the receiver node's public key, after which only nodes that have the receiver's private key may decode the information sent by the sender node. Senders encrypt text messages using their private keys and broadcast them to the rest of the network using a digital signature. The receiver decrypts the message with the help of the sender's public key in order to verify that it was sent by the sender. Asymmetric encryption algorithms such as SHA256, RIMPED160, RSA, Elgamal, Rabin, D-H, and ECC are only a few examples of the many options available.

Existing Applications of Blockchain (Who is Using Blockchain and How?)

Apart from any other buzz technology in the modern age of technology, blockchain has the potential to disrupt any market. This could be for a variety of reasons, including reducing overall operating costs, resolving cybersecurity issues, delivering identity and access control technologies, facilitating collaboration between private and public institutions, enhancing and simplifying data management to provide desired outcomes, such as creating a more streamlined insurance sales and management system or implementing a robust health-record information system to prevent spying attempts and so on.

HOW IS BLOCKCHAIN USED TO IMPROVE CYBERSECURITY?

Blockchain technology complements current attempts to protect networks, communications, and data. To hold permanent data, blockchain uses cryptography and hashing, and several emerging cyber protection solutions that make use of similar techniques. To validate information or store encrypted data, the majority of current security mechanisms depend on a single trusted authority (Taylor et al., 2020). As a consequence, the infrastructure is susceptible to attack; multiple bad actors may concentrate their resources on a specific target in order to conduct DoS attacks, extract data via theft or blackmail, or inject malicious data. Blockchains provide an advantage over current authentication measures that is they are decentralised and may not need the power of belief of any specific party or network or network (Taylor et al., 2020); the framework may not require trust since each node, or user, has a full copy of all the historical information accessible, and additional details may only be added to the chain of previous information to the blockchain through reaching majority agreement (Taylor et al., 2020).

Blockchain Use Cases for Cybersecurity

But how does this technology provide cybersecurity? This is a one-of-a-kind technology that may be used in a variety of ways to serve as the most secure means of transacting on an online platform. The BT is commended for ensuring information integrity, according to design and expectations. It may be beneficial to a variety of industries if utilized correctly. One of the greatest applications of BT's integrity assurance is in the development of network security solutions for a variety of different technologies. The following are potential prospective use cases for blockchain to improve network security:

Securing Private Messaging

Recently, many attacks have occurred on social platforms such as Twitter and Facebook. These attacks caused millions of records to be erased, and client data fell into unacceptable hands, leading to data leakage. If blockchain technology is well implemented in these messaging systems, such future cyber-attacks can be prevented (Legrand, 2020). The number of individuals joining social media is increasing, leading to an increase in the number of social media platforms. A significant number of metadata is gathered throughout these interactions. To secure their services and data, the majority of social networking sites' users use weak, unreliable passwords. The majority of messaging companies want to utilise the blockchain to secure user data, which is a more sophisticated alternative than the end-to-end encryption they presently use. Standard security procedures may be created using blockchain technology (Legrand, 2020). The blockchain may be utilised to create a uniform API architecture that enables cross-messenger communication.

Blockchain is being used by start-ups like Obsidian to protect private information shared in chats, messaging applications, and social media (Drinkwater, 2018). Unlike WhatsApp and iMessage, which use end-to-end encryption, Obsidian's messenger uses blockchain to protect users' metadata. To use the messenger, the user would not need to use email or any other form of authentication. Since metadata is spread at random in a ledger, it cannot be gathered in a centralised location from which it may be corrupted. Engineers at the Défense Advanced Research Projects Agency (DARPA) are currently working with blockchain in order to establish a stable and impenetrable messaging service (Drinkwater, 2018). One can expect Blockchain to evolve in the near future, as it is based on secure, authenticated communications.

IoT Security

Edge devices such as thermostats and routers are increasingly being used by hackers to gain access to the entire system. The current fascination with artificial intelligence (AI) makes it easier for hackers to gain access to entire systems like home automation via edge devices like "smart" switches. Many of these IoT devices offer rough security features in most instances (Legrand, 2020). In this scenario, the blockchain may be utilised to decentralise the management of such comprehensive systems or equipment, thus ensuring their security. This method will give the device the ability to make safety decisions on its own. By detecting suspicious commands in unknown networks and performing operations on them, it does not rely on central administrators or authorities to make edge devices more secure. Usually, hackers will invade the device's central management and take complete control of the device and system. The Blockchain can make such attacks more difficult to carry out by decentralizing the authorization system for such devices (even if it is possible).

Securing DNS and DDoS

Individuals who utilize target resources (such as network resources, servers, or websites) are denied access to or service to the target resources in Distributed Denial of Service (DDoS) attacks. The resource system may be shut down or have its speed reduced as a result of these attacks. The entire Domain Name System (DNS), on the other hand, is highly centralized, making it an ideal target for hackers looking to compromise the link between IP addresses and website names. This type of attack renders a website inaccessible, monetizes it, and even redirects users to other fraudulent sites (Legrand, 2020). Fortunately, by decentralizing DNS entries, the blockchain can be used to mitigate this type of attack. The Blockchain will remove susceptible single points abused by hackers by using decentralized solutions.

The Mirai botnet demonstrated how easily critical internet infrastructure may be hacked. By taking down the domain name system (DNS) service provider for most popular websites, the attackers were able to block access to Twitter, Netflix, PayPal, and other services (Drinkwater, 2018). Nebulis is a new project that examines the concept of a distributed DNS that never fails in the face of a spike in requests (Drinkwater, 2018). Nebulis utilises the Ethereum blockchain and the Interplanetary Filesystem (IPFS), a distributed alternative to HTTP, to register and address domain names. We see vital networks like DNS at the core of the internet creating grounds for a large-scale outage as well as hacking against organisations (Drinkwater, 2018). As a result, a more trusted DNS architecture based on blockchain methods will greatly assist the internet's core trust infrastructure.

Decentralising Medium Storage

Commercial data theft and hacking are quickly becoming a major source of worry for corporations. The majority of businesses still rely on centralised storage. Hackers simply need to exploit one weakness to get access to all of the data contained in these systems. Criminals get access to sensitive and private data (such as corporate financial data) as a result of this kind of assault. Sensitive data may be safeguarded via blockchain by guaranteeing a decentralised type of data storage (Legrand, 2020). Hackers will find it more difficult, if not impossible, to get into the data storage system using this mitigation technique. Many storage service providers are looking at how blockchain might help secure data from hacker assaults.

The Provenance of Computer Software

Blockchain can be utilised to guarantee the integrity of software downloads to prevent external intrusions. As far as blockchain technology is concerned, the hash value will be permanently saved in the database in the blockchain. The data stored in the technology cannot be changed or muted; subsequently, by comparing it with the hash value in the hash table, the blockchain can more effectively verify the integrity of the software (Legrand, 2020).

Cyber-Physical Infrastructure Verification

The integrity of information produced by cyber-physical systems has been compromised due to data manipulation, system misconfigurations, and component failures. However, blockchain technology's data integrity and verification capabilities may be utilised to verify the condition of any cyber-physical infrastructure (Legrand, 2020). By using the blockchain to generate information about infrastructure components, it is possible to ensure a complete chain of custody for those components.

Protecting Data Transmission

Blockchain may be used in the future to prevent unauthorised access to data during transmission (Legrand, 2020). Information transmission may be secured by using the technology's full encryption capabilities to prevent hostile actors, whether it is an individual or organisation, from gaining access to it. The reliability and integrity of information sent via the blockchain will be enhanced as a result of this approach. Malicious hackers will alter or totally erase data during transmission, creating a large gap in inefficient communications systems (e.g., email).

Diminish Human Safety Adversity Caused by Cyber-attacks

Unmanned military equipment and public transportation have lately been introduced as a result of technological advancements. These autonomous vehicles and weaponry rely entirely on the Internet to operate since it allows data to be sent from sensors to remote control databases (Legrand, 2020). Hackers, on the other hand, have struggled to penetrate and get access to networks like automobile Car area networks (CAN). When these networks are hacked, hackers have complete control over critical vehicle systems. Human safety will be jeopardised as a result of such events. However, many adversities can be avoided by verifying any data entering and passing through such systems on the blockchain (Legrand, 2020).

Using the Blockchain for Cybersecurity: Pros and Cons

Major Cons

Although the blockchain has a lot of potential as a cybersecurity measure, it also comes with a lot of risks. Let's take a closer look at the major disadvantages of blockchain technology that should be considered before deciding to use it to improve security:

Challenges of Scalability: Blockchain networks have varying thresholds, such as block volume and transaction size processed per second. As a result, one needs to look at the scalability of the blockchain network they are considering.

The current limits for Bitcoin are 1 MB of data and up to 7 transactions per second (TPS). Block generation on the Ethereum network is limited to 7 to 15 TPS (Yatsenko & Sotnichek, 2021). Other networks, on the other hand, claim to have much greater transaction capability. For example, Ontology claims to be able to reach 4,000 to 12,000 TPS depending on the environment, while the Futurepia network claims to be able to reach 300,000 TPS in laboratory testing (Yatsenko & Sotnichek, 2021).

Cyberattack Vulnerability: In spite of the fact that blockchain technology reduces the likelihood of malicious interference, it is not a panacea for all cyber risks. The blockchain has flaws in node correspondence (the eclipse attack), consensus processes (the 51 percent attack), and code vulnerabilities (Yatsenko & Sotnichek, 2021). If attackers are successful in exploiting either of these vulnerabilities, the security of the entire system may be jeopardised.

Reliance on Private Keys: Blockchains are dependent on the usage of private keys, which are lengthy sequences of random numbers generated automatically by a wallet. Unlike user passwords, private keys are designed to interact with the blockchain and cannot be retrieved. All data encrypted with a user's private key is almost likely unrecoverable if the user's private key is lost.

Blockchain Literacy: Despite the growing success of blockchain technologies, there is still a scarcity of qualified blockchain developers and cryptography experts. Blockchain architecture requires a wide variety of skills, as well as a comprehensive understanding of the different technologies, programming languages, and resources.

Issues with Adaptability: While blockchain technology may be utilised in almost every industry, certain businesses may have difficulty integrating it into their operations (Yatsenko & Sotnichek, 2021). It is hard to enforce blockchain technology to supply chain systems, for example, because re-implementing supply chain logic on a blockchain could take a long time. Companies should consider this before introducing blockchain technology since blockchain applications could require the complete replacement of established systems.

High Costs of Operation and Customisation: A blockchain requires a significant amount of computing power and storage. This, in contrast to existing non-blockchain systems, may result in greater marginal costs.

Lack of Governance: The operation and usage of blockchain technologies in general, and distributed ledger technologies in particular, are not adequately regulated or governed on a worldwide scale. Many countries, including Malta and the United States, have either passed or are in the process of implementing laws relating to cryptocurrencies. The legal and economic uses of blockchains and smart contracts are already being regulated in several jurisdictions throughout the United States, due to frameworks established by governments (Yatsenko & Sotnichek, 2021).

These are the key blockchain disadvantages to consider before using this technology to boost the cybersecurity of the product. Nevertheless, the ultimate scope of potential drawbacks may differ depending on the sector you operate in and the additional problems you choose to address utilising the blockchain.

Major Pros

Increased Consumer Confidence: A blockchain provides data protection and accountability, which will assist companies in gaining the trust of their clients. Apart from that, data owners will be granted full control over their personal information in many present blockchain networks, including the power to decide who will have access to it and when.

Data Storage Security: Blockchain archives are permanent, and any modification made to them is clear and irreversible. As a consequence, data stored on a blockchain is safer than data maintained in traditional digital or physical archives.

User Confidentiality: The client or organisations confidentiality is very high on the blockchain network because of the public key cryptography that is used to authenticate users. Some blockchain-based companies, on the other hand, take this technology a step further and enhance it. For example, Guardtime developed a Keyless Signature Infrastructure (KSI) that enables users to verify the validity of their signatures without disclosing their keys (Yatsenko & Sotnichek, 2021).

Encrypted Data Transfers: The blockchain enables data and financial transactions to be completed quickly and securely. Smart contracts, for example, allow for the automatic execution of multi-party agreements.

No Single Point of Failure: Permissionless blockchain networks have no common point of failure because they are decentralised and hence more resilient than traditional structures. If a single node is hacked, the blockchain's process or security will not be jeopardised. This implies that even if the system is exposed to DDoS assaults, it will continue to operate properly due to multiple copies of the ledger. 'Private blockchains,' on the other hand, are unable to offer you this advantage.

Transparency and Traceability of Data: Since blockchain transfers are digitally signed and time-stamped, network users can accurately trace the history of transactions and monitor accounts at any point in time (Yatsenko & Sotnichek, 2021). This functionality also enables a business to provide accurate statistics about assets or product delivery.

Top Blockchain Use Cases for Cybersecurity

The blockchain, by its very existence, delivers powerful cybersecurity solutions to start-ups and businesses in a variety of fields.

Finance

The immutability of data and transaction integrity is the most valuable aspects of a blockchain in the finance sector. Transactions stored on the blockchain are more open and safer than standard digital or paper documents. To maintain the security of customer information, some banking organisations, such as ING Group, use blockchains and, in particular, zero-knowledge range proof solutions. To secure user data, Q2, a virtual banking network, employs blockchain and machine learning (Yatsenko & Sotnichek, 2021).

Many blockchain networks have smart contracts, which allow for the automated implementation of agreements between several parties when all of the requirements of the agreements are fulfilled. Pledge arrangements and deposits are common examples of such agreements.

Healthcare

Healthcare organisations, just like the finance industry, will benefit enormously from using blockchains for safely storing and easily sharing medical data. BurstIQ, for example, is a blockchain-based network that assists healthcare facilities in safely storing patient data and sharing it between departments and organisations in near real-time.

A blockchain can also be used to create encrypted messaging systems for quick and easy contact between patients and institutions in administrative and non-urgent medical situations.

Real Estate

Blockchains are being used by real estate networks to solve two big problems: maintaining secure data storage and automating key processes like validating land ownership and transferring funds.

A blockchain enables land ownership and payment history to be kept permanent and transparent. This technology is used by StreetWire and ShelterZoom to make data processing easier for real estate companies (Yatsenko & Sotnichek, 2021).

A blockchain also provides reliability and automation, all of which are critical for real estate companies to operate successfully. Smart contracts are used by companies like SMARTRealy and Propy to sell, purchase, and rent real estate (Yatsenko & Sotnichek, 2021). Smart contracts guarantee that transactions between several parties are executed quickly, securely, and completely automatically.

Supply Chain

Blockchains are being used by global corporations such as Walmart, BMW, and FedEx to improve digital access and financial accountability. To simplify the review of a supply chain's performance and processes, a blockchain will store tamper-proof records of all operations, transfers, and freight details.

Asset authentication can also be done using blockchain platforms. Businesses are shifting their emphasis away from centralised authorities and toward trusted models focused on algorithms, according to Gartner. The blockchain is a perfect example of this kind of model.

Governance

Many government procedures, including tax collection, information governance, elections, and so on, will benefit from blockchain technology. Catena, a blockchain-based framework for monitoring government budgets, is used by the Canadian government (Yatsenko & Sotnichek, 2021).

In the case of elections, a blockchain may be used to expedite vote counting while still ensuring the accuracy of the results. Since all data records are immutable, it is almost impossible to tamper with electronic voting on the blockchain. Maintaining the privacy of a voter's preference while validating their identification, on the other hand, can be difficult.

BLOCKCHAIN APPLICATIONS IN HEALTH CARE FOR COVID-19 AND BEYOND

The COVID-19 (pandemic) has had a wide-ranging effect on governments, populations, and people, ranging from school closures to healthcare insurance problems, not to mention the loss of life (Banafa, 2020). Well before the COVID-19 crisis, emerging technology was increasingly altering how we learn, build skills, and function. The increasing use of online classes, virtual recruiting, collaborative software, and remote jobs demonstrates this. If "social distancing" becomes more prevalent in a world where digital globalisation persists unabated, these phenomena will inevitably escalate and become the new standard (Kersey, 2020). As the global digital economy expands on top of a huge internet universe, seamless communication between people, organisations, and gadgets will become more important, requiring solutions that boost trust and transparency. (Kersey, 2020). As governments scramble to resolve these issues, several blockchain-based strategies can assist in dealing with the global health crisis (Pressgrove, 2020).

One of the continuing problems in the early stages of the global pandemic has been a lack of reliable data (IMNOVATION, n.d.). Not only because of the disinformation but also because of the abundance of various voices and data sources. Based on common standards, having a reliable and robust system to transmit information has always been one of the biggest needs of the government, organizations and society as a whole. And it seems that blockchain may be a valuable asset (IMNOVATION, n.d.).

Contact tracers, which send this information to prospective contacts by phone or mail and tell them to be checked, have traditionally been used by public health departments. When the figures aren't as large as they were in the COVID-19 pandemic, this strategy works. Furthermore, these techniques were formulated prior to the advent of cell phones (Khurshid, 2020). Communication tracing applications for COVID-19 are an obvious public health option due to the sheer ease of mobile app development and universal access to mobile phones (Khurshid, 2020). The need to ensure data protection and privacy for consumers is one of the key issues associated with the use of these applications (Daly & Cunningham, 2020). Blockchain could be capable of addressing these concerns about privacy. A blockchain ledger may be used as a supplement to monitoring systems to record details about users' activities and share the data with other ledger members (Daly & Cunningham, 2020).

The use of a blockchain network will secure users' identities by encrypting data by using anonymous identifiers. Instead of usernames and passwords, each user will be given a special, secure digital identity to maintain and exchange their personal information. Users would have complete discretion of the details they want to exchange if private key technology was used. Furthermore, since the blockchain database is immutable, all shared data will be safe and secure and will not be tampered with (Daly & Cunningham, 2020).

The COVID-19 pandemic has prompted large-scale data coordination and management. To begin with, these data are usually sensitive, yet they must be easily verifiable and controlled in a transparent manner. However, if these data management platforms provide central authorities full access to the data, then privacy problems could arise, which could be counterproductive.

To address these concerns, Garg et al. (2020) created a blockchain-based movement pass based on smart contracts and tokens (token-based movement passes), which eliminates the requirement for personal information for verification (Garg et al., 2020). Separately, Xu et al. (2021) developed a practical blockchain platform (with data acquisition via IoT) that can desensitize a user's identification and location information using its hash function, protecting the identity of COVID-19 patients and public privacy in a decentralized environment (Xu et al., 2021). These examples demonstrate how blockchain technology can help solve the problem of collecting verifiable yet anonymous tracking data. Furthermore, the adoption of health and immunity certificates may be required to undertake rapid, widespread testing and vaccination programs. For cross-border verification of COVID-negative or immunity status, blockchain technology can provide a secure and decentralized environment. In addition, blockchain can enable a secure, decentralized, peer-to-peer network that might be used for telemedicine initiatives such as test kit management and medical data sharing among trustworthy stakeholders.

Many aspects of life have been impacted by the COVID-19 pandemic, including healthcare, finance, politics, economics, and education. Blockchain has the potential to play a key role in the post-COVID-19 world's administration. It is anticipated that the main features of blockchain will be beneficial in a wide range of applications including contact tracking and disaster relief as well as patient information dissemination and e-government. Other applications may include supply chain and online education management as well as immigration management, production management, electronic monitoring, and contactless distribution (Kalla et al., 2020). However, a number of obstacles must be overcome before blockchain can be completely used for these purposes, including legal, protection, safety, latency, throughput, scalability, and resource consumption issues (Kalla et al., 2020).

Apart from COVID-19, blockchain applications in digital health have been described in a variety of other crucial health-care domains, including authentication and electronic medical record management, clinical trial research and consent management, health-care insurance claims processing, research data transfer and AI model development, genomics, supply chain encryption for medical supplies, and mobile health and IoT.

CONCLUSION

Blockchain technology is expected to be a new field of business transactions between untrusted entities. Through encryption, transparency, and decentralised smart contracts and smart ledgers, it can be ensured that it supports verification, identification, authentication, integrity and immutability. Blockchain technology creates decentralised databases with chronologically linked and duplicated digital ledgers and distributes transactions over a large network of untrusted entities. It also provides independent verification guarantees, thereby eliminating reliance on a central authority. In addition, because there is no central authority, blockchain services can provide better security for systems distributed between different entities, and even if there are malicious insiders, abuse and supervision can be immutable. As a result of the blockchain's fundamental features of data encryption, immutability, transparency and auditability as well as its operational flexibility (not including single points of failure), it has the potential to aid in the improvement of cyber defences by preventing fraudulent activities through a consensus mechanism and detecting data tampering.

The precarious condition developed by the COVID-19 pandemic has highlighted the need for a single-source Blockchain-based pandemic health record management system to solve a variety of current and future challenges. The most important question to overcome the previously identified problems is blockchain; however, there are several concerns that need to be resolved by international health organisations, heads of states, and international policymakers to implement government to government digital health service-related policy, data transmission act, health policy, issues of digital connectivity, digital inequity and digital divide that are prevalent in the world's least-developed and developing nations. This pandemic crisis provides an excellent chance for mankind to unite all nations, regardless of their divisions, under a common flag to ensure the global health protection and to combatCOVID-19 and other pandemics (Azim et al., 2020).

While many people still believe in traditional transaction methods, the transition is unavoidable when blockchain facilitates safe transfers throughout the network. Blockchain features can improve the reliability and suitability of networks in nearly every aspect of life (Rathore et al., 2021, p. 357). The government should enact more rules regulating this technology, and corporations should use it to raise people's living standards (Rathore et al., 2021, p. 357).

Cybersecurity is one of the most dynamic markets, with new threats emerging almost every day (Gupta, 2018). While the future of cybersecurity will still be an unpredictably difficult challenge for global leaders, it is important to plan for emerging threats and security innovation in order to maintain clear customer and stakeholder confidence.

Blockchain is a perfect solution in the cybersecurity arsenal because it combines block-building algorithms and hashing to improve data security as transactions of any value are processed in the distributed network. Blockchain is influencing cybersecurity solutions in a variety of ways (Gupta, 2018). Businesses should utilise hundreds of apps (both internal and cloud-based) to fulfil a range of business requirements as a result of cloud computing and other digital advancements. Both end-users and businesses benefit from this because it lowers the risk of data breaches.

Hundreds of billions of data records are breached per year. As a result, comfort and flexibility are likely to be surpassed by privacy and protection in the coming digital age (Gupta, 2018). As stated earlier, blockchain is all about ensuring data protection of sensitive information, and blockchain is certain to be a big draw for many enterprise applications looking for improved security and privacy.

REFERENCES

Azim, A., Nazrul Islam, M., & Spranger, P. E. (2020). Blockchain and novel coronavirus: Towards preventing COVID-19 and future pandemics. *Iberoamerican Journal of Medicine*, 2(3), 215–218. doi:10.53986/ibjm.2020.0037

Banafa, A. (2020, June 22). *Blockchain Technology and COVID-19*. OpenMind. https://www.bbvaopenmind.com/en/technology/digital-world/blockchain-technology-and-covid-19/

Bayuk, J. L., Healey, J., Rohmeyer, P., Sachs, M., Schmidt, J., & Weiss, J. (2012). *Cyber Security Policy Guidebook* (1st ed.). Wiley & Sons. doi:10.1002/9781118241530

CompTIA UK. (2017). *The UK Cybersecurity Landscape 2017 and Beyond: A Report*. CompTIA. https://connect.comptia.org/content/whitepapers/the-cybersecurity-landscape

Daly, M., & Cunningham, M. (2020, July 1). *How Blockchain is helping in the fight against Covid-19*. Lexology. https://www.lexology.com/library/detail.aspx?g=8b5ef0f0-05b3-4909-b5d5-da7bd57f0381

Drinkwater, D. (2018, February 6). *6 use cases for blockchain in security*. CSO Online. https://www.csoonline.com/article/3252213/6-use-cases-for-blockchain-in-security.html

Garg, C., Bansal, A., & Padappayil, R. P. (2020). COVID-19: Prolonged Social Distancing Implementation Strategy Using Blockchain-Based Movement Passes. *Journal of Medical Systems, 44*(165), 165. Advance online publication. doi:10.100710916-020-01628-0 PMID:32780276

Gupta, R. (2018). *Hands-On Cybersecurity with Blockchain: Implement DDoS protection, PKI-based identity, 2FA, and DNS security using Blockchain.* Packt Publishing.

Hill, M., & Swinhoe, D. (2021, July 16). *The 15 biggest data breaches of the 21st century.* CSO Online. Retrieved November 26, 2021, from https://www.csoonline.com/article/2130877/the-biggest-data-breaches-of-the-21st-century.html

IMNOVATION. (n.d.). *How Blockchain is Helping to Fight the Coronavirus.* Retrieved 11 May 2021, from https://www.imnovation-hub.com/society/blockchain-help-coronavirus/

Kalla, A., Hewa, T., Mishra, R. A., Ylianttila, M., & Liyanage, M. (2020). The Role of Blockchain to Fight Against COVID-19. *IEEE Engineering Management Review, 48*(3), 85–96. doi:10.1109/EMR.2020.3014052

Kersey, J. (2020). *How Blockchain Technology & Self Sovereign Identity is Enabling The New Normal Post COVID-19.* Tata Consultancy Services. https://www.tcs.com/perspectives/articles/covid-19-how-blockchain-technology-and-self-sovereign-identity-enables-the-new-normal-of-remote-learning-training-and-working

Khurshid, A. (2020). Applying Blockchain Technology to Address the Crisis of Trust During the COVID-19 Pandemic. *JMIR Medical Informatics, 8*(9), e20477. doi:10.2196/20477 PMID:32903197

Legrand, J. (2020, September 4). *The Future Use Cases of Blockchain for Cybersecurity.* Cyber Management Alliance. https://www.cm-alliance.com/cybersecurity-blog/the-future-use-cases-of-blockchain-for-cybersecurity

Piscini, E., Dalton, D., & Kehoe, L. (2017). *Blockchain and Cybersecurity: An assessment of the security of blockchain technology.* Deloitte. https://www2.deloitte.com/tr/en/pages/technology-media-and-telecommunications/articles/blockchain-and-cyber.html

Pressgrove, J. (2020, March 11). *Blockchain Emerges as Useful Tool in Fight Against Coronavirus.* GovTech. https://www.govtech.com/products/blockchain-emerges-as-useful-tool-in-fight-against-coronavirus.html

Rathore, V. S., Kumawat, V., & Umamaheswari, B. (2021). The Rising of Blockchain Technology and Its Adoption in India. In V. S. Rathore, N. Dey, V. Piuri, R. Babo, Z. Polkowski, & J. M. R. S. Tavares (Eds.), *Rising Threats in Expert Applications and Solutions. Advances in Intelligent Systems and Computing* (1187th ed., pp. 351–357). Springer. doi:10.1007/978-981-15-6014-9_40

Shad, M. R. (2019). Cyber Threat Landscape and Readiness Challenge of Pakistan. *Strategic Studies, 39*(1), 1–19. https://www.jstor.org/stable/10.2307/48544285

Taylor, P. J., Dargahi, T., Dehghantanha, A., Parizi, R. M., & Choo, K. K. R. (2020). A systematic literature review of blockchain cyber security. *Digital Communications and Networks, 6*(2), 147–156. doi:10.1016/j.dcan.2019.01.005

Tunggal, A. T. (2021, November 15). *The 60 Biggest Data Breaches*. UpGuard. Retrieved November 26, 2021, from https://www.upguard.com/blog/biggest-data-breaches

Xu, H., Zhang, L., Onireti, O., Fang, Y., Buchanan, W. J., & Imran, M. A. (2021). BeepTrace: Blockchain-Enabled Privacy-Preserving Contact Tracing for COVID-19 Pandemic and Beyond. *IEEE Internet of Things Journal, 8*(5), 3915–3929. doi:10.1109/JIOT.2020.3025953

Yatsenko, M., & Sotnichek, M. (2021, February 4). *Blockchain for Cybersecurity: Pros and Cons, Trending Use Cases*. Apriorit. https://www.apriorit.com/dev-blog/462-blockchain-cybersecurity-pros-cons

Chapter 12
The Cryptocurrency "Pump-and-Dump":
Social Media and Legal and Ethical Ambiguity

Brady Lund

Emporia State University, USA

ABSTRACT

This chapter describes the author's personal experience as a member of a crypto-trading "pump-and-dump" group – groups organized on Reddit and Discord channels that use social media to spread positive misinformation about a cryptocurrency in order to temporarily inflate its value and collect huge profits. It discusses the nature of cryptocurrency marketplaces, social networking related to crypto, the pump-and-dump phenomenon, its social and economic impacts, and ethical concerns. Following the rise in the value of Bitcoin and the WallStreetBets/GameStop saga in December 2020 and January 2021, these pump-and-dump groups used the frenzy surrounding "get rich quick" investing to generate inordinate profits off of these ambitious individuals' losses. Rallying around a shared philosophy and profit motive, these groups utilized social media disinformation campaigns to fool new crypto investors in squandering their funds, often while failing to acknowledge the legal and ethical conundrum of stealing from the poor and ambitious.

INTRODUCTION

In January 2021, the "GameStop saga" became major news, while at the same time Bitcoin reached peak levels. It led to a peak frenzy of inexperienced investors who sought to "get rich quick," and there were plenty of sharks wait to prey on the fresh herd. The GameStop trading bonanza was a once-in-a-lifetime event. Major hedge funds had bet heavy on the stock to deprecate in value. Some savvy investors took notice. When you short a stock, you borrow and sell a certain number of shares at a specific price, hoping then that the price of the stock drops such as that when it comes time to return the shares that you borrowed, you can purchase them at a lower price and pocket the difference as profit. When you short,

DOI: 10.4018/978-1-7998-8641-9.ch012

though, you must always return what you borrow, regardless of where the price goes. So, if you short the entire quantity of GameStop shares in existence, and then a bunch of twenty-year olds with a Visa card buy up the shares in the meantime and inflate the price, the hedge funds are going to have to pay whatever inflated price those shares reach. Ultimately, the GameStop saga confirmed for many what they already thought: that game is rigged against them. The trading platforms barred the stock from being traded, causing the price to artificially drop and bailing out the hedge funds. However, these new investors had tasted the thrill of making serious profit for doing next-to-no work and, like true gambling addicts, many did not turn away completely from the game, but simply looked for looser slots.

Crypto tokens, or coins, are quantities of a digital asset (analogous to "shares" in a company), tracked on a ledger, that act as a form of completely-virtual currency (Narayanan et al., 2016). These tokens are created using blockchain technology: These "assets" are created through mining, a process whereby computer networks around the world compete to verify crypto transactions the fastest, consuming a lot of energy in the process (making crypto mining an unprofitable venture for many). Exchanges of crypto coins are tracked on an electronic ledger, which is where the verification of transactions occurs. Records of crypto ownership are often stored in "wallets," or a physical space (like a certain software) where the keys (code/password that identify ownership of an amount of crypto) are stored. However, many crypto traders today, particularly amateurs, simply allow the crypto marketplaces to store their currency for them (though this, of course, increases risks to privacy and security of the coin).

As the GameStop saga moved to a close, many of those who "got hooked" on the experience sought a new outlet to make large profits on short-term investments. Enter the world of crypto. Bitcoin had already nearly tripled in value in the month leading up to GameStop, and a robust market of thousands of cheaper crypto coins with seemingly boundless potential existed at the ends of everyone's fingertips. Investing sites like Robinhood had made it possible to purchase crypto on their platforms (as easily as purchasing regular stock in company), but there are plenty of crypto-specific marketplaces in operation as well – with perhaps the most well-known being Coinbase (the eTrade of the cryptosphere). This marketplace is most people's entry into the world of crypto investing, before the move on to other marketplaces with more diverse coin offerings (Coinbase is limited to only about 40 different coins). Traffic to these marketplaces grew, and simultaneously the Reddit groups for investing and crypto grew abuzz with activity. Opportunities seemed aplenty – and it was the perfect situation for the pump-and-dump groups to thrive.

CRYPTOCURRENCY

Cryptocurrency is a digital currency that is created and maintained (generally) using decentralized blockchain technology (Lee, Guo, & Wang, 2018; Narayanan et al., 2016). Cryptocurrency, in itself, is not anything physical. It is just a ledger of transactions that are validated by "miners," who (in Bitcoin's "proof of work" set-up) race to solve cryptographic puzzle, with the solver having the right to verify blockchain transactions and, in exchange for their efforts, receiving compensation in the form of that cryptocurrency. When one purchases a crypto token, they are really purchasing a stake on that blockchain – not too dissimilar from purchasing stock in a company. However, unlike with stock shares, which represent an ownership share in an actual company, ownership in cryptocurrency (in most cases) does not represent ownership over any tangible asset. Because the value of cryptocurrency is not tied to any physical asset and instead relies on a belief among investors in its value, the cryptocurrency market can be volatile and susceptible to manipulation.

Legal Concerns with Cryptocurrency

Cryptocurrency itself poses several legal and ethical risks, as noted in recent legal and scholarly literature. Presently, cryptocurrency lacks any government oversight or regulation (Nestertsova-Sobakor et al., 2019). That is part of the intrigue of cryptocurrency for many investors: they want a new economy that is not based on, or susceptible to, government control (Vishwakarma, Khan, & Jain, 2018). Of course, governments themselves want to maintain economic controls – for reasons that are both magnanimous (economic insecurity threatens the livelihoods of the public) and narcissistic (it is more difficult to maintain power without some economic control). Governments are just now exploring ways to regulate cryptocurrency and proposed solutions may have taxation implications for cryptocurrency investors and legal ramifications for the operators of cryptocurrency marketplaces (Prytula et al., 2021).

One significant challenge with the legal regulation of cryptocurrencies is that new coins are being created constantly. If a government attempts to regulate a coin, investors can just switch to another. For this reason, it is much more practical to regulate the marketplace – Binance, Coinbase, Crypto.com – than any currency itself (Inozemtsev, 2020). Enforcement of this type of regulation, however, is inconsistent among countries (Drozd, Lazur, & Serbin, 2017; Cvetkova, 2018). In the United States, for instance, the main Binance trading platform (Binance.com) is blocked due to the United States' government's accusation that Binance was improperly using assets and attempting to avoid regulation (Khatri, 2020). In some countries though, like Pakistan and Ukraine, the sale of cryptocurrency is illegal, which means that these marketplaces are also banned (Bachynskyy & Radeiko, 2019; Grabowski, 2019). These approaches have their own loopholes. New marketplaces can spring up in place of shuttered ones and cryptocurrency can be stored locally in "wallets" in order to avoid seizure of assets.

Given the desires of nations, and the vast amount of capital invested in cryptocurrency (over one trillion U.S. dollars, or more than 1/100 of the global annual GDP), it is likely that legal challenges will continue to arise and evolve. Just in the year 2021, China has enacted new restrictions on cryptocurrency and cryptomining (the process of validating cryptocurrency transactions in exchange for compensation in that currency) and India has aimed to follow suit (Kumar, 2021). The implications of cryptocurrency for international trade has yet to be fully explored. Given the fact that cryptocurrency transactions are impossible to trace, the potential for criminal activity is significant. One example of how cryptocurrency is used to support criminal activities is discussed in this chapter: the cryptocurrency pump and dump.

What is a Pump-and-Dump?

A pump-and-dump is a scheme where a relatively small group of people come together with the goal of defrauding a much larger group of an investment by manipulating the value of a stock (Huang & Cheng, 2015). They do this in (essentially) three steps: first, they purchase a large number of shares in the target stock at the lowest possible price; next, they hype up the stock on social media or email (or, historically, through word-of-mouth or phone calls) through spam messages with disinformation about the potential of the stock (e.g., "it is going to jump 1000% overnight!"); finally, as people flock to purchase the stock and the price rises, the scammers sell off all their shares for a tremendous profit. Meanwhile, the new investors are purchasing those shares at the inflated rate, assuming that the value will continue to grow, only to find that it quickly plummets and leaves them with significant loses.

Pump-and-dump schemes are generally considered to be unlawful price manipulation (i.e., fraud), but are not heavily policed – in part because they are hard *to* police (Tillman & Indergaard, 2005). These are generally white-collar crimes (which makes the current developments in the cryptosphere even more fascinating, given that it is being done mostly by blue-collar and no-collar workers). It is difficult to conclusively prove what is intentional and malicious manipulation unless there is some kind of "smoking gun." Instead, the market rules for trading were designed so that these schemes would be more difficult to pull off (at least until sites like Robinhood – which allowed for quick purchases of small amounts of shares – came around).

What makes cryptocurrency a good target for these pump-and-dump schemes? It lacks regulation almost completely. It is decentralized. The rules that govern how the crypto can be used, and how much will be created, are dictated by the owners of the crypto, not dissimilar from a stock holding. Most importantly, the craze over cryptocurrency, sparked mostly by the media coverage of Bitcoin, led to thousands of different crypto coins being created, and the market for these coins was and is still very volatile (Lee et al., 2018; Liu & Tsyvinski, 2018). 50% shifts in price from one day to the next are not uncommon, so pump-and-dump schemes are not difficult to pull off, nor are they too blatantly obvious as to raise serious negative publicity.

This chapter is not the first publication to discuss the cryptocurrency pump-and-dumps. There have been several technical papers on the topics, such as those by Kamps and Kleinburg (2018), Mirtaheri et al. (2019), and Xu and Livshits (2020). Corbet et al. (2020) discuss hacking of crypto markets among other crypto cybercrime concerns. Unlike those other articles, though, this article presents a first-hand narrative of my experiences as an integrated member of one of these pump-and-dump groups.

MECHANISMS OF ACTION: REDDIT, DISCORD, AND BINANCE

It is like gambling mixed with social networking with a touch of "sticking it to the suckers." Within Reddit, there are massive ecosystems of individuals interested in investing, both in stocks and in cryptocurrencies, and subreddits for topics like "Cryptopumping." The major forums on Reddit are kind of like the Facebook wall of the pump-and-dump schemes. This is where the pumps are advertised after they have already started. The major forces behind the pumps have already bought in and use Reddit posts as their marketing platform to promote their pumps. Reddit does a fair bit of policing of posts, and many groups self-police as well. The real action behind a pump-and-dump generally occurs at a deeper level, not on Reddit but on Discord, a private messaging service. Telegram is another popular service that is used in the same way (Nizzoli et al., 2020). Users on Reddit will invite others to join their Discord group, or sometimes open invites will be posted in a Reddit forum. The following narrative is based on the author's own experience as a member of a cryptopumping group.

In the typical medium-sized Discord, there are chats for stocks and crypto pumps, as well as a few long term investment projects. The long-term projects are selected because the group believed in the project's mission and saw long-term investment potential. The term "100X" will be used to denote an investment that was seen as having the potential to increase in value by 100 times over the course of the next few years (generally, 2025 was seen as the "finish line"). Short-term pumps are seen as ways to quickly increase the value of a stock or crypto by 100-200%, then quickly take those profits and invest in another pump. Members of the Discord will seek out cryptocurrencies that had a low or undervalued "market cap" – i.e., the total value of all of that crypto token that is owned. There are thousands of different crypto tokens in circulation that can be purchased from various marketplaces, so plenty of options existed. If a crypto has a market cap of $10 million or so, this is a good spot, because it meant that it has sufficient investment to show that investors had interest but is low enough that the price could easily be manipulated.

To begin a pump, a large segment of the Discord will agree to a coin. These members will then purchase large quantities of that coin at its lowest cost. Price trends for the coin could be viewed on Coin Market Cap, which is kind of like the Yahoo Finance of crypto. Binance is a marketplace that is commonly used to purchase crypto, because it is widely-known and available and, unlike some crypto markets, it allows for stop-limit trading, where crypto can be bought or sold at a specified price after the market reaches another specific price. For instance, one might set a stop-price order to purchase $1000 in Stellar (a popular crypto) at the price of $0.45 per token when the market price of Stellar reaches $0.44 per token. One would do this if they anticipated (but were not entirely sure) the market quickly rising, paying a premium for the token to ensure that the buy is processed before the price rises above the $0.45 level.

After a coin is purchased, members of the Discord will take to social media – particularly Reddit, but also Twitter and YouTube – to advertise a pump, saying things like, "invest in Stellar now. Price is going to the moon!" These pumps were fairly successful in early 2021, because there were many uninitiated users on the major Reddit forums like r/WallStreetBets and r/Cryptocurrency, due to the media frenzy and social media promotion around the GameStop stock sage and the Dogecoin cryptocurrency promoted by Elon Musk. People who were late to those two events but were intrigued by the idea of "getting rich quick" off of investing, flooded to Reddit in this wake. They could be convinced that, if they set up a Binance account and invested in a particular coin, they could see their profits "go to the moon" with a 10, 20, 100X growth. In reality, the growth, even in the biggest pumps, never reached that high. The biggest jump for Bitcoin was 4X, Dogecoin had a 10X jump for a brief moment, most others never got higher than a 300% jump. That level of increase over the course of a couple of days is nothing to scoff at, but it was not going to turn someone who invested $100 into a millionaire overnight, as they may have thought.

Of course, many of those who invest never will see any increase at all. They are the marks. The people making the 300% increase are those from the Discord group who have invested before the pump began. The first few members of the pump from outside the Discord will also see good returns (if they dumped at the right time) but most people jump on the pump right as the Discord members are starting the "dump." The dump is where the people jumping on the pump after seeing that the coin had gained 3X value in a day started being sold the coin of the Discord members, who were now raking in their profits. The skyrocketing price reaches its peak and starts to fall. Some investors will say it was just a small correction in the price before it would continue shooting up "to the moon." They will only see their investment continue to drop in value. Those who invested at the 3X price, expecting it to rise to a 30X price, are now left with a coin worth only 1/3 of what they paid for it. This is how the game works. Stealing from the suckers, turning a $100 investment into a $200 profit, and then turning around and doing the same thing again.

This is not to say that there is no risk for the pump-and-dumpers. It is indeed like gambling because the pump does not always work. The members are not always successful in convincing the average joes surfing Reddit to invest in their coin – if a batch has gotten burned enough times, they will turn away, and leave the pumpers waiting for the next batch to crop up. In these cases, pumpers have to turn on each other. Those who pull out fast enough can recoup their investment. Those who do not will take a loss on the coin. But there is always a next coin coming down the pike where one can earn it all back. Part of the fun is not just bringing in a profit: it is the comradery of being a member of this group where you could pull one over people, like information age street hustlers. One can make friends with a bunch of anonymous figures on the Internet, work together to pull off a heist, and then laugh about how big their profits were for a "day's work."

The Ethics of the Crypto Pump-and-Dump

Though I am a crypto investor, I did not directly participate in a pump-and-dump scheme, though I was, for several months in early 2021, a member of several pump-and-dump Discord channels and I would frequently participate in discussions held on these boards. I even recommended a coin once for a pump-and-dump that the group selected. These groups were intriguing not just because of what they do but because of how they are structured: with named leadership that had little actual control in a democratic system of suggesting and voting, but nonetheless held considerable sway over the decisions of the other group members. Many of the members fell that they have a righteous justification for their actions as a member of the group. As one anonymous member of a Reddit group posted,

We have all been inoculated with the power to change our future for the better. Something that has been inherently taken from us in one form of another over the past year. Yet, while we sit at home or at work, we watch our world burn, our jobs taken, our freedoms slashed. We hear our governments rationalize with us as to why they need more money from us and decide which businesses need to close. While behind a thinly veiled curtain, they pump cash to the wealthiest, greed ridden corporations, and financial institutions all over the world.

At some point, though, it becomes evident what these pump-and-dump schemes really were: theft in broad daylight – a pyramid scheme, a con, a hustle, a crime. And this theft is not perpetrated against some wealthy banker in all likelihood, it is perpetrated against other common people who are looking to make a profit on a promising crypto coin. This seems antithetical to what the WallStreetBets/GameStop traders claimed as their mission, that they were fighting back against the millionaire and billionaire hedge fund managers who were destroying companies and other investors with their own brand of market manipulation. That is not what is being done with the pump-and-dump schemes. It is all about the profit and, while the group members often justify their actions, like in the example above, by suggesting that it is necessary to fight against a financial system that is rigged against them, that is not actually what they were doing – they are not fighting against the financial system, they are stealing from one another.

One time, I posted a comment in one of the chats about the ethics of the pump-and-dump approach, "if we know the price is going to drop, then we know someone must be losing money. Can we actually feel okay about the fact that we are making money by tricking others and taking it from them?" These types of questions never really appeal to the group, though. The philosophy is reserved for a few members/ leaders who will ramble about it from time-to-time in order to motivate people – not unlike a football coach yelling at their players – but the average pump-and-dump investor seemingly has a fairly simple investing-mind, one that is trained to seek out the next opportunity to produce a profit. Some might say, "I'm investing my last $100," not realizing – or perhaps not caring – that another person saying the same thing just lost their last $100 as a victim to the scheme. Others will argue, "crypto pump-and-dumps aren't illegal," completely avoiding the true point of the question.

Nonetheless, there is a fair number of people who agree with my stance. There are "more ethical" groups that emerged that are "pump-and-hold" rather than pump-and-dump. The pump-and-hold name is a bit of a misnomer. These groups aim to create a pump that will inflate the price of a coin, but then only sell off about 25% of their coin at the inflated price, hoping that the overall price of the coin will drop only a little and then stabilize at a new elevated level, at which point they can sell off the remainder of the coin without feeling that they were swindling people. For instance, one might buy Stellar at $0.23, inflate the price to $0.71, sell off 25% of their balance at this profit level, have the price drop to $0.57 and then stabilize, at which point they can sell off a good chunk of their remaining bounty. These pump-and-hold schemes are perhaps not actually ethically superior to the pump-and-dump ones, but they do make the members of these groups feel better about their actions, which is all that is important, pragmatically, for these schemes to continue.

A lesser (perhaps) ethical concern is the use of the ill-gotten funds by some members of the group. Crypto is the currency of choice for many of the hidden services available on the "dark web." Much like with crypto, there is positive potential with the dark web, certainly for privacy purposes, but the idea of members advertising their use of their profits on illegal services, on purchasing pornography, etc. on these forums with no rebuke seems problematic, if expected.

THE LEGALITY OF PUMP-AND-DUMP SCHEMES

The legality of pump-and-dump operations can vary from country to country (Siering, 2019). In most developed countries it is prohibited to participate in these schemes, though it is difficult to police. Authorities would need to uncover the identities of members of pump-and-dump groups and then also supply evidence that they actually participated in the scheme. One of the most notable cases where participants in a pump-and-dump scheme were prosecuted was the Enron scandal at the start of the 21st century. In this case, major investors and executives in the company participated in inflating the stock price of Enron and then selling off their shares before the price cratered. At the end of the year 2000, the average price for a share of Enron stock was over $80. By the Fall of 2001, the average price was under $1. The fraud perpetrated to sustain this operation was discovered by authorities in late 2001 (Chambers, 2002). Because of the bureaucracy in place within the large organization, there was a substantial trail of evidence. This type of trail is less evident in the case of the cryptocurrency pump-and-dump, as the communication is more decentralized and the target (cryptocurrency instead of stocks) is far less regulated.

In the United States, there are several laws related to securities fraud that have been used to prosecute pump-and-dump schemes. The Securities Act of 1933 and the Securities Exchange Act of 1934 allow the Securities Exchange Commission to prosecute any attempts to defraud or manipulate market securities. "Securities" here tends to be the key word that cryptocurrency pump-and-dumpers use to justify the legalities of their schemes. A security is just a representation of an ownership/position, while cryptocurrency not representative of a physical ownership in anything. There have not really been any specific laws passed to regulate the cryptocurrency-type markets that trade a real commodity but do so at a rapid rate like a stock exchange.

According to Strickler (2021), the type of activity that occurred with the GameStop saga and other pump and dump schemes could qualify as price manipulation under the Securities Exchange Act of 1934, where manipulation is defined as, "a series of transactions to induce the purchase or sale of a security by others" (para. 3). However, Strickler concludes that there is likely insufficient evidence to prosecute the GameStop investors under the current law, since the law was designed to protect individuals from institutions (not the other way around) and there is little evidence that the investors intended to deceive anyone (the did the pump but were very clear and open about it). The case is somewhat different for crypto pump and dumpers, since they do intend to deceive. However, the existing law is still too ambiguous to adequately address the prosecution of crypto pump and dumpers to where crackdowns are feasible. Nations that want to pursue enforcement must consider enacting specific legislation that addresses the unique asset that is cryptocurrency.

CONCLUSION

In many ways, the democratization of online investing has been a tremendous boon to the average person. A low-wage worker can download an app like Binance or Robinhood and invest just a few dollars in a high-risk/high-reward crypto token that may, within days, double or triple in value. However, this type of investment is not really investing at all. It is not much more than gambling – selecting a coin and hoping that its price will jump (Liu & Tsyvinski, 2018). In trying to gain an advantage in this system by jumping on a supposedly "hot" coin, many investors are losing non-trivial amounts of money as victims to a culture of pump-and-dump schemers.

While it would be easy to write-off the schemers as common con-artists, it is evident that beyond the scheming, participation in these groups is a point of social connection. There is a sense of freedom in the level of anonymity that can be attained on the social media sites like Reddit and Discord, and the idea of democratically participating in the system of debating, selecting, and promoting a coin, while also pocketing a profit, is intriguing to many. They have a sense of morality, but it is a sense of morality that may not be too distinct from that of a street criminal, that it is okay to engage in these schemes because you have been economically repressed. That one can connect with others that feel the same way, and together earn a considerable profit, is liberating. After all, are they not simply doing the same types of things that Wall Street investors do every day, at much higher levels and too much greater harm? That was the whole idea behind the GameStop and WallStreetBets saga: major hedge funds had bet on and were working to accelerate the company (and its investors') demise, but the common man took notice and fought back, making the hedge funds pay dearly. However, the difference between the GameStop saga and the pump-and-dump crypto schemes is that the latter targets the average man, not the billion dollar hedge funds. It turns the romantic, robin hood-esque idea of taking from the rich and giving to the poor into a perversion where the poor are simply taking from the more-oblivious poor.

The truly fascinating aspect of this saga is that it is difficult to ever stop the cycle of pump-and-dumps from continuing. Participants utilize a number of fake accounts, messages among pump-and-dump groups occur on private channels, and the objects of the exchange were purposely designed to preserve anonymity as they are exchanged. As long as there are suckers who think they can "get rich quick" off of crypto, there will be groups that will take advantage of them. Nonetheless, the illegality of these schemes, and the severe penalties handed out for past pump-and-dump offenses, should serve as a warning to those who would consider participating in one. Awareness of these schemes and investment/financial literacy for new crypto investors, as well as appeals to the morals of these schemers, can make a quick, tangible impact. While cryptocurrency has exciting potential and investing in these coins in a marketplace can be a fun and profitable activity, these bad actors threaten to cause irreparable harm to the legitimacy of the crypto ecosystem in the eyes of the public.

REFERENCES

Bachynskyy, T., & Radeiko, R. (2019). Legal regulations of blockchain and cryptocurrency in Ukraine. *Hungarian Journal of Legal Studies, 60*(1), 3–17. doi:10.1556/2052.2019.60102

Chambers, D. (2002). Enron the symptom, not the disease. *The Public, 2*(2). https://web.archive.org/web/20060622102124/http://publici.ucimc.org/mar2002/32002_7.htm

Corbet, S., Cumming, D. J., Lucey, B. M., Peat, M., & Vigne, S. A. (2020). The destabilizing effects of cryptocurrency cybercriminality. *Economics Letters, 191*, 108741. Advance online publication. doi:10.1016/j.econlet.2019.108741

Cvetkova, I. (2018). Cryptocurrencies legal regulation. *BRICS Law Journal, 5*(2), 128–153. doi:10.21684/2412-2343-2018-5-2-128-153

Drozd, O., Lazur, Y., & Serbin, R. (2017). Theoretical and legal perspective on certain tyes of legal liability in cryptocurrency relations. *Baltic Journal of Economic Studies, 3*(5), 221–228. doi:10.30525/2256-0742/2017-3-5-221-228

Grabowski, M. (2019). *Cryptocurrencies: A primer on digital money*. Routledge. doi:10.4324/9780429201479

Inozemtsev, M. I. (2020). Digital assets in the United States: Legal aspects. *Lecture Notes in Networks and Systems, 139*, 514–522. doi:10.1007/978-3-030-53277-2_61

Kamps, J., & Kleinburg, B. (2018). To the moon: Defining and detecting cryptocurrency pump-and-dumps. *Crime Science, 7*(1), 18. doi:10.118640163-018-0093-5

Khatri, Y. (2020). *Binance has begun to block U.S. users from accessing its exchange platform*. Retrieved from https://www.theblockcrypto.com/post/84020/binance-blocking-us-users-exchange-email-2

Kumar, R. (2021). *Is it really possible to completely ban cryptocurrency in India?* Retrieved from https://www.msn.com/en-in/news/other/is-it-really-possible-to-completely-ban-cryptocurrency-in-india-check-experiences-from-other-countries/ar-AARfjiU

Lee, D. K., Guo, L., & Wang, Y. (2018). Cryptocurrency: A new investment opportunity? *Journal of Alternative Investments, 20*(3), 16–40.

Liu, Y., & Tsyvinski, A. (2018). *Risks and returns of cryptocurrency* (Working paper 24877). National Bureau of Economic Research.

Mirtaheri, M., Abu-El-Haija, S., Morstatter, F., Ver Sleeg, G., & Galstyan, A. (2019). *Identifying and analyzing cryptocurrency manipulations in social media*. Arxiv Pre-print: 1902.03110. Retrieved from https://arxiv.org/abs/1902.03110

Narayanan, A., Bonneau, J., Felten, E., Miller, A., & Goldfeder, S. (2016). *Bitcoin and cryptocurrency technologies*. Princeton University Press.

Nestertsova-Sobakar, O., Prymachenko, V., Valentyn, L., Bereznyak, V., & Sydorova, E. (2019). Legal approaches to the regulation of cryptocurrency and business ethics of ICO in the European Union. *Journal of Legal, Ethical and Regulatory Issues*, *22*(2), 1–6.

Nizzoli, L., Tardelli, S., Avvenuti, M., Cresci, S., Tesconi, M., & Ferreara, E. (2020). Charting the landscape of online cryptocurrency manipulation. *IEEE Access: Practical Innovations, Open Solutions*, *8*, 113230–113245. doi:10.1109/ACCESS.2020.3003370

Prytula, A., Lutsyk, V., Sviatoshniuk, A., Tkalia, O., & Kalachenkova, K. (2021). Cryptocurrency in transnational offences: Criminal and civil legal aspects. *Amazonia Investiga*, *10*(46), 209–216. doi:10.34069/AI/2021.46.10.21

Siering, M. (2019). The economics of stock touting during Internet-based pump-and-dump campaigns. *Information Systems Journal*, *29*(2), 456–483. doi:10.1111/isj.12216

Strickler, T. (2021, September 22). Game on: GameStop, market manipulation, and its implications. *Kentucky Law Journal Online*. Retrieved from https://www.kentuckylawjournal.org/blog/game-on-gamestop-market-manipulation-and-its-implications

Tillman, R. H., & Indergaard, M. L. (2005). *Pump and dump: The rancid rules of the new economy*. Rutgers University Press.

United States' Congress. (1934). Securities Act of 1934, 15 U.S.C. 77a-77mm 1934.

Vishwakarma, P., Khan, Z., & Jain, T. (2018). Cryptocurrency, security issues and upcoming challenges to legal framework in India. *International Research Journal of Engineering and Technology*, *5*(1), 212–215.

Xu, J., & Livshits, B. (2020). The anatomy of a cryptocurrency pump-and-dump scheme. *Proceedings of the 28th USENIX Security Symposium*. Retrieved from https://www.usenix.org/conference/usenixsecurity19/presentation/xu-jiahua

Chapter 13
Considerations for Blockchain–Based Online Dispute Resolution

Madhvendra Singh
Ministry of External Affairs, India

Nitya Jain
Panag and Babu Law Office, India

ABSTRACT

Blockchain is an indestructible ledger technology with a permanent digital footprint which is bringing about disruptions in almost every aspect of life. Since its inception, blockchain was deployed to eliminate human cost and effort and bring in decentralisation of power and control. With the overburdening of cases in national court systems, alternate dispute resolution is today the preferred mechanism for resolving private commercial disputes, outside of courts, especially arbitration. Resolution of commercial disputes plays a major role in the economic growth of any nation. Success of any system calls for a comprehensive approach consisting of five building blocks: the legal basis, the organisational setup, human excellence, communications, and management of change. It is also a hypothesis that the courts in the future will be more like a service rather than a location, with courtrooms being online/virtual, and customer-centric providers leading the market space. Resolution of commercial disputes will become more competitive and differentiated on the international front.

INTRODUCTION

Emergence of Online Dispute Resolution as a Mechanism for Resolving Disputes

Today, Online Dispute Resolution (ODR) has emerged as a preferred form of dispute resolution that utilizes technology and the internet. Initially, ODR programs were focused on relatively small claims and

DOI: 10.4018/978-1-7998-8641-9.ch013

simpler issues. With rapid innovation in the virtual spectrum, ODR is now being applied to large-scale disputes, where participants can conduct the proceedings online through video conferencing platforms like Zoom, Google, Microsoft, and Cisco, which have tailormade suites to meet the requirements of its category of customers. They use real time transcription, break out rooms, document management with OCR search, online document forensics and cloud services for ease of access. They now ensure GDPR compliance, conduct statistical audits and execute digital payments, for which they now have integrated technology suites bringing together blockchain, artificial intelligence, smart contracts, and cloud servers.

ODR has no standard description. Several use the word only to apply to private conflict settlement structures, while others provide courtroom technologies, such as e-filing case management applications, video conferencing and electronic record production as permitted by the UNCITRAL Arbitration Rules. In its 2017 Technical Notes, The United Nations Commission on International Trade Law (UNCITRAL), described ODR as follows:

ODR encompasses a broad range of approaches and forms (including but not limited to ombudsmen, complaints boards, negotiation, conciliation, mediation, facilitated settlement, arbitration and others), and the potential for hybrid processes comprising both online and offline elements. As such, ODR represents significant opportunities for access to dispute resolution by buyers and sellers concluding cross-border commercial transactions, both in developed and developing countries (UNCITRAL, 2017).

In brief, ODR methods, its templates and implementations differ widely, but they all use innovative technologies to achieve more effective dispute resolution. Today, most arbitral institutions aim to implement strategies for greater cost and time efficiencies in arbitration and virtual evidencing, and hearings are increasingly preferred. The onset of COVID-19 pandemic and social distancing measures have resulted in physical court systems to function at sub-optimal capacities. ODR has magically emerged just at the right time as the panacea for the problems that were being faced by the clients seeking efficient resolution of their commercial disputes.

Owing to the need for secure storage of data and saving time and cost, blockchain started to emerge as a technology in 1991. It came to be known as a credible solution after the publication of white paper on Bitcoin by Satoshi Nakamoto (Nakamoto, 2008) in 2008 (Anderson, 2018). It is deemed to be the most groundbreaking technologies that will fundamentally reshape how we live, work, and interact. Blockchain technology has today helped form a safe, secure, and automated platform for exchange of data and money.

Blockchain can be described as a peer-to-peer network of computers, encrypted and decentralized ledger systems for sharing data (Döngel, 2020). It stores data in immutable records, called blocks that are chained together. It can be portrayed as an interlinked platform that maintains accounts wherein the blocks are interconnected and encrypted to safeguard the security and privacy of data in the blocks. Essentially, blockchain is used to eliminate the need of a third-party intermediary by forming a distributed and verifiable data system (Aayog, 2020). It creates a universal database which is present and spread across the computers of all users, called as nodes. No individual node can alter or change this database until it gets consensus and approval from all other nodes in that network (Weinstein et al., 2019, pp. 1-17). Each user or node has its own copy of the data and if one node changes its local copy, the other nodes can reject it. This makes a blockchain system virtually hack- proof or impossible to corrupt the information stored as that would need hacking all connected computers at simultaneously. It can be used for vast purposes including banking, sales, management of information, collecting evidence etc.

Blockchain is premised on certain principal characteristics that result in synchronized and decentralized construction of an immutable and anonymous database of transactions (Valentina et al., 2018).

Blockchain however suffers from low efficiency, and that is the reason it isn't implemented widely except for the cryptocurrency trade. As an example, the number of transactions performed by Bitcoin is smaller than 6, whereas, PayPal and Visa performs 193 and 1,667 transactions per second respectively. The efficiency could be increased by utilizing relay network, directed acrylic graph, increasing block-size, witness segregation, cross-chain swap, side-chain, state-channel as in the lightening network for Bitcoin, and transactions information compression technique like Mimblewimble. Private or consortium blockchains can bypass efficiency bottlenecks as compared to the public blockchains.

The advantages of decentralisation by Blockchain are largely weighed down due to concerns of efficiency, privacy, reversibility, certainty, scalability and overnance. The cost of these concerns can be mitigated from the way the blockchain is implemented. Though in many cases, these costs can be completely eliminated, it is unlikely for others. One important concern with respect to the implementation of blockchain is the paradox of privacy vs transparency. Most blockchain based consensus protocols necessitate a considerable amount of transparency for ledger contents and a possible trade - off with the user's privacy. If a validating node cannot monitor the balance of an account or the internal state of a smart contract, it would be hard for the node to check if the account is overspent or even how the smart contract can respond when invoked. Person participants' level of data access varies as well. Both users in permissionless blockchains, such as Ethereum, may view all details. In permissioned blockchains, only validators have this extent of access, and some are limited by organisation or by function.

Online Dispute Resolution as a Service

Advantages of using disruptive technologies like AI or blockchain in dispute resolution mechanisms are multifold. For instance, blockchain is a stable framework on which smart contracts are executed. This makes the contracts more reliable and business relationships more stable. Again, it is almost impossible to hack a blockchain network, so transactions and disputes related data are secure and highly confidential. The process of adjudication using AI is free from discrimination as a machine cannot hold biases or cannot differentiate unless the algorithm itself commands so. In this context the objectivity of AI upholds the value of due process. AI can assist perfectly in long term project work. For example - Construction contracts are based on a series of sub-contracts, and smart contracts can help in managing the chain. Further, the novel concept of settlement averages, proposed by Madhvendra Singh, has been proven quite beneficial for counsels (Singh, 2020). The settlement averages tool helps estimate the probability of success in any arbitration or litigation, based on previous data and interpretation of facts. It can also predict on what amount the parties should settle. This can save a lot of cost, effort and time of both parties and counsel. The deployment of AI and blockchain in dispute resolution has been proven beneficial, and innovations in legal tech are on a rapid surge.

Existing Regulatory Framework for Blockchain

One of the major concerns surrounding use of AI & blockchain is the lack of universal regulatory framework. Some scholars suggest that the blockchain technology is in its tender stage and it shouldn't be over regulated as it may result in restricted organic growth (Piers et al., 2018, pp. 283-289). There are only a few scattered national regulations and rules. For instance, recently the UK's Financial Conduct Authority (FCA) circulated important instructions for crypto asset-related businesses. Gibraltar was the first jurisdiction to introduce a purpose-built Distributed Ledger Technology (DLT) regulatory framework which allows a legal record of online ledgers being used. In France, the PACT bill of law, voted on April 11, 2019, looks over a new framework for Initial Coin Offerings (ICOs) and Digital Assets Service Providers (DASP). These technologies engage in virtual assets and currencies on behalf of their clients. In 2019, Switzerland issued a draft bill that includes three crypto-friendly initiatives, and the government has been developing a systematic blockchain policy. The regulations are mostly in their formative stage. Presently, there are no signs of an international convention that may direct the future of blockchain technology.

However, the lack of a regulatory framework has not impeded the thriving usage of blockchain in multiple spheres. Blockchain has recently emerged as a viable solution for a wide range of problems apart from just peer to peer ledger keeping and digital cash. Deployment of blockchain technology in ODR is one such example. In November 2019, the UK Jurisdiction Task Force issued its Legal Report on the Position of Cryptoassets and Smart Contracts, which expressed that Cryptoassets are property and the smart contracts are contracts under the English Law. Now UK Jurisdiction is publishing the Digital Dispute Resolution Rules for incorporation into the on-chain digital relationships and smart contracts. They allow for:

1.   Arbitral or expert dispute resolution in very short periods
2.   Arbitrators to implement decisions directly on-chain using a private key
3.   Optional anonymity of the parties

BLOCKCHAIN AND AI IN ARBITRATION: A CREDIBLE MECHANISM

Today it is a celebrated idea that the whole process of arbitration can go online through blockchain and use of AI (Piers et al., 2018, pp. 283-289). Blockchain in arbitration is being used to resolve disputes based on decentralized execution of programmable contracts known as smart contracts. Advantages of using blockchain technology in arbitration are security, transparency and confidentiality. For smoothness and automation, smart contracts include arbitration agreements along with the contractual duties of parties. As soon as there is a breach, smart contracts can take care of services such as issue of notice, formation of neutral arbitral tribunal and compilation of amount in damages and compensation etc. without engagement of any intermediary (Resolution, 2019). By using smart contract technology, parties can allow for a self-executing arbitral award. In such an arrangement, an arbitrator shall act as third party 'oracle' whose course will affect the enforcement of the contract (Consultation, 2019, p. 31). Use of AI and blockchain technology simultaneously can help to form a safe, confidential and automatic platform for arbitral proceedings (Schmelzer, 2020). However, blockchain technology has a limited scope as it can only cover the procedural aspects of the proceedings. The sections below will analyze the application of blockchain and AI in various legs of an arbitration proceeding.

CodeLegit (Reuter, 2017) has proposed a Blockchain Library that can be embedded in the Smart Contract code. It has also proposed Blockchain Arbitration Rules to which parties will consent in their legal agreement. The Blockchain Arbitration would merge the capabilities of Smart Contracts with the advantages of arbitration. When incorporated into the Smart Contract, the Blockchain Library will be used as emergency halt in the event that a conflict occurs between the parties and they decide to take it to court. When triggered, the library would halt the Smart Contract's execution and give the parties time to settle their disagreement. The calling function would be *#pauseAndSendToArbitrator()*.

Figure 1. The execution of CodeLegit arbitration library

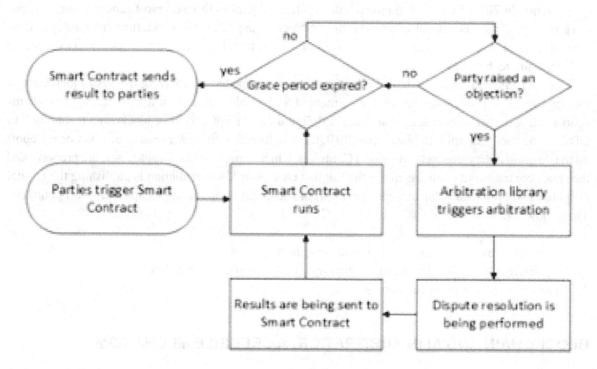

The code execution can be described as follows:

1.   The contract or the agreement between two or more parties is executed on a smart contract that utilises the Codelegit Library inserted in the arbitration clause of the contract,
2.   This library is triggered on the breach of the contract as also if a party feels the Smart Contract code is not running correctly,
3.   The performance is halted and execution suspended,
4. The Smart Contract starts the proceedings, and a message is sent to Codelegit for appointment of arbitral Tribunal.

Beginning the Arbitration – Appointment, Submissions and Pleadings

Parties in litigation or arbitration, exchange pleadings via email and most communications from courts and arbitrators are in electronic form. Testimonies and arguments in a hearing are routinely tracked via software that promptly transcribes what the counsel, witness, and arbitrator are saying. So, using technology and the internet is not a novel phenomenon in dispute resolution. Taking it one step higher, blockchain and AI are also being used in various legs of the arbitration process. Some of the examples are - the use of big data for discovery, easy document management, document forensics, enabling access to information instantaneously like summons /e-discovery, witness determination with less human intervention etc. The next section discusses the intertwining of blockchain and ODR and its impact on the whole arbitral procedure.

- Notice of Arbitration

The foremost step that initiates the arbitration proceedings is the notice that initiating party sends to the other. In offline arbitrations, the notice of arbitration is sent out via hard copy or sometimes by e-mail. When parties are operating on a smart contract, as soon as the dispute arises, the arbitration agreement/ clause/ code is triggered and the notice or the submission agreement is transferred on the blockchain itself, creating a permanent record of it. On the other hand, if the parties are not operating under a smart contract, generally the claimant may create a simple blockchain network which would be accessible to all the stakeholders in arbitration. The notice can be provided to parties using this platform.

- Appointment of the Arbitral Tribunal

The second stage is the appointment of an Arbitral Tribunal. AI can aid in appointing and assisting the Arbitrator. Through classification and analysis of available data, AI can suggest who can be the best adjudicator for resolving disputes of a specific nature. For this, history of case laws, outcomes, specialization, availability of an arbitrator can be looked upon (Paisley & Sussman 2018). *Jus Mundi* is one such international platform that offers AI powered legal search, due diligence and a diverse pool of arbitrators. These platforms reduce privacy concerns, increase accountability, and foster diversity in arbitrator selection by making key information about arbitrators' past decision are made available via the publication of AI Reports. For an arbitrator, AI can help in deciding disputes by providing auto-generated briefs or reviewing a large number of documents presented by the parties, and telling which document is relevant and in which sequence (predictive coding) (Westgaver & Turner 2020). Further, the tribunal is also the part of the blockchain setup, so when all the documents are exchanged by the parties, they are shared to all the stakeholders including the arbitrators. The reference terms defined among the parties can be programmed to become self-executing smart legal contracts that will be eventually resolved as and when the documents are filed and the witness statements are exchanged. Essentially this will eliminate the need of a third party and will help in assisting the arbitrator. AI can also help arbitrators in doing case management and streamlining the process of arbitration. For example, AI can check the availability of an arbitrator, manage time and cost of award etc. Further AI can also be used to check the validity of an award by looking at facts and legal mandates governing the disputes by using special algorithms (Bhattacharya, 2019).

- Pleadings and Submissions

The pleadings including the. statement of claim, statement of defense, counterclaim, reply to counterclaim, and further submissions can be uploaded to the blockchain and are therein they are automatically served upon the parties and the tribunal and accordingly acknowledgement is automatically generated (Piers et al., 2018, pp. 283-289). The documents can be sorted and meaningful briefs can be generated by use of AI for the better understanding of the tribunal. Keyword searches and cross references can be easily generated and hyperlinked for ease of access and bringing in coherence in the documents.

- Taking of Evidence

Evidence is a very critical aspect of any kind of dispute; governing the collection of evidence and determination of evidence are necessary components of both national and international commercial arbitration. Each arbitrator is supposed to be acquainted with the law regulating the proof, the *lex loci arbitri* and its background. In a blockchain and AI based arbitration, the evidence taking process is quite intriguing. Various technologies and novel techniques can be employed to make evidence taking smoother and quicker. In a blockchain dispute resolution process, smart contract conflicts can include proof of proprietary software and/or hardware. The idea that parties will want to ensure confidentiality of their disagreements would encourage the parties to restrict their disclosure and make their anonymous details available. Notably, one can't alter facts documented on a blockchain. Further, a blockchain can also act as a central award server, which can promote attempts to identify and implement the decision of the dispute (Argerich et al., 2020). For instance, parties should submit papers and presentations electronically, and they are immediately sent to all stakeholders., possibly on a blockchain (Piers et al., 2018, pp. 283-289). In a blockchain based dispute resolution platform, once the evidence exchanged is uploaded on the blockchain, they are immutable and accessible to all stakeholders. (Piers et al., 2018, pp. 283-289). Further, AI can be used for the document forensics and scientific detective work together to find cases of theft and statistical mismatch. Witness conferencing, cross-examination, and oral testimony taking can both be performed conveniently using integrated video conferencing suites, or even though trials are done manually, they can also be transmitted on blockchain and stored for procedural integrity. (Piers et al., 2018, pp. 283-289). Further, all oral submissions get transcribed in real time and are available to the counsel during witness cross examination, which enhances time efficiency and reduces costs in arbitration hearings. AI with gesture recognition tools can advise the counsel if a witness is lying. These gesture recognition tools are deep learning algorithms that are trained to identify and correlate meaningful gestures from a pre-built library of 'gestures' (Simon, 2021). Moreover, there is no scope of manipulating or contradicting anything stated during gathering of evidence or witness examination as a blockchain is immutable, the chances of evidence tampering are minimal (Piers et al., 2018, pp. 283-289).

- Enforcement and Challenges of Awards and Interim Measures

After the exchange of documents and presentation of pleadings, the next stage in an arbitration proceeding is either seeking interim measures or enforcement in case the award is rendered. The foremost question that pops up in case of a blockchain based arbitration is – whether the agreement itself is enforceable under the New York Convention (NYC) (Convention on Recognition and Enforcement of Foreign Awards, 1958). In that regard, blockchain based arbitration can be categorized as, i.e., on-chain arbitrations and off-chain arbitrations.

In case of an On-chain arbitration, an arbitral award is automatically executed by a smart contract without the involvement of a third party. It works on the "if-then" command wherein as soon as the "if" condition of the dispute is fulfilled, the "then" condition executes the award. As a result of the automatic execution, the need of enforcement is eliminated (Argerich et al., 2020). As and when the award is rendered, the funds (often virtual currencies) are conveyed to the winning party. As the assets are already transferred, there arises no need for examination via an enforcement process. This process removes the dependence on the State or judiciary for enforcement of awards and allows for automatic and self-enforceable arbitration awards (Gencosmanoglu, 2020). However, this kind of process is unfit for complicated contracts. Where contracts contain multiple parties, various clauses and subjective conditions, the on – chain algorithm might not be that effective to conclude a fair outcome.

Enforcement of an Off-chain arbitration award is a bit more complex. Herein, the execution is not automatic, and parties have to present themselves before a tribunal or jury, as explained in the case Kleros or Juris. Herein the award is rendered using the game theory tactics and by incentivizing the Jurors using crypto tokens.

- The issues under the New York Convention

Art II of the NYC primarily dictates the validity and arbitrability of an arbitration agreement. It reads –

"1. Each Contracting State shall recognize an agreement in writing under which the parties undertake to submit to arbitration all or any differences which have arisen, or which may arise between them in respect of a defined legal relationship, whether contractual or not, concerning a subject matter capable of settlement by arbitration.

2. The term "agreement in writing" shall include an arbitral clause in a contract or an arbitration agreement, signed by the parties or contained in an exchange of letters or telegrams.

3. The court of a Contracting State, when seized of an action in a matter in respect of which the parties have made an agreement within the meaning of this article, shall, at the request of one of the parties, refer the parties to arbitration, unless it finds that the said agreement is null and void, inoperative or incapable of being performed." (Convention on Recognition and Enforcement of Foreign Awards, 1958).

Art II (2) states the need for the arbitration agreement to be in writing and the scope is limited to telegrams or letters. In a blockchain based arbitration, the arbitration agreement is nothing, but codes exchanged in an electronic form. So, if strictly interpreted, electronically exchanged arbitration agreements fall outside the scope of Art II (2). This issue was discussed and clarified by the 2006 UNCITRAL recommendations wherein it was stated that an interpretative reorientation of the Art II should include exchange via electronic means (Paulsson, 2020). In any case as per Art 31 of the Vienna Convention on Law of Treaties, (The United Nations, 1969) a treaty should be interpreted in consonance with its object and purpose. The objective of the NYC is to facilitate arbitration proceedings and eventual enforcement. In the modern world usage of telegram is outdated, most document exchange takes place electronically. If a liberal interpretation is not adopted and modern trade practices are not taken into account, the treaty will not be in coordination with its principal objective. An interpretative reorientation opens opportunities for blockchain based arbitrations agreements to be included in the ambit of the Art II of the New York Convention.

In any case, the electronic equivalence for written agreements and awards becomes feasible when the purpose behind the particular form requirement is observed – which was to produce legible information. This is the approach chosen by Article 6(1) of the 1996 UNCITRAL Model Law on Electronic Commerce (EC-ML) and Article 9(2) of the 2005 UN Convention on the Use of Electronic Communications in International Contracts (Electronic Communications Convention). As per these provisions, the requirement of written form set out by law is satisfied by a data message if the information stored within is available and functional for reference purposes (UNCITRAL Model Law on Electronic Commerce, 1996). These provisions highlight the intent behind any 'in writing' requirement, it is simply to produce legible information, and in that case original documents available in the form of secure blocks can surely be used.

Article IV of the NYC requires that copies of the arbitration agreement and awards must be certified, and signatures authenticated for the purpose of enforcement (Convention on Recognition and Enforcement of Foreign Awards, 1958). In this case using Blockchain based arbitration is extremely beneficial. In a blockchain based arbitration, all the documents are stored in a permanent ledger and are accessible to all the stakeholders. So, it is possible for the parties and the arbitrators to access the original documents at the time of enforcement. Also, as the data is authentic, there is no need of duly certified copies and signatures. This saves the parties from technical fusses that submitting certified copies entails under Art IV (Gencosmanoglu, 2020).

- The Form and Method of Award

Article IV (1)(a) NYC requires that *'[t]he duly authenticated original award or a duly certified copy thereof' be supplied to court with the application for its recognition and enforcement'* (Convention on Recognition and Enforcement of Foreign Awards, 1958). In case of blockchain based dispute resolution platforms, the question is not only of the 'form' in which the award will be rendered, but also about how the Jurors have reached that award. The functioning of the Jurors is based on crypto incentives. However, the incentives work in a way that the decision rendered by a single arbitrator has to be in consonance with the decision of the majority. Forcing arbitrators to predict the outcome of other arbitrators and agree for the plurality, even though the arbitrator believes the award may be different, is often troublesome. This is also in conflict with notion of impartiality that Blockchain based arbitrations ensue. It could also raise difficulties at the stage of enforcement of the award in case of off chain arbitrations (Szczudlik, 2020). Again, the form in which the award is produced is in conflict with the age old treaties – the NYC and UNCITRAL Model law.

Overall, opting out of State regulations, as in escaping enforcement because of automatic execution can also be problematic. One the primary difficulty that seems to arise from adoption of blockchain in international arbitration is the concept of 'Stateless justice'. Even though the major objective of arbitration is party autonomy over process and least involvement of state entities, the fundamental integrity in enforcing justice that the state plays in international arbitration cannot be ignored (Firmin, 2020). So, legitimacy which state provides seems to be lost in blockchain with individual parties taking enforcement into their own hands. This could be seen as undermining the international accords (Ast, 2017).

Conclusively, whilst enforcement in case of an on-chain arbitration is not an issue, off-chain arbitrations are uncertain. The application of the NYC is unclear regarding the automated enforcement of blockchain based arbitral awards. More so, the position of 'State' in a blockchain based arbitration is also ambiguous. It is high time for UNCITRAL to issue guidelines for blockchain based arbitrations and its enforcement.

BLOCKCHAIN BASED ODR PLATFORMS

Numerous Blockchain based ODR Platforms have taken the Blockchain & AI based arbitral proceeding to the next level. Most of these platforms use cryptocurrency as an incentive and often result in fast and fair outcomes. For instance, *Kleros*, launched in 2018, is a next-gen, quasi-judicial platform that transcends the boundaries of traditional dispute resolution. It is a smart-contract based dispute resolution system for disputed transactions and agreements between parties. It is a very good example of how all the limbs of an arbitration proceeding can efficiently function online. *Kleros* is based on crowdsourcing which means that it uses the wisdom of the crowds and game theory, and is often paralleled to a traditional Jury system (Ast, 2017).

For instance, a person is hired for a job, and the employer and employee use a smart contract to seal the deal. They also choose *Kleros* as the dispute resolution protocol for their contract. Now, the funds are locked in the contract, and upon the emergence of a dispute, the *Kleros* arbitration process will kick start. Primarily a tribunal will be formed randomly from a pool of crowd sourced jurors. Then the details of the parties and the dispute will be sent to the jurors. Post this, the jurors vote on the case and when the vote is counted, the party with the majority votes is considered the winner. Based on these results, the smart contract is executed, and funds are transferred to the winning party. Overall, it offers a rights-based dispute resolution process, which results in a binary, dichotomous resolution in favor of one party and against the other (Eniy & Katsch, 2019).

The principles on which *Kleros* stands, resonates with the core principles of blockchain technology i.e. decentralized and fair dispute resolution, with a quick and automatic enforcement of award Eniy & Katsch, 2019). *Kleros* also has an appeals mechanism, which uplifts integrity of the platform. Another example of a quasi-judicial dispute resolution system is *Juris*, that was launched in 2019. It is a blockchain based dispute resolution platform that operates on smart contracts and is powered by human mediators and arbitrators globally. The judgment that is rendered is binding and enforceable. When the jurists pronounce their judgment, the contract is automatically modified and currency tokens are transferred to the winning party (Kerpelman, 2018). Another striking feature of these quasi-judicial blockchain based platforms is the automatic selection of arbitrators that entails independence and impartiality. Taking the example of *Kleros*, it deploys blockchain technology to guarantee transparency and fairness in the selection process of the arbitrators, called jurors. The game theory mechanics are used to predicate on important concepts, and their very own *Pinakion* (PNK) token structures the incentive model for jurors to act independently and carefully within the system. The jurors that vote with the majority of jurors – receive part of the arbitration fee and Jurors who don't vote with the majority – have part of their staked PNK transferred to jurors who did. To change the outcome of a court decision and attacker would have to bribe more than 50% of token holders or buy more than 50% of supply. Lastly by conducting the attack also devalue the token significantly (Paisley & Sussman 2018).

Further, the appellate mechanism ensures impartiality as each new appeal has twice the number of original jurors plus one, so the appeal fees rise exponentially and deter users from endlessly appealing or bribing jurors because the cost is too high as more appeals increase (Piers et al., 2018, pp. 283-289). Furthermore, only when both jurors have voted and their ballots have been confirmed would the votes become transparent, such that jurors can not manipulate or be swayed by the actions of other jurors. Similarly, Juris also enshrines the principles of transparency and fairness while the appointment and workings of the jurors. Juris appoints anonymous jurors to resolve a case, who are incentivized using its own crypto currency called JRS Tokens. Juris goes a step ahead in advancing the parties' needs and distributes the jurors into 3 categories - high jurists, good standing jurists and novice jurists, based on quality of their decision making. In case, the parties need a fast track solution, a group of anonymous jurors also provide legal opinion (Piers et al., 2018, pp. 283-289).

EFFICIENCY AND SECURITY OF BLOCKCHAIN SYSTEMS

Despite its pitfalls, blockchain is regarded as the best method of storing data since each block is mirrored and validated with the agreement of all stakeholders. Since there is no other person involved, no network administrator or boss, the risk of data breach is insignificant. (Piers et al., 2018, pp. 283-289). Blockchain technology is applauded for its secure, encrypted system which is almost impossible to hack. Blockchain in arbitration proposes to shift from the current cloud based storage system which enables management of large archives of documentations. But the question of the efficiency of blockchain to ensure security and privacy related concerns of translational data persists (UribarriSoares, 2018).

According to the 'impossibility trinity,' no blockchain technology can attain correctness, decentralisation, and cost savings all at the same time (Abadi & Brunnermeier 2018). Though centralised ledgers are correct and cost efficient, the owners can collect monopoly rent and are incentivized to uphold credibility by franchise value. Distributed ledgers, on the other hand, reward nodes that produce blocks. The use of Proof of Work to pick these nodes compromises cost effectiveness. Information transition between forks and miner rivalry may lead to fork competition, which eliminates the monopoly rent issue but introduces inconsistency and ambiguity. If the economic value of blockchain networks grows, so will the number of malicious attacks. The use of public blockchains on a broad scale can be approached with caution. Governments and corporations, on the other hand, have had cheaper data security solutions than public blockchains.

The parties, institutions and arbitrators during an arbitration exchange various information which are sensitive in nature owing to which cyber security is turning out to be a major issue in international arbitration. Parties across jurisdictions communicate through multiple web platforms using various media portals, including unencrypted email. A major chunk of such information with documents move across national borders via an unsecured channel raising issues regarding international data transfers, leading to increased relativity of cyber-attacks (Duprey & Ziadé 2018).

In order to minimize such risks, parties should therefore agree on an acceptable minimum level of security against unauthorized access by third parties. Where parties are willing to use virtual data rooms or a commercial platform for the purposes of data transmission, inquiry should be made by the parties checking whether the service providers are using encrypted databases for secure transmission and storage. The terms and conditions regarding confidentiality and data security should also be checked by the parties and see whether both of them agree to the same (International Chamber of Commerce, 2017).

When data has a personal identity of the user attached to it which may disclose someone's personal information, data protection issues emerge. Transparency of transactions on a blockchain server is also a concerning problem, since it can be incompatible with privacy requirements in some cases. Probable permission problems can occur when using a public blockchain, which may make an individual's personal data available, especially to individuals who may not have access to the data, either inside the territorial limits or across boundaries. Even so, even private blockchains will cause issues with cross-border data transfer and data subjects' rights to rectify. In all cases, the data privacy requirements of legal jurisdictions will be important (Wilson, 2018).

CHALLENGES AND BARRIERS

ODR has been embraced by the legal sector globally. In these dynamic times, especially with the advent of Covid 19 pandemic, ODR seems like the future of dispute resolution. It fulfills its promises of efficiency, security and convenience (Heiskanen, 2017). Today, blockchain and AI have taken ODR to a whole new level with increased confidentiality, stability and ease of work. The questions that remains is, is using blockchain & AI actually that easy and accessible? Are the shortcomings glaring at us right in the face while we celebrate the innovation? If blockchain was so convenient to use, why isn't it widespread yet? The next section will explore some challenges that come with the usage of blockchain and AI for reliable ODR.

- Legal Barriers

Blockchain technology has evolved at a tremendous rate. Its transnational nature, often termed as "terra nullis", has made it hard to regulate. Regulating AI and blockchain is one thing and recognizing award based on AI and blockchain, another. The binding impact of smart contracts varies as per three major factors: the specific use case; the type of smart contract being used; and the law applicable to the contract (Shehata & Partners, 2019). Generally, there are uncertainties on the point if an arbitration agreement written on blockchain is valid or not? This is because law specifically mandates that an arbitration agreement must always be in writing (UNCITRAL, 1958). Similarly, will an award by AI be valid or not, since AI is not a person in the eye of the law (Nelson, 2016); (Franklin 2020). These problems can be mitigated either by creating new conventions to recognize the use of technology in arbitration or by using 'soft laws', like UNCITRAL guidelines, clarifying position on these issues (Argerich & Taquela 2020). The second option seems more practical as the pace by which technology is progressing it is difficult to develop a 'hard law' with same speed. One of the primary difficulties that seems to arise from implementation of blockchain in international arbitration is the concept of 'Stateless justice', that lack the fundamental endorsement by the state.

- Trust Barriers

ODR has become common modern day dispute resolution system. Especially post COVID 19 pandemic, hearings, including cross-examination of witnesses, are streamed live online, with participants participating remotely and a judge observing over computer monitors. There really are no court clerks or transcribers, and the records are produced electronically using speech recognition software. The average person will also watch the trial live on a web stream. (Norton Rose Fulbright, 2017). However, ODR is still not used extensively to its full potential. The primary issue that humans have with ODR and AI is lack of trust and the fear of the unknown. Legal professionals are taking their time in developing reliability on ODR. While ODR techniques are deemed suitable for small scale claims like online shopping disputes, lawyers often avoid using 'too much' technology in larger claims.

Other than trust issues, using ODR becomes sketchy as the place of proceeding and the issue of jurisdiction are often uncertain questions. There is high risk of enforcement being challenged because of virtual evidence taking. Often the party puts authenticity in issue and presses on hard copy evidence taking, which is still perceived to be more reliable as a source. There is a lack of expertise in using technology in the international legal fraternity. Beyond the absence of consistent fair process provisions, another unanswered issue with regards to ODR is compliance of the outcome by the parties, unless the outcome is legally enforceable. At last, there is always a threat of hacking and intrusion, which increases the risk of evidence tampering.

- Expertise and Training of Stakeholders

One of the major restrictions in using this technology is the technological barrier of the parties. For moving to completely automated blockchain technology based dispute resolution, it is required to use sophisticated tools such as algorithm based platforms, crypto currency (if enforcement is also directly through blockchain) etc. This forces the parties who are not comfortable with these sophisticated technologies to opt out of this process.

The limited use of blockchain today is owing to the fact that there exists a lack of expertise and skill. An illustrative situation could be one where two parties are at different levels of business standards and one has a much superior setup to appoint and run these arbitrations through blockchain, while the other suffers due to lack of knowledge on the subject matter. Eventually lack of know-how makes it difficult for it to deal in blockchain and AI compared to dissimilarly situated opposite parties. When the internet was invented in the year 1969, for more than two decades, it had a very limited user base due to required skills and expertise to use the internet. Public awareness was lacking, and to run something like an email required a mastered skill set. With the origination of the World Wide Web in the 1990's, the situation saw a global change, which made internet browsing more convenient for the browsers. Blockchain technology holds a similar future.

Lack of trust, convenience and expertise is a huge hurdle for the use of blockchain. Let alone the issues of thefts, the jargons used in blockchain and AI setups are highly technical, and therefore difficult to understand for the non-experts. There is a real challenge that discourages people by using words like fork, nodes, proof of operation, on-chain and off-chain, hash, DAO, smart contracts, and even blockchain. crypto currencies (Eniy & Katsch, 2019). If this position as stated is true, the blockchain of today as it stands, is less of the internet of the 90's rather the internet of the 70's and 80's.

- Lack of Institutional Framework

Though Blockchain based dispute resolution is on a rise, there is no particular legal framework that may regulate it. There are numerous provisions for ODR but none for blockchain based proceedings. For example the LCIA Arbitration Rules (2014), encourage the parties and arbitral tribunals to conduct the proceedings by any means, including by a telephone conference call, a video-conference, or an exchange of e-communications (London Court of International Arbitration Rules, 2014). Similarly, The AAA Arbitration Rules (2013) also refer to the use of videoconferencing and the arbitrators can also permit the presentation of facts by alternate means such as video conferencing, internet correspondence, telephone conferences, and other methods other than in-person presentation (American Arbitration Association Rules, 2013); (Piers et al., 2018, pp. 283-289).

Regulation of blockchain based arbitration becomes a problem because cyber space is often called the 'terra nullis'. Potential blockchain dispute settlement can include municipal and transnational disputes involving not only private entities and businesses, but also international organisations, states, and other agencies., therefore a universal convention seems like a distant idea for now. Conflict of laws will remain an area of study for some time where blockchain based systems are concerned.

- Competition with Traditional Methods

The greatest barrier that Blockchain and AI based ODR faces is that currently it is far behind the traditional dispute resolution. The users don't trust the new system. Users fear that with this technologically robust system, they will lose control over the process. Smart contracts, for example, circumvent and neglect the legal model, in contrast to standard paper and e-contracts. Their end aim is not judicial enforcement. Instead of hiring attorneys to prepare complex jargon-filled paper papers, parties use technology to draught agreements in code so that there is no doubt over the parties' commitments. Smart contracts, on the other hand, are programming codes that have "if/then" clauses that outline each duty and eventuality. Smart contracts, through auto-enforcement, will improve the efficiency of several types of agreements. (Evans, 2019). This means that smart contracts largely eliminate the need for the complicated and costly means of traditional contract systems. However, this automatic execution might make parties feel that they have been pushed from the driver's seat to back seat.

This might happen because a set of codes cannot comprehend or recreate the human perspective and comprehend the subjectivity that every case entails. For instance, even though *Kira-* a machine learning based contract review tool, can read a contract's clauses, so it cannot ascertain the individual intentions of the user behind the clauses. To a similar extent, *ROSS* – another machine learning based tool, cannot consider the 'human factor' when answering a legal issue. How does online dispute resolution deal with imperfection of lives specifically, dealing with the human emotions and reflexes? For instance, in cases of breach sometimes parties do not want to enforce the breach so as to save the business relationship, but it is impossible for machines to understand this subjective intent. A smart contract will simply enforce the breach and trigger the remedy. Secondly, how do people trust the blockchain ODR system and how are we going to build that trust? For instance, a lawyer client relationship which is essentially based on trust. Can clients still have the same trust based relationship with a machine? Thirdly, there are ethical and security problems, there will also be fear of hacking. Furthermore, if we closely observe smart contracts are not so smart. Eventually, it is humans who have to create a code for smart contracts in the first place. Again, there are problems of time and cost, lack of computer literacy, the issue of training the arbitrators, issues surrounding confidentiality and data protection that make parties go back to their first love – traditional dispute resolution.

Blockchain technology is evolving at a tremendous speed. Every entity wants to use this secure and stable platform to their advantage. Today, blockchain based dispute resolution platforms are not limited to jury-based systems that may be open to all sorts of disputes. Recently, there has been a rise in tailor made blockchain based dispute resolution platforms that entities deploy for resolving specific natured disputes. For instance, as banks and financial institutions indulge in Distributed Ledger Technology (DLT), they encounter unique sets of disputes. In that regard, banks look for robust dispute resolution mechanisms that are settled in advance and adjusted to work efficiently with DLT and can offer a necessary escape valve while ensuring flexibility. In this case, they may set up a permissioned blockchain in which the administrator has the authority to erase or undo transactions. A conflict settlement provision signed by blockchain users would expressly restrict when this capacity can be used, ostensibly restricting it to comply with instructions by an arbitrator. This reduces the likelihood of managers being involved in customer conflicts. (Nortan Rose Fulbright, 2019). Another example can be IBM, which has launched blockchain based smart contracts into the Global Financing Unit and have reported that they have cut 75% of their resolutions with blockchain (Dalton, 2020).

Tailor made dispute resolution mechanism has entered not only the banking or trade sector, but it is also there in finance, construction and blockchain trading itself. With these kinds of innovation and advancements, soon more and more entities may come up with their own versions of dispute resolution mechanisms, cut out for their respective industry and needs.

CONCLUSION

Few drawbacks exist in every evolving technology. The advantages offered by blockchain and AI based dispute resolution mechanism far outweigh the temporary drawbacks. Moreover, technology is the most democratic and decentralized system that removes the biased intervention of third-party humans. There exists numerous solutions and breakthroughs in this spectrum as legal-tech grows at a tremendous rate. There is no need for AI to take over the whole process of adjudication. Blockchain technology is not necessarily here to replace humans, but to assist them. We can use technology where humans are absent, and humans can always be used to verify.

One of the significant but harmless concern is the need for subjectivity in the process of adjudication. Development of neutral networks on psychological profiling of the human brain utilizing contractual models and evolving concepts like explainable AI (XAI) are being explored, and the need for programming commercially subjective tactics is higher than ever. Further, it is about time for law schools to introduce coding and technology in the curriculum and modify the traditional contract learning and to keep up with the changing times. Legal professionals need to be technologically literate, and this is what the clientele demands today.

There is a pressing need for a proper legislation based on working protocols, which is not restricted to national boundaries but is universal. This calls for an international convention that deregulates the use of blockchain and AI in the legal sphere, making it more acceptable. But a full-fledged convention seems like a distant dream, at the moment, given the transnational nature of the blockchain technology, guidelines from UNCITRAL on the usage of blockchain and AI for reliable ODR would be a good place to start.

We must remember that the number of people that use internet in India is 40%, whereas people with access to justice is only 15%. That makes it quite clear that the internet must be used to full potential to provide everyone the easy access to justice. Blockchain and AI are therefore the tools to make justice delivery a service and transport customers at the center stage.

REFERENCES

Aarni, H. (2017). The Technology of Trust: How the Internet of Things and Blockchain Could Usher in a New Era of Construction Productivity. *Construction Research and Innovation, 8*(2), 66–70. doi:10.1080/20450249.2017.1337349

Aayog. (2020). *India report.* Blockchain The India Strategy Part-I.

Adam, J. K. (2018, March 21). *A non-technical overview of the Juris dispute resolution system.* Juris. https://medium.com/jurisproject/a-non-technical-overview-of-the-juris-dispute-resolution-system-62e28eec509d

American Arbitration Association Rules. (2013). *Commercial Including Procedures for Large, Complex Commercial Disputes Arbitration Rules and Mediation Procedures*. Retrieved from https://adr.org/sites/default/files/Commercial%20Rules.pdf

Claire, M. D. W., & Olivia, T. (2020). *Artificial Intelligence, A Driver For Efficiency In International Arbitration – How Predictive Coding Can Change Document Production*. Kluwer Arbitration Blog. http://arbitrationblog.kluwerarbitration.com/2020/02/23/artificial-intelligence-a-driver-for-efficiency-in-international-arbitration-how-predictive-coding-can-change-document-production/

Colin, R. (2017). Designing a Global Online Dispute Resolution System: Lessons Learned from eBay. *University of St. Thomas Law Journal, 13*, 354.

Convention on Recognition and Enforcement of Foreign Awards. (1958). Art. II Para. 1 & 2.

Convention on Recognition and Enforcement of Foreign Awards. (1958). Art IV.

Convention on Recognition and Enforcement of Foreign Awards. (1958). Art. II Para (1 & 2). Delos Dispute Resolution. *Introduction to Blockchain technology*. https://delosdr.org/index.php/2019/09/26/introduction-to-blockchain-smart-contracts/

Convention on Recognition and Enforcement of Foreign Awards. (1958). Art IV(1) (a).

Deren, D. (2020). *Blockchain Technology as Tool against Infringement of Copy Right on Photograph*. Tilburg University. http://arno.uvt.nl/show.cgi?fid=149345

Emily, W. (2018). *Blockchain for Hospitality*. Hospitality Technology Next Generation.

Federico, A. (2017). *A Protocol for a Decentralized Justice System*. Kleros. https://medium.com/kleros/kleros-a-decentralized-justice-protocol-for-the-internet-38d596a6300d

Francisco, U. S. (2018). The use of New Technologies and Arbitration. *The American Review of International Arbitration, 7*, 84.

Guillermo, A., María, B. N. T., & Juan, J. (2020). *Could an Arbitral Award Rendered by an AI System be Recognized or Enforced*? Kluwer Arbitration Blog. http://arbitrationblog.kluwerarbitration.com/2020/02/06/could-an-arbitral-award-rendered-by-ai-systems-be-recognized-or-enforced-analysis-from-the-perspective-of-public- policy/?doing_wp_ cron=1595473104. 80 26199340820312500000.

Idil, G. (2020). *Blockchain, Smart Contract and Arbitration*. Erdem & Erdem. http://www.erdem-erdem.av.tr/publications/newsletter/blockchain-smart-contracts-and-arbitration/

International Chamber of Commerce. (2017). *Information Technology in International Arbitration- Report of the ICC Commission on Arbitration and ADR*. Author.

Jack, W. N. (2016). *Machine Arbitration and Machine Arbitrator*. Young ICCA Blog. https://www.youngicca-blog.com/machine-arbitration-and-machine-arbitrators/

Jason, W., Alan, C., & Parke, C. (2019). *Promoting innovation through education: The blockchain industry, law enforcement and regulators work towards a common goal*. Blockchain Laws and Regulations 2019(17). Global Legal Insight.

Joseph, A., & Markus, B. (2018). *Blockchain Economics*. Princeton University.

Josh, F. (2020). *Blockchain and International Arbitration: Opportunities and Challenges*. Vocal Media. https://vocal.media/theChain/blockchain-and-international-arbitration-opportunities-and-challenges.

Katarzyna, S. (2020). *"On-chain" and "off-chain" arbitration: Using smart contracts to amicably resolve disputes*. Newtech Law. https://newtech.law/en/on-chain-and-off-chain-arbitration-using-smart-contracts-to-amicably-resolve-disputes/

Kathleen, P., & Edna, S. (2018). Artificial Intelligence Challenges and Opportunities for International Arbitration. *NYSBA New York Dispute Resolution Lawyer, 11*, 36.

Kim, F. (2020). *AI Technology and International Arbitration: Are Robot Coming for Your Job*. CIArB Blog. https://www.ciarb.org/news/ai-technology-and-international-arbitration-are-robots-coming-for-your-job/

London Court of International Arbitration Rules. (2014). Retrieved from https://www.lcia.org/dispute_resolution_services/lcia-arbitration-rules-2014.aspx

Madhvendra, S. (2020). *Blockchain and AI-is the cocktail right for Arbitration*. Bar & Bench. https://www.barandbench.com/columns/policy-columns/blockchain-ai-is-the-cocktail-right-for-conduct-of-arbitration#

Marike, R. P. P. (2020). *The Blockchain ADR: Bringing International Arbitration to the New Age*. Kluwer Arbitration Blog. http://arbitrationblog.kluwerarbitration.com/2018/10/09/blockchain-adr-bringing-international-arbitration-new-age/?doing_wp_cron=1596338917.2967860698699951171875

Michael, R. (2017). *CodeLegit Conducts First Blockchain-based Smart Contract Arbitration Proceeding*. CodeLegit.

Mike, D. (2019). *Dispute Resolution: How Blockchain Platforms Can Help Settle Conflict*. Bitrates. https://www.bitrates.com/news/p/dispute-resolution-how-blockchain-platforms-can-help-settle-conflict

Nivin, S. (2021). *How does AI recognise your hand gestures and movements?* Mantra AI. https://www.mantra.ai/blogs/ai-in-gesture-recognition/

Norton Rose Fulbright. (2017). *Online Dispute Resolution and Electronic Hearing*. Author.

Norton Rose Fulbright. (2019, November). *Blockchain dispute risks for banks*. Author.

Orna, R. E., & Ethan, K. (2019). Blockchain and the Inevitability of Disputes: The role for Online Dispute Resolution. *Journal of Dispute Resolution, 2019*(2), 47–75.

Pierre, D., & Roland, Z. (2018). *International arbitration and the rise of innovative tech*. International Chamber of Commerce. https://iccwbo.org/media-wall/news-speeches/guest-blog-international-arbitration-rise-innovative-tec/

Piers, M., & Aschauer, C. (Eds.). (2018). *Arbitration in the digital age : the brave new world of arbitration* (pp. 283–289). Cambridge University Press. doi:10.1017/9781108283670.015

Piers, M., & Aschauer, C. (Eds.). (2018). *Arbitration in the digital age : the brave new world of arbitration* (pp. 283–289). Cambridge University Press. doi:10.1017/9781108283670.015

Rayan, B. (2019). *The Fifth Arbitrator? Analysing the Potential Role of Artificial Intelligence and Blockchain Technology in the International Arbitration Industry.* The Board Room Lawyer. https://theboardroomlawyer.wordpress.com/2019/07/24/the-fifth-arbitrator-analysing-the-potential-role-of-artificial-intelligence-and-blockchain-technology-in-the-international-arbitration-industry/

Ron, S. (2019). AI and Blockchain: Double hype or Double value. *Forbes.* https://www.forbes.com/sites/cognitiveworld/2019/10/24/ai-and-blockchain-double-the-hype-or-double-the-value/?sh=5dbc565f5eb4

Sarah, A. (2018). The Missing Link Between Blockchain and Copyright: How Companies Are Using New Technology to Misinform Creators and Violate Federal Law. *North Carolina Journal of Law & Technology*, 19.

Satoshi, N. (2008). *Bitcoin: A Peer-to-Peer Electronic Cash System.* https://www.bitcoin.com/bitcoin.pdf

Shehata & Partners. (2019). *Blockchain Based Smart Contracts: An Overview.* Author.

The LawTech Delivery Panel, 3. *Consultation on the status of cryptoassets, distributed ledger technology and smart contracts under English private law.*

The United Nations Vienna Convention on the Law of Treaties (1969). Treaty Series, 1155, art 31.

Tonya, M. E. (2019). The Role of International Rules in Blockchain-Based Cross-Border Commercial Disputes. *Wayne Law Review*, 65.

UNCITRAL Model Law on Electronic Commerce, Guide to Enactment, para. 50; Explanatory note by the UNCITRAL secretariat on the United Nations Convention on the Use of Electronic Communications in International Contracts. 143 et seq.

United Nations Commission on International Trade Law. (2017). *UNCITRAL Technical Notes on Online Dispute Resolution.* United Nations.

Valentina, G., Fabrizio, F., Claudio, D., Chiara, P., & Víctor, S. (2018). Blockchain and Smart Contracts for Insurance: Is the Technology Mature Enough? *Future Internet*, *10*(2), 20. doi:10.3390/fi10020020

KEY TERMS DEFINITIONS

Arbitration: An alternate method of dispute resolution that is conducted outside of courts with the free will of the parties, where the award has the force of law for enforcement, and which is adjudicated by private arbitrators appointed by the mutual agreement of parties.

CodeLegit: A program library for use in smart contract codes and used to legitimize software.

Cryptocurrency: Digital asset used as a method of exchange stored in an online ledger form.

Interim Measures: Short term measures granted by a tribunal/ court until a final decision is made in a case in a matter being adjudicated.

Kleros: Kleros is an open-source online dispute resolution protocol which uses blockchain crowdsourcing to adjudicate disputes.

ODR: Online dispute resolution is a technology assisted system of adjudication of disputes online either fully automated traditionally by private arbitrators and assisted by technology suites.

Smart Contract: An instruction based transactional code which is used to self-execute conventional contracts between two parties.

Tech Nation: A legal Tech startup in UK that supports and enables legal services and dispute resolution systems.

Chapter 14
A Decade in Pixels:
Analyzing Incidents of State-Sponsored Surveillance From the Last Decade

Abhishek Vats
MAIMS, Guru Gobind Singh Indraprastha University, India

Claudia Masoni
New York University, USA & Siena University, Italy

ABSTRACT

State surveillance is the act of using technology like sensors, social media analytics, predictive policy systems, etc. to store, monitor, and/or analyze information about the targeted individual. In the age of Big Data and AI State surveillance is an ad hoc practise. This chapter intends to inform the readers about the harmful ramifications of indiscriminate mass surveillance by Governments. This chapter sheds light on incidents like NSA Leak, Cambridge Analytica and the surveillance of Uyghur Muslims in China. This chapter also discusses the impact of mass surveillance and human rights violations and the resultant chilling effect. Finally, this chapter recommends that to regulate surveillance, universal regulations striking a balance between privacy rights and surveillance coupled with strong domestic laws could be instrumental in preserving human rights.

INTRODUCTION

State Surveillance is the act of employing technology like sensors (thermal imaging systems, computer vision chips, surveillance-enabled light bulbs etc.), data analytic software (predictive policy systems, social media analytics etc.) (Sharma, 2021) with the objective of collecting, monitoring, storing and retaining sensitive data with or without the consent of the targeted individual (Sharma, 2021). This can be done either by Government servants or organizations acting under the direction of the Government. State Surveillance also includes using internet surveillance like- decryption tools, spyware to name a few. Another common method of gaining intelligence/ information is using audio/video recording devices which can be body worn, drone based. (Sharma, 2021).

DOI: 10.4018/978-1-7998-8641-9.ch014

We are living in the age of surveillance. The digital technologies that have revolutionized our lives has also created a detailed shadow of our lives on record, available as data. The Governments across the world have shown great promise to acquire such personal data sometimes in the name of security and national interest and some other reasons which are too ambiguous (Richards, 2013). While autocratic regimes have long been the antagonist when talking about surveillance, today even democratic countries do not shy away from indiscriminate surveillance of their citizens (Richards, 2013).

This Chapter intends to inform the reader of the magnitude of the problem with increased capabilities and potential avenues for state surveillance in light of the advent of newer and more sophisticated technologies. It will also broadly explore the methods and technological tools employed for state surveillance at present. Specifically, the Chapter will lay emphasis on the significant increase in the capabilities and frequency of surveillance purportedly, in the interest of national security and counter-terrorism efforts. The Chapter will also attempt to build a narrative around the key contemporary events like the Edward Snowden NSA Leak, Cambridge Analytica and the mass surveillance in China such events have influenced the conversation around state surveillance across the globe.

The English noun surveillance comes from the French verb sur-veillir, which is related to the Latin term vigilare (Marx, 2015). Vigilare loosely translates to something threatening lurking beyond the watchtower and town walls but the vigilant can successfully ward off the threat (Marx, 2015). A breakdown of these terms justifies the first thought that people have about surveillance i.e association of surveillance with policing activities and security agencies. Surveillance today has exceeded the bounds and limitations of "traditional surveillance" techniques.

Professor David Lyon has effectively captured the essence of surveillance. He mentions that surveillance is primarily about power but it also imbibes personhood. Lyon defines surveillance as "the focused, systematic and routine attention to personal details for purposes of influence, management, protection or direction" (Lyon 2007). Lyon's definition highlights four noteworthy characteristics of surveillance. Focused relates to the focus / aim on learning more about individuals, systematic highlights that surveillance is intentional and not random. Thirdly, routine highlights that it is an ordinary administrative apparatus and finally, variety of purposes – surveillance can be used for a wide range of purposes like totalitarian domination, crushing dissent or protecting civil liberties of individuals to name a few.

Today, the means and methods of sharing information have significantly changed, the technological developments have taken us from mails to e-mails, from wired phones to our one-stop mobile phones. The advent of internet has contributed largely to dissemination of information at a fast pace. Thus, today the outflow of information and ideas is unprecedented (United Nations, 2013). At the same time the techniques of surveillance have also developed and transformed, whenever a new technological outlet was discovered, along with it developed the means to spy, control or monitor its usage (United Nations, 2013). With the advent of technological advancements, we witness that not only the outlets or techniques of surveillance have changed but also what all can be monitored (United Nations, 2013). Internet has also contributed to the creation and accumulation of a large amount of metadata which includes personal information about individuals, their location or even information about the messages sent or received (United Nations, 2013). Metadata is easily accessible in today's digital age as their disclosure or usage isn't often properly regulated and the present legislations are outsmarted by the technical means of surveillance as they are far superior and can easily permeate any regulatory hinderance.

In a world where surveillance is a reality, it can be adjudged both a threat and a response to threat (Marx, 2015), the question whether surveillance is good or bad isn't the correct one to ask. Plainly put, like any other technology, the qualities, benefits and harm of surveillance remain the same rather it's how the technology is used that categorizes surveillance as good or evil. Surveillance is very broad and has a catena of forms. However, in this chapter, the focus is solely on the indiscriminate and involuntary surveillance by Government (includes persons acting under statutory authority, on the order of the government or government servants). The word indiscriminate here refers to the tendency to collect data on everyone without any prejudice for example- In the case of surveillance of a mafia boss or a terrorist, a distinction is made between a law-abiding citizen and a terrorist or threat to public tranquility and the surveillance may be justified in the interest of public safety. However, when surveillance is indiscriminate, the tools are used to monitor, store and analyze information about everyone regardless of any parameters.

Surveillance becomes involuntary when a person's meta data is being mined, stored, analyzed and shared in the absence of their consent. The word involuntary highlights lack of consent, meaning that the party being watched either refused to give their consent or subsequently revoked it. Consent here also imbibes lack of knowledge and the possibility of not being able to give consent because the party is not aware that it is being watched.

The "new surveillance" includes computer matching, big data, GPS, electronic work monitoring, video camera, DNA analysis, drug testing and monitoring through social media and cell phones (Marx, 2015). This new form of surveillance is very sophisticated that it can accumulate more data, extend the possibilities and reach of our traditional surveillance capacities, has little visibility which may allow it to solicit information with compliance or even involuntarily while the subject remains unaware (Marx, 2015). To breakdown all the outlets which are exercised for surveillance today is definitely a herculean task. Some of these forms may even be omnipresent and often presumed to be omnipotent.

The new surveillance can be understood as the scrutiny of individual groups by using technical means to extract or create information (Marx, 2015). Here, "technical means to extract and create information" refers to the fact that such techniques may help in going beyond what is voluntarily offered by our senses unaided by technology (Marx, 2015). To simplify, "extract and create" refers to new surveillance's ability to overcome logical or strategic borders which allow a more liberal access to personal information (Marx, 2015). Further, create refers to the fact that data reflect the output of a measurement tool (Marx, 2015). The tool itself reflects a decision about what to focus on and the results are an artifact of the way they were constructed.

While digital surveillance technologies are becoming more prominent and invasive, the measures to regulate its prowess seem to be virtually non-existent. Today, State agencies are not shy about accessing metadata from a wide range of sources (United Nations, 2019). Such access may often be free from judicial authorization and any oversight which means that often surveillance may not be backed by a warrant or an order of competent judicial or any supervisory authority. Similarly, such mass surveillance programs are also extra-territorial in nature (United Nations, 2019). Extra-territorial here refers to the capacity to extract data on a foreign national in a different country without having to permeate the territorial boundaries physically. Data protection is a global issue, where any computer or device from anywhere on the planet can be tapped or attacked by any individual regardless of geographical boundaries (United Nations, 2019). Thus, surveillance has become an ad hoc practice which isn't in total control today.

Barack Obama, the former President of The USA recognized the Big Data – surveillance link when he called for a "comprehensive review of Big Data and privacy" on 17 January 2014, following the NSA leak (White House, 2014). The onset of social media has also contributed to the creation and flourishing of "surveillance state", social media websites are not only used for commercial purposes but are not crucial for security purposes too. One could define this emphasis on accumulating data as "datafication" (Bertolucci, 2013), which captures the essence of data being central to certain businesses (Bertolucci, 2013).

Taking inspiration from a number of sources, Rob Kitchin shared some crucial characteristics of Big Data which include- huge volume, consisting of terabytes or petabytes of data; high velocity, being created in or near real time; extensive variety, both structured and unstructured; exhaustive in scope, striving to capture entire populations of systems; fine-grained resolution, aiming at maximum detail, while being indexical in identification; relational, with common fields that enable the conjoining of different data-sets; flexible, with traits of extensionality (easily adding new fields) and scalability (the potential to expand rapidly) (Kitchin, 2014: 262).

With the onset of Big Data analytics, two big players have also taken seats on the bandwagon these players are the Governments and Commercial surveillance. Bruce Schneier in his article related the Big data as a phenomenon similar to "Big Pharma" or "Big Oil" (Schneier, 2012), Here big signifies the economic worth of data as a commodity. Viktor Mayer-Scho"nberger and Kenneth Cukier (2012) argue that the new data management techniques have permitted analysis beyond "rows and tables", quoting this as the "Big Data revolution" they highlight that companies collect huge volumes of data because they have a "burning financial incentive to make use of them". Hence, it can be said that the position of data as a commodity on the market place is quite apparent in a fast pace technological world. The large extent of surveillance can be credited to Government and Private Sector collaboration. Private sectors often possess the incentives and skills to satisfy the surveillance needs of the Government (United Nations, 2019). While the intentions of the companies for developing the applications or servers could be legitimate, how the Governments may authorize the use of such technology can be detrimental to the civil liberties of the people.

State surveillance can also be practiced through censorship. The Government has the capacity to block or alter communication to dominate the flow of information between individuals. For example- A state can impose restrictions on results generated by online search engines, they can also block websites or disable social media website and content. Further, they may also block access to internet altogether. By removing information from the public eye, the government can effectively silence dissent and criticism. The government can also remove reports of abuse of civil liberties of the citizens or any authoritative action and protect itself from public scrutiny. Further, the government may restrict or intercept any communication necessary for coordination of collective action and obstruct dissemination of information which the public can use to form policy opinions (Hayes and Reineke 2007; King, Pan, and Roberts 2013; Gunitsky 2015).

While Surveillance is about being watched, it can also broadly include what one person is allowed to perceive. What people perceive can help influence their reaction. Cases of information manipulation by Governments by fabricating information for strategic purposes is not uncommon (Gunitsky 2015). Examples of manipulation includes production of fake news and its amplification on social media platforms, dissemination of propaganda and restricting access to Government data. Such false information may be used to shape the political attitudes of citizens (Geddes and Zaller 1989) and for countermobilizing a regime's support base (Gunitsky 2015).

We are oblivious to such vehement surveillance operations and their direct repercussions on our lives, especially in this day and age of social media, virtual studies and smart phones. The storage of metadata can lead to plethora of information on individuals both past and present, and can lead to elaborate surveillance. Such data when analyzed can be highly invasive (United Nations, 2013). The world is becoming increasingly dependent on technology and we notice that fresh and undiscovered tools of surveillance cannot be comprehensively identified.

Therefore, there exist concerns about the State's capacity to employ such sophisticated technology, using stored metadata in manners which are stifling the civil liberties is concerning for the citizens (Bhandari & Sane, 2018). A report commissioned by the White House mentioned that predictive policing software should be used judiciously otherwise they can become tools of discrimination (Bhandari & Sane, 2018). At the same time, the vast extent of surveillance leads to a chilling effect in the form of "psychological restraint" which hampers the citizens' ability to think and act freely (Bhandari & Sane, 2018).

Non-State Social Media and corporate giants like Facebook, Amazon, Google etc collect and store their users' consumer data which includes their location, consumer behavior, name to name a few (Bhandari & Sane, 2018). A study even highlighted that a user's Facebook likes can be used to predict a user's ethnicity, political opinions, sexual orientation, religion and other information with reasonable accuracy (Bhandari & Sane, 2018). Today data has become very valuable that data has emerged as the 'new currency' and thus there is a rise in "surveillance capitalism" (Bhandari & Sane, 2018). Under this regime of surveillance capitalism, personal data is bought and sold to third parties. Private Corporations have the resources to store and analyse our online activity to deduce our location, actions and thoughts and very often they work in collaboration with the State machinery (Bhandari & Sane, 2018).

ANALYZING SURVEILLANCE FROM CONTEMPORARY EXAMPLES

Mass Surveillance practices actually came to light following the infamous National Security Agency of The USA (NSA Leak). The NSA was the first of its kind Exposé, which shocked the world with its revelations about the indiscriminate and holistic mass surveillance by the USA along with UK, Canada, New Zealand and Australia.

The NSA Leak

Edward Snowden, an ex-CIA agent provided classified information to a U.K-based newspaper the Guardian about the indiscriminate and vast surveillance capacities of the 'Five Eye Alliance' (USA, UK, Australia, New Zealand and Canada). By doing so, Snowden helped unmask the indiscriminate surveillance practices of the US, UK government in collaboration with "sister organizations" from Australia, Canada and New Zealand. On June 5th 2013, the Guardian published a few revelations making the NSA leak a public outbreak (Amnesty International & Privacy International, 2015). In December, 2013, the Editor-in-chief of the Guardian revealed that only 1% of the information supplied by Snowden was made public through their articles (BBC News, 2013).

It was also revealed that NSA collected the metadata on millions of customers who used Verizon. The existence of such records has also been confirmed by Congressional Intelligence Committee. Acknowledging the extent of this program, the Director of National Intelligence compared the NSA program to "a library with literally millions of volumes of books" (Alhinnawi et al., 2015). The Government Communications Headquarters of the UK (GCHQ) and NSA started programs like TEMPORA and Upstream respectively, under such programs they intercepted transatlantic undersea internet cables (Amnesty International & Privacy International, 2015). This provided them access to a large volume internet traffic (Amnesty International & Privacy International, 2015). Canada, one of the members of the Five Eyes

Alliance, intercepted information on websites like Rapidshare and Megaupload, through the Communications Security Establishment Canada (CSEC) (Amnesty International & Privacy International, 2015). At the same time the agency also intercepted and stored emails to analyze them (Amnesty International & Privacy International, 2015). Similarly New Zealand through the Government Communications Security Bureau (GCSB) employed satellite interception to record data transmitted via phone and internet in the Asia Pacific region (Amnesty International & Privacy International, 2015). All the data that was collected was shared with the Five Eyes.

The Washington Post on June 6th 2013 reported that NSA and FBI are directly tapping central servers of nine leading US internet companies (Gellman et al., 2013). By doing so, they are extracting audio, video chats, photos, documents, emails etc and therefore, they are able to extract information on foreign targets/citizens (Gellman et al., 2013). Such data mining ranges from online communications to phone calls and other activities on the phone and computers. The NSA surveillance program impacted millions of American and international citizens. The documents shared by Snowden through the Guardian revealed that companies like Facebook, Microsoft and Google were participating with government agencies like - NSA, GCHQ to handover personal data of individuals stored with their servers (Amnesty International & Privacy International, 2015). A wild fixture of the surveillance programs by the Five Eyes nations was the XKeyscore which gave the NSA agents the power to store and process information regarding the browsing history, emails and social media activities of those being watched, infact nobody from a Federal Judge to the President were off-limit (Alhinnawi et al., 2015). Further, personal text and calls transmitted in countries like Kenya, Mexico and the Philippines were routinely intercepted by the Five eye nations (Amnesty International & Privacy International, 2015). In October, 2013 it was revealed that NSA was tapping Angela Merkel's phone (the ex- Chancellor of Germany) (BBC News, 2013a). The information provided by Snowden has also highlighted that under programs like MYSTIC and SOMALGET call recordings on about 250 million people from Mexico, Kenya, Bahamas, Afghanistan, the Philippines have been collected (Amnesty International & Privacy International, 2015).

The US intelligence officials initially mentioned that programs like PRISM and other similar initiatives surveillance operations under NSA helped prevent around 54 terrorist acts (Rollins & Liu, 2013). Time and again the intelligence authority extended national interest as the triumphant end to justify their means. However, in an interview in January 2014 Snowden explained that several incidents of surveillance were motivated solely by industrial espionage (Alhinnawi et al., 2015). At the same time, reports also highlighted that NSA agents misused the spyware technology to spy on their lovers on the internet (Perez, 2013). The Intelligence officials have placed reliance on domestic legislation to justify their ambitious data mining undertakings like- Section 215 of the Patriot Act and Section 702 of Foreign Intelligence Surveillance Act (FISA). The officials also highlighted that such drastic measures were taken pursuant to the domestic legislation to take proactive action as taking judicial orders time and again could overwhelm the judiciary and also prove detrimental to State interests (Rollins & Liu, 2013). Senators Ron Wyden and Tom Udall criticized such stance on June 19, 2013 and highlighted that such information could be easily taken through a regular court order, as the law allows expedient authorization under urgent circumstances (Rollins & Liu, 2013). They discarded the arguments which stated that collecting data in bulk is more convenient and contended that convenience alone does not justify the collection of metadata on millions of Americans as such information can be obtained through less intrusive modes (Rollins & Liu, 2013). Mass surveillance when arbitrary, is in violation of Right to Privacy and Fundamental rights human rights like- Freedom of speech and expression. Indiscriminate hoarding of information/metadata on people without any legitimate grounds of concerns is a violation of one's privacy.

Looming Consequences of the NSA Leak

After the controversy, the response from the US Government officials wasn't sympathetic towards Snowden. On the flip-side we notice that the public recognizes Snowden as a hero. In fact, a petition launched on 9th July, 2013 calling for the grant of free and absolute pardon for the crimes committed by Snowden for blowing the whistle on NSA (Zabarenko, 2013). This petition also secured 167,954 signatures (Rhodan, 2015).

Snowden has also been decorated with several grand awards for blowing the Whistle on the NSA surveillance activities. In August, 2013 he received the German "Whistle Blower Prize", in October 2013, he was awarded the Sam Adams Award (which is given to intelligence officers who have stood up for integrity and ethics) (Alhinnawi et al., 2015). The US received a lot of criticism from its biggest allies particularly from the European Union, Swedish politician Cecilia Malmstrom mentioned in 2013 that the NSA leak controversy has severed the trust and confidence between USA and the EU and she further called upon the US to restore these relations (Croft, 2013). The Highest Court of Justice of the EU, The European Court of Justice criticized the US as being an unsafe space for sharing data (McLaughlin & McLaughlin, 2015). One of the most significant impact of the NSA leak has been the swift change in legislation, particularly the giant steps taken by the EU to combat US surveillance prowess. The EU recognized the lacunae in the protection offered by the law and took upon national security policies diligently. As response to the NSA leak and large scale surveillance, the EU's General Data Protection Regulation (GDPR) came into effect on May 25, 2018 (European Union - Data Privacy and Protection | Privacy Shield, n.d.). The one of its kind legislation has been a massive step to ensure that the citizens across EU have a lucid idea about how their personal information is being used and pursue a remedial action in case their privacy rights were violated.

The Cambridge Analytica

Donald Trump's 2016 US presidential election has been accused to have spread rumours, propaganda and disinformation. Even Christopher Wylie, a former Cambridge Analytica contractor and the Whistle-blower in this case even stated that- "To be clear, the work of Cambridge Analytica is not equivalent to traditional marketing," (RYAN, 2018) Wylie said. "Cambridge Analytica specialized in disinformation, spreading rumors, kompromat and propaganda." (RYAN, 2018) Further, Trump's campaign reportedly deterred 3.5 million black Americans from voting through dark adverts (Sabbagh, 2020). The campaign's goal was to dissuade voters from backing Hillary Clinton and the dark adverts specifically portrayed Hillary as unsympathetic to African Americans (Sabbagh, 2020).

Strategic Communications Laboratories, the Parent Company of Cambridge Analytica and Global Science Research's founder Aleksandr Kogan were working together for the creation of Facebook user's profiles based on the data collected by Kogan's survey (Boldyreva et al., 2018). UK based Academic researcher Aleksandr Kogan had formulated a survey for his research project (Monika, 2020). The Survey was disseminated to the public through Facebook, where it was sent to 3 Lakh (300,000) Americans to analyse their personality traits. Kogan used Amazon Mechanical Turk and provided an opportunity for the surveyees to make money ($1 to $2) just by filling the survey (Boldyreva et al., 2018). The Survey contained questions where the surveyees had to either agree to a preposition or disagree with it (Monika, 2020). Upon Signing in with the Facebook account Kogan received personal information like- The birth date, the location/ address and their Facebook likes. Since the survey required the users to login with their Facebook account, this step automatically also made the surveyee's Facebook Friends' information available to the data collectors. This way one user provided access to approximately 340 other users and their personal information without their knowledge of consent.

This information was analyzed as per a five factor model – dispositional model of personality, which can deduce information about a person's benevolence, openness or the opposite of such traits (Boldyreva et al., 2018). Compiling all this information Kogan produced a psychometric model which could be called a personality profile of the survey takers (Monika, 2020). Cambridge Analytica a company in the USA collaborated Kogan to use his research to support Donald Trump's political campaign. Kogan combined the personalities he created with the users' voters records and sent this data to Cambridge Analytica. This partnership between Kogan and Cambridge Analytica managed to procure a users' Facebook Friends' data through similar methods (Monika, 2020). As of 2017, GSR reports claimed Cambridge Analytica had access to almost 30 Million Facebook users' information (Boldyreva et al., 2018). The ambition of this alliance led them to successfully mine data on over 87 million Facebook users (Boldyreva et al., 2018).

American politicians like Ted Cruz and Ben Carson had paid Cambridge Analytica $ 750,000 and $ 220,000 as revealed by the documents from the Federal Election Commission (Boldyreva et al., 2018). Facebook also expressed concerns about Cambridge Analytica after it started to make headlines. Consequently, Facebook launched an investigation into the matter and Facebook representatives reported that as per their investigation there was no trace of any illegal activity. Facebook's CEO Mark Zuckerberg remarked that since nobody's password was leaked or stolen nor the systems were broken into this did not amount to data breach (Zabarenko, 2013). On March 16, 2018 Facebook stated that even though Cambridge Analytica promised to destroy all the data they did not take any action to that effect.

Developments after Cambridge Analytica

After Donald Trump was successfully elected in 2016. The Cambridge Analytica was shut down in 2018. The now- defunct firm took part in influencing Donald Trump's Campaign for Presidency and several other elections around the globe. As a penalty for their complicit behaviour, Facebook had to pay a fine of £500,000 (about $643,000) to the UK's Information Commissioner's Office (Zialoita, 2019). However, Facebook did not admit its liability (Zialoita, 2019).

After the Scandal, Facebook pledged to improve and made a series of amendments in their business tools. They made efforts to make sure that businesses use the platform with prudence. Facebook also revoked API access to numerous third party apps to ensure that the efforts to mine data are minimized (Otlowski, 2021). Facebook also removed tens of thousands of applications from their platform following the Cambridge Analytica scandal. The company also highlighted that they made this decision as numerous applications were inappropriately sharing the data acquired from their platform (Rodriguez, 2019). Many social media networks including Facebook and Twitter have allowed the users to edit and remove their data from such platforms. Google also announced their commitment to block any third-party cookies from accessing Chrome (Otlowski, 2021). Chrome is a very popular browser and has a significant market share, around 70% people use Chrome via desktops/computers and around 41% use it on mobile phones (Otlowski, 2021). Such steps can help in improving the user experience and safety online but there is definitely a very long way to go.

The NSA Leak and the Cambridge Analytica incident have explained the sheer impact of state surveillance in the west. The unmasking of such incidents brought data protection on the forefront of the Western policy making. While the West seems to have been taking steps to minimize the infiltration of privacy, Asian countries like China are using surveillance technology for ethnic cleansing of Uyghur Muslims. The NSA leak was an incident of indiscriminate surveillance, where everyone was under the watchful eye of the Five eye nations, lets observe it in contrast to the religious or ethnic centric surveillance prevalent in China today.

SURVEILLANCE REGIME IN CHINA

Chinese Government launched the Golden Shield Project in the 2000s to develop a pan-China network for information collection, along with command centers who were responsible for analysing such information. Further, in 2003 the country adopted the British model called- "Intelligence-Led Policing" (Schwarck, 2017). This ensured that intelligence was front and center to all strategic and operational decision making. China since the 2000s has placed emphasis on "stability maintenance" to masquerade their surveillance agenda (Human Rights Watch, 2018). During the 2008 Olympics, China invested immense resources towards security, to ensure that they were able to police and break up protests. This also included censoring internet. To add fuel to fire, protests by Tibetans across the Tibetan Plateau followed by the riots in Urumqi, the capital of Xinjiang prompted more investments in mass surveillance technologies (Human Rights Watch, 2018).

The mass surveillance tactics of the Chinese Government have been developing to permeate the Chinese society for a long time. The Chinese Government issues a unique national identification card to all their nationals which is paramount for accessing several private and public services. At the same time, sophisticated technology allows the government to use public CCTV cameras, monitor calls and identify locals who may pose political threats (Human Rights Watch, 2018). At the same time, China is aggressively trying to pierce into the surveillance markets. China's approach to make surveillance technology accessible is quite shrewd. They provide/encourage soft loans to Governments to purchase their equipment. In this manner, China is subsidizing and popularizing the purchase of advanced repressive technology. China's surveillance technology is spreading worldwide with companies like Huawei, Hikvision, Dahua, and ZTE supplying surveillance tech in 63 countries approximately (Feldstein, 2019). China has managed to sold surveillance tools in Uzbekistan, Laos, Kenya, Mongolia and Uganda (Feldstein, 2019). It is worth noting that around 36 of these 63 countries are a part of the Belt and Road Initiative. Huawei alone supplies surveillance technology to around 50 countries (Feldstein, 2019).

One must remember that China is not alone in the race to supply sophisticated surveillance technology. Various U.S companies like IBM, CISO and Palantir are responsible for supplying surveillance gear in 32 countries. Various other democracies around the globe like- France, Germany, Israel, Japan are crucial stakeholders in the proliferation of surveillance technology (Feldstein, 2019). Huawei, a Chinese company is aggressively marketing their surveillance technology in Sub-Saharan Africa and they provide not only ongoing technological support but also assist in operating and management of these systems (Feldstein, 2019). Further, Huawei technicians helped the Government in spying on their political opponents in Uganda and Zambia. They employed tactics to decrypt communications, track cell data for location/whereabouts and also monitored their social media (Feldstein, 2019). In this way,

China is able to spread the surveillance technology across the globe and in this way, it has managed to arm various regimes with the power to control, monitor and accumulate data on their respective citizens.

Many believe that China is vehemently advocating for "authoritarian tech" and experts maintain that Chinese companies are closely involved in this ambition of the Government. Therefore, this partnership between Chinese companies and the Government are trying to spread and promote the Chinese governance model across the globe (Feldstein, 2019). For example, countries like Zimbabwe and Venezuela are importers of Chinese surveillance technology (Feldstein, 2019). While Chinese technology may not be the ipso-facto reason for such violations. It is believed that ordinarily, these countries wouldn't have had access to such high technology in the absence of China's involvement.

Mass Surveillance in Xinjiang

The Muslim population in China is dominated by the Hui and Uyghur Muslims. Uyghurs claim Xinjiang as their ancestral home and a walk through the "modernizing" Xinjiang's local areas is telling of the cultural imprints of these ethnic communities (ARM, 2020). In the contemporary times, the continued extreme "Hanification" policies of the Chinese Government has led to communal rifts between the Muslim communities (Uyghurs in particular) and the Han Chinese (ARM, 2020) as Chinese Communists believe Muslims to be a threat to Chinese culture and Communism.

Speaking of these extreme measures it is believe that under China's Strike Hard Campaign, the Xinjiang authorities are collecting metadata like- biometrics, DNA samples, iris scans, blood types etc of the Muslim residents of Xinjiang area (ARM, 2020. Such information is collated for all Muslim residents between the age of 12 to 65 (ARM, 2020). This information is further stored into a centralized database. China's surveillance model is different than NSA's model because China's model is only focusing on Muslim communities, whereas NSA resorted to indiscriminate surveillance.

In the past, Uyghurs and the Government have seen periods of violence like in 1990s the Uyghurs were responsible vehicular attacks and self-immolation in Beijing. In October 2013, a mass knifing incident at Kumming railway station and following the year in March 2014, a bomb attack at Urumqi railway station. The Chinese Government considered these attacks to be the advent of jihadi tactics in Xinjiang (Millward & Peterson, 2020). The Communist Party claims that mass surveillance is necessary to counter the three evils- Separatism, Terrorism and Extremism. Therefore, the Government is not shying away from monitoring Uyghurs 24 hours and 7 days a week (Human Rights Watch, 2018). While, the surveillance technology can be useful in curbing societal menace, as through monitoring activities, the police can anticipate potential crime, violent protests and other such disruptive activities, the surveillance is conducted over Uyghurs alone, the Han Chinese population (which amounts to 35% of the total population in the area) is not subjected to such measures. This seems rather arbitrary (Millward & Peterson, 2020).

With the revival of Strike Hard policy in May 2014, "stability maintenance" became as center-piece of Chinese policies in Xinjiang. Following which, the mobile phones of Uyghurs were hacked for real-time mass surveillance. (Millward & Peterson, 2020). A "de-extremification" ordinance was passed and old legislation was renewed with vaguely worded justifications to detain and prosecute the Muslim communities like Uyghurs, Kazakhs and Kyrgyz people living in Xinjiang region. They are detained for practices relating to or being symbolic to Islam (Millward & Peterson, 2020). The Mass Surveillance progressed at a rapid pace with the arrival of Chen Quanguo (Xinjiang Party Secretary) in 2017. Under his regime, a large number of new security personnel were deployed in Xinjiang and "Convenience Police

Stations" were created for grid policing (Millward & Peterson, 2020). These police stations were backed by sophisticated technology for gathering meta data including social media and religious practices, gait print to name a few (Millward & Peterson, 2020). All this information was used to issue identity cards.

The Integrated Joint Military Operations Platform known as the IJPOP has been created by China Electronics Technology Company. All the metadata collected by the security personnel has been cultivated and stored in the IJPOP system. The IJPOP is equipped with sophisticated AI which uses algorithms to predict behaviour or the likelihood of extremism, criminal behaviour ((Millward & Peterson, 2020). The authorities use the AI's predictions to sort individuals for imprisonments or other punitive measures based on the computational racist findings (Millward & Peterson, 2020). Few examples of these "suspicious activities" include having more than two children, not using the front door or having minimal social relations with neighbours (Millward & Peterson, 2020).

The International Consortium of Investigative Journalists revealed after pursuing classified Chinese documents that the IJOP flagged almost 24,421 persons as suspicious in Kashgar, Khotan, Akshu and Kizilsu districts. While 706 of these were arrested as criminals, around 15,683 residents were sent to reformation camps or educational camps (Millward & Peterson, 2020). These educational camps have come under severe scrutiny, as these camps are used as incubators to "Han-ify" Uyghurs in Xinjiang area by. Additionally, Wechat conversations of Uyghurs have been revisited or surveilled (Millward & Peterson, 2020). In fact they have been used as evidence by the security personnel to justify their punitive measures. They transcribed the chats, voice memos and images exchanged between Uyghurs and looked for keywords like "Allah" or "Quran" to justify their decision to employ surveillance. In light of such evidence cumulatively, in Xinjiang almost 350,000 people were prosecuted in 2017-2018 alone (Millward & Peterson, 2020).

If accounts of people who have fled China are to be believed, the Xinjiang education camps provide three levels of confinement from reformation schools to prison-like situations. A lot of Uyghur, Kazakh, Kyrgyz, and Uzbek are present in these camps, living a sentence for alleged extremism (Millward & Peterson, 2020). The said communities have been detained in these camps for mundane Islamic practices like- veiling, fasting or owning Quran, additionally other mundane activities which attracted detention orders include - having too many children and having foreign contacts (Millward & Peterson, 2020). The camps are said to "re-educate" the prisoners by forcing them to renounce Islamic and Uyghur culture and learning more about Chinese culture, and learning Mandarin (Millward & Peterson, 2020). Further, it is also reported by the escapees that they were subjected to physical and sexual violence, they lived in unsanitary conditions and were also subjected to forced sterilization through IUD implantation (Millward & Peterson, 2020). Therefore, we can objectively notice the harmful ramifications of Mass Surveillance. AI technology holds so much power in today's day and age where we are essentially living virtually. The Governments have been equipped with so much of information and the means to use it as they deem fit, therefore it becomes imperative to inquire into the expected and normative role that the Governments ought to play in the interest of their citizens.

AN ASPHYSIATING RESULT OF SURVEILLANCE: THE CHILLING EFFECT

Professor Neil M. Richard stated that, "To protect our intellectual freedom to think without state oversight or interference, we need what I have elsewhere called "intellectual privacy" (Richards, 2013).

The NSA leak is responsible for starting a global discourse on surveillance. In amassing such a meticulous data repository. The Five eye nations clearly violated numbers Human Rights legislations. Article 12 of the Universal Declaration of Human Rights (UDHR) provides for freedom from any inter-ference with one's privacy, family life, home or correspondence. This right even protects reputation. The indiscriminate surveillance by the Five eye nations under NSA leak clearly and arbitrarily permeated all walls and left no room for privacy by taping phone calls, emails, location and other components of individual metadata.

The NSA also disrespected ideas of sovereignty and mined data extra-territorially against unaware foreign nationals which included even politicians. The Five eyes routinely exchanged the data obtain by them and in this way breached the trust of their citizens by sharing personal data as a commodity. However, NSA leak was not the end of data surveillance. In fact despite the warnings of Snowden, the US despite criticism did not curb their surveillance and data mining ambitions.

Three very common measures to dissuade people from exercising their rights can broadly understood to include:

1. The adoption of deliberately ambiguous legal provisions; (Pech, 2021)
2. The arbitrary enforcement of these provisions against the most vocal critics of the autocratic minded authorities of the day—be they opposition politicians, journalists, judges, prosecutors, lawyers, academics or civil society groups—if only to "send a message" to the public at large; (Pech, 2021)
3. The adoption of disproportionate sanctions, as this will in turn further discourage people from exercising their rights and/ or obligations and therefore limit the need for future arbitrary enforce-ment of the relevant legal provisions whose lack of foreseeability is intentional (Pech, 2021).

The growing trend of collection and analysis of big data is automated, continuous, inexpensive and opaque (van Dijck, 2014). This helps the corporations or authorities to make profits from data trading and ostensibly, the state is able to improve national security. However, these surveillance techniques may create a fear of constantly being watched, thereby potentially deterring people from acting or speaking freely. Surveillance thus leads to self-censorship, conformity (which may be involuntary) and obedience (which may be anticipatory and/or forced).

Surveillance is against the exercise of our civil liberties. Surveillance allows the spectator or watcher (this should be understood as the one using surveillance tools) to invade our privacy and peek into our thoughts, conversations, views, tastes and preferences (Richards, 2013), it also enables them to store such metadata. Further, with the use of sophisticated tools, the spectator may also analyze our thoughts and make predictions based on the metadata collected (Richards, 2013).

Cambridge Analytica revealed how rampart and sometimes involuntary data mining coupled with predictive analysis technology Was employed to influence the election result in the USA. Cambridge Analytica is also one of the biggest data mining scandals that came to light in the last decade. Cambridge Analytica combined the power of Big data analysis with the data mining operations of the firm. The data analysis helps in making predictions about a person after collating and studying the data about an individual through their Facebook interactions (their likes, comments, posts shared and communication).

The Cambridge Analytica incident has led to a popular societal uproar where the citizens of USA realized just how powerful surveillance technologies are. Many believe Cambridge Analytica strikes hard at the civic duty and liberty of citizens to choose their representatives. Compromising the results of any election is a grave violation of Article 25 of International Covenant on Civil and Political Rights

1976 (ICCPR) which states that no country (which is a signatory of the Covenant) will without unreasonable restrictions intervene with the right of an individual to participate in opportunities in public affairs directly or through their chosen representatives. At the same time, this right also includes right to vote and to be elected. In light of such a right, the Trump Campaign meddled with the rights of American citizens to vote by dissuading them through dark advertisements.

One impact of NSA leak, the Cambridge Analytica and the mass surveillance of Muslims in China has been the interference with freedom of thought and expression. This interference is manifested by routinely surveilling personal metadata, private conversations (texts and calls), social media posts to name a few. This is in clear violation of Article 19 of ICCPR 1976 which provides for freedom of speech and expression of opinions. When a person is aware that they are being watched or there is a possibility that they are being watched, they will restrain from expressing their views and opinions fearing prosecution or retaliatory state action. Article 18 and 19 of the UDHR provide for a similar right wherein freedom of religious beliefs is manifested under Article 18 and Article 19 talks about freedom of expression of opinions and also the freedom to gain information from media and other frontiers.

The idea of speech or expression being 'chilled' is a popular and nuanced term in the journalism arena. This metaphor suggests an obstruction of communication, an idea that a person or organization has been made physically colder by restricting their right to freedom of expression (Richards, 2013). The chilling effect is not an esoteric legal metaphor: journalists and campaign groups cite it frequently. It can, but does not have to mean, an outright obstruction of human rights relating to speech. 'Chilling' does not necessarily mean to make ice cold; the metaphorical suggestion of temperature suggests a scale of deterrence from cool to freezing (Towned, 2017). In the presence of rampart surveillance citizens cannot perform their important civil duties or demand re-instatement of their civil rights, this leads to chilling effect on the exercise of our civil liberties (Richards, 2013). Free and independent media is very responsible to keep a check on arbitrary practices and laws of a regime. However, when the media outlets are under a chilling effect they will not report with accuracy fearing strict sanctions and penalty.

The surveillance in China has broken all the barriers of what can be achieved by surveillance. With surveillance piercing every household in the name of keeping law and order we notice that the disproportionate and prejudicial surveillance of Muslims within China is a nightmare come true. The surveillance in China expands to not only monitoring their lives but also using their activities as proof for their detention and subsequent mistreatment in the "Hanification" centers. Incidents of forced sterilization are in clear violation of Article 10 and Article 12 of International Covenant on Cultural and Economic Rights (CESR) 1976. Article 10 provides that family is the fundamental unit of society and it should be protected. Further Article 12 of CESR provides for the pledge of the Nation States to provide highest attainable standards of physical and mental health.

By detaining Uyghur Muslims and other Muslim groups in reformation camps, China is trying to erase their cultural identity which is a stark violation of Article 27 of the ICCPR which aims to protect the cultural, linguistic and religious expressions of minority communities in a nation. At the same time, China's actions are also in contravention of the Convention against Torture and other Cruel treatment 1984.

An interesting consideration in surveillance techniques deals with the power dynamics of the watcher vis-à-vis the watched (Richards, 2013). This disparity exposes the weaker party (generally the persons being watched) to discrimination, blackmail, coercion and even malicious prosecution. Mass surveillance by Governments may lead to arbitrary arrests and prosecutions targeting those in dissent and the data collected by surveillance may be furnished as proof.

Chilling effect manifests in individual's behaviour, which on a large scale can cause grave societal impacts. For example- A person fearing prosecution would never express dissent against a political party/ regime, which would lead to a collective decline in participation in the common democracy practices. An absence of more deliberations or opinions can lead to oppressive or imperfect policies and regulations.

This act of self-censorship is also an element of 'chilling effect' where exercise of fundamental rights is curtailed. This can consequently jeopardize individual autonomy, democratic participation and individual well being in digital societies (Véliz, 2020). However, chilling effect is not an inevitable or only consequence of surveillance. Infact, some people might react differently for example- some people might decide to improve protection of their data (Chou and Chou, 2021) or or engage in or engage in sousveillance (Mann and Ferenbok, 2013). Chilling effect is one of many reactions to the volatile and complicated system of digital communication in the digital age.

When individual communication is routinely intercepted and observed, in that case individuals will be discouraged from expressing any dissent or even efforts to mobilize collective action against Governments. The real harm of surveillance is not just the huge data that Governments hold but how that data is analyzed on some AI biases to generate predictions about events or "inherent deviant" behaviour. Here inherent deviant behaviour refers to the potential of anti-state or terrorist or criminal predisposition which the AI predicts through behvaiour analysis and based on such future contingencies the Government takes surveillance or punitive actions. All these incidents only substantiate the existence of a chilling effect, where by the individuals are under a psychological restraint and aren't truly free to exercise their rights, remedies and duties.

In the absence of transparency and effective control over mass surveillance, the gradual normalization may lead to feelings of resignation despite feeling uneasy. This would minimize the scope for any respite as people would be afraid to take collective actions to transform the model of governance of surveillance technologies. Governance alternatives should no longer assume that individuals are in a position of control to make informed choices according to their preferences for trading personal data for benefits they receive (Draper, 2017). Individuals who are aware about the mass surveillance may care a great deal about negative consequences, but may feel powerless and the consequential "decision not to engage may be a justifiable act of self-preservation" (Draper and Turow, 2019: 1828).

Countries like China, USA and UK are permanent members of the United Nations Security Council (UNSC), these countries themselves are responsible for unprecedented human rights violations. At the same time, since they possess the Veto power, any collective security measure by the UNSC against them is very improbable to pass. When surveillance through use of digital media becomes the de facto non-negotiable routine practise, chilling effect on digital communication is detrimental, as already discussed, a person would not be able to exercise their fundamental rights to the fullest and the surveillance may also intervene with any efforts to collectively oppose any bad regulation. The long term risks of excessive mass surveillance definitely warrant more academic attention.

THE WAY FORWARD

The public became aware about mass surveillance as a result of the NSA leak which happened 8 years ago and the true prowess of AI based Surveillance in 2021 is still a mystery. We have seen how surveillance and analyzing metadata can be used for stalking, profiling, monitoring and even for hampering electoral results etc. But the people of China are living the real horror of AI surveillance followed by prison like reformation camps. Many countries resort to surveillance under the guise of national interest and often use surveillance disproportionately. Since 2013, the discussions to protect data have become more frequent, with the EU creating protective laws for storing, analyzing and collecting data, a totally different shift can be seen in India and China, with frequent censorship and surveillance operations

It is crucial that the Governments realize their symbiotic partnership with the citizens who have put them in power. The Government has to ensure that they perform their functions in good faith and protect the rights of their citizens instead of piercing the privacy veil for minutest of reasons (United Nations, 2019). In light of such aspirations, the Government cannot side-line the Constitution and create menace for citizens. The UN Special Rapporteur in their 2019 report mentioned the following steps as detrimental in restoring the trust between the citizens and the government.

Governments while deploying surveillance technology, ought to be mindful that they are doing so in accordance with the law and that the surveillance is not outside the boundaries of the domestic legal system. The Governments should only authorize the surveillance for grave criminal offenses and make sure that no person's right of privacy is not infringed arbitrarily (United Nations, 2019). At the same right, the Government should ensure that they allow the citizens the freedom to hold opinions and to express them without forced censorship or interference and the same time ensure that they do not arbitrarily interfere with the media/journalists (United Nations, 2019). This would ensure that people have the freedom to access information. Failure to protect the right to freely express their thoughts could lead to chilling effect on the general public.

It is not sufficient that the surveillance is only allowed in certain cases, the surveillance should also be exercised proportionately, otherwise the surveillance measures may go beyond the reasonable scope (United Nations, 2019). Uncontrolled surveillance even if legally warranted can lead to invasion of privacy and other fundamental rights like Right to Life and Right to Equality. The Government must not exclude the role of an independent and impartial judiciary in a Constitutional democracy. Therefore, surveillance operations should be subjected to the judiciary's approval (United Nations, 2019). This can help in setting appropriate limitations with regards to scope and manner of surveillance.

The discourse surrounding surveillance technology is far from over. A branch of study called surveillance studies is shaping up and analyzing the human rights violation and invasive consequences of state surveillance. Impartial journalism and freedom of expression can help in mitigating draconian and arbitrary measures of pro-surveillance governments. At the same time the role of the stakeholders, NGOs and educational institutions is more imperative now than ever. As only educated and sensitized citizens would be able to recognize and tackle arbitrary surveillance. An international legal system setting standards of surveillance and privacy rights backed by strong domestic laws and an independent judiciary can help in vindicating the citizens.

REFERENCES

Alhinnawi, B., Edel, D., Incze, G., Priom, M., & Syed, E. (2015). The Snowden Revelations and Their Effects on European IT- Related Decisions and Decision - Making Processes. *Proceedings of the 2015/16 Course on Enterprise Governance and Digital Transformation.* https://www.researchgate.net/publication/305368725_THE_SNOWDEN_REVELATIONS_AND_THEIR_EFFECTS_ON_EUROPEAN_IT--RELATED_DECISIONS_AND_DECISION--MAKING_PROCESSES

Amnesty International & Privacy International. (2015). *Two Years After Snowden Protecting Human Rights In An Age of Mass Surveillance*. https://www.amnesty.org/en/documents/act30/1795/2015/en/

Arm. (2020). Mass Surveillance and Muslims in China. *Chinese Law and Religion Monitor*. https://www.researchgate.net/publication/343706635_mass_surveillance_and_muslims_in_china

Barbara, G., & John, Z. (1989). Sources of popular support for authoritarian Regimes. *American Journal of Political Science*, *33*(2), 319–347. doi:10.2307/2111150

BBC News. (2013, December 3). *Only 1% of Snowden files published - Guardian editor*. BBC News. https://www.bbc.com/news/uk-25205846

BBC News. (2013a, October 27). *NSA: New reports in German media deepen US-Merkel spy row*. BBC News. https://www.bbc.com/news/world-europe-24692908

Bertolucci, J. (2013). Big Data's new buzzword: Datafication. *Information Week*. Available at: www.informationweek.com/big-data/big-data-analytics/bigdatas-new-buzzword-datafication/d/d-id/1108797?/

Bhandari, V., & Sane, R. (2018). Protecting Citizens from the State Post Puttaswamy: Analysing the Privacy Implications of the Justice Srikrishna Committee Report and the Data Protection Bill, 2018. *Socio Legal Review, 14*(2), 143–169. https://papers.ssrn.com/sol3/papers.cfm?abstract_id=3251982

Boldyreva, E., Grishina, N., & Duisembina, Y. (2018). Cambridge Analytica: Ethics And Online Manipulation With Decision-Making Process. *The European Proceedings of Social & Behavioural Sciences*. https://www.europeanproceedings.com/files/data/article/95/4063/article_95_4063_pdf_100.pdf

Büchi, M., Festic, N., & Latzer, M. (2022). The Chilling Effects of Digital Dataveillance: A Theoretical Model and an Empirical Research Agenda. *Big Data & Society*, *9*(1). Advance online publication. doi:10.1177/20539517211065368

Chou, H.-L., & Chou, C. (2021). How teens negotiate privacy on social media proactively and reactively. *New Media & Society*. Advance online publication. doi:10.1177/14614448211018797

Croft, A. (2013, July 6). *EU threatens to suspend data-sharing with U.S. over spy reports*. https://www.reuters.com/article/us-usa-security-eu-idUKBRE9640JJ20130705

Draper, N. A. (2017). From privacy pragmatist to privacy resigned: Challenging narratives of rational choice in digital privacy debates: Challenging rational choice in digital privacy debates. *Policy and Internet*, *9*(2), 232–251. doi:10.1002/poi3.142

Draper, N. A., & Turow, J. (2019). The corporate cultivation of digital resignation. *New Media & Society*, *21*(8), 1824–1839. doi:10.1177/1461444819833331

European Union - Data Privacy and Protection | Privacy Shield. (n.d.). *Privacy Shield Framework*. Retrieved June 10, 2021, from https://www.privacyshield.gov/article?id=European-Union-Data-Privatization-and-Protection

Feldstein, S. (2019, September). *The Global Expansion of AI Surveillance*. Carnegie Endowment for International Peace. https://carnegieendowment.org/files/WP-Feldstein-AISurveillance_final1.pdf

Hayes, A. F., & Reineke, J. B. (2007). The effects of government censorship of war-related news coverage on interest in the censored coverage: A test of competing theories. *Mass Communication & Society*, *10*(4), 423–438. doi:10.1080/15205430701580581

Human Rights Watch. (2018, September). *China's Algorithms of Repression Reverse Engineering a Xinjiang Police Mass Surveillance App.* https://www.hrw.org/report/2019/05/01/chinas-algorithms-repression/reverse-engineering-xinjiang-police-mass

King, G., Pan, J., & Roberts, M. (2013). How censorship in China allows government criticism but silences collective expression. *The American Political Science Review*, *107*(2), 326–343. doi:10.1017/S0003055413000014

Kitchin, R. (2014). Big Data and human geography: Opportunities, challenges and risks. *Dialogues in Human Geography*, *3*(3), 262–267. doi:10.1177/2043820613513388

Lyon, D. (2007). *Surveillance Studies: An Overview*. Polity.

Lyon, D. (2014). Surveillance, Snowden, and Big Data: Capacities, consequences, critique. *Big Data & Society*, *1*(2), 1–11. doi:10.1177/2053951714541861

Mann, S., & Ferenbok, J. (2013). New media and the power politics of sousveillance in a surveillance-dominated world. *Surveillance & Society*, *11*(1/2), 18–34. doi:10.24908s.v11i1/2.4456

Marx, G. (2015). Surveillance Studies. *International Encyclopedia of the Social & Behavioral Sciences*, 733–741. https://web.mit.edu/gtmarx/www/surv_studies.pdf

McLaughlin, J., & McLaughlin, J. (2015, October 6). *Top European Court Rules That NSA Spying Makes U.S. Unsafe For Data*. The Intercept. https://theintercept.com/2015/10/06/top-european-court-rules-that-nsa-spying-makes-u-s-unsafe-for-data/

Meyer-Scho̎nberger, V., & Cukier, K. (2012). *Big Data: A Revolution that will Transform How we Work, Think and Live*. Mariner.

Millward, J., & Peterson, D. (2020, September). China's system of oppression in Xinjiang: How it developed and how to curb it. *Global China*. https://www.brookings.edu/wp-content/uploads/2020/09/FP_20200914_china_oppression_xinjiang_millward_peterson.pdf

Monika, K. (2020, April). *Case Study on Cambridge Analytica embezzling on Facebook users data*. Legal Desire. Retrieved July 10, 2021, from https://legaldesire.com/case-study-on-cambridge-analytica-embezzling-on-facebook-users-data/

Otlowski, A. (2021, September 3). Two Years Later: Cambridge Analytica and Its Impact on Data Privacy | HIPBlog. *The Hip, B2B*. Retrieved July 10, 2021, from https://www.hipb2b.com/blog/two-years-later-cambridge-analytica-and-its-impact-on-data-privacy

Pech, L. (2021). *The concept of chilling effect its untapped potential to better protect democracy, the rule of law, and fundamental rights in the EU*. Open Society European Policy Institute. https://www.opensocietyfoundations.org/uploads/c8c58ad3-fd6e-4b2d-99fa-d8864355b638/the-concept-of-chilling-effect-20210322.pdf

Perez, B. C. E. J. R. (2013, September 28). *NSA: Some used spying power to snoop on lovers – CNNPolitics*. CNN. https://edition.cnn.com/2013/09/27/politics/nsa-snooping/index.html

Rhodan, M. (2015, July 28). White House Responds to Petition Urging Obama to Pardon Edward Snowden. *Time*. https://time.com/3974713/white-house-edward-snowden-petition/

Richards, N. (2013). The dangers of surveillance. *Harvard Law Review*, *126*, 1934–1965. https://harvardlawreview.org/wp-content/uploads/pdfs/vol126_richards.pdf

Rodriguez, S. (2019, September 20). *Facebook has suspended tens of thousands of apps after Cambridge Analytica investigation*. CNBC. https://www.cnbc.com/2019/09/20/facebook-suspended-tens-of-thousands-of-apps-after-cambridge-analytica.html

Rollins, J. W., & Liu, E. C. (2013, September). *NSA Surveillance Leaks: Background and Issues for Congress* (No. R43134). Congressional Research Services. https://sgp.fas.org/crs/intel/R43134.pdf

Ryan, T. I. M. (2018). *Whistleblower: Cambridge Analytica Targeted Minority Voters to Stay Home*. CourtHouse News Service. Retrieved February 2, 2022, from https://www.courthousenews.com/whistleblower-cambridge-analytica-targeted-minority-voters-to-stayhome/#:~:text=WASHINGTON%20%28CN%29%20%E2%80%93%20The%20former%20research%20director%20for,voters%20at%20home%20during%20the%202016%20presidential%20election

Sabbagh, D. (2020, August 28). Trump 2016 campaign "targeted 3.5m black Americans to deter them from voting." *The Guardian*. https://www.theguardian.com/us-news/2020/sep/28/trump-2016-campaign-targeted-35m-black-americans-to-deter-them-from-voting

Schneier, B. (2012). *Liars and Outliers: Enabling the Trust that Society needs to Thrive*. Wiley.

Schwarck, E. (2017, December 8). *Behind the Golden Shield: China Reforms Public Security Intelligence*. Jamestown. Retrieved July 10, 2021, from https://jamestown.org/program/behind-golden-shield-china-reforms-public-security-intelligence/

Seva, G. (2015). Corrupting the cyber-commons: Social media as a tool of autocratic stability. *Perspectives on Politics*, *13*(1), 42–54. doi:10.1017/S1537592714003120

Sharma, I. (2021, February). *A More Responsible Digital Surveillance Future*. Federation of American Scientists. https://uploads.fas.org/2021/02/Digital-Surveillance-Future.pdf

United Nations. (2013, April). *Report of the Special Rapporteur on the promotion and protection of the right to freedom of opinion and expression (A/HRC/23/40)*. https://www.ohchr.org/Documents/HRBodies/HRCouncil/RegularSession/Session23/A.HRC.23.40_EN.pdf

United Nations. (2019, May). *Report of the Special Rapporteur on the promotion and protection of the right to freedom of opinion and expression (A/HRC/41/35)*. https://documents-dds-ny.un.org/doc/UNDOC/GEN/G19/148/76/PDF/G1914876.pdf?OpenElement

Van Dijck, J. (2014). Datafication, dataism and dataveillance: Big data between scientific paradigm and ideology. *Surveillance & Society*, *12*(2), 197–208. doi:10.24908s.v12i2.4776

Véliz, C. (2020). *Privacy Is Power: Why and How You Should Take Back Control of Your Data*. Bantam Press.

White House. (2014). *Big Data and the future of privacy*. Available at: www.whitehouse.gov/blog/2014/01/23/bigdata-and-future-privacy/

Zabarenko, D. (2013, June 10). *"Pardon Edward Snowden" petition seeks White House response*. https://www.reuters.com/article/us-usa-security-petition/pardon-edward-snowden-petition-seeks-white-house-response-idUSBRE95910820130610

Zialoita, P. (2019, October 30). *NPR Cookie Consent and Choices*. NPR. Retrieved July 10, 2021, from https://choice.npr.org/index.html?origin=https://www.npr.org/2019/10/30/774749376/facebook-pays-643-000-fine-for-role-in-cambridge-analytica-scandal

Chapter 15
A Survey on Privacy–Preserving Data Publishing Models for Big Data

Jayapradha J.

Department of Computing Technologies, SRM Institute of Science and Technology, Kattankulathur, India

Prakash M.

Department of Data Science and Business Systems, SRM Institute of Science and Technology, Kattankulathur, India

ABSTRACT

Big data deals with massive amounts of data with various characteristics and intricate structures. The vast amount of data collection in big data has led to lots of security and privacy threats. Big data evolution and the need for security and privacy in big data have been covered in the study. Big data taxonomy framework, the privacy laws, and acts have also been analyzed and studied. Various privacy-preserving data publishing models and their attack models have been thoroughly studied under the categories of 1) record linkage model, 2) attribute linkage model, 3) table linkage model, and 4) probabilistic model. Furthermore, the trade-off between privacy and utility, future directions, and inference from the study have been summarized. The study gives insights into various techniques in privacy-preserving data publishing to address the problems related to privacy in big data.

INTRODUCTION

The word 'Big Data' has started ruling the recent computing trade. (Keith, 2017) states that John Graunt dealt with the massive information for analysis and was the first to work with statistics. (Mark, 2013) states that in 1880, handling and processing data became very tedious for massive data sets. Providentially, in 1881, Herman Hollerith, an American, invented the Punch Cards Tabulating Machine. The Tabulating Machine reduced the duration of work from years to months. In 1927, Fritz Pfleumer, developed a method for storing information magnetically on tape. The technique to store information was a magnetic

DOI: 10.4018/978-1-7998-8641-9.ch015

strip that replaced wire recoding technology. In 1943, the British invented Colossus, the data processor, to identify the patterns in messages. It further reduced the duration of the work from weeks to hours. In 1945, John Von Neumann laid the foundation for the establishment of today's computer architecture. In 1952, computers were created, operated independently and dealt with the National Security Agency for decrypting messages. In 1969, the creation of ARPANET paved the way for the internet. As the ARPANET was not efficient, the technology moved to NSFNET to improve efficiency and speed. In 1965, the US government proposed data centers to store information. Due to privacy invasion, the first data center project was called off. Microcomputers were introduced in 1977 and became the milestone in the progression of the internet and later big data. In the beginning, the computers' costs were not affordable. Thereafter, prices were decreased, and now computers have become "reasonable consumer goods." Tim-Berners-Lee introduced the "World Wide Web in 1989," and the CERN announced that WWW would be free for the World in 1993.

The Theory of the Internet of Things (IoT) was proposed in 1999. The current situation is such that the world is nothing without the transmission of data. IoT constitutes automation, wireless communication, sensors, the internet, GPS and embedded systems. Unfortunately, IoT is prone to hacking. The development of artificial intelligence and machine learning is to focus on security issues in IoT. Owing to free access to the World Wide Web, the data transmission and flow of information became high. In 2005, Roger Mougalas named the massive data as big data as he couldn't handle and process it with the traditional tools. Then, various tools were discovered to handle big data, and the Hadoop open-source software was the first and foremost software. Another issue raised was how the data could be stored though magnetic strips were in use. Hence, cloud data storage came in. CompuServe was the first cloud service that offered 128k data space for the customers. Now, big data is revolutionizing the whole world with its technology.

BIG DATA

The word Big Data has been in existence since the early 1990s. Enterprise Big Data Framework (2019) discussed in their article that big data is not new; it has existed for a few decades. Over the centuries, data has been analyzed and decision-making has been done for numerous purposes. Around 300 BC, ancient Egyptians tried to analyze data in the library of Alexandria. Besides, the Roman Empire used statistics for managing the information of soldiers during wars. Though ancient Egyptians have used data analysis and statistics, the increase in the quantity, speed and variety of data has become very large in the past two decades only. The big data timeline can generally be subdivided into three phases. Figure 1 demonstrates the big data timeline that is divided into three phases.

The core part of the phase1 is Database Management Systems and Data Warehouses. It mainly deals with storing, extracting and analytical processing techniques. It laid the foundation for big data analysis and analytics using ETL, online statistical analysis, data mining and online analytical processing. Big Data phase 2 started from the early 2000s, handled the unstructured data, and made a secure place in different analyses such as social media, social network, sentiment analysis, web content and opinion mining. It also dealt with semi-structured data. The growth of information in social networks and social media required powerful tools, techniques and technologies to extract interesting patterns from unstructured data. Phase 2 helped the organizations resolve the crisis and to come up with a solution. In big data phase 3, although the unstructured data played a significant role in the analysis and analytics, the mobile and sensor devices started extracting valuable information. Due to the rise of data collection through sensor-based devices, IoT was popularly developed during phase 3.

The authors (Poornima and Pushpalatha, 2018) and (Simon, 2016) discussed that the combination of data collected from various sources such as mobile phones, sensors, tablets, social media and social networks creates tidal waves of data. To deal with the vast volume of data, Doug Laney coined three V's of Data Management: Volume (base of big data, constitute every piece of data), Velocity (quick flow of information) and Variety (data from different sources).

Figure 1. Big data timeline

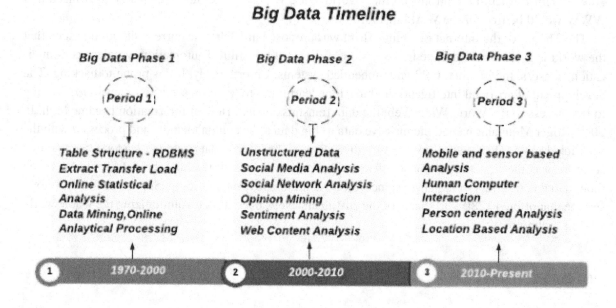

Later, other data scientists further extended three V's with various factors such as 1) Data Variability (loading of the inconsistent flow of data into the database) 2) Veracity (Consistency and accuracy of data) 3) Complexity (different format of sources for the same info) 4) Value (insights and interpretations to transform data into useful information). The V's and C describe the big data and its characteristics, as shown in Figure 2.

Figure 2. V's and C of big data

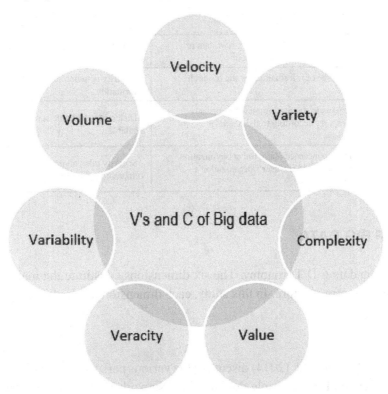

NEED FOR PRIVACY AND SECURITY IN BIG DATA

The author (Harsha et al., 2016) discussed privacy and security issues. With the increase in electronic data, more importance has been given to achieve security and data privacy. Numerous organizations have turned up ethical guidelines to impose legal requests to handle their data to achieve security and privacy. US Department of Health and Human Services (2015) announced that in recent times, both the public and private sectors have started considering the privacy and security guidelines as essential to avoid risk related to big data. (Prakash and Singaravel, 2014) discussed that all organizations should give importance to privacy and security. Without privacy and security protection tools, many organizations don't come forward to use big data services. (Jayesh et al., 2017) and (Oracle, 2019) discussed in their work that organizational privacy is more complex than individual privacy. Big Data privacy and safety play a significant role in all the phases, such as the Generation phase, Storage, Data Processing, etc. Table 1 clarifies the significant difference between privacy and security.

Table 1. Dissimilarities between privacy and security

S. No.	Privacy	Security
1	Data Privacy is about governing how data is composed, stored, shared and used.	Data Security is about protecting data from various attackers.
2	Proper usage of information for the research purpose.	Security is maintaining the secrecy and integrity of information.
3	No worldwide standard framework, privacy guidelines vary according to the needs of organizations.	Different worldwide standard security frameworks are available.
4	Privacy is concerned about the anonymization of data to safeguard the user's/organization's information.	Security talks about various attacks and vulnerabilities in the network.

TAXONOMY OF BIG DATA

Figure 3 shows the big data 6-D Taxonomy. The six dimensions constitute the main aspects needed to create a significant data infrastructure. In this study, each dimension of big data is focused.

Data

Is all data equivalent? Praveen et al. (2014) discussed the various perspectives of data, infrastructure and storage. Data are generated from multiple domains like Network Security, Social Networking, Visual Media, Sensor Data, Retail, Finance and Large Scale Science. Data can also be mapped with the degree of structure of an enterprise; they are 1. Structured data (Geo-data) 2. Semi-Structured data (E-mails) 3. Unstructured data (Video, Audio). Data can be classified into three types 1. Real-Time (Dynamic data) 2. Near Real-Time (Advertisement) and 3. Batch (Historical data). The data in a properly structured schema adapts a database model. The relational data typically represents the structured data. In unstructured data there are no pre-defined schema or structure and it will not be in an organized form. The unstructured data typically refers to the hefty text, i.e., long paragraphs. It may also include raw data such as images, video, audio, pixels data, blogs, documents, sensor data, pdf files, powerpoint files, spreadsheets and word documents. The semi-structured data fall amongst the structured data and unstructured data. The data domains are categorized as follows 1. Network security 2. Social Networking 3. Visual media 4. Sensor data 5. Retail 6. Finance and 7. Large-scale science.

Figure 3. Big data 6-D taxonomy

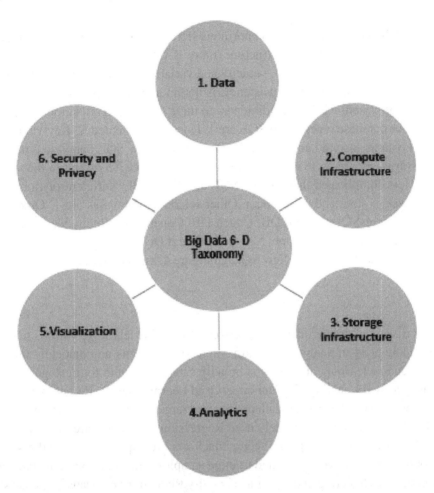

Compute Infrastructure

The Hadoop ecosystem is the most popularly used system in big data for parallel processing, whereas different approaches have been used for parallel processing in various domains. The two main infrastructures are 1. Hadoop and 2. Spark. The batch processing uses Hadoop and real-time processing uses Spark. Hadoop comprises different components 1. Pig, 2. Hive, 3. Hbase, 4. Flume, 5. Lucence, 6. Avro, 7. Zookeeper and 8.oozie. The taxonomy of various processing architectures differs with latency. The two different latency are 1. Low Latency (Stream Processing) and 2. High Latency (Batch Processing). Apache Hadoop and S4 can be adopted as effective frameworks for Map-reduce in Batch Processing. SAP Hama, Giraph, Pregel can be utilized for parallel bulk synchronization in Batch Processing. The streaming process addresses the computational load parallelization. High latency can tolerate the late generation of results. If an application does not need the result immediately, then the system is said to be in high latency.

Storage Infrastructure

Big Data handles 6 V's and 1 C, which need enormous storage. Various databases are required to store massive data. A scalable horizontal infrastructure (more RAM and HDD can be added) is needed to handle the volume, velocity, variety, value, veracity and variability of data. Though different databases are used, properties such as atomicity, consistency, isolation and durability (ACID) properties should be maintained. Storage structure is broadly divided into three databases 1. Relational (SQL), 2. No SQL and 3. New SQL. The database types of No SQL are 1. Document oriented, 2. Key-value stores, 3. Bigtable inspired, 4. Dynamo inspired and 5. Graph oriented. The new SQL database type is In-Memory. Data complexity varies according to the standards of the database. According to the survey, the relational database is less complicated than the No SQL and New SQL. Different platforms are followed by different databases to store and access data. Other relational databases are 1. Oracle, 2. SQL-lite, 3. MySQL and 4. PostgresSQL. Mongo DB, Couch DB, Couch base, Redis, Memcached, Aerospike, Riak, Cassandra, Voldemort, Hbase, Graph, Neo4j and Orient DB are the different databases of NoSQL. Hstore and VoltDB are the databases of New SQL. In Figure 4, big data security framework is depicted.

Analytics

Kevin (2012) has discussed probabilistic perspectives of machine learning. Various machine learning algorithms are widely used in analytics to learn interesting patterns automatically and for inferring knowledge. The machine learning algorithm is broadly categorized into four categories 1. Supervised Learning, 2. Unsupervised Learning, 3. Semi-supervised Learning and 4. Re-enforcement. Supervised learning methods work with the labeled data and known targets. The most common algorithms are 1. Regression and 2. Classification. The widely used Regression algorithms are Polynomial and MARS. Decision Trees, Naive Bayes and Support Vector Machines are supervised algorithms. Unsupervised learning does not have pre-defined classes and training samples. The most common algorithms of unsupervised learning are 1. Clustering and 2. Dimensionality Reduction. K-means and Gaussian Mixtures are the Clustering Algorithms. The famous Principle Component Analysis algorithm comes under Dimensionality Reduction. Semi-supervised is the mixture of both data that is labeled and unlabeled. Active and Co-training are semi-supervised algorithms. Reinforcement balances between exploration and exploitation. Markov's decision process and Q-learning come under the reinforcement algorithm.

Visualization

Han (2012) discussed and explained the various visualization techniques in his textbook. Visualization methods are categorized into the subsequent kinds 1. Spatial Layout Visualization, 2. Abstract/summary visualization and 3. Interactive/Real-time visualization. The spatial layout deals with the characteristics of points at specific coordinates. Line and bar charts and plots are common techniques in spatial layout. Abstract/summary visualization is used for processing billions (huge) of data. It helps out in data-driven insights for enterprises. Binning and clustering methods fall under Abstract/summary visualization.

Figure 4. The framework of big data security

Data	Compute Infrastructure	Storage Infrastructure	Analytics	Visualization	Security & Privacy
Network security · Intrusion Deduction · APTs **Social Networking** · Sentiment Analysis · Social Graph **Visual Media** · Scene Analysis · Image/Audio understanding **Sensor Data** · Weather · Anomaly detection **Retail** · Behavioral Analysis **Finance** · High Frequency trading **Large Scale Science** · Bioinformatics · High energy physics	**Batch** · MapReduce · Hadoop · S4 · Bulk Synchronous parallel · Hama · Giraph · Pregel **Streaming** · Info sphere · Storm · Spark	**Relational** · Oracle · Sql-lite · MySql · PostgresSQL **NoSQL** · Document Oriented · MangoDB · CouchDB · CouchBase · Key-Value stores In-Memory · Redis · Memcached · Aerospike · Dynamo inspired · Riak · Cassandra · Voldemort · Big table inspired · Hbase · Cassandra · Graph Oriented · Giraph · Neo4j · OrientDB **NewSQL** · In-Memory · HStore · VoltDB	· Supervised · Regression · Polynomial · MARS · Classification · Decision trees · Naïve Bayes · SupportVeet or Machines · Unsupervised · Clustering · K-means · Gaussian mixture · Dimensionality reduction · Principle component analysis · Semisupervised · Active · Co-training · Re-enforcement · Markov decision process · Q-learning	· Spatial Layout · Charts & Plots · Line & Bar Charts · Scatter Plots · Trees & Graphs · Tree Maps · Arc Diagrams · Forced-graph drawing · Abstract or Summary · Binning · Data Cubes · Histogram Binning · Clustering · Hierarchical Aggregation · Interactive or Real-time · Microsoft Pivot Viewer · Tableau	**Infrastructure** · Secure computation in distributed programming frameworks · Security best practices for non-relational data **Data privacy** · Privacy preserving data mining and analytics · Cryptographically enforced data centric security · Granular access control **Data Management** · Secure data storage and transaction logs · Granular audits · Data provenance **Integrity and reactive security** · End-point validation and filtering · Real-time security monitoring

The binning of data can be done through data cubes and histogram binning. Hierarchical Aggregation is used for clustering. Real-time user interaction can be adapted by Interactive/Real-time visualization. Microsoft Pivot Viewer and Tableau are the most popular tools used in Interactive/Real-time visualization.

Security and Privacy

(Chang et al., 2018) elaborated on the security and privacy issues. The issues of security and privacy in big data are broadly classified under four umbrellas 1. Infrastructure Security 2. Data Privacy, 3. Data Management and 4. Integrity and reactive security. The infrastructure of big data should cover data storage and its distributed architecture. Protecting data is the essential thing to ensure that information is not re-identified. Managing data includes the management of storage, audits and investigations of data. Data flow from various domains and sources should be integrated and secured. There are multiple forms of data flowing for integration, such as streaming, graph, scientific data, web data, retail and financial data.

DATA PRIVACY LAW AND ACT TIMELINE

The author (Kevin, 2010) discussed the prospect of having various privacy laws and their benefits. Providentially, privacy laws and regulations are made standard by the company to ensure the privacy of the end-user data. This study aims to look at the first privacy law act and the various acts proposed by the government. In Figure 5, the complete timeline of the privacy law and act is depicted. In 1974, the US established practice to manage the data collection, governance, management, maintenance, usability and broadcasting of information. The primary aim of the privacy act was to maintain the restrictions on data made by government agencies. The individuals are given rights to access only their records, and modification can also be given for that particular record. No agency should disclose the individual logs to other agencies or other individuals.

In 1996, HIPAA was proposed for health care. HIPAA enforces the tenet that health information records need not be disclosed to any agency or individual. The three security rules HIPAA comply with are 1. Administrative Requirement, 2. Physical Security requirement and 3. Technical Security Requirement. The regulatory requirement ensures that a patient's records are not disclosed to any unauthorized authorities. Physical Security Requirement helps to prevent theft of devices that maintain the information of patients. Technical Security Requirements protect the networks from information breaches. In 1999, the US asked financial institutions about their customer's data privacy. It also stated that the customers should be informed about their data security and privacy and the proposed GLB Act. The ultimate goal of this act is to make customers' financial data non-public.

COPPA, 2002 Act was proposed by the US. It was designed to restrict data usage of children under 12 years old by various agencies and website services. It was recommended mainly to limit the internet marketers, to collect the data of the children under 13 who visited their websites. The act aimed to protect children from hazardous individuals. In 2000, (HIPAA, 2002) privacy rule extension concentrated on safeguarding individual health records and personal information. Patients had been given rights to access, examine and even correct the documents on request. Patients also can claim a copy of their health records. In 2002, the US passed SOX to maintain shareholders' privacy from fraudulent agencies; hence, all government enterprises must adhere to SOX. In 2002, the US passed the FISM act. The government assigned responsibilities to various agencies to maintain the security and privacy of the government information. The fundamental aim was to protect the data from multiple data breaches. In 2013, ISO proposed a framework ISO27001 to enable each organization to safeguard their assets such as employee details, company details, intellectual property, revenue details and other confidential details. In 2018, the European Union passed the GDPR to protect its citizens and their economic data. In 2020, the CCP act was passed to enforce rules on collecting data for businesses.

Figure 5. Data privacy law and act timeline

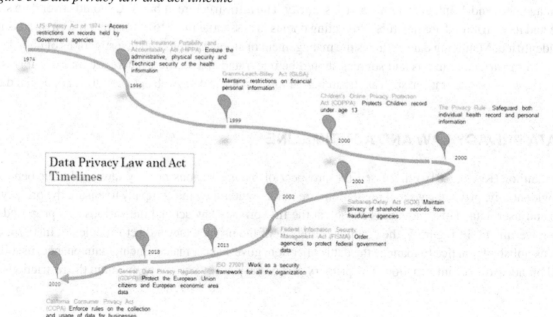

EXISTING MODELS FOR PRIVACY-PRESERVING DATA PUBLISHING (PPDP)

Privacy-Preserving becomes the most critical component in big data. Many privacy preservation techniques have been recommended and applied to eradicate the disclosure-control problem. Unfortunately, not all the methods are scalable and optimal. So to overcome the flaws, many techniques have been proposed. Such few traditionally existing privacy-preserving methods are discussed here.

De-Identification

De-identification is the most fundamental approach among the privacy preservation techniques. The key objective of de-identification is to guard the individual's identity against being exposed. Data anonymization is a technique used for de-identification. It sanitizes the information for protection. Data anonymization either encrypts the data or hides the information in the datasets. By performing data anonymization, the individual data remains anonymous in the dataset. Mehmet (2018) studied and suggested that the de-identification method is not the best for big data since the protection level is low due to the following factors:

- The de-identification process has ample flexibility.
- No efficient algorithms have been proposed to eliminate the risk of re-identification.
- The de-identification doesn't guarantee data anonymity.

A few standard terms used in the above three methods are

- **The Quasi-identifier attribute** was introduced by Tore Dalenius in 1986. It combines attributes used to identify the individual data by relating it with other external records. For example, age, gender, date of birth, zip code, etc., can be combined with other records to re-identify the individuals.
- **Sensitive Attributes** are personal information, which users usually don't disclose. Ex. Income.
- **Insensitive data** are not private information. The most general data are considered as insensitive. Ex. Gender.
- **An equivalence class** is a group of records that should have the same quasi-identifier values on each.

K-Anonymity

(Samarati and Latanya, 1998) introduced the k-anonymity model. Previously, many organizations, banks, life insurance agencies and other institutions selected their customers and employees based on their medical records. The question that arises here is from where they get the medical records without the individual's consent. Such a concept is called snooping. Many organizations just sell their customers' data to the third party by removing the direct identifiers such as individual name, address and mobile number assuming the data is anonymous. Thus the confidentiality is maintained without knowing the risk in it. Though, the individual record can be re-identified by connecting with the remaining attributes like zip code, sex, gender, and other characteristics.

(Latanya,1997) discussed the three challenges faced while providing anonymous data such as 1. Anonymity lies in the hand of the beholder 2. Uniqueness and rare information that lies in the dataset and 3. Degree of anonymity. The larger the record, the greater the anonymity of data, lessen the chance of re-identification. The voters' list and the medical history are related to identifying the persons. Voters list of 54,805 includes the date of birth and gender. Even though the data is considered anonymous by masking or removing the name, address, telephone number, the record can be re-identified using the date of birth or gender or both date of birth and gender. In the voter's record, 12% have the exact date of birth, 29% have unique records when date of birth and sex are combined and 69% records are exclusive with the birth and five-digit zip code. So, 97% of the individuals were re-identified when the date of birth and full zip code are combined. To solve the above problem, Samarati and Latanya introduced k-anonymity.

Figure 6 depicts the linking of records using a quasi-identifier to re-identify data. For the re-identification of an individual, the concept suppression and generalization are introduced in k-anonymity to avoid linking records. In k-anonymity, the data sanitization is done by 1) Generalization (values of attributes are given in the range of values) and 2) Suppression (certain values of the attribute are substituted by "*"). The disclosed database represents the k-anonymity if any individual tuple is unidentifiable from at least k-1 individuals relating to the quasi identifier. In Table 2, three tables are representing the patient's original table to be disclosed, a k-anonymized table and an identification table.

Figure 6. Linking of records using a quasi-identifier to re-identify data

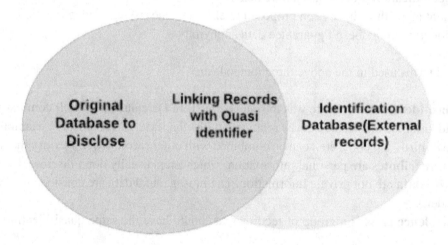

In each table, each tuple represents the individual record and the column represents the attributes. In all three tables, the sensitive attributes, insensitive attributes, identifying attributes and quasi-identifier are represented. (Khaled and Fida, 2008) stated that the primary objective of k-anonymity is to guard the values of the sensitive attribute (i.e., disease). The insensitive attributes sex, age and postal code represent the quasi identifier. The rules of k-anonymity are as follows:

1. The individual records of the dataset are divided into classes of the minimum occurrence of k.
2. Within each group of records, the quasi identifier (insensitive attributes) should be similar. It can be done through:
    a. Suppression (either delete the entry or mark it as "*")
    b. Generalization (replace it with the range of values).

3. No modifications are made to the values of the sensitive attributes.

The disclosed (k-anonymized) database represents the 2-anonymity. The identification database is the external record that is obtained from the journalist database. The journalist database is matched with the k-anonymity table to identify the name.

Table 2. k-anonymity model for the medical dataset

Identifying Variable	Sensitive Attribute	Quasi identifier (Insensitive Attribute)		
Name	Disease	Gender	Age	Zip code
John	Heart	M	31	12345
Paul	Heart	M	33	12346
Bill	Diabetes	M	45	12144
Freda	Cancer	F	40	12155
Douglas	Stomach Cancer	M	42	12156
Bob	Stomach Cancer	M	35	12157

Original Database to Disclose

2-Anonymization

Sensitive Attribute	Quasi identifier (Insensitive Attribute)		
Disease	Gender	Age	Zip code
Heart	*	3*	1234*
Heart	*	3*	1234*
Diabetes	*	>=40	121**
Cancer	*	>=40	121**
Stomach Cancer	*	>30	1215*
Stomach Cancer	*	>30	1215*

Disclosed (k-anonymized) Database

Identifying Variable	Quasi identifier (Insensitive Attribute)		
Name	Gender	Age	Zip code
John	M	31	12345
Paul	M	33	12346
Bill	M	45	12144
Freda	F	40	12155
Douglas	M	42	12156
Bob	M	35	12157
Henry	M	33	13158
Joe	F	26	14152
Nina	F	33	14153
Alex	M	28	14157
Kathy	F	25	15100
Almond	M	50	15150
Zipf	M	52	15153

Identification Database

Though k-anonymity is useful for group-based anonymity and is simple, it's prone to few attacks. When the attacker has little knowledge about records, it's easy to gain the information from the dataset by the following attacks.

- **Homogeneity Attack** occurs when the k records in a dataset comprise the same value. The sensitive attribute values of k records can be identified even though the dataset is anonymized using the k-anonymity model.
- **Background Knowledge attack** occurs when the attacker knows the k-records, and the attacker can be able to re-identify the value of the sensitive attribute when combined with quasi-identifier.

Due to these attacks, there is no guarantee that k-anonymity will provide a secured disclosure of data. The authors (Khaled and Fida, 2008) and (Sofya and Adam, 2010) discussed and implemented the k-anonymity model for the medical dataset, as shown in Table 2.

l-Diversity

Though k-anonymity is very simple and effective, it leads to homogeneity and background attacks. So as an extension of k-anonymity to overcome the disadvantages, (Machanavajjhala et al., 2006) proposed the concept of *l*-diversity. *l*-diversity provides privacy, stating that even the person disclosing the data to the third party does not become aware of the information possessed by the individuals. In Table 3, the *l*-diversity concepts ensure *l* "well represented" values for all the sensitive attributes, making the quasi-identifiers unpredictable in every equivalence class. In Table 3, 3-diversity disclosed data for the medical dataset is depicted. Implementing *l*-diversity is not always possible due to the distribution and variety of data. (Ram et al., 2018) stated that the *l*-diversity also has limitations and is prone to few attacks, such as skewness and similarity attacks.

- **Skewness attack** occurs when the dissemination of data is crooked into limited equivalence classes; the semantic closeness of the data in the equivalence class leads to the disclosure of sensitive attributes.
- **Similarity attack** occurs due to the similarity of the data. For example, if the attacker recognizes that Freda is 40 years old and resides in zip code 12155, then Freda falls under the disease-cancer category compared to others in the table. So the intruder can quickly identify that Freda has some disease related to cancer.

Table 3. 3-Diversity disclosed data for the medical dataset

Identifying Variable	Sensitive Attribute	Quasi identifier (Insensitive Attribute)		
Name	Disease	Gender	Age	Zipcode
John	Heart	M	31	12345
Paul	Heart	M	33	12346
Bill	Diabetes	M	45	12144
Freda	Cancer	F	40	12155
Douglas	Stomach Cancer	M	42	12156
Bob	Stomach Cancer	M	35	12157

Original database to disclose

Sensitive Attribute	Quasi identifier (Insensitive Attribute)		
Disease	Gender	Age	Zipcode
Heart	*	>30	12***
Heart	*	>30	12***
Diabetes	*	>30	12***
Cancer	*	>=35	1215*
Stomach Cancer	*	>=35	1215*
Stomach Cancer	*	>=35	1215*

3-diversity Disclosed Data.

(Keerthana et al., 2017) studied and stated that though l-diversity overcomes the difficulty in k-anonymity, the *l*-diversity also doesn't guarantee privacy in attribute disclosure due to a variety of data and the semantic relationship between the sensitive attributes. Prakash and Singaravel (2018) state that privacy is achieved by making the dissemination of sensitive attributes in each equivalence class similar to the dissemination of sensitive attributes in the whole table.

T-Closeness

(Ninghui et al., 2007) proposed t-closeness, which is an advancement of *l*-diversity. A threshold t is set in the concept of t-closeness. The information gain of the intruder measures privacy. The lesser information gained by the intruders, the higher the privacy. The table is partitioned into equivalence classes. The granularity of data representation is reduced in t-closeness. An equivalence class ensures t-closeness by measuring the distance between the sensitive attribute and the equivalence classes. The attributes of the whole table are no longer more significant than the threshold t. All the equivalence classes in the table should have t-closeness. Earth Movers Distance (EMD) is a distance metric to estimate the distance between two distributions. It is also called the "Wasserstein metric." EMD measures the distance between the sensitive attributes and all the other attributes in the table. EMD calculates the distance between elements in the equivalence class and table but does not reveal how it calculates between the two distributions. The distance measure differs according to the type of data in the table as follows. 1) The distance between the two numerical data is measured by ordered length. 2) Distance between categorical values is measured using equal distance (always 1) and categorical attributes can also be measured using hierarchical distance. (Caitlin, 2019) explained the distance measure for the numerical attributes with an example, as shown in Table 4.

1) The intruder will have some belief about the table and its sensitive attributes before its release. Such knowledge is called a Prior belief (B1).
2) After the table release, intruders will get different insights called Posterior belief. In t-closeness, the measure of information gain is the difference between Prior belief (B1) and Posterior belief (B2).
3) Sensitive attribute distribution in the entire table is denoted as GD (Global Distribution).
4) Sensitive attribute distribution in an equivalence class is denoted as PL.

Table 4. Disclosed dataset with t-closeness for the medical dataset

ID	Quasi identifier (insensitive attribute)		Sensitive Attribute	
	Zip code	Age	Salary	Disease
1	47679	28	3K	Heart
2	47602	21	4K	Ulcer
3	47678	25	5K	Cancer
4	47905	42	6K	ulcer
5	47909	50	11K	flu
6	47906	45	8K	Dengue
7	47609	31	7K	Dengue
8	47673	35	9K	Ebalo
9	47601	33	10K	Cancer

Disease database to be disclosed

ID	Quasi identifier (insensitive attribute)		Sensitive Attribute	
	Zip code	Age	Salary	Disease
1	476**	2*	3K	Heart
2	476**	2*	4K	Ulcer
3	476**	2*	5K	Cancer
4	4790*	>40	6K	ulcer
5	4790*	>40	11K	flu
6	4790*	>40	8K	Dengue
7	476**	3*	7K	Dengue
8	476**	3*	9K	Ebola
9	476**	3*	10K	Cancer

3-diversity table

ID	Quasi identifier (insensitive attribute)		Sensitive Attribute	
	Zip code	Age	Salary	Disease
1	4767*	<40	3K	Heart
2	4767*	<40	5K	Cancer
3	4767*	<40	9K	Ebola
4	4790*	>40	6K	ulcer
5	4790*	>40	11K	flu
6	4790*	>40	8K	Dengue
7	4760*	>20	4K	Ulcer
8	4760*	>20	7K	Dengue
9	4760*	>20	10K	Cancer

0.167t-closeness for numerical attribute salary and 0.275t-closeness for the disease.

The distance measure between the numeric attributes depends on the sequential order of the number of values.

PL1= {3k, 4k, 5k}

GD={3k,4k,5k,6k,7k, 8k, 9k,10k,11k}

Probability Mass for all the pairs to transform PL1 to GD =1/9((3-3)+(3-4)+(3-5)+(4-6)+(4-7)+(4-8)+(5-9)+(5-10)+(5-11))/8=0.375

[Note: For numerical attribute, Elements of GD needs to be accessed sequentially to achieve minimum work]

PL2= {6k, 8k, 11k}

GD={3k,4k,5k,6k,7k, 8k, 9k,10k,11k}

Probability Mass for all the pairs to transform PL2 to GD = 0.617

D [Pl1, GD] =0.375 and D [PL2, GD] =0.617 (i.e.) P2 has less privacy information.

The above calculation is a sample for numerical attributes. Table 4 gives a clear example of t-closeness for the medical dataset. t-closeness cannot handle any V's of big data as it is challenging to compute the closeness of massive amounts of data using the Earth Movers Distance (EMD). It also cannot handle real-time or streaming data.

E - Differential Privacy

(Dwork et al., 2006) proposed the ε-differential privacy model. Differential Privacy collects and shares the aggregated data of users, ensures their privacy and is considered an extension of (c,t)-isolation. The main goal of differential privacy is to include noise in the aggregated query result. The comparison of post and pre- belief about the victim is avoided here. (Nguyen, 2019) states that by applying differential privacy algorithms, government agencies could disclose the demographic information of individuals to the public without any information breach and loss of secrecy. Differential Privacy guarantees that intruders can learn only about the presence of an individual record and not anything more than that. (Charlie, 2017) has discussed a metric in differential privacy. The vital metric in differential privacy is Epsilon (ε), and it is used as a privacy loss metric. The parameter ε controls the degree of changes. For lesser privacy loss, the parameter should be less. If the ε is high, it indicates frequent changes, which may lead to more privacy loss.

Though we need lesser ε for better privacy, the decrease in ε leads to a decreased accuracy. If an algorithm has 0-differential privacy, it may protect the dataset well, but the output accuracy is very low. The output will have only noise instead of information. So there should be a balance between privacy protection and precision, which can be achieved by differential privacy. An analyst without having prior knowledge cannot work out the output in differential privacy. (Rick and Peter, 2003) have explained the perturbation techniques. Unlike anonymization, data are not modified in differential privacy. An intermediate wall acts as a security for the database. An analyst cannot query the database directly. The intermediate wall gets the query to compute the function and displays the result to analysts by adding noise. However, the noise will be detected and the output can be analyzed by the analyst. (Anjana and Nikita, 2014) have depicted the flow of differential privacy workflow.

Figure 7. Differential privacy flow

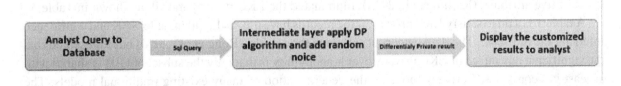

The point "estimation from repeated queries" is the vital drawback of differential privacy. If the intruder can make n number of queries to the differential privacy database, the intruder can assess the sensitive attribute through the multiple answers fetched from the repeated queries. Repeated queries to the database can breach privacy easily. Also, the research states that differential privacy cannot provide good results for complex queries; also, differential privacy computational cost is high. The process flow of differential privacy is shown in Figure 7.

(A, K)-Anonymity

(Raymond et al., 2006) introduced a concept called (α, k)-anonymity. It is an advancement of the k-anonymity model. Similar to the above models, the two privacy goals of (α, k)-anonymity are 1) To cover up individual identification 2) To cover up the linking of records. In (α, k)-anonymity, α is a fraction, and k is a whole number. k and α are the user-specified thresholds for the tables. After anonymizing data for disclosing, the sensitive attribute frequency value in the equivalence class (ec) should not exceed α, i.e., ec<= α. Wong proposed Global and Local recoding methods in (α, k)-anonymity. An optimal global recoding and efficient local recoding method were proposed in (α, k)-anonymity. In Global recoding, an attribute will have uniform values after anonymization. (Ton and Leon, 1995) proved that due to global recoding, the dataset is over-generalized and much information is skewed, which results in information loss. Local recoding is implemented to overcome data distortion due to global recoding. In local recoding, the values are anonymized at different levels by using a generalization process. The local recoding algorithm is four times faster and has three times less than global recoding in data distortion. The local recoding is also called a top-down approach. A table satisfies (α, k) - anonymized if the table's view satisfies the property of α–disassociation and k-anonymity for quasi-identifier.

LKC Privacy

(Mohammed et al., 2009) proposed a concept called LKC Privacy. The models seen so far have records and attribute linkages, which usually anonymize the records and attributes by generalizing the dataset, dividing it into equivalence classes and ensuring that each class has at least k records concerning QID. The sensitive records in the equivalence classes are diversified by obscuring the records. (Aggarwal, 2005) stated that when the dataset has high dimensionality, the data anonymized by k-anonymity leads to high utility loss. The above problem is called the "Curse of Dimensionality." LKC privacy is proposed to preserve privacy as well as the utility. To anonymize the high dimensional data, the three thresholds L, K and C are defined. Usually, the intruder cannot have all the information about the target victim's QID as it is impossible in real-time. The intruder's knowledge about the victim QID is assumed to be at most L values. The central insight of the LKC privacy is to ensure that the various combinations of the QID are made. i.e., QIDn $\subseteq$ QID with utmost length L in table T is shared with at least k records. Make sure the confidence of sensitive attribute S is less than or equal to C. The L, K and C are thresholds and S is the sensitive attribute. (Rashid et al., 2014), illuminated the LKC privacy model, as shown in Table 5.

A table T is said to satisfy LKC privacy, if the records have qid <=L, qid in table >=K and confidence inferring the qid <=C. The data owner sets all three thresholds. (Rong et al., 2020) have presented that the significant advantage of LKC privacy over k-anonymity is that only the subset of QID is shared with at least k records. LKC privacy model is the generalization of many existing traditional models. The methods k-anonymity, confidence bounding, (α, k)-anonymity, *l*-diversity are the entire exceptional cases of LKC privacy. LKC provides the right balance between privacy-preserving and utility preserving. If the threshold L and K increase and C decrease, both privacy and utility can be preserved. LKC privacy prevents both record and attribute linkages.

The patient database is considered in Table 5, as it is highly dimensional. Suppose the traditional privacy-preserving methods such as k-anonymity, (α, k)-anonymity, confidence bounding, *l*-diversity are applied to the patient data. In that case, the records are highly generalized or suppressed, which leads to more utility loss. So, in this case, LKC privacy methods can be applied. In Table 5, the three

QID's are job, sex and age. As per the intuition of LKC, the combination of QID are QID1=job, sex. QID2=sex, age. QID3=age, job. The PID is just for further verification; it will be detached when the data is published. The very significant algorithm applied in LKC Privacy is High Dimensional Top-Down Specialization (HDTDS) to achieve privacy on a large dimensional relational database. HDTDS is an extension of Top-Down Specialization. Earlier, the HDTDS cannot be applicable for privacy-preserving data mining; it was applied only for privacy-preserving data publishing. Later (Rahul and Shilpa, 2018) implemented the LKC privacy model on data mining.

Table 5. The anonymized process of the LKC privacy model

PID	Quasi identifier Job	Age	sex	Class Blood Transfuse	Sensitive Disease
1	Plumber	34	M	Y	Handicapped
2	Teacher	58	M	N	Migraine
3	Welder	34	M	Y	Handicapped
4	Doctor	24	M	N	Vascular
5	Carpenter	58	M	N	Asthma
6	Plumber	44	M	Y	Migraine
7	Teacher	24	M	N	Asthma
8	Doctor	58	F	N	Migraine
9	Teacher	44	F	N	Asthma
10	Carpenter	63	F	Y	Vascular
11	Technician	63	F	Y	Migraine

Original Medical data

PID	Quasi identifier Job	Age	sex	Class Blood Transfuse	Sensitive Disease
1	Technical	[30-60]	M	Y	Handicapped
2	Professional	[30-60]	M	N	Migraine
3	Technical	[30-60]	M	Y	Handicapped
4	Non-Technical	[1-30]	M	N	Vascular
5	Technical	[30-60]	M	N	Asthma
6	Technical	[30-60]	M	Y	Migraine
7	Professional	[1-30]	M	N	Asthma
8	Professional	[30-60]	F	N	Migraine
9	Professional	[30-60]	F	N	Asthma
10	Non-Technical	[60-99]	F	Y	Vascular
11	Technical	[60-99]	F	Y	Migraine

Anonymized data (L=2, K=2, C=0.5)

(K, E) – Anonymity

(Qing Zhang et al., 2007) introduced a concept (k, e) - anonymity. It is also an advancement of k-anonymity. The existing methods such as k-anonymity and *l*-diversity address only the categorical sensitive values. Zhang addressed the concept of protecting sensitive numerical attributes ex: credit score. The method t-closeness also deals with numeric sensitive attributes, whereas it does not deal with aggregated query result accuracy. The main goal of (k, e)-anonymity is to address the accuracy of aggregate query results with balanced and utility. The privacy goal of (k, e)-anonymity is to make an equivalence class with at least k values and bring the sensitive attribute groups larger than the threshold e. The threshold e is called an error, which is the difference between the maximum and minimum value of the sensitive attribute in each equivalence class. Also, after the data are grouped into equivalence classes, the data inside each equivalence class will be shuffled. The objective of (k, e)-anonymity is to have k values less than e. The threshold e prevents the intruder from identifying the sensitive attribute of an individual in a tapered range. A permutation-based method is proposed to handle the accuracy of the aggregate query resulting in privacy-preserving data publishing.

Applying permutation (k, e)-anonymity guarantees privacy similar to the generalization method and provides accurate aggregation results. Though the (k, e)- anonymity provides good privacy, in case the range of sensitive attribute values is very narrow, then the intruder can easily predict the sensitive attribute value.

Table 6. Sample dataset of (k, e)-anonymity (k=3, e=2000)

Quasi identifier		Sensitive		Quasi identifier		Sensitive		Quasi identifier		Sensitive
Age	Gender	Salary		Age	Gender	Salary		Age	Gender	Salary
21	M	84,000		21	M	84,000		21	M	86,000
22	M	85,000		22	M	85,000		22	M	84,000
53	M	86,000		53	M	86,000		53	M	85,000
27	F	89,000		27	F	89,000		27	F	90,000
53	M	90,000		53	M	90,000		53	M	89,000
37	M	91,000		37	M	91,000		37	M	91,000
49	F	92,000		49	F	92,000		49	F	92,000
a. Raw data				**b. Partitioned Data**				**c. Shuffled Data**		

(Bowonsak and Juggapong, 2014) proposed an incremental model for the concept (k, e)-anonymity. In Table 6a, the first table represents the original data that needs to be disclosed. According to (k, e) anonymity privacy goals, the two thresholds, k and e, are set. Let the k value be 3 and e be 2000 (the difference between the minimum and maximum value of the sensitive attribute in each class). In Table 6b, the raw table is partitioned into equivalence classes according to the thresholds. In Table 6c, the data are shuffled to break the link between QID and sensitive attributes.

Personalized Privacy

(Xiaokui and Yufei, 2006) introduced the concept of personalized privacy. The data is released to the third party for various purposes such as analyses, research, etc. The data owner removes the identifying attribute like name, id before disclosing the data to the third party. Though the identifying variables are eliminated, other attributes can reveal the person's identity when combined with the external records. Generally, generalization and suppression are the conventional approaches used for anonymizing the table. The aim of the personalized privacy method is that an individual can fix his/her limit of exposing data to others. The personalized method uses a tree taxonomy that can be accessed by the public. All the sensitive attributes are organized in the leaf node and the intermediate nodes hold the parent name that describes the disease. For example, if the child nodes are Covid and SARS with the intermediate node as "Deadly disease," then the individual can set the guarding node as a deadly disease to permit others to view only the intermediate node deadly disease. The above technique can be applied to both categorical and numerical QID. Personalized privacy uses a new approach called SA-generalization (SA-Sensitive Attributes).

The main advantage of personalized privacy is authorizing the individuals to define the threshold. The threshold imposed by an individual is called a "Guarding Node." Though record owners possess permission for their records, they are unaware of the sensitive attribute value distribution in the entire table or QID group before the data is disclosed. The lack of such information may lead to a high-level guarding node setup, which leads to high utility loss.

However, the individual guarding node-set is still not precise. (Jianfeng et al., 2018) proposed a concept (α, ε)-anonymity, an extension of personalized privacy. The (α, ε)-anonymity is used to deal with specific data based on lossy-join. In Table 7, all the QID {age, sex, zip code} are generalized along with the sensitive attribute. Tuple no: 4, Jai alone does not want any privacy because he does not mind disclosing his disease flu. So the generalized value for flu is the same .i.e. disease is directly displayed. The remaining tuples are substituted with range of values for the sensitive attribute to remain anonymous.

Table 7. Sample dataset of both QID and SA generalizations for the medical dataset

Identifying Variable	Quasi identifier			Sensitive Attribute	Guarding node
Name	Age	Sex	zip code	Disease	
John	5	M	12000	Eye disorder	Eye Disease
Paul	9	M	13000	Viral Bronchitis	Respiratory infection
Bill	7	M	14000	Eye Infection	Eye Disease
Jai	12	F	22000	Flu	flu
Dora	13	F	25000	pneumonia	Respiratory infection

Original data with guarding node.

Identifying Variable	Quasi identifier			Sensitive Attribute
Name	Age	Sex	zip code	Disease
John	[1-10]	M	[10000-20000]	Eye Disease
Paul	[1-10]	M	[10000-20000]	Respiratory infection
Bill	[1-10]	M	[10000-20000]	Eye Disease
Jai	[11-20]	F	[20000-30000]	flu
Dora	[11-20]	F	[20000-30000]	Respiratory infection

Result of both QID and SA Generalization.

Table 8. Privacy models and its attack model for privacy-preserving data publishing (PPDP)

S.no	Privacy Methods	Attack Model				Anonymization Method	Author	Year
		RL	AL	PA	TL			
1	k-anonymity	Yes				Generalization Suppression	Samarati and Sweeny	2002
2	*l*-diversity	Yes	Yes			Generalization Suppression	Machanavajjhala	2006
3.	t-closeness		Yes	Yes		Generalization Suppression	Li	2007
4.	ε-Differential Privacy			Yes	Yes	Data Perturbation	Dwork	2006
5.	(α, k) anonymity	Yes	Yes			Suppression.	Wong and Wang	2006
6.	LKC Privacy	Yes	Yes			Generalization Suppression did with the subsets of QID	Mohammed and Fung	2009
7.	(k, e)- anonymity		yes			Permutation based method	Zhang	2007
8.	Personalized Privacy		yes			SA Generalization	Xiao	2006

Four attack models have been studied in the paper. 1) Record Linkage Model, 2) Attribute Linkage Model, 3) Table Linkage Model and 4) Probabilistic Model Under each model, different types of attack models have been discussed. Table 8 has listed out the different privacy models and their attack models for privacy-preserving data publishing.

THE CLASSIFICATION OF PRIVACY-PRESERVING TECHNIQUES

The existing privacy preservation techniques are classified into three types 1) Data anonymization, 2) Data perturbation and 3) Data encryption. We cannot apply all kinds of privacy-preserving techniques for all types of applications. The study has discussed data anonymization and perturbation only, but in Table 9 and Table 10, the classification of all the three techniques and the performances are also discussed. The data encryption technique is just defined in Table 9 and Table 10. (Fang et al., 2017) have clearly described the privacy-preserving techniques and its performance estimates as shown in Table 9 &10.

Table 9. The classification of privacy-preserving techniques

Privacy Preservation Technique	Uniqueness of technique	Technologies
Data anonymization technique	It sanitizes an individual's identity by suppression and generalization to protect the privacy of the relational table. It always tries to achieve balanced privacy and utility while disclosing the anonymized data.	k-anonymity, l-diversity, t-closeness, (X,Y)-anonymity, (X,Y)-linkability, (X,Y)-privacy, Personalized Privacy, FF-Anonymity, δ-Presence, (α, k)-anonymity, LKC Privacy, (k,e)-anonymity, Confidence Bounding.
Data perturbation technique	It distorts the value of the sensitive data by adding random noise, aggregated values, synthetic values generated based on the statistical properties of raw data. Research states that the data perturbation technique does not completely prevent the leakage of sensitive values.	(c,t)-isolation, ε-Differential Privacy, (d, γ)-Privacy, Distributional Privacy.
Data encryption technique	It uses encryption technique to hide the value of the sensitive attribute from adversaries. It is extensively used in distributed applications and guarantees privacy without data destruction. Encryption technique is not appropriate for big data as its computational overhead is higher.	Symmetric encryption, Public key encryption etc.

Table 10. Performance estimates of privacy-preserving techniques

Privacy Preservation Technique	Degree of Privacy	Computational Cost	Utility Preserving	Communication Overhead
Data anonymization	Low	Medium	Medium	Low
Data perturbation	Medium	Low	Low	Low
Data encryption	High	High	High	High

Utility vs. Privacy

(Felix, 2013) has discussed the need for utility and the importance of the trade-off between utility and privacy. There is always a controversy in the trade-off between privacy and utility. Several researchers state that privacy and utility are incompatible, whereas few say that privacy and utility can be compatible. Though several technologies exist for privacy preservation, balancing privacy and utility is always a big deal. (Tiancheng and Ninghui, 2009) compared various anonymization technologies and stated, "Even modest privacy gains require almost destroying the data-mining utility." Proper guidelines have been proposed to choose the right path to avoid the high utility loss while preserving privacy and overcoming the above problem. We always have a question as to what is called a utility loss. The utility loss is the loss of information in the dataset during data anonymization. To preserve privacy, few attributes are hidden/removed, which may lead to information loss. Also, the study provides the answer for the following question: when all the quasi-identifiers are eradicated, what is information (utility) loss? The utility loss is computed by the average utility loss for the large datasets. Balancing utility and privacy always remain complex and problematic. (Kato and Claude, 2013) stated that a small fine-tuned parameter could lead to achieving a balanced level of utility and privacy. An approach "Comparative x-CEG" is proposed based on the classification technique in machine learning. The parameter adjustments are carried out until there is minimal utility loss in the privacy preservation process.

Furthermore, achieving the most delicate balance between utility and privacy is still an intractable problem. (Vibhor et al., 2007) discussed the concerns in privacy during the data publishing process. The database is anonymized, and the tuple tu is related to an attacker's prior and posterior beliefs. Though lots of research and evolution of technologies are still evolving, balancing the utility and privacy has not been achieved. (Graham et al., 2013) reverse the idea of 'Privacy Attacks'. Comparative analysis of different anonymization and perturbation methods is conducted to find utility and privacy trade-offs. After the reverse of the trade-offs, differential privacy achieves the empirical privacy (notion used in 2013) for a fixed level of utility. (Graham et al., 2013) says that Anonymization results in the prevention of higher utility than data perturbation. (Andre and Martin, 2018) discussed the trade-off of privacy-utility in the health domain.

INFERENCE AND FUTURE DIRECTIONS

Big Data deals with large datasets with lots of trends, patterns that can be analyzed computationally for better decision making. The big data foundations, its evolution, the need for security and privacy were presented in the paper. Big Data taxonomy, data privacy law and act timelines were clearly elaborated. This study covered various privacy models and their attack models of privacy-preserving data publishing. The privacy-preserving data publishing models were categorized into four models viz. 1) Record Linkage Model, 2) Attribute Linkage Model, 3) Table Linkage Model and 4) Probabilistic Model. Each privacy model was explained with examples, merits and demerits. The classification of the different privacy techniques such as data anonymization, data perturbation and data encryption were compared and described. The study's inference is that all the proposed models and techniques in privacy-preserving data publishing resolve only the technical part of the problem. It is also equally significant to identify the non-technical issues confronted by the decision-makers while implementing various privacy-preserving technologies. Various organizations implement privacy-preserving models; however, individuals should also have privacy tools for personalizing the rights over their data. Though lots of models were developed and implemented, the models should be in such a way that those should be customized according to the emerging technologies. In the face of recent years, many organizations and academia have spent lots of effort on big data privacy preservation. Still, a trade-off between privacy and utility is undeniably challenging. Shortly, the key focus should be on remedying the challenges faced in big data privacy-preserving data publishing. The solution for the trade-off between privacy and utility is to customize the various privacy models, privacy-preserving policies and laws. As per the study, though various models have been implemented, k-anonymity is a foundation for all emerging privacy models.

REFERENCES

Nguyen, A. (2019). *Understanding Differential Privacy.* https://towardsdatascience.com/understanding-differential-privacy-85ce191e198a

Valdez & Ziefle. (2018). The Users' Perspective on the Privacy-Utility Trade-offs in Health Recommender Systems. *International Journal of Human-Computer Studies, 121,* 1–35.

Gosain, A., & Chugh, N. (2014). Privacy Preservation in Big Data. *International Journal of Computers and Applications, 100*(17), 44–47. doi:10.5120/17619-8322

Srisungsittisunti, B., & Natwichai, J. (2015). An incremental privacy-preservation algorithm for the (k, e)-Anonymous model. *Computers & Electrical Engineering, 41,* 126–141. doi:10.1016/j.compeleceng.2014.10.007

Keith, D. F. (2017). *A brief history of Big Data.* https://www.dataversity.net/brief-history-big-data/#

Lustig. (2019). *T-closeness: Privacy beyond k- Anonymity and l-diversity.* https://www.ics.uci.edu/~projects/295d/presentations/295d-tcloseness

Cabot, C. (2017). *An Introduction to Differential Privacy.* https://www.infoq.com/articles/differential-privacy-intro/

Aggarwal, C. C. (2005). On k-anonymity and the curse of dimensionality. *Proceedings of the 31st International conference on Very Large Databases (VLDB).*

Dwork, C., McSherry, F., Nissim, K., & Smith, A. (2006). Calibrating Noise to Sensitivity in Private Data Analysis. In H. T. R. Shai (Ed.), Lecture Notes in Computer Science: Vol. 3876. *Theory of Cryptography* (pp. 265–284). Springer. doi:10.1007/11681878_14

Mark van Rijmenam, D. (2013). *A short History of Big Data.* https://datafloq.com/read/big-data-history/239

Enterprise Big Data Framework. (2019). *A short history of Big Data.* https://www.bigdataframework.org/short-history-of-big-data/

Wu. (2013). Defining Privacy and Utility in Data Sets. *Law Review Corolado, 84,* 1117-1177.

Cormode, G., Procopiuc, C. M., Entong, S. D. S., & Yu, T. (2013). Empirical privacy and empirical utility of anonymized data. *IEEE 29th International Conference on Data Engineering Workshops (ICDEW).*

Gardiyawasam Pussewalage, H. S., & Oleshchuk, V. A. (2016). Privacy preserving mechanisms for enforcing security and privacy requirements in E-health solutions. *International Journal of Information Management, 36*(6), 1161–1173. doi:10.1016/j.ijinfomgt.2016.07.006

Han, J., Kamber, M., & Pei, J. (2012). *Data mining: Concepts and techniques* (3rd ed.). Elsevier.

Surana, J., Khandelwal, A., Kothari, A., Solanki, H., & Sankhla, M. (2017). Big Data Privacy Methods. *International Journal of Engineering Development and Research, 5*(2), 979–983.

Xia, J., Yu, M., Yang, Y., & Jin, H. (2018). Personalized Privacy-Preserving with high performance: (α, ε)-anonymity. *Proceedings of the IEEE Symposium on Computers and Communications.*

Mivule, K., & Turner, C. (2013). A Comparative Analysis of Data Privacy and Utility Parameter Adjustment, Using Machine Learning Classification as a Gauge. *Procedia Computer Science, 20*, 414–419. doi:10.1016/j.procs.2013.09.295

Rajendran, K., Jeyabalan, M., & Rana, M. E. (2017). A study on k-anonymity, l-diversity, t-closeness Techniques focusing medical Data. *International Journal of Computer Science and Network Security, 17*, 172–177.

Aquilina, K. (2010). Public security versus privacy in technology law: A balancing act? *Computer Law & Security Review, 26*(2), 130–143. doi:10.1016/j.clsr.2010.01.002

Murphy, K. P. (2012). *Machine Learning: A Probabilistic Perspective*. The MIT Press.

El Emam, K., & Dankar, F. K. (2008). Protecting Privacy Using k-Anonymity. *Journal of the American Medical Informatics Association, 15*(5), 627–637. doi:10.1197/jamia.M2716 PMID:18579830

Sweeney, L. (1997). Weaving technology and policy together to maintain confidentiality. *The Journal of Law, Medicine & Ethics, 25*(2), 98–110. doi:10.1111/j.1748-720X.1997.tb01885.x PMID:11066504

Prakash, M., & Singaravel, G. (2018). Haphazard, enhanced haphazard and personalised anonymisation for privacy preserving data mining on sensitive data sources. *International Journal of Business Intelligence and Data Mining, 13*(4), 456–474. doi:10.1504/IJBIDM.2018.094983

Prakash, M., & Singaravel, G. (2014). An Analysis of Privacy Risks and Design Principles for Developing Countermeasures In Privacy Preserving Sensitive Data Publishing. *Journal of Theoretical and Applied Information Technology, 62*, 204–213.

Machanavajjhala, A., Gehrke, J., Kifer, D., & Venkita Subramaniam, M (2006). ℓ-diversity: Privacy beyond k-anonymity. *Proceedings of the 22nd International Conference on Data Engineering*.

Kayaalp, M. (2018). Modes of De-identification. In *AMIA Annual Symposium Proceedings*. U.S. National Library of Medicine, National Institutes of Health.

Li, N., Li, T., & Venkatasubramanian, S. (2007). t-Closeness: Privacy Beyond k-Anonymity and l-Diversity. *IEEE 23rd International Conference on Data Engineering*.

Mohammed, N., Fung, B. C. M., Hung, P. C. K., & Lee, C.-K. (2009). Anonymizing healthcare data: A case study on the blood transfusion service, *ACM SIGKDD International Conference on Knowledge Discovery and Data Mining*. 10.1145/1557019.1557157

Murthy, Bharadwaj, Subrahmanyam, Roy, & Rajan. (2014). Big Data Working Group. In *Big Data Taxonomy*. Cloud Security Alliance (CSA).

Protecting Children's Privacy under COPPA: A Survey on Compliance. (2002). Federal Trade Commission-Protecting America's Consumers.

Protecting personal Health Information in Research: Understanding the HIPAA Privacy Rule. (2002). Department of Health and Human Services.

Zhang, Q., Koudas, N., Srivastava, D., & Yu, T. (2007). Aggregate query answering on anonymized tables. *Proceedings of the 23rd IEEE International Conference on Data Engineering (ICDE)*.

Pandey, R., & Jain, S. (2018). A Hybrid Approach to Preserving Privacy in Data Mining using L-K-C and personalized Privacy. *International Journal of Innovative Research in Computer and Communication Engineering*, *6*, 1191–1198.

Ram Mohan Rao, P., Murali Krishna, S., & Siva Kumar, A. P. (2018). Privacy preservation techniques in big data analytics: A survey. *Journal of Big Data*, *33*(1), 1–12. doi:10.118640537-018-0141-8

Khokhar, R. H., Chen, R., Fung, B. C. M., & Lui, S. M. (2014). Quantifying the costs and benefits of privacy-preserving health data publishing. *Journal of Biomedical Informatics*, *50*, 107–121. doi:10.1016/j.jbi.2014.04.012 PMID:24768775

Wong, R. C.-W., Li, J., Fu, A. W.-C., & Wang, K. (2006). (α, k)-anonymity: An enhanced k-anonymity model for privacy preserving data publishing. *Proceedings of the 12th ACM International Conference on Knowledge Discovery and Data Mining.*

Wilson, R. L., & Rosen, P. A. (2003). Protecting Data through 'Perturbation' Techniques: The Impact on Knowledge Discovery in Databases. *Journal of Database Management*, *14*(2), 14–26. doi:10.4018/jdm.2003040102

Wang, R., Zhu, Y., Chang, C.-C., & Peng, Q. (2020). Privacy-preserving High-dimensional Data Publishing for Classification. *Computers & Security*, *93*, 1–10. doi:10.1016/j.cose.2020.101785

Poornima, S., & Pushpalatha, M. (2018). A survey of predictive analytics using Big Data with data mining. *International Bioinformatics Research and Applications*, *14*(3), 269–282. doi:10.1504/IJBRA.2018.092697

Samarati & Latanya. (1998). Protecting privacy when disclosing information: k-anonymity and its enforcement through generalization and suppression. *Harvard Data Privacy Lab,* 1-19.

Securing the Big Data Life Cycle. (2019). *MIT Technology Review.*

Walkowiak, S. (2016). *Big Data Analytics with R, Leverage R programming to uncover hidden patterns in your Big Data.* Packt Publishing.

Raskhodnikova, S., & Smith, A. (2010). *Algorithmic Challenges in Data Privacy.* Lecture Notes.

Li, T., & Li, N. (2009). On the Tradeoff between Privacy and Utility in Data Publishing. *Proceedings of the 15th ACM SIGKDD International Conference on Knowledge Discovery and Data Mining.*

de Waal & Willenborg. (1995). Information loss through global recording and local suppression. *Netherland Official Statistics*, 17- 20.

US Department of Health and Human Services. (2015). *Health Insurance Portability and Accountability Act.* https://www.hhs.gov/hipaa/for-professionals/index.html

Rastogi, Suciu, & Hong. (2007). The Boundary between privacy and utility in data publishing. *VLDB Endowment*, 1-12.

Fang, W., Xue, Z. W., Zheng, Y., & Zhou, M. (2017). A Survey of Big Data Security and Privacy Preserving. *IETE Technical Review*, *34*, 544–560.

Chang, W. L., Roy, A., & Underwood, M. (2018). *NIST Big Data Interoperability Framework, Security and Privacy.* https://www.nist.gov/publications/nist-big-data-interoperability-framework-volume-1-big-data-definitions-version-2

Xiao, X., & Tao, Y. (2006). Personalized privacy preservation. *ACM International Conference on Management of Data, 34,* 1-12.

Chapter 16
Critical Appraisal of Challenges to Online Consumer Fissures in Information Technology Law in India

Unanza Gulzar

https://orcid.org/0000-0002-2275-6154

NorthCap University, India

ABSTRACT

Despite the shift in e-commerce in India, there are inadequate laws to protect a person over the internet. The chapter highlights that the Information Technology (Amendment) Act, 2008, incorporated Section-A, which validates just e-commerce including e-shopping but does not include attendant principles of its formation, which gave rise to a number of questions. The chapter also discusses the loopholes and lacunas in the Information Technology Act relating to online consumers and the Indian Contract Act for formation of contracts that cannot be made equally applicable to online contracts, leaving consumers in a position where they cannot bargain. Further, the author has evaluated and analysed cases filed by consumers in terms of challenges they face. Lastly, the chapter came up with certain suggestions keeping in view unfilled space.

INTRODUCTION

Technology today has fundamentally transformed the way the commerce and enterprises were dealt by society. The presence of technology world-wide particularly internet has reached to new businesses and billions of new potential consumers (Snider, 1992). By this, electronic commerce commonly known as e-commerce have developed and is one of the wildest developing region around the world and India's greatest increasing and mainly electrifying means for business communications. While being able to access global markets, e-commerce has enabled businesses to bypass the traditional intermediaries in domestic jurisdictions. Besides, owing to its lower transaction costs, e-commerce has caused a steady

DOI: 10.4018/978-1-7998-8641-9.ch016

upsurge in the figure of sellers and suppliers in the marketplace, thus increasing diversity and competition in the market.

Electronic commerce as an indication of globalisation represents critical periphery of achievement in the virtual world across the globe. Today Internet development has led to a mass of fresh growth for example limited restrictions for corporations as customers turn exclusively towards internet to purchase products at possible meagre price (Beck, 2001). Further, internet being an effectual medium of changing straightforward behaviour of doing commerce. However, electronic commerce is preferable rather useful because of numerous reasons, say for example, access to products, which may not be accessible otherwise, becomes quite convenient. That is true particularly in rural areas. Besides, it acts as an effective mode of entering into transactions, for consumers as well as retailers and it has made cheaper cross-border transactions which could not have been anticipated earlier.

The term e-commerce of which online shopping (word online shopping is invented by Michael Aldrich an English tycoon in the year 1979) is a component, is the performance of purchasing or vending merchandises, services, or other information done through an e-network to consumers. Further, "it is classified as distance contracts, which means that the trader (service provider, seller) and the consumer (natural person who is acting for purposes which are outside his trade, business or profession), in lack of their simultaneous, actual and physical presence enter into contract not by meeting in person (e.g. in commercial premises, market, open-air market, via trade agent etc.), but only in an electronic way (European consumer centre, 2015)." 1n 1960's first time electronic commerce was presented through an Electronic Data Interchange (commonly known as EDI) on Value Added Networks (Susheela, 2014). Today it acts as guiding the business with the assistance of electronic mass media, creating the practice of Information Technology likewise Electronic Data Interchange.

In India development of E-commerce currently is a crucial component of its trade expedition strategy. Since the economic reformation happened in India after 1991 as a consequence of introduction of economy to merge with world economy, the necessity to enable international trade both over procedure and policy reorganisations has become the basis of India's trade and financial rules. Over the past decade internet with its web-technologies has brought technological revolution. Online shopping as a part of this revolution became extensively used across the globe general in trade and specific in Indian economy (Ray, 2011).

"As a symbol of globalization, e-commerce represents the cutting edge of success in this digital age and it has changed and is still changing the way business is conducted around the world. The commercialization of the Internet has driven e-commerce to become one of the most capable channels for inter-organizational business processes. Consequently, Internet growth has led to a host of new developments, such as decreased margins for companies as consumers turn more and more to the internet to buy goods and demand the best prices (Nissan, 2009)." Internet has precisely been an operative device in altering the straightforward ways of doing business. However, e-commerce is preferable rather useful because of numerous reasons, say for example, access to products, which may not be accessible otherwise, becomes quite convenient. That is true particularly in rural areas. Besides, it acts as an effective mode of entering into transactions, for consumers as well as retailers.

Moreover, online shopping a component of e-commerce has, in the recent years, gained a huge momentum. The internet has made possible for a seller to open a shop through a web portal, which can be even run from his home, and a consumer or shopper to place an order right from his home (Tkacz & Kapczynski. 2009), Besides, there is no speculative geographic boundaries, little functioning expenses and healthier excellence of services, no requirement of actual set up of any establishment, larger reach of shoppers, without moving physically and choosing goods from different vendors (Seybold, 2006) Indian Government had already recognised the requirement of emergence of information technology and its infrastructure as they are crucial to the development of finance. As a corollary, the government, over the last two decades, articulated open-minded guidelines, substantially successful, for the growth and progress of an industry of the Information technology. "Approximately today in India there are around 80 million Internet operators. Though significantly lesser than worldwide point of reference (typically 31% of the aggregate people), yet the figures signal the booming start of the Indian e-business success. (Majid, 2013).

Today in this period of Pandemic the e-commerce has played exponential role as it was seen that two years back only 13.6 percent sales occurred via online but today number has crossed 19.5 percent and will be in future around 48.5 percent (Kakaria, 2021).

DEVELOPMENT OF ELECTRONIC COMMERCE

In India e-commerce are likely persist an extraordinary development. Number of reasons are lucidly associating the development of E-commerce around the globe, and more specifically in India. Furthermore, this swiftness of development of e-commerce in India is incredible. There are numerous reasons which led the growth of e-commerce like easily accessible and financially cheap qualities of internet, increasing use of tablets, smartphones, and for professionals with their busy schedule etc. The growth of internet in India is tremendous as it holds first rank in it but China is having largest electronic commerce market followed by USA all around the globe. Further, as per the report of ASSOCHAM-Forrester study, annual growth of e-commerce in China is 18% but at the same time India is having tremendous annual growth of 51% (Chaudhary, 2002) Moreover, in India the estimations of future in online sales is expected to be welcoming as the as it is anticipated to reach $120 billion by 2020. Keeping in view proclivity of Indians towards Mobile phones and thereby increasing sales of mobile phones which have, percentage of e-commerce sales is growing day by day. (E-commerce in India, 2017).

THE TRENCHES – DETERMINATIONS AND CONSEQUENCES

The electronic commerce in India is highly hostile as it is a field where chief electronic commerce actors struggling amongst themselves in enlarging their province. The e-commerce sites like Amazon, Snapdeal and Flipkart have shown mega sales on their sites but the competition is increasing, thereby price cutting is high in number. At the same time Snapdeal is the most unfortunate rival because by confronting different backlashes and polemics throughout its being into existence (Laudon, 2016).

The Amazon is providing better quality and services than flipkart thereby is ahead of it in the line of competition of best downloaded app rating by 'App Annie'. However, 'Amazon Prime' is the most successful and had gained Leading status in e-commerce market compared to 'Flipkart First', thereby Amazon is ahead of Flipkart. However, Snapdeal is now improving after learned from its mistakes. The 'Unbox Zindagi' campaign is a step towards restructuring its own identity (E-commerce in India – Growth and Statistics, 2017).

ONLINE SHOPPING IN INDIA: STATISTICS AND FACTS

In 2018, an electronic shopping in Asia Pacific region the number has reached to one billion mark for the very first time ever which accounted for 60% of all users of internet in this region. India in continuation of emerging Asian market have showed positive projections for the online shopping. Presently in India, dynamic e-commerce including online shopping dispersion stands only 28% which needs plenty of improvement. However, India's retail e-commerce including online shopping CAGR is expected to touch 23% in 2021 from 2016 (Statista, 2018). In 2018 the revenue from e-commerce purchase amount to US$474353 million. Further, internet users shopping online will grow to 73.5% in the year 2022 from 70.0% in the year 2018. (Statista, 2018).

However, according to recent statistics by the year 2020 approximately 329.1 million Indians are expected to make online purchasing and hiring services. It means by then in India almost 70.7% of internet users will buy goods online. Moreover, majority are males who make purchasing online and this reflects growth of revenue as well. However, in the year 2020, female digital buyers are estimated to reach 42% of all internet shopping from 20% in 2015. Further, Indian retail e-commerce are expected to grow tremendously in the year 2016 from 16 billion US dollars to 45 billion US dollars in 2021. In India in the year 2016 net online shopping sales were 437.7 billion US dollars found on Amazon.in followed by Flipkart and Snapdeal. (Statista, 2018). "According to Grant Thornton, e-commerce in India is expected to be worth US$ 188 billion by 2025. With a turnover of $50 billion in 2020, India became the eighth-largest market for e-commerce, trailing France and a position ahead of Canada (IBPF, 2021)."

According to NASSCOM, despite COVID-19 challenges/disruptions, India's e-commerce market continues to grow at 5%, with expected sales of US$ 56.6 billion in 2021.

However, mobile phones are considered one of the promising online shopping platform as 23% of internet users expressed mobile phones as a purchasing instrument in India in the year 2016 and this has spaced India as leading electronic marketers for mobile shopping penetration. Moreover, according to recent statistics almost 27% of online purchasers purchased via smartphones on monthly basis and 24% on weekly basis. Further, in terms of value, sales from mobile commerce is expected to raise 63.5 billion US dollars by the year 2020. (Statista, 2018)

LITERATURE REVIEW

Given that the phenomenon of e-commerce is only recent to the whole world including India, there is a dearth of scholarly writings which can explore the challenges it poses to consumers besides offering legal ways to tackle them. So far, the research has been confined to rather a historical point of view. At the most, the authors have given a textbook analysis of the issues. The enormity of this new way of formation of contracts calls for its deep understanding on both sociological and legal counts. This impels the researcher to examine the existing laws related to contracts executed electronically.

Habul (2001), focussed on a question including that why a traditional market have been changed into virtual market? The most commonly reasons cited by him for shopping online is convenience and comparison of prices. Moreover the capability of electronic commerce is that a person need not to leave his home and goods or services are provided to him at doorstep. Moreover he cites reasons why the number of internet users who are shopping online goods or services is increasing day by day.

However, Tim Gerlach, (2005) in his article analysed that despite being trendy, allowing ease and quickness and received with a huge response by consumers both in urban and rural areas, online shopping cannot be said to be full proof. Rather it has become easy target for the evildoers. Online shopping poses a wide range of challenges from the consumer protection perspective, ranging from invasion of privacy to jurisdictional issues. He discusses all these challenges in detail.

Gregory Karp, (2009) explores that electronic commerce can be a best friend of elegant customers with the capability to without doubt evaluate shops and can look for relaxations and can buy with a few clicks on mouse. A customer can now easily compare prices and can look for discount offers

Forrester, (2012) analyse that there are hundred crore wireless subscribers and six crore smart phone users in India. There are 145 million internet users and they spend 20-25 hours /month for online shopping (Also McKinsey 2012). This is one of the reason why shoppers get attracted. However the author gives statistical data in his book on online shopping in India. Techno Pak (2012) discussed in their report that how the earlier people were afraid to purchase online and how the trend is changing from online to offline purchasing. Further the total retail size in India is 455 billion dollar. Out of this organised retail is thirty four billion dollar seven percent of total retail).

Dr. Jyoti Ratan, (2013) argues in detail that how the amount of trade has grown extra-ordinary with widespread internet usage and how the globe has now became a global market by shifting traditional world into virtual world. Further, paced special emphasis on advantages for both vendor and vendee in the sense that vendor can have reach to any corner of world and simultaneously the purchaser is having exceptional choices. Effectiveness to a great extent is enlarged, paper work abridged, time period concise and payment narrowed. Moreover the author focuses on Information Technology Act 2000.

Moreover according to Juneesh k, (2014) discusses the problems which the online shoppers are facing those are like receiving damaged products, wrong products, delay in delivery of products or fails to receive any product at all which is eventually affected on consumer's right. Further, approximately 40% of internet users around the world purchase products through online medium via different apparatus and this indicates greater than 1 billion purchasing over internet and is anticipated to grow endlessly.

Moreover, Katherine Arline, (2015) gives the historical perspectives of online shopping and further explains the different concepts of Electronic Commerce. It further analyses that with the beginning of internet machinery, the nature of e-commerce, its evolution have taken form and rotate dramatically. Further, medium of the E-commerce grow with the enlarged accessibility of internet entrance and the beginning of famous internet vendors in the 1990's and early on 2000's. In 1995 Amazon started functioning as a book delivering trade in Jeff Bezo's Garagr. At the same time in 1997 EBay exploded Beanie Babis Frenzy and in 1995 enabled customers to vend online against each other and which in 1995 launch online.

However, Farooq Ahmed (2015), evaluates in detail that how the Shopper as a consumer suffers despite having enumerable laws in India like Indian Contracts Act, 1872, Consumer Protection Act, 1986, Information Technology Act, 2000. Despite all these laws certain queries are raised which needs to be answered from the Indian Perspective by the agencies are: what are the questions related to formation of contract created by IT Act? How far the Indian Contract Act, is stretchy sufficient to contain these questions and to offer for their settlement? Does the IT Act include questions left cover by the Contract Law? How far the main principles of contract formation been changed by the Information Technology Act? What questions are left for courts to decide?

RESEARCH GAPS

Online Commerce or E-commerce, certainly, affords us transactions that otherwise would not be possible. However, as experience shows, it is not immune to consumer harm either. It is evident that much progress has been made in jurisdictions like United Kingdom and USA with respect to the protection of consumers on the Internet. Very little attention, however, has been paid to the online consumer protection in India. Further, despite the increasing growth of annual rate of e-commerce, India is far behind in protecting consumers which are discussed as under:

Electronic Commerce Issues under Information Technology Act, 2000

The issues under Information Technology Act, 2000 related to electronic commerce are as under:

- One of objective of Information Technology Act, 2000 reiterated by Information Technology (Amendment) Act, 2008 is to legalize the electronic commerce. At the same time in the IT Act 2000 there was no provision which validated electronic contracts despite the fact that under article 11 in the Model law there was direct provision to this effect. The IT (Amendment) Act now provides under section 10-A that *"where in a contract formation, the communication of proposals, the acceptance of proposals, the revocation of proposals and acceptances, as the case may be, are expressed in electronic form or by means of an electronic record, such contract shall not be deemed to be unenforceable solely on the ground that such electronic form or means was used for that purpose"*.

This provision makes it aptly clear that e-contracts are valid and enforceable but without laying down the principles of formation of contract which can give rise many questions than the solutions provided for the same by the amendment.

Are Common law principles followed by the Indian Courts to interpret provisions of the Indian Contract Act, applicable to the Electronic Contracts also? Are electronic contracts now exclusively dealt under IT Act? Has the IT Act provided additional requirement for the formation of electronic contacts? Has the IT Act in any way changed or modified substantive provisions relating to the Contract formation?

Further, one of the requisite under section 10 of Indian contract Act, 1872 is mutual consent of both the persons which must be offeror and offeree as provided under Section 2 (a) and (b) and the person equally includes both legal and natural person (under section 3 (43) of the General Clauses Act, 1897) but at the same time the word computer does not fall in any of the two class. Therefore any agreement performed by an independent computer will not fall under the above definition. Therefore two options would have been available before passing the IT Act to legislatures. One to embrace computers as parties second to treat computers as an agents. But the court *in State Farm Mutual Automobile insurance company v. Brockhorst,* support of treating computers as the agents.

In traditional contracts common law courts have clarified difference between dichotomy of offer and Invitation to treat. But it is equally difficult to prove on websites carrying such statements. Now the question arises are those statements simply an offer or information provider to customer. The distinction between invitation to treat and offer on websites is difficult to prove, the reason being that these sites are structured in such manner that acceptance means goods are in accumulation and proposal can be involuntarily withdrawn. At the same time there is an argument that vendor may refuse to sell off his products to certain or persons. (Toralf, 1998). Therefore every statement has to be interpreted by the words used and practice of deal.

- The phrase 'incorporation by reference' is used for a condition to refer a document where its provisions are defined somewhere else. Communication over internet is structured in a technique that huge messages are communicated with concise information to information detailed at other place. In such a situation question arises that does the terms by incorporation by reference form a part of actual agreement and if yes under what conditions?

The Information Technology Act is silent on conferring legal status on such terms. Infact it was not even in original United Nations Commission on Trade Law model but was later realised and express provisions to such an extent was incorporated in the Model law by Article 5 *bis UNCITRAL* and such type of provision is missing in IT Act.

Also, due to the significant difference amongst physical contracts and electronic contracts, the tests developed by courts in traditional contracts like standard form of contracts may be unsuccessful whilst applied to electronic contracts. Moreover the terms and conditions must always be brought to the notice of other party but at the same time opinions differ in electronic contracts (Rowe, 1999).

The 2008 amendment in IT Act, 2000 reveals the mounting significance of an Internet in the life of any Indian. The foremost concerns which are observed, into comprise privacy, slashing, authority regulating and sentences for transgressors. Nevertheless, the IT Act, does not emphasis on the protection of shoppers and is of restricted significance of shoppers shopping over Internet.

At the same time, under IT Act, 2000, if the oppressed shopper wants to file a complaint then the appropriate authority is "Adjudicating officer" as there is no specific provision for online shoppers to deal with as adjudicating authority is the general authority to deal with cyber frauds. However after an analysis of IT Act, 2000 and its procedure for online shoppers, it is perceived as:

- The first point is that if shopper wants to get the remedy under IT Act, then it is difficult to avail because online shoppers are outside the purview of said Act. Even if we perceive that online shoppers are impliedly covered still procedural framework is lacking.
- Most of the online shoppers suffer for instance in terms of receiving defective or expired goods, making a payment for the product not delivered or receiving goods of substandard quality. At the same time resolving their dispute in the traditional court become very difficult for online transactions and over and again impractical reason is complicated technicalities intricate in resolving internet disputes.
- Online shoppers usually don't keep proper documentation at the time of filing of consumer complaint the reason is shoppers usually don't maintain website record of online vendors, their e-mail, URL address, telephone number.
- Online shoppers usually in cheating are not having knowledge about the remedy available to them and those who are having are very reluctant in enforcing remedy because of the procedural complications and by this reason most cases go unreported.
- Most of the web portals at the time of transaction demand details of credit card or Personal identification number from shopper and if personal information is leaked then to prove such fraud together with documentation becomes very difficult.

Lack of knowledge about the IT laws among online shoppers is also missing which led e-commerce frauds more and more and implementation of "Due Diligence Requirements" also are the reason for unfamiliarity of its application. Further, IT Act is the sole Act governing electronic commerce in India. However this law directs ever entrepreneurs of electronic commerce must confirm "Cyber Law due diligence" and the IT law in India provides civil and criminal liabilities for "Non Observance of Due Diligence".

CHALLENGES AND ISSUES TO ONLINE SHOPPING

Apart from above problems, there is the revolution in the modes of business which has thrown newer challenges to the consumer, like, invasion of privacy, insecure payment methods, jurisdictional issues etc discussed as under:

Invasion of Privacy

To make a case of Privacy intrusion in the arena of e-shopping, it is submitted that the chain of computers through network forming internet has assisted masses to come closer and made various communications possible that were considered personal once. The reason being that internet users were asked information which is highly personal which may vary from an individual's preferences to monetary details to shopping behaviours to family details without letting the consumer to know the reason for its collection. In deed these enterprises creates a comprehensive personal profile of a consumer in consequence of activities carried out over the internet and user will not object unless and until he will release its repercussions. Therefore, the policies must be such to afford functional protection to e-consumers especially engaging in cross-border transactions effectively to sensitive data (Majid, 2013). For instance, the when a person visits particular website to shop there he is required to fill up with certain details like his date of birth, phone number and other details etc. but what is the guarantee to the said user that his information won't get exposed to some unidentified being. So, the privacy violation here includes breach of trustworthy information, medical history, monetary details, tracking the activities of consumer by installing cookies, sending spam emails, unreasonable examination on workers activity (Susheel, 2011).

Issues Vis-à-Vis Jurisdiction

Internet has made our world smaller in the past aeon in e-market. Further, internet has the ability to cross frontiers which has made jurisdictional void which is to be filled up. "In international transactions many challenging questions plea for answers. Like, where can the plaintiff file a case? Law of which country will apply? For instance, a shopper who lives in India possibly will purchase a couple of fabrics as of a professional situated in United Kingdom through the website of professional" (Gerlach, 2005). "On the face of it, such professional will have contacts to dual nations i.e., India and United Kingdom. Likewise, contacts to another nations may too rise; for instance, if the website of the UK professional is maintained by a machine server located in the USA, or bought fabrics have been synthesized by an establishment in China. It is possible that dealer and purchaser might be living in two diverse nations and the business is situated in the third nation. Therefore in case of differences, questions arise which nation is having jurisdiction? Of which nation's law is applicable? How the judgement will be implemented? (Meehan, 2018)."

In India Jurisdictional matters are obtained by any of the following like when cause of action arises, what is the "place of residence" or "place of business"? But the "cause of action" is a personal test among the three and is utmost possible to be deliberated in electronic commerce subjects. The aforementioned looks that Section 13 of the IT Act, 2000 is never in synchronization with section 11 of CP Act (Consumer Protection Act), 1986. Section 13 delivers, "wherever an instigator (offeror here) or the Receiver (offeree) has more than one place of business then principal place of business shall be deemed as the place where the electronic record have been dispatched or acknowledged." The place of business will obtain the jurisdiction of the court and in case there is a disagreement amongst them concerning agreement shaped by electronic means, at that time the case intend to be in the law court in the interior the limited restrictions of whose jurisdiction, foremost domicile of professional of the contrasting party is located.

In contradiction of it, the CP Act lays, that a shopper can file a grievance contrary to the opposed in a District Forum inside the native boundaries of whose jurisdiction the contrary party, has a division workplace. Therefore, it seems that there is an ostensible skirmish between the said sections as section 13 is likely to cause inconvenience to the shoppers particularly where the conflicting person has main office outside India.

Digital Payment Botches and Discreet Payment Methods

E-sopping is vulnerable to the methods of electronic payments. The reason is at each mechanism of payment there is an involment of an intermediary to assist in transaction. This is because he is having relationship with vendor, vendee or both depending on methods of transactions. At times a party may not be familiar that there is an involment of intermediary. The main advantage of this mechanisms is that they are resourceful and pragmatic selection as they helps the vendor to buy from anywhere.

The distress of e-payments every time appears in the air via e-communications whether a consumer paying through credit/debit card or other modes of online payment. The problem arises when the payment didn't gets transferred in sellers account due to mechanical issues or ambiguous internet link. "Besides recovering this sum is whatever nevertheless a swift course; a person has to notify the website and at that time have to wait round 7-10 days earlier the sum is reimbursed in their account. But then again this condition is gradually enlightening as the segment is concentrating further on cashless businesses and shoppers are receiving extra information and paying online (Mittal, 2017)."

Delayed Delivery of a Product

Deferment in the transportation of product suffers to continue at the extreme common whinge of shopper. The portals with respect to the time of transportation does not give any guarantee to the shopper. Thus it is submitted, in this background that these online portals must give security and they must be held accountable as otherwise it amounts to deficiency of services under CP Act of India.

Week Remark System

The online portals hardly provide any redressal grievance mechanism for redressing the complaint of shopper. However, they only mention their number, address and e-mail. At times they didn't even retort therefore places shopper in the distress.

Other Legal Issues Online Consumer Face

There are no adequate laws, protecting the online consumer, in place in India. It is true, that the provisions of the laws, for example, The Consumer Protection Act, 1986, The Indian contract Act, 1872, The Sale of Good Act, 1930, which apply to off-line transactions, also do apply to those concluded online also. Yet, they, surely, are inadequate in the overall protection of the shopper in the online transactions as there are number of loopholes present.

Yet another concern with respect to online shopping is the complexity of contractual terms the sellers employ in the agreements. Remember, the Indian Contract, while prescribing the method and form by which agreements are formulated and then executed, also lays down certain criteria for the contracting parties under section 10 to enter into a valid and binding contract like that of (a) competence of parties (b) lawful consideration (c) free consent (d) lawful object (e) intention to create legal relations. But, in e-commerce transactions (online shopping), what happens is that the contractual terms are already set by the seller and the consumer is only required to click on an 'Ok,' 'I Agree' or 'I Accept' button to enter into a contract. Therefore, with this shift in the means of entering into a contract, the user is generally being afforded the choice of accepting or rejecting the agreement and acceptance alone entitles them to access the services. There is no opportunity for negotiations of terms, therefore, leaving the consumer in a position where he can't bargain. Interestingly, the primary purpose of the terms and conditions is to absolve the service provider from all forms of liability like in case of the defect in goods, deficiency in the overall services etc. This has limited the scope of remedies available to the consumers. Delay in the delivery of goods also happens to be the most common grievance among the consumers in case of online shopping. However, the term consumer defined under Consumer protection Act 1986, does not cover online consumer. Moreover, given that the average length of these contractual terms and conditions is, more often than not, tedious, it is not humanly possible for an ordinary internet user to read them before clicking on the 'I Agree' button. A simple perusal of the different terms and conditions imposed by the online business sellers on the consumer clearly indicate that a large number of terms are against some established fundamental legal principles recognized under different laws like Indian Contract Act 1872, the Sale of Goods Act, 1930 and The CP Act, 1986 This rings true in other jurisdictions as well.

Keeping in consideration the requirement of documentary evidences it is likewise problematic to usage of the Consumer Protection Act, 1986 to decide e-Shopping grievances, because in e-Shopping accessibility of documentary evidences is circumscribed. Moreover, ever since there is no geographical restrictions for Internet, instituting Internet jurisdiction is so far one more problematic job. Prosecuting a trader in overseas is time consuming, challenging, costly and it cannot be known from website where the vendor is founded. Besides, it is difficult task to know which law of the nation is applicable to an agreement, the law of the nation where the Products were transported or the law of the nation where products were purchased. Action under law will take in to initiate court proceedings against vendor in his country thus can cause inconvenience to shopper to a large level (Roger, 2012).

Non-Bargainable nature and privacy invasion of E-Shopping agreements are others zones of shopper disappointment. Further, shoppers cannot take recourse to traditional systems of complaint redressal mechanism as a vendor is frequently unidentified with no physical site or address.

Table 1. Maximum number of complaints submitted relating to online shopping 2018-2019

Complaint against online Web portals	Number of complaints lodged
Amazon	246
Snapdeal	596
Flipkart	363
Shopclues	307
Airtel	283
Vodafone	487
Tata Docomo	249
PaTm	412
Whaay.com	450
Shopclues.com	306

Source: Indian Consumer Court Forum

Maximum Number of Complaints Lodged

- 01 April 2018 (www.asgtool.asendiahk.com). A shopper ordered Smart TV 123 for rupees 3295 but does not received the product.
- 01 April 2018 (www.ebay.in). A shopper purchased wireless earphone but received damaged, non-functional product. On complaint does not received any response.
- 30, March 2018 (www.ebay.in). A shopper purchased LG Q6 for an amount of rupees 13450 but received second hand product.
- 28 March2018 (www.stylishstop.com). A shopper purchased a smart watch from the website but does not received the product despite payment already made.
- 28 March, 2018 (www.rumpeach.com). A shopper purchased 5 sarees in two different orders and paid 789 and 1197 but does not received any order at all.
- 27 March, 2018 (www.wristBuddy.com). A shopper placed an order for KW 9X Android 5.1 Bluetooth Smartwatch for rupees 3040. On opening the box it was found product of an amount 1500 with less features.
- 26 March, 2018 (www.salesshop.biz). A shopper ordered a power bank for an amount 1140 but received defective product not in a workable position.
- 26 March, 2018 (www.shopmartshop.com). A shopper was contacted that he has been selected for some draw contest but he is required to make a shopping of rupees 3000 and he will get gift of 28000. Later called him again that he won 5, 20,000 but have to pay link up charge of rupees 19000. On payment neither gift not payment was made.
- 26 March, 2018 (www.snapdeal.com). A shopper placed an order of Veyron Sports Car 1.18 and paid 1699 rupees. Later cancelled the order but did not received any refund.

- 25 March, 2018 (www.bigsaleweb.com). A shopper placed an order for shoes but received wrong product.
- 25 March, 2018 (www.amazon.in). A shopper ordered 32 GB dual pen drive but only received 32 GB pen drive. Thereby supplied him wrong product.
- 23 March, 2018 (www.eloda.biz.com). A shopper placed an order for wallet but received fake product.
- 21 March, 2018 (www.snapdeal.com). A shopper placed an order for jeans but received product of poor quality.
- 20 march, 2018 (www.amazon.In). A shopper placed an order for philips BRE201 for an amount of rupees 2590 but on immediate cancellation only 1590 have been credited but not rest of amount.

FUTURE OF E-COMMERCE

It is seen that there will be huge rise in e-commerce especially in this pandemic. "Truth be told, Web based Business in 2021 is greater, and furthermore the world has combined business thoughts of online business stores insurgency and with over 1.92 billion individuals purchasing things on the web, a web based business store has a ton of possible purchasers. This makes it a beneficial undertaking for those wishing to track down a decent type of revenue. Rise of M-Commerce- Mobile commerce, also known as wireless E-commerce, is every financial activity including ownership by consuming goods and services, which are finished by a mobile device, are wireless commerce (Shewale, 2021)."

CONCLUSION AND SUGGESTIONS

If we talk of future as per the study conducted by ASSOCHAM, in India the number of online consumers in the year 2016, was 69 million and 100 million in the year of 2017 and which is expected to reach to 65% by the end of 2018 (E-commerce in India – Growth and Statistics, 2017)). Keeping in view the rising rate, it is submitted that the fate of electronic commerce will revolve to around the theory of survival of the fittest. Further, in near future the electronic commerce entrepreneurs will come in clash against each other for shares in the market and at the same time it will be very hard for new entrepreneurs to compete with giant marketers unless they will come up with some new ideas and construct something which may be new, novel and distinct. The outlook of electronic commerce seems intense in India and development is on plan.

Keeping in view fast-tracking progression of e-commerce because of an enjoyments and satisfactions of customers over the internet without any definite protection. It is therefore suggesting following measures:

1. The term 'consumer' defined under Consumer Protection Act, 1986 should now include even the term online consumer.
2. Necessary amendment should be made were IT Act, 2000 and Contract Act, 1872 must not clash against each other.
3. IT Act 2000 needs to be amended and a chapter should be incorporated On Electronic commerce.
4. Amicable settlement of all defies in trans-border market particularly in jurisdictional matters.

5. Restricted terms should be mentioned in online transactions and other party must be given opportunity to negotiate.
6. The Information Technology Act needs to be amended to decide the legal validity of the concept of Incorporation by reference.

REFERENCES

Ahmed, F. (2015). *Cyber law*. New Era Publishing House.

Beck, S., & Lynch, A. (2001). Profiles of Internet buyers in twenty countries evidence for region specific. *Journal of IBS, 1*(32), 725–748.

Majid, B. (2013). Consumer protection Concerns in e-commerce: Indian perspective. *International Journal of Law and Policy Review*, (2), 157.

Chaudhary, A., & Kuilboer, (2002). *E-Business and E-Commerce Infrastructure*. New York: McGraw-Hill.

European Consumer Centre. (n.d.). Retrieved on July 28, 2019, from http://magyarefk.hu/en/useful-information/online-shoping/the-definition-of-online-shopping.html

E-Commerce in India – Growth and Statistics. (2017). Retrieved on August 23, 2019, from, https://www.codilar.com/blog/e-commerce-in-india-growth-and-statistics

E-Commerce and Online Shopping in India - Statistics & Facts. (2018). *Statista Research Department*. Retrieved on July 17, 2019 https://www.statista.com/topics/2454/e-commerce-in-india

Forrester. (2012). Trends in Indians e-commerce market. *International Journal of Advanced Scientific Research & Development, 3*(2), 145.

IBPF. (2021). *India Brand Equity Foundation*. Retrieved from https://www.ibef.org/industry/ecommerce.aspx

Karp, G. (2009). *Personal Finance Writer for the Morning Call*. Tribune.

Habul. (2001). Consumer decisions making in online shopping environments: the effects of interactive decisions aid. *Marketing Science, 4*, 34.

Rowe, H. (1999). Internet-enabled commerce; International Issues for Business Lawyers. *Journal for Intellectual Property*, (2), 542.

Rattan, J., & Rattan, V. (2013). *Cyber laws and Information Technology*. Bharat Publishing House.

Arline. (2015). *What is E-Commerce*. Merger Insight. Retrieved on August 25, 2019 from, https://www.businessnewsdaily.com/4872-what-is-e-commerce.html

Juneesh, K. (2014). Online shopping problems and solution. *New Media and Mass Communication, 23*, 1-5.

Laudon, K., & Traver, G. (2016). *E-commerce: Business, Technology, and Society*. Pearson Publication.

Roger, M. (2012). *The Legal and E-Commerce Environment Today*. Thomas Learning.

Meehan. (2018). The continuing Conundrum of International Internet Jurisdiction. Int'l & Comp. L. Rev, 31, 42.

Susheel, B., & Mahalakshmi, V. (2011). Legal Issues in E-Commerce Transactions: An Indian Perspective. *International Journal on Recent and Innovation Trends in Computing and Communication*, 4(11), 185.

McKinsey. (2012). *The Social Economy: Unlocking Value and Productivity Through Social Technologies*. Mc Kinsey Global Institute.

Nissan, D. (2009). *Future Shop*. The Penguin Press.

Sarbapriya, R. (2011). Emerging Trends of e-commerce in India: Some crucial Issues, Prospects and Challenges. *Computer Engineering and Intelligent System*, 5(2), 19.

Seybold, P. (2006). *Customers.com*. Crown Business Random Publishing House.

Snider, J. H., & Ziporyn, T. (1992). *Future Shop: How New Technologies Will Change the Way We Shop and What We Buy*. St. Martin's Press.

State Farm Mutual Automobile insurance company v. Brockhorst 453 F. 2nd 533 (10 Cir. 1972

Susheela, M. (2014). *E-commerce Management*. University of Calicut.

Tarun, M. (2017). Common problems faced by customers while shopping online. *Empower Your Business, 5*, 124. Retrieved August 13, 2019, from https://yourstory.com/2017/04/common-problems-online-shopping/

Taniya, C. K. (2021). *An overview of E-commerce in 2021: Growth, hits, and misses*. Times of India. Retrieved December, 21, 2021, from https://timesofindia.indiatimes.com/blogs/voices/an-overview-of-e-commerce-in-2021-growth-hits-and-misses/

Techno Pak. (2012). *India's Attractiveness as a key Sourcing to Destination*. New Delhi: Outlook Textiles and Apparels Publication.

Gerlach, T. (2005). Using Internet Content Filters to Create E-Borders to Aid International Choice of Law and Jurisdiction. *World Law Review*, 5, 32.

Tkacz, E., & Adrian, K. (2009). *Internet —Technical Development and Applications*. Springer-Verlag Heidelburg Publications. doi:10.1007/978-3-642-05019-0

Toralf, N. (1998). Distance Selling in a Digital Age. *Journal of Communication Law*, 3(4), 33.

Shewale. (2021). *Future of E-commerce in India-2021*. Retrieved from https://www.researchgate.net/publication/351441684_Future_of_E-commerce_in_India-2021

KEY TERMS AND DEFINITIONS

Consumer: Means a person who sells or purchases goods for a consideration.

Digital Payment: Means paying electronically to a person for any purchase.

Due Diligence Requirements: It means an investigation or audit of a potential investment consummated by a prospective buyer.

E-Commerce: Means selling or purchasing over internet.

Intermediary: Any person, who on behalf of another person receives, stores, or transmits that record or provides any service with respect to that record and includes telecom service providers, network service providers, internet service provider.

Jurisdiction: Legal power or authority; the area in which this power can be exercised by administrators.

Prosecution: The process of officially charging somebody with a crime and of trying to show that he/she is guilty, in a court of law.

Chapter 17
OTT Platforms and Their Distributorship Agreement With Content Makers:
A Study From the Perspective of Competition Law and Policy in India and Other Jurisdictions

Swati Bajaj Seth

Department of Law, Maharaja Agrasen Institute of Management Studies, India

ABSTRACT

The OTT platform is a new market in itself. The growth of this new internet-based industry has brought atrocious competition in the broadcast industry. They effort to distinguish them from their competitors by getting exclusive content from the creators. This exclusivity though not per se appears to be anti-competitive but it raises apprehensions of its negative effect on the market. In fact, these agreements demonstrate interdependence of market players to sustain and reach consumers in the market. The competition laws of many jurisdictions refer to the anti-competitive nature of vertical agreement as ex post unlike cartel (horizontal agreements) which are per se void. The chapter discussed the distribution chain where vertical relationship in the form of agreement or integration is generally developed. The present chapter explains the nature of exclusive distribution agreement or exclusive screening license in the broadcast industry.

INTRODUCTION

This chapter explains in detail the evolution of OTT platforms in general as well as in India and how its demand increased among the society. The focus of the chapter is basically on the competition concerns related to OTT platforms in means of their distribution agreement with the content maker/creator. The author has discussed the vertical relationship between the two parties and their possible anti-competitive

DOI: 10.4018/978-1-7998-8641-9.ch017

impact in the market. The author has also discussed the customary practices used to be followed by the content maker/ film producers for distribution of their work to reach to the society.

The objective of current chapter is to analyze the vertical relationship between the content creator and OTT platforms from the perspective of competition laws. The methodology followed by the author is completely doctrinal. The author has studied this aspect from global perspective and practices followed in major trending jurisdictions.

BACKGROUND

Concept of OTT Platform and its Evolution

OTT or Over-the-top platform is a "novel budding trend" in the broadcasting sector which has given hilarious competition to the cable TV or satellite programming. OTT does not require any system operator and it distributes contents to the consumer in the form of video, audio, calls or messaging directly via internet. It is an online television or streaming television where the viewers are required to either download the Apps of these OTT platforms like Amazon Prime, Netflix, Disney + Hot star, Zee5 *etc.*, or they can get their access through their websites also. It is popularly known as subscription-based video-on-demand service (SVoD) as it requires subscription fees by the viewers on daily basis, monthly basis or annual basis. The US FCC has defined OTT as, "any entity that provides video programming by means of the Internet or other Internet Protocol (IP)-based transmission path where the transmission path is provided by a person other than the OVD. An OVD does not include an MVPD inside its MVPD footprint or an MVPD to the extent it is offering online video programming as a component of an MVPD subscription to customers whose homes are inside its MVPD footprint."

OTT platforms have proved to be a boon for the media and entertainment industry. It has brought a new apparatus for video streaming by the consumers. A shift from the days of VCR then Cable TV to DVR and Satellite Radio to Smartphones and OTT has been a tremendous success of digitalization all over the world. The evolution of OTT platforms has never been easy as it requires the appropriate use of smartphones or other digital devices and its knowledge to the users. In fact, the traditional people have always remained a challenge for all innovative incipient object; however, COVID 19 in way of pandemic has been proved a boon for OTT platforms as all other traditional video streaming mechanisms were locked down. The base of OTT platforms lies in video streaming. The video streaming services were made possible only because of DCT video compression and ADSL data transmission. DCT stands for 'discrete cosine transform' (Sundaravel E. and Elangovan N, 2020). It is a technology which transforms a signal or image from the spatial domain to the frequency domain in which severance can be branded. ADSL stands for 'asymmetric digital subscriber line'. It is a technology which enables faster data transmission. These two technologies made streaming services possible and this ultimately led to the launch of the YouTube in 2005. In 2017, the YouTube came with YouTube TV which allows the viewers to see live telecast of their programs. Simultaneously, many online video streaming channels begin where the TV programs and other videos were made available. These channels started evolving and became a tool wherein the people could purchase the content they want to see as per their time. This is called 'video-on-demand' service.

India's first live stream app was launched by Digivive in 2010 through a mobile app called nexGtv. Though, the first India's own OTT platform came in the form of BIGFlix which was launched by Reliance industries in 2008. Based on the on-demand services it provides, it is also termed as "personal blockbuster theatre".

Boon in OTT Scenario

OTT platforms like Netflix, Prime, Disney+ Hotstar, *etc.* are now a days have become an unavoidable part of people's life across the world. Especially during the time of pandemic when due to COVID 19 virus the theaters and other offline entertainment platforms got shut down in line of complete lockdown, these OTT platforms fluke stand out. Everyone started watching their programs on these platforms. In fact, a new rage of watching *web series* which people barely used to watch previously became the flawing subject of dialogue at every household and a medium of entertainment. In a research work published on research gate, it has been mentioned that, "technological advancements have made the movie or TV watching more convenient through online streaming or Video on Demand (VoD) services. VoD refers to streaming of video content over the Internet, through applications typically referred to as Over-The-Top (OTT). Viewers can access video content through OTT apps in any Internet-connected device like a Smartphone, smart TV, tablet, desktop computer, laptop, *etc.* Unlike traditional media, streaming services tell varied stories that are not restricted by censors, box office or demographic. It gives a viewing experience with greatly improved sound and visual quality, provided the consumers have a stable Internet." OTT has attracted its audience by making available videos as per their age and interest. Like Disney+ Hot Star has provided a separate link for Kids TV or for News and Discovery *etc.*

OTT has not only proved a benediction to the people but it has also fetched an opportunity to the content maker such as producers and directors of new movies and series to distribute their work and exhibit them through these OTT platforms. This transported a boom in the life of these platform proprietors. In simple terms, OTT platforms has brought an innovation in the cable television industry. As OECD policy roundtable suggest that, "Technological developments affect the conditions of competition as they alter: the range and quality of services; the underlying costs; the extent of barriers to entry (new technologies provide new means by which the market is contested); the ability of customers to switch suppliers; and pricing mechanisms (technological developments allow for provision of pay per view services). Therefore, digitisation generally reduces barriers to entry".

According to the report (News18, 2019), in the span of three years 40 OTT companies have entered into this business. Besides being new in the market, the platform has left its nascence at very earliest. Almost every individual having access to Smart-Phone has installed at least one OTT App. In fact, there is a tie-up among telecom companies and OTT platforms and also between Smart-Phone Companies and OTT platforms as the App comes pre-installed on the mobile handset. India's entertainment and media market is growing at the fastest rate and it is expected to reach at Rs. 451,373 cr. till 2023. The Partner & Leader – Entertainment & Media of PwC India Mr. Rajib Basu said that India has become a global market for OTT platforms as the same has already reached at its maturity stage in western market. The exact highlight of the report says that, "India's OTT video market will grow at a 21.8% CAGR from INR 4464Cr in 2018 to INR 11976Cr in 2023. Subscription video on demand will increase at a 23.3% CAGR from INR 3756Cr in 2018 to INR 10708Cr in 2023. The potential of India's enormous scale will become reality during the forecast period with its OTT video market overtaking that of South Korea to become the eighth-biggest market in the world by 2023". (PwC Report, 2019-2023)

AGREEMENT BETWEEN CONTENT MAKER (PRODUCERS/ DIRECTORS) AND DISTRIBUTORS

Process of Film Distribution

The content maker or the producer/ director and the distributors are having vertical relationship with each other in the chain of entertainment industry. The producers create the content by doing investment and recover the same by displaying their content to the consumers through distributors such as theaters, OTT platforms, DVDs, *etc*. The entire income received from the consumers is divided among the producers and the distributors according to the agreed ratio. The distribution agreement also specifies the rights and obligation of the content maker and distributor with respect to the work such as copyright, display rights, conditions related to further distribution, *etc*.

The distributor buys the distribution rights from the producers either at the beginning or at the final preview by entering into a licensing agreement. Thereafter, the distributors screen the movies to the consumer through theaters. However, with the advent of online video screening through OTT platforms, the role of the theaters has diminished. Now, the platform screens the movies directly on their platforms and can charge subscription fee from the viewers.

Explaining Distribution Chain

Creation of a movie or a web series or any entertainment content is a task of multiple people working at different channels of production chain. It requires investor, screen-writer, producer, director, cast and crew and also distributors. The relationship between a producer or content creator and the distributor falls in vertical chain. However, this vertical relationship can be created either through an integration or an agreement. In integration, there exists a combination of two industries in a supply chain; whereas, in agreement there exists a license and apart from the terms and conditions of license agreement the parties do not carry any rights or obligations towards each other (Raychaudhuri, T., 2011).

A producer of services requiring to sell its services to consumer may carry out the same through two ways either by carrying production and distribution itself (by way of vertical integration) or it may use the services of a commercial agent to find customers (Whish, R. & Bailey, D. 2018). Continuing with the same, they explained that "vertical integration can be achieved internally by setting up retail outlets or by establishing subsidiary companies to which the task of distribution is entrusted". In case producer wants to avail the services of a commercial agent and it can be done by way of entering into contracts on the producer's behalf. According to the experts, "commercial agency is a more common feature of distribution in continental Europe".

When Vertical Agreement can be Anti-Competitive?

Vertical agreements are not anti-competitive *per se*. In fact, these agreements demonstrate interdependence of market players to sustain and reach consumers in the market. Hence, the enterprises either enters into an agreement with the other enterprises in their vertical chain or they flinch into vertical integration by either acquiring or by combining their businesses. The competition laws of many jurisdictions refer anti-competitive nature of vertical agreement as *ex post* unlike cartel (horizontal agreements) which are *per se* void (Lorenz, M., 2013). The Indian competition law specifically provides a list of vertical agreements which if entered into by the enterprises then it would be considered as anti-competitive if they cause any appreciable adverse effect on competition such as "tie-in arrangements, exclusive supply agreement, exclusive distribution agreement, resale price maintenance, refusal to deal, *etc."*

EU Law

The EU Competition Law (Article 101, TFEU) has also faced long controversies in appreciating the possible harm of vertical agreements in the market. The block exemption regulations in its Article 1(1) (a) defined vertical agreements as, "agreement or concerted practice entered into between two or more undertakings each of which operates, for the purpose of the agreement or concerted practice, at a different level of the production or distribution chain, and relating to the conditions under which the parties may purchase, sell or resell certain goods or services".

According to the *"Guidelines on Vertical Restraint"* issued by European Commission, vertical agreements do not involve a combination of market power. In the case of *Allianze Hungaria*, the European Commission highlighted that "vertical agreements are likely to raise competition concerns only where there is a degree of market power at the level of the supplier or the buyer or at both levels". Hence, vertical agreements are often less damaging than horizontal agreements as they do not involve a combination of market power. However, in vertical agreements competition concerns can arise if there is huge market power at one side i.e., either on supplier side or on the distributor side. Under the EU law, Article 101 (1) of TFEU covers the anti-competitive effects of vertical agreements. However, the Treaty gives certain exemption to the vertical agreements from being declared as illegal and void under Article 101(3) read with EU Regulation No. 330/2010 (Commission Regulation, 2010)

The regulation provides for "block exemption" to vertical agreements from being declared as anti-competitive. However, to claim these exemptions certain requirements needs to be fulfilled such as there should not be any "hardcore" restrictions in the agreement; the market share cap of 30 per cent for both suppliers and distributors; obligations not to compete during the contract; obligations not to compete after termination of the contract; and, the exclusion of specific brands in a selective distribution system (Sundaravel E. and Elangovan N., 2020).

The block exemptions as provided under the regulations has been designed in a manner where is tries to manifest all restrictions of competition in vertical agreements as qualifying for exemption. The regulations have adopted the approach based on both the terms of agreement as well as market power of the parties to the agreement. The regulations also acknowledge the fact that the agreements may have an impact on Interbrand competition only from a certain degree of market power (Sundaravel E. and Elangovan N., 2020).

Further, the guidelines on vertical restraints provides for possible benefits of vertical agreements to competition; such as, "exclusive distribution agreement may help to avoid the free-riding understood as situation in which distributors use free-ride promotion and investment efforts of other distributors and offer the same products for lower prices since they have lower cost". Furthermore, "vertical agreements may provide local distributors with territorial protection which enables them to make 'first time investments' and open up new markets for the product at issue".

US Law

The United States has also given favorable treatment to vertical agreements in their anti-trust law. Vertical agreements need to be differentiated from horizontal agreements as it does not generally enter into between rivals. In fact, vertical agreements are pro-competitive as they combine the services providers which is for the betterment of the consumers. However, he has not denied that such agreements can be harmful for market competition especially when they are not efficiency-enhancing (Douglas Melamed A., 1998).

Vertical Agreements and Rule of Reason

The Sherman Act of 1890 does not restrict any restraint unless it appears unreasonable. In other words, those restraints are restricted which might affect economy. In modern jargon, the courts are applying "Rule of reason while considering whether a contract 'harness' competition or, instead, 'destroys' it, by creating or exercising market control. Some agreements are so clearly damaging that the courts criticize it with little analysis, considering it 'unreasonable per se'. Most agreements bear such criticism, and undergo more cautious inspection, which courts call 'the Rule of Reason'." The Courts, scholars and the enforcement agencies have given a three-step test to govern analysis under Rule of Reason, "Firstly, a plaintiff must establish a prima facie case by indicating that the restraint exhibit physical anticompetitive harm, which generally consists of actual adverse appreciable effects on the competition such as increased price or reduced output. Secondly, the defendants must establish that their agreement exhibits pro-competitive benefits which overshadow the harm implied in plaintiff's prima facie case. Thirdly, even though the defendants can make such a presentation, the plaintiff can still accomplish by proving that the defendants can achieve the same benefits by way of a less restrictive trade practises. This three-step test helps courts distinguish those agreements that 'harm' or 'destroy' competition, by creating or exercising market power, from those that encourage it" (Lorenz, M., 2013).

Further, under US law, few principles of analysis have been developed to determine competitive reasonableness under *Re Cardizem CD Antitrust Litigation,* "certain conduct that are clearly anti-competitive which are per se unreasonable. Here it is required to prove that only conduct occurred and not its competitive unreasonableness and accused are excluded from justifying the restraint as reasonable; the contract, combinations or conspiracies in restraint of trade that are not per se illegal are considered under rule of reason. The rule of reason inspects and balances various factors relating to competition in taking account whether particular business practise have pernicious effect on competition.". In *Arnold, Schwinn & Co. case* the Supreme Court held that "vertical restrictions laid by manufacturers on geographical territories were per se illegal". However, the decision was reversed in *Continental T.V Inc. case* that, "vertical non price restrictions imposed by manufacturers on its distributors are to be examined under rule of reason".

The U.S Department of Justice and Federal Trade Commission Antitrust Guidelines for Collaborations among Competitors (April 2000) provides that, "if participants of economic activities made an agreement which is reasonably related to combination and its pro-competitive advantages, the agency examines the agreement under rule of reason though it is of type that might be considered per se illegal".

HITCHES PERCEPTIBLE IN AN AGREEMENT BETWEEN CONTENT MAKER AND OTT DISTRIBUTORS

The agreement entered into between the content maker and the distributors was not restricted or exclusive to any single entity. In fact, the content maker used to display their work on every screen be it single screen or multiplexes. The distributors rights were limited to the display and profit sharing and the copyright of the content still remined with its creator.

Exclusive Distributorship Agreement/Exclusive Streaming Licenses

Exclusivity may result in foreclosure of market. However, all exclusive agreements do not harm market competition even if they create restraints. These agreements as define under Sec. 3(4) of the Indian Competition Act, are not *per se* anti-competitive. They can be anti-competitive only when they fall in the described five categories in the Act and cause harm to the market competition. Amongst those five categories, one is 'exclusive distributorship agreement' which implies an agreement to limit, restrict or withhold the supply of goods or allocate any area or market for the disposal or sale of goods. The law provides for certain factors which helps the enforcement authorities in determining the potential anti-competitive impact of such agreements. The factors embrace creation of entry barriers, driving existing competitors out of the market, foreclosure of competition, *etc.* These factors are the blend of both "for and against" aspects. The crux of providing such factors is to analyze the context and consequence of agreement (Lorenz, M., 2013).

An exclusive distributorship agreement may result in restrictions on the supplier as well as on the distributor to not to deal or compete with other market players. According to the EU Guidelines on Vertical Restraint, "the possible competition risks with exclusive distribution are mainly reduced intra-brand competition and market partitioning, which may facilitate price discrimination in particular". The European Court of Justice (ECJ) in *Société Technique Manière* explained that the jurisprudence of the European Competition Law, an exclusive distribution agreement do not necessarily fall within the scope of Article 101(1) of the Treaty.

Whether Exclusive Streaming License or Exclusive Distributorship Rights Given by the Content Creator to the Distribution Channel (Broadcasters) can be Anti-Competitive?

Doctrine of "Restraint of Trade"

The philosophy laid down under competition laws of numerous jurisdictions is based on common law principles. Even though, the Sherman Act of US is considered as the initiation of enacting competition laws in the country, but the basis of competition law is based on the principles against 'restraint of trade'. Any act either by way of an agreement or done by a single economic entity if results into restrictions in trade for other players in the market then it would be harmful for the economic growth of a country. The US has recognized this common law principle in its Sherman Act and it was explained by Chief Justice White in a very famous case of *Standard Oil.* The doctrine of restraint of trade is also explained beautifully by Lord Morris in *Harper's Garage case* as, "In general the law recognizes that there is freedom to enter into any contract that can be lawfully made. The law lends its weight to uphold and enforce contracts freely entered into. The law does not allow a man to derogate from his grant. If someone has sold the goodwill of his business, some restraint to enable the purchaser to have that which he has bought may be recognized as reasonable (Douglas Melamed A., 1998). Some restraints to ensure the protection of confidential information may be similarly regarded…but when all this is fully recognized yet the law, in some circumstances, reserves a right to say that a contract is in restraint of trade and that to be enforceable it must pass a test of reasonableness. In the competition between various possible principles applicable…public policy will give it priority".

The relationship between doctrine of restraint of trade and competition law has also been explained by European Commission in *W.W.F case*. However, it's approach is different from US. According to the EC, the common law's method was limited to discover the restraint between the parties; however, competition law's slant is much bend towards the effect of anything on the market and its competition.

Rule of Reason Approach in Case of Exclusive Screening License/ Exclusive Distribution Agreement between OTT Platforms and Content Creator

The producer or directors when creates the content, they get copyright over their work which gives them exclusive right to use and exploit their work. Hence, giving a streaming right to the broadcaster is also their own discretion. The broadcasters or distributors either gets the streaming license before finality is given to the content or they may also get the license after evaluating the work. As a result, an agreement is entered into between the content creator and the broadcasters.

Now-a-days, with the emerging trend of releasing the content through OTT platforms, the streaming license is given by the content creators to the OTT platforms for viewership. Due to pandemic and lockdown, the traditional content releasing practices got halt and the creators found OTT platforms as a new and direct apparatus of reaching viewers/consumers. No-doubt, OTT platforms have given benefit and comfort to the content producers as well as consumers. Now, the viewers can enjoy new movies or web-series from the comfort of their home by paying the subscription fee to the concerned OTT platform.

Though, numerous movies and series when displayed on the OTT platforms they are shown along with a tag line such as Amazon Original or Netflix Original or Zee5 Original, *etc*. What does the term 'Original' mean here?

Besides, the web-series or movies are displayed only on any one OTT platform. For instance, if any movie or web-series is shown on Netflix then the same will not be displayed on any other platform. They are exclusively streamed on any one OTT platform and not on any other. Is it because the content maker wants to get their work displayed by the dominant or strong OTT platforms? Or Is it a condition imposed by OTT platforms on the content maker (if so, does this makes it an anti-competitive behavior or can it be protected under the umbrella of effective competition)? Or whether the content providers are giving exclusive license of distributorship to the distributors? Can these agreements be called as anti-competitive? Another arena which needs to be focused upon is does these OTT platforms have their own in-house production or does they create content to be displayed exclusively on them?

OTT platforms have transformed their character to a cavernous level. Beginning with streaming video-on-demand and television programs they started releasing new web-series or films. They enter into contract with the content creators for viewership rights as protected under respective intellectual property rights. This raises competition among the OTT companies. They compete with respect to prices; they compete with respect to content. Even though there are many OTT companies which creates their own content and then show it on their platform exclusively; however, many OTT companies enters into exclusive contracts with content creator and show them on their platforms. These exclusive streaming agreements are not *per se* anti-competitive. However, they can become anti-competitive if they effect market and its competition. This kind of practices often raises the apprehension that what kind of efficiency an exclusive streaming license or agreement is yielding in the broadcast industry.

Impact on Consumers

The success of these OTT platforms is certainly in the hands of consumers. The consumers pay subscription fee on daily, weekly, monthly or yearly basis to these platforms. In fact, providing reasonable subscription plans or offers is one of the aspects between these platforms to strive with each other (Furht B., eds, 2006). However, the consumers for the sake of their entertainment 'needs' to take subscription of all the OTT platforms because they are unable to get all the content on one single platform. Hence, can this be called as consumer grievance or consumer exploitation?

CONCLUSION

According to the Porter's Diamond theory on National Competitive Advantage, competition is one amongst the many factors which enhance efficiency amongst the market players. The countries' competition policies usually object to fetch superlative out of the troop and for that the policy do not intent to protect competitors but intent to protect market competition. Henceforth, while curbing or barring any bustle which can destruct competitors, the competition policy needs to ensure that the activity should not impair or damage market competition. Because, if it does damage competition then the act would be considered as anti-competitive and if it does not then the act would be considered as pro-competitive. Also, competition law and policy promote pro-competitive activities as they lead to economic growth (Furht B. eds,2006).

Considering the above norms, vertical restraint has received a compassionate handling under the competition law and policy of many jurisdictions. Where on the one hand, vertical integration has been considered as an inorganic growth of the industries; there on the other hand vertical agreements are analysed on the basis of 'rule of reason'.

The relationship between OTT platforms and content creators falls under vertical chain. Their agreement appears to be pro-competitive at the *per se* level as it is the requirement of their business. However, agreement providing exclusive streaming rights to a distributor appears illogical because it not only restricts the business of other distributors but it also snatches options from the consumer. Suppose a film producer has given the streaming rights to only one distributor say Netflix and Netflix is streaming the same with the tagline Netflix Original then the same video would not be available on any other OTT platform (distributor) and the consumers if want to see the film then they have to take the paid subscription for the platform.

Although this doesn't appear unethical as the distributors needs to compete with each other and they are competing on content. However, suppose if either the distributor or the producer is having strengthening position in the market then such kind of vertical agreements can leave dire impact on the market. Hence, market share of the players is an important and unavoidable aspect of determining the pros and cons of vertical agreements.

RECOMMENDATIONS

The principle of "Rule of reason" has not been specifically mentioned under the law related to vertical agreements or vertical restraints under Indian competition law. However, in numerous cases the principle has been applied by the Commission. Such as *Deustche Post Bank Home Finance ltd. case, Mahindra and Mahindra v. Union of India,* etc. The principle has become an avoidable tool of investigation while dealing with allegations of anti-competitive vertical agreements. However, the law related to the vertical agreements is very ambiguous under Indian law. It does not provide any rules or regulations to determine the over-cross of that thin line difference between anti-competitive vertical agreement and pro-competitive vertical agreement. Like, the EU provides exemption regulations and Guidelines on vertical restraint and the US has defined set of precedents explaining the application of rule of reason on vertical agreements. Hence, Indian law also required certain guidelines for the same (Nijhavan, G. & Dahiya, S., 2020).

Also, OTT platforms are the emerging market having already achieved a settled space in people's life. Henceforth, it has become crucial to understand the nature and functioning of these platforms and to regulate them to the extent requires. Over-regulation may affect their growth in future. Also, considering the fact that unlike US, in India OTT platforms are at the stage of growth and is yet to reach at its maturity stage. Any mistake with respect to its over-regulation or de-regulation can leave a negative impact on its life cycle and can bring decline before saturation. Hence, the Indian competition law also requires to adopt a balancing approach between pro-competitive and anti-competitive effects of vertical agreements like European Union and USA.

REFERENCES

Lorenz, M. (2013). *An Introduction to EU Competition Law*. Cambridge University Press. doi:10.1017/CBO9781139087452

Whish, R., & Bailey, D. (2018). *Competition Law* (9th ed.). Oxford Publication. doi:10.1093/law-ocl/9780198779063.001.0001

Raychaudhuri, T. (2011) Vertical Restraints in Competition Law: The Need to Strike the Right Balance Between Regulation And Competition. *NUJS L. Rev., 4*(609).

FCC. (2016). Annual Assessment of the Status of Competition in the Market for the Delivery of Video Programming [Seventeenth Report; MB Docket No. 15-158; DA 16-510] (PDF) (Report). Washington, DC: Federal Communications Commission (FCC).

Furht, B. (Ed.). (2006). *Encyclopedia of Multimedia*. Springer. doi:10.1007/0-387-30038-4

ISO/IEC 10918-1, Information Technology — Digital Compression and Coding of Continuous-Tone Still Images: Requirements and Guidelines, 1994

Nijhavan, G. & Dahiya, S. (2020). Role of Covid as a catalyst In Increasing Adoption of OTTs In India: A Study Of Evolving Consumer Consumption Patterns And Future Business Scope. *Journal of Content, Community & Communication.*

Sundaravel, E., & Elangovan, N. (n.d.). *Emergence and future of Over-the-top (OTT) video services in India: an analytical research.* Available at: https://www.researchgate.net/publication/341558182_Emergence_and_future_of_Over-the-top_OTT_video_services_in_India_an_analytical_research

OECD Policy Roundtables. (2013). *Competition Issues in Television and Broadcasting.* Available at https://www.oecd.org/daf/competition/TV-and-broadcasting2013.pdf

PwC Report. (2019 – 2023). *Global Entertainment & Media Outlook.* Available at https://www.pwc.in/press-releases/2019/global-entertainment-and-media-outlook-2019-2023.html

Case C-32/11 EU:C:2013:160; *Allianz Hungária Biztosító Zrt. and Others v Gazdasági Versenyhivatal*

Commission Regulation (EU) No 330/2010 of 20 April 2010 on the application of Article 101(3) of the Treaty on the Functioning of the European Union to categories of vertical agreements and concerted practices; available at https://data.europa.eu/eli/reg/2010/330/oj

Douglas Melamed, A. (1998). *Exclusionary Vertical Agreements, Speech Delivered before American Bar Association.* Available at https://www.justice.gov/atr/speech/exclusionary-vertical-agreements#N_6_

Sec. 3(4), Indian Competition Act, 2002

Sec. 19(3), Indian Competition Act, 2002

Esso Petroleum Ltd. v. Harper's Garage (Stourport) Ltd., [1968] AC 269

Standard Oil Company v. United States, 221 US 1 (1911)

United States v. Arnold, Schwinn & Co. 388 U.S 365 (1967)

Continental T.V Inc. v GTE Sylvania Inc 433 U.S 36 (1977)

Chapter 18
Mapping the Changing Contours of Electronic Evidence in India

Utkarsh Maria
Supreme Court of India, India

Anant Vijay Maria
Supreme Court of India, India

ABSTRACT

The courts have gone on a discourse starting from admissibility of CDs as evidence to the latest being that of WhatsApp Chats. The author of this chapter will map the changing discourse of electronic evidence in India and its evolution in India. The author will discuss the normative discourse with respect to electronic evidence and its applicability, which will be followed by the legal dynamics during such evolution and in the third part argue the current trend of decisions. The author will further provide for the current policy and future changes which need to be imbibed in order to make the law more robust.

INTRODUCTION

The current need in the modern and technologically advanced world requires newer measures to control and regulate the misuse of technology. The need for appreciating electronic evidence in light of excessive usage and techno crimes being committed has created havoc, and the idea that comes forth is that of the use of electronic evidence vis a vis establishment of rules to authenticate documentary evidence (Ryder, 2009). The need arises from the standpoint view that the standards or thresholds that are evolved for the purpose of primary and secondary evidence with respect to paper documents cannot be stretched to apply to digital evidence. The difficulty in the evolution of such principles for the purpose of electronic evidence initially led to the provision being introduced with respect to a mechanism wherein the requirement of a mandatory certificate for the purpose of authenticity with respect to electronic evidence is required.

DOI: 10.4018/978-1-7998-8641-9.ch018

The current difficulty arises due to the ruling made by the Apex court in the judgment of *Arjun Panditrao Khotkar* v. *Kailash Kushanrao Gorantyal*, wherein the Court opined that it is mandatory to provide the certificate for the purpose of the authenticity of the electronic evidence, as well as the owner's authentication as a witness. Thus, the Apex Court in this distinguished the primary and secondary evidence with the requirement of the Section 65-B (4) certificate for the latter.

1.   Admissibility and Authenticating Evidence

The primary statute for reference for authenticating and admitting evidence will be the Evidence Act, 1872, which provides for the admission of documents. It requires that there should be compliance of the proof of contents with the help of primary and secondary evidence. This further creates a contextual definition of what is secondary evidence. It contains certified copies, mechanically processed documents wherein the accuracy is insured, an oral account of someone who had witnessed the documents to lead admissibility in the Court of law, etc. The Act additionally envisages a situation wherein such secondary evidence should be considered authentic and admissible only when the original documents are in possession of the person and when the existence is not in dispute or when the original is lost, subject to its movability or is a public document, etc.

2.   Authenticating and admissibility of Electronic Evidence

The originally envisaged Evidence Act did not provide for the shift in technology and the advent of electronic evidence and its related challenges. One of the more significant challenges that emerged in ever-increasing digital/ electronic transactions is the admissibility and authenticating of such electronic evidence. The ever-growing need for evidence law required provisions for the recognition of Courts of law and other streams. (Karia,2008) Thus, the law amended and introduced the authenticating legal structure and framework by virtue of Section 65A and Section 65B.

The Court in State of *Anvar P.V. v. P.K. Basheer* analysed this issue at large. The Court utilised the admissibility of electronic evidence and the process of authenticity. In addition, they referred to the Statement of Objects and Reasons of the Information and Technology Act, 2000, wherein it states that the new system of communications has changed the way we live and thus created a revolution in the way people transact business. Thus, it creates a new revolution for evidence production before the Court.

The Court consequently relies upon Section 59 and 65A of the Evidence Act in order to state that the documentary evidence by way of electronic evidence has to rely upon the admissibility regime laid down under Section 65B of the Act. (Karia,2015) Therefore, compliance is required as it consecrates the electronic evidence which is collected from the computer. This is furthered by the non-obstante clause and noting that for it to be considered as a document, it has to be compliant to conditions laid down in clause (2). The conditions as mentioned are laid down as:

a.   There should be lawful control over the computer, which is used to produce evidence that stores, or processes information required for daily activity.

b.   The information contained in the electronic record is stored and regularly fed into the computer.

c.   The computer was, for the significant part working correctly, and even if there was some minor, it could not affect the authenticity or accuracy of the contents.

d.   The record should be a direct reproduction of the source as used in the ordinary course.

The abovementioned requirements are supplemented with further requirements under clause (4) in the event the conditions are mentioned, which are the requirement of a certificate, it should describe the manner of production of electronic evidence, particulars of the device and compliance, as well as certificate, must be signed by a person occupying a responsible position with respect to the relevant device. (Vaidialingam,2015) The certificate ought to be produced can state that it is to the best of his knowledge and belief to ensure his liability. This, of course, has to be produced with the electronic record, which can be a hard drive, pen drive, CD, etc. The guidelines and requirements are stringent as it is believed that electronic records can be tampered with easily and may cause the miscarriage of justice. (Sethia, 2016)

The question with respect to the use of printouts as well as any output from an electronic record first came before the Court as a challenge to Section 65-B before the Supreme Court in the *State (NCT of Delhi)* v. *Navjot Sandhu*, wherein the Court was called to examine the authenticity of evidence without the requirement of a certificate. The Court held in affirmative by relying on secondary evidence under other provisions such as section 63 and 65 of the Evidence Act for the purpose of proving electronic records. This was supplemented with the fact that the officer responsible for the records so provided can assert the same by a witness who identifies the signature on the certificate or spoke of the facts based on her personal knowledge. Thus, the first case itself set the tone for deviation from such a formal certificate requirement due to the existence of impossibility. (Gupta, 2021). However, this, when fast-forwarded to the 3 Judge Bench decision in *Anvar*, seems to be negated as the Court asserted on the requirement of certificates under Section 65B (4) of the Act to admission such electronic evidence.

The Court further went on to define Section 65B as a complete code. Thus, no breach or digression can occur from this stated position for the purpose of authenticity and admission of the election speeches and announcements during the election brought before the Court in the instant case. The Court revisited the issue when they were examining the issue again in the decision of *Tomaso Bruno* v. *the State of U.P.*, where the three Judges Bench attempted to reverse the stand to the previously stated regime in Navjot Sandhu decision, thus again allowing the secondary evidence to be used for authenticating the electronic record under the Act. The only problem with the decision was that it was *per incuriam* as it did not respond to the decision in Anvar. The two-judge bench went further with the stated position as held in the case of *Sonu* v. *State of Haryana*, where a 65-B(4) certificate was held to be the sole proof for the purpose of the electronic record. The Court further in *Shafhi* tried to reverse the stated position as to overrule the applicability of the mandatory rule in Anvar, where the party does not have any control over the device in such a case the requirement as provided under Section 65 B(4) can be relaxed.

ARJUN PANDITRAO JUDGMENT

The recent case that settles the dispute regarding authenticity and admissibility is a three-JudgeBench decision in *Arjun Panditrao Khotkar* v. *Kailash Kushanrao Gorantyal*. The facts of the case being that election was challenged of MLA of State Legislative Assembly wherein the respondent is the one who was defeated in the election. He alleged that the respondent had improperly filed his nomination papers before the Election commission as he did not file them during the requisite time, i.e. before 3.00 p.m. on 27-9-2014. The respondent relied on CCTV footage within and outside the R.O.'s office in order to buttress his argument. The High Court had directed the Election Commission to produce the Video copy in the CD of the two days in question. The recording in question clearly showed that nomination papers were filed past the deadline. However, the R.O. office did not produce the mandatory certificate under

Section 65B (4) of the Act. This was despite multiple requests made by the respondent for the production of the same for the purpose of authenticity. The questions thus arose whether this electronic evidence can be utilised and admitted in the absence of the mandatory certificate under Section 65B (4). An official from R.O. gave evidence, and during her cross-examination, she admitted to non-tampering, collection of CD and entered in record and was used often by the authorities. The H.C. held that since Section 65B does not prohibit oral evidence, thus the compliance of Section 65B was duly done.

The matter thus went in appeal before the Supreme Court, the primary defence that was used as the judgment in *Anvar P.V.* v. *P.K. Basheer*, wherein the Court had previously held that written, and signed certificate under Section 65B (4) was a sine qua non for the purpose of admitting electronic evidence for the purpose of adjudication. However, meanwhile, The Apex court in Shahfi v State of H.P. made it non-mandatory for certificate requirement under Section 65B (4) in the 'interest of justice. This conflict was to be decided by a three-judge bench in the Arjun Panditrao case. The Apex Court upheld the ruling of Anvar, wherein Section 65B was considered to be the governing law of electronic evidence. Thus, it excludes all other provisions of the Act. The Court concluded the following:

1. The Court overruled the judgment in Tomaso Bruno as per incuriam and Shafhi Mohammad to be fallacious and incorrect in law and was therefore overruled.
2. The clarification that they gave was if the individual is the owner of the digital device in question can step into the witness box and prove that the concerned device, on which the original information is first stored, is owned and/or operated by him. However, if it belongs to a network and a computer system and cannot be brought before the Court, mandatory compliance of Section 65B(4) needs to be done. The Court further clarified the stance with "The last sentence in Anvar P.V. (supra) which reads as "...if an electronic record as such is used as primary evidence under Section 62 of the Evidence Act..." is thus clarified; it is to be read without the words "under Section 62 of the Evidence Act,..." With this clarification, the law stated in paragraph 24 of Anvar P.V. (supra) does not need to be revisited."
3. The Court also gave general directions to telecom companies to store and maintain CDR for the relevant period to produce the certificate at the appropriate stage. These directions shall apply in all proceedings till rules and directions under Section 67C of the Information Technology Act and data retention conditions are formulated for compliance by telecom and internet service providers.
4. Likewise, appropriate rules for preservation, retrieval, and production of electronic records, should be framed as indicated earlier, after considering the report of the Committee constituted by the Chief Justice's Conference in April 2016.

THE MANDATORY CERTIFICATE REQUIREMENT: REVISITED STANCE?

The Court in the Arjun Panditrao cases has had the opportunity to settle the dust finally. However, the opportunity was passed in by the Court. The Court does not detail the issue while previously the Court in Anvar decision had gone in charting the entire historical aspect with respect to Section 65B. This can be considered a great dub as the Court accepts the charted position as laid down in Anvar while in Arjun Panditrao does not examine it. The Court does not go into the objective as to the mandatory requirement of the Section 65B certificate and subsequently what could be the policy imperative in ignoring Section 65B(2) requirement of providing oral or secondary evidence.

Further, In Anvar, the Court draws a comparison with Section 69 of the Police and Criminal Evidence Act, 1984 (PACE) in the United Kingdom. The Court observes that in the U.K., there exist no apparent distinction between various category of evidence with respect to electronic evidence in terms of reliability and admissibility exist anymore to post the Reg v Shepherd decision of the House of Lord. The Court was called upon to examine the issue of placing reliance on computer-generated till rolls which was relied upon by the prosecution as crucial evidence. The defendant argued that the evidence is not authentic and reliable without the certificate. The Court rejected this contention of mandatory certificate use wherein the person responsible should give a mandatory certificate. However, in case of lack of availability in such a case, oral evidence can be led to prove the content. The Court diluted the requirement by saying that in the majority of cases, the oral evidence can be led by the person operating the computer instead of the certificate required under the Act. (Bajpai,2021) This missed opportunity by the Court might be costly as the future is full of electronic and digital evidence.

THE PRIMARY-SECONDARY EVIDENCE RULE: AN INVESTIGATION

In declaring Section 65B as a complete code, the Court operates independently relied upon the non-obstante in clause (1) to provide overriding effect with respect to digital evidence. The Court in Arjun Panditrao categorically held the abovementioned position. However, the problem lies with the incorrect justification, as the best proof for any document is the document itself. This theory generally is in line with the primary evidence rule. In the absence of primary rule lies the secondary rule, which can be utilised subject to fulfilment of certain conditions. The same can be evaluated through the prism of Section 63 as well as Section 65. Although section 65B provides for the conditions under the Act for electronic evidence, it includes a non-obstante clause in sub-section (1) so that it can provide a deeming fiction for all electronic records to be considered as proof of the contents of the original record itself. Unfortunately, the Supreme Court fails to consider this aspect in *Arjun Panditrao*.

The Court fails to answer the question what if there is a person able to testify as to the operating condition while but due to the current situation and requirement of the content of the certificate and its mandatory nature, there exist no one to give this certificate, how to rectify this anomaly. This part was considered by the Delhi High Court decision in *Kundan Singh* v. *State*. The Court accepts such ocular statements to corroborate, but the Court does not recognise the issue for consideration in the instant decision.

However, this is not all. There is another way in which this primary-secondary dichotomy constrains the understanding of the Court on electronic evidence and, thereby, the mandatory need for a certificate. In the Arjun Panditrao decision, the Court observed:

"Quite obviously, the requisite certificate in sub-section (4) is unnecessary if the original document itself is produced. This can be done by the owner of a laptop computer, a computer tablet or even a mobile phone by stepping into the witness box and proving that the concerned device, on which the original information is first stored, is owned and/or operated by him. In cases where "the computer", as defined, happens to be a part of a "computer system" or "computer network" (as defined in the Information Technology Act, 2000) and it becomes impossible to bring such network or system to the Court physically, then the only means of proving information contained in such electronic record can be in accordance with Section 65-B(1), together with the requisite certificate under Section 65-B(4)."

The Court could have considered various rules for various kinds of electronic evidence or allowed the case-to-case basis to be more inclusive and more pragmatic than a formalistic tokenism view. (Vinod, 2020) The Court also examined the electronic evidence through the lens of unique code versus general law wherein they stated that Section 65B would supersede the secondary evidence law, which is section 63 read with section 65. The Court observes the following in Anvar judgment in para 22:

"**22.** The evidence relating to electronic record, as noted hereinbefore, being a special provision, the general law on secondary evidence under Section 63 read with Section 65 of the Evidence Act shall yield to the same. *Generalia specialibus non-derogant*, a special law will always prevail over the general law. It appears that the Court omitted to take note of Sections 59 and 65-A dealing with the admissibility of an electronic record. Sections 63 and 65 have no application in the case of secondary evidence by way of electronic record; the same is wholly governed by Sections 65-A and 65-B. To that extent, the statement of the law on admissibility of secondary evidence pertaining to electronic record, as stated by this Court in *Navjot Sandhu case* [*State (NCT of Delhi)* v. *Navjot Sandhu*, (2005) 11 SCC 600: 2005 SCC (Cri) 1715], does not lay down the correct legal position. It requires to be overruled, and we do so. An electronic record by way of secondary evidence shall not be admitted in evidence unless the requirements under Section 65-B are satisfied. Thus, in the case of CD, VCD, chip, etc., the same shall be accompanied by the certificate in terms of Section 65-B obtained at the time of taking the document, without which the secondary evidence pertaining to that electronic record is inadmissible." This clearly showcases how the Court does not want to diverge from the formal requirements as laid down in Section 65B and go on the lines of other countries such as the U.K. and Singapore.

COMPARATIVE ANALYSIS

The U.S.

In the United States, they use the Federal Rules of Evidence (FRE), which were brought in a force of 1-12-2017 for the purpose of production of electronic evidence and its recognition. Two systems flows, the one under Rule 901 or the self-authentication under Rule 902, whereunder a certificate of authenticity will elevate its status. The fact can be noted with decision in *Lorraine* v. *Markel American Insurance Co.* [*Lorraine* v. *Markel American Insurance Co.*, 241 FRD 534 (2007)] wherein Paul Grimm, J. dealt with the issue of admissibility of emails in insurance dispute, he laid down a test which constitutes "Whenever ESI is offered as evidence, either at trial or in summary judgment, the following evidence rules must be considered: (1) is the ESI relevant as determined by Rule 401 (does it have any tendency to make some fact that is of consequence to the litigation more or less probable than it otherwise would be); (2) if relevant under Rule 401, is it authentic as required by Rule 901(*a*) (can the proponent show that the ESI is what it purports to be); (3) if the ESI is offered for its substantive truth, is it hearsay as defined by Rule 801, and if so, is it covered by an applicable exception (Rules 803, 804 and 807); (4) is the form of the ESI that is being offered as evidence an original or duplicate under the original writing rule, of if not, is there admissible secondary evidence to prove the content of the ESI (Rules, 1001-1008); and (5) is the probative value of the ESI substantially outweighed by the danger of unfair prejudice or one of the other factors identified by Rule 403, such that it should be excluded despite its relevance." The relevance of the abovementioned can be noted with the amendment as passed in 2017 by the federal government for the purpose of recognition and admissibility of electronic evidence.

The general provision is thus Rule 901 for generality. However, it is rule 902 which lays down the special regime for self-authentication of evidence. This is to be viewed with the fact that in no circumstances is Federal Rule 902 withstanding or excluding the provision of Rule 901. Thus making the regime robust, even giving the option to opt-out of self-authentication and to follow the general rule under Federal Rule 901. The Judges in the United States federal Court have utilised the Daubert Test wherein the question of admissibility of scientific or technical evidence is ascertained. The test has five components to it which are: whether the technique can be and has been already tested, whether has it been published and reviewed by other peers, the error commission rate on such evidence's admission, standards which maintain and govern the operation of the same and whether has it gained scientific communities acceptance in general. This test single-handedly determines the reliability of digital evidence in the courts. The guidelines of the same were extended in The Kumho Tire v. Carmichael, which gave the extension to include any form of technical evidence. The safeguard provided under FRE Rule 702 lays down the guidelines for the purpose of qualification of experts while also minimising negative bias in testimony.

The U.K.

It is evident that the Indian Evidence Act had generally utilised Section 5 of the UK Civil Evidence Act, 1968 for the purpose of incorporating Section 65B under the evidence law. In general comparison, the language, structure as well as essence seems to be para materia to UK Civil law. However, the recommendations made by the Law Commission (U.K.) made in 1993 led to the repeal of Section 5 of the 1968 Act. This amendment in 1995 gave new life to electronic records in the U.K. as the regime was more robust and comprehensive in comparison to the provision under the unamended 1968 Act. (Rangarajan, 1972)

For the purpose of Criminal Law, the evidence required is provided under the Police, and Criminal Evidence Act, 1984, wherein Section 69 provides for the admissibility of evidence and lays down three requirements which are: (*i*) that there are no reasonable grounds for believing that the statement is not inaccurate because of improper use of the computer; (*ii*) that at all material times the computer was operating properly; and (*iii*) that the additional conditions specified in the rules made by the Court are also satisfied.

This was, however, repealed by Section 60 of the Youth Justice and Criminal Evidence Act, due to the recommendations made by the Law Commission in June 1997 under its report titled "Evidence in Criminal Proceedings: Hearsay and Related Topics". The current legislative movement for admission of digital includes two most important legislation, which is the Criminal Justice Act 2003, the Regulation of Investigatory Powers Act 2000, the Computer Misuse Act 1990, etc. The first is the usage of section 117 of the Criminal Justice Act 2003, which rules the roster with respect to the admissibility of communication data and its admissibility, which is supplemented with a due warrant under law. There is, however, a different regime under section 17 of the Regulation of Investigatory Powers Act 2000, which provides for non-admission of such evidence unless it has been duly acquired from a foreign enforcement agency and has been made available for U.K. Courts. The obvious question that arises is that of intercepted data. Section 78 of the Police and Criminal Evidence Act 1984 categorically provide for its usage for intelligence purpose and is inadmissible, which denotes that unfairly acquired evidence is not admissible under law.

The U.K. stands out from its European counterpart with respect to admissibility rules as it is more stringent and stricter in its implementation. U.S. has also admitted a similar model to the U.K.; however, its variation is very different. E.g., the evidence seizing, and its authorisation are much more strict, and the chain of custody needs to be maintained while also if anything beyond the scope of a warrant is found is inadmissible in law which is not the case in the U.K.

The judges employ three considerations in the U.K. before deciding on the admissibility of digital evidence, which is regarding best evidence, search warrants, and reliability:

1. Best Evidence

The concept of the "best evidence" rule provides for the preference of an original copy of a document as a better form of evidence. This rule was implemented during the era where facsimile was inadmissible and was considered secondary evidence in the event the original evidence was in existence and could be acquired. The central notion was to utilise the best possible information and thus the advent of the rule. This rule, however, went through a transformation when computers and technology made sure that the copy so made was an identical and effective replica. The shift in rule led to the discovery of new rules for admissibility wherein the authenticity could be effectively be proved. The digital evidence has further expanded jurisdiction in order to preserve the original one as it removes the possibility of any sort of modification.

2. Search Warrants

The admissibility of digital evidence in the U.K. necessitates the requirement of proper authorisation for which the investigating agency needs to obtain proper search warrants or subpoenas for the purpose of search and seizure. In the process of getting a warrant from the Court, the investigators need to show reasonable cause, i.e., the commission of the crime, evidence of the crime, and the place at which it likely will be present. Search warrants in the U.K. can be limited and expanded in scope, which is there are several types of warrants such as "specific premises warrants", all-premises warrants", and "multiple entry warrants". In the event that the investigators discover new evidence which is not part of the warrant, they still need to get a new or second warrant, and the primary warrant will be not sufficient as it exceeds the scope. E.g., if the investigators have to use the data on the computer, they would require two warrants, one for the computer and one for the files as per 117 of Criminal Justice Act 2003

Position in Canada

In Canada, the Bar Association organised a conference in 1974, which was in succession to a similar conference of Commissioners on Uniformity of Laws in 1918. Moreover, in 1988 Committee adopted to resolve and proposed the law more similar to model law on Uniform Electronic Evidence, and the recommendations of the Uniform Law Conference later took shape in the form of amendments to the Canada Evidence Act, 1985. Which under Sections 31.1 and 31.2 of the said Act deals with authentication of electronic documents. Further, Sections 31.3 and 31.6(1) of the Canada Evidence Act, 1985 provide for similar requirements under Section 65-B of Evidence Act, 1872. However, there is a critical difference that includes the induction of electronic evidence if it does not suit the adverse party.

Standardisation of Digital Evidence

There have been calls for standardisation for the purpose of digital evidence collection, wherein standard such as ISO/IEC 27037:2012 was formulated for handling and using of digital evidence, which involves "identification, collection, acquisition, and preservation of potential digital evidence that can be of evidential value."

This creates a standard handling process in the event of digital evidence handling for the organisation for the purpose of disciplinary procedures and the exchange of potential digital evidence between jurisdictions. ISO/IEC 27037:2012 which lays down the digital storage standard on various digital devices such as phones, navigation systems, CCTV, etc.

The second such standard is that of ISO/IEC 27043:2015, wherein various models are suggested for the purpose of the investigation process with respect to digital evidence. This covers the entire stage from pre-incident until closure and includes security breaches, unauthorised access, data corruption, and system crashes.

CONCLUSION

The way digital evidence is making its way into the Courtroom is unprecedented due to the extensive use of technology and its substitute. The fact further challenges such as digital ledgers as well as Bitcoin will create further challenges to the existing regime and its mandatory requirement of the Section 65B certificate. The Court needs to balance the rights such as the exclusion of evidence v/s the manipulation of the electronic record. The lack of new-age measures leaves more questions and debates than the answer. This also becomes a problem as the prosecution can face problems someday in establishing a case critical in the national interest. The insufficient recognition of secondary evidence might create legal issues.

Supreme Court in Anvar made it mandatory with respect to the admissibility of electronic evidence a certificate under Section 65B. This is to ensure no manipulation and strict authenticity is maintained but comes at a cumbersome cost as well as sustainability with respect to the best evidence rule. This affects our legal systems and the treatment it gives to electronic evidence and will inevitably affect trials and other mechanisms of dispute resolution and hence, the more extensive process of justice delivery.

REFERENCES

Anvar P.V. v. P.K. Basheer, (2014) 10 SCC 473

Arjun Panditrao Khotkar v. Kailash Kushanrao Gorantyal, (2020) 7 SCC 1

Bajpai, P. (2021). Admissibility of CCTV Evidence. *Jus Corpus Law Journal*, *2*(1), 432–444.

Gupta, N. (2021). Relevancy and Admissibility of Electronic Evidence. *Jus Corpus Law Journal*, *1*(4), 143–158.

Karia, T., Anand, A., & Dhawan, B. (2015). The Supreme Court of India Re-Defines Admissibility of Electronic Evidence in India. *Digital Evidence and Electronic Signature Law Review*, *12*(0), 33–37. doi:10.14296/deeslr.v12i0.2215

Karia, T. D. (2008). Digital Evidence: An Indian Perspective. *Digital Evidence and Electronic Signature Law Review*, *5*, 214–220.

Mason, S. (2012). *Electronic Evidence*. Butterworths Law.

R v. Spiby (1990) 91 Cr App R 186 CA

Rangarajan, S. (1972). The Anglo-Saxon Experiment Concerning the Rule against Reception of Hearsay Evidence and What it may Mean to us. *Journal of the Indian Law Institute*, 26–52. https://www.scconline.com/DocumentLink/m5t8Gl90

Ryder, R. D., & Madhavan, A. (2009). Regulating Indian Cyberspace The Battle for Control in the New Media Version 2.0. *Convergence*, *5*(2), 250–256.

Seth, H. (2021). Impossibility Exception to the Section 65-B(4) Electronic Evidence Certificate, 2021 SCC OnLine Blog Exp 42.

Sethia, A. (2016). Rethinking Admissibility of Electronic Evidence. *International Journal of Law and Information Technology*, *24*(3), 229–250. doi:10.1093/ijlit/eaw005

Shafhi Mohd. v. State of H.P., (2018) 5 SCC 311

Sonu v. State of Haryana, (2017) 8 SCC 570

State (NCT of Delhi) v. Navjot Sandhu, (2005) 11 SCC 600

Tomaso Bruno v. State of U.P., (2015) 7 SCC 178

U.S. Supreme Court, Daubert v. Merrell Dow Pharmaceuticals Inc., United States Reports, vol. 509, pp. 579–601, 1983.

Vaidialingam, A. (2015). Authenticating Electronic Evidence: Sec. 65B, Indian Evidence Act, 1872. *NUJS Law Review*, *8*(1-2), 43–66.

Vaidialingam, A. (2015). Authenticating Electronic Evidence: §65B, Indian Evidence Act, 1872, (2015). *NUJS L Rev.*, *8*(43).

Vinod, V. (2020). Snag of Electronic Evidence. *RMLNLUJ, 12*, 166.

Chapter 19
The Vulnerability of Children in Cyberspace

Vibhuti Nakta

https://orcid.org/0000-0001-6627-4803
Panjab University, India

Ekta Sood
HIMCAPES College of Law, India

ABSTRACT

The internet is a tremendous tool. It allows users to chat, read, play, and be entertained while viewing content from around the world. It's vibrant, diverse, and provides instant access to knowledge on any topic. Although the internet has many advantages, it still has some drawbacks. The internet can be a dangerous place for anyone, but children and teenagers are particularly at risk. Online dangers can have severe, expensive, and even tragic consequences, ranging from cyber bullies to social media posts that can come back to haunt them later in life. Children can unintentionally expose their families to cyber attacks by downloading malware that gives cyber criminals access to their parents' bank accounts or other sensitive information. The internet can be a dangerous place for children due to cyberbullying, sexual communication, identity theft, scams, and exposure to adult content. The chapter is an attempt to view in detail the possible menace of cyber crime, its types, and the national and international conventions and legislations on the same.

INTRODUCTION

Technology is an integral part of our existence in today's world. Our lives are embedded in the layers of it. It becomes almost impossible to reconcile our existence in the absence of technology considering its multifarious benefits. Internet usage has been rapid in our country which has enabled newer avenues with each passing day in the areas of entertainment, infotainment, education, health, business, etc. However, despite all the positives it has multifarious drawbacks as well. Especially because in today's time various illegal activities are committed using the internet as a tool whether directly or indirectly. It

DOI: 10.4018/978-1-7998-8641-9.ch019

is quite certain that in the future warfare will be carried out using the internet as a weapon. A report of the International Telecommunications, 2019 illustrated in the Global Cyber Security Index 2018 established that today, about half of the world's population is connected to the internet. As per the statistics almost 3.9 billion people i.e., almost 51.2 per cent of the population is using the internet. While it is an important development considering the future of the internet, it also raises the concern to have a much more secure environment for cyber users. As per a report by 2023, there will be 70 percent internet penetration, thus implying an increased need for a secure cyber environment (Maqsood & Rizwan, 2019). As per the reports of Internet World Statistics (Internet usage and World Population Statistic, 2019), India is the second-largest user of the internet after China. India by 2019 had more than one billion of its population using the internet. While there are figures which are griming which show that the increase of unethical activities using the internet has also been manifold. Cybercrime can thus be defined as an activity that is unlawful and which uses the computer as a tool or instrument or target or either of these. The crimes committed using the internet are faceless and invisible which makes it all the more challenging and cumbersome to investigate such crimes (Ministry of Home Affairs, 2019). The cyber-crimes can be classified into three categories:

Computer as a "Tool" for Cybercrime

In this category of crime, 'computer' is used as means of committing cybercrime. Here the computer is used as the main source for committing cybercrime. It includes credit card frauds, electronic fund transfer frauds, ATM frauds, telecommunicating frauds, e-Commerce frauds, etc.

Computer as a "Target" for Cybercrime

This form of cybercrime is much more sophisticated and requires computer knowledge. In this type of cybercrime, the crime is committed on a computer while using an external source which is also a computer. The main motive of such crime is to steal information, data, software, etc. it includes, unlawfully accessing Government records, intellectual property crimes, stock transfer fraud, sabotaging computer information, system, or networks, etc.

Computers as "Incidental" to Cybercrime

In these types of crimes, computers are only part of transactional fraud and play a small part in committing such crimes. It includes stalking, hacking, gambling, insurance frauds, pornography, phishing, smishing, etc.

CHILDREN IN CYBERSPACE

As per reports till October 2020, almost 4.66 billion people actively used the internet, which equates to more than 60% of the world's population. Undeniably internet has changed how we think and has changed the manner of communication. The population using the internet has increased constantly and has surged further especially post the current pandemic. The entire world has come to a standstill because of the pandemic and everything is either shifted or is shifting over the internet. The work-from-home culture has increased, the meetings are being scheduled online and education has shifted online. Therefore, the vulnerability of children in cyberspace has increased immeasurable. In the past, children were the most vulnerable targets of cyber-attacks which continue to grow owing to the increased digital presence. It is a wrongful notion that children using the internet within the precincts of their homes are safe. The threats of cyberspace are present everywhere. Cyber dangers include hazards to privacy, exposure to unsuitable content, financial frauds, and so on. With the number of attacks on the rise, the disguising internet veil makes it harder to track down the perpetrators and hold them responsible. A child, as per the United Nations Convention on the Rights of the Child, is someone under the age of eighteen. However, there cannot be an umbrella categorization concerning cybersecurity as children of various age groups are exposed to different cybercrimes. Hence, there is a need to develop a broader framework for the protection of children in cyberspace.

Children today are subject to various threats on the internet which broadly include child pornography, sexual harassment, sexual grooming, and cyberbullying. Other threats include racial abuse and hate, online gaming addiction, online violence, and online fraud and deception. Most children today are unaware of the grave dangers posed by the cyber world and the realization of victimization comes only after they have been violated (Faiza, 2020).

MEANING OF CYBERCRIME

The usage of the term 'cyber' became widely accepted by the 1980s. It was a few years earlier to the same when the term 'cybernetics' was coined by Norbert Wiener in 1948. The word cyber-crime is a conjunction of two words 'cyber' and 'crime'. It is an act or omission done through the computer as a medium. The action takes place in a virtual space; therefore, it is usually difficult to trace the perpetrator and owing to lack of information such crimes often go unreported. Also, the infrastructure is not much developed especially in the developing countries to tackle the situation adequately. As per A. Giles, cybercrimes are crimes of the real world carried out through computers, and yet there is no difference between crimes in the actual world and the cyber world, the only difference is the medium through which the crimes are committed (Gilles, 2015).

DEFINITION OF CYBERCRIME

The word cybercrime is a misnomer, which is used as a generic term that described activities of criminal nature using computers. Under India, the term "cybercrime" is yet to be defined in the Indian Penal Code and the Information Technology (Amendment) Act, 2008. The UN manual on avoidance as well as the balance of computer-related criminal defines cybercrime (Clough, 2010) as "computer wrong done has been able to entail pursuits which have been regular for nature, like crime, fraud, forgery, and mischief, many of that have been generally subject all over to criminal sanctions." In general cybercrimes are those crimes wherein the computer is either an object or is used as a tool to commit an offence. The crimes committed can be multifarious and multifaceted which are used against different sections of individuals i.e., persons of any age group and any social and economic background can become the targets of cybercriminals. There are three categories of individuals that primarily are the target for cybercrime i.e., the Government, property, and individuals.

1. Government: these are the least frequent cybercrimes, and the most serious because they involve a crime against the government. Hacking government websites, military websites, and government data and records are all part of it. Cyber terrorism is a term used to describe such crimes.
2. Property: these are usually committed against individuals by gaining access to personal information and confidential records such as bank details, card details, etc. these usually cause monetary losses to an individual.
3. Individuals: these involve the distribution of defamatory, malicious, private information of an individual illegally. This includes cyber-stalking, pornography, trafficking, etc.

Table 1. Commonly cybercrimes can be differentiated into two categories i.e.

Network-related or device-related crimes	Crimes involving the use of technology to engage in illegal activity
Viruses	Phishing Emails
Malware	Cyberstalking
DoS Attacks	Identity Theft
Social engineering	Online Scams
Botnets	Exploit Kits
PUP	Prohibited Illegal Content

IMPACT OF CYBERSPACE ON CHILDREN

According to UNICEF, at least 71% of the adult population in the world utilizes the web. People's lives have indeed been significantly impacted by the digital world, which has become an essential part of their daily routine. Adolescents between the ages of 8 and 28 spend 44.5 hours a week on screens, according to the latest study from the US National Library of Medicine National Institutes of Health (NIH), and at least 23% of children claimed to be addicted to video games online. One out of every three active users of the internet is a child or a minor. One might consider cyber-attacks as trivial as there is minimal physical impact however the social, emotional, and psychological impact that it has is immeasurable. Children are the most susceptible and vulnerable to such attacks. Especially in today's time when families are getting smaller, parents have almost negligible time to spend with their children and the recent pandemic has all increased the usage of the internet amongst all age groups and especially the children. This makes it important that we should all learn about cybersecurity and awareness. Cybersecurity helps us in building a cyber conducive behaviour and makes us aware of the threats that are in cyberspace. Children most importantly need to learn the same as they are most susceptible to sharing personal photographs and videos in absence of knowledge concerning the maintenance of privacy and confidentiality. In absence of such information, children are vulnerable thus making them victims of unwarranted crimes (Faiza, 2020).

CYBERCRIMES AND CHILD ABUSE

Children are the most fragile members of society as they lack maturity and experience to deal with the world therefore, they can be easily manipulated. The reason why children are an easy target are:

1. They are trusting: it is not very difficult for a perpetrator to win over the trust of a child and lure them into illegal activities.
2. They don't react like adults: usually, a child who is a victim of cybercrime can be threatened easily or the child becomes ashamed and hesitant to speak clearly about the incident to anyone.
3. Lack of understanding concerning the abuse: children do not understand abuse and criminal activity; therefore, they continue to be harassed and abused over a long duration of time.

Threats to Children in the Age of Digitization

1. Cyber Grooming: in this, the cyber-criminal builds a bond with the child using social media, gaming platforms, or any other online platform. Once the child trusts the cyber-criminal completely, then he would take advantage of the child or use the child to do illegal activities.
2. Cyber Bullying: it is yet another means to threaten and harass a child. The child is usually harassed using obscene and abusive language by sending the abusive child content.it can severely impact the emotional and psychological well-being of a child. It includes intimidation and threats and cyberstalking.
   a. Intimidation and threats: causing fear in the mind of a person to injure a person's property or reputation.
   b. Cyber Stalking: to monitor the movement of a person including collecting information and tracking them to blackmail the person or threaten to injure a person's property or reputation.
   c. Cyber Morphing: using a computer to change one image into obscene content and putting it online.
3. Child Trafficking: as per UNICEF it means illegally enticing, a person who is under the age of 18 years for recruitment, transfer, harbouring, etc. in the present times the traffickers are using cyberspace to entice a child into trafficking.
4. Online Sexual Abuse of Children: Sexual abuse means forcing, luring, or persuading a child to take part in sexual activity, this may take place without actual physical contact and physical force. In cyberspace exposing a child to inappropriate content or sexually soliciting a child using force, threat, etc. thus forcing a child into sexual conversations or favours.
5. Online Sexual Exploitation: Children vulnerable to exploitative situations and relationships are lured using gifts, money, affection, and attention in return for sexual favours or activities. This can happen online as well wherein young children are forced to:
   a. send sexually explicit images;
   b. participate in sexual activities using webcam or camera;
   c. participate in sexual conversations (UNICEF, 2017).

Online sexual exploitation is largely done using Child Sexual Abuse Material (CSAM). This is commonly known as child pornography is material or literature showing acts of sexual abuse or indecent representation of children through animations, comic strips, and graphics

Table 2.

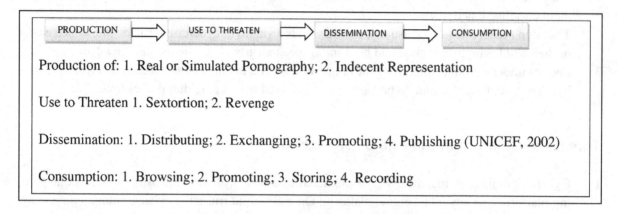

Production of: 1. Real or Simulated Pornography; 2. Indecent Representation

Use to Threaten 1. Sextortion; 2. Revenge

Dissemination: 1. Distributing; 2. Exchanging; 3. Promoting; 4. Publishing (UNICEF, 2002)

Consumption: 1. Browsing; 2. Promoting; 3. Storing; 4. Recording

6. Online Frauds: this can be classified into 4 categories:
    a. Hacking: accessing without authorization or permission or preventing someone from accessing his account or device.
    b. Phishing: when a person claims falsely that he or she is a genuine enterprise or a person to commit hacking or to gain the personal information of the victim.
    c. Identity Theft: Stealing unique credentials of a person such as a password, OTP, login information, etc.
    d. Cheating using impersonation: to take someone's identity to commit cheating online.
7. Online Transaction Fraud: Children typically do not have their bank accounts, but they do utilize their parents' accounts for online transactions such as shopping, gambling, and online payments. The criminal usually is in search of a victim using fraudulent schemes and benefits and children easily fall into the trap of such allurement.
8. Online Gaming: Online gaming is becoming increasingly popular as it is entertaining within the walls of the home. However, these are becoming increasingly unsafe as it is today not merely restricted only to playing games, but people in the game can share thoughts. To access the upgraded version purchase and transactions need to be made. Thus, making users vulnerable to online fraud. There is a risk of viruses, spam, etc. when installing such games which can lead to cyberbullying and the information uploaded can be misused by the criminal.

INTERNATIONAL CONVENTIONS AND NATIONAL LAWS TO ENSURE CYBER SAFETY OF CHILDREN

International Level

1. Convention on the Rights of the Child (1989)

It was signed on November 20, 1989. It is an international treaty concerning the civil, cultural, economic, political, social, and health rights of children. A child below the age of eighteen years comes within the scope and ambit of the said Convention. The Convention contains 41 Articles. The main principles are:

a. non-discrimination;
b. the best interest of the child;
c. the right to survival and development and respect for the views of the child.

The Convention defines a child as: '... any human being below the age of 18 years unless the law which applies on such child has reduced the minimum age criterion. The Convention considers child rights at par with human rights and recognizes:

a. Children rights are: right to life, right against discrimination, right to dignity, right to mental and physical wellbeing, security against slavery, exploitation, torture, etc.;
b. Children rights to nationality and identity;
c. Children right to education, health, decent living standard, right to live with parents;
d. Children rights to secure refuge;
e. Right to develop intellectually, emotionally, and physically;
f. Right against exploitation, mistreatment, kidnapping, etc.
    2. Optional Protocol to the Convention on the Rights of the Child on the Sale of Children, Child Prostitution and Child Pornography (2001)

The Optional Protocol was ratified on May 25, 2000, and came into force on January 18, 2002 (OHCHR, 2020). The optional protocol's goal is to safeguard children from being sold, prostituted, or subjected to pornography. Thus, securing and protecting children against economic exploitation and protection against works that are injurious to the health of a child along with physical, mental, social, and moral wellbeing. As per the preamble, the protocol is intended to achieve the purposes of certain articles in the Convention on the Rights of the Child and to take proper measures to protect the child.

Article 1 of the protocol requires state parties to secure the rights and interests of child victims from trafficking, pornography, labour, and prostitution.

As per Article 2 Sale of children means when a child is transferred or transacted for consideration from one person to another; child prostitution means using a child for sexual exploitation or an activity for a consideration, and child pornography includes representation of a child in real or simulated explicit activity or representing a part of child for sexual purposes.

Article 3 directs the state to lay down penal laws for acts mentioned under Article 2. as per article 3 w.r.t sale of a child defined under section 2 offering, delivering or accepting a child for organ transfer, child labour or sexual exploitation, exporting, importing, disseminating child or his pictures will also be made punishable by the State.

The mention of the optional protocol is pertinent here since all the said activities such as pornography, prostitution, and sale of children are done using cyberspace.

3.   Convention on Cybercrime (2001)

It is also known as the Budapest Convention. The Convention is the first international treaty that deals with copyright infringement, child pornography, fraud relating to computers, hate crimes, etc. (Martha, 2011).

It is the only binding multilateral treaty instrument to fight cybercrime. The Council of Europe drafted the Convention in 2001 with active participation from its observer states. It gives a framework for international cooperation between state parties to the treaty. The convention is open to countries that are not members of the Council of Europe. The Convention is a substantive multilateral agreement. The object of which is protection against cybercrime with help of harmonizing legislation. The Convention is supplemented by an Additional Protocol adopted in 2003. The main purpose of the Convention is to ensure a common policy on cybercrimes by fostering international cooperation. The Convention aims to harmonize the laws of domestic laws on cybercrimes, establishing a regime of international cooperation that is fast and effective and providing the necessary powers requisite for investigating the crimes committed using the computer.

The convention attempts to cover crimes of interference and interception of data, illegal access, and the criminal misuse of devices. Including offences committed using computers such as fraud, transmission, distribution, and production of child pornography.

The offences covered under the Convention can be classified into

"(1) offences against the confidentiality, integrity, and availability of computer data and systems; (2) computer-related offenses; (3) content-related offences; and (4) criminal copyright infringement" (Clough, 2014).

Cybercrimes not included under the Convention are identity theft, sexual grooming of children, and unsolicited spam and emails.

4.   Convention on the Protection of Children Against Sexual Exploitation and Sexual Abuse (2007):

It is a multilateral agreement of the Council of Europe under which governments have agreed to make certain types of child sexual abuse illegal. It is one of the first international conventions to address child sexual abuse at home. It was signed on October 25th, 2007 at Lanzarote, Spain. It came to force on July 1st, 2010 and has 47 Council of Europe member States out of which 38 States have signed and ratified and the remaining 9 have signed without ratification.

The Convention criminalizes the use of information technology for committing acts of:

a.   access child pornography,
b.   distribute child pornography,
c.   solicit children for sexual purposes and

d.   child prostitution.

The main features of the Convention are as follows:

a.   Criminalization of conduct relating to child pornography;
b.   Criminalizes any acts that coerce a child to engage in pornographic performances, which includes live streaming of child abuse and sextortion;
c.   Criminalizes activities of committing sexual activity with a child using threat force coercion or taking undue advantage of one's position to force a child into a sextortion;
d.   Criminalizes the act of exposing a child to the activity of sexual nature;
e.   Criminalizes anyone aiding an offender or abetting a child into such activity.
    5.   Resolution 2011/33 of the Economic and Social Council on the Prevention, Protection, and International Cooperation Against the Abuse and/or Exploitation of Children by New Information Technologies:

The United Nations, Economic, and Social Council issued a Resolution i.e. ECOSOC Resolution 2011/33". It lays stress that today newer technologies are being used to commit exploitation of children. Further, the Resolution highlights that developments in the field of technology have enabled the uprising of crimes such as possession, production, and distribution of material and images concerning children and these may be both audio and visual leading to increased sexual abuse and cyberbullying of children.

6.   Rio De Janeiro Pact to Prevent and Stop Sexual Exploitation of Children and Adolescents

The Rio de Janeiro Pact to Prevent and Stop Sexual Exploitation of Children and Adolescents:
Also known as the "Pact of Rio De Janeiro" was the result of World Congress III. Even though the paper is not legally binding, it addresses essential issues of child and adolescent sexual exploitation as well as state-level responses. It focuses on the online and other technological exploitation of children and adolescents (UNICEF, 2008).

National Level

The Constitution of India, 1950 has provisions concerning children's rights. Clause 3 of Article 15 enables the state to make specific laws for children to secure their interests. Article 21A (The Constitution of India, 1950- 86th AA) establishes that "State shall provide free and compulsory education to all children within the ages of 6 to 14 years, in such a manner as the State may by law determine". Under Article 45 of the Constitution, it will be the duty of the State that children under the age of 14 should receive early childhood care and education. According to Article 51 (k) of the Constitution, all parents and guardians are responsible for providing education and opportunities to children aged 6 to 14. In addition, the laws governing and protecting the rights of children are:

1.   Indian Penal Code, 1860;
2.   Juvenile Justice (Care and Protection of Children) Act, 2000;
3.   Information Technology Act, 2000;
4.   Protection of Children from Sexual Offenses Act, 2012

5. Notifications:
    a. "GSR 314(E) dated 11 April 2011: Information Technology (Intermediaries Guidelines) Rules, 2011"
    b. "GSR315(E) dated 11 April 2011: Information Technology (Guidelines for Cyber Café) Rules, 2011"
        1. To whom the Acts apply

In India, anyone under the age of 18 is considered a potential victim of cybercrime. As per section 2 (1) (d) of the POSCO "child" is anyone who has not completed 18 years of age.

The Explanation to section 67B of the IT Act child are persons who are below 18 years of age.

2. The offence of Child Pornography

Child pornography in India is criminalized under The Indian Penal Code (IPC), the Information Technology Act (IT Act), and the Protection of Children from Sexual Offenses Act (POSCO).

Section 67B of the IT Act penalizes displaying minors in a sexually explicit act, as well as depicting children in an obscene, indecent, or sexually explicit manner. Section 67B (a) lays prohibition on publication or transmission that may cause publication of material that contains sexually explicit material. Anyone who develops texts, digital photographs, gathers, downloads, advertises, promotes, swaps, or distributes information in electronic form that depicts children in an indecent or sexually explicit manner is punishable under Section 67B (b) of the Act. Enticing, encouraging, or cultivating minors into an online relationship with one or more children is also illegal under section 67 B(c) of the Act. This section covers all behaviours that could offend any reasonable adult who uses computer resources. As a result, under section 67 B(d) of the IT Act, anyone who abuses a child will face a penalty. Section 67 B(e) makes it illegal to record abuse of oneself or others with minors on an electronic device. Electronic publication and transmission of obscene material are punishable under section 67 of the IT Act, whereas publication and transmission of sexually explicit material are punishable under section 67 A of the IT Act. In IPC under section 292(2) the selling, distributing, publishing, or circulating material that is sexually explicit or is grossly indecent. Section 292 A of IPC makes publication, printing, selling, circulation of written documents or indecent material in any periodical, newspaper, etc. Section 293 of the IPC penalizes the selling, distribution, circulation, etc. of written material that is obscene and indecent to persons under the age of twenty.

Section 13 of the POSCO Act elaborates the offence where a child is used for pornographic purposes, the punishment for the same is given under section 14 of the Act. Section 15 of the same act criminalizes the storing of material that is indecent or is sexually explicit and the same is also used for commercial purposes.

3. Defining Pornography under Indian Legislation

Obscenity is defined under section 67 of the IT Act under section 292(1) and section 292(1) of the IPC. The material can be considered obscene in any form if it is vulgar or appeals to voyeuristic interest, or if its overall effect tends to corrupt a person.

Written material, paintings, drawings, representations, and the like are exempt from section 67 (B) of the IT Act, and the exception to section 292 of the IPC lays that if the publication is justified for public interest or is in the benefit of science, art, literature, or learning, or if the material is kept for literary or religious purposes.

a.   Child Pornography and its forms

"Minor pornography in any form" covers the use of "material in any form" that employs a child for sexual enjoyment, according to section 13 of POSCO. It also includes depicting a child's sexual organs, portraying a child indecently or obscenely, and depicting a youngster engaged in a real or simulated sexual act. Minor pornography in any form, as defined under section 15 of the Act, is pornographic material in any form that involves a child, and anyone who stores such material for commercial purposes will be penalized. Under section 13 of POSCO, the term "media in whatever form" refers to advertisements broadcast on television, the internet, or any other electronic or printed medium.

The interpretation of "use of a child" in section 13 of the POSCO Act is characterized as "engaging a child using an electronic, print, computer, or any other technology to prepare, transmit, produce, publish, etc.

b.   Child pornography in electronic form

Under section 67 B means any material in electronic form depicting children engaged in an explicit or sexually provocative act, representing a child obscenely or indecently. Under section 2(1) (r) of the IT Act "information in electronic form means" any information which is generated, received, sent, or stored using media, computer memory, film, microfiche, or any other similar device. The term 'information' under section 2(1)(v) means and includes data, messages, images, sound, videos, computer programs, software, database, etc.

4.   Criminalization of accessing or downloading child pornography images

The IT Act under section 67B (b) makes browsing and downloading of any material in any electronic form, which represents children in an indecent or obscene, or sexually explicit manner as illegal.

5.   Criminalization for possessing child pornography

As per section 15 of the POSCO Act storing pornographic material for commercial purposes is an offence. In India, even possession or storage of child pornography without any intention to distribute is an offence.

Apart from this section 292 (2)(a) of IPC even though not specifically applies to child pornography criminalizes possession of obscene material and objects for hire, sale, distribution, etc.

6.   Criminalization for possessing virtual images and sexually exploitative representations of children

Section 67(B)(b) of the IT Act specifically punishes any person who creates or collects or browses, downloads, promotes, advertises, etc. textual or digital images in electronic form that depicts children explicitly or obscenely.

Any representation of a child in a sexually exploitative manner in a pamphlet, paper, writing, drawing or painting, etc. is covered under section 67B of the IT Act.

7. Criminal liability of children involved in pornography

As per section 34(1) of the POSCO Act any child who commits an offence under the Act will be punished as under the provisions of the Juvenile Justice Act.

8. Criminal liability of associations and companies

Any association or company that commits an offence in contravention of the provisions of the IT Act will be fined under section 85 of the IT Act, which includes a penalty for neglect, acquiescence, or connivance by the director, secretary, or management under section 85(2) of the IT Act.

9. Extraterritorial jurisdiction over child pornographic offences when the alleged offender resident of India

IPC under section 4 provides that, *"The provisions of this Code apply also to any offence committed by any citizen of India in any place without and beyond India."* The Explanation to Section 4 of the IPC states that the word "offence" includes any act undertaken outside of India that would be criminal under this Code if committed in India.

Apart from this, the Supreme Court of India has ruled that citizens of Indian nationality who have committed offences abroad can in some cases be tried in India as per the provisions of IPC section 4.

10. Recognition to extraterritorial jurisdiction over child pornographic offences when the victim is a resident of India

As per IT Act section 75 (1) subject to the provision of subsection (2) the Act will be made applicable to any offence or omission which is perpetrated outside of India's borders, irrespective of the nationality of the person. Section 75(2) for offences covered under subsection (1) the act should be committed by using a computer or network located in India.

11. Confiscation of assets used for commission of child pornographic offences Indian law

Section 76 of the IT Act empowers the State to confiscate any medium which is used to commit a cybercrime, these include computers, computer systems, floppies, compact disks, accessories.

12. Section 19 (1) of the POSCO establishes that whenever any person even if a child either is apprehensive of an offence under the said Act is likely to be committed or has the knowledge that an action under the provisions of this Act has been committed, such person or child will inform the local police or special juvenile police unit. As per section 32 of the Juvenile Justice Act, any child who needs care and protection will be protected by the Child Welfare Committee by one of the following:

    a. Childline or any voluntary organization, or voluntary organization recognized by the state;

    b.   Social worker

    c.   Public spirited person

    d.   Public servant;

    e.   A police officer or special juvenile police unit;

    f.   Child himself.

13.   Internet Service Providers to report child pornography

There is no explicit provision that requires the ISP providers to report an offence of child pornography however section 20 of POSCO requires any person who is in the knowledge of sexual exploitation of a child to report Special Juvenile Police Unit or the local police. These persons may include media, lodge, hotel, club, studio, etc. Apart from this section 21 of the POSCO lays down punishment for failing to report any act as mentioned under section 20.

In India, there are no specific provisions in the legislation that mandate ISPs to report child pornography, Section 79 of the IT Act and Information Technology (Intermediaries Guidelines) Rules establish intermediaries' liability for making third party content available mentioned under section 79 (1) of the IT Act. It protects intermediaries from being made liable for transmitting 3rd party information, data, or communication links made available by them, as long as they exercise due diligence as per section 79 (2) of the IT Act and observe the Information Technology (Intermediaries Guidelines) Rules. Section 79 (3) of the IT Act provides that an intermediary will be liable for acts of a third party if:

a.   the intermediary has abetted or conspired or induced or aided the commission of the unlawful act provided under the IT Act; or

b.   when the intermediary fails to disable or remove access to the material even when notified by the appropriate Government or agency.

The Information Technology (Intermediaries Guidelines) Rules under Section 3 (4) mandates such intermediaries, on whose computer system any information is stored or published or hosted, upon receiving information either on their own or on the information of a victim in writing or through email which is signed with an electronic signature, on any such information mentioned in Section 3 (2) of these Rules, to 1) disable within 36 hours such information and 2) preserve such information for at least 90 days for investigation purposes. The information shall include information that: 1) violates any law for the time being in force according to Section 3 (2) (b),(c), and (e); 2) is obscene or pornographic or 3) harms minors in any way.

14.   Telephone helplines to report child abuse- Childline India, a non-profit organization dedicated to the welfare of children in general, has a special hotline for reporting incidences of child abuse.

15.   Provisions for data retention and preservation

The Information Technology Act contains two Sections that lay provisions on data retention and preservation requirements for intermediaries, Section 67C of the IT Act lays down that intermediaries will secure and retain such information for a duration specified in such format and manner as prescribed by the Government. Section 79 (2) (c) of the IT Act gives exemption to intermediaries from liability for the content of the third party provided they observe due diligence in their duties and observe the guidelines prescribed by the Central Government. The IT (Guidelines for Cyber Café) Rules were issued to exercise the powers under Section 79 (2) of the IT Act. As a part of their duty established under the Act, the cybercafe acting as an intermediary is required to observe due diligence and retain data and are responsible for storing: the history of websites using computer resources at cybercafe; logs of proxy servers for at least one year after the IT (Guidelines for Cyber Café) Rules, section 5.

16. Legislation for criminalizing online grooming

The word online grooming is not used in explicit terms in India, however, acts that constitute online grooming are covered under sections 11 and 12 of POSCO. Section 11 lays that any person is deemed to commit sexual harassment if he with sexual intent constantly and repeatedly follows watches, follows, or contacts a child directly or through a digital platform. Punishment for the same is under section 12. To address the problem of online grooming IT Act under section 67 B(c) punishes anyone who induces, coerces, entices a child into an online relationship. Section 67 B(d) makes facilitation of child abuse online an offence.

17. Requirement of photo identity for users of computers in cyber cafes

After the introduction of Section 4 of the IT (Guidelines for Cyber Café) Rules, cybercafés are prohibited to allow the usage of computer resources without the production of a photo identity to establish the identity of the user. The documents permitted for establishing identity are: 1) identity card of school or college; 2) unique identification (UID) or aadhar card 3) passport; 4) permanent account number (PAN) card issued by any income-tax authority;5) voter identity card; 6) photo identity card issued by the employer or any government agency; 7) driving license issued by the appropriate government; or 8) photo credit card or debit card issued by a bank or post office.

Section 4 (2) of the IT (Guidelines for Cyber Café) Rules further establishes that the cybercafé will keep a record of user's photo identity by either storing a photocopy or a scanned copy of the same and the record will be maintained for at least one year by the cyber cafes as per section 4(2). As per section 4(3) of the rules, the cybercafé owner may photograph the user using a webcam established on the cybercafé to establish the identity. Apart from this as per section according to Section 6 (5) of the Rules all computers in the cybercafé are required to have commercially available filtering software to avoid, access to websites on pornography, including child pornography or obscene information Rules. As per section 6(7) of the rules, the cybercafes are mandated to put in a conspicuous place of the cybercafe regarding disallowing pornographic sites and viewing or downloading such information.

18. The 2013 National Policy for Children lays a duty upon the State to, "protect children from any form of harm, neglect, violence and abuse, deprivation, stigma, discrimination, exploitation which shall include sexual and economic exploitation, abduction, sale, abandonment, separation, or pornography, alcohol, trafficking, and substance abuse, or any other activity that takes undue advantage of them, or harms them or impacts their development" (ICMEC & World Bank, 2015)

19. The main law concerning crimes against children committed with aid of ICTs in India is the IT Act. Section 67B (b) of the IT Act establishes liability for downloading or browsing any material in electronic form that depicts children in an indecent or obscene or sexually explicit manner.

20. Criminalization of 1) child trafficking for pornography, and 2) advertising child sex tourism

There is no separate provision for criminalizing child trafficking for pornography. However, under IPC section 370 criminalizes child trafficking for sexual exploitation. Section 370 (1) of IPC makes traffic a person for exploitation an offence. Furthermore, Explanation 1 to Section 370 (1) of IPC says that "exploitation" will include sexual exploitation in any form.

When the offence involves the trafficking of a minor, it is penalized under Section 370 (4) of the IPC by harsh imprisonment for a term not less than ten years, with the penalty of life imprisonment and a fine. In addition, the other provisions under IPC that criminalizes child trafficking and related offences are:

a. to procure a minor girl below the age of 18 years (366A);
b. section 366B prohibits the importation of girls under the age of 21 from Jammu and Kashmir to any other state or from a foreign country to any part of India; and
c. selling or buying of a minor girl below 18 years of age for prostitution, etc. (Sections 372 and 373).

No law or provision in India criminalizes advertising child sex tourism online. However, Section 67B (b) of the IT Act criminalizes the advertisement or promotion of explicit material in any electronic form that depicts children in an indecent or sexually explicit or obscene manner.

The Government of India has also ratified the Code of Conduct for Safe & Honorable Tourism, 2010, it is not a legally binding instrument but lays guidelines for preventing sexual exploitation of women and children and sex tourism.

21. India does not have any legislation on cyberbullying. In 2012 a survey was conducted by Microsoft in which 53% of Indian children reported having experienced cyberbullying (Redmond, 2012).
22. Criminalizing sexting

Sexting is the act of sharing, exchanging, or transferring sexually explicit messages, images, or videos of oneself to others, usually between mobile phones. It could also mean using a computer or other digital device. Consent refers to voluntarily agreeing to something. It's entirely up to you whether or not you sext and how far you go. If you agree to sext with someone, it does not mean you agree to them sharing your sext with anybody else or engaging in any other sexual activity with them. The word Sexting is not explicitly used in Indian legislation; however, Section 67 of the IT Act lays criminalizes persons engaged in publication or transmission of obscene materials in electronic form. Section 67A of the IT Act criminalizes persons engaged in the publication or transmission of materials containing sexually explicit acts.

23. India has ratified the following International Conventions:
     ◦ India ratified the Optional Protocol to the Convention on the Rights of the Child on the Sale of Children, Child Prostitution, and Child Pornography on August 16, 2005.
     ◦ Worst Forms of Child Labour Convention, 1999 (No. 182)
     ◦ Convention on the Rights of the Child on December 11, 1992.
24. Punishments

Table 3.

Offense	Penalty
Online Grooming	1) Imprisonment for a term extending to 3 years and a fine (Protection of Children from Sexual Offenses Act) (2) Imprisonment up to 5 years and a fine (IT Act)
Showing Pornography to anyone under 20	(1) Imprisonment up to 3 years and a fine (2) Repeated: Imprisonment up to 7 years and a fine
Trafficking of children to produce pornography	Imprisonment for a term of not less than 10 years but may extend to life and a fine
Possessing child pornography	(1) Up to 2 years imprisonment and a fine (Penal Code); (2) Up to 3 years imprisonment and/or a fine (Protection of Children from Sexual Offenses Act)
Selling child pornography	(1) Up to 2 years imprisonment and a fine (2) Repeated Max. 5 years imprisonment and a fine
Offering child pornography	(1) Imprisonment up to 5 years and a fine (IT Act) (2) Imprisonment up to 2 years and a fine (Penal Code)
Importing, Exporting child pornography	Up to 2 years imprisonment and a fine
Distributing, Disseminating child pornography	Up to 5 years imprisonment and a fine
Producing child pornography	(1) Up to 5 years imprisonment and a fine (IT Act) (2) Imprisonment extending to 2 years and a fine (Penal Code)

CONCLUSION AND SUGGESTIONS

Child safety is an important concern, it should be taken seriously if remain unchecked it may lead to dangers both online and offline. Thus, what can be ultimately be said about the Indian laws dealing with child safety in cyberspace is ambiguous as there are multiple provisions on similar issues in different legislations thus benefitting the wrongdoers. Section 67B of the IT Act, 2000 and section 13-15 of POCSO Act, 2012 deal with the same subject matter. The provisions of IPC are redundant and futile in comparison to new acts namely IT and POCSO Act. The need of the hour is that the laws concerning online offences under different laws should be consolidated. New legislation on the specific subject is a solution to the ambiguities created. As has been stated in *Kamlesh Vaswani* v. *Union of India* (2013, WP (C) No. 177.), the government must direct all internet service providers to ban sites that display pornographic content. Similar has been recommendations from the Bombay High Court Committee on 'Protecting Children from Online Pornography' appointed by the then *Hon'ble Chief Justice B.P. Singh* and *D.Y. Chandrachud J* of Bombay High Court in the case of *Mr Jayesh S. Thakkar and anr.* v. the *State of Maharashtra* (2001, Bombay HC, WP No. 1611), to discuss the ways how to control and monitor online child pornography. Among other recommendations by the committee, one was that the Cyber Cops must be specially trained to have a better check on online offences.

After reviewing and analyzing the issue at hand, the conclusion remains that child pornography is not only a crime specific to an individual, it is a crime against society at large. It is both a legal and a social wrong against public morality and conscience. Children are the most vulnerable part of our society therefore child-related crimes such as child pornography which involves aggravated sexual abuse, cyberbullying, child trafficking, etc. can be considered as the most heinous crimes. The main reason for the thriving of this issue is the growing technological advancements, growing cyberspace, and easy accessibility of technology. Hence a check on internet browsing especially done by children is the need of the hour which can be done by the government and the parents. More than the government it is the parents who should keep a vigil on the activities of the child and constantly monitor and guide them.

As regards the laws, the Indian legislature must make a comprehensive and uniform law on the subject matter laying strict punishments. Regulatory bodies must be set up to monitor and regulate the content browsed on the internet. An expert committee must be set up comprising experts from the field of law, technology, and human rights. Ultimately what must be kept in mind is that it is the "best interest of the child" which must be given paramount consideration and child pornography and sexual exploitation is its enemy.

REFERENCES

Clough, J. (2010). *Principle of Cyber Crime*. Cambridge University Press. doi:10.1017/CBO9780511845123

Gilles. (2015). *Cyber Crime –Key Issues and Debates*. Routledge.

ICMEC & World Bank. (2015). *Protecting Children from Cybercrime*. https://www.icmec.org/wpcontent/uploads/2015/10/Protecting_Children_from_Cybercrime_-_Legislative_Responses_in_Asia_to_Fight_Child_Pornography__Online_Grooming__and_Cyberbullying_2015.pdf

Jonathan, C. A. (2014). World of Difference: The Budapest Convention on Cybercrime and the Challenges of Harmonization. *Monash University Law Review. Monash University. Faculty of Law, 702*. https://www.monash.edu/__data/assets/pdf_file/0019/232525/clough.pdf

Maqsood, A., & Rizwan, M. (2019). Security, Trust, and Privacy in Cyber (STPC Cyber). *International Journal of Scientific and Research Publications*, *9*(2), p8682. doi:10.29322/IJSRP.9.02.2019.p8682

Ministry of Home Affairs. (2019). *Cyber Crime Reporting Portal*. Government of India.

OHCHR. (November 12, 2020). *Sexual Violence Against Children Online*. https://www.ohchr.org/_layouts/15/WopiFrame.aspx?sourcedoc=/Documents/HRBodies/CRC/GCChildrensDigitalEnvironment/2020/others/swiss-foundation-protection-of-children-2020-114.docx&action=default&Default ItemOpen=1

Redmond. (2012). *Online Bullying Is a Top Concern Among Youth*. https://news.microsoft.com/2012/06/26/online-bullying-is-a-top-concern-among-youth/

Rias, M. L. (2011). *The European Union Criminalizes Acts of Racism and Xenophobia Committed through Computer Systems*. Archived Wayback Machine.

Sarwar, F. (2020). *Harmful Impact of the Internet on Children*. https://timesofindia.indiatimes.com/readersblog/lifecrunch/harmful-impact-of-the-internet-on-children-27202/

Statistics, W. I. (2019). *Internet Usage Statistics the Internet Big Picture*. https://www.internetworldstats.com/stats.htm

UNICEF. (2002). *Handbook on Crime against Children.* https://scpsassam.org/wp-content/up-loads/2018/01/UNICEF-Handbook-for-Law-Enf-Agencies-Handbook-on-Cyber-Crimes-against-Children.pdf

UNICEF. (2008). *Rio de Janeiro Pact at Rio de Janeiro Pact to Prevent and Stop Sexual Exploitation of Children and Adolescents.* http://www.unicef.org/protection/Rio_Declaration_and_Call_for_Action.pdf

UNICEF. (2017). *Children in Digital World.* https://www.unicef.org/media/48601/file#:~:text=ICTs%20are%20intensifying%20traditional%20childhood,streaming%20of%20child%20sexual%20abuse

KEY TERMS AND DEFINITIONS

Botnets: Botnets are networks from compromised computers that are controlled externally by remote hackers. The remote hackers then send spam or attack other computers through these botnets. Botnets can also be used to act as malware and perform malicious tasks.

Cyberstalking: This kind of cybercrime involves online harassment where the user is subjected to a plethora of online messages and emails. Typically, cyberstalkers use social media, websites, and search engines to intimidate a user and instill fear. Usually, the cyberstalker knows their victim and makes the person feel afraid or concerned for their safety.

DDoS Attacks: These is used to make an online service unavailable and take the network down by overwhelming the site with traffic from a variety of sources. Large networks of infected devices known as Botnets are created by depositing malware on users' computers. The hacker then hacks into the system once the network is down.

Exploit Kits: Exploit kits need a vulnerability (bug in the code of software) to gain control of a user's computer. They are ready-made tools criminals can buy online and use against anyone with a computer. The exploit kits are upgraded regularly similar to normal software and are available on dark web hacking forums.

Identity Theft: This cybercrime occurs when a criminal gains access to a user's personal information to steal funds, access confidential information, or participate in tax or health insurance fraud. They can also open a phone/internet account in your name, use your name to plan a criminal activity, and claim government benefits in your name. They may do this by finding out users' passwords through hacking, retrieving personal information from social media, or sending phishing emails.

Online Scams: These is usually in the form of ads or spam emails that include promises of rewards or offers of unrealistic amounts of money. Online scams include enticing offers that are "too good to be true" and when clicked on can cause malware to interfere and compromise information.

Phishing: This type of attack involves hackers sending malicious email attachments or URLs to users to gain access to their accounts or computer. Cybercriminals are becoming more established and many of these emails are not flagged as spam. Users are tricked into emails claiming they need to change their password or update their billing information, giving criminals access.

Prohibited/Illegal Content: This cybercrime involves criminals sharing and distributing inappropriate content that can be considered highly distressing and offensive. Offensive content can include but is not limited to, sexual activity between adults, videos with intense violence, and videos of criminal activity. Illegal content includes materials advocating terrorism-related acts and child exploitation material. This type of content exists both on the everyday internet and on the dark web, an anonymous network.

PUPs: PUPS or Potentially Unwanted Programs are less threatening than other cybercrimes but are a type of malware. They uninstall necessary software in your system including search engines and pre-downloaded apps. They can include spyware or adware, so it's a good idea to install antivirus software to avoid malicious downloads.

Social Engineering: Social engineering involves criminals making direct contact with you usually by phone or email. They want to gain your confidence and usually pose as a customer service agent so you'll give the necessary information needed. This is typically a password, the company you work for, or bank information. Cybercriminals will find out what they can about you on the internet and then attempt to add you as a friend on social accounts. Once they gain access to an account, they can sell your information or secure accounts in your name.

Chapter 20
Artificial Intelligence:
The Need of the Hour

Ramit Rana

Step Next Legal, Advocates and Legal Consultants, India

Apurva Bhutani

Maharaja Agrasen Institute of Management Studies, Department of Law, Guru Gobind Singh Indraprastha University, India

ABSTRACT

We currently live in the "big data" era in which we have the ability to collect massive amounts of data that are too onerous for a single individual to process. Artificial intelligence has already proven to be beneficial in a variety of industries, including technology, banking, marketing, and entertainment. For example, transportation, including the transition to self-driving, or autonomous cars, has been one of the most transformative transformations. Another example is that of Amazon. It suggests other clothes or products you might like based on some of your searches. Even Netflix predicts which movies you may like to watch next. AI is also being used in a variety of sectors that we aren't aware of, such as credit card fraud detection and mortgage loan approval, with more uses on the way. Artificial intelligence is beginning to have an impact on our lives in a variety of ways. Thus, this chapter will analyse the important issues and challenges in the area of AI.

INTRODUCTION

Artificial intelligence (AI) is an area of technological science that focuses on assisting machines in finding solutions to complicated problems in a more human-like way. This generally includes borrowing traits from human intelligence and making use of them as algorithms in a computer friendly manner (Kumar, 2021). As the term implies, artificial intelligence basically refers to the intelligence that is transferred through humans to machines using technology and innovation. It refers to computational technologies that can replace human intelligence in the execution of certain tasks. The first use of the term "artificial intelligence" came in the year 1956 by an American scientist, John McCarthy who is also referred to as

DOI: 10.4018/978-1-7998-8641-9.ch020

the "Father of AI" (Kumar, 2019). John McCarthy also came up with a programming language called LISP which is still used to program computers in AI. LISP allows the computer to learn (Musil, 2011). Induction of robot Kerala Police for police work (Unnithan, 2019), existence of a robot-themed restaurant in Chennai (Porur, 2019) and autonomous prediction by the famous E-commerce company, Amazon.com based on your past preferences explored on the platform evinces that we have advanced into the age of AI. In fact, Siri and Alexa, which are more advanced forms of AI, have become our personal assistants that we use in our everyday lives to feel comfortable.

Artificial intelligence and technology are interwoven and complement each other wholly. It is pertinent to note that technology has not only aided artificial intelligence but has also made it more efficient. Therefore, artificial intelligence is a truly transformative computer science achievement that has already become a core component of all current as well as modern applications and will undoubtedly make its way into practically every industry in the coming years. (Anyoha, 2017). This is both a danger and an opportunity. Researchers, for example, have trained computer models to better recognise a person's personality characteristics than their peers based solely on what Facebook posts they liked and the websites they visited (Morin, 2014). Undoubtedly, digital footprints have enabled us to track one's behaviour, likes, preferences, and even movement (P Kosinski et al., 2013).

It is very crucial to learn to harness the benefits while minimizing the downsides anytime we work with technology. AI has gotten a lot of recognition in recent years. It has become more accessible to us because of technological advancements made possible by the Internet and telecommunications. As a result of these breakthroughs, as well as due to the curiosity about the technology's potential socioeconomic and ethical implications, AI has moved to the forefront of many current discussions. Industry investment in artificial intelligence is increasingly growing and policymakers are busy figuring out what the technology could mean for their people and how it can be used in the best possible way. AI is also influencing and changing the way people engage with the Internet. Internet's power is only going to grow in the near future. AI also has the potential to change the way humans interact with one another, not only with the digital environment. In clear terms, artificial intelligence will not only reach almost every industry, such as entertainment, shopping, social networking, banking, education, information technology and mass media but will also have a significant effect on them. Artificial Intelligence-based applications are already in use in healthcare diagnostics, targeted treatment, transportation, public safety etc and they will most certainly expand in the coming years. Artificial Intelligence, just like the Internet, is changing our perceptions of the surrounding world and has the potential to be a new source of economic development. Artificial Intelligence is infiltrating our lives in ways we don't normally notice; we're just becoming better at it, and we're seeing it in every facet of our life, from medical to transportation to the distribution of power. It will almost certainly result in an economy that is far more productive and efficient (Ito et al., 2016). However, if correctly harnessed, technology has the potential to generate great wealth for individuals, but it also has the potential to introduce human error into a lot of work. Many of AI's potential health-care applications would be about detecting and treating ailments, as well as assisting senior citizens in living fuller, healthier lives. It will certainly aid the funding of large-scale, much-needed public health initiatives. In the end, it seems that in coming years, it would be impossible for us to survive without AI.

ARTIFICIAL INTELLIGENCE: CONCEPT AND NEED

Artificial intelligence applications offer huge benefits and have the potential to transform and evolve any and every industry. Let's look at a few of them. The phrase "human error" was coined because people have been known to make mistakes since the dawn of time, whereas machines, if properly programmed, do not commit these errors. Artificial intelligence makes decisions based on previously gathered data and a set of algorithms. As a result, errors are reduced, and the possibility of improving precision and accuracy increases. One of the most major advantages of artificial intelligence is that it enables us to circumvent many of humanity's risky constraints by creating an AI Robot that can perform risky activities on our behalf. The Robot can be used to replace humans and can be sent to Mars for research, to disarm a bomb, to explore the deepest parts of the oceans, to mine coal and oil, and to deal with any type of natural or man-made calamity.

Humans are designed in such a way that they can take time off to recharge and prepare for a new day at work, and they even have weekly off days to keep their professional and personal lives separate. However, unlike humans, we can use AI to make machines work 24 hours a day, seven days a week with no breaks, and they even require rest to function (Global, 2021). In addition, humans perform a lot of repetitive labour in their daily lives, such as double-checking documents for flaws and so on. Artificial intelligence may now be used to efficiently automate these monotonous jobs and even remove them from people's schedules, allowing them to be more creative.

Due to AI, digital assistants are now being used extensively by some of the world's most well-known companies with the aim of engaging with customers efficiently and to reduce the need for human employees. Many websites also make use of digital assistants to help consumers find what they're looking for. People can talk to them about what they're looking for. In fact, some chat bots are designed in such a way that it's difficult to determine if you're chatting to a human or a computer (Ramos, 2018). Computers can make better decisions and complete jobs faster than humans by combining AI and other technologies. While a human considers a range of emotional and practical variables before making a decision, an AI-powered machine will focus on the work at hand and produce results more quickly and efficiently. Furthermore, AI aids various technologies in almost every domain, while assisting humans in addressing the majority of complex problems.

AI AND IT'S IMPACT

However Artificial Intelligence also brings with itself some major concerns that cannot be ignored and few of them are elaborated as under.

The majority of AI tools are in the hands of profit-driven enterprises or power-hungry governments, and values and ethics are frequently lacking from these automated systems that make decisions for humans. These processes are interrelated on a global scale and are difficult to monitor or manage. Because of its efficiency and other economic benefits, artificial intelligence technology will continue to pose a threat to all aspects of human work. While some people are optimistic about new work chances, others are worried about mass job losses, growing economic inequities, and societal upheavals. Many people feel that artificial intelligence can improve human capacities, while there is also a huge chunk of people who believe that their increasing reliance on machine-driven networks will erode their ability to think for themselves, or operate independently of automated systems, and connect successfully with others.

Due to the complexity of the engineering needed, constructing AI-based machines, computers, and other devices is extremely expensive. Additionally, the exorbitant cost does not end there, as repair and maintenance costs can go into the thousands of dollars. In a well-known example, Apple paid more than $200 million for Siri to enter the mobile search market (Schonfeld, 2010). Moreover, as machines become smarter, it's evident that AI-based software programmes will need to be updated on a frequent basis to keep up with the changing environment's requirements. Furthermore, if the software completely fails, retrieving deleted codes and reinstalling the system could be a nightmare owing to the time and money required.

Machines are indisputably superior to humans in terms of efficiency. Human intellect, on the other hand, is a natural gift that cannot be programmed into a computer, making the replacement of humans with AI is basically unachievable, at least in the near future. As a result, no machine, no matter how modern or intelligent, will ever be able to take the position of a human. Although the idea of being replaced by machines is terrifying, it is still a long way off. Machines are undoubtedly more logical but they are devoid of emotions and moral values. They lack the ability to form bonds with other people, which is a necessary skill for leading a group of people. The ability of human brain strengthens and develops with age and experience and this is one of the most astonishing aspects of the species. The same cannot be true of AIs, as they are machines that do not improve with experience and instead begin to wear out over time. It is important to remember that computers cannot alter their responses in accordance with the changing situations. The core concept on which AIs are built is the repetitive nature of labour with constant input. As a result, every time the input changes, the AIs must be re-evaluated, re-trained, and re-built. Furthermore, machines lack the ability to comprehend ethical or legal concepts, they are unable to discern what is correct or incorrect since they have been programmed to operate under specified parameters only, as a result they are unable to make decisions in the face of an unknown or unexpected situation. Artificial intelligence (AI) is not designed to do creative tasks. As a result, it should be obvious that AIs lack creativity and originality. Even if they can assist you in inventing and constructing something unique, they will never be able to match the human brain. Their power to be innovative is restricted by the person who programs and instructs them. Basically, AIs can grow to be skilled robots, but they will by no means have the cognitive capacities of a human mind. This is because, in contrast to skills, which can be taught and mastered, abilities are natural and can only be developed.

Another critical issue that needs to be addressed is the lack of laws and regulations governing artificial intelligence. There is, admittedly, a legal and regulatory void in the Artificial Intelligence system. The ill-defined features of this as-yet-unknown realm of technology make foreseeing and enacting a rigorous set of laws or regulations difficult and onerous. For example, if an autonomous self-driving automobile is involved in an accident, who would be held responsible? Questions like these are likely to occur and represent a dilemma. As a result, legal measures or rules are urgently required. A legal definition of the phrase Artificial Intelligence is also required. Also, some means must be found to assure that the emergence of digital super-intelligence is symbolic of mankind.

Even if it was created by him alone, man is afraid of anything overpowering or surpassing him or his intelligence, yet Artificial Intelligence should be approached with optimism. It's improbable that such a creature will try to exterminate us first. 'By 2022, Artificial Intelligence could produce 58 million net new jobs,' according to the World Economic Forum (Cann, 2018).

ROLE OF AI

We now live in the "big data" era, in which we may collect vast volumes of data that are too difficult for a single person to process. Artificial intelligence has already shown its worth in a number of fields, including technology, banking, marketing, and entertainment (Anyoha, 2017). For example- transportation, including the transition to self-driving, or autonomous cars, has been one of the most transformative transformations. Another example is that of Amazon, it suggests other clothes or products you might like based on some of your searches, even Netflix predicts which movies or shows you may like to watch next based on your previously watched list. AI is also being used in a variety of sectors that we aren't aware of, such as credit card fraud detection and mortgage loan approval, with more uses on the way (Bailey, 2018). Artificial intelligence is beginning to have an impact on our lives in a variety of ways, from the discovery of new materials to the development of new drugs — A.I. has already aided in the development of Covid-19 vaccines by narrowing the field of possibilities for scientists to search (Smith, 2021).

- **AI and Health**

Artificial intelligence (AI) will strive to keep you healthy at all times. Thanks to sensors in your home that constantly test your breath for early cancer indications, nanobots will swim through your bloodstream, eating plaque in your brain and dissolving blood clots before they can trigger a stroke or heart attack. It will track your immune responses, proteins, and metabolites over time to build a long-term picture of your health that doctors may use to see what's going on inside your body. Your doctor will compare your symptoms to thousands of other cases stretching back hundreds of years if you become unwell. (TaltyS, 2018). The health-care business is a great platform for AI systems in certain ways, as well as a perfect example of its possible implications. In this knowledge-intensive industry, data and analytics are employed to improve medicines and practises. The amount of data collected, which includes clinical, genetic, behavioural, and environmental data, has skyrocketed. The main goal of health-related AI applications is to investigate the links between preventative and treatment techniques and patient outcomes. (Taylor, 1998). Furthermore, hospitals are looking to AI technologies to assist them with operational activities such as cost-cutting, improving patient satisfaction, and meeting staffing and labour requirements (Kent, 2018). Even the US government is pouring billions of dollars into AI research and development in the healthcare sector. Clinical decision support systems make for a significant percentage of the healthcare industry's AI deployment focus. Machine learning algorithms improve as more data is collected, allowing for more reliable responses and solutions. As the AI market grows, major corporations such as Apple, Google, Amazon, and Baidu have established their own AI research departments, as well as set aside millions of dollars for the acquisition of smaller AI-based start-ups. Furthermore, a growing number of automakers are using machine learning into their machines. (Quan, 2018). Even, BMW, GE, Tesla, Toyota, and Volvo have all launched new research programmes to evaluate a driver's essential data to ensure that they are alert, paying attention to the road, and not impaired by drugs or emotional discomfort. (Quan, 2018). Artificial intelligence continues to increase its ability to diagnose more patients successfully in places where doctors are few. Many innovative technical firms, such as SpaceX and the Raspberry Pi Foundation, have helped impoverished countries gain access to computers and the internet (Zahra et al., 2018). Advanced machine learning algorithms can now allow patients to get accurately diagnosed, whereas previously they had no way of knowing if they had a life-threatening disease or not, thanks to the growing capabilities of AI over the internet. AI can lessen the need for outsourcing while also enhancing medical treatment in developing countries with limited resources. AI can not only help diagnose patients in areas where healthcare is scarce, but it can also improve the patient experience by searching through data to find the best treatment for them (Guo & Li, 2018). However, massive volumes of data must be collected in order to effectively train machine learning and utilise AI in healthcare. In most situations, however, obtaining this information comes at the sacrifice of patient privacy, which is not well appreciated by the general public. According to a survey conducted in the United Kingdom, 63 percent of the population is unwilling to share personal information in order to improve artificial intelligence. As a result, the lack of actual, accessible patient data is a roadblock to AI in healthcare research and deployment. Since AI relies only on the data it gets as input, it's critical that this data accurately depicts patient demographics. These algorithms may contain inadvertent bias, which could increase socioeconomic and healthcare inequities.

- **AI and Entertainment**

In recent years, Artificial Intelligence (AI) has had a tremendous impact on the entertainment industry. Artificial intelligence has already made its way into our everyday life. AI technology companies are rapidly altering the entertainment industry while also providing fantastic solutions for the professional world. We are all on the cusp of a technological revolution that will change our lives forever. Artificial intelligence will be used in marketing sectors such as design, film promotion, and advertising in the entertainment business. The most effective marketing and advertising tactics will be devised by intelligent algorithms. All marketing processes might be made many times faster by using predictive analytics and AI. Audience targeting, ad plan development, and other tasks can be handled by AI-powered marketing solutions. For example- Using artificial intelligence, IBM generated a trailer for the horror movie Morgan. Algorithms examined 100 common horror films, audio, and visual features to create a list of the most outstanding and memorable moments that must be included in a trailer. So, instead of weeks of human labour, a 6-minute trailer was created in just one day (Parker, 2020). In a variety of ways, artificial intelligence (AI) is influencing marketing and advertising. AI enables for the customisation of internet experiences at the most fundamental level. This enables the material to display the content that customers are most likely to be interested in. Advertisers are finding it easier to target their adverts because of advances in machine learning and the huge volumes of data being generated. They have the capacity to supply customers with personalised and dynamic advertisements on a large scale. For both organisations and consumers, personalised advertising has numerous advantages. It has the ability to increase sales and marketing activities return on investment for businesses. Spotify and Netflix, two of the most popular music and video streaming services, are this effective because they appeal to a diverse group of people with different tastes and interests. These businesses use AI and machine learning algorithms to analyse individual user behaviour and demographics in order to recommend what they might like to watch or listen to next, guaranteeing that they are always amused. As a result, these AI-powered platforms deliver content that is tailored to the user's specific tastes, resulting in a highly personalised experience (Shah, 2020). International media publishing houses must change their content so that it may be consumed by people from all over the world. In order to do so, they must provide proper multilingual subtitles for their video content. Human translators may spend hundreds, if not thousands, of hours painstakingly creating subtitles for a variety of programmes and films in a variety of languages. Furthermore, locating the human resources required to translate material into specific languages may be difficult. Human translation, on the other hand, is susceptible to errors. Media companies are looking to

AI-based solutions to address these concerns. Several websites, in addition to legitimate news pieces, publish and broadcast fake news in order to agitate the public about specific events or societal issues. Artificial intelligence is assisting in the discovery and control of such content, as well as supporting online platforms, such as social media site owners, in the moderation or removal of such content before its distribution. Not just text, but also photos and movies, are created using deep fake technology. We may, however, use the deep fake detection tool to find fraudulent images and videos and report them to regulatory authorities so that they can take appropriate action (Cogito, 2021).

As competition and the desire for efficiency continue to develop in the entertainment industry, AI's influence will only grow in the coming years. Artificial intelligence is expected to drive more innovation in the entertainment industry in the future. As seen by recent advancements, artificial intelligence has already become an important part of our life, influencing how we interact and interpret the world. Artificial Intelligence may be found in almost every part of our life, from our personal mobile devices to larger industries like business and entertainment. Artificial Intelligence has also had a lasting impression on the entertainment industry. Real-time user interphase visuals have been developed, laying the path for even more advanced improvements in the future.

- **AI and Education**

Grading coursework and exams for professional courses in schools and college can be challenging even when professors share the responsibility. Even in the primary grades, teachers frequently find that grading consumes a significant amount of time that could otherwise be spent interacting with students, planning lessons, or working on professional development. While artificial intelligence will never be able to completely replace human grading, it is getting close. Teachers may now automatically grade all types of multiple-choice and fill-in-the-blank exams, and automated grading of student's written work could be on the way shortly. Teachers may be oblivious of gaps in their lectures and educational materials that lead to students' confusion about specific subjects. This problem can be solved with artificial intelligence. For example- In Coursera, which is a huge open online course provider, when a large number of students submit incorrect answers to a homework assignment, the system alerts the teacher (Staff, 2014). While there are obvious benefits that a human teacher can provide and computer cannot, still more people may be educated in the future by tutors who only speak binary. Children can now benefit from artificial intelligence-based tutoring software that can assist them with fundamental math, writing, and other disciplines. These programmes can teach children the fundamentals, but they are not meant to help them develop higher-order thinking abilities or creativity, which real-world teachers usually encourage. This still does not rule out the possibility that in the future, AI educators may be able to fulfil these responsibilities. Advanced tutoring systems may not be a faraway fantasy given the high pace of technical innovation over the last few decades. On a national level, UNESCO is developing an AI readiness self-assessment framework to assist its Member States in assessing their preparedness to embrace and integrate AI technology in all areas relevant to education. For each country, a profile would be prepared to showcase its strengths and weaknesses, as well as detailed recommendations for how to overcome them (Fengchun, 2021). The project's ultimate goal is to assist key players in education systems around the world in achieving their objectives, being prepared, and having the capacity to use AI to ensure that everyone has access to inclusive, egalitarian, high-quality education, as well as opportunities for lifelong learning. The adoption of cutting-edge AI technologies opens up new ways to interact with students having learning disabilities. AI enables individuals with unique difficulties to attend school. Any group of students can benefit from artificial intelligence technologies because lectures/lessons are adapted according to the needs of different learning groups. Students may now avoid comparing themselves to one another as they can have personalised study material altered in accordance with their needs. Previously, a student would have contacted a teacher for help in front of the entire class, but now it is sufficient to put a query into a personal virtual assistant and receive an instant response. These opportunities provided by AI tools put personal progress first, reducing stress in the classroom. As machine learning algorithms improve and become more precise, the education sector will rely more on technology to provide a holistic learning environment for students and will also help teachers and students to interact in a better way. While the future of AI in education is unknown, we can be certain that students of all abilities and limitations will have a better chance of learning and exhibiting their abilities. As additional AI tools are developed, students will be able to better plan their career paths and work toward their goals. Educational institutions can generate wiser future generations by investing a considerable amount in artificial intelligence.

- **AI and E-Commerce**

For decades, traditional analytics has served the data-driven retail industry well. On the other hand, Artificial Intelligence (AI) and Machine Learning (ML) have introduced a whole new level of data processing that leads to more in-depth business insights. Data scientists could open up a new world of possibilities for business owners by discovering anomalies and connections from hundreds of Artificial Intelligence/Machine Learning models. Artificial intelligence companies raised $1.8 billion in 374 deals between 2013 and 2018, according to CB Insights. To stay ahead of the competition, Amazon persuaded business leaders to contemplate adopting artificial intelligence in retail — both physical stores and e-commerce methods. Over 28% of traders have already deployed Artificial Intelligence/Machine Learning solutions (Chuprina & Kovalenko, 2018). Checkout-free stores have already been implemented by Amazon AI. Your Amazon account will be debited when you leave the store with your items. Amazon plans to establish more AI-powered stores like Amazon Go, which employs only six to twenty people (Chuprina & Kovalenko, 2018). AI chat-bots improve customer service, search, gives notifications about new collections, and recommends related products. If a buyer has already purchased a black hoodie, a chat-bot can recommend a matching pants or shoes to complete the look. When shopping online, we may see product results that are not only irrelevant, but also foreign, making the search extremely inconvenient. This is where artificial intelligence (AI) comes into play. To address this issue, AI typically employs NLP, or natural language processing, to contextualise and improve search results. Not only that, but AI makes use of visual search as well (Martin, 2019). Many businesses are utilising artificial intelligence to boost sales and give the greatest shopping experience to their clients. For example, Amazon's digital shopping assistant "AR View" use augmented reality to allow customers to virtually place items in their own homes before making a purchase (Willems, 2020).

- **AI and banking**

A digital revolution is sweeping many industries, including banking, especially in the aftermath of demonetization. Traditional banking has evolved, and more banks are integrating new technologies such as artificial intelligence (AI), cloud computing, and block chain to reduce operating costs and boost efficiency. Banks are on the verge of an artificial intelligence revolution, despite the fact that it is still in its infancy. The AI industry will improve and develop, resulting in more productivity at a lower cost. Managers in all businesses will have to lift their game when it comes to skill development. There's no denying that the recent push toward digitalization is having a significant impact on traditional banking models. It has, however, exposed the institutions to a growing number of cyber security threats and vulnerabilities. In order to create an active defence system against cybercrime, banks are increasingly looking to emerging technologies such as blockchain and analytics.AI can also help in determining a customer's spending pattern, allowing for the creation of personalized strategies for them. The banking sector benefits from AI's excellent security; AI mobile applications can make transactions faster and safer. The customer and the banks both benefit from AI because it saves time, it aids in the reduction of human mistake, it aids in the development of a strong and loyal consumer base. It facilitates the passage of huge cash inflows and outflows. It facilitates cashless transactions from any location and at any time. Therefore, Artificial Intelligence is gaining extensive popularity, and banks are experimenting with and integrating it to change the way clients are assisted.

- **AI and sports**

There aren't many things in this world that can't be measured. Thanks to data analytics and artificial intelligence, anything can now be tracked and predicted with pinpoint accuracy. Sports are rich in quantifiable characteristics, making them a suitable venue for AI applications. In recent years, artificial intelligence applications in sports have become more popular than ever before. Artificial Intelligence will continue to advance in the field of sports as a result of its significant effect and rising abilities. Analysts and coaches must evaluate a plethora of data points pertaining to individual players and group performances in order to judge a player's performance in any sport, which is exceedingly difficult and often impossible to do; this is where Artificial Intelligence comes into play. By using artificial intelligence to find relationships between qualitative traits and quantitative data, and then assessing those variables to forecast the players qualitative value, the process becomes much faster and more convenient. Artificial Intelligence can be used to spot trends in an opponent's strategy, strengths, and weaknesses while preparing for a game. This enables coaches to devise detailed game strategies based on their assessment of the opposition, and thus increases the chances of victory. Artificial intelligence will significantly improve sports competitiveness. With stronger sensors and algorithms, it will be able to anticipate competition outcomes more accurately. AI will have an impact on advertisers, sports corporations, franchise owners, coaches, and game strategists. Consequently, with such a diverse set of uses, it's possible that the entire sports industry will be keen to include AI in order to gain a competitive advantage.

AI and Intellectual Property Rights

When we talk about Intellectual Property laws, the first thing that comes in mind is that it grants exclusive rights to inventors/creators so that they can benefit from the work generated by them. Things that are able to be created by the use of Artificial Intelligence require protection because such things hold a very high value. Intellectual Property law provides protection to the unique, distinctive and novel ideas, it inspires people to think out of the box and get credit for it, it allows people to monopolise their unique innovation, thus motivating people to innovate and create. However, Artificial Intelligence has sparked a lot of discussion and debate in the area of intellectual property. The patentability of AI-related ideas, proprietary difficulties around inventorship, and a lack of suitable laws and standards have all raised some unanswered questions. To understand the prospect of AI-related inventions becoming patentable, one must first appreciate that an AI-related invention is a combination of several inventions. A computational, mathematical, or algorithmic method, or a combination of the two, could be used. One could argue that copyright laws would protect the algorithm once it was coded, but because copyright laws do not cover the unique concept behind the expression, the AI creation cannot be fully protected. However, if a machine can self-learn and effectively do a task without being expressly programmed, the question becomes whether the natural person's first thought is sufficient to be credited as the named inventor. Artificial Intelligence has already had a considerable impact on the development, production, and distribution of economic and cultural goods and services, and will continue to do so in the future. One of the main purposes of IP policy is to promote innovation and creativity in the economic and technological sectors, which is where AI and IP collide frequently.

Is AI Influencing the Society?

Another major concern is that AI does not become so adept at performing the task for which it was built, that it crosses ethical or legal boundaries. While the AI's original objective and goal was to benefit humanity, it would have a negative impact on civilization if it chose to achieve the desired goal in a destructive (but efficient) manner. Artificial intelligence has the potential to greatly improve workplace productivity while also supplementing the work that humans can do. AI frees up human labour to focus on jobs that need creativity and empathy, among other qualities, when it takes over monotonous or dangerous work that could have been performed by humans only earlier. When people do work that they enjoy, their happiness and job satisfaction is also likely to increase. With the introduction of autonomous transportation and AI affecting our traffic congestion concerns, not to mention the various ways it will boost on-the-job productivity, our society will gain countless hours of production. Humans will be able to spend their time in a variety of ways now that they are no longer bound by uncomfortable commutes. Artificial intelligence will also boost our ability to detect and solve illegal crimes and activities. Facial recognition software is now catching up to fingerprint scanners in terms of popularity. AI's use in the judicial system brings up a lot of options for figuring out how to make the technology work without infringing people's privacy. Artificial intelligence is more likely to have a positive impact on society than a negative one, even despite the various learning opportunities and difficulties that will arise as the technology grows into new and almost all applications. Artificial intelligence (AI) is revolutionising economies, promising more productivity, efficiency, and cost reductions. It makes people's lives better by providing them with more accurate forecasts and judgments. There are many more advancements and luxuries that we will be seeing in the future because of Artificial Intelligence.

In recent years, artificial intelligence has advanced tremendously. Recently developed technologies, such as machine learning and deep learning, have emerged from laboratories to do tasks that were previously thought to be unattainable to computers, such as picture recognition, satisfactory translation of a basic text etc. These technologies are already present in our smart phones and make up a significant portion of them. (Schmidt et al., 2019). Artificial intelligence has indeed made our lives easier

CONCLUSION

If we thought of machine ridden lives in the 90s like we had been showed in the Hollywood movies namely MATRIX, we would have been subjected to nothing but laughter. But times have changed or better to say, we have advanced into the transitional phase allowing us to think of reality beyond our imagination. Lives have become easier but did we ever dare wonder at what cost? I'm afraid, absolutely not. Today we have started to become dependent for switching on a bulb to playing out music on Alexa. These AI can solely operate on the predefined data by which they learn further which has no boundary. It stores everything and outputs on the basis of our requirements. The global data security framework and associated privacy aspects are still in the premature stage. Despite of that, we heavily lean in favour of surrendering our personal as well as sensitive personal information at the mercy of using various AI tools. Even if we don't wish to give in our valuable data, there are AI tools which we cannot use unless we provide basic information. It is more or less quid pro quo of digital advancement. One can't avail something in AI if he/she is not ready to give up his data. But the problem doesn't end here. Instances like Cambridge Analytica are no more fantasy. Whistle blowers like Edward Snowden and Julian Assange have already highlighted at large how we are put under pervasive surveillance without our knowledge and consent. The authors believe societies are well aware of misuse of big data by tech giants, corporate entities as well the State, but the real question is are we really concerned? Aren't we agreeing to surrender even further as and when required? Authors wish to state so because the time when we would come across applications and machines which would require us to provide more and more information to provide us preferences and their consequential operations is not too far. And the worst part, it's INEVITABLE!

The authors have already highlighted in aforementioned parts how AI has successfully secured its place in almost every sector, mainly the one which are directly linked to the common man such as healthcare and banking. They also believe that unless a strong data protection mechanism such as General Data Protection Regulation (GDPR) is put into action globally, data leaks, abuse of data and data theft cannot be avoided. Therefore, it is important for the policymakers to look into with immediate attention and provide clarities to various ambiguities associated with Artificial Intelligence.

REFERENCES

Kumar, V. (2021, June 5). *What is Artificial Intelligence? Functions, 6 Benefits, Applications of AI.* GetupLearn. Retrieved July 29, 2021, from https://getuplearn.com/blog/artificial-intelligence/

Kumar, S. (2019, November 25). *Advantages and Disadvantages of Artificial Intelligence.* Towards Data Science. Retrieved January 14, 2022, from https://towardsdatascience.com/advantages-and-disadvantages-of-artificial-intelligence-182a5ef6588c

Musil, S. (2011, October 24). *John McCarthy, creator of Lisp programming language, dies.* clnet. Retrieved January 14, 2022, from https://www.cnet.com/news/john-mccarthy-creator-of-lisp-programming-language-dies/

Unnithan, P. S. G. (2019, February 20). *India's first RoboCop: Kerala Police inducts robot, gives it SI rank.* IndiaToday. Retrieved January 22, 2022, from https://www.indiatoday.in/trending-news/story/india-first-robocop-kerala-police-inducts-robot-gives-si-rank-1460371-2019-02-20

Porur. (2019, February 6). *In this Chennai restaurant robot waiters serve customers, speak to them in Tamil and English*. IndiaToday. Retrieved November 15, 2021, from https://www.indiatoday.in/india/story/in-this-chennai-restaurant-robot-waiters-serve-customers-speak-to-them-in-tamil-and-english-1449122-2019-02-06

Anyoha, R. (2017, August 28). *Can Machines Think?* SITN. Retrieved November 20, 2021, from https://sitn.hms.harvard.edu/flash/2017/history-artificial-intelligence/

Morin, A. (2014, October 31). *What Your Facebook Use Reveals About Your Personality And Your Self-Esteem* [web log]. Retrieved July 29, 2021, from https://www.forbes.com/sites/amymorin/2014/10/31/what-your-facebook-use-reveals-about-your-personality-and-your-self-esteem/?sh=6cf70ee9321f

Kosinski, P. M., Stillwell, D., & Graepel, T. (2013, April 9). *Private traits and attributes are predictable from digital records of human behavior*. PNAS. Retrieved July 29, 2021, from https://www.pnas.org/content/110/15/5802

Ito, J., Dadich, S., & Obama, B. (2016, August 24). Barack Obama, Neural Nets, Self Driving Cars, And The Future of the World. *Wired*. Retrieved July 29, 2021, from https://www.wired.com/2016/10/president-obama-mit-joi-ito-interview/

Global. (2021, October 19). *Advantages and Disadvantages of Artificial Intelligence*. iCert Global. Retrieved November 25, 2021, from https://www.icertglobal.com/advantages-and-disadvantages-of-artificial-intelligence/detail

Ramos, D. (2018, April 16). *Voice Assistants: How Artificial Intelligence Assistants Are Changing Our Lives Every Day*. smartsheet. Retrieved November 25, 2021, from https://www.smartsheet.com/voice-assistants-artificial-intelligence

Schonfeld, E. (2010, April 29). *Silicon Valley Buzz: Apple Paid More Than $200 Million For Siri To Get Into Mobile Search*. TechCrunch. Retrieved November 26, 2021, from https://techcrunch.com/2010/04/28/apple-siri-200-million/

Cann, O. (2018, September 17). *Machines Will Do More Tasks Than Humans by 2025 but Robot Revolution Will Still Create 58 Million Net New Jobs in Next Five Years*. World Economic Forum. Retrieved November 26, 2021, from https://www.weforum.org/press/2018/09/machines-will-do-more-tasks-than-humans-by-2025-but-robot-revolution-will-still-create-58-million-net-new-jobs-in-next-five-years/

Bailey, B. (2018, December 20). *AI Market Ramps Everywhere*. Semiconductor Engineering. Retrieved November 26, 2021, from https://semiengineering.com/what-is-artificial-intelligence/

Smith, C. S. (2021, March 9). A.I. Here, There, Everywhere. *New York Times*. Retrieved November 26, 2021, from https://www.nytimes.com/2021/02/23/technology/ai-innovation-privacy-seniors-education.html

Talty, S. S. (2018, April). *What Will Our Society Look Like When Artificial Intelligence Is Everywhere?* Smithsonian. Retrieved November 26, 2021, from https://www.smithsonianmag.com/innovation/artificial-intelligence-future-scenarios-180968403/

Taylor, P. (1998, January 10). *Guide to Medical Informatics, the Internet and Telemedicine; Cyber-medicine*. thebmj. Retrieved November 26, 2021, from https://www.bmj.com/content/316/7125/158.1

Kent, J. (2018, August 8). *Providers Embrace Predictive Analytics for Clinical, Financial Benefits*. Health IT Analytics. Retrieved November 26, 2021, from https://healthitanalytics.com/news/providers-embrace-predictive-analytics-for-clinical-financial-benefits

Quan, X. I. (2018, November 20). *Understanding the Artificial Intelligence Business Ecosystem*. IEEE Xplore. Retrieved November 28, 2021, from https://ieeexplore.ieee.org/document/8540793

Zahra, S. A., Brewer, J., & Cooper, M. (2018, April). *Artificial Intelligence (AI) for Web Accessibility: Is Conformance Evaluation a Way Forward?* ACM Digital Library. Retrieved November 27, 2021, from https://dl.acm.org/doi/abs/10.1145/3192714.3192834

Guo, J., & Li, B. (2018, August). *The Application of Medical Artificial Intelligence Technology in Rural Areas of Developing Countries*. PMC. Retrieved November 27, 2021, from https://www.ncbi.nlm.nih.gov/pmc/articles/PMC6110188/P

Parker, S. (2020, January 10). *How AI is Transforming the Entertainment Industry*. readwrite. Retrieved November 28, 2021, from https://readwrite.com/2020/01/10/how-ai-is-transforming-the-entertainment-industry/

Shah, R. (2020, June 27). *Applications of AI in the media & entertainment industry*. PHRAZOR. Retrieved November 28, 2021, from https://phrazor.ai/blog/applications-of-ai-in-the-media-entertainment-industry

Cogito. (2021, April 8). *Application of Artificial Intelligence in Media & Entertainment with Use Cases*. Cogito. Retrieved November 28, 2021, from https://www.cogitotech.com/blog/application-of-ai-in-media-entertainment-use-cases/

Staff, T. T. (2014). *10 Roles For Artificial Intelligence In Education*. Teach Thought. Retrieved November 29, 2021, from https://www.teachthought.com/the-future-of-learning/roles-for-artificial-intelligence-in-education/

Fengchun, M. (2021). *AI and education: Guidance for policy-makers*. UNESCO.

Chuprina, R., & Kovalenko, O. (2018). *The Value of Artificial Intelligence for Retail in 2022*. SPD Group. Retrieved November 28, 2021, from https://spd.group/artificial-intelligence/ai-for-retail/

Martin, S. (2019, October 25). *Top 12 Ways AI is Revolutionizing the Online-Shopping/E-commerce Trends*. Towards Data Science. Retrieved November 30, 2021, from https://towardsdatascience.com/top-12-ways-ai-is-revolutionizing-the-online-shopping-ecommerce-trends-9c3e98ef519c

Willems, I. (2020, June 20). *Using AI to create a personalized shopping experience in online retail*. DM EXCO 22. Retrieved January 12, 2022, from https://dmexco.com/stories/using-ai-to-create-a-personalized-shopping-experience-in-online-retail/

Schmidt, J., Marques, M. R. G., Botti, S., & Marques, M. A. L. (2019, August 8). *Recent advances and applications of machine learning in solid-state materials science*. NPJ. Retrieved January 7, 2022, from https://www.nature.com/articles/s41524-019-0221-0#citeas

Compilation of References

A Brief History of Cryptocurrency. (2020). CryptoVantage.

Aarni, H. (2017). The Technology of Trust: How the Internet of Things and Blockchain Could Usher in a New Era of Construction Productivity. *Construction Research and Innovation*, *8*(2), 66–70. doi:10.1080/20450249.2017.1337349

Aayog. (2020). *India report*. Blockchain The India Strategy Part-I.

Abadi, J., & Brunnermeier, M. (2018). *Blockchain Economics*. Princeton University. Retrieved on the 24.01.2019 from https://scholar.princeton.edu/sites/default/files/markus/files/blockchain_paper_v3g.pdf

Acarer, T. (2020). Ülke Güvenliğimizde Alınabilecek Makro Siber Güvenlik Önlemleri. *Uluslararası Bilgi Güvenliği Mühendisliği Dergisi*, *6*(2), 61–71.

Acqua Minerals Limited. v. Pramod Borse & Another, AIR 2001 Del 463

Adam, J. K. (2018, March 21). *A non-technical overview of the Juris dispute resolution system*. Juris. https://medium.com/jurisproject/a-non-technical-overview-of-the-juris-dispute-resolution-system-62e28eec509d

Adediran, A. (2020), Cyberbullying in Nigeria: Examining the Adequacy of Legal Responses. *International Journal for the Semiotics of Law - Revue internationale de Sémiotiquejuridique*, (34), 29.

Adeshina, O. (2020). *Popular Hacking Group "Anonymous" Allegedly Hacks Nigerian Government Websites*. https://nairametrics.com/2020/10/15/endsars-popular-hacking-group-anonymous-allegedly-hacks-nigerian-govt-websites/

Aggarwal, C. C. (2005). On k-anonymity and the curse of dimensionality. *Proceedings of the 31st International conference on Very Large Databases (VLDB)*.

Agrawal, S. (2019). *Government localises 'critical' & 'sensitive' personal data*. Retrieved from The Economic Times: https://economictimes.indiatimes.com/news/politics-and-nation/government-localises-critical-sensitive-personal-data/articleshow/72376594.cms?from=mdr

Agrawal, M., & Mishra, P. (2012). A comparative survey on symmetric key encryption techniques. *International Journal on Computer Science and Engineering*, *4*(5), 877.

Ahmad, L., & Firasath, N. (2021). *Agriculture 5.0: Artificial Intelligence, IoT and Machine Learning*. CRC Press. doi:10.1201/9781003125433

Ahmed, F. (2015). *Cyber law*. New Era Publishing House.

Aktan, E. (2018). Büyük veri: Uygulama alanları, analitiği ve güvenlik boyutu. *Bilgi Yönetimi*, *1*(1), 1–22. doi:10.33721/by.403010

Alam, M. A. (2020). *A Neoteric Smart and sustainable farming environment incorporating block chain-based artificial intelligence approach in Crypto Currencies and Blockchain Technology Applications*. John Wiley and Sons.

Alhinnawi, B., Edel, D., Incze, G., Priom, M., & Syed, E. (2015). The Snowden Revelations and Their Effects on European IT- Related Decisions and Decision - Making Processes. *Proceedings of the 2015/16 Course on Enterprise Governance and Digital Transformation*. https://www.researchgate.net/publication/305368725_THE_SNOWDEN_REVELATIONS_AND_THEIR_EFFECTS_ON_EUROPEAN_IT--RELATED_DECISIONS_AND_DECISION--MAKING_PROCESSES

Allen, G. (2019). *Understanding China's AI Strategy*. The Center for a New American Security (CNAS). https://www.cnas.org/publications/reports/understanding-chinas-ai-strategy

Allison, G., & Schmidt, E. (2020). *Is China Beating the U.S. to AI Supremacy?* Belfer Center for Science and International Affairs. https://www.belfercenter.org/publication/china-beating-us-ai-supremacy#footnote-027

Almarabeh, H., & Suleiman, A. (2015) The Impact of Cyber Threats on Social Networking Sites. *International Journal of Advanced Research in Computer Science, 10*(2).

Alogo, U. (2021). *West Africa: 'Nigeria Lost N5.5 Trillion to Cybercrimes in 10 Years*. Retrieved from https://allafrica.com/stories/202104260948.html

Alsahafi, A. Y. A., & Gay, B. V. (2018). An overview of electronic personal health records. *Health Policy and Technology, 7*(4), 427–432. doi:10.1016/j.hlpt.2018.10.004

Alsenoy, B. V. (2017) Reconciling The (Extra)Territorial Reach Of The GDPR With Public International Law. Data Prevention And Privacy Under Pressure Transatlantic Tensions, EU Surveillance, And Big Data, 77-100.

American Arbitration Association Rules. (2013). *Commercial Including Procedures for Large, Complex Commercial Disputes Arbitration Rules and Mediation Procedures*. Retrieved from https://adr.org/sites/default/files/Commercial%20Rules.pdf

Amnesty International & Privacy International. (2015). *Two Years After Snowden Protecting Human Rights In An Age of Mass Surveillance*. https://www.amnesty.org/en/documents/act30/1795/2015/en/

Anderlini, J. (2019). How China's smart-city tech focuses on its own citizens. *Financial Times*. https://www.ft.com/content/46bc137a-5d27-11e9-840c-530737425559

Anvar P.V. v. P.K. Basheer, (2014) 10 SCC 473

Anyoha, R. (2017, August 28). *Can Machines Think?* SITN. Retrieved November 20, 2021, from https://sitn.hms.harvard.edu/flash/2017/history-artificial-intelligence/

Aquilina, K. (2010). Public security versus privacy in technology law: A balancing act? *Computer Law & Security Review, 26*(2), 130–143. doi:10.1016/j.clsr.2010.01.002

Arjun Panditrao Khotkar v. Kailash Kushanrao Gorantyal, (2020) 7 SCC 1

Arline. (2015). *What is E-Commerce*. Merger Insight. Retrieved on August 25, 2019 from, https://www.businessnewsdaily.com/4872-what-is-e-commerce.html

Arm. (2020). Mass Surveillance and Muslims in China. *Chinese Law and Religion Monitor*. https://www.researchgate.net/publication/343706635_mass_surveillance_and_muslims_in_china

Árnason. (2015). *Cryptocurrency and Bitcoin: A possible foundation of future currency why it has value, what is its history and its future outlook*. Verslunarfélag Reykjavíkur.

Arya. (2018). *What Is Blockchain Technology?* [Video presentation]. Edureka. https://www.youtube.com/watch?v=QCvL-DWcojc//transaction works

Assembly, U. G. (1990). *Guidelines for the regulation of computerized private data files.* Academic Press.

Assembly, U. G. (1948). Universal declaration of human rights. *UN General Assembly, 302*(2), 14–25.

Assenmacher, K., & Krogstrup, S. (2018). *Monetary Policy with Negative Interest Rates: Decoupling Cash from Electronic Money.* International Monetary Fund.

Ayakoroma, F. B. (2008). #Endsars: Popular Hacking Group, Anonymous Allegedly Hacks Nigerian Govt. Websites Reinventing the Pollical Process in Nigerian Video Films: A Critical Reading of Teco Benson's "The Senator". *Nigerian Theatre Journal., 14*(2), 1–21.

Ayhan, B. (2017). *Digitalization and Society.* Peter Lang Gmbh, Internationaler Verlag Der Wissenschaften. doi:10.3726/978-3-653-07022-4

Ayözger, A. Ç. (2016). *Elektronik Haberleşme Sektöründe Kişisel Verilerin Korunması.* İstanbul Üniversitesi Sosyal Bilimler Enstitüsü, Doktora Tezi.

Azim, A., Nazrul Islam, M., & Spranger, P. E. (2020). Blockchain and novel coronavirus: Towards preventing COVID-19 and future pandemics. *Iberoamerican Journal of Medicine, 2*(3), 215–218. doi:10.53986/ibjm.2020.0037

Babich & Hilary. (2018b). *Distributed Ledgers and Operations: What Operations Management Researchers Should Know about Blockchain Technology.* Georgetown McDonough School of Business Research Paper No. 3131250.

Bachynskyy, T., & Radeiko, R. (2019). Legal regulations of blockchain and cryptocurrency in Ukraine. *Hungarian Journal of Legal Studies, 60*(1), 3–17. doi:10.1556/2052.2019.60102

Bailey, B. (2018, December 20). *AI Market Ramps Everywhere.* Semiconductor Engineering. Retrieved November 26, 2021, from https://semiengineering.com/what-is-artificial-intelligence/

Bajpai, P. (2021). Admissibility of CCTV Evidence. *Jus Corpus Law Journal, 2*(1), 432–444.

Balogun, N. A., Awodele, T. A., Bello, O. W., Oyekunle, R. A., & Balogun, U. O. (2017). Impact of Social Networks on the Increase of Cyberbully Among Nigerian University Students in Ilorin Metropolis. *Journal of Science and Technology, 8*(2), 102–111.

Banafa, A. (2020, June 22). *Blockchain Technology and COVID-19.* OpenMind. https://www.bbvaopenmind.com/en/technology/digital-world/blockchain-technology-and-covid-19/

Banerjee, A. (2018). Blockchain technology: Supply chain insights from ERP. In *Advances in Computers* (Vol. 111). Elsevier.

Barbara, G., & John, Z. (1989). Sources of popular support for authoritarian Regimes. *American Journal of Political Science, 33*(2), 319–347. doi:10.2307/2111150

Bashir, I. (2018). *Mastering Blockchain: Distributed ledger technology, decentralization, and smart contracts explained* (2nd ed.). Packt Publishing Ltd.

Basu, A. (2020). *Key Global Takeaways From India's Revised Personal Data Protection Bill.* Retrieved from Law Fare Blog: https://www.lawfareblog.com/key-global-takeaways-indias-revised-personal-data-protection-bill

Bayuk, J. L., Healey, J., Rohmeyer, P., Sachs, M., Schmidt, J., & Weiss, J. (2012). *Cyber Security Policy Guidebook* (1st ed.). Wiley & Sons. doi:10.1002/9781118241530

BBC News. (2013, December 3). *Only 1% of Snowden files published - Guardian editor.* BBC News. https://www.bbc.com/news/uk-25205846

BBC News. (2013a, October 27). *NSA: New reports in German media deepen US-Merkel spy row.* BBC News. https://www.bbc.com/news/world-europe-24692908

BBC. (2021). *Obinwanne Okeke: Nigerian Email Fraudster Jailed for 10 Years in US.* Available at https://www.bbc.com/news/world-africa-56085217

Beck, S., & Lynch, A. (2001). Profiles of Internet buyers in twenty countries evidence for region specific. *Journal of IBS, 1*(32), 725–748.

Beijing, A. I. (2019). Principles. *Datenschutz Datensich, 43*(10), 656. doi:10.100711623-019-1183-6

Benjamin, M. (2021). *How much will the Artificial Intelligence Act cost Europe?* Center for Data Innovation. https://www2.datainnovation.org/2021-aia-costs.pdf

Berentsen, A., & Schär, F. (2018). *A Short Introduction to the World of Cryptocurrencies.* https://www.researchgate.net/publication/322456542_A_Short_Introduction_to_the_World_of_Cryptocurrencies

Bertolucci, J. (2013). Big Data's new buzzword: Datafication. *Information Week.* Available at: www. informationweek.com/big-data/big-data-analytics/bigdatas-new-buzzword-datafication/d/d-id/1108797?/

Bertot, J. C., Jaeger, P. T., & Hansen, D. (2012). The Impact of Polices in Government Social Media Usage; Issues, Challenges And Recommendations. *Government Information Quarterly, 29*(1), 30–40. doi:10.1016/j.giq.2011.04.004

Bhandari, V., & Sane, R. (2018). Protecting Citizens from the State Post Puttaswamy: Analysing the Privacy Implications of the Justice Srikrishna Committee Report and the Data Protection Bill, 2018. *Socio Legal Review, 14*(2), 143–169. https://papers.ssrn.com/sol3/papers.cfm?abstract_id=3251982

Bieker, F., Friedewald, M., Hansen, M., Obersteller, H., & Rost, M. (2016). A process for data protection impact assessment under the European general data protection regulation. *Annual Privacy Forum*, 21–37.

Bilir, F. (2021). Kişisel Verilerin Korunması Kişinin Kendisinin Korunmasıdır. *TRT Akademi, 6*(11), 172–181.

Bindra, J. (2019). *The Tech Whisperer: On Digital Transformation and the Technologies that Enable It.* Penguin Random House India Private Limited.

Biswas, P. (2021). *Maharashtra: Blockchain tech to get farmers faster finance.* The Indian Express.

Blackman, R. (2020). *A Practical Guide to Building Ethical AI.* https://hbr.org/2020/10/a-practical-guide-to-building-ethical-ai

Bloomberg Finance L.P., (BF) vs. Mr. Kanhan Vijay, INDRP/110 (2009)

Boldyreva, E., Grishina, N., & Duisembina, Y. (2018). Cambridge Analytica: Ethics And Online Manipulation With Decision-Making Process. *The European Proceedings of Social & Behavioural Sciences.* https://www.europeanproceedings.com/files/data/article/95/4063/article_95_4063_pdf_100.pdf

Borky, J. M., & Bradley, T. H. (2019). Protecting information with cybersecurity. In *Effective Model-Based Systems Engineering* (pp. 345–404). Springer. doi:10.1007/978-3-319-95669-5_10

Boss, S. R., Galletta, D. F., Lowry, P. B., Moody, G. D., & Polak, P. (2015). *What Do Systems Users Have to Fear? Using Fear Appeals to Engender Threats and Fear that Motivate Protective Security Behaviors.* Rochester, NY: Social Science Research Network. Retrieved from https://papers.ssrn.com/abstract=2607190 doi:10.25300/MISQ/2015/39.4.5

Bovaird, C. (2017, September 1). *Why Bitcoin Prices Have Risen More Than 400% This Year*. Retrieved from https://www.forbes.com/sites/cbovaird/2017/09/01/why-bitcoin-prices-have-ris en-more-than-400-this-year/#15d4160f6f68

Boxall, L. (2020). *Exceptional Exceptions to Consent*. Data Protection Excellence Network. https://www.dpexnetwork.org/articles/exceptional-exceptions-consent/

Bozkurt, H. (2019). *Kişisel verilerin işlenmesinin hukuki boyutu*. Kadir Has Üniversitesi, Yüksek Lisans Tezi.

Bradford, A. (2020). *The Brussels Effect: How the European Union Rules the World*. Oxford University Press. doi:10.1093/oso/9780190088583.001.0001

Brattberg, E., Csernatoni, R., & Rugova, V. (2020). *Europe and AI: Leading, Lagging Behind, or Carving Its Own Way?* Carnegie Endowment for International Peace. https://carnegieendowment.org/2020/07/09/europe-and-ai-leading-lagging-behind-or-carving-its-own-way-pub-82236

Brethenoux, E., Dekate, C., Hare, J., Govekar, M., Chandrasekaran, A., & Rich, C. (2018). *Predicts 2019: Artificial Intelligence Core Technologies*. Gartner. https://www.gartner.com/en/documents/3894131

Büchi, M., Festic, N., & Latzer, M. (2022). The Chilling Effects of Digital Dataveillance: A Theoretical Model and an Empirical Research Agenda. *Big Data & Society*, *9*(1). Advance online publication. doi:10.1177/20539517211065368

Burman, A. (2020). *Will India's Proposed Data Protection Law Protect Privacy and Promote Growth?* Retrieved from Carnegie India: https://carnegieindia.org/2020/03/09/will-india-s-proposed-data-protection-law-protect-privacy-and-promote-growth-pub-81217

Bygrave, L. A. (1998). Data prevention pursuant to the right to privacy in human rights treaties. *International Journal of Law and Information Technology*, *6*(3), 247–284. doi:10.1093/ijlit/6.3.247

Bygrave, L. A. (2002). *Data protection law*. Wolters Kluwer Law & Business.

Byun, J.-W., & Li, N. (2008). Purpose based access control for privacy protection in relational database systems. *The VLDB Journal—The International Journal on Very Large Data Bases*, *17*(4), 603–619.

Cabinet Office of Japan. (2019). *Social Principles of Human-centric AI*. https://www8.cao.go.jp/cstp/stmain/aisocial-principles.pdf

Cabot, C. (2017). *An Introduction to Differential Privacy*. https://www.infoq.com/articles/differential-privacy-intro/

Cann, O. (2018, September 17). *Machines Will Do More Tasks Than Humans by 2025 but Robot Revolution Will Still Create 58 Million Net New Jobs in Next Five Years*. World Economic Forum. Retrieved November 26, 2021, from https://www.weforum.org/press/2018/09/machines-will-do-more-tasks-than-humans-by-2025-but-robot-revolution-will-still-create-58-million-net-new-jobs-in-next-five-years/

Case C-32/11 EU:C:2013:160; *Allianz Hungária Biztosító Zrt. and Others v Gazdasági Versenyhivatal*

Casey, M., Crane, J., Gensler, G., Jonson, S., & Narula, N. (2018). *The Impact of Blockchain Technology on Finance: A Catalyst for Change*. International Center for Monetary and Banking Studies. https://www.sipotra.it/old/wp-content/uploads/2018/07/The-Impact-of-Blockchain-Technology-on-Finance-A-Catalyst-for-Change.pdf

Cashell, B., Jackson, W. D., Jickling, M., & Webel, B. (2004). The economic impact of cyber-attacks. *Congressional Research Service Documents*, CRS RL32331, 2.

Castro, D., & Chivo, E. (2019). *Want Europe to have the best AI? Reform the GDPR*. International Association of Privacy Professionals. https://iapp.org/news/a/want-europe-to-have-the-best-ai-reform-the-gdpr/

Cemil, K. (2011). Avrupa Birliği veri koruma direktifi ekseninde hassas (kişisel) veriler ve işlenmesi. *Journal of Istanbul University Law Faculty, 69*(1-2), 317–334.

Chadha, A., Kumar, V., Kashyap, S., & Gupta, M. (2021). Deepfake: An Overview. In *Proceedings of Second International Conference on Computing, Communication, and Cyber Security* (pp. 557-565). Springer. 10.1007/978-981-16-0733-2_39

Chai, S., Bagchi-Sen, S., Rao, H. R., Upadhyaya, S.J., & Morrell, C. (2009). Internet and Online Information Privacy: An Exploratory Study of Preteens and Early Teens. *IEEE Transactions on Professional Communication, 52*(2), 167-182. doi:10.1109/TPC.2009.2017985

Chambers, D. (2002). Enron the symptom, not the disease. *The Public, 2*(2). https://web.archive.org/web/20060622102124/http://publici.ucimc.org/mar2002/32002_7.htm

Chang, W. L., Roy, A., & Underwood, M. (2018). *NIST Big Data Interoperability Framework, Security and Privacy.* https://www.nist.gov/publications/nist-big-data-interoperability-framework-volume-1-big-data-definitions-version-2

Channels, T. V. (2021). *Court Sends Two Internet Fraudsters to Two Years in Prison.* Available at https://www.channelstv.com/2021/07/19/court-sends-two-internet-fraudsters-to-two-years-in-prison/

Charan, P. (2015). A Survey of the Prominent Effects of Cybersquatting in India. *International Journal of Information Security and Cybercrime, 4*(1), 47–58. doi:10.19107/IJISC.2015.01.07

Chaudhary, A., & Kuilboer, (2002). *E-Business and E-Commerce Infrastructure.* New York: McGraw-Hill.

Chawla, V. (2020). Why We Shouldn't Underestimate South Korea In The Race To AI Supremacy. *Analytics India Mag.* https://analyticsindiamag.com/why-we-shouldnt-underestimate-south-korea-in-the-race-to-ai-supremacy/

Chiemela, Q. A., Ovute, A. O., & Obochi, C. I. (2015). The Influence of the Social Media on the Nigerian Youths: Aba Residents Rxperience. *Journal of Research in Humanities and Social Science, 3*(3), 12–20.

Cho, H., Im, J., & Kim, D. (2016). A metadata service architecture providing trusted data to global food service. *2016 IEEE World Congress on Services (SERVICES)*, 64–67. 10.1109/SERVICES.2016.39

Chou, H.-L., & Chou, C. (2021). How teens negotiate privacy on social media proactively and reactively. *New Media & Society.* Advance online publication. doi:10.1177/14614448211018797

Chowdhury, A. R. (2020). *Domain Name Protection: Is Your Interest Legitimate?* ALG India. https://www.algindia.com/domain-name-protection-is-your-interest-legitimate/

Chuprina, R., & Kovalenko, O. (2018). *The Value of Artificial Intelligence for Retail in 2022.* SPD Group. Retrieved November 28, 2021, from https://spd.group/artificial-intelligence/ai-for-retail/

Cisco. (2019). *What is cybersecurity?* Available at https://www.cisco.com/c/en/us/products/security/what-is-cybersecurity.html#~how-cybersecurity-work

Citron, D. K., & Chesney, R. (2019). Deep Fakes: A Looming Challenge for Privacy, Democracy, and National Security. *California Law Review, 107*, 1753–1801.

Claire, M. D. W., & Olivia, T. (2020). *Artificial Intelligence, A Driver For Efficiency In International Arbitration – How Predictive Coding Can Change Document Production.* Kluwer Arbitration Blog. http://arbitrationblog.kluwerarbitration.com/2020/02/23/artificial-intelligence-a-driver-for-efficiency-in-international-arbitration-how-predictive-coding-can-change-document-production/

Clark, D. (2010). Characterizing cyberspace: Past, present and future. *MIT CSAIL. Version, 1*, 2016–2028.

Clarke, L. (2021). *The EU's leaked AI Regulation is ambitious but disappointingly vague.* https://techmonitor.ai/policy/eu-ai-Regulation-machine-learning-european-union

Clement, J. (2020). *Number of social network users worldwide from 2010 to 2023.* Academic Press.

Clough, J. (2010). *Principle of Cyber Crime.* Cambridge University Press. doi:10.1017/CBO9780511845123

CNN. (2020). *He Flaunted Private Jets and Luxury Cars on Instagram. Feds Used His Posts to Link Him to Alleged Cybercrimes.* Available at https://edition.cnn.com/2020/07/12/us/ray-hushpuppi-alleged-money-laundering-trnd/index.html

Çobansoy, G. (2020). *İnsan hakları açısından kişisel verilerin korunması sorunu* (Master's thesis). Maltepe Üniversitesi, Sosyal Bilimler Enstitüsü.

Cogito. (2021, April 8). *Application of Artificial Intelligence in Media & Entertainment with Use Cases.* Cogito. Retrieved November 28, 2021, from https://www.cogitotech.com/blog/application-of-ai-in-media-entertainment-use-cases/

Colin, R. (2017). Designing a Global Online Dispute Resolution System: Lessons Learned from eBay. *University of St. Thomas Law Journal, 13,* 354.

Commission Regulation (EU) No 330/2010 of 20 April 2010 on the application of Article 101(3) of the Treaty on the Functioning of the European Union to categories of vertical agreements and concerted practices; available at https://data.europa.eu/eli/reg/2010/330/oj

CompTIA UK. (2017). *The UK Cybersecurity Landscape 2017 and Beyond: A Report.* CompTIA. https://connect.comptia.org/content/whitepapers/the-cybersecurity-landscape

Continental T.V Inc. v GTE Sylvania Inc 433 U.S 36 (1977)

Convention on Recognition and Enforcement of Foreign Awards. (1958). Art IV(1) (a).

Convention on Recognition and Enforcement of Foreign Awards. (1958). Art IV.

Convention on Recognition and Enforcement of Foreign Awards. (1958). Art. II Para (1 & 2). Delos Dispute Resolution. *Introduction to Blockchain technology.* https://delosdr.org/index.php/2019/09/26/introduction-to-blockchain-smart-contracts/

Convention on Recognition and Enforcement of Foreign Awards. (1958). Art. II Para. 1 & 2.

Coran, S. J. (2001). The Anticybersquatting Consumer Protection Act's In Rem Provision: Making American Trademark Law the Law of the Internet? *Hofstra Law Review, 30,* 169–196.

Corbet, S., Larkin, C. J., Lucey, B. M., Meegan, A., & Vigne, S. (2019). *Cryptocurrency Architecture and Interaction With Market Shocks.* https://papers.ssrn.com/sol3/papers.cfm?abstract_id=3369527

Corbet, S., Cumming, D. J., Lucey, B. M., Peat, M., & Vigne, S. A. (2020). The destabilizing effects of cryptocurrency cybercriminality. *Economics Letters, 191,* 108741. Advance online publication. doi:10.1016/j.econlet.2019.108741

Cormode, G., Procopiuc, C. M., Entong, S. D. S., & Yu, T. (2013). Empirical privacy and empirical utility of anonymized data. *IEEE 29th International Conference on Data Engineering Workshops (ICDEW).*

Council, N. R. (2003). *Government data centers: Meeting increasing demands.* National Academies Press.

Croft, A. (2013, July 6). *EU threatens to suspend data-sharing with U.S. over spy reports.* https://www.reuters.com/article/us-usa-security-eu-idUKBRE9640JJ20130705

Cvetkova, I. (2018). Cryptocurrencies legal regulation. *BRICS Law Journal*, 5(2), 128–153. doi:10.21684/2412-2343-2018-5-2-128-153

Cyber Help Line. (2019). *Cyber Stalking*. https://www.thecyberhelpline.com/guides/cyber-stalking

Cybersquatting Examples Everything You Need to Know. (2020). Retrieved from: https://www.upcounsel.com/cyber-squatting-examples

Cybersquatting. (2018). *JUSTIA*. Retrieved from: https://www.justia.com/intellectual-property/trademarks/cybersquatting/

Daily Post Newspaper. (2021). *Two Internet Fraudsters Convicted in Lagos, Forfeit Assets to FG*. Available at https://dailypost.ng/2021/08/09/two-internet-fraudsters-convicted-in-lagos-forfeit-assets-to-fg/

Dalmia, V. P. (2017). *Data Protection Laws In India - Everything You Must Know*. Retrieved from Mondaq: https://www.mondaq.com/india/data-protection/655034/data-protection-laws-in-india--everything-you-must-know

Dal, U. (2019). Article. *Kişisel Verileri Koruma Dergisi*, 1(1), 21–33.

Daly, M., & Cunningham, M. (2020, July 1). *How Blockchain is helping in the fight against Covid-19*. Lexology. https://www.lexology.com/library/detail.aspx?g=8b5ef0f0-05b3-4909-b5d5-da7bd57f0381

Danezis, G., Domingo-Ferrer, J., Hansen, M., Hoepman, J.-H., Le Metayer, D., Tirtea, R., & Schiffner, S. (2015). Privacy and data protection by design-from policy to engineering. *ArXiv Preprint ArXiv:1501.03726*.

Dargan, S., & Kumar, M. (2020). A comprehensive survey on the biometric recognition systems based on physiological and behavioral modalities. *Expert Systems with Applications*, 143, 113114. doi:10.1016/j.eswa.2019.113114

Das, P. (2020). Critical Analysis of Interpretation of Article 21 of the Constitution. *International Journal of Law, Management and Humanities*.

Daws, R. (2021). *Amazon will continue to ban police from using its facial recognition AI*. Artificial Intelligence News. https://artificialintelligence-news.com/2021/05/24/amazon-continue-ban-police-using-facial-recognition-ai/

de Arimatéia da Cruz, J. (2020). The Legislative Framework of the European Union (EU) Convention on Cybercrime. The Palgrave Handbook of International Cybercrime and Cyberdeviance, 223–237.

De Búrca, G. (2013). After the EU Charter of Fundamental Rights: The Court of Justice as a human rights adjudicator? *Maastricht Journal of European and Comparative Law*, 20(2), 168–184. doi:10.1177/1023263X1302000202

de Waal & Willenborg. (1995). Information loss through global recording and local suppression. *Netherland Official Statistics*, 17- 20.

Deloitte Asia Pacific Limited. (2020). *Deloitte Asia Pacific Privacy Guide 2020-21*. https://www2.deloitte.com/mm/en/pages/risk/articles/ap-privacy-guide-2020-2021.html

Deo, S. (2019). Cybersquatting: Threat to Domain Name. *International Journal of Innovative Technology and Exploring Engineering*, 8(6S4), 1432–1434. doi:10.35940/ijitee.F1291.0486S419

Deren, D. (2020). *Blockchain Technology as Tool against Infringement of Copy Right on Photograph*. Tilburg University. http://arno.uvt.nl/show.cgi?fid=149345

Deshpande, S. (2020). Cyber squatting – A study of Legal framework in India. *International Journal of Law. Management & Humanities*, 3, 1825–1835.

Determann, L. (2019). Privacy and Data Protection. *Московский Журнал Международного Права*, 1, 18–26.

DeVries, P. D. (2016). *An Analysis of Cryptocurrency, Bitcoin, and the Future. International Journal of Business Management and Commerce.*

Different types of cryptocurrencies available in the digital world. (2020). *The European Business Review.*

DiGiacomo, J. (2015). *An overview of Cybersquatting Laws.* Revision/Legal. https://revisionlegal.com/copyright/copyright-infringement/an-overview-of-cybersquatting-laws/

Dimov, D. (2017). *Latest trends in Cybersquatting.* INFOSEC. https://resources.infosecinstitute.com/topic/latest-trends-in-cybersquatting/

Directive, E. U. (1995). 95/46/EC of the European Parliament and of the Council of 24 October 1995 on the prevention of individuals with regard to the processing of private data and on the free movement of such data. *Official Journal of the EC, 23*(6).

Douglas Melamed, A. (1998). *Exclusionary Vertical Agreements, Speech Delivered before American Bar Association.* Available at https://www.justice.gov/atr/speech/exclusionary-vertical-agreements#N_6_

Dourado, E., & Brito, J. (2014). Cryptocurrency. *The New Palgrave Dictionary of Economics.* https://www.researchgate.net/publication/298792075_Cryptocurrency

Dr. Reddy's Laboratories Limited v. Manu Kasouri, 2001 PTC 859 (Del).

Draper, N. A. (2017). From privacy pragmatist to privacy resigned: Challenging narratives of rational choice in digital privacy debates: Challenging rational choice in digital privacy debates. *Policy and Internet, 9*(2), 232–251. doi:10.1002/poi3.142

Draper, N. A., & Turow, J. (2019). The corporate cultivation of digital resignation. *New Media & Society, 21*(8), 1824–1839. doi:10.1177/1461444819833331

Drinkwater, D. (2018, February 6). *6 use cases for blockchain in security.* CSO Online. https://www.csoonline.com/article/3252213/6-use-cases-for-blockchain-in-security.html

Drozd, O., Lazur, Y., & Serbin, R. (2017). Theoretical and legal perspective on certain tyes of legal liability in cryptocurrency relations. *Baltic Journal of Economic Studies, 3*(5), 221–228. doi:10.30525/2256-0742/2017-3-5-221-228

Dülger, M. V. (2018). İnsan hakları ve temel hak ve özgürlükler bağlamında kişisel verilerin korunması. *İstanbul Medipol Üniversitesi Hukuk Fakültesi Dergisi, 5*(1), 71-144.

Dwork, C., McSherry, F., Nissim, K., & Smith, A. (2006). Calibrating Noise to Sensitivity in Private Data Analysis. In H. T. R. Shai (Ed.), Lecture Notes in Computer Science: Vol. 3876. *Theory of Cryptography* (pp. 265–284). Springer. doi:10.1007/11681878_14

E-Commerce and Online Shopping in India - Statistics & Facts. (2018). *Statista Research Department.* Retrieved on July 17, 2019 https://www.statista.com/topics/2454/e-commerce-in-india

E-Commerce in India – Growth and Statistics. (2017). Retrieved on August 23, 2019, from, https://www.codilar.com/blog/e-commerce-in-india-growth-and-statistics

El Emam, K., & Dankar, F. K. (2008). Protecting Privacy Using k-Anonymity. *Journal of the American Medical Informatics Association, 15*(5), 627–637. doi:10.1197/jamia.M2716 PMID:18579830

Emily, W. (2018). *Blockchain for Hospitality.* Hospitality Technology Next Generation.

Enterprise Big Data Framework. (2019). *A short history of Big Data*. https://www.bigdataframework.org/short-history-of-big-data/

Ervin Warnink v Townend, [1979] A.C. 731

Esso Petroleum Ltd. v. Harper's Garage (Stourport) Ltd., [1968] AC 269

European Commission – Press Release. (2021). *Europe fit for the Digital Age: Commission proposes new rules and actions for excellence and trust in Artificial Intelligence*. https://ec.europa.eu/commission/presscorner/detail/en/ip_21_1682

European Commission, Directorate-General for Communication. (2018). *A definition of AI: Main capabilities and scientific disciplines*. https://digital-strategy.ec.europa.eu/en/library/definition-artificial-intelligence-main-capabilities-and-scientific-disciplines

European Commission. (2018). *Communication From The Commission To The European Parliament, The European Council, The Council, The European Economic And Social Committee And The Committee Of The Regions 25ᵗʰ April, 2018. COM(2018)237*. https://eur-lex.europa.eu/legal-content/EN/TXT/PDF/?uri=CELEX:52018DC0237&from=EN

European Commission. (2018). *Coordinated Plan on Artificial Intelligence (COM(2018) 795 final)*. https://eur-lex.europa.eu/resource.html?uri=cellar:22ee84bb-fa04-11e8-a96d-01aa75ed71a1.0002.02/DOC_1&format=PDF

European Commission. (2020). *Communication from the Commission to the European Parliament and the Council - two years of application of the General Data Protection Regulation*. https://ec.europa.eu/info/law/law-topic/data-protection/communication-two-years-application-general-data-protection-regulation_en

European Commission. (2020). *EU-US: A new transatlantic agenda for global change*. https://ec.europa.eu/commission/presscorner/detail/en/IP_20_2279

European Commission. (2020). *On Artificial Intelligence: A European Approach to Excellence and Trust*. https://ec.europa.eu/info/publications/white-paper-artificial-intelligence-european-approach-excellence-and-trust_en

European Commission. (2021). *Communication: 2030 Digital Compass: The European way for the Digital Decade. Brussels, 9.3.2021 COM(2021) 118 final*. https://eur-lex.europa.eu/legal-content/en/TXT/?uri=CELEX%3A52021DC0118

European Commission. (2021). *Coordinated Plan on Artificial intelligence Review* (COM(2021) 205 final). https://eur-lex.europa.eu/resource.html?uri=cellar:01ff45fa-a375-11eb-9585-01aa75ed71a1.0001.02/DOC_1&format=PDF

European Commission. (2021). *Proposal For A Regulation Of The European Parliament And Of The Council Laying Down Harmonised Rules On Artificial Intelligence (Artificial Intelligence Act) And Amending Certain Union Legislative Acts*. https://digital-strategy.ec.europa.eu/en/library/proposal-Regulation-laying-down-harmonised-rules-artificial-intelligence

European Consumer Centre. (n.d.). Retrieved on July 28, 2019, from http://magyarefk.hu/en/useful-information/online-shoping/the-definition-of-online-shopping.html

European Data Protection Board. (2021). *EDPB & EDPS call for ban on use of AI for automated recognition of human features in publicly accessible spaces, and some other uses of AI that can lead to unfair discrimination*. Press Release statement 2021_05. https://edpb.europa.eu/news/news/2021/edpb-edps-call-ban-use-ai-automated-recognition-human-features-publicly-accessible_en

European Digital Rights. (2021). *Open letter: Civil society call for the introduction of red lines in the upcoming European Commission proposal on Artificial Intelligence*. https://edri.org/wp-content/uploads/2021/01/EDRi-open-letter-AI-red-lines.pdf

European I. P. R. Helpdesk. (2017). *Domain Names and Cybersquatting*. Retrieved from: https://www.ipoi.gov.ie/en/commercialise-your-ip/tools-for-business/domain-name-and-cybersquatting.pdf

European Parliament, Panel for Future of Science and Technology. (2020). *The ethics of artificial intelligence: Issues and Initiatives*. Author.

European Parliament, Panel for Future of Science and Technology. (2020). *The ethics of artificial intelligence: Issues and Initiatives*. https://www.europarl.europa.eu/RegData/etudes/STUD/2020/634452/EPRS_STU(2020)634452_EN.pdf

European Parliament, Panel for Future of Science and Technology. (2020). *The impact of the General Data Protection Regulation (GDPR) on artificial intelligence*. https://www.europarl.europa.eu/RegData/etudes/STUD/2020/641530/EPRS_STU(2020)641530_EN.pdf

European Parliament. (2017). *European Parliament resolution of 16 February 2017 with recommendations to the Commission on Civil Law Rules on Robotics*. Resolution No. P8_TA(2017)0051 dated 16th February, 2017. https://www.europarl.europa.eu/doceo/document/TA-8-2017-0051_EN.html

European Parliament. (2021). *Tackling Deepfakes in European Policy*. Panel for Future of Science and Technology. https://www.europarl.europa.eu/RegData/etudes/STUD/2021/690039/EPRS_STU%282021%29690039_EN.pdf

European Union - Data Privacy and Protection | Privacy Shield. (n.d.). *Privacy Shield Framework*. Retrieved June 10, 2021, from https://www.privacyshield.gov/article?id=European-Union-Data-Privatization-and-Protection

Evans, M., & Mathews, W. (2019). New York Regulator Probes UnitedHealth Algorithm for Racial Bias. *The Wall Street Journal*. https://www.wsj.com/articles/new-york-regulator-probes-unitedhealth-algorithm-for-racial-bias-11572087601

Fairfield, J. A. T. (2021). *Runaway Technology: Can Law Keep Up?* Cambridge University Press. doi:10.1017/9781108545839

Fang, W., Xue, Z. W., Zheng, Y., & Zhou, M. (2017). A Survey of Big Data Security and Privacy Preserving. *IETE Technical Review*, *34*, 544–560.

FAO (Food and Agriculture Organization) of the United Nations. (2019). *International Telecommunication Union, E-agriculture in action: Blockchain for agriculture: Opportunities and challenges*. Food & Agriculture Org.

Farell, R. (2015). *An Analysis of the Cryptocurrency Industry*. Wharton Research Scholars. https://repository.upenn.edu/wharton_research_scholars/13

FCC. (2016). Annual Assessment of the Status of Competition in the Market for the Delivery of Video Programming [Seventeenth Report; MB Docket No. 15-158; DA 16-510] (PDF) (Report). Washington, DC: Federal Communications Commission (FCC).

Federico, A. (2017). *A Protocol for a Decentralized Justice System*. Kleros. https://medium.com/kleros/kleros-a-decentralized-justice-protocol-for-the-internet-38d596a6300d

Feeney, M. (2021). *Deepfake Laws Risk Creating More Problems Than They Solve*. Regulatory Transparency Project of the Federalist Society. https://regproject.org/wp-content/uploads/Paper-Deepfake-Laws-Risk-Creating-More-Problems-Than-They-Solve.pdf

Feigenbaum, E. (2020). *Assuring Taiwan's Innovation Future*. Carnegie Endowment for International Peace. https://carnegieendowment.org/files/2020-Feigenbaum-Taiwan_Innovation.pdf

Feldstein, S. (2019, September). *The Global Expansion of AI Surveillance*. Carnegie Endowment for International Peace. https://carnegieendowment.org/files/WP-Feldstein-AISurveillance_final1.pdf

Fengchun, M. (2021). *AI and education: Guidance for policy-makers*. UNESCO.

File, I. (2012). *Proposal for a Regulation of the European Parliament and of the Council on the Prevention of Individuals with Regard to the Processing of Private Data and on the Free movement of Such Data (General Data Prevention Regulation)*. General Data Prevention Regulation.

Finnell, K. O. (1979). Computer Crime-Senate Bill S. 240. *Mem. St. UL Rev., 10*, 660.

Foley, S., Karlsen, J. R., & Putniņš, T. J. (2018). *Sex, Drugs, and Bitcoin: How Much Illegal Activity Is Financed Through Cryptocurrencies? Review of Financial Studies*. Published.

Forrester. (2012). Trends in Indians e-commerce market. *International Journal of Advanced Scientific Research & Development, 3*(2), 145.

Fox, D. (2008). *Property Rights in Money*. Oxford University Press.

Francis, O., & Naku, D. (2021). *Man Bags Two-Year Jail Term For Currency Counterfeiting*. Available at https://punchng.com/two-internet-fraudsters-jailed-six-years-in-rivers/

Francisco, U. S. (2018). The use of New Technologies and Arbitration. *The American Review of International Arbitration, 7*, 84.

FrankenfieldJ. (2021). *Altcoin*. https://www.investopedia.com/terms/a/altcoin.asp

Franklin, A. W. (2012). Management of the problem. In S. M. Smith (Ed.), *The maltreatment of children* (pp. 83–95). MTP.

Franks, J. (2019, January). *Cryptocurrencies and Monetary Policy*. International Monetary Fund.

Frowein, J. A. (1950). European Convention on Human Rights. *Encyclopedia of Public International Law, 2*, 188-196.

Furht, B. (Ed.). (2006). *Encyclopedia of Multimedia*. Springer. doi:10.1007/0-387-30038-4

G20 Ministerial Statement on Trade and Digital Economy. (2019). https://www.mofa.go.jp/files/000486596.pdf

Ganti, V., & Das Sarma, A. (2013). Data cleaning: A practical perspective. *Synthesis Lectures on Data Management, 5*(3), 1–85. doi:10.2200/S00523ED1V01Y201307DTM036

Gaolub, K. (2018). *History of Social Media in Nigeria and the World*. https://www.legit.ng/1209780-history-social-media-nigeria-world.html

Gardiyawasam Pussewalage, H. S., & Oleshchuk, V. A. (2016). Privacy preserving mechanisms for enforcing security and privacy requirements in E-health solutions. *International Journal of Information Management, 36*(6), 1161–1173. doi:10.1016/j.ijinfomgt.2016.07.006

Garg, C., Bansal, A., & Padappayil, R. P. (2020). COVID-19: Prolonged Social Distancing Implementation Strategy Using Blockchain-Based Movement Passes. *Journal of Medical Systems, 44*(165), 165. Advance online publication. doi:10.100710916-020-01628-0 PMID:32780276

Gellert, R., & Gutwirth, S. (2013). The legal construction of privacy and data protection. *Computer Law & Security Review, 29*(5), 522–530. doi:10.1016/j.clsr.2013.07.005

Gerlach, T. (2005). Using Internet Content Filters to Create E-Borders to Aid International Choice of Law and Jurisdiction. *World Law Review, 5*, 32.

Gerstner, E. (2020). Face/Off: "Deepfake" Face Swaps and Privacy Laws. *Defense Counsel Journal, 87*(1), 1–14.

Ghode, P. (2020). *Blockchain, the doorway to transforming agri sector*. The Hindu BusinessLine.

Gieseke, A. (2020). "The Weapon of Choice": Law's Current Inability to Properly Address Deepfake Pornography. *Vanderbilt Law Review, 73*(5), 1479–1516.

Gilles. (2015). *Cyber Crime –Key Issues and Debates*. Routledge.

Global. (2021, October 19). *Advantages and Disadvantages of Artificial Intelligence*. iCert Global. Retrieved November 25, 2021, from https://www.icertglobal.com/advantages-and-disadvantages-of-artificial-intelligence/detail

Google inc. v. Gulshan Khatri, Case no. 8 of 2011. https://www.registry.in›show-doc›id=googleein

Google Inc. v. Herit Shah (Shah), Case No. D2009-0405 (2009)

Gordon, S. (2021). *What Is Cyberstalking?* https://www.verywellmind.com/what-is-cyberstalking-5181466

Gosain, A., & Chugh, N. (2014). Privacy Preservation in Big Data. *International Journal of Computers and Applications, 100*(17), 44–47. doi:10.5120/17619-8322

Goundar, S. (2020). *Blockchain Technologies, Applications And Cryptocurrencies: Current Practice And Future Trends*. World Scientific.

Government of Japan, Cabinet Office. (2021). *Sixth Science, Technology and Innovation Basic Plan*. https://www8.cao.go.jp/cstp/english/sti_basic_plan.pdf

Government of Japan, Cabinet Office. (n.d.). *The 5th Science and Technology Basic Plan, Human-centered society that balances economic advancement with the resolution of social problems by a system that highly integrates cyberspace and physical space*. https://www8.cao.go.jp/cstp/kihonkeikaku/5basicplan_en.pdf

Government of Japan. (2020). *Integrated Innovation Strategy 2020*. https://www8.cao.go.jp/cstp/english/strategy_2020.pdf

Government of Taiwan. (n.d.a). *AI for Industrial Innovation*. https://ai.taiwan.gov.tw/actionplan/ai-for-industrial-innovation/

Government of Taiwan. (n.d.b). *AI International Innovation Hub*. https://ai.taiwan.gov.tw/actionplan/ai-international-innovation-hub/

Government of Taiwan. (n.d.c). *AI Pilot Project*. https://ai.taiwan.gov.tw/actionplan/ai-pilot-project/

Government of Taiwan. (n.d.d). *AI Talent Program*. https://ai.taiwan.gov.tw/actionplan/ai-talent-program/ Last Accessed 24th July, 2021.

Government of Taiwan. (n.d.e). *Cabinet plans to develop the Nation's AI Industry*. https://ai.taiwan.gov.tw/news/cabinet-plans-to-develop-the-nations-ai-industry/

Government of Taiwan. (n.d.f). *Test Fields and Regulatory Co-creation*. https://ai.taiwan.gov.tw/actionplan/test-fields-and-regulatory-co-creation/

Govindrajan, V. (2019). *How India Plans to Protect Consumer Data*. Retrieved from Harvard Business Review: https://hbr.org/2019/12/how-india-plans-to-protect-consumer-data

Grabowski, M. (2019). *Cryptocurrencies: A primer on digital money*. Routledge. doi:10.4324/9780429201479

Granzen, A. (2021). *How will Singapore ensure responsible AI use?* GovInsider. https://govinsider.asia/digital-gov/achim-granzen-forrester-ai-drives-the-evolution-of-technology-and-data-governance/

Greenberg, A. (2017, January 25). Cryptocurrency Monero Is Skyrocketing Thanks to Darknet Druglords. *Wired*. https://www.wired.com/2017/01/monero-drug-dealers-cryptocurrency-choice-fire/

Greenleaf, G. (2018). 'Modernised' Data Prevention Convention 108 and the GDPR. *Data Prevention Convention*, 108, 22-3.

GreenleafG. (2018). *Global Convergence of Data Privacy Standards and Laws: Speaking Notes for the European Commission Events on the Launch of the General Data Protection Regulation (GDPR) in Brussels & New Delhi, 25 May 2018*. UNSW Law Research Paper No. 18-56. Available at https://ssrn.com/abstract=3184548 doi:10.2139/ssrn.3184548

Guillermo, A., María, B. N. T., & Juan, J. (2020). *Could an Arbitral Award Rendered by an AI System be Recognized or Enforced?* Kluwer Arbitration Blog. http://arbitrationblog.kluwerarbitration.com/2020/02/06/could-an-arbitral-award-rendered-by-ai-systems-be-recognized-or-enforced-analysis-from-the-perspective-of-public-policy/?doing_wp_cron=1595473104. 80 26199340820312500000.

Guo, J., & Li, B. (2018, August). *The Application of Medical Artificial Intelligence Technology in Rural Areas of Developing Countries*. PMC. Retrieved November 27, 2021, from https://www.ncbi.nlm.nih.gov/pmc/articles/PMC6110188/P

Gupta, A. (2021, June 30). *Made gains from cryptocurrencies? Know the income tax implications*. Moneycontrol. https://www.moneycontrol.com/news/business/personal-finance/made-gains-from-cryptocurrencies-know-the-income-tax-implications-7106151.html

Gupta, D. (2015). *Biomteirc Data: History and Evolution*. Thompson Reuters.

Gupta, N. (2021). Relevancy and Admissibility of Electronic Evidence. *Jus Corpus Law Journal*, *1*(4), 143–158.

Gupta, R. (2018). *Hands-On Cybersecurity with Blockchain: Implement DDoS protection, PKI-based identity, 2FA, and DNS security using Blockchain*. Packt Publishing.

Gür, B. A. (2019). Uluslararası Hukuk ve AB Hukuku Boyutuyla Kişisel Verilerin Yurt Dışına Aktarılması. *Marmara Üniversitesi Hukuk Fakültesi Hukuk Araştırmaları Dergisi*, *25*(2), 850–872.

Habip, O. (2013). Elektronik Ortamda Kişisel Verilerin Korunması, Bazı Ülke Uygulamaları Ve Ülkemizdeki Durum. *Uyuşmazlık Mahkemesi Dergisi*, (3), 1–38.

Habul. (2001). Consumer decisions making in online shopping environments: the effects of interactive decisions aid. *Marketing Science*, *4*, 34.

Haday, L. (2012, March 13). Biomteric Data: Stages and steps in the making. *Technology Bites*, 23-31.

Hamnnon, J. (2013). *Functions of Biomteirc Data: Scope redefined*. Springer.

Han, J., Kamber, M., & Pei, J. (2012). *Data mining: Concepts and techniques* (3rd ed.). Elsevier.

Hann, M. (2017). *Fingerprinting and Anthropology: Connection and disconnection*. Thomson Reuters.

Hao, K. (2020). *We read the paper that forced Timnit Gebru out of Google. Here's what it says*. https://www.technologyreview.com/2020/12/04/1013294/google-ai-ethics-research-paper-forced-out-timnit-gebru/

Hao, K. (2021). Deepfake Porn is Ruining Women's Lives. Now the Law may finally ban it. *MIT Technology Review*. https://www.technologyreview.com/2021/02/12/1018222/deepfake-revenge-porn-coming-ban/

Härdle, Harvey, & Reule. (2019). *Understanding Cryptocurrencies*. International Research Training Group 1792.

Hasbro, Inc. v. Clue Computing, Inc., 66 F. Supp. 2d 117 (1999)

Hathaway, O. A., Crootof, R., Levitz, P., Nix, H., Nowlan, A., Perdue, W., & Spiegel, J. (2012). The law of cyber-attack. *California Law Review*, 817–885.

Hatipoğlu, S. (2019). *Kişisel Verilerin Korunması ve İdarenin Sorumluluğu, Trakya Üniversitesi Sosyal Bilimler Enstitüsü, Yüksek*. Lisans Tezi.

Hawkins, S. M., Yen, D. C., & Chou, D. C. (2000). Disaster recovery planning: A strategy for data security. *Information Management & Computer Security*, 8(5), 222–230. doi:10.1108/09685220010353150

Hayes, A. F., & Reineke, J. B. (2007). The effects of government censorship of war-related news coverage on interest in the censored coverage: A test of competing theories. *Mass Communication & Society*, 10(4), 423–438. doi:10.1080/15205430701580581

He, D., Habermeier, K., Leckow, R., Haksar, V., Almeida, Y., Kashima, M., Kyriakos-Saad, N., Oura, H., Sedik, T. S., Stetsenko, N., & Yepes, C. (2016, January). *Virtual Currencies and Beyond: Initial Considerations*. International Monetary Fund. https://www.imf.org/external/pubs/ft/sdn/2016/sdn1603.pdf

Heikkila, M. (2021a). *Europe throws down gauntlet on AI with new rulebook*. Politico. https://www.politico.eu/article/europe-throws-down-gauntlet-on-ai-with-new-rulebook/

Heikkila, M. (2021b). *Ex-Google chief: European tech 'not big enough' to compete with China alone*. Politico. https://www.politico.eu/article/ex-google-chief-eric-schmidt-european-tech-not-big-enough-to-compete-with-china-alone/

Henkoğlu, T. (2017). Kişisel Verileriniz Ne Kadar Güvende? Bilgi Güvenliği Kapsamında Bir Değerlendirme. *Arşiv Dünyası*, (18-19), 36–47.

Hickok, E., Mohandas, S., & Paul Barooah, S. (2018). *The AI Task Force Report - The first steps towards India's AI framework*. The Center for Internet and Society. https://cis-india.org/internet-governance/blog/the-ai-task-force-report-the-first-steps-towards-indias-ai-framework

High-Level Expert Group on Artificial Intelligence (AI HLEG). (2019). *Ethics Guidelines for Trustworthy AI*. https://digital-strategy.ec.europa.eu/en/library/ethics-guidelines-trustworthy-ai

High-Level Expert Group on Artificial Intelligence (AI HLEG). (2020a). *Policy and investment recommendations for trustworthy Artificial Intelligence*. https://digital-strategy.ec.europa.eu/en/library/policy-and-investment-recommendations-trustworthy-artificial-intelligence

High-Level Expert Group on Artificial Intelligence (AI HLEG). (2020b). *Assessment List for Trustworthy AI (ALTAI)*. https://digital-strategy.ec.europa.eu/en/library/assessment-list-trustworthy-artificial-intelligence-altai-self-assessment

High-Level Expert Group on Artificial Intelligence (AI HLEG). (2020c). *Sectoral Considerations on the Policy and Investment Recommendations*. https://digital-strategy.ec.europa.eu/en/library/assessment-list-trustworthy-artificial-intelligence-altai-self-assessment

Hileman, G., & Rauchs, M. (2017, April). *Global Cryptocurrency Benchmarking Study*. Cambridge University Press.

Hill, M., & Swinhoe, D. (2021, July 16). *The 15 biggest data breaches of the 21st century*. CSO Online. Retrieved November 26, 2021, from https://www.csoonline.com/article/2130877/the-biggest-data-breaches-of-the-21st-century.html

Hitesh Bhatia v. Kumar Vivekanand, Case No. 3207/2020.

Hoffman, Ibáñez, & Simperl. (2020). *Toward a Formal Scholarly Understanding of Blockchain-Mediated Decentralization: A Systematic Review and a Framework*. doi:10.3389/fbloc.2020.00035

Holbrook, J. (2020). *Architecting Enterprise Blockchain Solutions*. John Wiley & Sons. doi:10.1002/9781119557722

Holtmeier & Sandner. (2019). *Cryptocurrencies and the Future of Money*. Academic Press.

Höne, K., & Eloff, J. H. P. (2002). Information security policy—What do international information security standards say? *Computers & Security*, *21*(5), 402–409. doi:10.1016/S0167-4048(02)00504-7

Hong, H., Pradhan, B., Xu, C., & Bui, D. T. (2015). Spatial prediction of landslide hazard at the Yihuang area (China) using two-class kernel logistic regression, alternating decision tree and support vector machines. *Catena*, *133*, 266–281. doi:10.1016/j.catena.2015.05.019

Hopland, C., Dorwart, H., & Zanfir-Fortuna, G. (2020). *Singapore's Personal Data Protection Act shifts away from a consent-centric framework*. Future of Privacy Forum. https://fpf.org/blog/singapores-personal-data-protection-act-shifts-away-from-a-consent-centric-framework/

Houben, R. (2018, July). *Cryptocurrencies and Blockchain*. European Parliament. https://www.europarl.europa.eu/cmsdata/150761/TAX3%20Study%20on%20cryptocurrencies%20and%20blockchain.pdf

Hua, J., & Bapna, S. (2013). The economic impact of cyber terrorism. *The Journal of Strategic Information Systems*, *22*(2), 175–186. doi:10.1016/j.jsis.2012.10.004

Huang, Z., Su, X., Zhang, Y., Shi, C., Zhang, H., & Xie, L. (2017). A decentralized solution for IoT data trusted exchange based-on blockchain. *2017 3rd IEEE International Conference on Computer and Communications (ICCC)*, 1180–1184.

Human Rights Watch. (2018, September). *China's Algorithms of Repression Reverse Engineering a Xinjiang Police Mass Surveillance App*. https://www.hrw.org/report/2019/05/01/chinas-algorithms-repression/reverse-engineering-xinjiang-police-mass

Humble, K. (2020). International law, surveillance and the protection of privacy. *International Journal of Human Rights*.

Ibikunle, F. & Eweniyi, O (2013). Approach to Cyber Security Issues in Nigeria: Challenges and Solution. *International Journal of Cognitive Research in Science, Engineering and Education, 1*(1).

IBPF. (2021). *India Brand Equity Foundation*. Retrieved from https://www.ibef.org/industry/ecommerce.aspx

ICMEC & World Bank. (2015). *Protecting Children from Cybercrime*. https://www.icmec.org/wpcontent/uploads/2015/10/Protecting_Children_from_Cybercrime_-_Legislative_Responses_in_Asia_to_Fight_Child_Pornography__Online_Grooming__and_Cyberbullying_2015.pdf

Idil, G. (2020). *Blockchain, Smart Contract and Arbitration*. Erdem & Erdem. http://www.erdem-erdem.av.tr/publications/newsletter/blockchain-smart-contracts-and-arbitration/

IMNOVATION. (n.d.). *How Blockchain is Helping to Fight the Coronavirus*. Retrieved 11 May 2021, from https://www.imnovation-hub.com/society/blockchain-help-coronavirus/

Index, B. L. (2018). *Data breach database*. Academic Press.

Infocomm Media Development Authority. (2018). *Composition of the Advisory Council on the Ethical Use of Artificial Intelligence ("AI") and Data*. https://www.imda.gov.sg/news-and-events/Media-Room/Media-Releases/2018/composition-of-the-advisory-council-on-the-ethical-use-of-ai-and-data

Inozemtsev, M. I. (2020). Digital assets in the United States: Legal aspects. *Lecture Notes in Networks and Systems*, *139*, 514–522. doi:10.1007/978-3-030-53277-2_61

Integrated Innovation Strategy Promotion Council Decision. (2019). *AI Strategy 2019*. https://www.kantei.go.jp/jp/singi/ai_senryaku/pdf/aistratagy2019en.pdf

Intermatic v. Toeppen, 947 F. supp 1227 (N.D.I ll. 1996)

International Chamber of Commerce. (2017). *Information Technology in International Arbitration- Report of the ICC Commission on Arbitration and ADR*. Author.

International Institute of Communications. (2020). *Artificial Intelligence in the Asia-Pacific Region*. https://www.iicom.org/wp-content/uploads/IIC-AI-Report-2020.pdf

Internet and Mobile Association of India v. Reserve Bank of India, Writ Petition (Civil) No.528 of 2018.

Internet Society. (2000). *History of Internet in Africa*. Available at https://www.internetsociety.org/internet/history-of-the-internet-in-africa/

Interstellar Starship Services, Ltd. v. Epix, Inc, 304 F.3d at 947

ISO/IEC 10918-1, Information Technology — Digital Compression and Coding of Continuous-Tone Still Images: Requirements and Guidelines, 1994

Ito, J., Dadich, S., & Obama, B. (2016, August 24). Barack Obama, Neural Nets, Self Driving Cars, And The Future of the World. *Wired*. Retrieved July 29, 2021, from https://www.wired.com/2016/10/president-obama-mit-joi-ito-interview/

Jack, W. N. (2016). *Machine Arbitration and Machine Arbitrator*. Young ICCA Blog. https://www.youngicca-blog.com/machine-arbitration-and-machine-arbitrators/

JainS. (2015). Cyber Squatting: Concept, Types and Legal Regimes in India. https://ssrn.com/abstract=2786474 doi:10.2139/ssrn.2786474

Jarmanning, A. (2020). *Boston Bans Use Of Facial Recognition Technology. It's The 2nd-Largest City To Do So*. WBUR News. https://www.wbur.org/news/2020/06/23/boston-facial-recognition-ban

Jason, W., Alan, C., & Parke, C. (2019). *Promoting innovation through education: The blockchain industry, law enforcement and regulators work towards a common goal*. Blockchain Laws and Regulations 2019(17). Global Legal Insight.

Jing, T. W., & Murugesan, R. K. (2020). Protecting Data Privacy and Prevent Fake News and Deepfakes in Social Media via Blockchain Technology. In *International Conference on Advances in Cyber Security* (pp. 674-684). Springer.

Jonathan, C. A. (2014). World of Difference: The Budapest Convention on Cybercrime and the Challenges of Harmonization. *Monash University Law Review. Monash University. Faculty of Law*, 702. https://www.monash.edu/__data/assets/pdf_file/0019/232525/clough.pdf

Joseph, A., & Markus, B. (2018). *Blockchain Economics*. Princeton University.

Josh, F. (2020). *Blockchain and International Arbitration: Opportunities and Challenges*. Vocal Media. https://vocal.media/theChain/blockchain-and-international-arbitration-opportunities-and-challenges.

Joshi, D. (2020). *India's Privacy Law Needs To Incorporate Rights Against The Machine*. Medianama. https://www.medianama.com/2020/05/223-indias-privacy-law-needs-to-incorporate-rights-against-the-machine/

Juneesh, K. (2014). Online shopping problems and solution. *New Media and Mass Communication, 23*, 1-5.

Justice K.S. Puttaswamy (Retd.) v. Union of India (2017) 10 SCC 1.

Kalla, A., Hewa, T., Mishra, R. A., Ylianttila, M., & Liyanage, M. (2020). The Role of Blockchain to Fight Against COVID-19. *IEEE Engineering Management Review, 48*(3), 85–96. doi:10.1109/EMR.2020.3014052

Kamps, J., & Kleinburg, B. (2018). To the moon: Defining and detecting cryptocurrency pump-and-dumps. *Crime Science, 7*(1), 18. doi:10.118640163-018-0093-5

Kania, E. (2018). *China's ambitions an Artificial Intelligence: A challenge to the future of democracy?* https://www. power3point0.org/2018/08/08/chinas-ambitions-in-artificial-intelligence-a-challenge-to-the-future-of-democracy/

Karia, T. D. (2008). Digital Evidence: An Indian Perspective. *Digital Evidence and Electronic Signature Law Review*, *5*, 214–220.

Karia, T., Anand, A., & Dhawan, B. (2015). The Supreme Court of India Re-Defines Admissibility of Electronic Evidence in India. *Digital Evidence and Electronic Signature Law Review*, *12*(0), 33–37. doi:10.14296/deeslr.v12i0.2215

Karimi, O., & Korkmaz, A. (2013). Kişisel Verilerin Korunması. *XViIII. Türkiye'de İnternet Konferansı*, 193-199.

Karp, G. (2009). *Personal Finance Writer for the Morning Call*. Tribune.

Katarzyna, S. (2020). *"On-chain" and "off-chain" arbitration: Using smart contracts to amicably resolve disputes*. Newtech Law. https://newtech.law/en/on-chain-and-off-chain-arbitration-using-smart-contracts-to-amicably-resolve-disputes/

Kathleen, P., & Edna, S. (2018). Artificial Intelligence Challenges and Opportunities for International Arbitration. *NYSBA New York Dispute Resolution Lawyer*, *11*, 36.

Kaur, R., Singh, S., & Kumar, H. (2018). Rise of spam and compromised accounts in online social networks: A state-of-the-art review of different combating approaches. *Journal of Network and Computer Applications*, *112*, 53–88. doi:10.1016/j.jnca.2018.03.015

Kayaalp, M. (2018). Modes of De-identification. In *AMIA Annual Symposium Proceedings*. U.S. National Library of Medicine, National Institutes of Health.

Keith, D. F. (2017). *A brief history of Big Data*. https://www.dataversity.net/brief-history-big-data/#

Kemp, S. (2021). *Digital 2021 Nigeria*. Available athttps://datareportal.com/reports/digital-2021-nigeria

Kent, J. (2018, August 8). *Providers Embrace Predictive Analytics for Clinical, Financial Benefits*. Health IT Analytics. Retrieved November 26, 2021, from https://healthitanalytics.com/news/providers-embrace-predictive-analytics-for-clinical-financial-benefits

Kersey, J. (2020). *How Blockchain Technology & Self Sovereign Identity is Enabling The New Normal Post COVID-19*. Tata Consultancy Services. https://www.tcs.com/perspectives/articles/covid-19-how-blockchain-technology-and-self-sovereign-identity-enables-the-new-normal-of-remote-learning-training-and-working

Keshavlal Khemchand and Sons Pvt. Ltd. v. Union of India Writ Petition (Civil) No. 901 of 2014.

Ketizmen, M., & Ülküderner, Ç. (2007). E-devlet uygulamalarında kişisel verilerin korun (ma) ması. *XII. Türkiye'de İnternet Konferansı*, 8-10.

Khanna, A., & Khanna, P. (2020). Where Asia is taking the world with AI. *Forbes*. https://www.forbes.com/sites/insights-ibmai/2020/05/21/where-asia-is-taking-the-world-with-ai/?sh=3669da577947

Khan, Z. H., Charan, P., Ansari, M. A., & Khan, K. H. (2015). Cybersquatting and its Effectual Position in India. *International Journal of Scientific and Engineering Research*, *6*, 880–886.

Khatri, Y. (2020). *Binance has begun to block U.S. users from accessing its exchange platform*. Retrieved from https://www.theblockcrypto.com/post/84020/binance-blocking-us-users-exchange-email-2

Khokhar, R. H., Chen, R., Fung, B. C. M., & Lui, S. M. (2014). Quantifying the costs and benefits of privacy-preserving health data publishing. *Journal of Biomedical Informatics*, *50*, 107–121. doi:10.1016/j.jbi.2014.04.012 PMID:24768775

Khurshid, A. (2020). Applying Blockchain Technology to Address the Crisis of Trust During the COVID-19 Pandemic. *JMIR Medical Informatics*, *8*(9), e20477. doi:10.2196/20477 PMID:32903197

Kietzmann, J., McCarthy, I. P., & Lee, L. W. (2019 in press). *Deepfakes: Trick or Treat*. Kelley School of Business, Indiana University Press.

Kim, F. (2020). *AI Technology and International Arbitration: Are Robot Coming for Your Job*. CIArB Blog. https://www.ciarb.org/news/ai-technology-and-international-arbitration-are-robots-coming-for-your-job/

Kindt, E. J. (2016). *Privacy and data protection issues of biometric applications* (Vol. 1). Springer.

King, G., Pan, J., & Roberts, M. (2013). How censorship in China allows government criticism but silences collective expression. *The American Political Science Review*, *107*(2), 326–343. doi:10.1017/S0003055413000014

Kitchin, R. (2014). Big Data and human geography: Opportunities, challenges and risks. *Dialogues in Human Geography*, *3*(3), 262–267. doi:10.1177/2043820613513388

Korkmaz, İ. (2016). Kişisel Verilerin Korunmasi Kanunu Hakkinda Bir Değerlendirme. *Türkiye Barolar Birliği Dergisi*, (124), 81–152.

Kosinski, P. M., Stillwell, D., & Graepel, T. (2013, April 9). *Private traits and attributes are predictable from digital records of human behavior*. PNAS. Retrieved July 29, 2021, from https://www.pnas.org/content/110/15/5802

Krishnamurthy, V. (2020). A Tale of Two Privacy Laws: The GDPR and the International Right to Privacy. *The American Journal of International Law*.

Kumar, P. R., & Deepamala, N. (2010). Design for implementing NetFlow using existing session tables in devices like Stateful Inspection firewalls and Load balancers. *Trendz in Information Sciences & Computing*, 210–213.

Kumar, R. (2021). *Is it really possible to completely ban cryptocurrency in India?* Retrieved from https://www.msn.com/en-in/news/other/is-it-really-possible-to-completely-ban-cryptocurrency-in-india-check-experiences-from-other-countries/ar-AARfjiU

Kumar, S. (2019, November 25). *Advantages and Disadvantages of Artificial Intelligence*. Towards Data Science. Retrieved January 14, 2022, from https://towardsdatascience.com/advantages-and-disadvantages-of-artificial-intelligence-182a5ef6588c

Kumar, V. (2021, June 5). *What is Artificial Intelligence? Functions, 6 Benefits, Applications of AI*. GetupLearn. Retrieved July 29, 2021, from https://getuplearn.com/blog/artificial-intelligence/

Kumar, A., Gupta, S. K., Rai, A. K., & Sinha, S. (2013). *Social Networking Sites and their Security Issues* (Vol. 3). International Journal of Scientific and Research Publications.

Küzeci, E. (2019). *Kişisel Verilerin Korunması*. Turhan Kitapevi. Yenilenmiş ve Gözden Geçirilmiş 3. Baskı.

Lamparello v. Falwell, 420 F.3d 309 (4th Cir. 2005)

LaRue, F. (2011). *Report of the Special Rapporteur on the promotion and prevention of the right to freedom of opinion and expression*. Frank La Rue. UN.

Laskai, L., & Webster, G. (2019). *Translation: Chinese Expert Group Offers 'Governance Principles' for 'Responsible AI'*. https://perma.cc/V9FL-H6J7

Laudon, K., & Traver, G. (2016). *E-commerce: Business, Technology, and Society*. Pearson Publication.

Laurence, T. (2019). *Introduction to Blockchain Technology*. Van Haren.

Lee, D. K., Guo, L., & Wang, Y. (2018). Cryptocurrency: A new investment opportunity? *Journal of Alternative Investments*, *20*(3), 16–40.

Legrand, J. (2020, September 4). *The Future Use Cases of Blockchain for Cybersecurity*. Cyber Management Alliance. https://www.cm-alliance.com/cybersecurity-blog/the-future-use-cases-of-blockchain-for-cybersecurity

Lei, Y., & Yucong, D. (2021). Trusted Service Provider Discovery Based on Data, Information, Knowledge, and Wisdom. *International Journal of Software Engineering and Knowledge Engineering*, *31*(01), 3–19. doi:10.1142/S0218194021400015

Li, N., Li, T., & Venkatasubramanian, S. (2007). t-Closeness: Privacy Beyond k-Anonymity and l-Diversity. *IEEE 23rd International Conference on Data Engineering*.

Li, T., & Li, N. (2009). On the Tradeoff between Privacy and Utility in Data Publishing. *Proceedings of the 15th ACM SIGKDD International Conference on Knowledge Discovery and Data Mining*.

Lieure, A. (2018). *Herd behaviour and information uncertainty: Insights from the cryptocurrency market*. Academic Press.

Liu, Y., & Tsyvinski, A. (2018). *Risks and returns of cryptocurrency* (Working paper 24877). National Bureau of Economic Research.

Li, X., Liang, X., Lu, R., Shen, X., Lin, X., & Zhu, H. (2012). Securing smart grid: Cyber attacks, countermeasures, and challenges. *IEEE Communications Magazine*, *50*(8), 38–45. doi:10.1109/MCOM.2012.6257525

London Court of International Arbitration Rules. (2014). Retrieved from https://www.lcia.org/dispute_resolution_services/lcia-arbitration-rules-2014.aspx

Lorenz, M. (2013). *An Introduction to EU Competition Law*. Cambridge University Press. doi:10.1017/CBO9781139087452

Loucks, J. (2018). Deepfakes and AI: Questioning artificial intelligence ethics and the dangers of AI. In *State of AI in Enterprise* (2nd ed.). Deloitte. https://www2.deloitte.com/us/en/pages/technology-media-and-telecommunications/articles/deepfakes-artificial-intelligence-ethics.html

Lustig. (2019). *T-closeness: Privacy beyond k- Anonymity and l-diversity*. https://www.ics.uci.edu/~projects/295d/presentations/295d-tcloseness

Lyon, D. (2007). *Surveillance Studies: An Overview*. Polity.

Lyon, D. (2014). Surveillance, Snowden, and Big Data: Capacities, consequences, critique. *Big Data & Society*, *1*(2), 1–11. doi:10.1177/2053951714541861

Machanavajjhala, A., Gehrke, J., Kifer, D., & Venkita Subramaniam, M (2006). ℓ-diversity: Privacy beyond k-anonymity. *Proceedings of the 22nd International Conference on Data Engineering*.

Madhvendra, S. (2020). *Blockchain and AI-is the cocktail right for Arbitration*. Bar & Bench. https://www.barandbench.com/columns/policy-columns/blockchain-ai-is-the-cocktail-right-for-conduct-of-arbitration#

Majid, B. (2013). Consumer protection Concerns in e-commerce: Indian perspective. *International Journal of Law and Policy Review*, (2), 157.

Makulilo, A. B. (2016). *African data privacy laws* (Vol. 33). Springer. doi:10.1007/978-3-319-47317-8

Malgieri, G. (2020). The concept of fairness in the GDPR: a linguistic and contextual interpretation. *Proceedings of the 2020 Conference on Fairness, Accountability, and Transparency*, 154–166. 10.1145/3351095.3372868

MandaviaS. A. (2019). https://economictimes.indiatimes.com/news/politics-and-nation/government-localises-critical-sensitive-personal-data/articleshow/72376594.cms?from=mdr

Manheim, K., & Kaplan, L. (2019). Artificial Intelligence: Risks to Privacy and Democracy. *Yale Journal of Law and Technology, 21*(106). https://www.trai.gov.in/consultation-paper-privacy-security-and-ownership-data-telecom-sector

Manish Vij v. Indra Chugh, AIR 2002 Del. 243.

Mann, S., & Ferenbok, J. (2013). New media and the power politics of sousveillance in a surveillance-dominated world. *Surveillance & Society, 11*(1/2), 18–34. doi:10.24908s.v11i1/2.4456

Maqsood, A., & Rizwan, M. (2019). Security, Trust, and Privacy in Cyber (STPC Cyber). *International Journal of Scientific and Research Publications, 9*(2), p8682. doi:10.29322/IJSRP.9.02.2019.p8682

Maras, M. H., & Alexandrou, A. (2019). Determining Authenticity of Video Evidence in the Age of Artificial Intelligence and in the Wake of Deepfake Videos. *International Journal of Evidence and Proof, 23*(3), 255–262. doi:10.1177/1365712718807226

Marike, R. P. P. (2020). *The Blockchain ADR: Bringing International Arbitration to the New Age.* Kluwer Arbitration Blog. http://arbitrationblog.kluwerarbitration.com/2018/10/09/blockchain-adr-bringing-international-arbitration-new-age/?doing_wp_cron=1596338917.2967860698699951171875

Mark van Rijmenam, D. (2013). *A short History of Big Data.* https://datafloq.com/read/big-data-history/239

Martin, S. (2019, October 25). *Top 12 Ways AI is Revolutionizing the Online-Shopping/E-commerce Trends.* Towards Data Science. Retrieved November 30, 2021, from https://towardsdatascience.com/top-12-ways-ai-is-revolutionizing-the-online-shopping-ecommerce-trends-9c3e98ef519c

Marx, G. (2015). Surveillance Studies. *International Encyclopedia of the Social & Behavioral Sciences,* 733–741. https://web.mit.edu/gtmarx/www/surv_studies.pdf

Mason, S. (2012). *Electronic Evidence.* Butterworths Law.

Mathis, T. (2016). *Blockchain: A Guide to Blockchain; The Technology Behind Bitcoin; Ethereum And Other Cryptocurrency.* Level Up Lifestyle Limited.

McKinsey. (2012). *The Social Economy: Unlocking Value and Productivity Through Social Technologies.* Mc Kinsey Global Institute.

McLaughlin, J., & McLaughlin, J. (2015, October 6). *Top European Court Rules That NSA Spying Makes U.S. Unsafe For Data.* The Intercept. https://theintercept.com/2015/10/06/top-european-court-rules-that-nsa-spying-makes-u-s-unsafe-for-data/

Md. Faruk v. State of Madhya Pradesh and Others (1969) 1 SCC 853.

Meehan. (2018). The continuing Conundrum of International Internet Jurisdiction. Int'l & Comp. L. Rev, 31, 42.

Mehmood, A., Natgunanathan, I., Xiang, Y., Hua, G., & Guo, S. (2016). Protection of big data privacy. *IEEE Access: Practical Innovations, Open Solutions, 4,* 1821–1834. doi:10.1109/ACCESS.2016.2558446

Meyer-Schönberger, V., & Cukier, K. (2012). *Big Data: A Revolution that will Transform How we Work, Think and Live.* Mariner.

Michael, K. (2016). RFID/NFC implants for bitcoin transactions. *IEEE Consumer Electronics Magazine, 5*(3), 103–106. doi:10.1109/MCE.2016.2556900

Michael, R. (2017). *CodeLegit Conducts First Blockchain-based Smart Contract Arbitration Proceeding*. CodeLegit.

Michigan. Audi AG v. D'Amato, 469 F.3d 534 (6th Cir. 2006)

Microsoft v. MikeroweSoft, (2004)

Mike, D. (2019). *Dispute Resolution: How Blockchain Platforms Can Help Settle Conflict*. Bitrates. https://www.bitrates.com/news/p/dispute-resolution-how-blockchain-platforms-can-help-settle-conflict

Millward, J., & Peterson, D. (2020, September). China's system of oppression in Xinjiang: How it developed and how to curb it. *Global China*. https://www.brookings.edu/wp-content/uploads/2020/09/FP_20200914_china_oppression_xinjiang_millward_peterson.pdf

Minevich, M. (2021). *European AI needs strategic leadership, not overregulation*. TechCrunch. https://techcrunch.com/2021/05/15/european-ai-needs-strategic-leadership-not-overRegulation/

Ministry of Home Affairs. (2019). *Cyber Crime Reporting Portal*. Government of India.

Ministry of Internal Affairs and Communications. (2017). *AI Utilisation Guidelines*. https://www.soumu.go.jp/main_content/000499625.pdf

Ministry of Internal Affairs and Communications. (2019). *AI Utilisation Guidelines*. https://www.soumu.go.jp/main_content/000658284.pdf

Ministry of Science and ICT, Government of Taiwan. (2016). *Mid-to Long-term Master Plan in Preparation for the Intelligent Information Society: Managing the Fourth Industrial Revolution*. http://english.msit.go.kr/cms/english/pl/policies2/__icsFiles/afieldfile/2017/07/20/Master%20Plan%20for%20the%20intelligent%20information%20society.pdf

Mirtaheri, M., Abu-El-Haija, S., Morstatter, F., Ver Sleeg, G., & Galstyan, A. (2019). *Identifying and analyzing cryptocurrency manipulations in social media*. Arxiv Pre-print: 1902.03110. Retrieved from https://arxiv.org/abs/1902.03110

Mishra, P. K. (2019). *Sustainable Agriculture and Natural Resource Management: Issues and Challenges*. DAYA Publishing House.

Mivule, K., & Turner, C. (2013). A Comparative Analysis of Data Privacy and Utility Parameter Adjustment, Using Machine Learning Classification as a Gauge. *Procedia Computer Science*, *20*, 414–419. doi:10.1016/j.procs.2013.09.295

Mohammed, N., Fung, B. C. M., Hung, P. C. K., & Lee, C.-K. (2009). Anonymizing healthcare data: A case study on the blood transfusion service, *ACM SIGKDD International Conference on Knowledge Discovery and Data Mining*. 10.1145/1557019.1557157

Monetary Authority of Singapore. (2019). *MAS Partners Financial Industry to Create Framework for Responsible Use of AI*. https://www.mas.gov.sg/news/media-releases/2019/mas-partners-financial-industry-to-create-framework-for-responsible-use-of-ai

Monika, K. (2020, April). *Case Study on Cambridge Analytica embezzling on Facebook users data*. Legal Desire. Retrieved July 10, 2021, from https://legaldesire.com/case-study-on-cambridge-analytica-embezzling-on-facebook-users-data/

Morin, A. (2014, October 31). *What Your Facebook Use Reveals About Your Personality And Your Self-Esteem* [web log]. Retrieved July 29, 2021, from https://www.forbes.com/sites/amymorin/2014/10/31/what-your-facebook-use-reveals-about-your-personality-and-your-self-esteem/?sh=6cf70ee9321f

Mota, S. A. (2003). The anticybersquatting consumer protection act: An analysis of the decisions from the courts of appeals. *Journal of Computer & Information Law*, *21*, 355–370.

Mr. Arun Jaitley v. The Network Solutions Pvt. Ltd, 181 (2011) DLT 716.

Mueller-Kaler, J. (2020). *Europe's third way*. Atlantic Council. https://www.atlanticcouncil.org/content-series/smart-partnerships/europes-third-way/

Mulligan, S. P., Freeman, W. C., & Linebaugh, C. D. (2019). *Data protection law: An overview*. R45631. Congressional Research Service. Https://Crsreports. Congress. Gov/Product/Pdf

Murphy, Murphy, & Seitzinger. (2015). *Bitcoin: Questions, Answers, and Analysis of Legal Issues*. Congressional Research Service. 7-5700.

Murphy, K. P. (2012). *Machine Learning: A Probabilistic Perspective*. The MIT Press.

Murthy, Bharadwaj, Subrahmanyam, Roy, & Rajan. (2014). Big Data Working Group. In *Big Data Taxonomy*. Cloud Security Alliance (CSA).

Musil, S. (2011, October 24). *John McCarthy, creator of Lisp programming language, dies*. c|net. Retrieved January 14, 2022, from https://www.cnet.com/news/john-mccarthy-creator-of-lisp-programming-language-dies/

N.R. Dongre v. Whirlpool Corporation, 1996 (16) PTC 583 (SC).

Najibi, A. (2020). *Racial Discrimination in Facial Recognition Technology*. Blog, Science Policy, Special Edition – Science Policy and Social Justice. Graduate School of Arts and Sciences, Harvard University. https://sitn.hms.harvard.edu/flash/2020/racial-discrimination-in-face-recognition-technology/

Nakamoto, S. (2008). *Bitcoin: A peer-to-peer electronic cash system*. Available at https://bitcoin.org/bitcoin.pdf

Nakamoto, S. (2008, October). *Bitcoin: A Peer-to-Peer Electronic Cash System*. https://bitcoin.org/bitcoin.pdf

Nambobi, M., Ruth, K., Alli, A. A., & Ssemwogerere, R. (2021). The Age of Autonomous Internet of Things Devices: Opportunities and Challenges of IoT. *Challenges and Opportunities for the Convergence of IoT, Big Data, and Cloud Computing*, 1–16.

Nambobi, M., Ssemwogerere, R., & Ramadhan, B. K. (2020). Implementation of Autonomous Library Assistants Using RFID Technology. In *Emerging Trends and Impacts of the Internet of Things in Libraries* (pp. 140–150). IGI Global. doi:10.4018/978-1-7998-4742-7.ch008

Narayanan, A., Bonneau, J., Felten, E., Miller, A., & Goldfeder, S. (2016). Bitcoin and Cryptocurrency Technologies: A Comprehensive Introduction (Illustrated ed.). Princeton University Press.

Narayanan, A., Bonneau, J., Felten, E., Miller, A., & Goldfeder, S. (2016). *Bitcoin and cryptocurrency technologies*. Princeton University Press.

Nestertsova-Sobakar, O., Prymachenko, V., Valentyn, L., Bereznyak, V., & Sydorova, E. (2019). Legal approaches to the regulation of cryptocurrency and business ethics of ICO in the European Union. *Journal of Legal, Ethical and Regulatory Issues*, 22(2), 1–6.

Netherlands Enterprise Agency. (2020). *Artificial Intelligence; an overview of policies and developments in Taiwan*. https://www.rvo.nl/sites/default/files/2020/04/AI-Developments-in-Taiwan.pdf

Nguyen, A. (2019). *Understanding Differential Privacy*. https://towardsdatascience.com/understanding-differential-privacy-85ce191e198a

Nijhavan, G. & Dahiya, S. (2020). Role of Covid as a catalyst In Increasing Adoption of OTTs In India: A Study Of Evolving Consumer Consumption Patterns And Future Business Scope. *Journal of Content, Community & Communication*.

Nissan, D. (2009). *Future Shop*. The Penguin Press.

Nivin, S. (2021). *How does AI recognise your hand gestures and movements?* Mantra AI. https://www.mantra.ai/blogs/ai-in-gesture-recognition/

Nizzoli, L., Tardelli, S., Avvenuti, M., Cresci, S., Tesconi, M., & Ferreara, E. (2020). Charting the landscape of online cryptocurrency manipulation. *IEEE Access: Practical Innovations, Open Solutions, 8*, 113230–113245. doi:10.1109/ACCESS.2020.3003370

No, G. C. (1988) *16: The right to respect of privacy, family, home and correspondence, and prevention of honour and reputation* (Art. 17). UN Doc HRI/GEN/1/Rev, 1.

Norton Rose Fulbright. (2017). *Online Dispute Resolution and Electronic Hearing*. Author.

Norton Rose Fulbright. (2019, November). *Blockchain dispute risks for banks*. Author.

O'Donnell, N. (2021). Have We No Decency? Section 230 and the Liability of Social Media Companies for Deepfake Videos. *University of Illinois Law Review, 2021*(2), 701–ii.

OCED. (1980). *OECD (Organization for Economic Co-operation and Development) guidelines on the prevention of privacy and transborder flows of private data*. Author.

OECD Policy Roundtables. (2013). *Competition Issues in Television and Broadcasting*. Available at https://www.oecd.org/daf/competition/TV-and-broadcasting2013.pdf

Oest, A., Safei, Y., Doupé, A., Ahn, G.-J., Wardman, B., & Warner, G. (2018). Inside a phisher's mind: Understanding the anti-phishing ecosystem through phishing kit analysis. *2018 APWG Symposium on Electronic Crime Research (ECrime)*, 1–12. 10.1109/ECRIME.2018.8376206

Ogunjobe, O. (2020). *The Impact of Cybercrime on Nigerian Youths*. Retrieved from https://www.researchgate.net/publication/347436728_THE_IMPACT_OF_CYBERCRIME_ON_NIGERIAN_YOUTHS

OHCHR. (November 12, 2020). *Sexual Violence Against Children Online*. https://www.ohchr.org /_layouts /15/WopiFrame.aspx?sourcedoc=/Documents/HRBodies/CRC/GCChildrensDigitalEnvironment/2020/others/swiss-foundation-protection-of-children-2020-114.docx&action=default&Default ItemOpen=1

Olenik, S., Lee, H. S., & Güder, F. (2021). The future of near-field communication-based wireless sensing. *Nature Reviews. Materials, 6*(4), 1–3. doi:10.103841578-021-00299-8 PMID:33680503

Olurounbi, R. (2021). *Nigeria Unemployment Rate Rises to 33%, Second Highest on Global List*. Available at https://www.bloomberg.com/news/articles/2021-03-15/nigeria-unemployment-rate-rises-to-second-highest-on-global-list

Omohundro, S. (2014). Crypto-Currencies, Smart Contracts, and Artificial Intelligence. *AI Matters, 1*(2), 19–21. doi:10.1145/2685328.2685334

Ong, T. (2018). *Facebook announces new European privacy controls, for the world*. The Verge. https://www.theverge.com/2018/4/18/17250840/facebook-privacy-protections-europe-world-gdpr

Organisation for Economic Cooperation and Development. (2019). *Committee on Digital Economy Policy, Recommendation of the Council on Artificial Intelligence adopted on. OECD/LEGAL/0449*. https://legalinstruments.oecd.org/en/instruments/OECD-LEGAL-0449

Orna, R. E., & Ethan, K. (2019). Blockchain and the Inevitability of Disputes: The role for Online Dispute Resolution. *Journal of Dispute Resolution, 2019*(2), 47–75.

Otlowski, A. (2021, September 3). Two Years Later: Cambridge Analytica and Its Impact on Data Privacy | HIPBlog. *The Hip, B2B*. Retrieved July 10, 2021, from https://www.hipb2b.com/blog/two-years-later-cambridge-analytica-and-its-impact-on-data-privacy

Ouaddah, A., Mousannif, H., Abou Elkalam, A., & Ouahman, A. A. (2017). Access control in the Internet of Things: Big challenges and new opportunities. *Computer Networks, 112*, 237–262. doi:10.1016/j.comnet.2016.11.007

Pandey, A. (2017). *Laws against cybersquatting*. IPleaders. https://blog.ipleaders.in/cyber-squatting/

Pandey, R., & Jain, S. (2018). A Hybrid Approach to Preserving Privacy in Data Mining using L-K-C and personalized Privacy. *International Journal of Innovative Research in Computer and Communication Engineering, 6*, 1191–1198.

Parker, S. (2020, January 10). *How AI is Transforming the Entertainment Industry*. readwrite. Retrieved November 28, 2021, from https://readwrite.com/2020/01/10/how-ai-is-transforming-the-entertainment-industry/

Parn, E. A., & Edwards, D. (2019). Cyber threats confronting the digital built environment. *Engineering, Construction, and Architectural Management, 26*(2), 245–266. doi:10.1108/ECAM-03-2018-0101

Payne, S. (2007). Qualitative methods of data collection and analysis. *Research Methods in Palliative Care*, 139–161.

Pech, L. (2021). *The concept of chilling effect its untapped potential to better protect democracy, the rule of law, and fundamental rights in the EU*. Open Society European Policy Institute. https://www.opensocietyfoundations.org/uploads/c8c58ad3-fd6e-4b2d-99fa-d8864355b638/the-concept-of-chilling-effect-20210322.pdf

Perez, B. C. E. J. R. (2013, September 28). *NSA: Some used spying power to snoop on lovers – CNNPolitics*. CNN. https://edition.cnn.com/2013/09/27/politics/nsa-snooping/index.html

Personal Data Protection Commission. (2018). *Discussion Paper on Artificial Intelligence (AI) and Personal Data - Fostering Responsible Development and Adoption of AI*. https://www.pdpc.gov.sg/-/media/Files/PDPC/PDF-Files/Resource-for-Organisation/AI/Discussion-Paper-on-AI-and-PD---050618.pdf

Personal Data Protection Commission. (2020). *Model Artificial Intelligence Governance Framework – Second Edition*. Accessible at: https://www.pdpc.gov.sg/-/media/Files/PDPC/PDF-Files/Resource-for-Organisation/AI/SGModelAIGov-Framework2.pdf

Petronio, S. (2004). Road to Developing Communication Privacy Management Theory: Narrative in Progress, Please Stand By. *Journal of Family Communication, 4*(3/4), 193–207. doi:10.120715327698jfc0403&4_6

Pierre, D., & Roland, Z. (2018). *International arbitration and the rise of innovative tech*. International Chamber of Commerce. https://iccwbo.org/media-wall/news-speeches/guest-blog-international-arbitration-rise-innovative-tec/

Piers, M., & Aschauer, C. (Eds.). (2018). *Arbitration in the digital age : the brave new world of arbitration* (pp. 283–289). Cambridge University Press. doi:10.1017/9781108283670.015

Pietsch, B. (2021). 2 Killed in Driverless Tesla Car Crash, Officials Say. *The New York Times*. https://www.nytimes.com/2021/04/18/business/tesla-fatal-crash-texas.html

Piscini, E., Dalton, D., & Kehoe, L. (2017). *Blockchain and Cybersecurity: An assessment of the security of blockchain technology*. Deloitte. https://www2.deloitte.com/tr/en/pages/technology-media-and-telecommunications/articles/blockchain-and-cyber.html

Ponavision v. Toeppen, 141 F.3e 1316 (1998)

Ponemon Institute. (2013). 2013 Cost of Cyber Crime Study: Global Report. Technical Report October, Ponemon Institute.

Poornima, S., & Pushpalatha, M. (2018). A survey of predictive analytics using Big Data with data mining. *International Bioinformatics Research and Applications, 14*(3), 269–282. doi:10.1504/IJBRA.2018.092697

Porur. (2019, February 6). *In this Chennai restaurant robot waiters serve customers, speak to them in Tamil and English.* IndiaToday. Retrieved November 15, 2021, from https://www.indiatoday.in/india/story/in-this-chennai-restaurant-robot-waiters-serve-customers-speak-to-them-in-tamil-and-english-1449122-2019-02-06

Prakash, M., & Singaravel, G. (2014). An Analysis of Privacy Risks and Design Principles for Developing Counter-measures In Privacy Preserving Sensitive Data Publishing. *Journal of Theoretical and Applied Information Technology, 62*, 204–213.

Prakash, M., & Singaravel, G. (2018). Haphazard, enhanced haphazard and personalised anonymisation for privacy preserving data mining on sensitive data sources. *International Journal of Business Intelligence and Data Mining, 13*(4), 456–474. doi:10.1504/IJBIDM.2018.094983

Premium Times. (2021). *52 Suspected Internet fraudsters Arrested in Benin, Six in Abuja.* Available at https://www.premiumtimesng.com/news/top-news/460807-52-suspected-internet-fraudsters-arrested-in-benin-six-in-abuja.html

Pressgrove, J. (2020, March 11). *Blockchain Emerges as Useful Tool in Fight Against Coronavirus.* GovTech. https://www.govtech.com/products/blockchain-emerges-as-useful-tool-in-fight-against-coronavirus.html

Protecting Children's Privacy under COPPA: A Survey on Compliance. (2002). Federal Trade Commission-Protecting America's Consumers.

Protecting personal Health Information in Research: Understanding the HIPAA Privacy Rule. (2002). Department of Health and Human Services.

Prytula, A., Lutsyk, V., Sviatoshniuk, A., Tkalia, O., & Kalachenkova, K. (2021). Cryptocurrency in transnational of-fences: Criminal and civil legal aspects. *Amazonia Investiga, 10*(46), 209–216. doi:10.34069/AI/2021.46.10.21

PwC Report. (2019–2023). *Global Entertainment & Media Outlook.* Available at https://www.pwc.in/press-releases/2019/global-entertainment-and-media-outlook-2019-2023.html

PwC. (2017). *Sizing the prize: PwC's Global Artificial Intelligence Study: Exploiting the AI Revolution.* https://www.pwc.com/gx/en/issues/data-and-analytics/publications/artificial-intelligence-study.html

Quan, X. I. (2018, November 20). *Understanding the Artificial Intelligence Business Ecosystem.* IEEE Xplore. Retrieved November 28, 2021, from https://ieeexplore.ieee.org/document/8540793

R v. Spiby (1990) 91 Cr App R 186 CA

Rahm, E., & Do, H. (2000). Data cleaning: Problems and current approaches. *IEEE Data Eng. Bull., 23*(4), 3–13. http://wwwiti.cs.uni-magdeburg.de/iti_db/lehre/dw/paper/data_cleaning.pdf%5Cnpapers2://publication/uuid/17B58056-3A7F-4184-8E8B-0E4D82EFEA1A%5Cnhttp://dc-pubs.dbs.uni-leipzig.de/files/Rahm2000DataCleaningProblemsand.pdf

Rajendran, K., Jeyabalan, M., & Rana, M. E. (2017). A study on k-anonymity, l-diversity, t-closeness Techniques focusing medical Data. *International Journal of Computer Science and Network Security, 17*, 172–177.

Ram Mohan Rao, P., Murali Krishna, S., & Siva Kumar, A. P. (2018). Privacy preservation techniques in big data analytics: A survey. *Journal of Big Data, 33*(1), 1–12. doi:10.118640537-018-0141-8

Ramos, D. (2018, April 16). *Voice Assistants: How Artificial Intelligence Assistants Are Changing Our Lives Every Day.* smartsheet. Retrieved November 25, 2021, from https://www.smartsheet.com/voice-assistants-artificial-intelligence

Rangarajan, S. (1972). The Anglo-Saxon Experiment Concerning the Rule against Reception of Hearsay Evidence and What it may Mean to us. *Journal of the Indian Law Institute*, 26–52. https://www.scconline.com/DocumentLink/m5t8Gl90

Raskhodnikova, S., & Smith, A. (2010). *Algorithmic Challenges in Data Privacy*. Lecture Notes.

Rastogi, Suciu, & Hong. (2007). The Boundary between privacy and utility in data publishing. *VLDB Endowment*, 1-12.

Rathore, V. S., Kumawat, V., & Umamaheswari, B. (2021). The Rising of Blockchain Technology and Its Adoption in India. In V. S. Rathore, N. Dey, V. Piuri, R. Babo, Z. Polkowski, & J. M. R. S. Tavares (Eds.), *Rising Threats in Expert Applications and Solutions. Advances in Intelligent Systems and Computing* (1187th ed., pp. 351–357). Springer. doi:10.1007/978-981-15-6014-9_40

Rattan, J., & Rattan, V. (2013). *Cyber laws and Information Technology*. Bharat Publishing House.

Rayan, B. (2019). *The Fifth Arbitrator? Analysing the Potential Role of Artificial Intelligence and Blockchain Technology in the International Arbitration Industry*. The Board Room Lawyer. https://theboardroomlawyer.wordpress.com/2019/07/24/the-fifth-arbitrator-analysing-the-potential-role-of-artificial-intelligence-and-blockchain-technology-in-the-international-arbitration-industry/

Raychaudhuri, T. (2011) Vertical Restraints in Competition Law: The Need to Strike the Right Balance Between Regulation And Competition. *NUJS L. Rev., 4*(609).

Rediff Communications Ltd. v. Cyberbooth & Another, AIR 2000 Bom 27

Redmond. (2012). *Online Bullying Is a Top Concern Among Youth*. https://news.microsoft.com/2012/06/26/online-bullying-is-a-top-concern-among-youth/

Reed, K. (2016). History and Technology: Intersecting lines in the spectrum. *International Journal of Anthropology*, 23–39.

Rekhi, K. S. (n.d.). *Analytical Positivism- Indian Perspective*. Retrieved from Legal Service India-E-journal: https://www.legalserviceindia.com/legal/article-4931-analytical-positivisim-indian-prespective.html

Rengel, A. (2014). *Privacy as an International Human Right and the Right to Obscurity in Cyberspace. Groningen Journal of International Law*. doi:10.21827/5a86a81e79532

Ren, W., Wan, X., & Gan, P. (2021). A double-blockchain solution for agricultural sampled data security in Internet of Things network. *Future Generation Computer Systems, 117*, 453–461. doi:10.1016/j.future.2020.12.007

Report of Indian Council of Food and Agriculture. (2020). *Agriculture and Indian Farmers: Issues and Road Ahead*. Author.

Reserve Bank of India. (2017, December). *Report of the Working Group on FinTech and Digital Banking*. https://rbidocs.rbi.org.in/rdocs/PublicationReport/Pdfs/WGFR68AA1890D7334D8F8F72CC2399A27F4A.PDF

Rhodan, M. (2015, July 28). White House Responds to Petition Urging Obama to Pardon Edward Snowden. *Time*. https://time.com/3974713/white-house-edward-snowden-petition/

Rias, M. L. (2011). *The European Union Criminalizes Acts of Racism and Xenophobia Committed through Computer Systems*. Archived Wayback Machine.

Richards, N. (2013). The dangers of surveillance. *Harvard Law Review, 126*, 1934–1965. https://harvardlawreview.org/wp-content/uploads/pdfs/vol126_richards.pdf

Roberts, H., Cowls, J., Morley, J., Taddeo, M., Wang, V., & Floridi, L. (2021). The Chinese approach to artificial intelligence: An analysis of policy, ethics, and Regulation. *AI & Society, 36*(1), 59–77. doi:10.100700146-020-00992-2

Rodriguez, S. (2019, September 20). *Facebook has suspended tens of thousands of apps after Cambridge Analytica investigation.* CNBC. https://www.cnbc.com/2019/09/20/facebook-suspended-tens-of-thousands-of-apps-after-cambridge-analytica.html

Roger, M. (2012). *The Legal and E-Commerce Environment Today.* Thomas Learning.

Rogers, R. W. (1975). A Protection Motivation Theory of Fear Appeals and Attitude Change. *The Journal of Psychology, 91*(1), 93–114. doi:10.1080/00223980.1975.9915803 PMID:28136248

Rollins, J. W., & Liu, E. C. (2013, September). *NSA Surveillance Leaks: Background and Issues for Congress* (No. R43134). Congressional Research Services. https://sgp.fas.org/crs/intel/R43134.pdf

Ron, S. (2019). AI and Blockchain: Double hype or Double value. *Forbes.* https://www.forbes.com/sites/cognitive-world/2019/10/24/ai-and-blockchain-double-the-hype-or-double-the-value/?sh=5dbc565f5eb4

Rossolillo. (2021). *Types of Cryptocurrency.* The Motley Fool.

Rouvroy, A. (2018). *Bureau Of The Consultative Committee Of The Convention For The Prevention Of Individuals With Regard To Automatic Processing Of Private Data* [ETS 108]. T-PD-BUR.

Rowe, H. (1999). Internet-enabled commerce; International Issues for Business Lawyers. *Journal for Intellectual Property,* (2), 542.

Rueckert. (2019). Cryptocurrencies and fundamental rights. *Journal of Cybersecurity.* doi:10.1093/cybsec/tyz004

Ryan, T. I. M. (2018). *Whistleblower: Cambridge Analytica Targeted Minority Voters to Stay Home.* CourtHouse News Service. Retrieved February 2, 2022, from https://www.courthousenews.com/whistleblower-cambridge-analytica-targeted-minority-voters-to-stayhome/#:~:text=WASHINGTON%20%28CN%29%20%E2%80%93%20The%20former%20research%20director%20for,voters%20at%20home%20during%20the%202016%20presidential%20election

Ryder, D. R. (2001). Guide to Cyber Laws (Information Technology Act, 2000: E-commerce, Data Protection & the Internet). Eastern Book Publisher.

Ryder, R. D., & Madhavan, A. (2009). Regulating Indian Cyberspace The Battle for Control in the New Media Version 2.0. *Convergence, 5*(2), 250–256.

Sabbagh, D. (2020, August 28). Trump 2016 campaign "targeted 3.5m black Americans to deter them from voting." *The Guardian.* https://www.theguardian.com/us-news/2020/sep/28/trump-2016-campaign-targeted-35m-black-americans-to-deter-them-from-voting

Salomon, A. (2019). UDHR and New Prospects. *Sustainability,* 230–247.

Samarati & Latanya. (1998). Protecting privacy when disclosing information: k-anonymity and its enforcement through generalization and suppression. *Harvard Data Privacy Lab,* 1-19.

Sarada, G., Abitha, N., Manikandan, G., & Sairam, N. (2015). A few new approaches for data masking. *2015 International Conference on Circuits, Power and Computing Technologies [ICCPCT-2015],* 1–4. 10.1109/ICCPCT.2015.7159301

Sarah, A. (2018). The Missing Link Between Blockchain and Copyright: How Companies Are Using New Technology to Misinform Creators and Violate Federal Law. *North Carolina Journal of Law & Technology,* 19.

Sarbapriya, R. (2011). Emerging Trends of e-commerce in India: Some crucial Issues, Prospects and Challenges. *Computer Engineering and Intelligent System, 5*(2), 19.

Sarwar, F. (2020). *Harmful Impact of the Internet on Children*. https://timesofindia.indiatimes.com/readersblog/lifecrunch/harmful-impact-of-the-internet-on-children-27202/

Satoshi, N. (2008). *Bitcoin: A Peer-to-Peer Electronic Cash System*. https://www.bitcoin.com/bitcoin.pdf

Satyam Infoway Ltd versus Sifynet Solutions, 2004 (3) AWC 2366 SC, AIR 2004 SC 3540

Schick, N. (2020). *Deep Fakes and the Infocalypse: What You Urgently Need to Know*. Octopus Publishing Group.

Schmidt, J., Marques, M. R. G., Botti, S., & Marques, M. A. L. (2019, August 8). *Recent advances and applications of machine learning in solid-state materials science*. NPJ. Retrieved January 7, 2022, from https://www.nature.com/articles/s41524-019-0221-0#citeas

Schneier, B. (2012). *Liars and Outliers: Enabling the Trust that Society needs to Thrive*. Wiley.

Schonfeld, E. (2010, April 29). *Silicon Valley Buzz: Apple Paid More Than $200 Million For Siri To Get Into Mobile Search*. TechCrunch. Retrieved November 26, 2021, from https://techcrunch.com/2010/04/28/apple-siri-200-million/

Schwarck, E. (2017, December 8). *Behind the Golden Shield: China Reforms Public Security Intelligence*. Jamestown. Retrieved July 10, 2021, from https://jamestown.org/program/behind-golden-shield-china-reforms-public-security-intelligence/

Scott, B. (2016, February). *How Can Cryptocurrency and Blockchain Technology Play a Role in Building Social and Solidarity Finance?* United Nations Research Institute for Social Development (UNRISD). https://www.unrisd.org/80256B3C005BCCF9/(httpPublications)/196AEF663B617144C1257F550057887C?OpenDocument

Scroxton, A. (2019). *Three Cyber Criminals Arrested in Nigerian BEC Investigation*. Available at https://www.computerweekly.com/news/252492711/Three-cyber-criminals-arrested-in-Nigerian-BEC-investigation

Sec. 19(3), Indian Competition Act, 2002

Sec. 3(4), Indian Competition Act, 2002

Securing the Big Data Life Cycle. (2019). *MIT Technology Review*.

Securities and Exchange Commission v. Trendon T. Shavers and Bitcoin Savings and Trust, Civil Action No. Civil Action No. 4:13-CV-416 (2014).

Semwal, S. K. (2011). Human Rights Jurisprudence in Indian Constitution. *The Indian Journal of Political Science*.

Sengupta, S., Kaulgud, V., & Sharma, V. S. (2011). Cloud computing security—trends and research directions. *2011 IEEE World Congress on Services*, 524–531. 10.1109/SERVICES.2011.20

Sen, J. (2015). Security and privacy issues in cloud computing. In *Cloud technology: concepts, methodologies, tools, and applications* (pp. 1585–1630). IGI Global. doi:10.4018/978-1-4666-6539-2.ch074

Seth, H. (2021). Impossibility Exception to the Section 65-B(4) Electronic Evidence Certificate, 2021 SCC OnLine Blog Exp 42.

Sethia, A. (2016). Rethinking Admissibility of Electronic Evidence. *International Journal of Law and Information Technology*, 24(3), 229–250. doi:10.1093/ijlit/eaw005

Seva, G. (2015). Corrupting the cyber-commons: Social media as a tool of autocratic stability. *Perspectives on Politics*, 13(1), 42–54. doi:10.1017/S1537592714003120

Seybold, P. (2006). *Customers.com*. Crown Business Random Publishing House.

Shad, M. R. (2019). Cyber Threat Landscape and Readiness Challenge of Pakistan. *Strategic Studies, 39*(1), 1–19. https://www.jstor.org/stable/10.2307/48544285

Shafhi Mohd. v. State of H.P., (2018) 5 SCC 311

Shah, H. (2019). Biometric Data: A complex mystery to resolve. Academic Press.

Shah, R. (2020, June 27). *Applications of AI in the media & entertainment industry.* PHRAZOR. Retrieved November 28, 2021, from https://phrazor.ai/blog/applications-of-ai-in-the-media-entertainment-industry

Shalini. (2021). Cybersquatting: The Domain Name Dispute. *Law Audience Journal, 2,* 69-85.

Sharma, H., Meenakshi, E., & Bhatia, S. K. (2017). A comparative analysis and awareness survey of phishing detection tools. *2017 2nd IEEE International Conference on Recent Trends in Electronics, Information & Communication Technology (RTEICT),* 1437–1442.

Sharma, I. (2021, February). *A More Responsible Digital Surveillance Future.* Federation of American Scientists. https://uploads.fas.org/2021/02/Digital-Surveillance-Future.pdf

Sharma, K. (2006). *Reimagining LPG in the post modern world.* Lexis Nexus.

Shashank. (2019). *How blockchain works.* Edukera.

Shawn, T. (2014). *Right to Privacy and contemporary world.* Thompson Reuters.

Shehata & Partners. (2019). *Blockchain Based Smart Contracts: An Overview.* Author.

Shewale. (2021). *Future of E-commerce in India-2021.* Retrieved from https://www.researchgate.net/publication/351441684_Future_of_E-commerce_in_India-2021

Shwed, K. (2015). History and its impact on technical know how. *The International Journal of Social Sciences (Islamabad).*

Siering, M. (2019). The economics of stock touting during Internet-based pump-and-dump campaigns. *Information Systems Journal, 29*(2), 456–483. doi:10.1111/isj.12216

Singh & Associates. (2012). *India: Cyber Squatting Laws in India.* Mondaq. https://www.mondaq.com/india/trademark/208840/cyber-squatting-laws-in%20india

Singh & Chawla. (2019). Cryptocurrency Regulation: Legal Issues and Challenges. *International Journal of Reviews and Research in Social Sciences,* 365-375.

Singh, H. P. (2018). Cyber squatting and the role of Indian Courts: A Review. *Amity Journal of Computational Sciences, 2,* 18-23. https://amity.edu/UserFiles/aijem/914%20-%202018_V02_I02_P017-021.pdf

Smith, C. S. (2021, March 9). A.I. Here, There, Everywhere. *New York Times.* Retrieved November 26, 2021, from https://www.nytimes.com/2021/02/23/technology/ai-innovation-privacy-seniors-education.html

Smith, H., & Mansted, K. (2020). What's a Deep Fake. Australian Strategic Policy Institute.

Snider, J. H., & Ziporyn, T. (1992). *Future Shop: How New Technologies Will Change the Way We Shop and What We Buy.* St. Martin's Press.

Somani, U., Lakhani, K., & Mundra, M. (2010). Implementing digital signature with RSA encryption algorithm to enhance the Data Security of cloud in Cloud Computing. *2010 First International Conference On Parallel, Distributed and Grid Computing (PDGC 2010),* 211–216. 10.1109/PDGC.2010.5679895

Song, D., Shi, E., Fischer, I., & Shankar, U. (2012). Cloud data protection for the masses. *Computer*, *45*(1), 39–45. doi:10.1109/MC.2012.1

Sonkar, S. (2021, May). *Privacy Delayed is Privacy Denied.* Retrieved from The Wire: https://thewire.in/tech/data-protection-law-india-right-to-privacy

Sonu v. State of Haryana, (2017) 8 SCC 570

Soper, S. (2021). Amazon employee fired by a robot: It's you vs machine's algorithm. *The Business Standard.* https://www.business-standard.com/article/international/amazon-employee-fired-by-a-robot-it-s-you-vs-machine-s-algorithm-121062801581_1.html

Spyridaki, K. (2021). *GDPR and AI: Friends, foes or something in between?* SAS Europe. https://www.sas.com/en_us/insights/articles/data-management/gdpr-and-ai--friends--foes-or-something-in-between-.html

Srisungsittisunti, B., & Natwichai, J. (2015). An incremental privacy-preservation algorithm for the (k, e)-Anonymous model. *Computers & Electrical Engineering*, *41*, 126–141. doi:10.1016/j.compeleceng.2014.10.007

Staff, T. T. (2014). *10 Roles For Artificial Intelligence In Education.* Teach Thought. Retrieved November 29, 2021, from https://www.teachthought.com/the-future-of-learning/roles-for-artificial-intelligence-in-education/

Stallings, W., & Brown, L. (2008). Computer security: Principles and practice. Pearson Education.

Standard Oil Company v. United States, 221 US 1 (1911)

Stangarone, T. (2019). COVID-19 Underscores the Benefits of South Korea's Artificial Intelligence Push. *The Diplomat.* https://thediplomat.com/2020/12/covid-19-underscores-the-benefits-of-south-koreas-artificial-intelligence-push/

Starbucks corporation v. Mohanraj, Case Number INDRP/118 (2009)

State (NCT of Delhi) v. Navjot Sandhu, (2005) 11 SCC 600

State Council of China. (2017). *A Next Generation Artificial Intelligence Development Plan.* New American. https://na-production.s3.amazonaws.com/documents/translation-fulltext-8.1.17.pdf

State Farm Mutual Automobile insurance company v. Brockhorst 453 F. 2nd 533 (10 Cir. 1972

State of Maharashtra v. Indian Hotel and Restaurants Association (2013) 8 SCC 519.

Statistics, W. I. (2019). *Internet Usage Statistics the Internet Big Picture.* https://www.internetworldstats.com/stats.htm

Stol, W., Leukfeldt, R., & Klap, H. (2013). 5 Policing a Digitized Society. *Cybercrime and the Police*, 61.

Strickler, T. (2021, September 22). Game on: GameStop, market manipulation, and its implications. *Kentucky Law Journal Online.* Retrieved from https://www.kentuckylawjournal.org/blog/game-on-gamestop-market-manipulation-and-its-implications

Sundaravel, E., & Elangovan, N. (n.d.). *Emergence and future of Over-the-top (OTT) video services in India: an analytical research.* Available at: https://www.researchgate.net/publication/341558182_Emergence_and_future_of_Over-the-top_OTT_video_services_in_India_an_analytical_research

Sun, G.-Z., Dong, Y., Chen, D.-W., & Wei, J. (2010). Data backup and recovery based on data de-duplication. *2010 International Conference on Artificial Intelligence and Computational Intelligence*, *2*, 379–382. 10.1109/AICI.2010.200

Sungya, L. (2018). *Identity Management: boon or curse?* University College of London.

Sun, Y., Zhang, J., Xiong, Y., & Zhu, G. (2014). Data security and privacy in cloud computing. *International Journal of Distributed Sensor Networks, 10*(7), 190903. doi:10.1155/2014/190903

Surana, J., Khandelwal, A., Kothari, A., Solanki, H., & Sankhla, M. (2017). Big Data Privacy Methods. *International Journal of Engineering Development and Research, 5*(2), 979–983.

Susheela, M. (2014). *E-commerce Management.* University of Calicut.

Susheel, B., & Mahalakshmi, V. (2011). Legal Issues in E-Commerce Transactions: An Indian Perspective. *International Journal on Recent and Innovation Trends in Computing and Communication, 4*(11), 185.

Swan, M. (2015). *Blockchain: Blueprint for a New Economy.* O'Reilly Media, Inc.

Sweeney, L. (1997). Weaving technology and policy together to maintain confidentiality. *The Journal of Law, Medicine & Ethics, 25*(2), 98–110. doi:10.1111/j.1748-720X.1997.tb01885.x PMID:11066504

Tade, O. (2021). *Poverty and Widening Inequality in Nigeria.* Available at https://www.vanguardngr.com/2021/07/poverty-and-widening-inequality-in-nigeria/

Talty, S. S. (2018, April). *What Will Our Society Look Like When Artificial Intelligence Is Everywhere?* Smithsonian. Retrieved November 26, 2021, from https://www.smithsonianmag.com/innovation/artificial-intelligence-future-scenarios-180968403/

Taniya, C. K. (2021). *An overview of E-commerce in 2021: Growth, hits, and misses.* Times of India. Retrieved December, 21, 2021, from https://timesofindia.indiatimes.com/blogs/voices/an-overview-of-e-commerce-in-2021-growth-hits-and-misses/

Tarun, M. (2017). Common problems faced by customers while shopping online. *Empower Your Business, 5,* 124. Retrieved August 13, 2019, from https://yourstory.com/2017/04/common-problems-online-shopping/

Tata Sons Limited and Anr Vs Fashion ID Limited, (2005) 140 PLR 12

Tata Sons Limited v. Manu Kishori & Others, 2001 IIIAD Delhi 545

Taulli, T. (2020). *How 5G will Unleash AI.* https://www.forbes.com/sites/tomtaulli/2020/05/08/how-5g-will-unleash-ai/?sh=59235be448c3

Taylor, P. (1998, January 10). *Guide to Medical Informatics, the Internet and Telemedicine; Cybermedicine.* thebmj. Retrieved November 26, 2021, from https://www.bmj.com/content/316/7125/158.1

Taylor, P. J., Dargahi, T., Dehghantanha, A., Parizi, R. M., & Choo, K. K. R. (2020). A systematic literature review of blockchain cyber security. *Digital Communications and Networks, 6*(2), 147–156. doi:10.1016/j.dcan.2019.01.005

Team Mogo. (2021). *History of Bitcoin.* Author.

Techno Pak. (2012). *India's Attractiveness as a key Sourcing to Destination.* New Delhi: Outlook Textiles and Apparels Publication.

Telecom Regulatory Authority of India. (2017). *TRAI's Consultation Paper on Privacy, Security and Ownership of the Data in the Telecom Sector.* https://trai.gov.in/sites/default/files/CIS_07_11_2017.pdf

Telford, T. (2019). *Apple Card algorithm sparks gender bias allegations against Goldman Sachs.* https://www.washingtonpost.com/business/2019/11/11/apple-card-algorithm-sparks-gender-bias-allegations-against-goldman-sachs/

Teymourlouei, H., & Jackson, L. (2016). Detecting and preventing information security breaches. *Proceedings of the International Conference on Security and Management (SAM),* 304.

The Declaration of the International Panel on Artificial Intelligence facilitating international collaboration on AI led in the most part by Canada and France. (n.d.). https://www.canada.ca/en/innovation-science-economic-development/news/2019/05/declaration-of-the-international-panel-on-artificial-intelligence.html

The Influence of Cryptocurrency on the World Economy. (2020). *The World Financial Review*. https://worldfinancial-review.com/the-influence-of-cryptocurrency-on-the-world-economy/

The Interpol. (2020). *Three Arrested as INTERPOL, Group-IB and the Nigeria Police Force Disrupt Prolific Cybercrime Group.* Available at https://www.interpol.int/en/News-and-Events/News/2020/Three-arrested-as-INTERPOL-Group-IB-and-the-Nigeria-Police-Force-disrupt-prolific-cybercrime-group

The LawTech Delivery Panel, 3. *Consultation on the status of cryptoassets, distributed ledger technology and smart contracts under English private law.*

The Legal Nature of Cryptocurrency. (n.d.). https://iopscience.iop.org/article/10.1088/1755-1315/272/3/032166/pdf

The National News. (2021). *More Than Email Scams: The Evolution of Nigeria's Cyber-Crime Threat.* Available at https://www.thenationalnews.com/world/africa/2021/07/22/more-than-email-scams-the-evolution-of-nigerias-cyber-crime-threat/

The Smart Nation and Digital Governance Office, Government of Singapore. (2019). *National Artificial Intelligence Strategy.* https://www.smartnation.gov.sg/docs/default-source/default-document-library/national-ai-strategy.pdf?sfvrsn=2c3bd8e9_4

The United Nations Vienna Convention on the Law of Treaties (1969). Treaty Series, 1155, art 31.

The US Department of Justice. (2019). *10 Men Involved in Nigerian Romance Scams Indicted for Money Laundering Conspiracy.* Available at https://www.justice.gov/opa/pr/10-men-involved-nigerian-romance-scams-indicted-money-laundering-conspiracy

Tillman, R. H., & Indergaard, M. L. (2005). *Pump and dump: The rancid rules of the new economy.* Rutgers University Press.

Tkacz, E., & Adrian, K. (2009). *Internet —Technical Development and Applications.* Springer-Verlag Heidelburg Publications. doi:10.1007/978-3-642-05019-0

Toivo-Think Tank. (2012). *Social Media- The New Power of Political Influence.* Centre for European Studies.

Tomaso Bruno v. State of U.P., (2015) 7 SCC 178

Tonya, M. E. (2019). The Role of International Rules in Blockchain-Based Cross-Border Commercial Disputes. *Wayne Law Review*, 65.

Toralf, N. (1998). Distance Selling in a Digital Age. *Journal of Communication Law*, 3(4), 33.

Trendov, N.M. (2019). *Digital Technologies in Agriculture and Rural Areas: Status report.* Food and Agriculture Organization of the United Nations, FAO.

TRPC. (2018). *Privacy in the Age of Artificial Intelligence.* Briefing Paper. https://trpc.biz/old_archive/wp-content/uploads/IIC.Singapore-AI.BriefingPaper.20Nov.pdf

Tunggal, A. T. (2021, November 15). *The 60 Biggest Data Breaches.* UpGuard. Retrieved November 26, 2021, from https://www.upguard.com/blog/biggest-data-breaches

U.S. Supreme Court, Daubert v. Merrell Dow Pharmaceuticals Inc., United States Reports, vol. 509, pp. 579–601, 1983.

Uba, J., & Agbakoba, O. (2021). *Cybercrimes and Cyber Laws in Nigeria: All You Need To Know.* https://www.mondaq.com/nigeria/security/1088292/cybercrimes-and-cyber-laws-in-nigeria-all-you-need-to-know

Uma, M., & Padmavathi, G. (2013). A Survey on Various Cyber Attacks and their Classification. *International Journal of Network Security, 15*(5), 390–396.

UNCITRAL Model Law on Electronic Commerce, Guide to Enactment, para. 50; Explanatory note by the UNCITRAL secretariat on the United Nations Convention on the Use of Electronic Communications in International Contracts. 143 et seq.

Understanding The Different Types of Cryptocurrency. (2021). SoFi.

UNICEF. (2002). *Handbook on Crime against Children.* https://scpsassam.org/wp-content/uploads/2018/01/UNICEF-Handbook-for-Law-Enf-Agencies-Handbook-on-Cyber-Crimes-against-Children.pdf

UNICEF. (2008). *Rio de Janeiro Pact at Rio de Janeiro Pact to Prevent and Stop Sexual Exploitation of Children and Adolescents.* http://www.unicef.org/protection/Rio_ Declaration_and_ Call_for_ Action.pdf

UNICEF. (2017). *Children in Digital World.* https://www.unicef.org/media/48601/file#:~:text=ICTs%20are%20intensifying%20traditional%20childhood,streaming%20of%20child%20sexual%20abuse

Union, T. (2001). International telecommunication union. *Yearbook of Statistics 1991–2000.*

United Nations Commission on International Trade Law. (2017). *UNCITRAL Technical Notes on Online Dispute Resolution.* United Nations.

United Nations Educational, Scientific and Cultural Organisation (UNESCO). (2021). *Draft Text of the Recommendation on the Ethics of Artificial Intelligence.* https://unesdoc.unesco.org/ark:/48223/pf0000377897/PDF/377897eng.pdf.multi

United Nations. (2013, April). *Report of the Special Rapporteur on the promotion and protection of the right to freedom of opinion and expression (A/HRC/23/40).* https://www.ohchr.org/Documents/HRBodies/HRCouncil/RegularSession/Session23/A.HRC.23.40_EN.pdf

United Nations. (2019, May). *Report of the Special Rapporteur on the promotion and protection of the right to freedom of opinion and expression (A/HRC/41/35).* https://documents-dds-ny.un.org/doc/UNDOC/GEN/G19/148/76/PDF/G1914876.pdf?OpenElement

United States v. Arnold, Schwinn & Co. 388 U.S 365 (1967)

United States v. Ulbricht, 31 F. Supp. 3d 540 (S.D.N.Y. 2014).

United States' Congress. (1934). Securities Act of 1934, 15 U.S.C. 77a-77mm 1934.

Unnithan, P. S. G. (2019, February 20). *India's first RoboCop: Kerala Police inducts robot, gives it SI rank.* IndiaToday. Retrieved January 22, 2022, from https://www.indiatoday.in/trending-news/story/india-first-robocop-kerala-police-inducts-robot-gives-si-rank-1460371-2019-02-20

US Department of Health and Human Services. (2015). *Health Insurance Portability and Accountability Act.* https://www.hhs.gov/hipaa/for-professionals/index.html

Uwem, A., Enobong, A., & Nsikan, S. (2013). Uses and Gratifications of Social Networking Websites among Youths in Uyo, Nigeria. *International Journal of Asian Social Science, 3*(2), 353–369.

Vaccari, C., & Chadwick, A. (2020). Deepfakes and Disinformation: Exploring the Impact of Synthetic Political Video on Deception, Uncertainty and Trust in News. *Safe Journal, 6*(1), 1–13. doi:10.1177/2056305120903408

Vaidialingam, A. (2015). Authenticating Electronic Evidence: §65B, Indian Evidence Act, 1872, (2015). *NUJS L Rev.,* *8*(43).

Vaidialingam, A. (2015). Authenticating Electronic Evidence: Sec. 65B, Indian Evidence Act, 1872. *NUJS Law Review,* *8*(1-2), 43–66.

Vakil, R. (2018). Constitutionalizing administrative law in the Indian Supreme Court: Natural justice and fundamental rights. *International Journal of Constitutional Law, 16*(2), 475–502. doi:10.1093/icon/moy027

Valdez & Ziefle. (2018). The Users' Perspective on the Privacy-Utility Trade-offs in Health Recommender Systems. *International Journal of Human-Computer Studies, 121,* 1–35.

Valentina, G., Fabrizio, F., Claudio, D., Chiara, P., & Víctor, S. (2018). Blockchain and Smart Contracts for Insurance: Is the Technology Mature Enough? *Future Internet, 10*(2), 20. doi:10.3390/fi10020020

Van Dijck, J. (2014). Datafication, dataism and dataveillance: Big data between scientific paradigm and ideology. *Surveillance & Society, 12*(2), 197–208. doi:10.24908s.v12i2.4776

Van Roy, V., Rossetti, F., Perset, K., Galindo-Romero, L., & Watch, A. I. (2021). National strategies on Artificial Intelligence: A European perspective, 2021 edition, EUR 30745 EN. Publications Office of the European Union. doi:10.2760/069178

Vanguard Newspapers. (2021). *Nigeria Drops in Transparency International Corruption Perceptions Index, ranks 149 out of 183 countries.* https://www.vanguardngr.com/2021/01/nigeria-drops-in-transparency-international-corruption-perceptions-index-ranks-149-out-of-183-countries/

Van, W. (2021). *Applying blockchain for climate action in agriculture: state of play and outlook.* Food & Agriculture Org.

Vardhan. (2019). *Blockchain Technology* [Video presentation]. Edureka. https://www.youtube.com/watch?v=QQcBvfP3KBw

Véliz, C. (2020). *Privacy Is Power: Why and How You Should Take Back Control of Your Data.* Bantam Press.

Vincent, J. (2021a). *China overtakes US in AI start-up funding with a focus on facial recognition and chips.* The Verge. https://www.theverge.com/2018/2/22/17039696/china-us-ai-funding-startup-comparison

Vincent, J. (2021b). *Artificial intelligence research continues to grow as China overtakes US in AI journal citations.* The Verge. https://www.theverge.com/2021/3/3/22310840/ai-research-global-growth-china-us-paper-citations-index-report-2020

Vinod, V. (2020). Snag of Electronic Evidence. *RMLNLUJ, 12,* 166.

Vishwakarma, P., Khan, Z., & Jain, T. (2018). Cryptocurrency, security issues and upcoming challenges to legal framework in India. *International Research Journal of Engineering and Technology, 5*(1), 212–215.

Viswanath, N. (2018). *The Supreme Court's Aadhaar Judgement And The Right To Privacy.* Retrieved from Mondaq: https://www.mondaq.com/india/privacy-protection/744522/the-supreme-court39s-aadhaar-judgement-and-the-right-to-privacy

Voigt, P., & Von dem Bussche, A. (2017). *The eu general data protection regulation (gdpr). A Practical Guide* (1st ed.). Springer International Publishing. doi:10.1007/978-3-319-57959-7

Walkowiak, S. (2016). *Big Data Analytics with R, Leverage R programming to uncover hidden patterns in your Big Data.* Packt Publishing.

Wang, W. (2019). *Reflecting on Chinese Artificial Intelligence and National Responsible Innovation.* https://cyberbrics.info/wp-content/uploads/2019/10/Reflecting-on-Chinese-Artificial-Intelligence-and-National-Responsible-Innovation.pdf

Wang, R., Zhu, Y., Chang, C.-C., & Peng, Q. (2020). Privacy-preserving High-dimensional Data Publishing for Classification. *Computers & Security*, *93*, 1–10. doi:10.1016/j.cose.2020.101785

Watkins, B. (2014). The impact of cyber attacks on the private sector. *Briefing Paper. Association for International Affair*, *12*, 1–11.

Webster, G., Creemers, R., Triolo, P., & Kania, E. (2017). *China's Plan to 'Lead' in AI: Purpose, Prospects, and Problems*. New America. https://www.newamerica.org/cybersecurity-initiative/blog/chinas-plan-lead-ai-purpose-prospects-and-problems/

Whish, R., & Bailey, D. (2018). *Competition Law* (9th ed.). Oxford Publication. doi:10.1093/law-ocl/9780198779063.001.0001

White House. (2014). *Big Data and the future of privacy*. Available at: www.whitehouse.gov/blog/2014/01/23/bigdata-and-future-privacy/

Willems, I. (2020, June 20). *Using AI to create a personalized shopping experience in online retail*. DM EXCO 22. Retrieved January 12, 2022, from https://dmexco.com/stories/using-ai-to-create-a-personalized-shopping-experience-in-online-retail/

Wilson, R. L., & Rosen, P. A. (2003). Protecting Data through 'Perturbation' Techniques: The Impact on Knowledge Discovery in Databases. *Journal of Database Management*, *14*(2), 14–26. doi:10.4018/jdm.2003040102

Winter, R. (2013). SSD vs HDD–data recovery and destruction. *Network Security*, *2013*(3), 12–14. doi:10.1016/S1353-4858(13)70041-2

WIPO Press Release. (2020). *WIPO's Anti-"Cybersquatting" Service: 50,000 Cases and Growing amid COVID-19 Surge*. Retrieved from: https://www.wipo.int/pressroom/en/articles/2020/article_0026.html

WIPO Press Releases. (1999). *WIPO Processes First Case Under Cybersquatting Procedure*. Retrieved from: https://www.wipo.int/pressroom/en/prdocs/1999/wipo_pr_1999_200.html

Withers, K. J. (2005). Electronically stored information: The December 2006 amendments to the federal rules of civil procedure. *Nw. J. Tech. & Intell. Prop.*, *4*, 171.

Wong, R. C.-W., Li, J., Fu, A. W.-C., & Wang, K. (2006). (α, k)-anonymity: An enhanced k-anonymity model for privacy preserving data publishing. *Proceedings of the 12th ACM International Conference on Knowledge Discovery and Data Mining*.

Works, V. Inc. v. Volkswagen of America, 238 F.3d 264 (4th Cir. 2001) Vodafone Group Plc v. Rohit Bansal, INDRP/052. https://www.registry.in/show-doc?id=vodafone_0.pdf

World Wrestling Federation Entertainment Inc. v. Michael Bosman, [1 N.C.J.L. & Tech. 3 (2000)]

Wu. (2013). Defining Privacy and Utility in Data Sets. *Law Review Corolado*, *84*, 1117-1177.

Xia, J., Yu, M., Yang, Y., & Jin, H. (2018). Personalized Privacy-Preserving with high performance: (α, ε)-anonymity. *Proceedings of the IEEE Symposium on Computers and Communications*.

Xiao, X., & Tao, Y. (2006). Personalized privacy preservation. *ACM International Conference on Management of Data*, *34*, 1-12.

Xiong, H. (2020). *Blockchain Technology for Agriculture: Applications and Rationale.* . doi:10.3389/fbloc.2020.00007

Xu, J., & Livshits, B. (2020). The anatomy of a cryptocurrency pump-and-dump scheme. *Proceedings of the 28th USENIX Security Symposium*. Retrieved from https://www.usenix.org/conference/usenixsecurity19/presentation/xu-jiahua

Xu, H., Zhang, L., Onireti, O., Fang, Y., Buchanan, W. J., & Imran, M. A. (2021). BeepTrace: Blockchain-Enabled Privacy-Preserving Contact Tracing for COVID-19 Pandemic and Beyond. *IEEE Internet of Things Journal, 8*(5), 3915–3929. doi:10.1109/JIOT.2020.3025953

Yadav, V. S., & Singh, A. R. (2020). A Systematic Literature Review of Blockchain Technology in Agriculture. *International Conference on Industrial Engineering and Operations Management.*

Yahoo Inc. v. Aakash Arora & Anr, 2000 PTC 209 (Del.).

Yao-Huai, L. (2020). Privacy and data privacy issues in contemporary China. In *The Ethics of Information Technologies* (pp. 189–197). Routledge. doi:10.4324/9781003075011-14

Yatsenko, M., & Sotnichek, M. (2021, February 4). *Blockchain for Cybersecurity: Pros and Cons, Trending Use Cases.* Apriorit. https://www.apriorit.com/dev-blog/462-blockchain-cybersecurity-pros-cons

YouTube LLC v. Rohit Kohli, Case no. INDRP/42. https://www.registry.in/show-doc?id=youtubeco_0.pdf

Zabarenko, D. (2013, June 10). *"Pardon Edward Snowden" petition seeks White House response.* https://www.reuters.com/article/us-usa-security-petition/pardon-edward-snowden-petition-seeks-white-house-response-idUSBRE95910820130610

Zahra, S. A., Brewer, J., & Cooper, M. (2018, April). *Artificial Intelligence (AI) for Web Accessibility: Is Conformance Evaluation a Way Forward?* ACM Digital Library. Retrieved November 27, 2021, from https://dl.acm.org/doi/abs/10.1145/3192714.3192834

Zhang, D., Mishra, S., Brynjolfsson, E., Etchemendy, J., Ganguli, D., Grosz, B., Lyons, T., Manyika, J., Carlos Niebles, J., Sellitto, M., Shoham, Y., Clark, J., & Perrault, R. (n.d.). *The AI Index 2021 Annual Report.* AI Index Steering Committee, Human-Centered AI Institute, Stanford University. https://aiindex.stanford.edu/wp-content/uploads/2021/03/2021-AI-Index-Report_Master.pdf

Zhang, Q., Koudas, N., Srivastava, D., & Yu, T. (2007). Aggregate query answering on anonymized tables. *Proceedings of the 23rd IEEE International Conference on Data Engineering (ICDE).*

Zhao, Y., Ge, W., Li, W., Wang, R., Zhao, L., & Ming, J. (2019). Capturing the Persistence of Facial Expression Features for Deepfake Video Detection. In *International Conference on Information and Communications Security* (pp. 630-645). Springer.

Zheng, Z., Xie, S., Dai, H.-N., Chen, X., & Wang, H. (2017). An Overview of Blockchain Technology: Architecture, Consensus, and Future Trends. Academic Press.

Zhu, B., Joseph, A., & Sastry, S. (2011). A taxonomy of cyber attacks on SCADA systems. *2011 International Conference on Internet of Things and 4th International Conference on Cyber, Physical and Social Computing,* 380–388. 10.1109/iThings/CPSCom.2011.34

Zialoita, P. (2019, October 30). *NPR Cookie Consent and Choices.* NPR. Retrieved July 10, 2021, from https://choice.npr.org/index.html?origin=https://www.npr.org/2019/10/30/774749376/facebook-pays-643-000-fine-for-role-in-cambridge-analytica-scandal

About the Contributors

Nisha Dhanraj Dewani has done her Ph.D. LLM (corporate law) and BA LLB from Jamia Millia Islamia University (India). She has practiced as a lawyer in Delhi High Court for 3 years. She has worked with reputed law firm and senior partners handling IPR matters for 2 years. In addition, she holds more than a decade experience in academics. Her major area of academic interest includes Intellectual Property rights, Cyber Law, International Commercial Law and Public International Law. She has many research papers in various national and international reputed law journals. She has received number of letters of appreciation not only from the academic institutions but from different law journals for her contributions. She is a resource person for IPR, corporate law and Cyber Law at many international forums including ACUNS, Italy and Nigeria. She has presented many research papers in various seminars and conferences. She has worked with UNICEF and many reputed NGOs. She has one edited international book to her credit. Presently she is working with the Department of Law, Maharaja Agrasen Institute of Management Studies, GGSIP University, India.

Zubair Ahmed Khan is a Ph.D. from Guru Gobind Singh Indraprastha University, New Delhi, India in the area of biodiversity law and biopiracy. His specialization is in IPR, Corporate Law, Criminal Law and Environmental Law. He is a member of the All India Law Teachers Congress, the Indian Institute of Public Administration and various academic bodies. He held the position of faculty coordinator of Legal Entrepreneurship and Incubation Cell, & ADR Cell at USLLS, GGSIPU and organized many conferences and seminars at school level. Dr. Khan is a resource person at national institutions like ICSI, NIOS and many law schools across the country. He is also a resource person at many international forums and law schools established in UK, Bangladesh, Indonesia, etc. Apart from participating and presenting papers in various seminars and conferences across the country and aboard, Dr. Khan has numerous publications in reputed national and international journals and authored three edited books to his credit.

Aarushi Agarwal is an alumna from Shri Ram College of Commerce, Delhi University, India. She passed her LL.B. and LL.M. degrees from Faulty of Law, Delhi University. She is pursuing her Ph. D from MAU, Baddi, Himachal Pradesh. She has worked as an Advocate associate with AAC law firm for five years. She holds litigation experience of more than five years in criminal, matrimonial and service matters. She has worked on various PILs on health and education related issues in association with Social Jurist NGO. Her areas of interest are Procedural Laws and Cyber law. She holds teaching experience of more than three years.

Mamta Sharma has been working as an Assistant Professor of Law in Gautam Buddha University, Greater Noida, India. She is also the Head of the department of School of Law, Justice and Governance. She has been teaching Contract Law, Arbitration, Labour Law and Criminology. She also owes to her credit more than dozens of publications in National and International journals.

Shaharyar Asaf Khan has more than 10 years of experience in academics. He has authored various research papers which have been published in UGC recognised and peer-reviewed journals and has also chapter contributions in various edited books. Dr. Khan has also presented papers in various International and national seminars and conferences. He has been invited as a Guest Speaker and Resource Person in various Law schools, NGOs and other forums. Dr. Khan is currently an Associate Professor in School of Law, Manav Rachna University, Faridabad, Haryana.

* * *

Charitarth Bharti is a lawyer and policy professional with expertise in matters of regulation of emerging technology with a focus on Data Protection and Technology Law. Charitarth has multiple years of experience in working in high stakes litigation and advisory with a variety of Government Agencies on legal matters as well as matters of import to businesses. From wearing the hat of a Policy Lead to a Member of Parliament as a part of the 2016-17 cohort of the prestigious Legislative Assistants to Members of Parliament (LAMP) Fellowship in India, he has worked with the office of the Central Government Standing Counsel and the Additional Solicitor General of India in representing the Government of India before the High Court of Delhi on various areas of law and governmental policy. At NUS, he earned a Masters in Public Policy Degree as a prestigious Li Ka Shing Scholar, researching on issues of emerging technologies and working with leading organisations in the domain. He currently works in the Privacy and Data Trusts practice of EY Canada based out of Toronto working on issues at the intersection of AI and Data Protection.

Apurva Bhutani is a final year law student at Maharaja Agrasen Institute of Management Studies, Department of Law, GGSIPU. She has a keen interest in Intellectual Property Laws. She believes in getting the job done while learning along the way. She has gained valuable experience by interning at various IPR law firms. She has been the content head and editor at Niti Manthan which is a research organisation. She is the student coordinator of the Internship and Placement Cell of her college and is also an active volunteer of the Legal Aid Committee.

Ersin Caglar is currently a senior lecturer at the European University of Lefke. He holds a PhD in Management Information Systems (MIS) from Girne American University. He also obtained his MBA in Business from the European University of Lefke (EUL). He teaches network, computing and information systems courses. His research interest is in the areas of information systems, social media, network security, cloud computing, cryptocurrency and IoT.

Parag Chatterjee received the B.E. degree in Computer Science & Engineering from the Karnatak University, Dharwad, India, in 1998 and received M.Tech. degree from IIEST Shibpur, Kolkata, India, in 2007. Since 2007, he has been with the Department of Computer Science & Engineering, Pailan College of Management & Technology, as Associate professor. His current research interests include Data ware Housing, Data mining and Wireless sensor. He has 2 publication in national and international journals.

Swarnendu Chatterjee is a Principal Associate in the Dispute Resolution team of Saraf and Partners and an Advocate-on-Record in the Supreme Court of India with vast experience of a decade. He has worked in many fields of law and his experience of a decade extends to virtually all aspects of litigation and arbitration. He has extensive experience in both domestic and international jurisdictions and has extensively advised on debt recovery, insolvency, banking and financial issues, service matters, matters of constitutional importance and commercial and corporate disputes and real estate in various Courts all over India. He has completed his B.B.A.LL.B(H) from the School of Law, KIIT University, Bhubaneswar, Odisha. He was awarded the Lex-Falcon Award in April 2021 in Dubai, for being one of the top 100 young achievers in the legal field in 2020-21. He has over 50 publications in the form of articles and blogs in various journals (both online and print) including SCC Online, IndiaCorpLaw and Bar and Bench, and other prestigious platforms.

Deren Fırat is currently Research Assistant at the Faculty of Law at Cyprus International Univerity (CIU). She is PhD Candidate in Law, specializing in International Criminal Law at CIU. She obtained her PgDip in Criminology and Criminal Justice from the University of Glasgow, UK. Her research interest is in the areas of International Law, Criminal Law, Criminology and Human Rights.

Unanza Gulzar is currently working as an assistant professor in school of law, the The NorthCap University. She has done her LL.B and LLM specializing in Business laws besides holding Bachelor's degree in science. She Has done her Ph.D. in e-commerce from India. She has qualified the U.G.C. NET twice and State eligibility test for lectureship in the year 2013. She has to her credit a Book on "Money Laundering in India: Legal Perspective". She has published more than 28 research papers in various national and international reputed law journals. She has received number of letters of appreciation from different law journals for her contribution. Besides, her articles have appeared in various newspapers/ Web-portals on a wide range of subjects from politics to typical legal matters. She has presented 35 research papers in various Seminars and conferences. With over more than 7 years of teaching experience, she has taught in Central University of Kashmir.

Balyejusa Gusite is an ambitious and focused web systems administrator and developer with a bias in specific fields like data mining, big data analytics, data science, data visualization, database management systems, machine learning, and automation systems. In these, am exacting professional experience and confidence as a road map towards the peak of the ICT career. In this process, I have worked on several systems like at Kampala International University where we developed the students-lecturer evaluation tool's front and back-end functionalities. Furthermore, the revamping of the university's website and embedding individual sites for the seven faculties or schools within the university. This was through the Dean school of computing and information technology and the DVC research and innovation in 2017. Currently, am pursuing a master of science in information systems from Kampala international university with research in the data mining arena.

Yılsev Hoca is PhD student at Cyprus International University (CIU). She worked as a research assistant in the field of public law at Cyprus International University for 3 years. Her research interest is in the areas of constitutional law, human rights, government systems, constitutional judgment and general public law.

Jayapradha J. was awarded a Bachelor of Technology in Electrical and Electronics Engineering in 2008 from SASTRA University, Thanjavur, and Master of Technology in Computer Science and Engineering in 2011 from SRMIST Chennai, Tamilnadu State, India. She has also awarded the University 3rd rank holder in the Master degree. She has published many research papers on machine learning, data mining and privacy. Her particular research area includes machine learning, databases and privacy. Currently, she works as an assistant professor in the Department of Computer Science and Engineering, SRMIST, Chennai, Tamilnadu, India. She also has three years of industrial experience in the Business Intelligence domain. She is a professional member in CSI, ISCA, and IAENG.

Nitya Jain completed her LLB from Nirma University and is an Associate working with the Litigation and Dispute Resolution Team at Panag & Babu Law Offices, Delhi, India.

Brady Lund is the author of several publications in top scholarly journals on topics including cybersecurity and the dark web. He is also co-author of four books on the topics of the accessibility, dark web, and information privacy and security.

Prakash M. received the Doctor of Philosophy from Anna University, Chennai, India. He received the Master of Technology degree in Information Technology from Anna University, Chennai, India. He is currently working as Associate Professor in the Department of Computer Science and Engineering, SRM Institute of Science and Technology, Kattankulathur, Tamil Nadu, India. He has 13 years of experience in teaching and learning. His research interest includes big data analytics, Databases and Security. He is a professional member of ISTE, IE(I), ISCA, IAENG, CSTA, IACSIT, and UACEE.

Utkarsh Maria is an advocate practising in the Supreme Court of India. He has several Supreme Court reported judgments to his credit. His interest includes Company Law, Insolvency Law and Civil Law. He actively reads on privacy, digital evidence and arbitration law.

Claudia Masoni is Specialised in Arts and Law. BA in Comparative literatures and Philology, LLM in International Human Rights Law and PhD in international law. She is an expert in the field of indigenous cultural rights and traditional knowledge. Also she is a Consultant in the field of law and researcher in cultural Anthropology, Theology Philosophy and Social sciences.

Vibhuti Nakta is Assistant Professor of Law at HIMCAPES College of Law.

Desmond Onyemechi Okocha, PhD, is a Social Scientist with specialisation in management and mass communication. He has over 15 years experience in consulting, research and lecturing. He obtained his B.A degree in Management from the United Kingdom, holds a M.A and PhD in Journalism and Mass Communication, both from India. Additionally, has PGDs in Education Management and Leadership and another in Logistics and Supply Chain Management. He was the pioneer National Knowledge Management and Communication Coordinator for the International Fund for Agricultural Development project in the Niger Delta. He is presently, a Senior Lecturer, Department of Mass Communication, Bingham

University, Nigeria. He is the Founder of Institute for Leadership and Development Communication, Nigeria. As an international voice, Dr. Okocha is a frequent speaker in conferences across continents. In 2018, he was invited to speak at Harvard University, USA, Vienna University, Austria, and at the MIRDEC-8th, International Academic Conference on Social Sciences, Portugal.

Shifa Qureshi is an undergraduate student of law at the Faculty of Law, Aligarh Muslim University, Aligarh, India. Her focus of research is in Public International Law, Constitutional Law, Commercial Law, Technology Law & Competition Law. She has recently served as Joint Editor of the AMU Law Society Review and is currently an Assistant Editor and Staff writer for JURIST, University of Pittsburgh, Pennsylvania, USA. She is also assisting Mr. Harsh Mahaseth (Lecturer and Assistant Dean (Office of Academic Affairs) at Jindal Global Law School) as an undergraduate Research Assistant. Their papers have been accepted for publication in SCOPUS-indexed journals.

Ramit Rana is a Practising Advocate at the Delhi High Court, and other lower Courts of Delhi. He possesses 7+ years of experience and currently he is working as a Partner at "Step Next Legal", Advocates & Legal Consultants. He worked as a Legal Manager in Agarwal Associates and also as a Senior Legal Associate in GP Global (formerly known as Gulf Petrochem). Prior to GP, he had also worked with RHA LEGAL. He has industry experience in Networking and Testing, as he had done B.Tech in Computer Science.

Sambhav Sharma is a final year student of law at Amity Law School, Delhi (affiliated to Guru Gobind Singh Indraprastha University), India. He has a penchant for legal writing and research. He has served as the Convenor of the Moot Court Society of his college and has earned merit in prestigious moot court competitions such as the Willem C. Vis International Commercial Arbitration Moot and the Philip C. Jessup Public International Law Moot. At present, he serves as an Associate Editor and India Correspondent for JURIST, University of Pittsburgh, Pennsylvania, U.S.A. He also holds several publications on leading domestic and international legal platforms.

Anurag Singh is an Associate Professor of Law in Meerut College, Meerut. He also done post graduation in Maths and also passed company secretary exams. He joined Meerut college in 2001 as a Lecturer.

Ramayni Sood is a final year law student at Amity Law School, Delhi (affiliated to Guru Gobind Singh Indraprastha University), India. She frequently writes on social and legal issues. She is an avid mooter and has participated in various Moot Court Competitions such as the John H. Jackson Moot Court Competition on International Trade Law and currently serves as the President of the Student Recruitment Council in her college.

Rajab Ssemwogerere is pursuing a Master's of Science in Computer Science from Makerere University (MUK) Kampala, Uganda, a Postgraduate Diploma in Management and Teaching at Higher Education from Islamic University in Uganda. He received his honors B.Sc. in Computer Science (2018) and a diploma in Computer science and Information Technology (2014) at the Islamic University in Uganda. Rajab gained certificates in Introduction to cybersecurity (2018) and an Introduction to the internet of things and digital transformation (2018) from CISCO networking Academy. Currently, he works as a research assistant in the Motion Analysis Research Lab as well as a computer lab officer based at the

Islamic University in Uganda. He Led a team of six that developed an autonomous smart office system that later won the Rector award at Islamic University In Uganda (2018). He has research interests in computer vision, Artificial intelligence (IoT) and Machine learning.

Manini Syali is pursuing PhD from USLLS, GGSIPU in Environmental Law. Did LLM from South Asian University. Published many papers in national as well as international journals.

Abhishek Vats is the Head of Research and Development at ASEAN Youth Organization and the Co-Founder of AYO Recent , Research Center. Abhishek is a final year student of BALLB program at Department of Law, MAIMS, Guru Gobind Singh Indraprastha University, Delhi. Abhishek has also been published in renowned International and National journals on topics related to International Human Rights law and International Economic Law, LGBTQIA+ rights in India. Through AYO Recent, Abhishek has led teams of researchers on contemporary issues related to International Relations, Migration and Refugee crisis, Rights of indigenous communities, Digital Literacy etc.

Anant Vijay Maria is an advocate practising in the Supreme Court of India. He has done his masters from NLU Delhi. He is practising in various commercial tribunals and High courts of the country. His PhD thesis is in corporate insolvency law. He has taken several guest lectures and has been a trainer in corporate law in many organizations. He has also authored several articles for various national and international journals.

Index

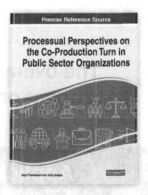

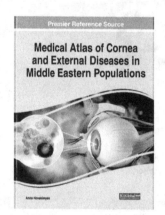

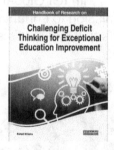

Have Your Work Published and Freely Accessible
Open Access Publishing

With the industry shifting from the more traditional publication models to an open access (OA) publication model, publishers are finding that OA publishing has many benefits that are awarded to authors and editors of published work.

Freely Share Your Research

Higher Discoverability & Citation Impact

Rigorous & Expedited Publishing Process

Increased Advancement & Collaboration

Acquire & Open

When your library acquires an IGI Global e-Book and/or e-Journal Collection, your faculty's published work will be considered for immediate conversion to Open Access *(CC BY License)*, at no additional cost to the library or its faculty *(cost only applies to the e-Collection content being acquired)*, through our popular **Transformative Open Access (Read & Publish) Initiative**.

Provide Up To **100%** OA APC or CPC Funding

Funding to Convert or Start a Journal to **Platinum OA**

Support for Funding an **OA Reference Book**

IGI Global publications are found in a number of prestigious indices, including Web of Science™, Scopus®, Compendex, and PsycINFO®. The selection criteria is very strict and to ensure that journals and books are accepted into the major indexes, IGI Global closely monitors publications against the criteria that the indexes provide to publishers.

Learn More Here:

For Questions, Contact IGI Global's Open Access Team at openaccessadmin@igi-global.com

www.igi-global.com

Printed in the United States
by Baker & Taylor Publisher Services